■ United States Holocaust Memorial Museum
Center for Advanced Holocaust Studies

# Documenting Life and Destruction
## Holocaust Sources in Context

**SERIES EDITOR**

Jürgen Matthäus

**CONTRIBUTING EDITOR**

Jan Lambertz

# DOCUMENTING LIFE AND DESTRUCTION
## HOLOCAUST SOURCES IN CONTEXT

This groundbreaking series provides a new perspective on history using firsthand accounts of the lives of those who suffered through the Holocaust, those who perpetrated it, and those who witnessed it as bystanders. The United States Holocaust Memorial Museum's Center for Advanced Holocaust Studies presents a wide range of documents from different archival holdings, expanding knowledge about the lives and fates of Holocaust victims and making these resources broadly available to the general public and scholarly communities for the first time.

BOOKS IN THE SERIES

1. *Jewish Responses to Persecution, Volume I, 1933–1938*, Jürgen Matthäus and Mark Roseman (2010)
2. *Children during the Holocaust*, Patricia Heberer (2011)
3. *Jewish Responses to Persecution, Volume II, 1938–1940,* Alexandra Garbarini with Emil Kerenji, Jan Lambertz, and Avinoam Patt (2011)
4. *The Diary of Samuel Golfard and the Holocaust in Galicia,* Wendy Lower (2011)
5. *Jewish Responses to Persecution, Volume III, 1941–1942,* Jürgen Matthäus with Emil Kerenji, Jan Lambertz, and Leah Wolfson (2013)
6. *The Holocaust in Hungary: Evolution of a Genocide*, Zoltán Vági, László Csősz, and Gábor Kádár (2013)

*A project of the*

## United States Holocaust Memorial Museum

SARA J. BLOOMFIELD
*Director*

## Center for Advanced Holocaust Studies

PAUL A. SHAPIRO
*Director*

JÜRGEN MATTHÄUS
*Director, Applied Research*

*under the auspices of the*

## Academic Committee
## of the
## United States Holocaust Memorial Council

ALVIN H. ROSENFELD, *Chair*

| | | |
|---|---|---|
| Doris L. Bergen | Peter Hayes | Michael R. Marrus |
| Richard Breitman | Sara Horowitz | John T. Pawlikowski |
| Christopher R. Browning | Steven T. Katz | Menachem Z. Rosensaft |
| David Engel | William S. Levine | George D. Schwab |
| Zvi Y. Gitelman | Deborah E. Lipstadt | James E. Young |

This publication has been made possible by
support from

The Gerald M. and Mary L. Fisch Fund
for Study of the Holocaust in Hungary

Claims Conference ועידת התביעות
The Conference on Jewish Material Claims Against Germany

The William S. and Ina Levine Foundation

The Blum Family Foundation

and

Dr. Alfred Munzer and Mr. Joel Wind

The authors have worked to provide clear information about the provenance of each document and illustration included here. In some instances, particularly for journals and newspapers no longer in print, we have been unable to verify the existence or identity of any present copyright owners. If notified of any items inadvertently credited wrongly, we will include updated credit information in reprints of this work.

**Documenting Life and Destruction**
Holocaust Sources in Context

# THE HOLOCAUST IN HUNGARY
## Evolution of a Genocide

Zoltán Vági, László Csősz, and Gábor Kádár

Foreword by Randolph L. Braham

Advisory Committee:

Christopher R. Browning
David Engel
Sara Horowitz
Steven T. Katz
Alvin H. Rosenfeld

AltaMira Press
in association with the United States Holocaust Memorial Museum
2013

For USHMM:
Project Manager: Mel Hecker
Translator: Zsófia Zvolenszky
Research Assistants: Greg Wilkowski, Kathryn Cornelius, Holly Robertson,
 Chris Henson, and Ryan Farrell

Published by AltaMira Press
A division of Rowman & Littlefield Publishers, Inc.
A wholly owned subsidiary of The Rowman & Littlefield Publishing Group, Inc.
4501 Forbes Boulevard, Suite 200, Lanham, Maryland 20706

Estover Road, Plymouth PL6 7PY, United Kingdom

Front cover: (top row, left to right) courtesy of FORTEPAN; USHMMA RG 39.013M, reel 25 (HJA XX-F-1, box D 6/1); USHMMPA WS# 28215, courtesy of Ivan Sved; (bottom row, left to right) image no. 1012010205385956, CENTROPA (www.centropa.hu); map produced by Béla Nagy, Institute of History of the Hungarian Academy of Sciences; courtesy of Yad Vashem Photo Archives, photo album FA268/49

Copyright © 2013 by AltaMira Press

British Library Cataloguing in Publication Information Available

Library of Congress Cataloging-in-Publication Data
Vági, Zoltán, author.
 The Holocaust in Hungary : evolution of a genocide / Zoltán Vági, László Csősz and Gábor Kádár.
   pages cm. — (Holocaust sources in context ; 6)
   Includes bibliographical references and index.
   ISBN 978-0-7591-2198-0 (cloth : alk. paper) — ISBN 978-0-7591-2200-0 (ebook)
  1. Jews—Persecutions—Hungary. 2. Holocaust, Jewish (1939-1945)—Hungary.
 3. Hungary—Ethnic relations. I. Csősz, László, author. II. Kádár, Gábor, author.
 III. Title.
 DS135.H9H587 2013
 940.53'1809439—dc23                                                    2013014479

*All rights reserved.* No part of this book may be reproduced in any form or by any electronic or mechanical means, including information storage and retrieval systems, without written permission from the publisher, except by a reviewer who may quote passages in a review.

∞™ The paper used in this publication meets the minimum requirements of American National Standard for Information Sciences—Permanence of Paper for Printed Library Materials, ANSI/NISO Z39.48-1992.

Printed in the United States of America

# Contents

Reader's Guide — xi
Abbreviations — xiii
Foreword by Randolph L. Braham — xvii
Acknowledgments — xxiii
Introduction — xxvii
Maps
   1. *The Consequences of the 1920 Trianon Peace Treaty* — xxxvii
   2. *Territorial Expansion of Hungary, 1938–1941* — xlii
   3. *Deportation of the Provincial Jews, Spring–Summer 1944* — liv
   4. *Antisemitic Mass Executions and Death Marches in Hungary, 1942–1945* — lxiv

**1 Laws against the Rule of Law** — **1**
   The "Jewish Laws" — 3
   The Impact of the Antisemitic Legislation — 16

**2 Discrimination, Radicalization, and the First Mass Murders** — **23**
   Bureaucratic and Illegal Antisemitism before 1944 — 24
   The First Mass Murders — 33
   Labor Service — 46
   Hungarian-German Relations and the "Jewish Question" — 61

viii  Contents

| | 3 | **Blitzkrieg against the Jews** | **71** |
|---|---|---|---|
| | | Stigmatization | 72 |
| | | Setting Up the Ghettos | 76 |
| | | Life in the Ghettos | 90 |
| | 4 | **Deportations from the Provinces and the Fate of the Budapest Jews** | **103** |
| | | Destruction of the Provincial Communities | 104 |
| | | The Strasshof Deportations | 120 |
| | | The Concentration of the Budapest Jews | 123 |
| | | Suspension of Deportations: July to August 1944 | 134 |
| | 5 | **The Arrow Cross Regime** | **147** |
| | | The Takeover | 148 |
| | | The Arrow Cross Movement: Its Leader and Ideology | 150 |
| | | Deportations Resumed: The Death Marches | 153 |
| | | Szálasi's Final Plan and the Budapest Ghettos | 157 |
| | | Terror outside the Ghettos | 169 |
| | | Jewish Voices from the Arrow Cross Era | 172 |
| | 6 | **Plunder** | **177** |
| | | The Machinery of Plunder: The Process and Agencies | 179 |
| | | The Effects of Plunder: Winners and Losers | 198 |
| | | Synagogues into Storehouses | 208 |
| | 7 | **In the Nazi Camps** | **213** |
| | | Auschwitz Getting Ready | 214 |
| | | On the "Jewish Ramp" of Auschwitz II–Birkenau | 217 |
| | | The Mass Murder of Hungarian Jews | 219 |
| | | Deported to Other Camps | 231 |
| | 8 | **Jewish Responses to Persecution** | **243** |
| | | Patterns of Individual Jewish Responses | 244 |
| | | Strategy of the Jewish Council | 254 |
| | | Zionist Responses | 265 |
| | | Thwarted Appeals | 272 |

| 9 | **Non-Jewish Reactions** | **279** |
|---|---|---|
| | Bystanders: Collaborators and Beneficiaries | 279 |
| | Bystanders: Solidarity and Rescue | 294 |
| | The Churches | 306 |
| | Intervention and the International Community | 313 |
| 10 | **Jews in Postwar Hungary** | **329** |
| | Liberation | 330 |
| | The Dimensions of Destruction | 335 |
| | To Leave or to Stay? | 340 |
| | Rehabilitation, Restitution, Pogroms | 341 |
| | Jews, Communists, Zionists | 351 |
| | The 1956 Revolution and Fight for Freedom | 355 |
| | The Kádár Era and Beyond | 358 |

*Tables*

1. *U.S. Army Equivalents of SS Ranks* — 367
2. *Changes in the Number and Percentage of Israelites within the Hungarian Population* — 368
3. *Territorial Expansion of Hungary, 1938–1941* — 369
4. *Administrative Structure of Hungary in 1944* — 370
5. *Number of Jewish Congregations in Post-Trianon Hungary and Carpatho-Ruthenia after World War II* — 371
6. *Concordance between Hungarian and Non-Hungarian Place Names* — 372

*List of Documents* — 375
*Bibliography* — 389
*Glossary* — 399
*Chronology* — 419
*Index* — 425
*About the Authors* — 441

# Reader's Guide

THIS VOLUME is part of the *Documenting Life and Destruction* series, designed to present original historical documents on the Holocaust within an explanatory narrative. It provides cogent clues about the context and distinctiveness of each selection, material hitherto largely inaccessible to an English-speaking public. The chapters for the most part move chronologically, highlighting developments of particular relevance to Hungary's unique position in the war and its political and social history. Other parts of the book, especially the glossary and bibliography, add further context for a better understanding of the subject.

The documents in this volume have been printed in a distinct format to set them apart from our commentary. We have reproduced the form and content of the originals as faithfully as possible, working to provide clear information about the provenance and copyright of each selection. We have retained emphases used by the authors of the actual documents and corrected obvious orthographical mistakes made by the authors of English-language texts. In cases where we could not print a document in its entirety, we have marked any omitted text with bracketed ellipses ([. . .]). For documents not clearly dated by those who produced them, we provide an estimated date in the header (in parentheses) based on indirect evidence drawn from the document itself or supplementary information.

All the documents in this volume have been translated from Hungarian unless otherwise noted. Many terms used by Hungarian commentators during the interwar period and the war carry complicated meanings that are often difficult to capture in English. Sometimes they represent distinct political configurations or the peculiar—often racialized—bureaucratic terms of a wartime regime. Sometimes, however, they simply constitute the distinctive vocabularies of sentiment, identity, mood, and so forth that pertain to every language. The nuances of particular terms can be important for understanding both the rhetoric of public appeals and the language of private reflection, and in some cases we have indicated the difficulty of translation by adding the original word or phrase in brackets after its English equivalent. Furthermore, owing to the difficulty of the Hungarian language, we have supplied references to all available English translations of published sources.

Geographical names also vary from language to language and have changed to reflect the shifting borders and power constellations of the 1930s and 1940s. We have worked to provide clear guideposts to track this varying, often shifting nomenclature. Table 6 on page 372 offers readers a basic guide to Hungarian place names and their equivalents in several other central European languages. A number of names, events, and organizations appear in boldface throughout the volume when they are first mentioned in a chapter. This indicates that readers can find further information on the highlighted term in the glossary at the end of the volume. Using the extensive resources of the U.S. Holocaust Memorial Museum's library and archives, we have also attempted to reveal the ultimate fate of each author of a document and persons mentioned in the document by their full names. Some of this information appears in the glossary and some of it in footnotes to the original documents. Regrettably, we were unable to unearth information on every individual mentioned, often in passing, in these pages.

Readers will find several further resources at the back of the volume to orient them to the complex events of this period. We include a series of tables outlining the shifting borders and administrative structures of Hungary, and a demographic profile of Hungarian Jews. In addition, we provide a basic chronology of critical events covered by this volume. Finally, the bibliography offers the reader an opportunity to explore in greater depth the topics touched on here.

# ABBREVIATIONS

(Bold indicates a Glossary term.)

| | |
|---|---|
| ABSM | Auschwitz-Birkenau State Museum (Miejsce Pamięci i Muzeum Auschwitz-Birkenau, Oświęcim) |
| AMH | Archives of Military History (Hadtörténelmi Levéltár, Budapest) |
| APH | Archives of Political History and the Trade Unions (Politka történeti és Szakszervezeti Levéltár) |
| | |
| BCA | Baranya County Archives (Baranya Megyei Levéltár, Pécs) |
| BdS | Befehlshaber der Sicherheitspolizei und des SD |
| BMA | Budapest Municipal Archives (Budapest Főváros Levéltára, Budapest) |
| BMTI | Historical Archives of the Ministry of the Interior (Belügyminisztérium Történeti Irattára, Budapest) |
| | |
| CENTROPA | Central Europe Center for Research and Documentation (www.centropa.org) |
| | |
| **DEGOB** | National Committee of Hungarian Jews for Attending Deportees (Magyarországi Zsidók Deportáltakat Gondozó Országos Bizottsága) |

| | |
|---|---|
| ELTE | Eötvös Loránd University, Budapest |
| ÉME | Association of Awakening Hungarians (Ébredő Magyarok Egyesülete) |
| | |
| GyMSCA | Győr-Moson-Sopron County Archives (Győr-Moson-Sopron Megyei Levéltár, Sopron) |
| | |
| HAHSS | Historical Archives of the Hungarian State Security (Állambiztonsági Szolgálatok Történeti Levéltára, Budapest) |
| HBCA | Hajdú-Bihar County Archives (Hajdú-Bihar Megyei Levéltár, Debrecen) |
| H&GS | *Holocaust and Genocide Studies* |
| HJA | Hungarian Jewish Archives (Magyar Zsidó Levéltár, Budapest) |
| HMC | Holocaust Memorial Center (Holokauszt Emlékközpont, Budapest) |
| HNA | Hungarian National Archives (Magyar Országos Levéltár, Budapest) |
| HSSPF | Higher SS and Police Leader (*Höherer SS- und Polizeiführer*) |
| | |
| IMT, NG | International Military Tribunal, Nuremberg Government |
| | |
| JNSZCA | Jász-Nagykun-Szolnok County Archives (Jász-Nagykun-Szolnok Megyei Levéltár, Szolnok) |
| | |
| KdS | Kommandeur der Sicherheitspolizei und des SD |
| KEOKH | National Central Authority for Controlling Foreigners (Külföldieket Ellenőrző Országos Központi Hatóság) |
| KMOF | National Superintendent of the Public Interest Labor Service System (Közérdekű Munkaszolgálat Országos Felügyelője) |
| | |
| MÁV | Hungarian State Railways (Magyar Államvasutak) |
| MÉP | Hungarian Life Party (Magyar Élet Pártja) |
| MMP | Hungarian Renewal Party (Magyar Megújulás Pártja) |
| MNSZP | Hungarian National Socialist Party (Magyar Nemzetiszocialista Párt) |

Abbreviations  XV

| | |
|---|---|
| NA | Hungarian National Army (founded in 1919) (Nemzeti Hadsereg) |
| NARA | U.S. National Archives and Records Administration |
| NCA | Nógrád County Archives (Nógrád Megyei Levéltár, Salgótarján-Balassagyarmat) |
| OZSSB | National Jewish Aid Committee (Országos Zsidó Segítő Bizottság) |
| PCA | Pest County Archives (Pest Megyei Levéltár, Budapest) |
| RSHA | **Reich Security Main Office** of the SS (Reichssicherheitshauptamt, Berlin) |
| ŠAB | State Archives in Bytča, Martin Branch (Štátny Archív Bytča, Pobočka Martin, Bytča) |
| SD | Sicherheitsdienst |
| SEK | **Sondereinsatzkommando Eichmann** |
| SS | Schutzstaffel |
| SzSzCA | Szabolcs-Szatmár-Bereg County Archives (Szabolcs-Szatmár-Bereg Megyei Levéltár, Nyíregyháza) |
| USHMM | United States Holocaust Memorial Museum (Washington, DC) |
| USHMMA | United States Holocaust Memorial Museum Archives |
| USHMMPA | United States Holocaust Memorial Museum Photo Archives |
| WCC | World Council of Churches |
| WVHA | SS-Business Administration Main Office (Wirtschafts-Verwaltungshauptamt, Berlin) |
| YVA | Yad Vashem Archive, Jerusalem |
| YVS | *Yad Vashem Studies* |
| ZCA | Zala County Archives (Zala Megyei Levéltár, Zalaegerszeg) |

# Foreword

PERHAPS NO other event in modern world history has been as thoroughly documented as the Holocaust—the destruction of nearly 6 million Jews of Europe during the Nazi era. A considerable proportion of this documentation pertains to the Hungarian chapter of the Holocaust. In early March 1944, when most of the Jews in Nazi-dominated Europe had already been murdered, Hungary, a member of the Axis alliance, still had a Jewish population of approximately eight hundred thousand, including close to one hundred thousand converts to Christianity identified as Jews under the racial laws then in effect. As patriotic "Magyars of the Israelite faith," the Jews had by that time convinced themselves that they would survive World War II relatively unscathed under the protection of the conservative-aristocratic government led by Prime Minister **Miklós Kállay**. Their conviction was reinforced not only by the positive news from the war fronts—Italy extricated itself from the Axis in late summer 1943, the Red Army was fast approaching the borders of Romania, and the Allies were triumphing in both Europe and the Pacific—but also by the considerable easing of the anti-Jewish climate in Hungary itself. They were further encouraged by the realization that the sweeping anti-Jewish laws, while still in effect, were no longer strictly enforced and that the Hungarian government had adopted a series of measures that clearly irritated Nazi Germany. The government consistently rejected the Nazis' demand for the implementation of the "Final Solution," put on trial a number of top-ranking military and **gendarmerie** officers for war crimes committed against Serbs and Jews, and sought the withdrawal of the remnant of the Hungarian Second Army from the Soviet front.

After the crushing defeat of the Hungarian forces near Voronezh in January 1943, followed by the destruction of the German and Romanian armies in and around Stalingrad shortly thereafter, the leaders of Hungary had become convinced that the Axis would lose the war. In the summer of that year, they embarked on a desperate effort to follow the example of Italy and extricate the country from the Axis alliance. Overlooking the geographic realities of their country and the bonds that tied together the wartime alliance between the Anglo-Saxons and the Soviet Union, the leaders of Hungary aimed to surrender exclusively to the western Allies. They had hoped not only to avoid a Soviet occupation—they feared bolshevism more than Nazism—but also to retain the territories they had acquired with the support of the Third Reich. Toward this end, in the late summer of 1943, they established "secret" contacts with several military and diplomatic representatives of the western Allies in Turkey and liberated Italy. The details of the "secret" negotiations were widely known in both Hungary and Nazi Germany. Hitler, who was fully briefed by his many spies and informers, decided to protect the Reich's national interests by occupying Hungary. Although he based his decision regarding the occupation, reached in February 1944, primarily on military-strategic considerations, Hitler never lost sight of the unsolved "Jewish question" in Hungary.

The occupation took place on March 19, 1944, without any resistance. Many among the Hungarians, especially the military and the rightist extremists, welcomed it. At first the Nazis in charge of the "Final Solution" were not absolutely sure that the new government they planned to install to replace the "pro-Jewish" Kállay government would be more cooperative in the drive to "solve" the "Jewish question." Given the dire economic, military, and international situation at the time, some among the Nazis feared that even a new, pro-German government might consider the "solution" of the Jewish question a domestic issue.

The hundred-man **Sondereinsatzkommando Eichmann** arrived in Hungary with contingency plans. To the unit's pleasant surprise, representatives of the newly established government of **Döme Sztójay**—all constitutionally appointed by **Miklós Horthy**, the head of state—outdid the SS in their eagerness to "solve" the "Jewish question." Aware of the fast-approaching Soviet forces, the new government placed the instruments of state power—the police, gendarmerie, and civil service—at the disposal of the Germans and Hungarians in charge of the "Final Solution." Since time was of the essence, the Nazis and their Hungarian accomplices acted swiftly and decisively. They were resolved to implement the "Final Solution" before the arrival of the Red Army.

It is an irony of history that the Jews of Hungary, who survived the first four and a half years of the war, confident that they—proud citizens of Hungary—would continue to be protected, were destroyed on the eve of Allied victory. Almost oblivious to what happened to the neighboring Jewish communities before the German occupation of Hungary, the Jews of that country were subjected not only to the fastest but also the most barbaric process of destruction in the history of the Holocaust. It is another irony of history that the chain of events that triggered the German occupation and the subsequent destruction of the Jews started with Hungary's quixotic attempts to extricate itself from the war. "In retrospect," to quote from an earlier study, "it appears that had Hungary continued to remain a militarily passive but politically vocal ally of the Third Reich instead of provocatively engaging in essentially fruitless, if not merely alibi establishing, diplomatic maneuvers, the Jews of Hungary might possibly have survived the war relatively unscathed."[1]

The German occupation of Hungary caught the Jews by surprise. Stunned and bewildered, they continued to hope that the new Hungarian government, which included several members of the Kállay government, would consider the Jewish question a domestic issue. They also found solace in the fact that Horthy had resolved to continue as head of state. However, they were unaware that Horthy had not only committed Hungary to the delivery of three hundred thousand Jewish "workers" to Germany but also decided not to become involved in Jewish matters. The Jews had also hoped that the new Hungarian leaders would resist the Nazis' demands because of the essential role the Jews were playing in the economy—an economy that was in the service of both the German and the Hungarian war effort. Finally, they tended to believe that, given the "imminent and inevitable" Allied victory, the new Hungarian leaders would not expose themselves to possible criminal prosecution for war crimes after the war.

Abandoned by the Hungarians in whom they had put their trust, the leaders of the Jewish community felt compelled to enter into negotiations with the SS. These proved basically fruitless, ending with the rescue of a limited number of Jews. The Jewish negotiators had hoped to drag out the discussions in a desperate effort to win the "race for time," pinning their hopes on the swift arrival

---

1. Randolph L. Braham, *The Politics of Genocide: The Holocaust in Hungary* (New York: Columbia University Press, 1981), 225–26.

of the liberating Soviet forces. The SS negotiators were fully aware of this tactic and played along. By negotiating and freeing a limited number of Jews, they would pocket a large amount of cash and valuables and lull the Jewish masses into submission, distracting their attention from the possibility of resistance. The SS held all the trump cards and continued to "negotiate" while proceeding with the implementation of the "Final Solution" according to a master plan they worked out in cooperation with their Hungarian accomplices.

The master plan called for the implementation of the "Final Solution" in Hungary in two distinct phases, the first lasting fifty-four days, the second fifty-six days. During the first phase, lasting from the March 22 appointment of the Sztójay government until May 15, the victims were subjected to an avalanche of anti-Jewish laws and decrees. They were totally isolated; they were deprived of their right to travel and to own or use any means of transportation and communication; they were forced to wear the yellow star and robbed of the remnant of their property. Then they were rounded up, placed into ghettos, and concentrated in entrainment centers. Few, if any, of the Jews had an inkling of the ultimate fate awaiting them. During the second phase, lasting from May 15 through July 9, approximately 440,000 of the Jews of Hungary were deported, more than 420,000 to Auschwitz-Birkenau, where most of them were murdered soon after their arrival. By July 9, when Horthy's decision three days earlier to halt the deportations took effect, all of Hungary (with the notable exception of Budapest) had become *judenrein*. By the end of the war, the Jews of Hungary had suffered nearly 560,000 fatalities, approximately 70 percent of its pre-occupation total.

The Holocaust brought an end to the once flourishing Jewish community of Hungary. Proud and overwhelmingly patriotic since their emancipation in 1867, the Jews played an important role in the advancement of the national interests and modernization of Hungary. They remained faithful and loyal to the Magyar cause even during the counterrevolutionary Horthy era. Partially because of this and partially because of the barbarity and speed with which the Jews of Hungary were destroyed on the eve of Allied victory, the Hungarian chapter of the Holocaust emerged as controversial in the history of the catastrophe that befell the Jews of Europe during the Nazi era. This is reflected not only in the large number of bibliographical references to scholarly and literary accounts but also in the many documentary collections published during the postwar era.[2]

---

2. See, e.g., Randolph L. Braham, ed., *Bibliography of the Holocaust in Hungary* (Boulder, CO: Social Science Monographs, 2011), with 934 pages and 5,685 references.

The first documentary collections on the Holocaust in Hungary were published in 1946, based on the documents the Hungarian Ministry of Foreign Affairs submitted to the Peace Conference in Paris. The communist regime that came to power two years later followed the leadership of the Soviet Union and sank the "Jewish question" and the issue of the Holocaust into the Orwellian black hole of history. The campaign in Hungary was somewhat less intensive, possibly because of the relatively large number of Jewish survivors still living in Budapest, among them a considerable number of professionals, including well-known historians and archivists. These managed, the prohibitions notwithstanding, to publish a relatively large number of highly valuable collections of documents relating to the Holocaust.[3]

This new source volume, *The Holocaust in Hungary: Evolution of a Genocide*, is an invaluable addition to the documentation of the catastrophe that befell Hungarian Jewry. Part of the *Documenting Life and Destruction* series, edited by Jürgen Matthäus, a highly respected member of the staff of the Center for Advanced Holocaust Studies (CAHS) of the United States Holocaust Memorial Museum, the volume is organized in ten chapters with documents covering all aspects of the Hungarian facet of the Holocaust, including the prewar and postwar periods. They range from those relating to violations of the rule of law and the spread of the scourge of venomous antisemitism to those dealing with the many problems confronting the surviving Jewish communities after the war. The authors of the volume—Zoltán Vági, László Csősz, and Gábor Kádár—are recognized experts on the Holocaust in Hungary and the authors of several seminal works. They are among the best of the new generation of Hungarian historians. With the publication of this sourcebook, CAHS director Paul Shapiro and the editor and authors have made an invaluable contribution to the documentation of the Holocaust in Hungary. This volume surely will be identified as an indispensable sourcebook for interested scholars and laypersons alike.

Randolph L. Braham
Distinguished Professor Emeritus
Graduate Center of the City University of New York

---

3. Ibid. See esp. references 2655–70.

# Acknowledgments

THIS VOLUME is the product of several years of hard work, and we would like to dedicate it to our daughters: Lea, Juli, and Nóra. While we spent countless hours researching and writing, the amazing women living with us were always there for us and stepped into the breach in both work and family obligations. We would like to thank them for their endless care, love, and patience. Mariann, Hajni, Christine: we could not have done it without you. We are grateful to the people without whose assistance and wisdom it would have been impossible to finish this volume. We are deeply indebted to Professor Randolph L. Braham (Graduate Center of the City University of New York) and Professor István Deák (Columbia University, New York), two world-renowned scholars of the Holocaust and 19–20th century Hungary, for great conversations, continuous guidance, and their personal and professional support. Special thanks go to the chief archivist of the Hungarian Jewish Archives, Zsuzsanna Toronyi, for her friendship and backing, no matter how complicated our inquiries and requests. We received great ideas from Ágnes Peresztegi, and Brigitta Prukner who revised our Hungarian texts. In the difficult phases of research and writing, we could always count on the kindness and problem-solving capabilities of Mariann Szeleczky. We would like to thank László Karsai and Judit Molnár for their many years of support and for the documents we have obtained from them.

For their support, we would like to thank the J. and O. Winter Fund, headed by Professor Braham, and the Memorial Foundation for Jewish Culture and its executive vice president, Jerry Hochbaum. We deeply appreciate the work of archivists and librarians, whose assistance has been and remains of vital importance. We felt as if we could always turn for help to Béla Sarusi Kiss and Csaba Fehér (Budapest Municipal Archives), Kálmán Radics and Mrs. Katalin Hajdu (Hajdú-Bihar County Archives), Géza Cseh and Mihály Szikszai (Jász-Nagykun-Szolnok Archives), Attila Seres (Hungarian National Archives), Árpád Tyekvicska and Zsolt Galcsik (Nógrád County Archives), Ernő Csekő (Győr-Moson-Sopron County Archives), and Pál Héjjas (Pest County Archives). We are grateful to Fruma Mohrer, chief archivist of the YIVO Institute for Jewish Research (New York City), for her kindness and help. We are also indebted to the chief archivist of the Stutthof Museum in Sztutowo (Poland), Danuta Drywa, and the scholars and leaders of the Auschwitz-Birkenau State Museum (Poland), Piotr Setkiewicz and Wojciech Plosa, for allowing us to conduct unhindered research in their archives.

The United States Holocaust Memorial Museum has long bolstered our professional careers. It is an honor that all three of us have been visiting fellows at that institution's Center for Advanced Holocaust Studies (CAHS). We are grateful to CAHS director Paul Shapiro and to Radu Ioanid, director of International Archival Programs. While researching in the USHMM archives and library, we could always count on the outstanding experts who work there. We were assisted on numerous occasions by our good friend, now retired archivist Ferenc Katona. We were also helped by Michlean Amir, Henry Mayer, Vincent Slatt, Ronald Coleman, and Steven Kanaley. We also would like to thank other staff of the USHMM's Library, Archives, Photo Archives, and Art and Artifacts Section, particularly Brad Bauer, Judith Cohen, Rebecca Erbelding, Nancy Hartman, Megan Lewis, Teresa Pollin, Susan Snyder, Anatol Steck, and Caroline Waddell. We are immensely thankful to our colleagues at CAHS who patiently read and corrected previous versions of this manuscript. Grateful acknowledgments are due to series editor and director of applied research, Jürgen Matthäus, and contributing editor, Jan Lambertz, for their tenacity and valuable contributions. We are also thankful to Mel Hecker, Emil Kerenji, Michael Gelb, Greg Wilkowski, Kathryn Cornelius, Holly Robertson, and Ryan Farrell for their tireless efforts to improve this text. Gwen Sherman and Wrenetta Richards provided vital administrative and other assistance. This publication has been supported in part by grants from the Conference on Jewish Material Claims Against Germany, the Tziporah Wiesel Fund, the William S. and Ina Levine Foundation, the Fisch Foundation, and Dr. Alfred Munzer and Mr. Joel Wind, for which we are grateful. At AltaMira Press we would like to thank Marissa Parks, Elaine McGarraugh, and Jennifer Kelland for their dedication to the project. We are grateful to the members of the USHMM's Academic Committee for their ongoing support, especially Professor Braham, the first and foremost scholar on this topic. We also greatly appreciate the work of Béla Nagy, Associate Research Fellow at the Institute of History of the Hungarian Academy of Science, who developed the maps used in the Introduction. Finally, thanks go to Holly Case (Ithaca), Tim Cole (Bristol), and Paul Hanebrink (New Brunswick) for their constructive comments and suggestions on an earlier draft of this book.

# INTRODUCTION
## Zoltán Vági and Gábor Kádár
### with contributions by László Csősz

## THE HOLOCAUST IN HUNGARY

In 1939 more than 10 million Jews lived in Europe. Over the next four years, the Nazis and their collaborators murdered over 4 million of them. In the Baltic states, the Ukraine, and Belarus and throughout the occupied Russian territories, *Einsatzgruppen* had slaughtered the majority of the Jewish population by 1942. The annihilation of 3 million Polish Jews was practically complete. Only a few hundred thousand slave laborers remained alive, languishing in labor camps and ghettos. In Axis-dominated western Europe, the size of the Jewish populations had significantly dwindled as a result of deportations to "the East." Southeastern Europe had been equally hard hit. After murdering about 250,000 people in the regions (re)taken from the Soviet Union, the Romanian government refused to deport Jews living within its original borders in 1942, as did Bulgaria. Beginning in March 1942, Slovakia sent fifty-eight thousand Jews to various extermination camps, but the transports were stopped that autumn. The Jews of Thessaloniki were deported in 1943, while German units and local regimes had killed off the Jewish communities in Serbia and Croatia even earlier. In the European countries allied with or controlled by the Nazis, one last major Jewish community had survived the war's first four and a half years almost entirely unharmed: the one in Hungary.

On March 19, 1944, however, the Germans occupied the country. The events of the following months were in many ways unique in the history of the Holocaust. In what amounted to a virtual blitzkrieg against the Hungarian

Jews, many were now murdered with unprecedented speed and efficiency. Nowhere else was the complete disenfranchisement and isolation of Jews carried out with greater speed. Forcing Jews to wear the yellow star and isolating and deporting them had taken years, even in Germany. After arriving in Budapest, fifty-six days (March 20–May 15) were sufficient for all such preparations for **Sondereinsatzkommando Eichmann** (SEK). Never before had this many people been deported this quickly. Years had not sufficed to fully complete the anti-Jewish "cleansing campaign" in France, the Netherlands, or Poland. In Hungary it took only another fifty-six days (from May 15 to July 9) to deport all the Jews from the country, except for the capital. For the first time, **Adolf Eichmann** directed an *Aktion* in the field. He hoped to beat the unofficial "record" set by SS-Major Hermann Höfle, who had deported Warsaw's Jews to Treblinka in fifty-three days in 1942.[1] Despite the approaching front lines and with just a handful of men assisting him, Eichmann sent off some 150 trains with 437,402 Jews on board in less than two months. Apart from a fraction of this number, about fifteen thousand individuals, all of them arrived at Auschwitz.

The many postwar accounts regarding Auschwitz differ vastly and include memories of survivors of various religions, nationalities, and ideological backgrounds, recollections of the camp's former commander, and testimonies of its SS officers.[2] But all share the assessment that Auschwitz experienced its most lethal days during the summer of 1944. According to Professor Raul Hilberg, "Hungary was going to lift Auschwitz to the top" among the camps.[3] The Birkenau "Death Gate" and "**Jewish ramp**" became widely known, universal symbols. They would certainly be less infamous if the unending stream of cattle cars carrying Hungarian Jews had not arrived there. The following numbers clearly illustrate the magnitude of the mass murder: Between 1940 and 1945, altogether 1.3 million people were deported to the Auschwitz complex, among

---

1. Testimony of Dieter Wisliceny. Quoted in Jenő Lévai, "The Hungarian Deportations in the Light of the Eichmann Trial," *YVS* 5 (1964): 84.
2. Compare Wiesław Kiełar, *Anus Mundi: Five Years in Auschwitz* (London: Allen Lane, 1981), 263; Hermann Langbein, *People in Auschwitz* (Chapel Hill: University of North Carolina Press in association with the USHMM, 2004), 48; Rudolf Höss, *Death Dealer: The Memoirs of the SS Kommandant at Auschwitz*, ed. Steven Paskuly (New York: Da Capo Press, 1996), 37; Jadwiga Bezwinska and Danuta Czech, eds., *KL Auschwitz Seen by the SS: Höss, Broad, Kremer*, 2nd rev. ed. (Oświęcim: Auschwitz-Birkenau State Museum, 1978).
3. Raul Hilberg, "Auschwitz and the 'Final Solution,'" in *Anatomy of the Auschwitz Death Camp*, ed. Yisrael Gutman and Michael Berenbaum (Bloomington: Indiana University Press in association with the USHMM, 1998), 88.

them 1.1 million Jews. Most of them (430,000) came from Hungary.[4] During the fifty-six months of Auschwitz's existence, the Nazis killed about 1.1 million people there; among them were 1 million Jews, 70,000 to 75,000 Polish gentiles, 21,000 Roma, 15,000 Soviet prisoners of war, and 15,000 members of the resistance, common criminals, people with mental disabilities, and gay men. One out of three victims arrived from Hungary over a period of just fifty-six days during the spring and summer of 1944. There are no graves in Birkenau. Still, this site is the largest cemetery in Hungarian history.

Throughout Europe, hundreds of thousands of collaborators supported the Nazis' persecution of Jews. Some were rabid antisemites, others just sought material advantages, and many persecuted the Jews simply by performing their administrative jobs. Although their motivations varied, one thing is certain: without their cooperation and knowledge of local areas, the "Final Solution" would have been far less deadly. In the Netherlands and Vichy France, the Nazis could count on help from the public administration and police when it came to implementing anti-Jewish laws, including arresting and deporting Jews. In Slovakia, Norway, and Italy, mainly the local extremist parties and their militias led the way in persecuting their Jewish compatriots. The Croatian Ustaše murdered Jews and Roma without any substantive German assistance. In the occupied territories, the Romanian army and **gendarmerie** killed about a quarter million Jews within their own sphere of control. Ukrainian SS guards staffed the extermination camps at Treblinka, Sobibór, and Bełżec, while in the Ukraine and the Baltic region thousands of local residents participated in pogroms or *Einsatzgruppen* mass murders.

Enthusiastic and efficient Hungarian support was essential for Eichmann, who arrived in Budapest without a complete and detailed plan for deporting the Jews. If the Hungarians had shown some resistance or demonstrated less willingness to collaborate, hundreds of thousands of people would have survived. The success of the Nazi plans required the intensive cooperation of the Ministry of the Interior, primarily Secretary of State **László Endre**.[5] As we shall see, the deportation of all Hungarian Jews resulted from a multiphase decision-making process. The Endre-Eichmann duo played a decisive role in making this

---

4. For the numbers of deportees from other countries, see Franciszek Piper, *Die Zahl der Opfer von Auschwitz* (Oświęcim: Staatliches Museum in Oświęcim-Brzezinka, 1993); Franciszek Piper, *Auschwitz, 1940–1945: Central Issues in the History of the Camp* (Oświęcim: Auschwitz-Birkenau State Museum), 3:11–12.

5. The Hungarian word *államtitkár* translates as "secretary of state," but the meaning has nothing to do with the U.S. cabinet position of the same name. *Államtitkár* is virtually a deputy minister, the second-ranking member of the staff of the ministry.

procedure more dynamic. They embodied perfectly the two forces that caused the deaths of almost two-thirds of the Hungarian Jews. One was the murderous Nazi antisemitism that created and operated the infrastructure of the Holocaust. The other was the specifically Hungarian-grown, race-protectionist, anti-Jewish platform that emerged at the turn of the century and came to dominate the country a few decades later. The combination of these two factors sealed the victims' fate.

Between 1941 and 1945 more than half a million Hungarian Jews were murdered. The Holocaust in Hungary was not only the final major chapter of the Nazi genocide but also the peak of its evolution. This volume presents selected sources and analyses on how this genocide came about, what drove it, and what it meant for those who were targeted. As with other volumes in this series, this book does not aim to be comprehensive; instead, it is intended to stimulate further research. Before we delve deeper into the documentation and the context within which it emerged, the following pages offer some basic background information to give readers a better understanding of this crucial phase in Holocaust and Hungarian history.

## ORIGINS OF A DIVERSE COMMUNITY

Jews first appeared in the area that would later become Hungary during the first centuries CE. Over the next one and a half millennia, however, they disappeared from the region from time to time. Thus, at the brink of the Holocaust, the majority of Jewish families living in Hungary had been in the country no longer than 100 to 150 years. Their ancestors arrived during the eighteenth and nineteenth centuries from three regions: eastern Austria and Vienna, Moravia, and Poland.[6]

Between 1869 and 1910, the Israelite population grew by 78 percent. (The term "Israelite" in this volume refers to Jews whose professed religion was Judaism, as opposed to those following Christianity. This differentiation is used widely in the targeted era of this work, especially by official statistics.) The wave of immigration, mainly a result of the extreme poverty in Galicia and the pogroms following the 1846 peasants' uprising in Poland, reached its peak between 1830 and 1870. Afterwards, the influx rate declined significantly.

---

6. About the history of the Jews in Hungary in the eighteenth and nineteenth centuries, see Géza Komoróczy, *A zsidók története Magyarországon* (Pozsony: Kalligram, 2012), 1:41–1188, 2:13–321.

Moreover, the rate of emigration exceeded the waning immigration rate.[7] From the last third of the nineteenth century, the dynamic rise in the Jewish population was primarily due to favorable demographics: high birthrates and decreasing mortality, especially in urban communities. From the early 1900s onward, however, the Jews' natural reproduction parameters showed a sharp decline.[8]

The economic strategies of the Hungarian Jews were not very different from those of other communities in the region. Premodern feudalism excluded them from land ownership and farming. They were therefore confined to large-scale trading and to financial transactions. This sector demanded a complex knowledge of market relations, flexibility, and employment of mobile capital strategies. Many ended up in the commercial and financial sectors, as well as in independent intellectual professions. In 1900, when Jews made up 5 percent of the Hungarian population, 57.9 percent of trade and bank employees, 48.3 percent of physicians, 34.1 percent of lawyers, and 23.8 percent of private engineers were Israelites. Moreover these figures included only those following the Jewish religion (Israelites) and therefore do not encompass Christians of Jewish origin.[9]

Increasingly broad layers of Jews became diligent actors and clear winners of capitalism. The government acted with goodwill toward them. This attitude was based on clear political consideration: the Hungarian Kingdom was such a multiethnic empire that the majority of its population was not even Hungarian. It is telling that in 1910, in forty of the seventy-one **counties**, Magyars constituted only a minority, while Romanians, Slovaks, Croats, or Germans (singly or together) exceeded them in number. Leading politicians hoped that through the Magyarization of hundreds of thousands of Jews, Hungarians could finally become the majority. By and large it meant that Jews would become Hungarian in language, culture, and identity and thereby secure a majority to the Hungarians. In return, they would receive free access to social, economic,

---

7. This was first noted by the antisemitic statistician Alajos Kovács, who was acknowledging his own research results with disappointment. Alajos Kovács, *A zsidóság térfoglalása Magyarországon* (Budapest: n.p., 1922). On this topic, see also László Varga, "Zsidó bevándorlás Magyarországon," *Századok* 1 (1992).

8. Yehuda Don and George Magos, "A magyarországi zsidóság demográfiai fejlődése," *Történelmi Szemle* 28 (1985): 439–41.

9. László Katus, "The Occupational Structure of Hungarian Jewry in the Eighteenth and Twentieth Centuries," in *Jews in the Hungarian Economy, 1760–1945. Studies Dedicated to Moshe Carmilly-Weinberger on His Eightieth Birthday*, ed. Michael K. Silber (Jerusalem: Magnes Press–Hebrew University, 1992), 102.

and cultural positions.[10] Many adopted the Hungarian language sooner and more widely than other minorities. By 1910, 77 percent of the entire Jewish population considered Hungarian their mother tongue.[11] Higher education played a key role in the marked social mobility of the Jews. Between 1867 and 1914, the ratio of Israelites in Hungarian-language secondary schools went up by 125 percent. In higher education this figure was 190 percent.[12] Another major path to integration was the army. Unlike in Russia or Germany, Jews were significantly overrepresented (18.7 percent) among officers of the joint Austro-Hungarian army.[13]

Many Jews stepping into the political and cultural arena adhered to the ideology of acculturation. Unlike in Poland and Romania, there were no Jewish parties or political movements organized on an ethnic-religious basis in Hungary. In the early 1900s Hungarians of the Jewish religion and/or ancestry constituted 20 to 25 percent of the members of parliament, and many of them (predominantly converts) reached high positions such as minister, state secretary, and mayor of Budapest.[14] On the other hand, few Jews went as far as complete assimilation: between 1896 and 1917 only around 1–1.5 percent of the Israelite population converted to Christianity.

After 1869, three liturgical-organizational branches emerged among the Jews: the pro-modernization **Neologue**, the anti-Reform **Orthodox**, and the **Status Quo Ante** communities. The state recognition of this official "schism" was a unique phenomenon in European Jewish history.

## ANTISEMITISM

Many were irritated by the rise of the Jews. After the 1848 Revolution against the Habsburgs, there were riots in over thirty towns in March and April: Jews were beaten or even killed, their shops and houses looted. Thousands, among them Hungarians, Germans, and Slovaks, participated in these atrocities and demanded expulsion of the Jews. The new, liberal government took

---

10. See, e.g., Viktor Karády, *Önazonosítás, sorsválasztás. A zsidó csoportazonosság történelmi alakváltozásai Magyarországon* (Budapest: Új Mandátum, 2001), 40–49.

11. Gyula Zeke, "Statisztikai mellékletek (1735–1949)," in *Hét évtized a hazai zsidóság életében I. rész*, ed. L. Ferenc Lendvai, Aniko Sohár, and Pál Horváth (Budapest: MTA Filozófiai Intézet, 1990), 190.

12. Ignác Romsics, *Magyarország története a XX. században* (Budapest: Osiris, 1999), 58.

13. István Deák, *Volt egyszer egy tisztikar. A Habsburg-monarchia katonatisztjeinek társadalmi és politikai története, 1848–1918* (Budapest: Gondolat, 1993), 219.

14. Romsics, *Magyarország története a XX. században*, 58.

steps to protect the Jews: government commissioners were sent and the military restored order.¹⁵ Despite the preceding atrocities, thousands of Jews fought in the Hungarian army during the upcoming war of independence against the Habsburgs and the invading Russians. To honor their contribution, in the last days of the uprising, the parliament eventually passed the law on emancipation on July 28, 1849. Because the Hungarians surrendered two weeks later, it did not come into effect and remained a symbolic gesture. After bloody retaliation, the years of absolutism descended on non-Jews and Jews alike.

The so-called Compromise of 1867 created a dual monarchy. The states of Austria and Hungary became allied under the same ruler, with joint ministries of defense, finance, and foreign affairs. The Austro-Hungarian monarchy was born with Emperor (in Hungary, King) Franz Joseph on the throne. That same year, the Hungarian parliament decided to codify the emancipation of the Jews. Eventually, after lengthy political and public debates, Act XLII of 1895 abolished all differences in the legal status of Jews and Christians. The civil and religious emancipation of the Jews was achieved in all respects.¹⁶

But as in France and Germany, the economic crisis of 1873 stirred up anti-Jewish sentiments in Hungary. In April 1875, Member of Parliament Győző Istóczy was already speaking about a worldwide Jewish conspiracy that threatened the country. He urged the government to halt the policy of emancipation. The prime minister rejected this idea as one that "would offend humanism, civilization, and justice." In 1878 Istóczy demanded the departure of Jews from Hungary and "a recreation of the Jewish state in Palestine."¹⁷

Anti-Jewish sentiments skyrocketed between 1882 and 1884 when, in the wake of the Tiszaeszlár blood libel case, a new wave of pogroms swept across the country. A little Christian girl went missing in this small eastern Hungarian village. In a rekindling of the old scapegoating of the Middle Ages, the Jews were accused of killing her and using her blood for their rituals. The defendants were acquitted in court, and the case was celebrated as a victory of reason over archaic superstition and antisemitism. However, Tiszaeszlár unleashed massive violence. Mobs in over two hundred cities and villages around the country attacked Jews and their property. In some counties civic rule was suspended. Troops moved in, and martial law was declared to stop the rampage. In Budapest the police

---

15. Béla Bernstein, *A negyvennyolcas magyar szabadságharc és a zsidók*, 3rd ed. (Budapest: Múlt és Jövő Kiadó, 1998), 25–54.

16. Act XLII of 1895 on the Israelite religion. Kálmán Csiky et al., eds., *Magyar Törvénytár. 1894–1895. évi törvényczikkek* (Budapest: Franklin, 1897), 305–6.

17. For the original script of these speeches, see *Istóczy Győző országgyűlési beszédei, indítványai és törvényjavaslatai 1872–1896* (Budapest: n.p., 1904), 1–16, 42–63.

fought a seven-day battle (August 7–13, 1883) with rioters who raided the Jewish shops and assaulted people. Istóczy took advantage of the surge in anti-Jewish passions and in 1883 established the National Antisemitic Party. This political formation managed to get seventeen nominees into parliament during elections the following year, but it was soon marginalized and lost its place in the legislature.[18]

At the turn of the nineteenth and twentieth centuries, a new form of political antisemitism emerged, integrating anticapitalist frustrations, xenophobic hatred, and religious anti-Judaism rooted in ancient superstitions. Politicians and journalists formulated social demands in opposition to Jewish capital. They defined the dissonances in society and the economy as a purely "Jewish" phenomena. The complete association of capitalism with the Jews proved to be the origins of a tragic mind-set. Otherwise progressive programs and concepts that recognized the need for social reforms started from the false axiom that only through anti-Jewish policies could the living conditions of the Hungarian population be improved. In addition, as the cornerstone for racial nationalism, Hungarian "Turanism" came into being. This pseudoscientific ideology strove to prove the existence and superiority of a unified Hungarian "race" and therefore inevitably incorporated an anti-Jewish aspect. In 1917, headed by the renowned scholar of geography, Count **Pál Teleki**, the Hungarian Racial Hygiene and Population Policy Association was established. It specialized in eugenics and "racial breeding."[19]

## THE REVOLUTIONS OF 1918–1919

Despite the strengthening of antisemitism, the situation of Jews during the dual monarchy era was still favorable. Unlike in Russia, with its pogroms, or Austria, with the rule of Vienna's antisemitic mayor Karl Lueger (a decisive role model for Adolf Hitler), antisemitism quite remarkably did not gain a foothold in Hungary's mainstream politics for a long time.

The defeat in World War I and the independence movements of various nationalities led to the dismantling of the Austro-Hungarian monarchy.

---

18. Jacob Katz, *From Prejudice to Destruction: Anti-Semitism, 1700–1933* (Cambridge, MA: Harvard University Press, 1980), 273–80.

19. János Gyurgyák, *A zsidókérdés Magyarországon* (Budapest: Osiris, 2001), 371–76, and Péter Bihari, *Lövészárkok a hátországban: középosztály, zsidókérdés, antiszemitizmus az első világháború Magyarországán* (Budapest: Napvilág, 2008), 184. Teleki later served as two-time prime minister in the interwar period and introduced anti-Jewish laws during both of his terms.

In October 1918, a revolution broke out in Budapest. Public order deteriorated again, and as if on schedule, this led to renewed anti-Jewish atrocities. In Kiskunfélegyháza, the party turned to bloodshed as people celebrated the end of the war in the streets. Drunken soldiers and civilians looted Jewish shops and houses. Some people, including women, were killed or injured. In Gyöngyös, locals and a drunken hussar company beat up several passersby and burglarized Jewish shops. In Bököny, two Jewish shopkeepers were beaten to death; in Tótkomlós, a rabbi was shot.[20]

These and other pogrom-like atrocities were by no means isolated incidents. The rationales varied, but the main features remained the same. The riots were accompanied by looting of Jewish homes and shops, and Jews were always among the victims of physical violence. According to data by Jewish organizations, 6,206 Jews were beaten and/or robbed in the space of a few months.[21] In many cases external military and policing assistance was needed to restore order.

In March 1919, Hungary became a communist dictatorship. Approximately 60 percent of the Hungarian Soviet Republic's leaders were Jewish by religion or ancestry. The internationalism of leftist ideologies lured them into renouncing their Jewish identity. They thought that in the new proletariat state their "class consciousness" would matter and not their ancestry, which they considered a burdensome heritage. Béla Kun, a leader of the Hungarian Soviet Republic, whom subsequent antisemitic propaganda portrayed as the embodiment of the "Jewish communist" stereotype, formulated this mind-set most succinctly: "My father was a Jew, but I did not remain a Jew, because I became a socialist, a communist!"[22] He and his communist leadership regarded as their archenemies not only the aristocrats but also the capitalists, industrialists, and bourgeoisie. Thus the communist "**Red Terror**" struck Jews and non-Jews alike. Some were arrested; others were executed. Jews were significantly overrepresented among the victims of the communist regime. Still, many Christians interpreted the communist dictatorship as simply a Jewish uprising.

---

20. For these incidents, see Tibor Iványosi-Szabó, ed., *Olvasókönyv Kiskunfélegyháza történetéhez* (Kecskemét: n.p., 1985), 327–47; Ágnes Orbánné Szegő, "A gyöngyösi zsidóság története a középkortól a holokausztig," in *Tanulmányok a holokausztról II*, ed. Randolph L. Braham (Budapest: Balassi, 2002), 295.

21. János Pelle, *A gyűlölet vetése. A zsidótörvények és a magyar közvélemény 1938–1944* (Budapest: Európa, 2001), 20.

22. Gyurgyák, *A zsidókérdés Magyarországon*, 98–103.

## THE HORTHY REGIME AND TRIANON

In the summer of 1919, Bolshevik rule collapsed. With the Entente's permission, the last commander of the Austro-Hungarian navy, Admiral **Miklós Horthy,** led his antirevolutionist troops into Budapest. Left on the scene without a serious rival, he was elected regent by the parliament on March 1, 1920. The emerging regime was a multiparty parliamentary system with strong autocratic features. The regent was elected for an indefinite period, the press was censured, and open elections (that is, nonsecret voting) were introduced in the provinces.[23]

A new wave of violence, known as the "**White Terror**," accompanied Horthy's seizure of power. Under the pretext of avenging "Jewish" Bolshevik rule, his paramilitary units killed people by the hundreds. Murders, lynchings, and torture took place at dozens of locations. In many cases, the local gentile population initiated pogroms. In Celldömölk, four Jews were murdered; in Diszel, nine. In Rácalmás-Kulcs, a Jew was tied to the tail of a horse, which then ran through the streets. Armed peasants dragged off an epileptic war veteran and his wife. In Tapolca in late August 1919, soldiers, railway workers, local residents, peasants, and even women and children attacked Jews. In Mezőszentgyörgy, Jews were given twelve hours to leave for Palestine. In Gyöngyös, in early 1920, they were attacked by a mob of two thousand.[24] Eventually, in order to consolidate his power, Horthy disbanded these units and restricted anti-Jewish violence. This wave of pogroms was the fourth since 1848 in a series of antisemitic riots spreading to a significant part of the country. This was the first time, however, that the authorities had not stepped up to protect the Jews. On the contrary, they demonstrated explicit hostility toward them.

Although the violence quieted down, the social tensions remained following the signing of the **Trianon Peace Treaty** in June 1920. The accord reduced the country's territory by two-thirds (from 280,000 square kilometers [109,000 square miles] down to 93,000 square kilometers [36,000 square miles]). Hungary's population shrank from more than 18 million to under 8 million. Suddenly 3.2 million Hungarians found themselves in Czechoslovakia, Romania, and the Kingdom of Serbs, Croats, and Slovenes (later Yugoslavia). Even the newborn Republic of Austria, another successor state of the

---

23. For a detailed description of the political system between the two world wars, see Levente Püski, *A Horthy-rendszer* (Budapest: Pannonica, 2006).

24. For thorough documentation on the antisemitic atrocities in 1919–1920, see HJA, RG PIH I-E, box B 10/3.

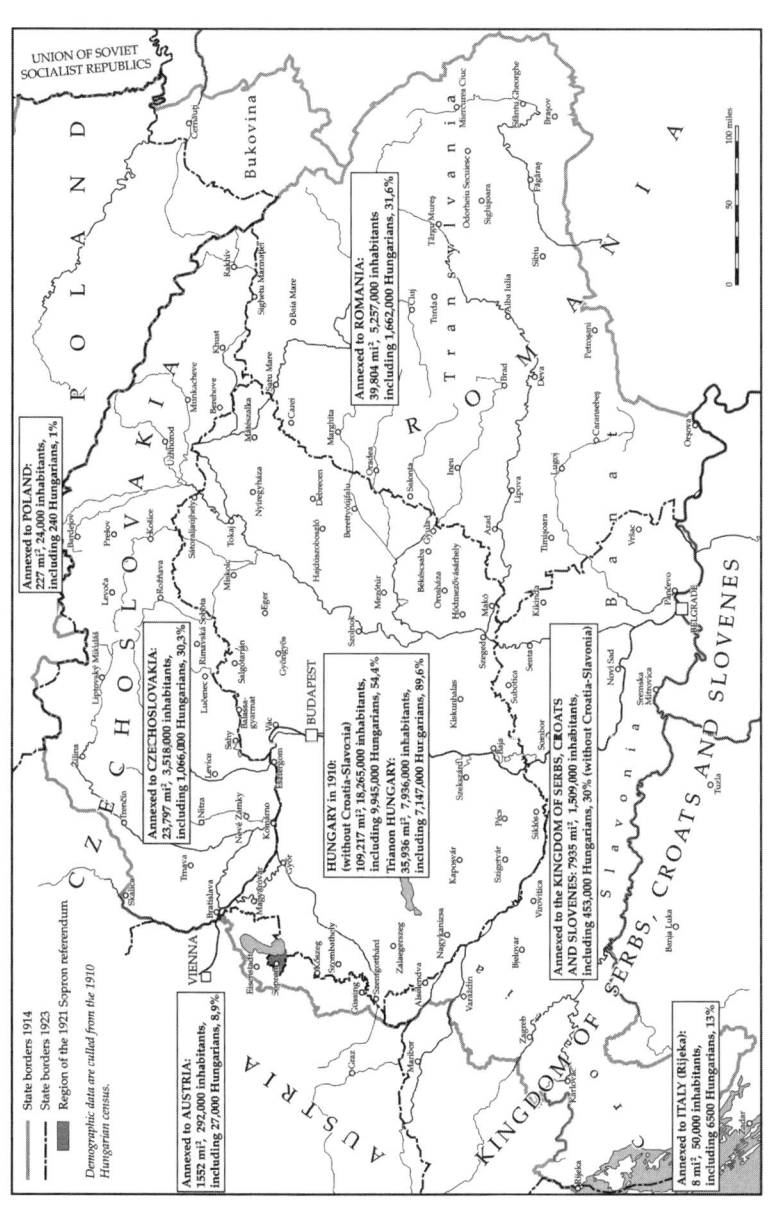

Map 1. The Consequences of the 1920 Trianon Peace Treaty
For a closer look at this map, go to: rowman.com/isbn/9780759121980.

Austro-Hungarian Empire, gained some Hungarian territories, as did Poland, a nation with traditionally friendly ties to Hungary. The new borders cut through homogenous ethnic communities and economically unified territories. They tore Hungary's transportation infrastructure in half and cut the country off from several of its traditional markets and cultural centers. In the wake of the treaty, basically one goal drove Hungarian internal and foreign policy for the next two decades: to nullify or at least alter Trianon.

## HUNGARY IN THE POST–WORLD WAR I ERA

In 1920, Hungary was home to less than half a million Israelites. As a consequence of the Trianon Peace Treaty, the demographic profile of the community changed. The treaty had left over half of Hungary's Jews outside the new country's borders, but their proportion within the population grew (see table 2, p. 368). Modernized, Hungarian-speaking Neologues became the majority. Jews were transformed into an urban community; over 40 percent lived in Budapest.[25] The Jewish population grew older on average, and its birthrate declined. Between 1920 and 1941, due to this demographic pattern, emigration (especially during the height of the antisemitic wave of the early 1920s), and the pressure to assimilate (including conversion to Christianity and entering into mixed marriages), the Israelite population shrank by almost seventy-three thousand people (15 percent).[26]

The Horthy regime identified itself as the antithesis to the revolutions, a "Christian" (not Jewish), national, and counterrevolutionary form of government. The ideology of the new system rested on antiliberalism, anti-bolshevism, and antisemitism. New right-wing organizations took root, infiltrating politics with their anti-Jewish agendas. One of the most important, the Association of Awakening Hungarians (ÉME), had a membership of several hundred thousand. At its general assembly on November 30, 1919, the ÉME demanded that European Jews be resettled elsewhere. According to estimates, one-fourth to one-third of the members of parliament belonged to ÉME by the early 1920s. At that time, even though outright mob violence against Jews was suppressed, antisemitism had become

---

25. Kovács, *A zsidóság térfoglalása Magyarországon*. See also Varga, "Zsidó bevándorlás Magyarországon," 60–61; László Gonda, *A zsidóság Magyarországon, 1526–1945* (Budapest: Századvég, 1992), 198–99.

26. Don and Magos, "A magyarországi zsidóság demográfiai fejlődése," 459.

firmly entrenched in state politics[27]; before long it was manifested in discriminatory legislation. Since the country, greatly reduced in size, needed far fewer doctors, engineers, and officials—and tens of thousands of now jobless officials had flooded in from the lost territories—the new government of Count Pál Teleki (founder of the former Hungarian Racial Hygiene and Population Policy Association) decided to cut back the number of intellectuals radically to the detriment of Jews. The general antisemitic mood prevalent in universities also exerted pressure in the political realm. On September 26, 1920, the national assembly passed one of the first anti-Jewish laws of interwar Europe. Act XXV of 1920, the so-called ***numerus clausus*** law, restricted the number of Jews admitted to institutions of higher education,[28] spelling the end of legal equality for Jews in Hungary.

Count **István Bethlen** was appointed prime minister in 1921. He and Regent Horthy soon strove to consolidate the regime. The paramilitary units were disbanded. Those who took their antisemitic rhetoric too far could be held accountable for "incitement against a denomination." By 1923, the situation had largely been normalized, although antisemitic physical assaults (especially at the universities) did not cease entirely. In 1928 (partly due to international pressure), the most discriminatory elements of the *numerus clausus* law were repealed. Bethlen successfully tried to drag Hungary out of political and economic isolation. Through international loans and adequate financial policies, the economy grew steadily and unemployment decreased. According to Bethlen, the "Jewish question" did exist; however, he planned to "solve" it not through negative discrimination against the Jews but rather through favoritism toward the Christian middle class. Horthy and Bethlen tried to normalize relations with the Jews, primarily because they had a profound need for the funds

---

27. For different proposals and about the political debate, see, e.g., Randolph L. Braham, *The Politics of Genocide: The Holocaust in Hungary* (New York: Columbia University Press, 1994), 1:30–31; Jenő Gergely, *Gömbös Gyula. Politikai pályakép* (Budapest: Vince, 2001), 88, 99–101; Gyurgyák, *A zsidókérdés Magyarországon*, 117–23.

28. The percentage of Israelites among university and college students had decreased from over 30 percent before World War I to 10.4 percent already by 1920. Due to the *numerus clausus*, it went down as low as 8 percent by 1927. On the *numerus clausus* and its impact, see Viktor Karády, *Iskolarendszer és felekezeti egyenlőtlenségek Magyarországon (1867–1945). Történeti-szociológiai tanulmányok* (Budapest: Replika Kör, 1997), 235–66; Romsics, *Magyarország története a XX. században*, 138, 180–84; Gyurgyák, *A zsidókérdés Magyarországon*, 117–23; Braham, *The Politics of Genocide*, 1:30–32; Mária M. Kovács, "The 1920 *Numerus Clausus* and Anti-Jewish Legislation after 1938 in Hungary," in *The Holocaust in Hungary: A European Perspective*, ed. Judit Molnár (Budapest: Balassi Kiadó, 2005), 130–42.

and experience of Jewish industrialists (the Weiss, Chorin, Kornfeld, Hatvany-Deutsch, Fellner, Goldberger, and Herzog families, among others). Without the assistance of the leading companies, the country's economic reorganization would have been impossible. But Bethlen was forced to resign in 1931 due to the global economic crisis.

With the start of the Great Depression, unemployment skyrocketed. In some industrial sectors, one in three workers lost his or her job. By 1932, national income had fallen by 44 percent, and industrial production decreased by 37 percent. The Depression pushed the agricultural sector to the verge of bankruptcy. The pauperized rural population's general standard of living decreased by one-third; with 55 to 75 percent of the population living around or under the poverty line, Hungary came to be referred to as "the country of 3 million beggars."[29] The government sought the means to remedy a growing social crisis, while its revenues decreased further and further. Meanwhile, the right-wing extremist opposition put forth a strong sociopolitical agenda that resonated with the public. It arose from the premise that the solution was the state-organized confiscation and wide-scale redistribution of all Jewish wealth. One tragic element of the history of the Horthy era is that social issues were submerged within a radical discourse about the "Jewish question."[30] During the economic crisis, the main question became how to manage growing tensions and needs in a period of reduced financial resources. Since the huge estates of the aristocracy and the church served as an essential base for the regime's feudal-conservative tenor, many on the right saw only one way to reduce social tensions: the expropriation of Jewish wealth.

In 1932 **Gyula Gömbös**, a former right-wing extremist and founder of the ÉME, was appointed prime minister. He stunned his followers and enemies alike when he proclaimed that he had revised his antisemitic worldview. Most likely, behind this sharp change of tone was the recognition that the country could not overcome the economic crisis if it declared war on Jewish industrialists. As an advocate of realpolitik, Gömbös did not want to risk this. Indeed, during his term (1932–1936) no anti-Jewish legislation was enacted.[31]

---

29. See Zsuzsa Ferge, *Fejezetek a magyar szegénypolitika történetéből* (Budapest: Kávé, 1998).

30. On this dichotomy of race protectionism and social policy, see Gábor Kádár and Zoltán Vági, *Hullarablás. A magyar zsidók gazdasági megsemmisítése* (Budapest: Jaffa, 2005), 73–82.

31. On Gömbös's political career, see Gergely, *Gömbös Gyula*, and József Vonyó, *Gömbös Gyula és a jobboldali radikalizmus. Tanulmányok* (Budapest, Pannónia, 2001).

Changes in the international arena during the 1930s also played their part in the country's drift to the right. All political forces and significant social groups supported a revision of the Trianon Peace Treaty in order to regain as many of the lost territories as possible. The rise of the German Nazis and their rejection of the Versailles Peace Treaty engendered a glimmer of hope for changing the situation at last. The positive image of the Third Reich was enhanced by the fact that Germany's economy and culture had a quite strong traditional influence in Hungary. In turn, Hungary's increasing German-Nazi orientation strengthened the extreme right even further. The process gained momentum when Nazi Germany arrived at the Hungarian border in 1938, having swallowed up Austria, and began its military expansion in September 1939.

## REANNEXATIONS AND ANTI-JEWISH LAWS

Between 1938 and 1941, with Italian and German support, Hungary regained about 40 percent of its territories lost after World War I.[32] Horthy owed all his successes to Hitler.

In the two **Vienna Awards**, Berlin put forth decisions that favored Budapest over Czechoslovakia and Romania. Germany's popularity and economic influence were on the rise. In early 1939, Hungary left the League of Nations and entered the Anti-Comintern Pact. In November 1940, Budapest joined the Tripartite Pact between Germany, Italy, and Japan. Eventually, in April 1941, the Hungarian government broke the Treaty of Eternal Friendship signed with Yugoslavia only four months earlier, and its troops marched across the border. Realizing that he could no longer prevent Hungary from entering the war, Prime Minister Pál Teleki (1939–1941) committed suicide. His successor, **László Bárdossy**, declared war on the Soviet Union when the Wehrmacht attacked Stalin's empire in June 1941.

By the late 1930s, increasing demand for "a legal solution to the Jewish question" in the Hungarian political arena tied in with other forms of discrimination. Chapters 1 and 2 address these developments in greater detail. The political leadership, which consisted of committed antisemites but not necessarily Nazis or Nazi supporters, yielded easily to the pressure and enacted the so-called First "Jewish Law" (Act XV of 1938) in May 1938, marking the

---

32. See table 3, p. 369 and map 2, p. xlii. When writing about the territorial expansion of Hungary from 1938 to 1941, we usually use the terms "regain" and "reannexation," since before World War I all these regions belonged to Hungary. Furthermore, these terms best reflect the Hungarian desire to have these areas under its control again—the cornerstone of understanding what happened between the two world wars.

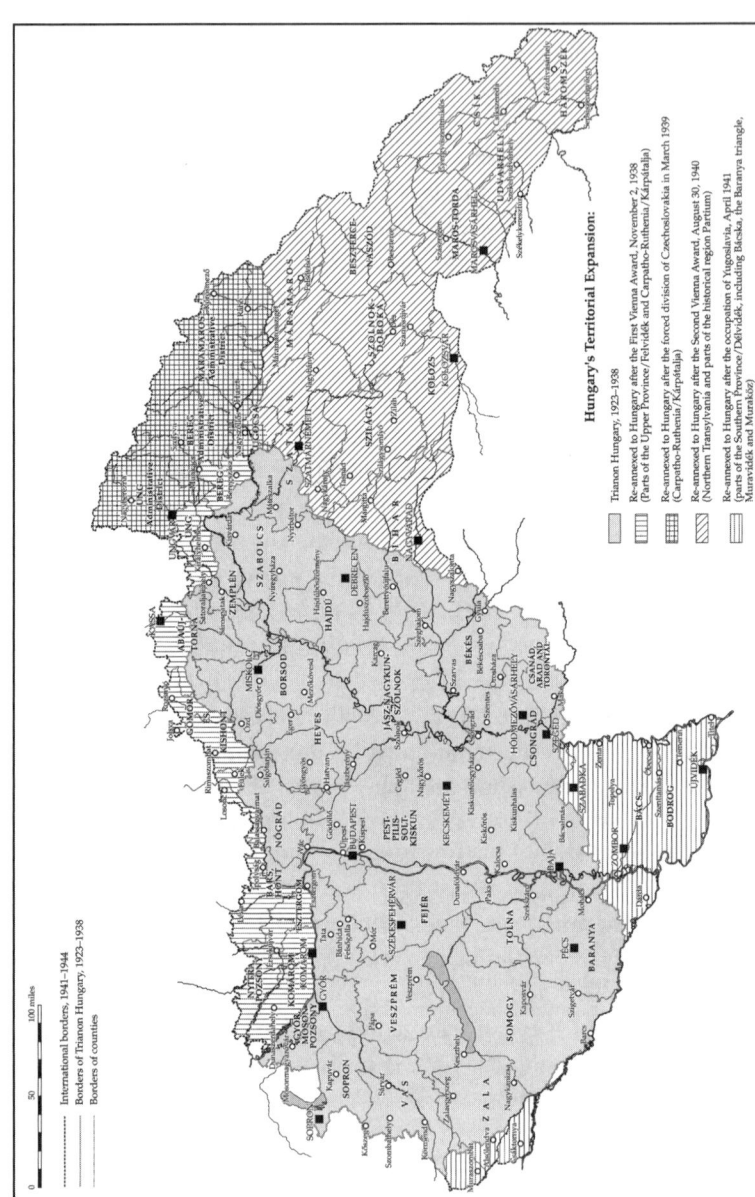

Map 2. Territorial Expansion of Hungary, 1938–1941

For a closer look at this map, go to: rowman.com/isbn/9780759121980.

beginning of a long list of codifications. The law aimed at reducing the proportion of Jews in business and various professions to a mere 20 percent over five years. Between May 1938 and March 1944 (that is, before the German occupation), the government passed twenty-two antisemitic acts. Some were explicitly discriminatory, others only implicitly so. Alongside these, 267 anti-Jewish ministerial and governmental decrees were issued.[33] In 1941, marriages and extramarital sex between Jews and non-Jews were banned. Estimates of the number of jobs lost by Jews by 1943 vary between forty and ninety thousand.[34] For a long time, Nazi Germany did not exert any sort of pressure on Hungary to enact anti-Jewish laws.[35] Antisemitic legislation was the product of an organic, essentially Hungarian development. As the Jews were pushed out of the Hungarian economy, many non-Jews benefitted: they unscrupulously lined their pockets under the cover of such slogans as "social justice" and "the protection of the Christian middle classes." Economic life had everywhere become embroiled in corruption, blackmail, and profiteering.[36]

In the areas occupied from 1938 to 1941, the ever-stricter anti-Jewish policies were implemented in an even more radical form. The army launched a series of operations against the Jews. When Hungarian troops marched into the Upper Province (Felvidék) in 1938, they immediately started to round up Jews. The following year, during the invasion of Carpatho-Ruthenia, they regularly beat up Jews, looted apartments, broke windows of houses, and even commited murders. Jewish firms were kept under strict surveillance; trade licenses were revoked en masse, even if in certain areas this meant severe disturbances in the provision of services and supplies. As Horthy's troops entered Northern Transylvania in 1940, Hungarian-speaking Jews lined the streets waving, throwing flowers to the soldiers. Soon the bitter realization dawned on them that these were not forces of the Austro-Hungarian monarchy, which they had

---

33. For details, see László Karsai, "Anti-Jewish Laws and Decrees in Hungary, 1920–1944," in *The Holocaust in Hungary*, ed. Molnár, 144–48. Besides the decrees published in official bulletins, several confidential decrees were in effect as well.

34. See Yehuda Don, "Economic Implications of the Anti-Jewish Legislation in Hungary," in *Genocide and Rescue: The Holocaust in Hungary, 1944*, ed. David Cesarani (New York: Berg 1997), 59; Ferenc Chorin, "Tanulmányok, cikkek, beszédek, feljegyzések, nyilatkozatok, levelek," in *Az Andrássy úttól a Park Avenue-ig. Fejezetek Chorin Ferenc életéből 1879–1964*, ed. Daisy Strasserné Chorin and András D. Bán (Budapest: Osiris, 1999), 112; Péter Sipos, ed., *Imrédy Béla a vádlottak padján* (Budapest: Osiris–Budapest Főváros Levéltára, 1999), 36.

35. Nathaniel Katzburg, *Zsidópolitika Magyarországon 1919–1943* (Budapest: Bábel, 2002), 194–95.

36. Viktor Karády, "Zsidótörvények és életfeltételek a szociális jelzők tükrében (1938–1943)," in *Zsidósas, asszimiláció polgárosodás. Tanulmónyok* (Budapest: Cserépfalvi, 1997), 280–81.

remembered with nostalgia. Romanians and Jews were killed in around twenty to thirty villages, and the new rulers introduced anti-Jewish laws. For military officers, maintaining any social relationships with Jews and even visiting their shops were strictly banned.[37] During the winter of 1940–1941, the army began arbitrary deportations. Jews were chased across the border to Romania or the Soviet Union. Some were sent back by patrols, others were arrested, and many civilians froze to death or simply disappeared into the forests.

In all countries under Nazi influence, the outbreak of the war brought radicalized policies regarding minority groups. Such policies appeared to offer a means of "solving" interethnic conflicts that had endured for centuries. Mass deportation, execution, and despoliation of civilians became an everyday routine. Removing minorities considered dangerous became an element of government programs: the Serbs in Croatia, the Muslim Pomacs in Bulgaria, and the Ukrainians in Romania were now endangered. All this was interconnected with anti-Jewish and often anti-Roma operations. The same phenomenon can be observed for Hungary as well. In 1941 the army prepared for an ethnic purge in the occupied Southern Province. The military planned to rob and expel 150,000 Serbs to zones occupied by the Germans. The Bárdossy government wanted to replace them with a Hungarian-speaking *Székely* population from Bukovina.[38] Twenty-five to thirty thousand Serbs were actually relocated to German-occupied Serb and Croat territories, and twelve thousand *Székelys* were resettled in their place. These intentions and actions were important precursors of the similar operations soon launched against the Jews: the 1941 expulsion of Jews with "unsettled citizenship" and the 1942 raid in the Southern Province, both culminating in mass murder.

Besides antisemitic legislation and the atrocities in the reannexed territories, the **Labor Service** constituted another discriminatory Hungarian government

---

37. For a detailed account and analysis, see Gyula Vargyai, *Magyarország a második világháborúban. Összeomlástól összeomlásig* (Budapest: Korona, 2001), 119–53. Cf. Mária Ormos, *Egy magyar médiavezér: Kozma Miklós* (Budapest: Polgart, 2000), 2:768–69; Bela Vago, "The Destruction of the Jews of Northern Transylvania," in *Hungarian-Jewish Studies*, ed. Randolph L. Braham (New York: World Federation of Hungarian Jews, 1966), 1:179; Loránt Tilkovszky, "A zsidótörvények mint a Holocaust előzményei," in *The Holocaust in Hungary: Fifty Years Later*, ed. Randolph L. Braham and Attila Pók (New York: Columbia University Press, 1997), 124.

38. Telegram from Oberkommando des Heeres to the German Ministry of Foreign Affairs, May 3, 1941. See Gyula Juhász et al., eds., *A Wilhelmstrasse és Magyarország. Német diplomáciai iratok Magyarországról 1933–1944* (Budapest: Kossuth, 1968), 581, 589–91; Enikő A. Sajti, *Délvidék 1941–1944. A magyar kormányok délszláv politikája* (Budapest: Kossuth, 1987), 40–52.

policy. Military labor service was a unique phenomenon in the history of World War II. Germany and most of its allies excluded Jews from their armies. By contrast, Hungary required Jews to perform unarmed military labor service. The Horthy regime did not want to draft those it considered "unreliable," such as communists, ethnic minorities, Jehovah's Witnesses, and, most of all, Jews into the armed service. At the same time, the government did not wish to leave them out of the war effort either. While discriminatory measures were implemented selectively against the regime's other target groups, every draft-age Jewish male was required to perform labor service.

An increasingly radical domestic political environment shaped the antisemitic agenda. In the governing party, the ratio of those who sympathized with the radicals gradually rose. Starting in the mid-1930s, supporters of the moderate former prime minister Bethlen were gradually pushed out of power. In 1939, in the last prewar elections, the **Arrow Cross**, National Socialist, and Race Protectionist parties did shockingly well, winning 30 percent of the vote.[39] Meanwhile, the anti-Jewish program of the governing party, renamed the Hungarian Life Party (MÉP), began adopting extreme right-wing rhetoric. About half of MÉP representatives essentially shared the radicals' views on the eve of the war.[40]

The dividing line between the radicals within and outside the governing party became increasingly blurred. When appointed prime minister in the spring of 1942, **Miklós Kállay** faced MÉP leaders demanding an antisemitic, pro-German political stance and threatening to overthrow him if he did otherwise.[41] One of the leading politicians of the era, **Béla Imrédy**, who formerly headed the Hungarian National Bank and served as prime minister in 1938–1939, established the pro-Nazi, anti-Jewish political formation called the Hungarian Renewal Party (MMP) in 1940. Barely four months before the German occupation, Imrédy went so far as to call upon Kállay to confiscate all Jewish assets and to ghettoize and mark the Jews with yellow stars.[42] Meanwhile, other right-wing extremist members of parliament delivered speeches about seizing the Jews' property and resettling them. Later they openly demanded that

---

39. György Földes and László Hubai, eds., *Parlamenti választások Magyarországon 1920–1998* (Budapest: Napvilág, 1999), 199.

40. Zsuzsanna Boros and Dániel Szabó, *Parlamentarizmus Magyarországon 1867–1944* (Budapest: Korona, 1999), 200.

41. Miklós Kállay, *Magyarország miniszterelnöke voltam, 1942–1944* (Budapest: Európa-História, 1991), 1:94–95.

42. For the memorandum of the MMP to Prime Minister Miklós Kállay dated October 1943, see Sipos, *Imrédy Béla a vádlottak padján*, 557, 565–66.

the Jews be killed as retaliation for Allied air strikes. Hardly any counterbalance remained. The liberal, social democratic, and agrarian smallholder anti-Nazi opposition held a mere 10 percent of seats in parliament.

At the latest, by the spring of 1943 Budapest was aware that the Germans' final goal was the destruction of the European Jews. While Jews all around the Nazi-controlled continent were being persecuted and murdered en masse, Hungarian foreign policy firmly rejected Berlin's "solution" to the "Jewish question." Kállay and Horthy used the same argument to refute what became increasingly energetic German reproaches. They said that while Hungary's anti-Jewish stance was unquestionable, further measures against the Jews would jeopardize Hungarian military production.[43] Of course, they would not reveal other considerations that came into play. They did not mention the exploratory talks they were carrying out with the western Allies for a peace treaty. Nor did they mention the military situation, which was becoming increasingly unfavorable for the Germans. They likewise chose not to cite the fact that Hungary's great rival, Romania, was not deporting its Jews, that Slovakian deportations had ceased in the fall of 1942, and that the Italians were not handing over their Jews either. In essence, the Kállay government's most important foreign policy goal was to hold on to the territories seized through the German alliance and, at the same time, leave open the possibility of switching sides in the event that the war's outcome was unfavorable for the Axis powers. The conservative governing circles were at heart antisemitic, but they did not wish to assist the Germans in the slaughter of the Jews.

As a result of the reannexations, Hungary's territory grew, as did its Jewish population. The 1941 census registered 725,000 Israelites; the number of converts to Christianity was estimated at 100,000.[44] Thus, in the first half of 1941, about 825,000 Jews lived in Hungary, making up about 5.6 percent of the total population of 14,683,323. At the end of 1943, approximately twelve to sixteen thousand Jewish refugees also lived in Hungary. They had arrived from Slovakia,

---

43. György Ránki, ed., *Hitler hatvannyolc tárgyalása 1939–1944. Hitler Adolf tárgyalásai kelet-európai államférfiakkal* (Budapest: Magvető, 1983), 2:83. See also **Sztójay's** note, December 2, 1942, in Juhász et al., *A Wilhelmstrasse és Magyarország*, 703.

44. József Kepecs, ed., *A zsidó népesség száma településenként (1840–1941)* (Budapest: Központi Statisztikai Hivatal, 1993), 32. According to the 1941 census, 61,548 Jews of the Christian religion lived within the borders of Hungary. Alajos Kovács, "A keresztény vallású, de zsidó származású népesség a népszámlálás szerint," *Magyar Statisztikai Szemle*, nos. 4–5 (1944): 95–108. Kovács stated that, for various reasons, at least forty thousand Jews of the Christian religion remained hidden, so an accurate estimate would be about one hundred thousand Hungarian Jews of a non-Israelite religion.

Bohemia and Moravia, Poland, Yugoslavia, Germany, and Austria.[45] The Labor Service caused the deaths of about twenty-five to forty thousand Jewish men, the summer 1941 deportations led to approximately fifteen thousand deaths, and the Újvidék massacre killed between seven hundred and one thousand people.[46] A few thousand people also emigrated during the war years. On the eve of the German occupation, a total of about 760,000 to 780,000 people considered Jewish resided in Hungary.

During the war, Hungarian Jews lived under continually deteriorating conditions. Tens of thousands perished in the Labor Service; others lost their jobs and social prestige. They were largely excluded from the universities and often humiliated by the public administration. Despite all of this, before the German occupation, one could see Jews in Hungary living a normal life compared to those in many other parts of Hitler's Europe. Young Zionist leader Rafi Benshalom, who arrived in Budapest from Slovakia in January 1944, was shocked: "For me, in Europe of 1944, this seemed like a fantasy [. . .] Jews seeking entertainment could still visit coffee houses, cinemas and theaters. While in Poland, hundreds of thousands of Europe's Jews were being annihilated and the whole world lived in fear."[47] Jews were disgusted by the Arrow Cross Party, Imrédy's pro-Nazi political formation, and the increasing antisemitic propaganda, but they respected the regent and trusted the government. In the spring of 1944, the majority of them hoped that the war would soon be over and their communities would survive.

## THE GERMAN OCCUPATION AND ITS CONSEQUENCES

When on March 19, 1944, the Wehrmacht occupied Hungary, Horthy ordered the army not to resist. At first the Germans contemplated an exclusively military solution: full-scale occupation, subjugation, and disarming of the Hungarian troops. According to the new German ambassador and plenipotentiary, **Edmund Veesenmayer**, such disarmament would generate a series of

---

45. Kasztner Report, YVA, 015H/35, I/19. According to Kinga Frojimovics's estimates, between 1933 and 1944 a total of twenty to twenty-five thousand Jewish refugees arrived in Hungary and spent some time in the country. Kinga Frojimovics, *I Have Been a Stranger in a Strange Land: The Hungarian State and the Jewish Refugees in Hungary, 1933–1945* (Jerusalem: Yad Vashem, 2007), 56.

46. For details, see chapter 2.

47. Rafi Benshalom, *We Struggled for Life: The Hungarian Zionist Youth Resistance during the Nazi Era* (Jerusalem: Gefen, 2001), 8–10.

problems. He worried about fatal political outcomes (Horthy's resignation, the formation of a united political opposition), significant logistical difficulties (the risk of a general strike), and even serious military consequences (the emergence of partisan movements). He warned Berlin that "for centuries the Hungarians have been the masters of passive resistance." One of his most powerful arguments against disarmament was that Germans might lose the Hungarians' willingness to cooperate. Ernst Kaltenbrunner, head of the Reich Security Main Office (RSHA), shared this view.[48] For these reasons, Hitler decided on a model built on broad collaboration. In exchange for the appearance of sovereignty, the Hungarians guaranteed the cooperation of the armed forces, law enforcement, and public administration.[49]

A five-hundred- to six-hundred-member Einsatzgruppe of the German Security Police (Sicherheitspolizei) accompanied the Wehrmacht troops as they marched in. Among them were members of the Sondereinsatzkommando directed by Adolf Eichmann. These forces were charged with suppressing potential or actual resistance. The Einsatzgruppe was led by SS-Standartenführer Hans Geschke, who was appointed chief commander of the Security Police and the Security Service in Hungary (Befehlshaber der Sicherheitspolizei und des SD, or BdS), with regional commandos spread out in the major towns and cities across the country. Based on a list prepared in advance, they arrested several hundred conservative, opposition, and anti-Nazi politicians, police officers, journalists, and economic leaders. Within just a few days, the Gestapo eliminated the core of the anti-German resistance, which had been rather weak from the outset. During the first days, the German and Hungarian police conducted surprise checks, arresting thousands of Jews at railway stations and in the open street. Through March 31, 3,364 individuals were dragged off to various detentions sites, prisons, and internment camps.[50]

Horthy relieved Kállay of his post on March 19 and three days later appointed Döme Sztójay, the pro-Nazi, antisemitic ambassador to Berlin, as prime minister. The new coalition cabinet consisted of the governing party (MÉP), joined by two far-right parties that had been in opposition until the occupation: Imrédy's MMP and the Hungarian National Socialist Party (MNSZP). Veesenmayer favored Imrédy and his party, while the MNSZP was

---

48. Veesenmayer's telegram to the German Foreign Office, March 24, 1944, in Juhász et al., *A Wilhelmstrasse és Magyarország*, 794–95.

49. György Ránki, *Emlékiratok és valóság Magyarország második világháborús szerepéről* (Budapest: Kossuth, 1964), 250–60.

50. Veesenmayer's telegram to the German Foreign Office, March 31, 1944, in Randolph L. Braham, ed., *The Destruction of Hungarian Jewry: A Documentary Account* (New York: Pro Arte for the World Federation of Hungarian Jews, 1963), 2:539.

the protégé of Heinrich Himmler.[51] The fact that the new government consisted of widely known politicians rather than new faces enhanced the appearance of legal continuity. In a cabinet soon expanded to ten members, eight were former ministers, and four had even been members of the Kállay administration. Surprisingly enough, the strongest far-right party was simply left out of the new government: the Germans deemed **Ferenc Szálasi**'s Arrow Cross Party unsuited to a Berlin-controlled cabinet.

As is shown in chapter 3, the critical question for the future of Jews became who would head the Ministry of the Interior, since it was in charge of the police and gendarmerie as well as public administration agencies. As a result of German pressure, radicals laid their hands on the post. **Andor Jaross**, an Imrédy supporter, became the new government's minister of the interior. The position of state secretary for political affairs went to an MNSZP leader and retired gendarme major, **László Baky**. Neither had any experience in public administration, however. For this reason, Jaross appointed an expert as state secretary in charge of the public administration: László Endre, the subprefect of Pest-Pilis-Solt-Kiskun County.

Endre had worked as a civil servant for twenty-five years and climbed his way up in the hierarchy. From 1924 he served as chief constable of Gödöllő, the largest district in the country. In 1938 he became a subprefect, heading Pest-Pilis-Solt-Kiskun County, the largest and most populous public administrative unit in Hungary.[52] Not only was Endre a competent professional, but his right-wing extremist convictions suited him politically for the new assignment. Several dozen counties and towns around the country adopted the strict anti-Jewish measures he initiated between 1939 and 1944. His radical antisemitism secured him a nationwide reputation and made him a particularly attractive figure for the new government.[53]

After the German invasion and still in his capacity as subprefect, Endre did not waste any time. Ahead of the government's antisemitic measures, he started

---

51. Draft memorandum of the RSHA, March 11, 1944, in Magda Ádám, Gyula Juhász and Lajos Kerekes, eds., *Magyarország és a második világháború. Titkos diplomáciai okmányok a háború előzményeihez és történetéhez* (Budapest: Kossuth, 1959), 447–51. Otto Winkelmann's note to Major Pál, November 14, 1945, in László Karsai and Judit Molnár, eds., *A magyar Quisling-kormány. Sztójay Döme és társai a népbíróság előtt* (Budapest: 1956-os KHT, 2004), 819–20.

52. For an explanation of the administrative terms, see table 4, p. 370.

53. For details on Endre's career, see Zoltán Vági, "Endre László: Fajvédelem és bürokratikus antiszemitizmus a közigazgatási gyakorlatban 1919–1944," in *Tanulmányok a holokausztról II*, ed. Randolph L. Braham (Budapest: Balassi, 2002), 81–153. For Endre's interwar activities, see chapter 2.

a private anti-Jewish campaign without any higher authorization. He immediately issued nine new regulations in Pest County on his own initiative.[54] On the morning of March 24, newly appointed Minister of the Interior Andor Jaross asked him to accept the position of state secretary. Endre's diary indicates that he first met Eichmann on March 29: "Afternoon [Pest] county hall. Eichmann and associates at my place. Jewish affairs advisors, dinner."[55] Over the next two days they met again.

On March 31, the party got out of hand: the drunk company was shooting off the Germans' submachine guns in the courtyard, and the SEK commander presented his own weapon to Endre as a gift.[56] This is how Eichmann remembered their relation: "Dr. Endre [. . .] became one of the best friends I have had in my life."[57] He correctly sensed that Endre's willingness to collaborate stemmed not from fear or calculation. Quite the contrary, as a committed antisemite chauvinist, he had been waiting for years for the opportunity to finally get rid of the Jews.[58] On the Hungarian side, Endre now had the final word in Jewish matters. As state secretary, he supervised the entire Hungarian public administration. Moreover, with Baky's blessing, informally from April and formally from mid-May, Endre took charge of ghettoization in Hungary, as well as the supervision of the police and the gendarmerie carrying out the deportations.[59]

---

54. Some of Endre's regulations: he banned the Jews' receipt of food coupons for sugar and lard (Decree nos. 4900/1944 and 4901/1944), ordered the confiscation of Jewish apartments and internment of "unreliable" Jews and communists, and confiscated the Jews' radios (Decree nos. 18.913/1944, 18.901/1944, and 18.903/1944); he initiated the withdrawal of trade licenses and permits from Jews (Decree no. 18.912/1944) and also began purging works by Jewish authors from libraries and shop windows. HNA P1434, fascicle 16, file "1944 március 21–22."

55. Entry for March 29, 1944, László Endre's diary, Endre Collection, in the authors' possession.

56. Entry for March 31, 1944, László Endre's diary, Endre Collection; Adolf Eichmann, *Ich, Adolf Eichmann. Ein historischer Zeugenbericht*, ed. Rudolf Aschenauer (Leoni: Druffel Verlag, 1980), 347, and "Eichmann Tells His Own Damning Story," *Life*, November 28–December 5, 1960.

57. "Eichmann Tells His Own Damning Story," *Life*.

58. Eichmann, *Ich, Adolf Eichmann*, 359.

59. Kádár and Vági, *Hullarablás*, 112–14. See also Prime Minister's Decree no. 3140/1944 about setting up a so-called special service in charge of the "resettlement" of the Jews, May 13, 1944, in Ilona Benoschofsky and Elek Karsai, eds., *Vádirat a nácizmus ellen. Dokumentumok a magyarországi zsidóüldözés történetéhez (1944 március 19–1944 május 15. a német megszállástól a deportálás megkezdéséig)* (Budapest: Magyar Izraeliták Országos Képviselete, 1958), 1:312–13.

According to the head of the Gestapo in Budapest, Alfred Trenker, Eichmann's most important contact was Endre.[60] Eichmann's deputy, Hermann Krumey, and the SEK's railway specialist, Franz Novak, were of the same opinion.[61] The Higher SS and Police Leader (*Höherer SS- und Polizeiführer*, HSSPF) in Hungary, Otto Winkelmann, stated that Eichmann did not even have to influence Endre much because the latter "fulfilled his task out of his own conviction."[62] At his trial in Jerusalem, Eichmann naturally tried to emphasize Endre's responsibility, since he had already been hanged by then. He claimed that "Laci did everything [. . .] He was the one taking care of the whole matter."[63] As Eichmann summarized his experiences in Hungary, Endre made his job easier "in a way that I could not have dreamed of before."[64]

## DEPORTATIONS: THE DECISION-MAKING PROCESS

Chapter 4 in this volume describes the ghettoization and deportation of the Hungarian Jews. The process involved a multiphase, evolving sequence of joint German-Hungarian decisions.[65] Among the many events of the increasingly radicalizing process, four strategic decisions of fundamental importance stand out. The first was a general, political one. It took shape at the beginning of the occupation. On March 18, Hitler demanded of Horthy that "they should solve the Jewish question" in Hungary. RSHA chief Kaltenbrunner repeated this expectation to future prime minister Sztójay.[66] The German demands for the introduction of the yellow star and the physical isolation of Jews had already been accepted in theory at a meeting of the new Hungarian ministers

---

60. Péter Bokor, *Végjáték a Duna mentén. Interjúk egy filmsorozathoz* (Budapest: RTV-Minerva, 1982), 94.

61. Ibid., 108; Krumey's testimony, Frankfurt, June 6, 1961, in *The Trial of Adolf Eichmann: Record of Proceedings in the District Court of Jerusalem* (Jerusalem: State of Israel, Ministry of Justice, 1994), 5:1940.

62. Winkelmann's testimony, Bordesholm, May 19, 1961, in *The Trial of Adolf Eichmann*, 5:1946.

63. Laci is a diminutive of Endre's first name, László.

64. Lévai, "The Hungarian Deportations in the Light of the Eichmann Trial," 89.

65. For details, see Kádár and Vági, *Hullarablás*, 105–46. For a different approach to a multiphase decision-making process, see Gerlach and Aly, *Das letzte Kapitel*, 249–69. For a critique of Gerlach and Aly's concept, see Kádár and Vági, *Hullarablás*, 123–24, and László Karsai, "A holokauszt utolsó fejezete," *Beszélő* 10 (2005): 74–91.

66. Sztójay's testimony, March 5, 1946, in Karsai and Molnár, *A magyar Qusiling-kormány*, 213.

on March 22, triggering the creation of anti-Jewish decrees and preparations for ghettoization.[67]

The second strategic decision took place on March 31, when Jaross approved the ghettoization plan that Endre and Eichmann had worked out during their previous meetings. The plan covered the entire country. It included the concentration of all Hungarian Jews in ghettos and collection camps. The Hungarian police and gendarmerie under the auspices of Eichmann's Sondereinsatzkommando were given the task of rounding up the internees and guarding these facilities.[68]

The third decision elevated the Holocaust in Hungary to a whole new register. The goal was no longer simply robbing, humiliating, and segregating the Jews in ghettos but initiating their deportation to the Reich. This, however, was only a limited action, affecting not all Hungarian Jews but only one hundred thousand deemed fit for manual labor to alleviate the German war industry's pressing shortage of workers. Regent Horthy, Prime Minister Sztójay, and the Ministry of the Interior, as well as the Ministry of Defense, had accepted it by April 13. Veesenmayer, who also requested directions about the transports' destination, informed Berlin of the decision. Nevertheless, the limited deportation never took place since the scope of the action was soon radically expanded.[69]

The last and final decision completed the evolution of genocide, setting the goal of total, comprehensive deportation targeting every Hungarian Jew and designating Auschwitz as their destination. Behind the scenes, Eichmann and Endre clearly initiated the decision. On April 22, the RSHA approved the scheme of taking up Jews capable of working according to the earlier limited deportation plan and reported that Eichmann would receive the necessary instructions later that day. However, the situation altered drastically in the next few hours. As a result of their parallel efforts, Eichmann and Endre managed to achieve a breakthrough. A summit was convened at the Szentkút estate of the Endre family. Besides the state secretary, Eichmann, and his legal advisor,

---

67. Sztójay's testimony, March 5, 1946, in ibid., 213–14.

68. See Endre's entries from late March, László Endre's diary. For details about the process, see Kádár and Vági, *Hullarablás*, 114–19.

69. For a description of the concept of and the events regarding the limited deportation, see, e.g., Veesenmayer's report to the German Foreign Office, April 14, 1944, in Juhász et al., *A Wilhelmstrasse és Magyarország*, 823; Veesenmayer's telegram to the German Foreign Office, April 15, 1944, in Braham, *The Destruction of Hungarian Jewry*, 1:343; Rolf Günther's report to Eberhard von Thadden, April 24, 1944, in ibid., 359–60; entries for April 12, 1944, László Endre's diary, Endre Collection, in the authors' possession; Endre's testimony before the people's court, short protocol, December 17, 1945, HAHSS, Endre-Baky-Jaross trial V-79802, 16.

Otto Hunsche, the participants included HSSPF Winkelmann, BdS Geschke, and the top officials at the Ministry of the Interior, Jaross and Baky. The parties negotiated about Eichmann and Endre's initiative and in a few hours reached a bilateral agreement regarding total, comprehensive deportation. Veesenmayer informed Berlin about the new developments on April 23, at 1:30 a.m.[70]

The Szentkút agreement was the final phase of the decision-making process regarding the fate of Hungary's Jews and represented a broad consensus. Berlin and Budapest both supported a total and comprehensive deportation. Hungarian and German offices enthusiastically joined the implementation process, which culminated in the mass murder of Hungarian Jews in Auschwitz II–Birkenau. Further important decisions were undoubtedly made over the upcoming weeks as well. On May 3 the perpetrators accelerated the deportations, and in late June they sent some fifteen thousand Jews to Austria instead of Auschwitz. At other junctures they rescheduled specific regional operations, rearranged train timetables, or altered the composition of certain transports. However, these steps always arose in the context of the fourth and final strategic decision delineated here. Later decisions were tactical in nature and should be interpreted as elements of the technical implementation of this plan.

As a result of this decision-making process, between May 15 and July 9, in the span of just fifty-six days, Hungarian authorities deported 437,402 Hungarian Jews on 147 trains—with the exception of fifteen thousand people, all to Auschwitz. Moreover, between April and August 1944 the German security police deported eleven to twelve thousand additional people, with little to no involvement by the Hungarian authorities (in so-called *Einzelaktionen*). Thus, altogether, close to 450,000 Jews were deported in this period; chapter 7 provides glimpses of their fate.[71]

Hungary's Labor Service units were not handed over for deportation during this time frame. This issue caused the most intense conflict between the Germans and the Hungarians during the deportations. The Ministry of Defense, the office with exclusive control over the labor servicemen, intended

---

70. Veesenmayer's report to the German Foreign Office, April 23, 1944, in Braham, *The Destruction of Hungarian Jewry*, 1:356. For the Szentkút meeting, see entry for April 22, 1944, László Endre's diary, Endre Collection, in the authors' possession. For the role of the meeting in the context of the final decision, see Kádár and Vági, *Hullarablás*, 136–38.

71. See Braham, *The Destruction of Hungarian Jewry*, 1:443. In his report dated July 9, Hungarian gendarme Lieutenant Colonel **László Ferenczy**, acting as liaison officer between the Hungarian Ministry of the Interior and the Sondereinsatzkommando, speaks of 434,351 "individuals of the Jewish race" deported on 147 trains between May 14 and July 9. See László Karsai and Judit Molnár, eds., *Az Endre-Baky-Jaross per* (Budapest: Cserépfalvi, 1994), 522.

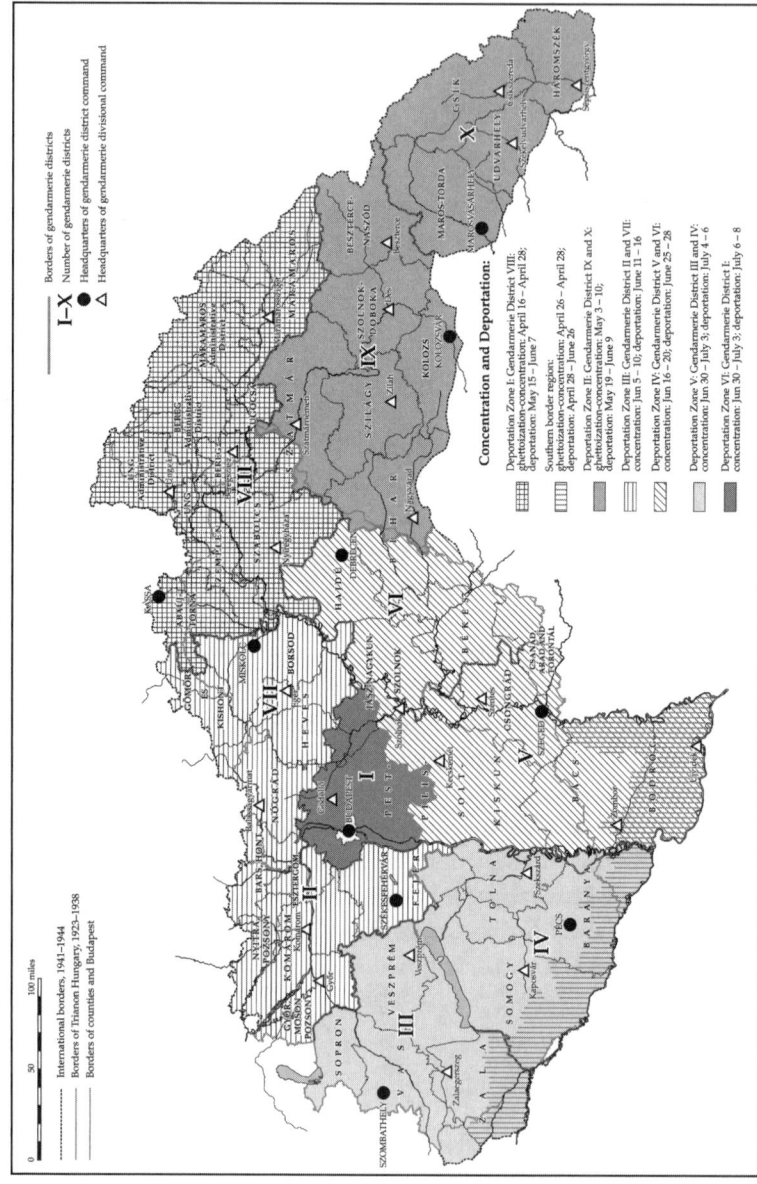

Map 3. Deportation of the Provincial Jews, Spring–Summer 1944
For a closer look at this map, go to: rowman.com/isbn/9780759121980.

to keep their labor capacity in the Hungarian realm. The army thus began sending call-up summons for the Labor Service to the Jews imprisoned in ghettos and collection camps. By pulling Jewish men out of these places, some high-ranking military officers were probably, in essence, defending the last remnants of Hungarian sovereignty from the occupying Germans. Others were intent on rescuing the men. In any case, the conflict saved thousands of people from the gas chambers.

By early July 1944 Jews had disappeared from the provinces. The last action would have been the deportation of the Budapest Jews. However, deterioration of the military situation, increasing international protests (for example, from Pope Pius XII, King Gustaf V of Sweden, and President Franklin D. Roosevelt), pressure from those around Horthy, and the widely circulated documents describing the mass murder at Auschwitz all combined to influence the regent at last to stop the deportations in early July 1944.[72] Moreover, he was also afraid that State Secretary László Baky had concentrated thousands of gendarmes around Budapest not to organize the deportation of the Jews in the capital but to overthrow him. Horthy thus forced the gendarmes out of the city by bringing in troops from the neighboring areas. Apart from the Budapest Jews and the Labor Service battalions (who, as mentioned, were not included in the spring and summer mass deportation campaign), Hungary was rendered "*Judenrein*" (free of Jews). For the time being, the remaining Jews were safe.

The lack of Hungarian cooperation immediately paralyzed the Germans. They did not give up though. Eichmann and his team deported 2,720 prisoners from two internment camps (Kistarcsa and Sárvár) in the second half of July. Nazi diplomacy increased pressure on the regent to restart the deportations. Finally, Horthy caved in and promised to give permission for a continuation in late August. However, when on August 23–24 Romania switched sides and turned against Germany, the situation changed radically: knowing that in the drastically deteriorated situation Berlin needed Hungarian support more than ever, Horthy dismissed the Sztójay-government, appointed a new cabinet with General **Géza Lakatos** as its head, and took deportations off the agenda.

## TRADITIONS AND ZEAL: COLLABORATION IN HUNGARY

Eichmann had had substantial experience throughout Europe regarding the collaboration of local authorities. In his memoirs written in Israeli prison, he

---

72. For details, see chapter 4.

praised the Hungarians with enthusiasm: "The apparatus of the Hungarian authorities worked with an efficiency that the authorities of other countries can rarely call their own [. . .] On several occasions, I would say to myself: Wow! Till now, you thought that in Germany, there is that certain precision reigning, and here you are seeing the same painstaking accuracy. I admired the Hungarian public administration, and not in the sense of how they managed their Jewish affairs, but more generally, from a bureaucratic perspective."[73] It is difficult to receive praise greater from an SS bureaucrat, and without a doubt, the Hungarians deserved it. Without them Eichmann could not have made a single move in the spring of 1944.

Officials in the pre-1944 era frequently adopted each other's (often illegal) anti-Jewish initiatives, contributing to the radicalization process. Socialized in the practice of **bureaucratic** and **illegal antisemitism**,[74] they became accustomed to the idea of Jews as second-class citizens. After 1938, the implementation of discriminatory measures became a matter of everyday paperwork for the public administration. Because of this, the German occupation did not seem like the start of a new era for Hungary's two hundred thousand civil servants, gendarmes, and policemen. For most it was simply a continuation of former anti-Jewish policies, albeit with different means.

To facilitate the smooth, uninterrupted participation of the apparatus, a thorough political "cleansing" began after the German occupation. Forty-one of the sixty-one government-appointed **county** and town prefects (67 percent) were removed.[75] Some resigned in protest, while Minister of the Interior Jaross dismissed and replaced others. Local purges commenced. Through the end of July, fifty-eight new chief constables were appointed, and twenty-five cities and towns installed new mayors. Nonetheless, the majority of high-ranking officials (60 percent of mayors, 80 percent of subprefects, and 75 percent of chief constables heading districts) remained in place.[76]

The majority of those who organized the forcible removal of half a million men, women, and children were apolitical civilians, simple civil servants: the central ministerial apparatus and the staffs of forty-one counties, three Carpatho-Ruthenian public administration districts, and many municipal

---

73. Adolf Eichmann, *Tárgyalástól ítéletig. Feljegyzések a börtönből* (Budapest: Trifer, 2000), 223.

74. For more on these terms, see chapter 2 and the glossary.

75. Veesenmayer's report to the German Foreign Office, May 11, 1944, in Juhász et al., *A Wilhelmstrasse és Magyarország*, 845.

76. László Csősz, "A Vészkorszak Jász-Nagykun-Szolnok vármegyében" (PhD diss., University of Szeged, 2010), 72.

authorities.⁷⁷ The tasks of seizing, inventorying, transporting, and assessing the value of confiscated Jewish goods were the responsibility of the country's forty-one financial directorates. Even following the occupation, they did not feel as though they were fulfilling the orders of clique-serving foreign interests. They were doing their jobs in an orderly manner, and, of course, many were lining their pockets with assets stolen from Jews.

The Germans were especially fascinated by the Hungarian gendarmes, a military-style formation that served the regime unconditionally, maintaining internal order.⁷⁸ Recruits were subjected to a careful selection process. Training put special emphasis on a militant, anticommunist worldview and indoctrination in a general xenophobic attitude, reinforcing prejudices against Jews and others.⁷⁹ In 1944, this had quite an effect. The gendarmes' reliability is reflected in the fact that after the occupation, the Germans saw no need to cleanse the organization. All commanders of the ten gendarmerie districts retained their offices. It is therefore not surprising that thousands of survivors' eyewitness accounts mention the gendarmes' brutality. They were notorious for beating Jews during ghettoization and the deportations. The cruelest among them were the gendarme detectives who searched for Jews' hidden valuables.⁸⁰

Compared to appraisals of the gendarmerie, assessments of the police are somewhat more nuanced. Among them, the enthusiastic implementers were fewer. One reason was that the police more often came in contact with local Jews whom they knew. By contrast, the gendarmes, purposely deployed in areas of the country away from their residences, were uninfluenced by personal sympathies. In Budapest, the massacres committed by the Arrow Cross outraged some policemen responsible for maintaining public order. They interfered on several occasions, rescuing Jews from the hands of Arrow Cross militiamen.⁸¹

Hungarians actually murdered less than 10 percent of the more than five hundred thousand victims of the Holocaust in Hungary. Apart from thousands

---

77. For the administrative structure of the country, see table 4, p. 370.
78. Judit Molnár, "Gendarmes before the People's Court," in idem, *The Holocaust in Hungary*, 651–52.
79. Financial abuses (fraud, embezzlement, etc.) were frequently illustrated through examples with individuals having Jewish names. If the crime committed was stealing or disorderly conduct, then the perpetrator was "naturally" Roma. See, e.g., *Csendőrségi Lapok*, July 15, 1938, 480; November 1, 1939, 751; January 1, 1941, 15; January 15, 1941, 45. Subsequent volumes show that this tendency grew even stronger once Hungary entered the war.
80. For examples of gendarme brutality, see chapters 4 and 5.
81. Gábor Kádár and Zoltán Vági, "Zsidók és nemzsidók. Szolidaritás és embermentés a vészkorszakban," in *Holocaust Füzetek* 10 (1998): 19–20.

of fanatical Jew haters (mainly bloodthirsty soldiers and officers in the army, gendarmes, and policemen, Arrow Cross extremists, Hungarian SS men, and so forth) the majority of radicals, race protectionists, and right-wing politicians of different parties (MÉP, MNSZP, MMP, and the Arrow Cross) did not want to kill the Jews. Following their own traditions, they "only" wanted to get rid of them for good and were happy that the Germans were willing to take on the "dirtiest part of the job." Nonetheless, in some way or another, hundreds of thousands took part in what many called the "de-Jewification of Hungary."

The majority of the Hungarian population did not want to kill the Jews either. They were just eager to seize their assets and positions. When the Jews were ultimately taken away, many people, as exemplified in chapter 6, fixated on their property; few asked any questions about the fate of former neighbors or colleagues. They did not wish the Jews dead, but the group's excision from Hungarian society and life was of great interest to hundreds of thousands of men and women. Chapter 8 provides a detailed account of the non-Jewish reactions to the antisemitic persecution.

## HORTHY'S RESPONSIBILITY

The issue of Horthy's role in and responsibility for the 1944 events remains complex and controversial. After some hesitation, he accepted the German occupation of his country. Military resistance was never a realistic option. Although most of the occupying troops were soon removed, Nazi military presence still remained a permanent threat. Moreover, due to border disputes, neighboring countries were always ready to launch anti-Hungarian operations. In addition, the majority of Hungarian generals, fearing the Red Army, considered it unthinkable to turn against their German allies. Another option was resignation. Horthy did not take this step either but instead withdrew from Jewish-related issues. New Jewish laws would have required his signature to go into effect, but it seems that he did not want to place himself in the compromising position of endorsing them. Instead he allowed rule by decree, by which the government could implement policies without his written consent. According to Sztójay's words at the March 29 government meeting, "[Horthy] granted complete freedom to the government [. . .] with regard to all Jewish decrees and regulations and in this respect, wished to exert no influence."[82]

---

82. Minutes of the meeting of the Council of Ministers, March 29, 1944, HNA K27, box 260.

Horthy thus remained in his position and appointed the members of the new government, who collaborated with the occupiers in all matters. Trusting the promises made by the Nazis, he hoped that by sacrificing the Jews, he could get the Germans to pull their troops out as soon as possible.[83] By staying in his position, he maintained the appearance of constitutional order and normality. Thus, from the perspective of the population and government officials, he legitimized cooperation with the Germans. After all, this broad collaboration led to the destruction of Hungary's provincial Jewish population. At the same time, it is also true that, had the regent resigned, Budapest's Jews and Jewish labor servicemen would most likely have been deported: the remaining one-third of the Hungarian Jews would not have survived the Holocaust.

This said, Horthy halted the deportations halfheartedly. In his early June memorandum to Sztójay, he had already demanded that certain groups of Jews be spared.[84] Three weeks later, at the June 26 Crown Council, he repeated his wish, but nothing happened. He finally ordered a halt to the deportations on July 6, but they continued until July 9. All this delay cost the lives of several tens of thousands of Hungarian citizens. In his memoirs Horthy claimed that he was not informed about murders of the deported Jews until early July.[85] His apologists would later invoke this remark to maintain that as soon as he learned the terrible reality, Horthy had immediately stopped the deportations. This claim has profound problems. On the one hand, he was well aware of the nature of the Nazis' Jewish policies long before the German occupation of Hungary. On the other hand, he had already decided to stop the deportation (of at least certain groups) in early June but did not act forcefully to implement this decision. Moreover, only Romania's defection in late August prevented the deportation of Budapest's Jews—and by this time, even Horthy himself conceded his awareness of what was going on at their destination.

The stopping of the deportations reveals two facts: first, that the Nazis were basically paralyzed without Hungarian assistance, and second, that the Regent was actually very powerful. Upon his command, Hungarian troops rolled into Budapest, and the gendarmes who were enthusiastically collaborating with the SD until then marched right out of the capital. Neither the SS

---

83. Miklós Szinai and László Szűcs, eds., *Horthy Miklós titkos iratai* (Budapest: Kossuth, 1962), 439. Jenő Rátz's testimony, March 7, 1946, in Karsai and Molnár, *A magyar Qusiling-kormány*, 245. On June 7, at the meeting between Hitler and Sztójay, the Führer reassured Sztójay that after "the solution of the Jewish question," he would remove his troops from Hungary. Ránki, *Hitler hatvannyolc tárgyalása 1939–1944*, 2:324.

84. See document 4-2.

85. Miklós Horthy, *Emlékirataim* (Budapest: Európa, 1992), 291.

nor the Wehrmacht ventured to initiate an armed conflict for the deportation of the Budapest Jews. This degree of determination, had it manifested itself a few weeks earlier, could have saved a lot of lives. Granted, at that earlier point, Horthy did not feel his power was in danger.

## HUNGARIAN JEWS IN AUSCHWITZ II–BIRKENAU

The Hungarian-German deportation agreement indicated that Auschwitz II–Birkenau would be the murder site of Jews deported from the country.[86] In early May, before his return to Auschwitz, former camp commander Rudolf Höss traveled to Budapest, where he consulted with Eichmann and the Hungarian State Railways (MÁV) about the deportation schedule. Höss was trying to slow the pace, for he knew that the crematoria had limited capacity and that Auschwitz was not prepared to handle the arrival of so many deportees. But Eichmann, not the least bit interested in these difficulties, cited Himmler's order. Endre, whom Höss probably also met in Budapest, held a similarly radical view. Höss found himself in a difficult position in Budapest: "I had to fight for each transport train that I wished to delay. Most of the time, I lost," he wrote in his memoirs.[87] Eventually, he achieved one concession: that instead of four trains every day (with forty to fifty cattle cars, each carrying three thousand to thirty-five hundred people), only five such trains would leave every two days.[88] But this schedule fell apart as soon as the deportations began. Beginning on May 8, Höss launched hasty measures to prepare Auschwitz for the influx of hundreds of thousands of people. The preparations were still ongoing when the first mass transports arrived on May 16, 1944. On that day the largest mass murder in the history of the Auschwitz complex began. It was called "Operation Höss," after its leader.

In the first two weeks the Hungarians sent almost twice as many transports as they had agreed on with Höss. At least fifty-eight trains were directed to Auschwitz, with 184,049 people aboard. On several days during this period, five to six transports arrived at the *Judenrampe*, unloading such overwhelming numbers that "selection" often became impossible. In some cases, the SS men performing the notorious selection process did not even have time to conduct the customary cursory examination of new arrivals. Tens of thousands were

---

86. For details regarding the fate of Hungarian Jews in Auschwitz, see chapter 7.
87. Höss, *Death Dealer*, 45–46, 241–42.
88. Ibid.

sent to camp blocks to be subjected to a selection process later.[89] Many arrivals were not tattooed and were shipped off to other camps without any registration procedure. Others were sent to smaller subcamps operating in the vicinity of Auschwitz.

After the first 116,000 Hungarian Jewish arrivals had undergone a "selection" process, it became clear that half of those capable of working were women. The chief of the SS-Business Administration Main Office (WVHA), SS-Obergruppenführer Oswald Pohl requested Himmler's approval to employ them in the paramilitary work corps Organisation Todt. The Reichsführer-SS agreed, and in a rather twisted manner, he suggested that their diet should include Hungarian garlic.[90] In reality, they had hardly anything to eat and were put into a half-completed section of the camp (BIII), the so-called Mexico sector, where extremely bad conditions reigned even by Birkenau standards.[91]

The SS used the new arrivals as a reserve workforce. Efficiency was low. The Nazis simply could not provide work for many of them. On August 29, 1944, of 17,662 prisoners in the Birkenau men's camp, only 58 percent were sent to work; 19 percent of the rest were sick, and no work could be secured for the remaining 23 percent. The situation did not improve. On October 2, 26,230 female prisoners were registered in Birkenau. Theoretically, all were fit for labor, but less than half (44 percent) were actually given any work. Due to deteriorating conditions, half (28 percent) of the remainder were sick, and the others (28 percent) were unemployed.[92] The situation had become wholly irrational: while factories and plants in Germany desperately waited for laborers, Hungarian Jews capable of working spent weeks in senseless roll calls. Not having enough to eat, many of them gradually lost their work capacity and were sent to be gassed. Rational economic objectives disappeared in the face of Auschwitz's real objective: murder.

---

89. Franciszek Piper, *Auschwitz: How Many Perished Jews, Poles, Gypsies . . .* (Oświęcim: Auschwitz-Birkenau State Museum, 1996), 24; Robert Jay Lifton, *The Nazi Doctors: Medical Killing and the Psychology of Genocide* (New York: Basic Books, 1986), esp. chs. 8–10.

90. See the correspondence of Pohl and Himmler, May 24–27, 1944, in Braham, *The Destruction of Hungarian Jewry*, 1:378–79, 391.

91. In April 1944, the WVHA halted the construction work in the Mexico sector. Danuta Czech, *Auschwitz Chronicle, 1939–1945* (New York: Henry Holz, 1997), 561.

92. Ibid., 699, 721.

A total of about 430,000 Jews of Hungarian citizenship were taken to Auschwitz in 1944.[93] Determining the number of Hungarian Jews murdered in Auschwitz is considerably more difficult, and postwar estimates vary substantially. Although the ratio of those fit to those unfit for work varied by transports, SS physicians left on average at most 20 to 30 percent of the incoming deportees alive. This means that out of the 430,000 Hungarian Jews arriving at Auschwitz, some 300,000 to 345,000 were gassed immediately. Many thousands more were murdered as a result of further selections or died owing to illness, forced labor, starvation, or harsh treatment in Birkenau and its subcamps. The death marches after the evacuation of the camp claimed further lives. So did forced labor and the infernal conditions reigning in other camps to which Hungarian Jews were sent from the Auschwitz complex in the period from May 1944 to January 1945. Thousands died immediately after the liberation of the camp system, unable to recover from illness and starvation or other forms of illtreatment. Ultimately, every third person killed in Auschwitz was a Hungarian citizen; the biggest group of victims at the largest Nazi death factory had come from Hungary.

## ARROW CROSS RULE IN HUNGARY

Following Horthy's attempt to exit the war by negotiating a cease-fire with the Soviets, on October 15, 1944, the Germans removed him and replaced him with Arrow Cross leader **Szálasi**. The army, the majority of law enforcement officers, and much of the administrative apparatus pledged their loyalty to the new government. On October 17, Eichmann returned to Budapest to complete the anti-Jewish campaign. Together with Arrow Cross Minister of the Interior **Gábor Vajna**, he agreed to resume the deportations by immediately handing

---

93. Between 1942 and 1944, hundreds of Jews who were citizens or residents of Hungary were sent to Auschwitz from occupied Europe. Their exact number is unknown. On April 29 and 30, 1944, 3,800 people were sent from Budapest prisons and the Kistarcsa and Bácstopolya internment camps. Some 422,000 to 423,000 came with the mass transports starting on May 16, while 15,000 were deported to Austria. On July 22 and 26, 2,720 Jews arrived. They were smuggled out by the Nazis from the Sárvár and Kistarcsa camps. Besides these, smaller groups were also sent to the camp all the way through October. On May 15, 31 people were sent to the camp; July 25, several dozen from Budapest; July 27, 5 people; July 30, 2 people; August 19, 16 people; August 22, 2 people; September 4, 5 people from Vienna; September 5, 5 people, and so forth. See the secret list of the resistance movement about the tattoo numbers issued in the A and B series, 1944, ABSM, D-RO/123.

over fifty thousand Jewish forced laborers.⁹⁴ Eichmann informed Veesenmayer that he considered this a first step only, and as soon as they reached the contingent specified in the agreement, he would come forward with a demand for another fifty thousand.⁹⁵

The deportations resumed on November 6. Due to a shortage of trains, most of the labor servicemen and Jews rounded up in Budapest were herded westward on foot in so-called death marches. The destination was no longer Auschwitz. Right around then, some time between October 30 and November 3, Himmler ordered a stop to the gassing in Birkenau, the last extermination center.⁹⁶ The systematic genocide therefore came to an end, even though tens of thousands more Jews would be murdered in the Nazi camp system through the spring of 1945. From this point on, the deportations indeed became primarily a workforce issue. Accordingly, Hungarian Jews were directed to work on the construction of the so-called *Südostwall*, a fortress system to be set up on the Reich's eastern frontier. The SS assumed supervision of the Jews at the border.

All in all, Arrow Cross authorities handed over some fifty to sixty thousand Jews to the Germans.⁹⁷ This number included Labor Service units and Jews rounded up in Budapest, most sent on death marches. In late November and early December, thousands more were deported in cattle cars. On November 21, Veesenmayer informed Berlin that Szálasi had decided that only men fit to work would be marched from the capital to the border, women would be transported in cattle cars, and those unfit for work would be placed in ghettos in Budapest. A further remark by Veesenmayer illuminated the significance of the decision: "Because of the impossibility of supplying cattle cars, in practice, this means that the transports would be stopped."⁹⁸ The large-scale marches were halted in November, and all deportations eventually stopped in early

---

94. Veesenmayer's telegram (no. 2996) to the German Foreign Office, October 18, 1944, in Braham, *The Destruction of Hungarian Jewry*, 2:506.

95. Veesenmayer's telegram (no. 3007) to the German Foreign Office, October 18, 1944, in Braham, *The Destruction of Hungarian Jewry*, 2:507.

96. For details about the issues surrounding the halting of the deportations, see Gábor Kádár and Zoltán Vági, *Self-financing Genocide: The Gold Train, the Becher Case and the Wealth of Hungarian Jews* (Budapest: Central European University Press, 2004), 225–30.

97. On the various estimates, see Tamás Stark, *Zsidóság a vészkorszakban és a felszabadulás után 1939–1955* (Budapest: Magyar Tudományos Akadémia Történettudományi Intézete, 1995), 26–29.

98. Veesenmayer's telegram to the German Foreign Office, November 21, 1944, in Braham, *The Destruction of Hungarian Jewry*, 2:532–33.

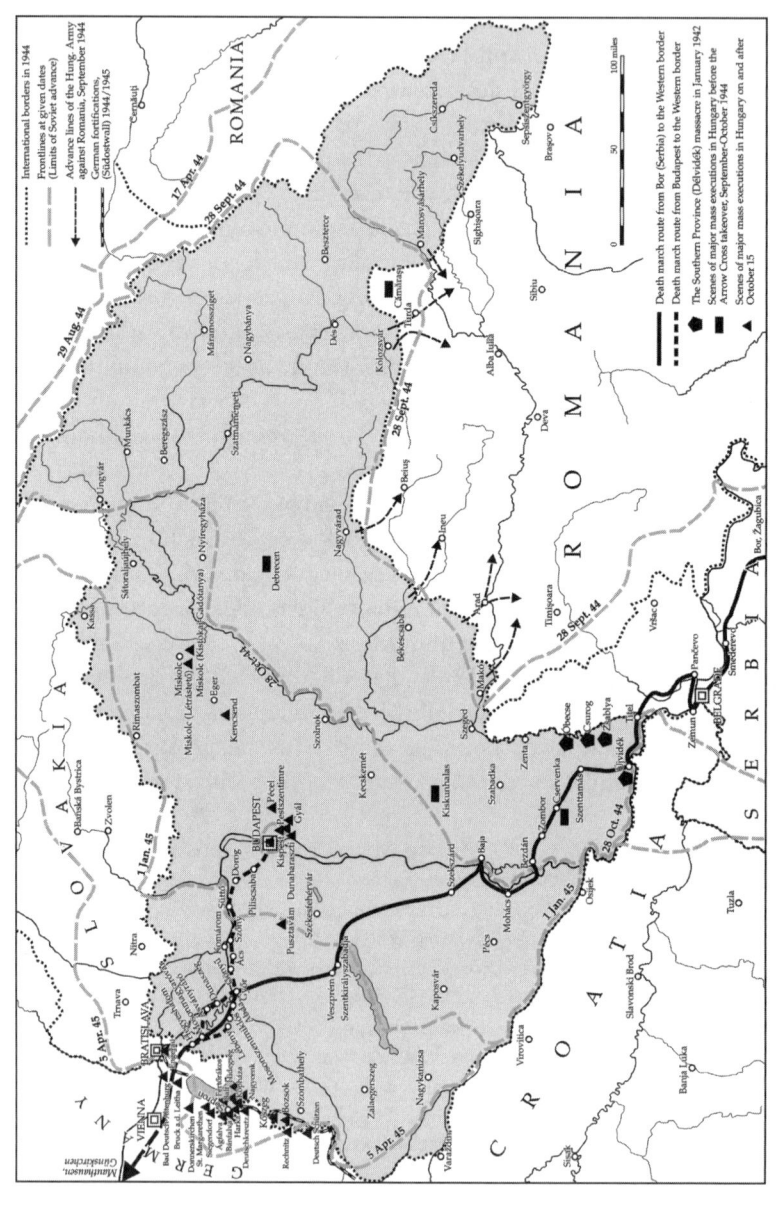

Map 4. Antisemitic Mass Executions and Death Marches in Hungary, 1942–1945
For a closer look at this map, go to: rowman.com/isbn/9780759121980.

December.[99] Against the explicit wishes of the Germans, the Jews remaining in Budapest were herded into two ghettos. The backdrop to this decision was Szálasi's Jewish policy, which proved quite surprising to the German Nazis.

Compared to the Horthy-appointed cabinet under Döme Sztójay, Ferenc Szálasi was far less enthusiastic about collaborating with the Germans on the Jewish question. Maneuvering in a narrow space, his government occasionally strayed from the Berlin line. In numerous matters (especially those concerning Jewish assets), the former regime had attempted to loosen the Germans' grip. However, with respect to the deportation of the Jews, it enthusiastically collaborated with the Germans. By contrast, Szálasi, the new leader, was far more willing to surrender Hungarian economic and military capacity but often held his ground stubbornly in Jewish matters. The Arrow Cross leader was a committed antisemite and envisioned the state he would create as free of Jews. However, this issue did not have the utmost priority on his political agenda.

Because Szálasi had foreign policy aspirations of his own, it was crucial that the neutral states officially recognize his rule. He was therefore willing to make compromises on the Jewish question, hoping for international recognition of his government. Chapter 9 attests to the fact that neutral diplomacy (that is, mainly on the part of representatives in Budapest of the Vatican, Switzerland, and Sweden) had been pressuring the Hungarian government since June or July: first in order to stop the deportations and then to prevent their resumption. The activities of the embassies intensified during the Arrow Cross era. Soon their actions grew into the most extensive diplomatic rescue operations in the history of the Holocaust. Szálasi had every reason to think that by fulfilling all German demands in Jewish matters, he would severely jeopardize his chances of gaining international recognition for his regime.

Szálasi's policies may seem "moderate" compared to the events of the spring and summer. The situation is more complex though. Arrow Cross units murdered some five to eight thousand Jews in Budapest and thousands more in the provinces from October 1944 through April 1945. As already mentioned, fifty to sixty thousand Jews were handed over to the Nazis. Following this, however—because of his perceived diplomatic interests—Szálasi was more resolute in resisting the Germans' demands concerning the Jews than his predecessor, Sztójay, or even Horthy himself up to late July 1944. The majority of the Budapest Jews therefore stayed in the country and were liberated by the Soviet army in early 1945.

---

99. The Budapest Gestapo sent off the very last transport to Buchenwald around Christmas.

## VICTIMS AND SURVIVORS

As the Soviets approached Auschwitz and other eastern camps, prisoners were evacuated westward. Hungarian Jews deported to the Auschwitz complex in the spring and summer of 1944 who had survived the selections were further transported to as many as six hundred different concentration camps and factories to work for the German military industry. In the early spring of 1945, the survivors of forced labor projects in western Hungary and eastern Austria were also sent into the Reich.[100] These groups—each comprising tens of thousands of people—converged in Mauthausen, Dachau, Sachsenhausen, Buchenwald, Gross-Rosen, Ravensbrück, Stutthof, and Bergen-Belsen concentration camps and hundreds of their subcamps. The once systematic Nazi mass murder now turned into a series of arbitrary killings. SS guards shot thousands of Hungarian Jews during death marches from one camp to another, while many prisoners escaped. Others died en masse on trains or in death marches that wandered through Germany for weeks on end.

Of the more than half a million Hungarian Jews deported in 1944 and 1945, only relatively few survived. At least 300,000 to 345,000 were murdered in the Birkenau gas chambers upon arrival. Thousands more died due to hunger, epidemics, forced labor, and selections throughout the Auschwitz complex. Additional tens of thousands perished in the Nazi web of concentration camps: in Mauthausen, Bergen-Belsen, Dachau, Mittelbau-Dora, Ravensbrück, Gross-Rosen, Neuengamme, Sachsenhausen, and hundreds of other main camps and subcamps.

When the survivors came out of the camps, many did not return to Hungary. Their families had been killed, communities destroyed, and assets seized. They felt that the country would never be their home again. Many decided to emigrate, mainly to countries further west or to Palestine. As indicated in chapter 10, others hoped for a new beginning and expected that the system replacing the Horthy regime would ensure them a normal life. But instead of freedom, old antisemitism and new threats lay in wait for them.

In the twentieth century, the Hungarian state frequently persecuted its own citizens in the name of various ideologies. Race protectionists and antisemites had started with the Jews, and the Arrow Cross included the Roma as well. But in the communist Eastern Bloc, after the war, it was the German minority's

---

100. For details about forced laborers working at the western border and about the subsequent fate of the survivors, see Szabolcs Szita, *Utak a pokolból. Magyar deportáltak az annektált Ausztriában 1944–1945* (Budapest: Metalon Manager Iroda, 1991).

turn. From 1946 to 1948, the new Hungarian authorities despoiled at least 147,000 to 170,000 ethnic Germans (*Svábs*), then put them into railway cars and sent them "back to Germany."[101] From 1948 on, aristocrats, "kulaks," capitalists, reactionaries, clerics, black marketers, and others were taken to different prisons and camps. As Hungarian author Sándor Márai wrote in his diary, "Yesterday the Jews, today the Svábs, tomorrow the bourgeoisie, and then those with flat ears."[102] Unlike in those parts of Europe that came under American, British, or French occupation, behind Soviet lines, a new chapter of suffering began—this time for both Jews and non-Jews.

---

101. Ágnes Tóth, "A magyarországi németek kitelepítése," *Kommentár* 5 (2007): 12–14.
102. Sándor Márai, *A teljes napló 1945* (Budapest: Helikon, 2006), 367.

# CHAPTER 1

# LAWS AGAINST THE RULE OF LAW

"CONCERNING THE Jewish question, for all my life, I have been an antisemite, I have never made any contact with Jews. I have found it intolerable that here, in Hungary, every single factory, bank, asset, shop, theater, newspaper, trade, etc. is in Jewish hands."[1] Regent **Miklós Horthy**, head of the Hungarian state between 1920 and 1944, wrote these words to Prime Minister **Pál Teleki** in 1940. Horthy's words are indicative of the system he created: his regime pursued anti-Jewish policies from its inception, and even in the periods when this was not manifested in explicit, open discriminatory steps, antisemitism remained one of its ideological cornerstones. The 1938 launch of a sequence of anti-Jewish laws therefore is not the starting point of Hungary's antisemitic tradition. Nor is 1920, when Horthy grabbed power in the midst of a destructive wave of pogroms. The roots go deeper than that.

In the second half of the nineteenth century, Jewish economic successes prompted negative sentiments, mainly from groups that were losers in the transition to a market economy. Among the discontented were landowners, who, lacking agricultural management knowledge, went broke after the liberation of the serfs and flocked into public administration, where they developed an anti-capitalist ethos[2]; Christian artisans who had lost their traditional, feudal privileges as the guild system was terminated in 1872; and stockholders bankrupted

---

1. Regent Miklós Horthy's letter to Prime Minister Pál Teleki, October 14, 1940, in Miklós Szinai and László Szűcs, eds., *Horthy Miklós titkos iratai* (Budapest: Kossuth, 1962), 260.
2. In Hungary, these impoverished noblemen were labeled gentries (*dzsentri*).

1

in 1873 as a result of the biggest global economic crisis of the nineteenth century, when the value of the Philadelphia, Vienna, and Budapest stock exchanges fell by almost 50 percent. The economic crisis boosted anti-Jewish sentiments in Hungary as well as in France and Germany. The primary target of criticism was the stratum of "alien" Jewish capitalists and financial entrepreneurs.

Besides the new anticapitalist platform, popular xenophobic hatred rooted in ancient superstitions and religious anti-Judaism was also present. This was manifested in the pogrom waves of the 1848 Revolution and the early 1880s. The liberal political elite suppressed the mob's violent outbursts and marginalized the antisemitic party created using the pogroms' momentum. However, at the turn of the twentieth century, political antisemitism flared up with renewed intensity. Christian socialism and clerical, antiliberal Catholicism played an important role in this process. In addition, in accordance with European trends, social Darwinist race theory emerged and served as an ideological basis for racial nationalism.

It is no exaggeration to say that antisemitism in Hungary was a well-developed ideology in all its components even before World War I. It was deeply embedded in international trends and enjoyed increasingly wide popularity. With Horthy's coming to power in 1920, it became one of the most important elements of the ruling ideology. The *numerus clausus* act, which restricted the number of Jews admitted to higher education, clearly marked this change. In the late 1930s the international political environment and the gradual radicalization of Hungarian inner politics resulted in a systematic series of anti-Jewish laws, which caused major material losses for the Jews. Estimates of the number of jobs lost by Jews by 1943 vary between forty and ninety thousand.[3] Moreover, the state significantly intruded into the most intimate spheres of peoples' lives by banning marriage between Jews and non-Jews, and by introducing a racial state definition of "Jewishness," hence depriving individuals of the right to choose their identities freely. This chapter lays out the provisions of the new legislation, while providing some account of the personal consequences of these

---

3. See Ferenc Chorin, "Tanulmányok, cikkek, beszédek, feljegyzések, nyilatkozatok, levelek," in *Az Andrássy úttól a Park Avenue-ig. Fejezetek Chorin Ferenc életéből 1879–1964*, ed. Daisy Strasserné Chorin and András D. Bán (Budapest: Osiris, 1999), 112; Péter Sipos, ed., *Imrédy Béla a vádlottak padján* (Budapest: Osiris–Budapest Főváros Levéltára, 1999), 36; Yehuda Don, "Economic Implications of the Anti-Jewish Legislation in Hungary," in *Genocide and Rescue: The Holocaust in Hungary, 1944*, ed. David Cesarani (New York: Berg, 1997), 59.

laws. How did Jews from different backgrounds and circumstances respond to the new restrictions?

## THE "JEWISH LAWS"

Enacting these laws required legislation to clarify who was considered Jewish. The text and commentary of the First "Jewish Law" (Act XV of 1938) did not define the term, but Article 21 of its enacting decree did.[4] This decree declared that Hungarian citizens were Jewish if they were members of the Israelite denomination; had converted to Christianity after July 31, 1919; had left the Israelite denomination before or after this date but not joined a Christian one; or were born after this date but had at least one parent who had been a member of the Israelite denomination on this date. The fall of the 1919 communist dictatorship served as the dividing date, reflecting the Horthy regime's claim that the Jews had caused the 1918–1919 revolutions. The legislators reasoned that it had been "advantageous" to be Jewish before and during those events. Therefore, they regarded conversions only that happened in that period as valid. Those who changed their religion after this date were not exempt from the law. Neither were those born Christian after July 31, 1919, who had one parent of the Israelite religion on the dividing date. In this way the act's definition of "Jewish" already contained many elements based on the idea of "race."

The bill that came to be known as the First "Jewish Law" was submitted to the parliament on April 8, 1938, by the Minister of Justice.[5] Discussion of the bill in the Lower House began on May 5, accompanied by lively interest from the public as well as the press, which at the time remained ideologically quite wide-ranging.[6] Along with the Jewish community, which published its objections in proclamations and pamphlets, non-Jewish intellectuals also raised their voices against antisemitic propaganda. On the morning of the first session, a manifesto by fifty-nine intellectuals appeared in the influential daily newspaper *Pesti Napló*. Those who signed the document included not only politicians but also a Catholic aristocrat, a Protestant pastor, well-known

---

4. Prime Minister's Decree no. 4350/1938. The codified measures described in this chapter were not officially titled "Jewish Laws"; yet already at the time this term had become the summary reference to anti-Jewish legislation.

5. *Az 1935. évi április hó 27-ére összehívott országgyűlés képviselőházának irományai* (Budapest: Athenaeum, 1938–1941), 10:273–82.

6. After 1920 the law ensuring freedom of the press remained in place, albeit with significant restrictions (Act XIV of 1914).

painters, writers, and publicists, and widely honored composers such as Béla Bartók and Zoltán Kodály.[7] The political affiliations of the protesters covered a broad spectrum, with the liberal and social democratic opposition joined by certain so-called folk intellectuals, who were not averse to anticapitalist expressions of antisemitism.[8] Accordingly, the manifesto rested on a mixture of arguments, elements of which also appeared in the speeches of members of parliament who objected to the bill.[9]

**DOCUMENT 1-1: Pronouncement of fifty-nine leading intellectuals and artists protesting the First "Jewish Law,"** *Pesti Napló*, **May 5, 1938, 2.**

A declaration by writers, artists, and scientists, addressed to Hungarian society and members of parliament.

[. . .] We, Hungarian writers, artists, and scientists, proponents of diverse worldviews and party affiliations, who work in a wide range of professions and jobs, each and every one of us having inherited the imperative to preserve and enrich our thousand-year-old Hungarian culture, we, each and every one of us descendants of Christian families, raise our voices with the self-evident unity and firmness of our human sense of justice, true Christianity, sensibility and patriotism, raise our voices on behalf of a principle—the legal equality of citizens—which the so-called "bill to secure social balance in a more efficient way," were it passed, would instantly erase from the Hungarian constitution.

[. . .]

The proposal humiliates Jewry less than it does the sons of the Christian middle class, when it assumes that they are expecting that their subsistence is secured through total ignorance of the sacred principle of

---

7. Béla Bartók (1881–1945) was a world-renowned concert pianist, one of Europe's leading composers, and a keen promoter of the study of Hungarian folk music. Opposed to the political developments in Europe in the 1930s, he moved permanently to New York. Budapest-born composer and musicologist Zoltán Kodály (1882–1967) promoted the preservation of folk music with Béla Bartók and others. See Benjamin Suchoff, *Béla Bartók: Life and Work* (Lanham, MD: Scarecrow Press, 2001); László Eősze, Mícheál Houlahan, and Philip Tacka, "Kodály, Zoltán," in *The Grove Dictionary of Music and Musicians*, ed. Stanley Sadie, 2nd ed. (New York: Macmillan, 2001), 13:716–26.

8. On the folk movement, see document 9-11(A).

9. For arguments about the law from debates in the Lower House, see *Az 1935 évi április hó 27-ére összehívott országgyűlés képviselőházának irományai*, 18:292–629 and 19:1–30.

legal equality of citizens: through deprivation of rights, through humiliating patronization, through coercion. [. . .]

Hungarians need all their strength in the crisis-ridden times—historic times—in which we are living today. The masters of the occupied territories are attempting to employ statistical tricks to separate those Hungarians who are of Jewish faith from the Hungarian people,[10] who have, apart from a very small number of exceptions, loyally shared the fate of Hungarians, their minority status and fate notwithstanding. How could we even inadvertently follow this example, excluding 400,000 of our fellow citizens from the Hungarian people?

[. . .] It is because of this inner command that we are now turning to the members of both houses of the legislature, to the Christian churches, to the professional and trade associations, to the unions and other bodies representing interest groups, to political, social, and cultural societies, and to the sensible and patriotic people of this country: they must demonstrate their self-esteem, bravery, and selflessness and stand up against the proposal that offends us all.

All of our contemporaries must realize the magnitude of the responsibility weighing upon them if—despite all conscientious objections—a law is passed, the thought of which must some day fill every Hungarian with shame!

The petition responded to the bill's historical and nationalist statements, raising similar arguments: it mentioned the achievements of the country's assimilated Jews. Moral, Christian approaches appeared as well; the petition argued the measure would demoralize the Christian middle class and go against the teachings of the churches by rendering the validity of a baptism contingent on its date or other secular considerations. The protesters also appealed to the principle of civic legal equality, the violation of which would create a dangerous precedent. Finally, left-wing counterarguments also cropped up, according to which the law directed attention away from social issues, affecting primarily those Jews who were poor, young workers, and those just entering the labor market.

The protesters represented a broad spectrum of intellectual traditions but lacked a significant base of followers. This became clear during the elections a year later (May 1939), when support for the antifascist, left-wing, and civic

---

10. This refers to the successor states (Romania, Czechoslovakia, and Yugoslavia) of the Austro-Hungarian monarchy that were given territories of the Hungarian Kingdom in accordance with the peace treaties after World War I. See map 1, p. xxxvii.

parties dwindled to under 10 percent. One reason for this was that in the meantime, due to the new "Jewish Law," many Jews had been stripped of their right to vote.[11] Subsequently, the opposition platform weakened further, and no similar, powerful joint proclamations were forthcoming. Because of the increasingly extreme right-wing atmosphere, some who had signed the manifesto emigrated shortly thereafter. For example, anti-Nazi composer and pianist Béla Bartók left for the United States in 1940. He settled in New York City and never returned to Hungary. During the war, one of his sons even served in the U.S. Navy.

The First "Jewish Law" (officially referred to as Act XV of 1938 on Securing Social Balance in a More Efficient Way) restricted the proportion of Jews in the press, theater, film, liberal professions (medicine, the law, and engineering), and white-collar careers at major industrial and commercial enterprises. Jews could henceforth comprise no more than one-fifth of the ranks of professional associations, in which membership became mandatory and exclusive. In the case of private companies, the law set a five-year deadline for its implementation. In activities deemed "of primary importance and for the public interest," the deadline was ten years.[12]

Contrary to what many expected, the law did not satisfy the extreme right, nor did it curb the anti-Jewish mood or public discourse. Instead it escalated tensions and hatred. Further legal measures promptly followed. Prime Minister **Béla Imrédy** organized a new mass movement, which gradually incorporated not only right-wing extremist voters but also their program. By November 1938 he had already declared a stronger and more fast-paced form of "self-defense" against the Jews. Its political manifestation was the bill of the Second "Jewish Law," submitted to parliament in December 1938. Not only was the new bill a stricter version of its precursor, but it differed qualitatively from it. Beyond providing a definition of "Jew," its aims and reasoning also changed markedly. Besides pushing Jews out of their economic positions, it now also placed the severe restriction of their political rights and forced emigration on the agenda. In February 1939, Pál Teleki succeeded Imrédy as prime minister. Teleki directed the vote on the bill in the parliament and also wrote the reasons attached to the act.

By passing the act, the government laid the groundwork for the gradual expulsion of the Jewish population. A separate government commissioner's office was planned to implement this goal, and negotiations began with Jewish

---

11. See document 1-2.
12. See the text of the law in Miklós Degré and Alajos Várady-Brenner, eds., *Magyar Törvénytár. 1938. évi törvényczikkek* (Budapest: Franklin, 1939), 132–44.

leaders. However, the outbreak of war thwarted execution of the plan.[13] Refugee policies simultaneously became stricter. Jews could not obtain Hungarian citizenship under any circumstances (Article 3). The law also permitted retroactive withdrawal of citizenship through naturalization from persons whose "living situation does not indicate that they will remain within the territory of the country."[14] This wording gave authorities a rather broad range of options for expelling refugees and other "undesirable elements." In 1941, this process led to the first mass murder of Jews during the Holocaust in Hungary.[15]

DOCUMENT 1-2: **Act IV of 1939 on the Limitation of Jewish Expansion in Public and Economic Spheres (Second "Jewish Law"), in Miklós Degré and Alajos Várady-Brenner, eds.,** *Magyar Törvénytár. 1939. évi törvényczikkek* **(Budapest: Franklin, 1940), 129–48.**

§ 1

With respect to the application of this law, all are considered Jewish who are members of the Israelite denomination at or prior to the date when this law goes into effect. Also considered Jewish are those who have at least one parent or at least two grandparents who are members of the Israelite denomination at or prior to the date when this law goes into effect. In addition, the offspring born to any persons listed above after this law has taken effect also count as Jewish.

[. . .]

§ 4

[. . .]

Jews have the right to vote for members of Parliament or municipal governing bodies and can be elected as members of Parliament or municipal governing bodies only if they themselves, as well as their parents, were born in Hungary (their grandparents must also have been born in Hungary if the parents were born after December 31, 1867),

---

13. See memoirs of **Samu Stern** in Nathaniel Katzburg, *Zsidópolitika Magyarországon 1919–1943* (Budapest: Bábel, 2002), 272–83. At his meeting with the Jewish leaders, Béla Imrédy designated a target number of one hundred thousand emigrants over five years. Ibid., 281.

14. "Naturalization" meant that a male person holding foreign citizenship, who stayed in the country and paid taxes for five consecutive years, could acquire Hungarian citizenship. On the acquisition of Hungarian citizenship, see Kinga Frojimovics, *I Have Been a Stranger in a Strange Land: The Hungarian State and the Jewish Refugees in Hungary, 1933–1945* (Jerusalem: Yad Vashem, 2007), 17–18, 39.

15. See chapter 2.

and—beyond satisfying other legally prescribed preconditions—they provide conclusive proof that their parents (and also their grandparents, if the parents were born after December 31, 1867) have been living in the territory of Hungary continuously since December 31, 1867.[16]

[. . .]

§ 5

Jews may not serve as officers or other employees of the state, of any municipal governing bodies, of any public body, public institution, or public utility company.

[. . .]

§ 9

In various professional associations, including those for lawyers, engineers, doctors, journalists, as well as the theater and cinema associations, Jews are admitted as members only if their number does not exceed a proportion of six percent of the total membership of the association. Alternatively, if the association is divided into sections and occupational groups, the number of Jewish members may not exceed six percent of the total membership of each section or group.

[. . .]

§ 14

No trade certificate or trade license for practicing a trade will be issued to a Jew until the number of trade certificates and licenses that have been issued to Jews in a given municipality drops below six percent of the total number of certificates and licenses in that municipality.

[. . .]

§ 22

The government is authorized to issue decrees regarding certain matters that would otherwise fall within the authority of the Parliament—specifically, matters such as the promotion of the emigration of the Jews and, in this connection, Jewish assets being moved abroad. The government may also issue decrees about customs, as well as other regulations deemed necessary for the protection of national assets in connection with the promotion of Jewish emigration.

[. . .]

---

16. The law specified the 1867 emancipation as the dividing line. In practice this meant that Jews had to obtain various types of documentation going back at times as far as a hundred years. This posed a problem for many, especially if they hailed from areas formerly separated from Hungary. For this reason, several Jews lost their right to vote and to hold office.

The text of the Second "Jewish Law" explicitly specified who would count as Jewish. Its rationale was primarily racial, but its basis was religious membership, given that no other workable criterion was available. All those were considered Jewish who, at or prior to the time the law came into effect, were themselves members of the Israelite denomination or had one parent or at least two grandparents who were members. Therefore, the law in theory did not affect Jewish families that had converted to Christianity for three generations. The law likewise did not apply to certain groups whose background was quite complicated, if they were born from "mixed" marriages and/or to parents who had converted to Christianity. Thus, the racial definition was not comprehensive, although the text and the commentaries made it clear that legislators considered Jewry a single, indivisible racial group, as well as a unified spiritual-emotional category. More threateningly, the legislative power concerning Jewish emigration was now placed in the hands of the government instead of the parliament. With this maneuver, the act sought to create a legal framework for pushing the Jews out of the country in the future more quickly and easily. The first two "Jewish Laws" can be considered independent, organically Hungarian developments. Hitler had not demanded them.

However, by the time the Third "Jewish Law" was issued in 1941, the increasing power of Nazi Germany generated a certain anti-Jewish rivalry among the satellite countries (Italy, Romania, and Slovakia) that resonated significantly in Hungary as well. Still, the Third "Jewish Law" was not enacted due to direct pressure from Germany. Instead, Prime Minister Pál Teleki favored pursuing a Jewish policy that afforded fewer exceptions and was based explicitly on racial categories. The "Race Protection Law" was another step in a policy of separating out Jews and preventing their acculturation and assimilation.

In June 1941, three days after the declaration of war against the Soviet Union, the government submitted the bill for the Third "Jewish Law" to parliament. The proposed goal was the "qualitative and quantitative" improvement of the population through various racial measures. The state made so-called marriage loans available only to those prospective marital partners deemed healthy. Those intending to marry now also had to provide medical certification proving they were in good health. The ban on marriage between Jews and non-Jews made up another component of these measures.

In the Lower House, the left-wing opposition to anti-Jewish legislation had by this time shrunk to a minimum; most of the votes against the bill came from right-wing extremist representatives. Naturally they did not oppose the government's intentions; they merely strove for an even more radical "arrangement" with a broader scope.[17] This time around, however, the heads of the Christian churches, who had supported the first two "Jewish Laws," united against the bill. At the same time, the churches' proclamations included antisemitic remarks and protested primarily against encroachments on their sphere of influence: religious jurisdiction over marriage and baptism. They were not against anti-Jewish policies as such; rather, they disapproved of the state's intrusion into what they considered their own domain.

DOCUMENT 1-3: **Act XV of 1941 on the Modification and Amendment of Act XXXI of 1894 on Marriage Law and the Necessary Related Race Protection Regulations (Third "Jewish Law"), in Miklós Degré and Alajos Várady-Brenner, eds.,** *Magyar Törvénytár. 1941. évi törvényczikkek* **(Budapest: Franklin, n.d. [1942]), 63–65.**

[. . .]

§ 9

It is forbidden for a non-Jew to marry a Jew.

A marriage between a Jewish woman and a non-Jewish foreign citizen is not subject to the prohibition under the present article.

Under the terms of this law, those are considered Jewish who have at least two grandparents who were born as members of the Israelite denomination, and—regardless of their ancestry—those who are themselves members of the Israelite denomination.[18] Those with two grandparents born as members of the Israelite denomination do not fall into the same category as Jews if they themselves were born as members of a Christian denomination, have remained so since, and both of their parents were, at the time of their marriage, members of a Christian denomination.

[. . .]

§ 14

A non-Jewish Hungarian citizen who marries a Jew; a Jew who marries a non-Jewish Hungarian citizen; and a Hungarian citizen who is a Jewish man marrying a foreign non-Jewish woman commits a crime in violation of the prohibition set out in Article 9 and shall be punished by up to five

---

17. János Gyurgyák, *A zsidókérdés Magyarországon* (Budapest: Osiris, 2001), 156–57.
18. This sentence refers to those who converted to Judaism.

years of prison, discharge from public service, and suspension of the exercise of political rights.[19]

[. . .]

§ 15
Jews commit an offense punishable by up to three years of prison, discharge from public service, and suspension of the exercise of political rights if
>    they have sexual intercourse with a decent,[20] non-Jewish woman who is a Hungarian citizen, or
>    they secure or attempt to secure a decent, non-Jewish woman who is a Hungarian citizen for themselves or another Jew for the purpose of sexual intercourse.

The action is a crime punishable by up to five years in prison, discharge from public service, and suspension of the exercise of political rights if the offender
1. committed the act through deceit, violence, or threat,
2. committed the act against a relative or someone entrusted or subordinated to him for education or supervision,
3. committed the act when the woman had not yet turned 21 years of age,
4. committed the act despite the fact that he had previously been punished for a similar offense and a ten-year period has not elapsed since completing the sentence for that offense.

---

19. The law prohibited the marriage of a Jewish man holding Hungarian citizenship and a non-Jewish woman of foreign nationality since the children from this marriage would gain Hungarian citizenship, and in this way "the number of offspring created by miscegenation, unwanted from a national point of view, would grow." See commentary in Róbert Vértes, ed., *Magyarországi zsidótörvények és rendeletek 1938–1945* (Budapest: Polgár, 1997), 150. The children resulting from a marriage of a non-Jewish Hungarian and a Jewish foreigner did not get Hungarian citizenship.

20. Decent (*tisztességes*) meant that the given female was not registered as a prostitute. Those women who were not registered prostitutes, but who regularly or occasionally had sexual intercourse with men in exchange for money, were also considered "not decent." Therefore, sexual relationships between them and Jewish men did not qualify as a crime. In a few cases, non-Jewish women bore the social stigma and falsely stated that they were "not decent" so that their Jewish partners would not be imprisoned. For the legal practice of "miscegenation" cases, see László Josefovits, *"Fajgyalázás," Az 1941: XV tc. 15 §-ának büntetőbírósági joggyakorlata* (Budapest: Feldmann, 1944).

The "Race Protection Law" came into effect on August 8, 1941. Its definition of "Jew" became the basis for further anti-Jewish measures. Gaining notoriety as the Third "Jewish Law," the act was even stricter than Germany's Nuremberg racial laws: Hungarian legislators had allowed for fewer exceptions than the Nazis.[21] Besides banning marriage between Jews and non-Jews, the law also regulated extramarital sexual relations, imposing a punishment only on relations between Jewish men and Christian women. At the same time, Christian males could continue their affairs with their Jewish lovers. When several representatives in the Lower House of parliament objected to this double standard, Ferenc Rajniss, representing the extreme right, responded (prompting considerable amusement), "There is a little bit of injustice in it."[22] Resistance by members of the Lower House—almost entirely Christian men—to restrictions on their own sexual freedom and privileges most likely lay behind this phenomenon.[23]

The law directly affected a few thousand people at most. Still, it had enormous significance, denying citizens a basic human right to choose a partner freely. While the previous laws were confined to the public sphere and to the means of earning a livelihood, with this move the state brutally interfered in the private lives of its citizens. The passages on the criminal consequences of breaking the law (Articles 11 to 15) reflected Nazi-style stereotypes and scapegoating of the morally corrupt, sexually criminal Jewish male engaged in extramarital relations, incest, seduction, trafficking in women, and prostitution. The

---

21. Both laws established exceptions for those with two Jewish grandparents; still, according to the Nuremberg Laws, individuals in this group were considered Jewish if they were Jewish by religion on September 15, 1935, whereas the Hungarian laws extended even to those who were born in the Jewish religion and later converted to Christianity. Thus, if a Hungarian who had two Jewish grandparents and was born in the Jewish religion converted, he or she was still subject to the law, whereas by contrast, a conversion prior to September 1935 could exempt German Jews who were in a similar situation. For a comparison of the two laws, see Raul Hilberg, *The Destruction of the European Jews*, 3rd ed. (New Haven, CT: Yale University Press, 2003), 2:856–59. Note that the treatment of "*Mischlinge*" in Nazi Germany remained in flux and became more radical over time.

22. Gyurgyák, *A zsidókérdés Magyarországon*, 155.

23. For more details about this phenomenon, see Gábor Kádár and Zoltán Vági, "Szex és faj. A nácik testpolitikája," *Magyar Narancs* 28 (July 2008): 13–15. Similarly, in numerous southern states of the United States, sexual relations between whites and people of color (not just African Americans) were long banned; yet juries and courts consisting of white men often treated a case more leniently if it involved a white man. On these histories, see, e.g., Peggy Pascoe, *What Comes Naturally: Miscegenation Law and the Making of Race in America* (New York: Oxford University Press, 2009).

credence given to these assumptions by the law further fueled the hatred of Jews that already permeated Hungarian society in significant ways.[24]

The first three "Jewish Laws" were followed by many others. One aimed at the confiscation of Jewish-owned agricultural real estate. The agrarian question was one of the most severe social problems of modern-day Hungary. The existence of large estates hindered modernization and the social mobility of the peasantry, which constituted the overwhelming majority of the population. Like other countries, Hungary introduced a land-reform law immediately after World War I to quell the hunger for land among the rural population.[25] Instead of requisitioning the large estates from the two pillars of the regime, the aristocracy and the Catholic Church, it seemed more practical to take over the lands of the (largely Jewish) middle-class. The Horthy regime handled the agrarian question much as it handled other social issues, in an antisemitic way. People of Jewish origin had owned nearly half the estates distributed to smallholders during the implementation of the 1920 reform.[26] By the end of the 1930s, the proportion of land owned by Jews was roughly equivalent to their proportion in society (5.2 percent).[27] However, due to the fact that the majority of the farms in "Jewish" hands were actually lease holdings, Jews' role in and profit from agriculture was much more significant than this figure suggests. The possibility of requisitioning Jewish-owned property was first made explicit in the Second "Jewish Law," which also severely restricted the rights of Jews to obtain land.

The law that went into effect on September 6, 1942, was the final stage of a two-decade-long process of "Aryanization" in the agricultural sector. Prime Minister **Miklós Kállay**'s government introduced the bill. An agricultural expert and a representative of the conservative large-estate-owning elite, Kállay

---

24. Nathaniel Katzburg, *Hungary and the Jews: Policy and Legislation, 1920–1943* (Ramat-Gan: Bar-Ilan University Press, 1981), 180–82.

25. Act XXXVI of 1920, in Gyula Térfy, ed., *Magyar Törvénytár. 1920. évi törvényczikkek* (Budapest: Franklin, 1921), 230–72.

26. Statement of reasons attached to the draft bill on Jewish-owned agricultural land and forests, *Az 1939. évi június hó 10-ére összehívott országgyűlés képviselőházának irományai* (Budapest: Athenaeum, 1941–1942), 8:146–48. Hungarian laws, decrees, and regulations usually, but not always, were (and are) issued with a so-called statement of reasons, in which a legislator explains the necessity of and interprets the contents of the given piece of legislation. It is not identical to the preamble (opening section) or the commentary of the laws, decrees, and regulations.

27. The total land (including forests) owned by Jews was about 830,000 cadastral holds (1,178,600 acres). See *Az 1939 évi június hó 10-ére összehívott országgyűlés képviselőházának irományai*, 8:148.

was aware of the political and economic risks of total expropriation. The bill was a gesture to appease both the Germans and Hungarian radicals, including Kállay's fellow party members. At the same time, the government intended to "outbid" the extreme right **Arrow Cross** opposition, which had gained mass support with promises of large-scale land reform. The preamble of the bill quoted in document 1-4 ensured an ideological grounding for the bill, which violated fundamental civil rights.

DOCUMENT 1-4: **Act XV of 1942 on the Jewish-Owned Agricultural Lands and Forests, in Miklós Degré and Alajos Várady-Brenner, eds.,** *Magyar Törvénytár. 1942. évi törvényczikkek* **(Budapest: Franklin, n.d. [1943]), 93–98.**

[Preamble]
[. . .]
Even before World War I, the conspicuous expansion of Jewry had caused uneasiness throughout other layers of Hungarian society. Since the end of the nineteenth century, efforts had been made to solve the political, social, and economic facets of the Jewish question. The Catholic People's Party had already taken steps against the expansion of the Jews, as well as the liberal political trends that served Jewish interests. However, major organized political aspirations aimed at curbing the territorial expansion of the Jews were only launched after the war that ended in 1918.

The principal goal of every struggle aimed at curbing Jewish expansion was to exclude Jewry from Hungarian land. Nothing could be viewed as more natural than this aspiration. Land cannot be compared to other assets. Land is not a commercial commodity, which is how the liberal conception of the preceding decades had endeavored to characterize it (and thereby "downgraded" it). The value of land cannot be measured solely in economic terms, because seedlings planted in the earth grow more than roots, they grow souls. For us Hungarians, land holds an extraordinary significance; the Hungarian land, which is our motherland, is a carrier of Hungarian life, Hungarian fate, our thousand-year history. Hungarian land stands in silent witness to our every joy and misery, to our every rise and downfall. It remains, to this day, not only a source of rights but also of associated duties—and those are no minor duties.

[. . .] If the state bars the ownership of land or lease holdings (in line with its financial possibilities and in an equitable manner) for those who are so different from members of the historical community due to their racial, spiritual, and moral capabilities that owing to these differences they, en masse, oppose the goals of the community, then in theory the state is not violating private property. On the contrary: by implementing those restrictive measures to protect the interest of the community, it returns property to the required ethical level.

[. . .]

*II. Prohibition on the acquisition of real estate*

§ 2

A Jew may not, through contract or auction, acquire agricultural land or forests (or land-use rights) and may not acquire real estate of any kind in small or large municipalities.[28]

*III. The requirement to surrender real estate*

§ 3

Jews shall be required to surrender the ownership of all of their agricultural land and forests (and surrender land use rights), as well as ownership of all their components and parts, and of agriculture- and forestry-related industrial factories and factory apparatus found on agricultural land and forests or associated with it. [. . .]

All those affected by the law were obliged to hand over their estates and any production facilities connected to them. If the estate exceeded five hundred *holds* (710 acres), the obligation included all animals and equipment as well. Compensation was to be made in the form of thirty-year treasury bonds, nonredeemable before the maturity date. The compensation offered was significantly less than the real value of the estates. Moreover, the decrees regulating the implementation left room to further restrict compensation, including the option of not giving any compensation whatsoever.[29] Acquiring an exemption from these laws was considerably harder than it had been under the Second "Jewish Law."

Official statements referring to an enormous number of Jewish estates created unreasonable expectations among the landless and smallholding peasantry. However, only estates under five *holds* (7.1 acres), about 3 percent of the approximately 750,000 *holds* (1.65 million acres) of expropriated land, were distributed among them. The estates and vineyards between five and one hundred *holds* (about 17.3 percent of the total amount of expropriated land), suitable for providing an independent existence, were put under the sole authority of the

---

28. The law's declared aim was to prevent "the ability of the Jews to re-enter into life of the rural communities." Paradoxically, this aim contradicted the antisemitic endeavor to stop the "Jewification" of the cities.

29. Prime Minister's Decree no. 3600/1943, June 22, 1943, in *Magyarországi Rendeletek Tára, 1943* (Budapest: Belügyminisztérium, 1943), 2:1403–58.

**Order of Vitéz.** Thus, the main beneficiaries of the expropriation process were members of the politically loyal Christian middle class, especially ex-servicemen, public servants, and officers, as well as members of civil associations, municipalities, and the churches. Corruption and nepotism flourished as a result.

Due to wartime economic and administrative difficulties (including a lack of non-Jewish agricultural experts), no final decision was made about the majority of the expropriated estates. After the German occupation, further efforts were made to increase the pace of expropriation. Allotments continued to be made to non-Jews until the arrival of the Soviet army. Besides depriving those thousands of Jewish families who earned their livelihoods from agriculture, the law also afflicted some non-Jewish groups, including the employees and workers of the liquidated Jewish estates.[30]

## THE IMPACT OF THE ANTISEMITIC LEGISLATION

The Jewish groups hit the hardest by the "Jewish Laws" included the lower middle class, craftsmen, retailers, state employees, white-collar workers, and above all young Jews in the provinces who had less training and were just entering the labor market. At the same time, major efforts were undertaken to circumvent the restrictions. If the laws had been taken at face value and applied immediately, the economy would have ground to a halt. For this reason, the authorities often turned their backs on attempts to bypass the laws, especially in economic branches of key importance, such as industries supplying the military.[31] Other efforts pulled in the opposite direction: civil and military officials often strove to enforce the regulations out of antisemitic zeal. In some areas this led to severe economic difficulties.

The laws also hurt quite a few Christian employees and clients of now shuttered Jewish-owned businesses. Still, for many non-Jews these years brought effortless economic advances. One illegal tactic that dodged the new restrictions—to the benefit of Jews and Christians alike—was the hiring of so-called

---

30. For details about the genesis and the implementation of the law, see László Csősz, "Land Reforms and Race Protection: The Implementation of the Fourth Jewish Law," in *The Holocaust in Hungary: A European Perspective*, ed. Judit Molnár (Budapest: Balassi, 2005), 180–97.

31. Viktor Karády, "Zsidótörvények és életfeltételek a szociális jelzők tükrében (1938–1943)," in *Zsidóság, asszimiláció, polgárosodás. Tanulmányok*, ed. Viktor Karády (Budapest: Cserépfalvi, 1997), 279–81.

*strómans* (literally "strawmen"). These were non-Jewish family members, acquaintances, or friends who agreed—in order to help but mostly in exchange for a sizable sum—to have a Jewish-owned shop or factory put in their name so that the company would not be subject to the Jewish laws.

The excerpts included in document 1-5(A–E) provide some indicators of how these new arrangements and new forms of discrimination affected the careers and daily lives of Jews. The first concerns a young man from Budapest whose career path was blocked by the antisemitic legislation. The author of the second testimony, Dr. Róbert Pap, was a wealthy lawyer in Szeged who turned sixty-five in 1939. He was among those whom the laws affected only indirectly. Still, the excerpt highlights communal and individual strategies for survival. A mark of social mobility among Jews was that many responded to the altered circumstances with flexibility: they attempted to cope by changing careers, retraining, or shifting their assets. The third excerpt, an interview with a young man from an **Orthodox** Jewish family in Munkács, reflects the Hungarian authorities' more radical Jewish policies in the occupied areas relative to their attitudes in **post-Trianon Hungary**.

DOCUMENT 1-5(A): **István Domonkos, recollections of the impact of the discriminatory laws on individuals, 2004–2005, CENTROPA (www.centropa.hu).**

> When my brother Péter got his high school diploma in 1938, the First Jewish Law came right away. As a result, no matter how talented he was, university studies were out of the question.[32] First, they tried to set him up with work in an office, but it was hard to find a decent job in that world governed by the Jewish Law, so at that point, our parents—along with other Jewish parents—got the idea [for us] to learn an industrial trade. My brother signed up at the Neumann electrician company as a student, an apprentice.

---

32. Although discrimination against Jewish applicants at universities had existed earlier, it was only with the Second "Jewish Law" that the *numerus clausus* was introduced yet again. On the *numerus clausus*, see the glossary.

DOCUMENT 1-5(B): **Portrait of Péter Domonkos, image no. 1011222232160678, CENTROPA (www.centropa.hu).**

This portrait shows Péter Domonkos in 1936. He was killed on the eastern front as a labor serviceman in 1943.[33] His brother, István Domonkos, survived the Holocaust in Budapest. As a high-ranking employee of the Central **Jewish Council**, their father, **Miksa Domonkos**, was one of the de facto leaders of the large Budapest ghetto at the turn of 1944–1945.

---

33. Péter Domonkos was born in 1919 in Budapest.

DOCUMENT 1-5(C): **Dr. Róbert Pap (1945),**[34] **recollections of the impact of the discriminatory laws on individuals, HJA, DEGOB Protocols, no. 3560.**

[. . .] In Szeged, the Jews found work in a variety of areas. Some of them were merchants, others craftsmen, but most of them were clerks and public servants. In general, they all lived well.

From 1938 onward, their economic circumstances went into gradual decline. The Chevra tried to help them with various forms of aid.[35] The Welfare Bureau of Hungarian Israelites was established,[36] and initially 50 percent of taxes would go into its budget to provide aid for the Jews[37]; later on, this was increased to 100 percent. There were also fund-raisers in Szeged to help the Jews in Budapest, and the money collected was used toward the goals of Hungarian National Jewish Aid Action.[38]

The misery-laden journey of the Jews began in 1939.[39] There was the First Jewish Law, at which point companies were allowed to keep their Jewish employees doing white-collar work only if their proportion did not exceed 20 percent of the white-collar workforce. This law did not yet have a dramatic impact because at most of the companies, the proportion of Jews was lower to begin with, so few people were affected by the decree.

After the Jewish laws were implemented, the Jews of Szeged could manage to make a living in the following ways: for example, a clerk who received his severance pay could invest his small capital in a business and could try to sustain himself that way. Congregations established workshops, retraining programs were organized, and unemployed workers were

---

34. Pap was head of the Szeged **Neologue** community, and after the March 1944 German occupation, he became the leader of the local Jewish Council. In June he fled from the Szeged ghetto and went into hiding in Budapest. He survived the Holocaust.

35. Chevra Kadisha (Holy Society) was the traditional charitable and burial society of Jewish communities.

36. The Welfare Bureau of Hungarian Israelites (MIPI) was a charity organization established in 1938 by the joint efforts of all three Jewish community networks: the National Office of Hungarian Israelites (Neologue), the Central Office of the Autonomous Orthodox Israelite Denomination of Hungary, and the National Alliance of the **Status Quo Ante** Communities. In 1939 the Zionists joined the organization as well. See Randolph L. Braham, *The Politics of Genocide: The Holocaust in Hungary* (New York: Columbia University Press, 1994), 1:89. The papers of the organization are held in HJA PIH-I F.

37. This refers to community taxes imposed by the Jewish communities on their members.

38. Hungarian National Jewish Aid Action (OMZSA) was a charitable effort connected to MIPI, launched in 1939. The papers of OMZSA are kept in HJA PIH-I K.

39. The "1939" is a typo; the actual date was 1938.

offered jobs. Women started to work at home; they would do needlework, they would weave yarn out of wool and angora wool, but their main income would come from renting apartments, providing room and board. [. . .]

DOCUMENT 1-5(D): **Ernő Galpert, personal recollections of the impact of the discriminatory laws on individuals, 2003, CENTROPA (www.centropa.hu).**

[. . .]
In 1938, the Germans handed over to the Hungarians the territories that had previously belonged to Hungary, including Carpatho-Ruthenia. Although the Hungarians thought they had been liberated, opinions on this issue were diverse. The Hungarian population greeted the situation with joy. Older Jews recalled that within the Austro-Hungarian Empire, Jews used to have a relatively large degree of freedom, and they hoped for the best until they figured out the situation. [. . .] With time it became clear that this country was no longer the old Hungary but a fascist country. Anti-Jewish laws went into effect. Jews were not allowed to own factories, shops, workshops. These properties were either handed over to a new owner, who had to be non-Jewish, or were seized by the state. Very few rich Jews managed to exempt themselves and keep their property; most had their licenses taken away and were stripped of all means of providing for their families. Supporting oneself became very difficult. My father had his trade license taken away. The owner of the workshop in which I worked also had his license taken from him, so the workshop closed down in 1940. My father and I had to look for jobs. The Roth paper factory was still operating at the time, and we were hired there.
[. . .]

DOCUMENT 1-5(E): **Portrait of Ernő Galpert, image no. 1012150900158492, CENTROPA (www.centropa.hu).**

Ernő Galpert is pictured here in 1939. His parents were deported and killed in Auschwitz, but he was drafted into the **Labor Service**. In late 1944 he was driven to eastern Austria on foot and worked there as a slave laborer.[40] The Red Army liberated him.

---

40. Austria as an independent state ceased to exist in 1938, when Nazi Germany occupied and annexed it under the name Ostmark. This volume uses the original name, Austria, in discussions of this territory.

Despite these losses and humiliations, few Hungarian Jews opted for the most obvious "dissimilation" and withdrawal strategies: emigration or conversion to Christianity. Emigration rarely proved an option, due both to external circumstances (the unwillingness of potential host countries to accept immigrants and fewer options owing to the spread of the war) and subjective factors (hesitation about leaving a home, relationships, and family). The "Jewish Laws" prompted another wave of Christian conversions, despite the fact that this action afforded questionable protection. The overall number of people changing religion ultimately remained insignificant.[41] The low number of emigrants and converts was—among other factors—partially rooted in the self-perception and self-identity especially prevalent among the Neologue Jews. They considered themselves Hungarians of the Jewish religion, true to both their country and their faith. Many responded to persecution by stressing their patriotic loyalty and achievements. They did so in part because going in the opposite direction would have meant reassessing integration strategies in place for several generations. The ideas of a shared fate, a shared mother tongue, and shared cultural values were important components of the Jewish Hungarian subculture, and giving them up would have meant substantial internal conflict. Many of the acculturated Jewish middle class believed in the existence of "another Hungary," one that rejected discrimination. Others held out hope for an improved situation and believed that the political elite was using a "double" or disingenuous rhetoric with the extreme right and the Nazis but would eventually step up to protect Jewish citizens.[42]

---

41. The number of conversions in 1938 was 8,584. This constituted 1.9 percent of the Israelite population (i.e., people of the Jewish religion) registered by the last prewar census in post-Trianon Hungary (1930). In 1941 this number came to 3,072 people (0.4 percent of the registered Israelite population in 1941), and in 1942 it amounted to 3,662 people (0.5 percent). Gyula Zeke, "Statisztikai mellékletek (1735–1949)," in *Hét évtized a hazai zsidóság életében*, ed. László Bányai et al. (Budapest: MTA Filozófiai Intézet, 1990), 1:195.

42. Viktor Karády, "Identity Strategies under Duress before and after the Holocaust," in *The Holocaust in Hungary: Fifty Years Later*, ed. Randolph L. Braham and Attila Pók (New York: Columbia University Press, 1997), 156–58.

## CHAPTER 2

# Discrimination, Radicalization, and the First Mass Murders

IN 1938 the Hungarian parliament officially launched antisemitic legislation. In the course of its implementation, provincial officials, the military, and police officers often initiated administrative procedures and proposals against Jews that exceeded even the strict provisions of the "Jewish Laws." This indicates that a significant number of civil servants and local extremists were ready to confront the Jews much more harshly than the parliament itself. During World War II this pressure—exerted by lower levels of the state upward and magnified by the Third Reich's increasing political influence and military power—continually radicalized the climate and public discourse. Measures that seemed unimaginable even in 1937 had become routine by 1941. The government launched an extensive "aryanization" program. In the framework of the so-called **Labor Service** system, Jews were first excluded from the armed service, then ended up in the hell of the eastern front without proper clothing or supplies, exposed to the brutality of their guards. In the summer of 1941, administrative steps against illegal emigrants resulted in the deportation of around eighteen thousand Jews to the Ukraine, where the SS executed most of them. Half a year later, a series of antipartisan actions produced a frenzy of killings of innocent civilians by the military and **gendarmerie** in the southern regions. At the same time, due mainly to foreign policy considerations, the Hungarian government denied German demands to ghettoize and deport the Jews. This chapter focuses on developments in the period between 1938 and 1944: the antisemitic measures of the local governments, Hungary's Labor Service, the first mass murders, and German-Hungarian negotiations around the "Jewish question."

## BUREAUCRATIC AND ILLEGAL ANTISEMITISM BEFORE 1944

Implementation of the "Jewish Laws" was not the only way antisemitic local officials could make the lives of Jews harder. Many found the means to do so even outside the framework of discriminatory legislation. **László Endre** offers a typical example, first as chief constable of Gödöllő between 1923 and 1937, then later as subprefect of Pest-Pilis-Solt-Kiskun County. Endre used a wide range of measures against the Jews, often based on forgotten and never revoked regulations, orders, and decrees with which compliance would have been virtually impossible. For example, the regulations pertaining to issuing of trade licenses included the condition that the petitioner had to be a Hungarian citizen. In most cases the authorities did not require certification of citizenship. However, Endre demanded that Jews produce proof that they and their ancestors had lived in Hungary since 1851. Moreover, he added that only original documents would be accepted as evidence; even certified copies were invalid. With Hungary's border changes and waves of migrants in the previous century, many petitioners quite clearly would never be able to comply with this strict stipulation, even if they were Hungarian citizens.[1] At other times, Endre ordered Jewish-owned restaurants and shops to close if the owner failed to abide by every minute detail of the public health regulations (which their Christian rivals likewise failed to observe). Endre was not the only official to pursue this practice. Based on a similar argument about the preservation of public health, the subprefect of Békés County shut down an **Orthodox** institution in Békéscsaba. The Zalaegerszeg Financial Directorate issued a directive about the administrative means of sabotaging petitions by Jews for liquor licenses.[2] We call this practice **bureaucratic antisemitism**, in the sense that although not explicitly anti-Jewish, these bureaucratic regulations were indisputably used for anti-Jewish purposes.

Another form of antisemitic administrative action consisted of authorities exceeding the discriminatory laws in effect, even violating them in order to implement their own anti-Jewish initiatives. This was **illegal antisemitism** (that is, it did not comply with the laws). An example was Endre's forbidding

---

1. For a detailed analysis of Endre's decree, see Zoltán Vági, "Endre László politikai pályája 1919–1945. Szélsőjobboldali elit, közigazgatási apparátus, zsidókérdés" (PhD diss., ELTE, 2003), 92–95.
2. Letter of the Zalaegerszeg Financial Directorate to the prefect of Zala County, August 2, 1938, in László Németh and Zoltán Paksy, eds., *Együttélés és kirekesztés. Zsidók Zala megye társadalmában, 1919–1945* (Zalaegerszeg: Zala Megyei Levéltár, 2004), 266–67.

Jewish merchants to sell their products at markets and fairs in 1940. Within a couple of months, five cities and nineteen **counties** all over the country had begun following his example. On another occasion, in 1941 he prohibited Jews from obtaining lard.[3] Again, numerous cities and counties followed his lead. Among them was Heves County, which in the summer of 1942 forbade Jews to purchase food before 9 a.m., that is, they were banned from shops during the busiest time of day.[4] Various appeals forced the Ministry of the Interior to start investigations concerning the legality of these decrees. The inquiries usually lasted years, during which these dubious measures remained in effect. In the end, the ministry annulled many of them because they proved illegal even within the standard established by existing anti-Jewish laws. The documents that follow record examples of these administrative manipulations.

Rimaszombat was a small town in the Upper Province with a largely Hungarian-speaking population, less than a mile from the Slovakian border. In June 1941, when Hungary declared war on the Soviet Union, the mayor issued a new regulation against local Jews. His decision was motivated by other municipal officials who did not consider the government-sanctioned antisemitism sufficient and probably also by a decree with a similar thrust issued two weeks earlier by the Slovak Ministry of the Interior.[5] At the same time, he proceeded in a "creative" manner, taking into account local circumstances and thus doing far more than just adopting examples. On June 30, 1941, the municipal government body of representatives unanimously passed the proposed regulation excerpted in document 2 1, put it into effect immediately, and requested approval for it only afterward. The body of representatives had one member of Jewish origin, who had exempted status. He was not allowed to speak or vote, given his "vested interest" in the matter.[6]

---

3. The regulations only excluded Orthodox Jews from access to the lard supply. Endre extended the scope of the decree to all Jews, even though some **Neologue** and many converted Jews did use lard in their kitchens.

4. Letters of the National Office of Hungarian Israelites to the Minister of the Interior and the Minister of Public Supply, September 1943, HJA XVI-A, box TA 9/3/4.

5. In addition to a shopping ban prior to 10 a.m., the Slovak order also banned Jews from using public baths and parks, as well as from being out on the streets past 9 p.m. It also ordered a ban on Jews and non-Jews visiting one another. See Decree of the Minister of the Interior, July 15, 1941, ŠAB, Presidential Documents of the Turčiansky Svätý Martin District Office, document 199/1941 (courtesy of Hana Klamkova).

6. Summary of the record of the meeting of the local government body of representatives, June 30, 1941, YVA, M 48, fascicle 3166, ŠOKA Rimavská Sobota, documents of the Mayor of Rimaszombat, document 4400/1941.

DOCUMENT 2-1: **City regulation and the attached statement of reasons, issued by the Rimaszombat municipal authorities, June 1941, YVA RG M 48, fascicle 3166, ŠOKA Rimavská Sobota, Documents of the Mayor of Rimaszombat, document 4400/1941.**

[. . .]

At the meeting of the body of representatives of the town of Rimaszombat, held on June 30, 1941, the following decision was passed under Public Administration Number 4400-1941 Meeting 112:

"Regulation by the town of Rimaszombat, to secure public supply and public order:

Article 1. Serving lard to Jews is forbidden throughout the area of the town of Rimaszombat.

Article 2. It is forbidden for Jews and for wholesale buyers to make purchases before 10 a.m.—either in person or through an authorized individual, a so-called "strohmann"[7]—at markets and at fairs. [. . .]

Article 4. Assembling in public places is prohibited for Jews. Two or more persons are considered an assembly.[8] Streets, squares, coffeehouses, restaurants, baths, etc., are considered public places. Theaters, traveling theaters, and social organizations and groups are not considered public places.

[. . .]

Statement of reasons attached to the regulation:

[. . .]

Spreading disturbing rumors and idle gossip are both acts of high treason; nonetheless, many become involved in this inadvertently, or out of selfish motives. Experience has shown that disturbing rumors are primarily started by Jews. Jews enjoy listening to foreign radio station programs in various languages and show great willingness to create disturbances by passing on the news they have heard there—news that had been broadcast with the intent to deceive. It therefore seems necessary to prevent this and where possible, to prevent Jews from discussing and passing on these frightening rumors.

With respect to this regulation, theaters, movie theaters, social organizations, and groups had to be excluded because, given the nature of these

---

7. See the glossary.
8. Redefining an assembly as the joint presence of two or more people contradicted a well-established legal principle based on Roman law that required at least three individuals for an assembly (*tres faciunt collegium*).

venues, the spreading of frightening rumors, etc., at these venues is difficult and because these venues are under permanent police supervision."
[. . .]

Article 4 affected the most basic everyday needs of Jews, for it pronounced that they could not stroll on the streets with their families, go to restaurants, or use the town's only operating public bath, which served as the congregation's ritual bath. The mayor justified the decision by alluding to the "whispering" and "subversive" propaganda of Jews listening to foreign radio stations. He claimed that the Jews harbored communist sentiments and had "brought about the war and are now hiding away in their nests so they can pounce on the bleeding body of the nation."[9] The statement of reasons attached to the regulation was even more specific[10]: it accused the Jews of outright treason. The irrational, purely ideological motivation showed in the fact that the regulation accused Jews of listening to radio broadcasts, when they had previously been ordered to turn their radios over to the authorities.[11] The regulation proved so contradictory in legal terms that a month later the Ministry of the Interior annulled it.[12]

When it came to taking the initiative in introducing discriminatory measures, the pioneering efforts of László Endre proved extremely influential. The case cited in document 2-2(A, B) is a classic example of the illegal antisemitic methods routinely deployed during World War II. The petition submitted by Gyömrő citizens offered a pretext for the subprefect to issue a regulation running against laws already in effect by appealing to the "public interest."[13] With the exception of local residents, he banned all Jews from every single beach and bath in the **county**. Complex motivations lay behind prohibiting Jews from using the baths. Besides "protecting Christian morals," it reflected the racist aspiration to segregate the "filthy Jews," along with a desire to secure cultural, recreational activities for non-Jews only.

---

9. Petition by Mayor Dr. László Éva addressed to the minister of the interior, seeking approval for the regulation, June 30, 1941, YVA M 48, fascicle 3166, ŠOKA Rimavská Sobota, documents of the Mayor of Rimaszombat, document 4400/1941.

10. Cf. chapter 1, note 26.

11. Appeal by Jewish local residents against the regulation, July 11, 1941, YVA, M 48, fascicle 3166, ŠOKA Rimavská Sobota, documents of the Mayor of Rimaszombat, document 4400/1941.

12. Ibid., Decision of the Minister of the Interior, July 28, 1941.

13. This is a municipality east of Budapest.

DOCUMENT 2-2(A): **Letter written by János K. (last name illegible) to the subprefect of Pest-Pilis-Solt-Kiskun County, László Endre, spring 1941, Pest County Archives IV/408/B, document 29.877/1941.**

The beach and swimming pool season is starting [. . .] Throughout the country, one finds several beaches and outdoor baths where the following foulness, a remnant of the Jewish-liberal world, can be observed: separate sunbathing sections exist for women and men, yet they would be completely naked everywhere, lying there like pigs [. . .] This is filthy wantonness, for it is unnecessary for one to expose and burn body parts to a Negro black [color],[14] the display of which befits none other than the Jewish ghetto spirit.

DOCUMENT 2-2(B): **Order of the subprefect of Pest-Pilis-Solt-Kiskun, No. 27.845/1941, May 1941, USHMMA RG 39.013M, reel 71 (HJA XXIV/C, box A 5/1).**

Sándor Dobossy, a resident of Gyömrő, along with 233 others has filed a complaint against the Jews, citing the Jews' intolerable behavior observed at baths and spas and requesting that they be banished from these venues.

Final Decision

With fellow petitioners, Sándor Dobossy, a resident of Gyömrő, filed a petition that is hereby sustained. Accordingly, individuals who are considered Jewish based on Article 1 of Act IV of 1939 are banned throughout the county from every bath, special climate sanatorium, health and holiday resort, specified as such in Articles 1–4 of Act XVI of 1929.[15] The aforementioned individuals may not visit the baths, sanatoria, health and holiday resorts described above and may not participate in the public use of these facilities.

The current prohibition does not apply to those individuals falling under paragraph 1 of Act IV of 1939 at their permanent or temporary residence who have such residence in a health or holiday resort location, provided that the location was already registered as their permanent or temporary residence prior to the publication of the current decision. However, even within their permanent or temporary residence, these individuals may

---

14. In the original: *néger-fekete*.
15. See document 1-2.

not use the pools, baths, sunbathing and entertainment venues open to the public; nor may they participate in the use of other facilities intended to enhance the comfort and entertainment of resort guests.

Statement of Reasons

According to the Statement of Reasons attached to Act IV of 1939 (Document no. 702 of the 1939–1940 Parliament), the morality and tradition of the Jews, going back several thousand years, have led to a worldview and behavior that is often different with respect to strangers. This worldview and behavior are an inherited attribute rooted in the Jewish race and therefore cannot be cast off easily.[16]

The observation cited above is demonstrated most clearly in the behavior of Jews at health and holiday resorts, behavior through which they aim to keep non-Jewish individuals who are strangers to them away from the health and holiday resorts.

Sándor Dobossy and the fellow petitioners' petition derives from the recognition of this unsustainable situation.

Because the moral conception rooted in the Jewish race is indeed so distant from and so antithetical to the Christian moral worldview, a reconciliation of the two is impossible, and because the Jews do not want to shed the worldview and behavior originating from their race, a radical change in their worldview and behavior cannot be expected, I must sustain the petition by Sándor Dobossy and fellow petitioners for the sake of the working Hungarian population of the county that seeks rest, recreation, relaxation, and healing.

However, I must also sustain the petition in terms of services and facilities available to the public. It cannot be permitted, after all, that individuals of Jewish race flood the holiday and spa resorts during the summer months, endangering the service provided to the indigenous population.

I order the publication of this decision in the *Official County Journal*. Appeals against the present decision can be submitted to His Excellency,

---

16. According to the statement of reasons of the May 1939 Second "Jewish Law" (written by Prime Minister **Pál Teleki**), the Jews represented not simply a race but a special "physiological, spiritual, mental, and emotional unity," with a collective character and deeply rooted features that were markedly different from those of non-Jews. Reasons attached to the bill, *Az 1935. évi április hó 27-ére összehívott országgyűlés képviselőházának irományai* (Budapest: Athenaeum, 1938–1941), 12:298–321.

the Hungarian Royal Minister of the Interior and to me within 15 days past the 8th day following its publication in the *Official County Journal.*

Budapest, May 5, 1941
vitéz Dr. László Endre [signed].[17]
Subprefect

Endre cited the interests of Christian citizens, but at the same time, he also de facto violated "Christian" interests. Banning Jewish visitors from county baths meant a sizable reduction in income for these institutions. These businesses, together with private individuals and the National Office of Hungarian Israelites, filed a joint appeal to the minister of the interior, who subsequently annulled the regulation on the grounds that restrictions concerning individual rights fell exclusively within the legislative purview of parliament.[18] It was characteristic of Endre's influence and the political atmosphere that despite the series of legal violations he committed, he maintained his position even after his decree was invalidated. It is also telling that other municipal authorities issued similar regulations, even after the Ministry of the Interior annulled Endre's decree: for example, in March 1943 Mayor of Szatmárnémeti László Csóka banned Jews from public baths (together with non-Jews infected with various sexually transmitted diseases).[19]

Measures exceeding the harsh provisions of antisemitic laws in effect were not the only results of local officials' tendency to try to radicalize the government's anti-Jewish policies. As document 2-3 shows, certain municipal bodies came up with complete plans to solve the "Jewish question." In addition, in many of them, radicals who considered the government's Jewish policy inadequate formed a majority. This was due in part to the general shift to the right in the political arena. Another factor was that after 1939, in all but a few large towns and cities, most Jewish representatives lost their membership in municipal bodies, and about 90 percent of Jewish citizens lost their right to vote. Local governments regularly submitted political initiatives or measures, hoping to influence legislators on the national level. The interactions and pressures exerted between various levels of power thus also shaped national Jewish policies.

---

17. Endre was the member of the **Order of Vitéz**.
18. Gábor Kádár and Zoltán Vági, *Hullarablás. A magyar zsidók gazdasági megsemmisítése* (Budapest: Jaffa, 2005), 66.
19. Ágnes Hegyi and Daniel Lőwy, "Szatmár County," in *The Geographical Encyclopedia of the Holocaust in Hungary*, ed. Randolph L. Braham and Zoltán Tibori Szabó (Evanston, IL: Northwestern University Press in association with the USHMM, 2013), 2:964.

Just a few days after **Miklós Kállay**'s government took office (March 1942), the Municipal Committee of Bihar County made clear what it expected from the government through a petition.[20] Retired general Sándor Báthory-Szűts, a typical representative of the locally born, traditional noble elite, submitted the proposal for the petition to the committee. He reasoned that a victorious ending to the war would, in the foreseeable future, bring "the only perfect solution" to the "Jewish question": the resettlement of Jews to a Jewish nation-state, to be designated at a later time. According to him, Hungarians must prepare for this. Among the basic tasks he mentioned were administrative preparations, a final and precise way to determine who counted as Jewish (including extensive restrictions on exemptions), and the total confiscation of Jewish assets. For the remaining period, he demanded the complete segregation of the Jews from Christian society "in space and time." He argued that this was the only way to protect society, particularly the youth, from the "infectious Jewish mentality."[21] The demands listed in the first three points of the petition had already been part of the government program for some time, so they were "only" calling for stricter and more consistent reinforcement. Subsequent points went much further, however.

DOCUMENT 2-3: **Minutes of a meeting of the Bihar County authorities, March 28, 1942, HBCA IV.B. 1406/b, box 284, document 16.978/1942.**

Prepared in Nagyvárad, on March 28, 1942, in the small council room of the County Hall, based on decision no. 82, county assembly 6228.sub-prefect/1942 of the Bihar County Committee, concerning an independent motion submitted by County Committee Member Vitéz Sándor Szüts on the subject of resolving the Jewish question [. . .]

The public of Bihar County is submitting a petition to the Hungarian Royal Government in order to underline the following points in the institutional solution of the Jewish question:

1.) The Hungarian Royal Government should immediately set up an agency with the appropriate powers, whose task is the practical preparation of the resettlement of Jews and its implementation.[22]

---

20. This county is in the eastern part of Hungary; most of its territory (along with the county seat Nagyvárad) was in the area regained from Romania in 1940.
21. Proposal by the Municipal Committee of Bihar County about resolving the Jewish question, HBCA IV.B. 1406/b., box 284, doc. 16.978/1942.
22. Setting up an authority to coordinate the forced emigration of Jews was planned since 1939. See document 1-2.

2.) The legislation should specify the definition of being Jewish in all details, one exclusively based on the definition given in Act XV of 1941,[23] that is to say, one based on the correct racial grounds.

3.) If the legislation permits any exceptions, they should be restricted to the following:

either a.) military decorations awarded for bravery in the 1914–1918 World War, or b.) counterrevolutionary feats during the revolutions and the foreign occupation.[24]

Fulfillment of either condition is to be accompanied by both an unblemished past and loyalty to the nation.

Should half-blood Jews come under these exceptions, their blood assimilation into the Hungarian people should be institutionally regulated.

4.) The Hungarian Royal Government should, without delay, freeze the assets and income of the Jews, as well as assets and incomes originating from Jews, and impose upon these:

a military-exemption capital levy and military-exemption tax,

a compensation capital levy and compensation tax, in order to compensate for the damages to the Hungarians for intellectual, physiological, and economic losses imposed by the Jewish liberal economic system,

a resettlement capital levy and resettlement tax, in order to cover costs associated with the preparation and implementation of the resettlement of the Jews, including the securing of job opportunities and living expenses—up until the resettlement is carried out—for Jews living in poverty.

5.) Until the resettlement is carried out the Hungarian Royal Government should segregate the Jews through laws and decrees from Christian, Hungarian economic and social life.[25]

[. . .]

Báthory-Szűts was presumably unaware that his proposal for a compensation tax was practically identical to the measure formulated at the meeting of

---

23. See document 1-3 for the definition of "Jew" in the antisemitic legislation.

24. This refers to the 1918–1919 revolutions and the era of Romanian rule in Transylvania (1918–1940).

25. The fact that Bihar County authorities acted as if such regulations had not been in force as of 1938 clearly shows that they found the antisemitic legislation weak and unsatisfactory.

top Nazi leaders following "*Kristallnacht*" in November 1938. This required the German Jews to pay 1 billion RM as "compensation for damages" during the disturbances. The resettlement tax likewise had a precursor. The Zentralstelle für jüdische Auswanderung (Central Office for Jewish Emigration), which **Adolf Eichmann** had set up in Vienna in 1938, implemented a similar model (paying for the emigration of poor Jews with wealthier Jews' assets). Báthory-Szűts's proposal for the military exemption tax argued that Jews kept reproducing, turning the war to their advantage, while Hungarians were making sacrifices on the battlefield, and their numbers were decreasing. He acted as if he did not know that all Jews were subject to a military service requirement and that thousands of labor servicemen were dying at the front. The proposal suggested that "social justice" considerations should determine how many of their assets Jews could keep and take with them to their new homes. Quite a number of other municipal governing bodies supported the letter addressed to the government.[26] Still, Kállay's government put this proposal aside.

## THE FIRST MASS MURDERS

In the regions that Hungary reannexed between 1938 and 1941 (see table 3, p. 369 and map 2, p. xlii]), the government and military administration pursued Jewish policies that were generally more radical than in the core territories.[27] They even initiated independent operations to remove Jews from these areas. Following the reannexation of the Upper Province in 1938, around three thousand Jews were expelled from the region.[28] After Hungary occupied Northern Transylvania, the army launched a series of actions in Csíkszereda and its vicinity, near the Romanian-Hungarian border. In late 1940, the military expelled twenty-four Jewish families, most of them born in the country, and

---

26. However, some of them refused to back the proposal. For example, the mayor of Debrecen declined to support it on the grounds that "solving the Jewish question is a government task . . . and its institutional solution has been projected by His Excellency, the Hungarian Royal Prime Minister." HBCA IV.B. 1406/b., box 284, doc. 16.978/1942.

27. For an analysis of the phenomenon, see Mária Ormos, *Egy magyar médiavezér: Kozma Miklós* (Budapest: Polgart, 2000), 2:736–37, 767–759; Gyula Vargyai, *Magyarország a második világháborúban. Összeomlástól összeomlásig* (Budapest: Korona, 2001), 119–53.

28. Kinga Frojimovics, *I Have Been a Stranger in a Strange Land: The Hungarian State and the Jewish Refugees in Hungary, 1933–1945* (Jerusalem: Yad Vashem, 2007), 73.

transported them to the other side of the border.²⁹ During the following summer, a significantly broader operation was launched, primarily targeting Jews who were not Hungarian citizens but also leaving several Jewish victims dead, as this chapter details.

The aggressive nationalism and antisemitism of much of the army led to increasingly radical steps during the war. The concrete result of this dangerous combination is evident in the number of civilian victims of the subsequent reannexation waves: in the Upper Province and in Carpatho-Ruthenia, a few dozen civilians were killed, while in Northern Transylvania, where sporadic guerrilla operations triggered army retaliations against civilian residents, the number of casualties rose to a few hundred.³⁰ A full-scale operation against certain ethnic groups occurred in the Southern Province: by 1942 tens of thousands of people (mostly Serbians) had been driven out and thousands killed. Traditional Hungarian-Romanian and Hungarian-Serbian interethnic conflicts were rekindled. In addition, Jews became an integral and central component in the image of the enemy. For this reason, although the Jews nowhere played a role in the anti-Hungarian attacks, large numbers of them fell victim to the occupying authorities' actions.

Many in the Hungarian-speaking Jewish population of the reannexed territories welcomed **Miklós Horthy**'s incoming army. The image reproduced in document 2-4 shows a representative of a Jewish community (a rabbi, the head of the community, or other leader) giving a speech at an event in Beszterce (Bistriţa) celebrating the reannexation of Northern Transylvania by Hungary in September 1940. (Nazi flags and the Italian banner can be seen in the background.) Those Jews enthusiastic about the territories returning to the "heartland" soon suffered disappointment.

---

29. Tamás Majsai, "The Deportation of Jews from Csíkszereda and Margit Slachta's Intervention on Their Behalf," in *Studies on the Holocaust in Hungary*, ed. Randolph L. Braham (New York: Columbia University Press, 1990), 113–63; Zoltán Tibori Szabó, "Csík vármegye zsidósága a betelepüléstől a megsemmisítésig," in *Tanulmányok a holokausztról III*, ed. Randolph L. Braham (Budapest: Balassi, 2004), 105–7.

30. Miklós Zeidler, *A revíziós gondolat* (Budapest: Osiris, 2001), 223–24.

DOCUMENT 2-4: **Photograph of a Jewish community representative at a commemorative event celebrating the reannexation of Northern Transylvania by Hungary, 1940 (Courtesy of FORTEPAN).**

Not restricted to passing and implementing anti-Jewish laws and decrees, Hungarian politics soon claimed the first Jewish lives. The first mass murder occurred in the summer of 1941. The primary targets were foreign Jews, but several people holding Hungarian citizenship also fell victim to the operation.

On the brink of World War II and during its initial phases, Budapest pursued a relatively tolerant refugee policy, primarily for diplomatic reasons. In the fall of 1939, despite a prevailing pro-German foreign policy trend, the government admitted over one hundred thousand Polish citizens. Refugees also arrived from the former countries of Austria and Czechoslovakia, among them, quite a few Jews.[31] However, this latter group became subject to an increased level of discrimination and bureaucratic strictness.[32] The major agency enforcing refugee-related policies was the National Central Authority for Controlling

---

31. Between 1933 and 1945, a total of about twenty to twenty-five thousand Jewish refugees arrived in Hungary. Frojimovics, *I Have Been a Stranger*, 56.

32. Tamás Majsai, "A kőrösmezei zsidódeportálás 1941-ben," *A Ráday gyűjtemény évkönyve* 4–5 (1984–1985): 61–62.

Aliens (KEOKH), which operated out of the public security department of the Ministry of the Interior. By the mid-1930s, the KEOKH had established a registry of Jews arriving from the east and often expelled them.[33] By 1941 a bureaucratic antisemitic approach had become widespread, according to which all Jews were considered alien until they verified their Hungarian citizenship.

As of early June 1941, high-ranking officials pushed to organize a large-scale action to expel "the unsuitable aliens residing in the country." The KEOKH issued the decree included in document 2-5 on July 12, 1941, fifteen days after Hungary declared war on the Soviet Union. The decree ordered law enforcement agencies to create a register of "unsuitable aliens." A week later, the Ministry of the Interior issued an order to deport foreigners shipped to collection sites across the country.[34] Between July 19 and August 15, about seventeen to eighteen thousand Jews were crowded into trucks and cattle cars and transported to collection camps in the border town of Kőrösmező and the neighboring Havasalja.[35] Contrary to others, this action was not an illegal excess committed by overzealous low-level local officials. The Ministry of Defense, the Army General Staff, the Ministry of the Interior, and the leaders of the KEOKH jointly supported the operation. The regent's commissioner of Carpatho-Ruthenia,[36] **Miklós Kozma**, obtained approval to proceed from Prime Minister **László Bárdossy** as well as Regent Horthy.[37]

---

33. A detailed account of the activity of the KEOKH is in Frojimovics, *I Have Been a Stranger*, 23–33.

34. Decree nos. 192/1 and 192/2 res. VII. b. of the Ministry of the Interior, July 19, 1941, in Zoltán Szirtes, *Temetetlen halottaink. Kőrösmező, Kamenyec-Podolszk, 1941* (Budapest: Kopint-Datorg, 1996), 12–14.

35. According to Mária Ormos's summary, 13,400 people were deported from Carpatho-Ruthenia and 4,000 from other areas. She believes that by July 16, the process of forcing Jews to move out of their homes to ghettos or collection camps had already begun. Ormos, *Egy magyar médiavezér*, 2:760–62. Data of the KEOKH and of the Welfare Bureau of Hungarian Israelites mention 17,656 and 17,560 individuals, respectively. Majsai, "A kőrösmezei zsidódeportálás 1941-ben," 68–69. According to the report of the Ungvár border police station, 17,306 Jews arrived at the Kőrösmező camp between July 15 and August 9. Frojimovics, *I Have Been a Stranger*, 123–24.

36. The position of regent's commissioner is not to be confused with government commissioner. The former was appointed by Regent Horthy, in this case to head the Hungarian administration in Carpatho-Ruthenia. The latter was appointed by the government to supervise certain specific issues throughout the country.

37. Ormos, *Egy magyar médiavezér*, 2:757–60. Kozma originally wanted to deport politically dangerous Ukrainian "agitators" as part of the operation, as well as Roma, but this plan was eventually given up.

DOCUMENT 2-5: **Decree of the Minister of the Interior, July 12, 1941, USHMMA RG 39.018M, disc 45, V-122.405 (HAHSS, file V-122.405).**

HUNGARIAN ROYAL MINISTER OF THE INTERIOR
   Re: Preparing a register of foreigners required to leave the country
*No. 192/res/1941*
VII/b
STRICTLY CONFIDENTIAL!
To the heads of first instance police authorities at their headquarters.[38]

In the light of the present foreign affairs situation, it has become possible to remove from the territory of the country unsuitable aliens and foreign citizens against whom the final expulsion order or denial of a residential permit have not, until now, been carried out effectively.

In the light of all of the important national political considerations, I emphatically call the attention of all leaders of the first instance police authorities to the fact that they are to submit to me the register of all such foreigners as soon as possible.

The report should contain the name of the foreigners and all data about their place of origin as well as data about their family members. If a family member subject to a final decision is not presently residing in the area under your control, then also provide the exact address of that person.

In light of the above, utmost care must be taken in the compilation of the report. The swift and effective execution of the question will in many respects be greatly assisted by the precise and careful measures taken by the first instance police authorities.

After the reports have come in, I shall issue an order concerning the foreigners to be removed, and in that order I shall also provide details about the implementation measures.

The report should be submitted directly to the address of Ministerial Department Councillor Vitéz Sándor Siménfalvy,[39] head of the National Central Authority for Controlling Aliens (Municipal District IX, 8 Fővám Square, first floor, 101).

*Budapest, 1941. July 12*

*From the decree of the minister:*
SÁNDOR SIMÉNFALVY
Ministerial Department Councillor

---

   38. That is, local police.
   39. Ministerial department councillor was a rank in the administrative structure usually held by officials heading up subdepartments in the ministries.

The main targets of the actions were refugees who had arrived in Hungary more recently. However, many Jewish citizens were also deported along with them. Because compilation of the lists was left to local authorities, this became a good opportunity for lower-ranking officials to show initiative—by going beyond orders—and deporting people who in fact had proper certificates, as well as exempted individuals, including pregnant women, the elderly, and the sick.[40] A telling example of such eagerness is the case of the Putnok chief constable described in document 2-6.

DOCUMENT 2-6: **Report of István Weiss on the activity of Putnok chief constable Imre Mogyoróssy in 1941, February 26, 1946, HBCA XXV.1, file 257/1947.**[41]

[. . .] On the afternoon of August 8, 1941, I was returning from a business trip, and while in Ragály, Chief Constable Mogyoróssy had the Ragály gendarme patrol unit arrest me and had them escort me all the way to Putnok through the intervening municipalities. Because it was late at night by then, a group of 88 people was already on its way toward the train station, and I, too, was hauled in. They did not even allow me to run home for the most basic items. The group included my 72-year-old mother, Mrs. Ödön Weiss, as well. The objective—or rather, the pretext—for our arrest and transfer to the Galician border: "uncertain citizenship." The objective: complete extermination. Because Chief Constable Mogyoróssy knew all too well that those who were pushed over the other side of the Polish border would hardly survive (and he obviously welcomed this outcome). I myself was born in Hungary, as were my late father and even my grandmother; my father and I were both Hungarian lawyers, so neither my mother nor I could be anything other than Hungarian citizens. But the other members of our group had also been born in Hungary, as were their ancestors. Most of them provided certificates to prove this, which the chief constable took away from them previously. There were also several people who showed their valid Hungarian citizenship certificates, issued by the Ministry of the Interior, with which they could prove their citizenship beyond a doubt, but the chief constable was depraved enough to

---

40. Majsai, "A kőrösmezei zsidódeportálás 1941-ben," 67–68; Tamás Majsai, "A Kamenyec-Podolszkij-i deportálás," *História* 16, no. 7 (1994): 29.

41. The authors have been unable to find additional information on Mogyoróssy.

take away these citizenship certificates, which were completely in order. Then, despite the fact that he knew better, he still arrested these people, filing the obviously false report that they were "Polish immigrants from Galicia." And he had them expelled, transferring them to the Hungarian border police stationed at Kőrösmező and Havasalja. Chief Constable Mogyoróssy was hardly bothered by minor details, such as the fact that even according to the laws in effect at the time, his method constituted a severe case of falsifying official documents, which is punishable by a prison sentence.

[. . .]

Victims were often rounded up at night. During the journey, which sometimes lasted an entire day, the authorities would not open the cattle cars even for the passengers to meet their basic bodily needs. At the collection camp, the deportees had no water and not enough food or sleeping space. Even the most minimal requirements for hygiene were absent. The Jews were transferred from the camps to Hungarian-occupied former Soviet territory without any food or supplies. The reception by the local Ukrainian population was quite hostile. Many deportees wandered around, trying to survive, facing starvation, killing sprees, robbery, torture, and murder. Several thousand made it to Stanislau,[42] where the Hungarian army initially protected the Jews. However, once the Germans took control of the town in late July, mass murder began, conducted in collaboration with the Ukrainian population. According to the testimony of the Adler sisters, who were among those deported, "many were thrown into the Dniester, women's breasts were cut off, children were cut in half, and quite a few people were buried alive."[43] Other deportees were taken to the ghettos of Nadworna and Kolomea. There the Jews from Hungary shared the fate of these ghettos' prisoners: most of them were massacred in the fall of 1941 or deported to the Bełżec extermination camp in the spring of 1942.

German authorities initially tried to send the Jews back to Hungary. Once it became clear that the Hungarians were unwilling to allow the deportees to return, the Higher SS and Police Leader (*Höherer SS- und Polizeiführer*) for occupied Ukraine, SS-Obergruppenführer Friedrich Jeckeln, recommended to Wehrmacht commanders that they "solve" the issue

---

42. Also spelled Stanisławów or Stanislav; today Ivano-Frankivsk, Ukraine.
43. HJA, DEGOB Protocols, no. 129.

before the civilian administration took over the territory on September 1, 1941. His suggestion was taken. Between August 27 and 30, Police Battalion 320, reinforced by members of Jeckeln's staff and an *Ordnungspolizei* unit and conducted with the help of Ukrainian militiamen, murdered 23,600 people: Jews from Hungary deported to the Kamenets-Podolski district and the majority of local Jews.[44] No more than two to three thousand deportees returned to Hungary.[45]

In Hungary many opposition politicians and church leaders protested against these events. Most active among them was Member of Parliament **Margit Slachta**. Although on August 9 Minister of the Interior Ferenc Keresztes-Fischer prohibited all further deportations, some fanatical local officials continued them for a few more days. The operation officially ended on August 15, when the KEOKH finally suspended it. Firm objections by the German authorities played a decisive role in eventually putting an end to the deportations.[46] The Germans saw the unorganized influx of thousands of Jews (in their eyes, saboteurs, spies, and enemies) as a serious public safety hazard.[47] Despite having suspended the deportations, the KEOKH did not give up: it repeatedly tried to continue and expand the operation. As a result, smaller Jewish groups were deported from the northeastern part of the country on several occasions during 1942.[48]

---

44. Progress reports on military operations nos. 66 and 80, August 28 and September 11, 1941, in Yitzhak Arad, Shmuel Krakowski, and Shmuel Spector, *The Einsatzgruppen Reports: Selections from the Dispatches of the Nazi Death Squads' Campaign against the Jews, July 1941–January 1943* (New York: Holocaust Library, 1989), 112–13, 128–29; Christopher R. Browning, with contributions by Jürgen Matthäus, *The Origins of the Final Solution: The Evolution of Nazi Jewish Policy, September 1939–March 1942* (Lincoln: University of Nebraska Press, 2004), 291; Dieter Pohl, "The Murder of Ukraine's Jews under German Military Administration and in the Reich Commissariat Ukraine," in *The Shoah in Ukraine: History, Testimony, Memorialization*, ed. Ray Brandon and Wendy Lower (Bloomington: Indiana University Press in association with the USHMM, 2008), 29–31.

45. Ormos, *Egy magyar médiavezér*, 2:758–64.

46. On Slachta, see the glossary. See also Szirtes, *Temetetlen halottaink*, 16; Ormos, *Egy magyar médiavezér*, 2:763.

47. Around the same time, a similar tug-of-war was going on between the German and Romanian authorities, who wanted to resettle Jews from the occupied areas of northern Bukovina and Bessarabia to territories beyond the Dniester River. See Radu Ioanid, *The Holocaust in Romania: The Destruction of Jews and Gypsies under the Antonescu Regime, 1940–1944* (Chicago: Ivan R. Dee in association with the USHMM, 2000), 115–38.

48. Majsai, "A kőrösmezei zsidódeportálás 1941-ben," 71–72.

The Kamenets-Podolski operation was the first mass murder of the Holocaust in which the number of victims was over ten thousand. It was also significant for another reason. The anti-Jewish policies of Germany's Romanian and Hungarian allies formed part of the "cleansing campaigns" that evolved into systematic genocide.[49] The events demonstrate that three years before the German occupation, officials at the highest levels of the Hungarian state and the governing party already considered the mass deportation of Jews to their deaths a legitimate political aspiration. The Germans made no demands whatsoever that the refugees be handed over. On the contrary, protests by German agencies stood in the way of the Hungarians moving larger numbers across the border.[50] The precision with which Hungarian public administration officials and the military fulfilled their duties, their overzealousness, the inhumane methods used in carrying out orders, and their cynical aloofness toward deportees' subsequent fate all foreshadow the events of 1944 in Hungary.

A rare document from the operation survived. Gyula Spitz, a Jewish truck driver of the Hungarian army, clandestinely took the photo reproduced in document 2-7.[51] (Note the outline of the steering wheel in the lower part of the image, behind which Spitz hid the camera.) Taken in Kamenets-Podolski (today Ukraine) at the end of August 1941, the photograph shows Jews deported from Hungary being herded to their place of execution. Unlike other Jews, Spitz was drafted into regular army service, probably because of his skill as a driver.[52] The protection this job afforded him did not last, for after they occupied Hungary,

---

49. Browning, *The Origins of the Final Solution*, 253–60, 268–91. For a detailed analysis of the qualitative leap, see Klaus-Michael Mallmann, "Der qualitative Sprung im Vernichtungsprozess. Das Massaker von Kamenez-Podolsk Ende August 1941," *Jahrbuch für Antisemitismusforschung* 10 (2001): 239–64.

50. At the same time, some members of the Hungarian army also protected Jews in some locations. The reports of *Einsatzgruppen* on several occasions mentioned the pro-Jewish (and pro-Polish) attitudes of the Hungarians. See progress reports on military operations, nos. 23, 67, and 74 (July 15, August 29, and September 5, 1941), in Arad et al., *The Einsatzgruppen Reports*, 26, 119, 126.

51. Spitz, a Hungarian Jew from Budapest, was a cab driver prior to his conscription into the Hungarian army, in which he served from 1940 to 1942. He was eventually arrested by the Germans and probably did not survive the war. See Gábor Miklós, "Örökre fülébe csengtek a jajkiáltások: Ötvenöt évig bujkáló fotódokumentumok Kamenyec-Podolszkról," in *Népszabadság* [*Magyar Tükör*], November 12, 1996, 8.

52. According to an undated report from the summer and autumn of 1941, out of the 7,719 drivers serving in the Hungarian army, 2,487 (32.2 percent) were Jewish, despite efforts made to replace them. AMH I.31. Ministry of Defense, documents of Presidential Department no. 1/b. 1941, file no. 59844.

the Germans arrested and deported him. He perished in the Mauthausen concentration camp.

DOCUMENT 2-7: **Photograph by Gyula Spitz of Jews being taken to the execution site in Kamenets-Podolski, August 1941, USHMMPA WS# 28215 (courtesy of Ivan Sved).**

In addition to deporting Jews with "uncertain citizenship," Hungarian authorities were involved in anti-Jewish mass murder long before the March 1944 German occupation. One atrocity took place in the so-called Southern Province. Hungary occupied this region in April 1941, when Yugoslavia collapsed under German military attack (see table 3, p. 369, and map 2, p. xlii). From early summer, intensive partisan activity emerged in the Bácska region. Local law enforcement units could not curtail these actions. Therefore, in late December 1941, Chief of the General Staff Ferenc Szombathelyi ordered a general raid, designating the region as a military operations zone. He entrusted the forces of the military district commander, Lieutenant General Ferenc Feketehalmy-Czeydner, with carrying out his order. In early January, several attacks on Hungarian patrols occurred in the Sajkásvidék region along the Danube, leaving numerous soldiers dead. Armed resistance was terminated in a few days, but the operation against the civilian population continued with help from civilian guards recruited from among Hungarian and German residents. The action culminated in mass executions, primarily targeting well-off Serbian farmers and intellectuals in order to seize their valuables.[53]

Soon thereafter military leaders launched another operation, this one wholly unprovoked. They viewed the situation as ripe for the "pacification" of the entire territory and for getting rid of "undesirable elements."[54] It was no accident that the raids coincided with the Budapest negotiations of German foreign minister Joachim von Ribbentrop and chief of the Supreme Command of the Wehrmacht Wilhelm Keitel (January 8 and 20, 1942). Hungary's wartime role became the main topic during the meetings. The Hungarians purposefully exaggerated the number of partisans and the magnitude of the danger they posed, striving to demonstrate that their troops were needed to protect the Hungarian borders and to prevent them from being sent to the eastern front.[55]

General Feketehalmy-Czeydner informed Budapest that the partisans had relocated to the most important town in the region, Újvidék. He soon received permission for an operation from the Army General Staff and the government. At dawn on January 21, 1942, troops led by the commander of Újvidék, Colonel József Grassy, cut off telegram and telephone connections and traffic into the town. A curfew and complete ban on any gatherings went into effect. The raid began. Locals accused of cooperation with the partisans, mostly Serbs, were selected from lists prepared in advance. Between twenty and fifty of them were executed after being sentenced to death in a court-martial conducted using Hungarian and German civilian recruits. Dissatisfied with the numbers, the command headquarters demanded "results." On the second day troops began arresting primarily the wealthy middle-class Jews living in Újvidék.

Some of the officers—such as Gendarme Captain Márton Zöldi—did more than simply carry out orders. With support, encouragement, and retroactive consent from their superiors, they initiated measures proactively. They encouraged the soldiers and gendarmes with alcohol, opportunities for plundering, and staged provocations. On the third day (Friday, January 23), the action turned into an uncontrolled bloodbath. Instead of targeted arrests, the perpetrators carried off entire families selected at random and looted their apartments.

---

53. Confidential report to the Ministry of the Interior about the raid in the Southern Province, HNA K149, item 1942-1, file 7128. See also Randolph L. Braham, *The Politics of Genocide: The Holocaust in Hungary* (New York: Columbia University Press, 1994), 1:214–15; Elek Karsai, *A budai vártól a gyepüig 1941–1945* (Budapest: Táncsics, 1965), 162–63.

54. Daily reports of the General Staff, January 6 and 12, 1942, in Enikő A. Sajti, *Délvidék 1941–1944. A magyar kormányok délszláv politikája* (Budapest: Kossuth, 1987), 154.

55. Ibid., 160–62; Karsai, *A budai vártól a gyepüig*, 92–108.

Some victims were killed in front of their houses, in the open street. Others were herded to execution grounds set up at six locations across town. Victims had to stand in line on the banks of the frozen Danube in the extreme cold until they were shot in the back of the neck. Their bodies were thrown into a hole cut into the ice with explosives.[56] Document 2-8 presents the recollections of events of a woman who was twenty-one years old at the time.

DOCUMENT 2-8: **Testimony of Julia Kolb about the Újvidék massacre (1945), USHMMA RG 39.013M (HJA, DEGOB Protocols, no. 761).**

> [. . .] We were living in **Újvidék.** One morning, we woke up realizing we were not allowed to leave the street and that we were surrounded by soldiers and machine guns. We were living on the edge of the town and did not know what was going on downtown. Soldiers checked our identification papers and told us that we should not walk around in the streets, and also that if we did not heed them when they ordered us to stop, they would have to shoot. Saturday morning the raid was over. One of my neighbors came out and told me that the entire town was covered in blood. I did not know what had happened to my parents and set out for town. I was horribly afraid that I would not find them alive. Along the way, there were bloody corpses lying on the road. I rang at my parents', and it was only when I heard my father's footsteps that my horrible fear dissipated. Many people we knew were executed. They sat on the cold pavement for 48 hours and then they were thrown into the Danube. Lots of our relatives died then. In some cases, a child disappeared and the parents survived, in others, the parents disappeared and a child was the only one left. The rabbi was also taken to the banks of the Danube, along the way, they kept beating him with a rifle butt. Suddenly an order came in that the killings had to stop. This is how the survivors escaped. Many had nervous breakdowns, many were driven insane. The famous Újvidék pogrom lasted three days.[57]

On January 22, the military leadership ordered the operation to stop. But the massacre did not end until 9 p.m. the next day. The announcement published by the town's military command did acknowledge that looting had taken

---

56. Braham, *The Politics of Genocide*, 1:217–18; HJA, DEGOB Protocols, no. 2740.
57. In 1944 Julia Korb was deported to Auschwitz. She was liberated in Torgau.

place and that innocent people had been murdered, but it suggested that combatting the alleged rebels justified all of these actions.

News of the mass murder reached Budapest immediately through reports by local government leaders and eyewitness accounts. The authorities received numerous petitions from Jews desperately searching for relatives who had been staying in Újvidék.[58] Several members of the left-wing opposition and the parliamentary representative of the Serbian minority strongly protested as soon as the first news arrived, but for a long time no attempt was made to investigate the incident.[59] It was delayed until the course of the war took a turn in 1943. As the government began preliminary peace explorations without the Nazis' knowledge, it simultaneously strove to improve its international reputation and therefore launched investigations regarding the massacre. Regent Horthy first had the investigations stopped on August 13, 1943. Then on October 11, he ordered courts-martial for three army officers and twelve gendarme officers. Proceedings were also initiated against two hundred lower-ranking soldiers and gendarmes.[60] In January 1944 the verdicts came in, but the four main perpetrators fled to Germany to escape accountability. (They returned to Hungary as high-ranking SS officers following the March 1944 German occupation.[61]) The defendants remaining in Hungary received ten- to fifteen-year prison sentences. The government began to issue financial compensation to relatives of the victims, but in a rather typical turn of events, Jews could not receive compensation even when their claims were acknowledged as just.[62] Various estimates exist for the number of victims. According to statistics prepared by the army, 3,340 people were shot to death. Among them were 2,550 Serbs and 743 Jews. During

---

58. Petitions by relatives of those who disappeared during the raid in the Southern Province, HNA K149, item 1942-1, file 6279; Ervin Hollós, *Rendőrség, csendőrség, VKF 2* (Budapest: Kossuth, 1971), 305–6.

59. See Member of Parliament Endre Bajcsy-Zsilinszky's memorandum of February 4, 1942, in Karsai, *A budai vártól a gyepüig*, 116–19.

60. Enikő A. Sajti and György Markó, "Ismeretlen dokumentum az 1942. januári délvidéki razzia résztvevőinek peréről. (1943 december 14–1944 január 14)," *Hadtörténelmi Közlemények*, no. 5 (1985): 426–56.

61. Lieutenant General Ferenc Feketehalmy-Czeydner went on to attain the highest rank that a foreigner ever reached in the SS, becoming an *SS-Obergruppenführer*. Colonel of the General Staff József Grassy became an *SS-Gruppenführer* and commander of the SS Division Hunyadi recruited in Hungary. Gendarme Captain Márton Zöldi joined the Gestapo. Following the German occupation, the convicts were retried and acquitted.

62. For details about the raid in the Southern Province and its consequences, see Enikő A. Sajti, *Délvidék 1941–1944,* 152–68, 174–88.

the raid 1,238 women, elderly people, and children were reportedly killed.[63] Jewish and Serbian sources recorded more victims.

## LABOR SERVICE

Following Nazi Germany's example of ignoring the provisions of the peace treaties drawn up at the conclusion of World War I, Hungary began reorganizing its own army in the late 1930s. As part of this initiative, the Act on National Defense (Act II of 1939) introduced a general system of compulsory military service.[64] A number of the act's stipulations affected Jews. Articles 87 through 94 instituted a national defense labor requirement. Article 230 stated that all males holding Hungarian citizenship or residing in Hungary (Jews and non-Jews alike) who were over twenty-one and had been deemed permanently unfit for armed military service could be required to perform labor service for a maximum of three months.[65] The national superintendent of the Public Interest Labor Service System headed the Labor Service organization, which operated as part of the Ministry of Defense. Provisions, equipment, and treatment of labor servicemen were initially the same as for soldiers. The Labor Service was thus not discriminatory at its inception. However, it did create the legal framework for the gradual introduction of anti-Jewish (and antiminority) restrictions.

Citing the Second "Jewish Law," which barred state employment for Jews, the Ministry of Defense ordered that Jews could not become officers or non-commissioned officers. Jews deemed fit for armed service had to be divided proportionately into the different military branches, while those deemed unfit had to be organized into separate units. In neither case were Jews allowed to serve in positions requiring special responsibilities (and carrying a lesser risk of death), such as those in the signal corps, as messengers, or in administrative posts.[66] At the same time, increasing numbers of Jews were forced into unarmed units, and from the spring of 1941 onward, Jews lost their right to carry arms.[67]

---

63. Ibid., 159–60.
64. Act II of 1939. Miklós Degré and Alajos Várady-Brenner, eds., *Magyar Törvénytár. 1939. évi törvényczikkek* (Budapest: Franklin, 1940), 6–128.
65. Paragraph 5 of Article 5 stipulated that under certain circumstances and on a strictly voluntary basis, girls and women could also join the Labor Service. However, until the **Arrow Cross** takeover in October 1944, Jewish women were not drafted.
66. Decree no. A.-1939-I.-26149 of the Ministry of Defense, September 23, 1939, in Elek Karsai, ed., *"Fegyvertelen álltak az aknamezőkön . . . " Dokumentumok a munkaszolgálat történetéhez Magyarországon* (Budapest: Magyar Izraeliták Országos Képviselete, 1962), 1:102–5.
67. Prime Minister's Decree no. 2870/1941, April 19, 1941.

Following the anti-Jewish legislation launched in 1938, some departments of the Ministry of Defense regularly urged more radical anti-Jewish measures than those proposed in the bills under discussion in the parliament.[68] In addition, from 1940 to 1942 the army enacted a wide range of instances of illegal antisemitism: the establishment of special companies, prohibiting Jews from acquiring military ranks, issuing official documents marked "Zs,"[69] ordering Jews to wear yellow armbands, and so forth.[70] At the time they were issued, these measures went beyond even the provisions of the existing anti-Jewish regulations. However, they were not revoked. On the contrary, governmental decrees and the law on the Labor Service in 1942 (see document 2-9) retroactively systematized and ratified them. As a result of the political radicalization spurred on by German victories and territorial expansion, the Labor Service system had by 1941 become an expressly antisemitic institution based on collective stigmatization and racial discrimination.

In addition to the Jews, some ethnic minorities, primarily Romanians and southern Slavs, were also deemed too unreliable for armed service.[71] Those considered dangerous from a national security perspective (mostly those holding left-wing views) were drafted into penal units and subsequently organized into special Labor Service companies. Among them were members of smaller denominations who refused armed service on religious grounds, for example, Jehovah's Witnesses.[72] By 1942 about one hundred thousand males (mostly Jews) served in Labor Service units.

Hungary joined the war against the Soviet Union in the summer of 1941. The Labor Service companies mainly worked constructing roads and bridges during the first months. By the spring of 1942, it had become clear that the war would be prolonged. The Second Hungarian Army was sent to the front line, with almost fifty thousand labor servicemen in its ranks. On March 17, Minister of Defense Károly Bartha issued a decree stipulating that in the event of mobilization, at least 10 percent of those drafted had to be Jewish. He also specified that in the territory for each army corps, Jews had to be drafted and sent to the military operations zone immediately.[73] Many were called up indi-

---

68. Krisztián Ungváry, *A magyar honvédség a második világháborúban* (Budapest: Osiris, 2004), 117.
69. "Zs" is the abbreviation for *zsidó*, or "Jewish" in Hungarian
70. On "illegal antisemitism," see p. 24 and the glossary.
71. Szabolcs Szita, *Haláleröd. A munkaszolgálat és a hadimunka történetéhez, 1944–1945* (Budapest: Kossuth, 1989), 14.
72. Karsai, *"Fegyvertelen álltak az aknamezőkön,"* 1:87.
73. Ibid., 1:58.

vidually rather than by age cohort, providing a prime opportunity for the abuse of power and individual vengeance.[74] On April 22, 1942, the Ministry of Defense issued a confidential order that 10 to 15 percent of those drafted had to be Jews who were "widely known because of their name or economic status." In these cases, the authorities need not observe the upper age limit of forty-two years for those sent to the front lines.[75] Among those drafted for labor service despite their age was journalist and Olympic gold medalist fencer Attila Petschauer. As an Olympic champion, he was exempt from the anti-Jewish laws. Still, he had to join the Labor Service.[76] He was murdered by his Labor Service guards on the eastern front in January 1943.

Prior to the German occupation in March 1944, about twenty-five to forty thousand Jewish labor servicemen died either on the front lines or in Soviet captivity.[77] Many fell victim to the brutality of Labor Service guards and officers, whose repertoire of cruelties exceeded those generally prevalent within the army. Withholding of food, blackmail, theft, and murder were everyday practices in numerous units. At times the army cleared minefields by herding labor servicemen through dangerous zones. On occasion long leashes were fastened to the necks of Jews, who were mocked as "1942-style minesweepers." In January 1943, in the midst of the chaos following the Soviets' destruction of the Second Hungarian Army, Jews often suffered the most. Both the Germans and the Hungarians considered them scapegoats. Retreating on foot through the extraordinarily harsh winter without provisions or support, many of them died in the snowfields. German soldiers or Ukrainian volunteers murdered others. The Hungarian military command ordered Labor Service guards to use weapons against such attackers,[78] but on other occasions, Hungarian army troops themselves committed mass murder. In April 1943 near the Ukrainian village of Doroshich, the soldiers set fire to the barrack of labor servicemen ill with

---

74. Vilmos Nagybaczoni Nagy, *Végzetes esztendők*, 2nd rev. ed. (Budapest: Kossuth, 1986), 99.

75. Karsai, *"Fegyvertelen álltak az aknamezőkön,"* 1:524–25.

76. Act IV of 1939, Article 2. See Degré and Várady-Brenner, *Magyar Törvénytár. 1939*, 130–31. Petschauer (1904–1943) won gold medals at the 1928 and 1932 Olympic Games as a member of the Hungarian sabre team.

77. For various estimates, see Ungváry, *A magyar honvédség*, 119–20; Tamás Stark, *Zsidóság a vészkorszakban és a felszabadulás után 1939–1955* (Budapest: Magyar Tudományos Akadémia Történettudományi Intézete, 1995), 76; László Varga, "A Holocaust és ami utána . . . ," in *The Holocaust in Hungary: Fifty Years Later*, ed. Randolph L. Braham and Attila Pók (New York: Columbia University Press, 1997), 518; Braham, *The Politics of Genocide*, 2:1298.

78. Karsai, *"Fegyvertelen álltak az aknamezőkön,"* 1:75–76. See also Ungváry, *A magyar honvédség*, 116–21.

typhoid fever. They shot down those who tried to escape with machine guns. About four hundred people died in the massacre.[79]

The brutality that escalated to murder can only partially be attributed to the sadism of individual Labor Service guards. Often the higher military command went beyond reigning anti-Jewish orders and, using special confidential orders that bypassed even official channels, encouraged guards' antisemitic sentiments. Yet instances of humane treatment remained in evidence as well. Some of the Hungarian officers protested against the mass murder of civilians and Jews and offered them protection in the areas they occupied.[80]

During 1943 the bidirectional politics of the Hungarian government influenced the labor servicemen's fate. On the one hand, Prime Minister Miklós Kállay and his diplomats cautiously began exploring the possibility of making peace with the Western Powers, an intention evidenced by orders easing the labor servicemen's situation. On the other hand, the government strove to appear an enthusiastic supporter of the German cause. It thus sent additional units to the front lines, including many from the Labor Service. As part of this effort the cabinet handed over sixty-two hundred labor servicemen to the German paramilitary labor corps Organisation Todt in July 1943 and May 1944. They were taken to work in copper mines and on railroad construction in and around Bor, Serbia.[81]

The most significant piece of legislation creating the legal framework of the Jewish Labor Service was Act XIV of 1942. This summarized and codified the practices of the past years and defined the situation of labor servicemen until the 1944 German occupation. According to this law, Jews fulfilled their military obligation exclusively through work in unarmed labor service. The military officers subject to the "Jewish Laws" lost their ranks. The department within the Ministry of Defense that handled staff matters provided the following explanation for the proposed measure: "Someone who is—as the law stipulates[82]— considered stigmatized by society because of his racial affiliation, stigmatized even within civilian society, cannot remain an officer."[83] The ministry was not

---

79. Braham, *The Politics of Genocide*, 1:334; HJA, DEGOB Protocols, nos. 221, 875, 2093, 2729, 2811, and 3028.
80. Braham, *The Politics of Genocide*, 1:323–28, 272–73; Karsai, *"Fegyvertelen álltak az aknamezőkön,"* 1:61–63.
81. Karsai, *"Fegyvertelen álltak az aknamezőkön,"* 1:86–87; Decree no. 11470. eln. KMOF–1943 of the Ministry of Defense, July 6, 1943; Karsai, *"Fegyvertelen álltak az aknamezőkön,"* 2:370–78.
82. The author is referring to the government's "Jewish Laws."
83. Karsai, *"Fegyvertelen álltak az aknamezőkön,"* 1:41.

addressing a pressing issue. Jews within the Hungarian army were few, even in the years prior to the war: in April 1939 just 2,292 Jews were in its ranks (2.24 percent of the force), and of these, only forty-one held a rank.[84]

As the bill was being drafted, the Ministry of Justice indicated that it wanted to follow the German example and exempt Jews from the military service requirement. The Ministry of Defense wanted just the opposite, to make military service compulsory for them. The soldiers argued that, on the one hand, the country should utilize the Jewish workforce to the maximum, while on the other, Jews should not be allowed to stay behind the front lines, engaging in "activities against the nation." The draft submitted by General Staff headquarters sought to subject to compulsory labor service even those non-Jews who had a Jewish spouse. As the act was debated in parliament, the far-right opposition put forth even more radical proposals, for example, the establishment of labor camps and ghettos for the Jews.

DOCUMENT 2-9: **Introduction to and articles of Act XIV of 1942 on the Modification and Extension of Act II of 1939 on National Defense and Act IV of 1938 on the Recognition of the Achievements of Combat Veterans of the 1914–1918 World War, in *1942. évi Országos Törvénytár* (Budapest: Magyar Királyi Belügyminisztérium, 1943), 76–89.**

[...]

The bill upholds the principle that Jews cannot perform armed service in the Hungarian army and must fulfill their military obligations through auxiliary military service. This principle and the declaration and implementation thereof with respect to the Hungarian army ensures uniformity with the provisions of the so-called "Jewish Laws,"[85] which are intended to secure the exclusion of the Jews from government, as well as public employment, and keep them from assuming the intellectual leadership of the country. Thus, no argument or extended explanation is needed to justify this bill's goal that the Jews should likewise be excluded from the armed sections of the Hungarian army. After all, the individual and the corporate life of the armed forces is the primary realm in which in every respect the requirements of the Hungarian national movement and the Christian moral conception must prevail uninterruptedly.

---

84. Proposal of Presidential Department "A" of the Ministry of Defense, April 4, 1939, in Karsai, *"Fegyvertelen álltak az aknamezőkön,"* 1:14–21.

85. See chapter 1.

It would, however, be misguided to opt for a decree that at this time would remove the Jews' military obligations, specifically, their obligation to serve in the army, and would thereby relieve them of the associated burdens. For this reason, auxiliary military service within the Hungarian army is the area in which training Jews can be of public utility; it is here that their physical disciplining and moral education can be carried out afterward with results that are—hopefully—not unfavorable from the public's point of view.

[. . .]

§ 3

(1) Jews do not receive "levente" training.[86]

(2) Jews who are subject to compulsory military service cannot perform armed service in the Hungarian army or in the gendarmerie.

[. . .]

§ 5

(1) Jews subject to compulsory military service will fulfill their military obligations through auxiliary military service.

(2) Those assigned to perform auxiliary military service will do so without rank or arm badge,[87] even if they previously held the rank of a commissioned officer or noncommissioned officer, or junior noncommissioned officer, or wore an arm badge; they may not sign up for reserve officer training. [. . .]

Between September 1942 and June 1943, anti-Nazi general **Vilmos Nagybaczoni Nagy** headed the Ministry of Defense; document 2-10(A) excerpts his postwar memoirs. Nagy tried to improve conditions for labor servicemen and attempted to put an end to incidents of arbitrary, cruel treatment. He strenuously insisted that individuals over age forty-two and those unable to work should be relieved from duty or not drafted at all. Going against previous practices, he made discharge after six months possible for Jewish labor servicemen and those from ethnic minorities. In his speeches in parliament, he demanded uniform treatment and humane methods, arguing—justifiably—that these served the interest of warfare. He initiated court-martial proceedings against officers who abused their powers.[88] In his decree issued in December 1942,

---

86. See the glossary.

87. An arm badge was a distinguishing mark on the uniforms of enlisted soldiers holding a high school diploma.

88. Nagy, *Végzetes esztendők*, 99–100; Karsai, *"Fegyvertelen álltak az aknamezökön,"* 1:77–79.

excerpted in document 2-10(B), he also imposed regulations concerning the rights of and social provisions for labor servicemen's family members.[89]

DOCUMENT 2-10(A): Memoirs of Minister of Defense Vilmos Nagybaczoni Nagy (1947), published in Vilmos Nagybaczoni Nagy, *Végzetes esztendők*, 2nd rev. ed. (Budapest: Kossuth, 1986), 99, 126, 132, 168.

[. . .] A few days after I assumed my duties, I already saw that the Jewish question was one of the toughest and gravest of problems that manifested all of its features within the army. [. . .] Labor Service companies were established for the Jews. The recruitment was not by age group, however, but with rounds of the so-called "SAS" call-up summons: "Hurry, Immediately, Hurry."[90] This gave rise to abuse of the gravest form. If someone had a conflict with a Jew, he would handle it by having that person called in for labor service, regardless of the person's age or social status.

This anti-Jewish sentiment reigned in the Ministry of Defense. And this sentiment became even more extreme as a result of the order regulating military duty relief from battlefield service. The order declared that Romanians, Serbs, and Jews were not allowed any form of preferential treatment and could not be relieved of their duties. [. . .]

Had the higher-ranking commanders supervised their deputies, making them feel that their superiors did not regard the labor servicemen as having been sentenced to death, as pariahs consigned to the ranks of animals, then the cruelties that led to the death of so many labor servicemen on Russian fields would have stopped or would not have happened at all. [. . .]

Jewish members of the workforce were removed at many firms due to pressure from military agencies, particularly Department 17/a of the Ministry of Industry. During these operations, even the department of mobilization of the Ministry of Defense was used. As a result, shortages arose at every juncture. For example, following my resignation, the production of rocket launchers only began after an eight-month delay; Jewish skilled workers in the machine industry had been removed from the factories, and it took a long time before new workers were recruited and trained.

The case of doctors is instructive here: Jewish doctors were called in without any deliberation. While the order specified that only one

---

89. Karsai, *"Fegyvertelen álltak az aknamezőkön,"* 2:330–37.

90. In Hungarian: *siess, azonnal, siess*. It meant that those who received the summons had to report for duty within a very short time.

doctor could be assigned to each Labor Service company, which consisted of about 220 men, it still happened on several occasions that 10 to 12 doctors ended up serving in a single unit. And instead of saving lives, they were assigned to ordinary physical labor. Meanwhile, some villages remained wholly without a doctor. Military units also experienced a shortage. As a result, many Hungarians in active combat did not receive appropriate treatment or medical assistance fast enough; many died because of minor injuries because trained doctors were elsewhere, breaking stones, digging trenches, cutting down forests, carrying lumber, working in railroad construction, or sweeping mines in front of the lines.

[. . .]

I would receive reports of the brutal treatment day after day. In many places, the Labor Service guards went wild—unfortunately, the reserve company commanders followed suit—they introduced such cruel treatment that decent Hungarian soldiers were appalled and filed reports. Because of the beatings, the extremely strenuous work, and the lack of adequate food, many labor servicemen died. These atrocities were established during military court investigations, and I tried as best I could to put an end to them.

[. . .]

DOCUMENT 2-10(B): **Decree of Minister of Defense Vilmos Nagybaczoni Nagy, December 19, 1942, in Elek Karsai, ed., "*Fegyvertelen álltak az aknamezőkön . . .*" *Dokumentumok a munkaszolgálat történetéhez Magyarországon* (Budapest: Magyar Izraeliták Országos Képviselete, 1962), 1:178–84.**

*Hungarian Royal Ministry of Defense*
*Decree no. 121.480. eln. KMOF—1942.*[91]

Confidential!
To be opened by the commander only!

[. . .]
*Budapest, December 19, 1942.*

At the end of this past November, I surveyed the Jewish labor servicemen working on the Transylvanian railroad construction.[92] I conducted

---

91. KMOF (National Superintendent of the Public Interest Labor Service System): head of the labor service system within the ranks of the Ministry of Defense.

92. This refers to construction of the "circular railroad" connecting the so-called **Székely** Land with other parts of the reannexed Northern Transylvania.

additional surveys through committees delegated to go to several backcountry locations where Jewish Labor Service companies were working.

I publish my conclusions from these surveys with the instructions that

[. . .]

*(b)* in the future, the commander in charge of every Labor Service company should emphasize that the work capacity and performance of Jews be enhanced through humane treatment, through having Jews examined who are unable to work or ill and sending them to the hospital.

### 1. STAFF OFFICERS

[. . .]

There are, however, officers who bring their personal attitudes into how they handle the treatment of the Jews; they no longer possess the objectivity that is necessary for commanders and must be expected of them. As a result, these officers implement impermissible ways of maintaining discipline and enhancing work performance and are therefore not suited to being commanders.

I have already had some of these officers replaced, and I order the military district headquarters that within their sphere of command, they replace officers with similar attitudes and behavior. [. . .]

### 2. THE LABOR SERVICE GUARD

[. . .]

The Labor Service guards are either too lenient with the workers or have a tendency toward cruelty. In general, their behavior reflects the attitudes of the headquarters and the company commander and the staff officers.

### 3. AUXILIARY WORKERS

[. . .]

In my Order no. 5584. M. 1b.—1942, I have already issued instructions that auxiliary workers who are over 42 years old be discharged. In several locations, this order has not yet been implemented. Immediate action must be taken toward this end.

[. . .]

Given their intelligence and good manual skills, they [those in the Labor Service] easily learn to perform even types of work to which they are wholly unaccustomed. Former Jewish officers and noncommissioned officers, former engineers, individuals who had previously, in civilian life, been employed as managers, directors, and foremen can be used quite well for supervising work.

Work performance is especially favorably influenced by a suitable and well-balanced diet, sanitary facilities, and suitable accommodations for securing restful sleep at night. [. . .]

At many locations, committees found auxiliary workers who were unable to work because of disabilities or physical infirmities. [. . .]

I will make specific arrangements concerning patients whose inability to work has been medically established, as well as concerning the replacement and accelerated review of those who, due to their physical weakness and infirmities, are evidently hindering the work associated with auxiliary labor service. [. . .]

[. . .]

### 5. ACCOMMODATION

[. . .]

At all times, accommodations must be appropriate to the weather.

[. . .]

The fate of Jews at the front line still depended largely on the attitudes of the local commanders. Under pressure from the far right and the Germans, Nagybaczoni Nagy resigned in June 1943. His successor, General **Lajos Csatay**, was more committed to Hungary's alliance with Germany, but he continued his predecessor's moderate policies toward the Jews.

The major reason behind the cruelty against labor servicemen—also mentioned in the memoirs of Nagybaczoni Nagy—was the rabid antisemitism of the higher-ranking commanders and reserve officers assigned to the companies. This greatly influenced the behavior of Labor Service guards. The radicalization of the Hungarian officer corps had already begun in the early 1930s. During that decade a generational turnover took place in the military leadership. Young followers of Prime Minister **Gyula Gömbös**, all committed pro-Germans and "race-protectionist" antisemites, seized several top positions. As their behavior in the territories reannexed after 1938 indicated, radicals in the army considered Jewry a fifth column, an alien component within the nation that was conspiring with the enemy. In the context of the barbaric warfare carried out on the eastern front, torturing and executing labor servicemen became patriotic, an everyday routine in many units.

DOCUMENT 2-11: **Diary entries of a Hungarian officer serving on the eastern front lines, November–January 1943, USHMMA RG 39.013M, reel 71 (HJA XXIV-C, box A 5/4).**[93]

[. . .]
1942. XI. 18
We woke up in good spirits. After washing up, we went down to the canteen. Another round of reassuring news. Spain has mobilized.[94] Yeah, if only we could get our hands on Roosevelt. Filthy Jews. [. . .]

1942. XII. 8
We work here as ordered. The mood is stirred up because frozen Jews are dragged around. They are dragging them barefoot, on a child's sled. 13 Jews fled to the Russians from auxiliary labor company no. 432[95]; the company was decimated. 17 were shot in the head. This is already the second such incident since I have been here. [. . .]

1942. XII.18
[. . .]
Court-martial hearing at noon. We sentenced to death Emil Gyémánt, a Jewish labor serviceman, for pretending to be sick.[96] What an unfortunate bloke he was. He deserved it; he hid for four days.

1942. XII. 19
Yesterday's execution by gunshot affected me. Although I do not regret it. They deserve it. Filthy Jews.
    [. . .]

---

93. The unidentified Hungarian officer served in Labor Service Battalion No. II in the region of Yablochnoye, Ukraine.

94. In July 1941, Spanish dictator General Francisco Franco agreed to send the Blue Division (División Azul), theoretically consisting of volunteers, to the eastern front line in order to support the "fight against bolshevism."

95. For the most part, the Soviets did not distinguish the labor servicemen from enemy soldiers. For them, it made essentially no difference in the war launched against them if someone was participating with a weapon or with a shovel. Jews were also regarded as prisoners of war; thus many of them were allowed to return home only after several years of Soviet captivity. Braham, *The Politics of Genocide*, 1:363–65.

96. Gyémánt (1908–1942) was a tradesman from Érsekújvár..

[1943.] I.15
We arrived in Ivanowka at 5 in the morning. What we saw on Kotschatowka Road was awful. Vehicle upon vehicle, crowds of people pushing each other, horse cadavers, frozen Jews.
[. . .]

In this period the command headquarters of the Second Hungarian Army authorized its men to decimate the Labor Service units in the event of attempted escapes. Since the service code did not include this method of imposing discipline, the measure was illegal.[97] Many nonetheless acted on this authorization. General Ferenc Szombathelyi, chief of staff from 1941 to 1944, did much to escalate the situation himself. After the war, he said, "The Jewish question had a disastrous effect on the army. [. . .] All values were reassessed. Cruelty turned into patriotism, atrocities into heroism, corruption into virtue. [. . .] Discipline divided into two kinds. One toward the Jews, where everything was permitted, and another sort of discipline, where one had to obey the rules. [. . .] Thus the discipline of the entire army was undermined; they would not obey if a command concerned the Jews."[98]

Document 2-12 provides an account of some of the extreme cruelty that surfaced in the Labor Service companies and went far beyond the humiliating practices customary in armies of the day. Particularly frequent targets of abuse were older people or those whose work capacity was limited, along with religiously observant Jews and intellectuals. Note that the acts described below were committed in a Labor Service company not on the front but in Hungary, where conditions and treatment were generally better.

DOCUMENT 2-12: **Sentence of the people's court in the city of Győr regarding the crime committed by Corporal Ferenc Varga and Private István Suri, August 2, 1945, in Elek Karsai, ed., "*Fegyvertelen álltak az aknamezőkön . . .*" Dokumentumok a munkaszolgálat történetéhez Magyarországon (Budapest: Magyar Izraeliták Országos Képviselete, 1962), 1:83–88.**

[. . .]
The people's prosecutor charged the defendants with committing the war crime [. . .] on the grounds that during the summer of 1942 as, respectively, corporal and private of the 102/4-6 Labor Service company, they

---
97. Ungváry, *A magyar honvédség*, 119.
98. Cited in Karsai, *"Fegyvertelen álltak az aknamezőkön,"* 1:65–66.

were in part perpetrator of and in part accomplice in the illegal torturing of labor servicemen.[99] Specifically:

In the midst of the summer heat, the defendants increased the work pace to the point that it became unbearable; the defendants beat those who could not keep up—mostly on bare body parts—sometimes with sticks and sometimes with prickly chestnut burrs fastened onto sticks. The defendants kicked and trod upon those who collapsed with their boots. The defendants also tormented the labor servicemen exhausted by work—making them perform exercises in the heat, forcing them to slap each other on the face. In the midst of the heat, the defendants would deprive people tormented by thirst of water [. . .]

[. . .] Defendants Ferenc Varga, as corporal and deputy foreman, and István Suri, as a private, both serving in the Labor Service guard at the 102/4-6 Labor Service company established in Komárom in the summer of 1942, subjected the labor servicemen to cruel, brutal, and inhumane treatment, among them a rabbi named Strasser, whom they beat up afterward. [. . .]

For their own entertainment, the defendants would select some labor servicemen, order them to lie down on the ground, and would completely cover them with soil so that only their heads remained free. The defendants would also force the labor servicemen to jump off tall, steep spots, to summersault backwards, to stand facing another serviceman, slapping his face.

[. . .] At one time, there was a diarrhea epidemic among the labor servicemen, at which point the defendants prohibited them from going to the toilet. On some occasions, if a labor serviceman defecated elsewhere, the defendants would push his nose into his own feces. On one occasion, they even forced a labor serviceman named Frankl from Komárom to eat his own feces because in his urgent need, he had defecated into the pig swill dish of the lieutenant colonel. The labor servicemen were often deprived of drinking water; some of them were called to the Labor Service guards' office on some pretext, and once there, they were beaten and then had their food confiscated on the pretext that it would be sent to the Red Cross, when in fact most of it was consumed by members of the Labor Service guard. [. . .]

After Romania changed sides in August 1944, the Wehrmacht started to evacuate the Balkans. The six thousand Jewish labor servicemen toiling in the Serbian copper mines in Bor were sent back toward Hungary in two waves. The first group left the camp on September 17. Yugoslavian partisans soon liberated the second wave. The three thousand members of the first group, which included

---

99. On people's courts, see the glossary.

Hungarian poet Miklós Radnóti,[100] were herded northward on foot (see map 4, p. lxiv). Treatment turned increasingly rough; the exhausted labor servicemen were regularly beaten and killed. On October 7–8, 1944, SS troops executed seven to eight hundred of them at Cservenka. By the time the death march reached the Austro-Hungarian border, Radnóti was completely exhausted from starvation and the long march. No longer able to move, the poet was shot and killed on November 9, 1944, at Abda by Hungarian soldiers escorting the group. The survivors of the first Bor wave were forced to march along the western border to concentration camps in the interior of the collapsing Reich. Radnóti's body was found only after the war during exhumation of the mass grave in which he lay. A small checkered notebook found in the pocket of his coat contained a sequence of poems he had written during his captivity and the death march. Among the powerful, tragic poems were also love poems to his wife, Fanni Gyarmati. Radnóti predicted his own death in his last poem, written on October 31, 1944 (document 2-13), a depiction of the execution of a fellow prisoner, violinist Miklós Lorsi.

DOCUMENT 2-13: **Miklós Radnóti, "Fourth Razglednica," private collection, Mrs. Miklós Radnóti.**[101]

> I fell next to him, his body turned over
> and it was stiff already, like a string about to snap.
> Shot in the back of the neck. "This will be your end, too,"
> I whispered to myself, "lie still,
> now, patience will blossom into death."
> "Der springt noch auf,"[102] I hear above me.
> Blood mixed with mud was drying on my ear.

Ten days later the poet met the fate he had foreseen.[103]

---

100. Miklós Radnóti (1909–1944), a poet, literary translator, and one of the leading figures of Hungarian literature in the twentieth century, was born into an assimilated middle-class Jewish family in Budapest and converted to Catholicism in 1943. He strongly identified with Hungarian language and culture and expressed his patriotism openly, despite being discriminated against and persecuted as a Jew.

101. *Razglednica* is Serbian for picture postcard. A version of this poem and others by him appeared in *Foamy Sky: The Major Poem of Miklós Radnóti*, ed. and trans. Zsuzsanna Ozsváth and Frederick Turner (Princeton, NJ: Princeton University Press, 1992), 118.

102. German for "he will still jump back up."

103. On the Labor Service in Bor, see Braham, *The Politics of Genocide*, 1:343–52; Tamás Csapody, *Bori munkaszolgálatosok* (Budapest: Vince, 2012); Anna Szele and György Szele, eds., *Kényszermunka, erőltetett menet, tömeghalál* (Budapest: Makkabi, 2004); Ferenc Andai, *Mint tanú szólni* (Budapest: Ab Ovo, 2003). On Radnóti's fate, see also Győző Ferencz, *Radnóti Miklós élete és költészete* (Budapest: Osiris, 2005), 628–700.

Other victims left few verbal accounts of their experiences in the service. Often the only traces of them remain faded family photographs or fragmented family stories preserved by survivors. The image reproduced in document 2-14 shows labor serviceman Aladár Barber in 1944.[104] During World War II, Barber was conscripted into the Labor Service several times. At the end of 1944, his unit was among those handed over to the Germans and taken to the western border of Hungary to build fortifications. Note the Hungarian national tricolor insignia on Barber's military cap.

DOCUMENT 2-14: **Photograph of labor serviceman Aladár Barber in 1944, USHMMPA WS# 10030 (courtesy of Charles and Herma Ellenboghen Barber).**

---

104. Barber was a resident of Budapest's District 6.

Due to severe conditions, a lack of food, and maltreatment by their Hungarian and German guards, thousands of labor servicemen perished. Barber died on January 15, 1945, in Sopronbánfalva. His wife was killed in Auschwitz. Only his son Károly found shelter in a safe house in Budapest, survived the war, and emigrated to the United States after the 1956 Revolution.

## HUNGARIAN-GERMAN RELATIONS AND THE "JEWISH QUESTION"

In March 1942, Miklós Kállay succeeded László Bárdossy as prime minister. With defeat seeming ever more likely, he was supposed to lead Hungary out of the war. It was Kállay's task to seek out contact with the Western Powers. An important component of the strategy of breaking with the Germans was rejection of the Nazis' Jewish policies. During his two-year term as prime minister, in complete agreement with Horthy, Kállay consistently resisted German demands to hand over and deport the Jews. Hungarian Jewry thus found itself in a unique situation. While across occupied Europe millions of Jews were being shot to death or gassed, in Hungary the yellow star was not introduced, ghettos were not set up, and trains were not routed to death camps. Most Hungarian Jews still remained physically safe, even if living under harsher daily conditions due to economic restrictions and disenfranchisement. (This, of course, did not apply to the labor servicemen in lethal danger and the victims of the atrocities described above.) The international environment favored the policies of Horthy and Kállay. Mussolini refused to allow deportations from Italy or from areas occupied by his troops. In the fall of 1942, the Romanian dictator Ion Antonescu stopped preparations to deport the Romanian Jews. France, led by Marshal Henri-Philippe Pétain, did not hand over most Jews with French citizenship, so predominantly refugees were dragged away.[105]

Even though Horthy and the government refused to deport the Jews, official propaganda assumed a harsh, antisemitic tone, and the parliament passed further anti-Jewish laws. This attitude was partially rooted in the political elite's own anti-Jewish sentiments and agenda. Budapest also wished to prove to Berlin that its antisemitism had not subsided.

While the Kállay cabinet did not hand its Jewish citizens over to the Nazis before the German occupation, it did abandon Hungarian Jews living abroad. Even though the government knew what awaited them in Nazi-occupied territories, it blocked the way back to the safety of Hungary. After passage of the

---

105. See Raul Hilberg, *The Destruction of the European Jews*, 3rd ed. (New Haven, CT: Yale University Press, 2003), 2:645–46, 792ff.

Second "Jewish Law," Hungarian political leaders were committed to making Jews emigrate. Consequently, the government did not want to allow the return of several thousand Jews. In 1942–1943, answering German demands, the cabinet set a final date eight times for transporting the Hungarian Jews living abroad back to Hungary, and it breached every single agreement.[106] Return was permitted for only a strictly selected, narrow group of different celebrities (artists, professionals, businessmen, and their relatives). For the regime in Budapest, Jews' assets were more important than their lives. While the Kállay government did its best to keep the Hungarian Jews living abroad out of the country, it also made every effort to gain access to their property.[107] This policy meant the death sentence for many of them.

On August 18, 1942, György Ottlik, editor in chief of the journal *Pester Lloyd*,[108] traveled to Italy and western Europe (Switzerland, Vichy France, and Germany) on a diplomatic mission. He wrote the report excerpted in document 2-15, informing the Ministry of Foreign Affairs about his meetings during the tour. This text offers important clues about what information was available to the Hungarian diplomatic corps about the expected outcome of the war. It also reveals awareness of the Jewish policy carried out in the territories under German influence, specifically about the purpose and implementation of the "Final Solution." In postwar trials and in memoirs, Hungarian politicians and high-ranking officials often defended themselves by claiming they thought the Germans were carting Hungarian Jews off to work in the Labor Service. In early July 1944, before the deportations were stopped, Prime Minister **Döme Sztójay** was still rejecting assertions by diplomats of neutral countries about mass murder and suggesting that these were fabricated rumors designed to spread fear.[109] But two years earlier, in September 1942, Ottlik had met with German diplomats along with Sztójay, who was serving as Hungary's ambassador to Berlin at the time. His report shows that in confidential circles, Sztójay was already talking openly in 1942 about murdering Jews by the hundreds of thousands.

---

106. László Karsai, "Magyar zsidók sorsa Nyugat-Európában 1942–1943," in *Magyarország a (nagy)hatalmak erőterében. Tanulmányok Ormos Mária 70. születésnapjára*, ed. Ferenc Ficher and József Vonyó (Pécs: University Press, 2000), 361.

107. For details, see Kádár and Vági, *Hullarablás*, 99–104.

108. The *Pester Lloyd* was established in 1854 as a German-language daily newspaper. It served as the semiofficial mouthpiece for Hungarian government politics between the two world wars and was intended for audiences abroad.

109. Minutes of the Council of Ministers, July 5, 1944, in Elek Karsai, ed., *Vádirat a nácizmus ellen. Dokumentumok a magyarországi zsidóüldözés történetéhez (1944 május 26–1944 október 15. A budapesti zsidóság deportálásának felfüggesztése)* (Budapest: Magyar Izraeliták Országos Képviselete, 1967), 3:63–64.

DOCUMENT 2-15: **György Ottlik's report to the Ministry of Foreign Affairs, October 10, 1942, HNA, Series K 64, fascicle 96, item 41, file 437/1942.**[110]

[. . .]
On the first day, straight away, I spent three hours at Mr. Ambassador Sztójay's. The main topics of our conversation were the following: I told him about my impressions, consulting with him about what I should tell the German gentlemen I would be meeting, and how I should put what I was to say; after this, he told me about his understanding of the military and the political situation, all in a spirit of optimism, of course, and he spent a long time dwelling on the Jewish question. He pointed out that the Germans have shifted away from their original standpoint that they would solve this problem after the war. Their reason for this, according to him, is that they do not want to carry the burden of resettling the Jews into the peace negotiations. For this reason, they want to make the Jews vanish from Europe. Beyond this, they have two further reasons for this radical "solution": the Jews are enemies with whom one cannot make a peace agreement—a peace agreement and coexistence are conceivable with the English or the Americans (a German diplomat told me the same thing), but the Jews remain mortal enemies, so it is "us or them." The other reason is that the Jews, with their mentality and network, are everywhere friends of the enemy; during the war, they must therefore be removed from all occupied areas and allied countries. An ally or a friend who provides shelter for Jews and protects them is not a friend but should be regarded as an enemy. This approach has now been launched in France as well. Soon, they will pose a question for us as well, for there are just two problems weighing down on Hungarian-German relations, heavy burdens indeed. One is our treatment of the German *Volksgruppe*[111]; this has been improving for now, and grievances have been pushed into the background.[112] The other problem is far more severe: the great influence and

---

110. First cited in Karsai, *A budai vártól a gyepüig*, 203–6.
111. This refers to ethnic Germans living in Hungary.
112. Sztójay's remark refers to constant tension caused by the pro-Nazi movements and elements of the German minority in Hungary who wished to gain independence from the Hungarian state and increase the influence of Nazi Germany. The government warded off these attempts with ever-decreasing success. For a detailed account, see Loránt Tilkovszky, *Ez volt a Volksbund. A német népcsoport-politika és Magyarország* (Budapest: Kossuth, 1978); Loránt Tilkovszky, *Hét évtized a magyarországi németek történetéből. 1919–1989* (Budapest: Kossuth, 1989).

role of the Jews in Hungary. As long as these continue, the Hungarians cannot be trusted. Sztójay would therefore consider it appropriate for Hungary to stop waiting until confronted with the question in a harsh manner. The country must speed up its changing of the guard and resettle a large portion of the Jewish population into occupied areas of Russia.[113] At first our Ambassador talked about 300,000 individuals, but then he lowered his estimate to 100,000. In response to my interjection, he made no secret of the fact that this move would not mean resettlement but murder.

During my response, I pointed out that we are not yet in a situation to take over the positions held by the Jews. In many places, in companies of varying sizes, I have an insider's perspective on what the real results of aryanization have been, and I must regrettably state that when it comes to intellectual productivity and diligence, Christian Hungarians, and especially the Hungarians of Hungarian origin, cannot, and perhaps do not even want to, keep up with the competition. They like income that requires no work and therefore favor the convenient position of a *Strohmann*.[114] To this Sztójay responded that if we do not make a move by ourselves, then the Germans will take the matter into their own hands after the war, remove the Jews, and put Germans in their places, and will do this even if "they perhaps win only a 75 percent victory, or a 50 percent one."

For my part, I emphasized that thinking about matters soberly, the takeover of the position of the Jewish capital, and economic replacement of the Jews would require at least a generation, thirty years—thirty years during which today's strong political and moral pressure would be maintained throughout. It is, so to speak, impossible to follow mobile capital, and it would simply disappear if there were threats and persecution. Forcing that solution would therefore lead to a rather severe economic crisis at a moment, during the last two or three years of the war, when we are supposed to be doing all we can to lift our economic, moral, and physical strength to the highest degree. If the Germans win—a total victory, not a 50 percent one, and I do not know what the latter is supposed to mean—then they will do whatever they please, and it will make no difference to what extent we try to please them beforehand. In terms of banishing 100,000 or 300,000 Jews, sentencing them to death, that would certainly be a fine gesture toward Germany. But it would not solve the

---

113. In Hungary the "aryanization" of Jewish property was widely called the "changing of the guard."

114. See the introduction to document 1-4 and the term *stróman* in the glossary.

Jewish question and would therefore do no more than impose the burden on the Hungarian state and its people of having used unprecedented brutality against its own citizens. This would lead to Hungary's inner disruption, while yielding no more than a 10 or 30 percent improvement. This is no way to rescue a nation. His Excellency the ambassador was shaking his head quite a bit as he acknowledged this argument of mine, which I supported with the claim that, to a reasonable extent, I myself do everything in my power to replace the Jews with genuine Hungarians, but I had never gone so far (nor would I be willing to) as to endanger the quality and therefore the very existence of the *Pester Lloyd*,[115] that is to say, incurring the loss of a Hungarian value, a Hungarian weapon. One can, and can only, replace one value with another. Only a revolution can go further than this, by destroying blindly at first, so it can subsequently build things in their place.

[. . .]

Ottlik's notes show that Sztójay was aware of the change in the Reich's Jewish policies after the turn of 1941–1942 and the motivations behind it. He thought that the rational move would be for Hungary to anticipate the Germans' demands, which were likely to grow stronger, and initiate the deportation of its Jewish citizens. Sztójay also made clear that participation in the pan-European solution in practice meant collaboration in a systematic genocide.

Following the 1943 turn in the war caused by the German defeat at Stalingrad, Hungary became an increasingly important component in the Reich's strategy, not because of its army, which was of modest combat value, but because of its geostrategic position and economic resources. Through its intelligence service, Berlin had precise information about the leading circles' diminishing enthusiasm for the German alliance. On April 16–17, 1943, at the German-Hungarian negotiations taking place at the Klessheim castle in Austria, Hitler and German foreign minister Joachim von Ribbentrop personally confronted Horthy about his government's "defeatist" behavior and "moderate" Jewish policies. Unprepared to counter these attacks, the regent did not give a substantive response at that time.[116] He did so three weeks later in the form of a letter, after he had consulted with the Council of Ministers and the Ministry of Foreign Affairs.

---

115. This is Ottlik's newspaper. See note 108 above.
116. For minutes of the meeting between Hitler and Horthy, see Randolph L. Braham, ed., *The Destruction of Hungarian Jewry: A Documentary Account* (New York: Pro Arte for the World Federation of Hungarian Jews, 1963), 1:218–28.

DOCUMENT 2-16: **Regent Miklós Horthy's letter to Adolf Hitler, May 7, 1943, in Miklós Szinai and László Szűcs, eds., *Horthy Miklós titkos iratai* (Budapest: Kossuth, 1962), 391–400.**[117]

Your Excellency,
Following the kind invitation of Your Excellency, on the 16th of this month, I traveled to the Klessheim castle in order to exchange, in accordance with our allied status and our mutual interests, our thoughts about questions concerning our cooperation.

Because I think it is of utmost importance that our countries maintain the same open and trusting relations we have had in the past, I consider it my duty to respond in some detail to the reproaches directed at me during our long conversations on this occasion.

According to one such reproach, the treatment of the Jews is allegedly much too lenient in Hungary. Concerning this question and without being presumptuous, I wish to cite the fact that at the time,[118] I was the first to raise my voice against the destructive behavior of the Jews, and I have ever since taken every measure to curb their influence.[119] This was a new trend at the time, and because of it, my country was boycotted by Germany, as well as the rest of the world. However, the measures that I undertook practically stripped the Jews of the opportunity to continue exerting their harmful influence on the public affairs of the country. The enormity of the difficulties that had to be overcome in the process is due to the fact that before this, commerce and industry were almost entirely in Jewish hands. At present, we have further measures underway aimed at gradually shutting out the Jews, and we will carry out their deportation as soon as conditions for their transportation are secured. [. . .]

In this letter Horthy continued with detailed assurances about his country's loyalty to the alliance and Hungary's commitment to joint goals in the war. Addressing the Jewish question, he briefly summarized the rationale that Hungarian diplomats had also used before in response to German demands: the indispensability of the Jews to the economy, technical difficulties impeding

---

117. Cf. the English translation appearing in Miklós Szinai and László Szűcs, eds., *The Confidential Papers of Admiral Horthy* (Budapest: Corvina, 1965), 249–50.
118. He means the immediate post–World War I era.
119. Horthy is referring to the introduction of the ***numerus clausus*** in 1920, which was one of the first anti-Jewish laws in Europe introduced after World War I. See the glossary.

the deportations, the regime's commitment to antisemitism from the very start, and so forth.[120]

**Edmund Veesenmayer** was at the time working within the German Foreign Ministry as the special commissioner for the southeastern region of Europe. During 1943 he paid two longer visits to Hungary, and in subsequent reports he provided detailed information about the political situation, offering suggestions about how the interests of the Reich might be served. Document 2-17 includes excerpts from his report following his second visit to Budapest in late November and December of 1943.

Like other Nazi leaders, Veesenmayer viewed the Hungarians with contempt. In the introduction to his report, he dealt with Hungarian history and the Hungarian collective spirit, unleashing a scathing criticism of what he saw as the country's backward social system and political unreliability. He concluded that fear and cowardice were the basic traits of Hungarian politicians and most Hungarian people. He urged that immediate steps be taken against the "center of sabotage" run by the Jews, who formed the "vanguard of bolshevism" and allied with the feudal aristocratic elite. His conspiracy theories, rabid antisemitism, and generally negative prejudices about the Hungarian population notwithstanding, Veesenmayer accurately assessed the situation and the chances of German intervention. He believed that Berlin had the power to occupy Hungary. If Germany chose to follow an aggressive course, the Hungarians would not resist, due to their foreign policy of isolation, their hostile neighbors, and last but not least, the pro-German leanings of the Army General Staff.[121] He also correctly predicted that the Germans could count on the "national opposition" (that is, the pro-Nazi extreme right), the hierarchical nature of the political culture, and the weakness of parliamentarianism in Hungary.

In his April 1943 report, Veesenmayer had already suggested that Kállay be replaced, but once the Hungarians made concessions and increased their war efforts following the Klessheim negotiations, German leaders were satisfied with the results, at least for the time being.[122] With the military situation

---

120. Miklós Szinai and László Szűcs, eds., *Horthy Miklós titkos iratai* (Budapest: Kossuth, 1962), 391–400.

121. Among Hungarian civil servants and the general staff, pro-German attitudes had a long-standing tradition independent of Nazi influence. This was due in part to joint foreign policy interests and economic ties, as well as military-technological interdependency.

122. Szinai and Szűcs, *Horthy Miklós*, 399.

deteriorating further and with information about new Hungarian diplomatic overtures to the Allies at hand, the Germans made preparations to occupy Hungary.[123]

**DOCUMENT 2-17: Report by Edmund Veesenmayer, representative of the German Foreign Office, on the political situation in Hungary, December 10, 1943, IMT, NG-5560 (translated from German).**

[. . .]

The Jew is Enemy No. 1. These 1.1 million Jews are all saboteurs against the Reich,[124] as are at least the same number of Hungarians—if not twice as many—who are the followers [*Trabanten*] of the Jews and act as their auxiliary troops and external cover in the realization of the Jews' grand plan aimed at sabotage and espionage.

[. . .]

It is astounding how well the Jews' system of relaying news operates. They know everything within 24 hours, even the most intimate goings-on in the Reich. There must be a system of illegal transmitters in Hungary, which functions brilliantly.[125]

[. . .]

Summary:

1.) The developments in Hungary have progressed to a point that requires quick and determined action.

2.) Because a solution of the Hungarian question ought to be—if at all possible—carried out together with the Regent and not without him, in this respect, too, the time has come to stop leaving the Hungarians more or less to their own devices.

3.) Hungary, as a most important transport area and a potential instrument of economic assistance to Germany, can and must be completely

---

123. They saw as political provocations not only the new round of "secret" negotiations but also the fact that those responsible for the Southern Province mass murders were put on trial in Hungary. Braham, *The Politics of Genocide*, 1:255–56.

124. Veesenmayer overestimated the size of the Jewish population, which was around 760,000 to 780,000, including those Christians who qualified as Jews according to the anti-Jewish laws.

125. It is not certain if Veesenmayer, an otherwise clearheaded foreign policy expert, actually believed this accusation, so typical of paranoid antisemitic propaganda, or if he was using such a baseless statement instrumentally.

integrated into the Reich's war economy, especially in the realm of agriculture.

4.) The current Hungarian government policy and propaganda have taken on a form that exhibits a veiled provocation toward the Reich. Failing to react to this would be construed as a sign of weakness, both on the part of the Hungarians, as well as our enemies, and would have a corresponding effect on those elements that are useful to us.

5.) An active policy by the Reich with the corresponding consequences by no means constitutes a danger for any later Reich policy. After all, the evolution of Hungary as a nation remains in an early phase, and it will take several decades for her to achieve a certain degree of maturity.

6.) There are no grounds to fear any serious, negative repercussions for any of Hungary's peripheral states allied with us,[126] for the Bolshevik danger hovers above the entire southeast region today.

7.) Tackling the Jewish question thoroughly should be the order of the day for a variety of reasons. Settling this question is a prerequisite for involving Hungary in the Reich's defensive and existential struggle.

[. . .]

Contrary to previous plans for an exclusively military solution, Veesenmayer suggested carrying out the occupation of Hungary in a "peaceful" manner without affecting the regent or the constitutional structure. This strategy was to be accompanied by the twin tools of threat and manipulation, under the supervision of a special commissioner of the Reich. Not surprisingly, Hitler appointed none other than Veesenmayer to the position of plenipotentiary and minister in Hungary on March 19, 1944.

---

126. He is referring primarily to sovereign satellite states (Romania and Bulgaria).

## CHAPTER 3
# BLITZKRIEG AGAINST THE JEWS

ON MARCH 19, 1944, the German army occupied Hungary. The reasons behind Hitler's decision to invade its reluctant ally were manifold. Berlin was with good reason concerned that Regent **Miklós Horthy** would follow the Italians' example and try to exit the war. Invasion would also enable takeover of the country's military production and reinforcement of the crumbling eastern front with Hungarian soldiers.[1] The Nazis' wish to solve the "Jewish question" in Hungary was one, but certainly not the most important, reason for the occupation. To use Randolph L. Braham's phrasing, the Holocaust in Hungary was a concomitant of a primarily military decision.[2]

After the occupation, the regent did not resign. He dismissed Prime Minister **Miklós Kállay** and, in accordance with the Germans' "wish," appointed a new government led by the pro-Nazi Hungarian ambassador to Berlin, **Döme Sztójay**. For the SS officer in charge of the "Final Solution," SS-Obersturmbannführer **Adolf Eichmann**, the collaboration of the Hungarian authorities was essential. He was thus pleasantly surprised when he found

---

1. On the reasons behind the occupation, see Gyula Vargyai, "Így döntöttek. A Magyarország német megszállását eredményező német katonai döntési mechanizmus," in *Magyarország 1944—A német megszállás*, ed. Gyula Vargyai and János Almási (Budapest: Nemzeti Tankönyvkiadó, 1994), 7–20; György Ránki, *1944 március 19. Magyarország német megszállása*, 2nd rev. ed. (Budapest: Kossuth, 1978), 7–93; Randolph L. Braham, *The Politics of Genocide: The Holocaust in Hungary* (New York: Columbia University Press, 1994), 1:381–89.

2. Randolph L. Braham, "The Holocaust in Hungary: A Retrospective Analysis," in *The Nazis' Last Victims: The Holocaust in Hungary*, ed. Randolph L. Braham, with Scott Miller (Detroit, MI: Wayne University Press in association with the USHMM, 1998), 36.

the new leadership of the Ministry of the Interior more than ready to deploy Hungary's complete public administration and law enforcement network in the anti-Jewish campaign launched immediately after the occupation. This chapter focuses on the first phase of this campaign: the disenfranchisement of Hungary's Jews and their physical isolation in ghettos and collection camps.

## STIGMATIZATION

The new government subjected Jews to a flood of new antisemitic decrees. These measures completely deprived them, practically overnight, of the rights that had remained intact under the "Jewish Laws." During the previous years, various public agencies had attempted to introduce these restrictions in the form of (illegal or semi-illegal) resolutions, regulations, and orders, as well as petitions addressed to the government.[3] **László Endre**, the newly appointed state secretary at the Ministry of the Interior, could rightfully claim that Hungary's policies, rather than merely copying the German example, were the culmination of an organically developed process spanning a quarter century.[4] Just a few days after the new government was set up, Jews were ordered to wear the yellow star. Their vehicles and phones were confiscated, and they were banned from several professions. Over the weeks to come, further decrees, issued one after the other, gradually pushed them out of society. They could not go to the cinema, theater, or restaurants with Christians. They were banned from the beaches and public bathhouses.[5] Their food rations were reduced. Jews received separate food stamps and could only shop during one or two hours each day.[6] A new requirement to hand over radios and bicycles was intended to restrict the flow of information to the Jewish community and the options for escape.[7]

---

3. See chapter 2.

4. See László Endre's statement in a radio broadcast of March 31, 1944, in Ilona Benoschofsky and Elek Karsai, eds., *Vádirat a nácizmus ellen. Dokumentumok a magyarországi zsidóüldözés történetéhez (1944 március 19–1944 május 15. A német megszállástól a deportálás megkezdéséig)* (Budapest: Magyar Izraeliták Országos Képviselete, 1958), 1:88–89.

5. Minister of the Interior's Decree no. 444/1944 about banning Jews from frequenting public baths. Minister of the Interior's Decrees nos. 500/1944 and 510/1944 about the ban on frequenting restaurants, bars, and entertainment venues. See *Budapesti Közlöny*, May 2, 1944, 1–2; May 20, 1944, 4.

6. Each Jew would receive a quota of thirty decagrams (less than 0.7 pounds) of sugar and cooking oil per month, and ten decagrams (about 0.2 pounds) of horse meat or beef per week. The food stamps issued up to that point then had to be handed in. Exchanging them meant a new round of registrations for the Jews. See Minister of Public Supply's Decree no. 108.500/1944, April 21, 1944; Benoschofsky and Karsai, *Vádirat a nácizmus ellen*, 1:228–31.

7. The most important order regarding the submitting of radios was Minister of Commerce and Transportation's Decree no. 217.300/1944, *Budapesti Közlöny*, April 21, 1944, 2.

Restrictions on travel made free movement impossible.[8] Decree after decree ensured confiscation of virtually all movable property and real estate belonging to Jews.[9] Between March and August 1944, the Sztójay government introduced over one hundred anti-Jewish decrees depriving Jews of their rights, assets, and freedom. Visible stigmatization was the first step toward complete physical isolation.

DOCUMENT 3-1: **Prime Minister's Decree no. 1240/1944 on the distinguishing mark of the Jews,** *Budapesti Közlöny*,[10] **March 31, 1944, 3.**[11]

[. . .]

1. §

(1) After this decree takes effect, all Jewish persons over the age of six are required when going outdoors to wear a canary-yellow, six-pointed star at least 10 × 10 centimeters in diameter,[12] made of cotton, silk, or velvet, affixed to an easily visible place over the left breast of their outer garments.

(2) The distinguishing mark mentioned in the previous article must be sewn on garments, so it cannot be easily detached.

2. §

In determining who is considered Jewish and non-Jewish with respect to the application of this law, Articles 9 and 16 of Act XV of 1941 are to be followed with the additional provision that those persons are also considered non-Jewish who satisfy the conditions set out in the last paragraph of Article 9, provided that they have not married (and up until they do not marry) a Jew or a non-Jew with one or two grandparents who were born as members of the Israelite denomination.[13]

[. . .]

---

8. Exceptions were doctors on duty or people with serious reasons for traveling (e.g., heading to work). See Prime Minister's Decree no. 1270/1944 on restricting the travel of Jews, *Budapesti Közlöny*, April 7, 1944, 4.

9. For details, see chapter 6.

10. *Budapesti Közlöny* (*Budapest Bulletin*) was the official government journal in which nonconfidential decrees were published.

11. The document was published in Benoschofsky and Karsai, *Vádirat a nácizmus ellen*, 1:52–55.

12. Approximately 4 × 4 inches.

13. "Up until they do not marry" means that the exemption loses validity once the person marries a Jew. For Act XV of 1941, see document 1-3; the last paragraph of Article 9 stipulated that a non-Jew and a Jew with two Jewish grandparents needed to obtain special permission from the government to marry.

4. §

(1) Those who do not obey the order set out in Article 1 commit an offense and will be sentenced to two months of confinement and in wartime, six months of confinement, provided that their action does not fall under a more serious offense.

[. . .]

The Central **Jewish Council** (the leading Jewish body set up by Eichmann) warned everyone to obey the decree.[14] Few Jews ultimately refused to wear the yellow star and were willing to take the great risk of going into hiding. The vast majority proved to be law-abiding citizens and followed the decree. In some places Jews sarcastically referred to the star as the "Sztójay medal."[15] In the wake of objections raised by the churches, the regulation was amended a few days later: exempted status was now also extended to Christian ecclesiastics of Jewish origin, to Jewish widows and orphans of Christian Hungarian soldiers who had fallen in the "recent war" (World War II), and certain groups of Jews in "mixed" marriages.[16]

In practice, violating the decree mostly meant "just" having to pay a fine. After German Plenipotentiary **Edmund Veesenmayer** found the penalties imposed insufficient, the Ministry of the Interior introduced further decrees ordering authorities to conduct stricter checks.[17] After that, law enforcement officials held yellow-star raids throughout the country, issuing fines when stars were not of the appropriate color, were not sewn on properly, were covered by a scarf or a bag, or were not worn inside a shop or workshop. Hundreds of people received fines, and several were jailed.[18]

Under such circumstances most Jews unsurprisingly obeyed the law and wore the yellow star, even on rare joyful occasions such as weddings. Imre Rosner (later

---

14. On the Jewish Council's attitude and strategies, see chapter 8.
15. Moshe Élijáhu Gonda, *A debreceni zsidók száz éve. A mártírhalált halt debreceni és környékbeli zsidók emlékére* (Tel Aviv: Debreceni Zsidók Emlékbizottsága, n.d [1970]), 242.
16. Prime Minister's Decree no. 1450/1944 supplementing the decree concerning distinguishing mark for the Jews, *Budapesti Közlöny*, April 5, 1944. The exemption applied to those who belonged to the Christian religion living with their non-Jewish spouses, as well as to the widows of non-Jewish spouses. However, if their children were considered "Jewish" according to the racial regulations, the exemption was null and void.
17. Minutes of the meeting of the Council of Ministers, April 14, 1944, HNA K27, box 260.
18. Judit Molnár, *Zsidósors 1944-ben az V. (szegedi) csendőrkerületben* (Budapest: Cserépfalvi, 1995), 47–48; László Csősz, "'Keresztény polgári érdekek sérelme nélkül . . .' Gettósítás Szolnokon 1944-ben," *Századok* 134 (2000): 644.

Rozsnyai) was born in a small village in northeastern Hungary. Around the age of twenty, he moved to Budapest. From 1940 on, Imre was drafted into the **Labor Service** several times. In Budapest he met Klára Krausz, a Budapest-born woman, the only child of Abraham and Margit Krausz. They got married after April 5, 1944, when all the Jews in Hungary were ordered to wear the yellow badge. The picture reproduced in document 3-2 was taken on their wedding day. Note the star on Imre's suit. Klára is covering her badge with her bouquet.

DOCUMENT 3-2: **Wedding portrait of Imre Rosner and his wife, Klára Krausz, 1944, USHMMPA WS# 27410.**

Shortly after this photo was taken, Klára and her parents found shelter in a Catholic convent. Imre's labor company stayed in Hungary and in December was sent to the Austrian border to build fortifications along with dozens of other units. As the Red Army approached, the labor servicemen were herded off to the Mauthausen concentration camp. The U.S. Army liberated Imre on May 5, 1945. Returning home, he was reunited with Klára and her parents in Budapest. After the anticommunist revolution in 1956, they faced a dilemma shared by tens of thousands of other families: leave the country or stay. The couple could not agree on what to do and finally divorced: Imre stayed in Soviet-occupied Hungary, while Klára emigrated to Canada with their daughter.

## SETTING UP THE GHETTOS

Stigmatization was just the beginning of the process of persecution, soon to be followed by physical isolation. On April 7, 1944, representatives of the Hungarian and German authorities assembled to work out the details of the Jews' ghettoization. Present were state secretaries of the Ministry of the Interior László Endre and **László Baky**, gendarme and police officers, Adolf Eichmann with one of his men, and representatives of the Hungarian army. A draft decree prepared by Endre and Eichmann was distributed. The document, issued by the Ministry of the Interior as Confidential Decree no. 6163/1944,[19] laid the ground for ghettoization.

DOCUMENT 3-3: **Minister of the Interior's Confidential Decree no. 6163/1944 on designating the residence of Jews, April 7, 1944, USHMMA RG 52.001M, reel 11 (HNA I).[20]**

>Hungarian Royal Minister of the Interior
>Number: 6163/1944. res.
>             Re: Designating residences for the Jews
>The Hungarian Royal government will within a short period of time cleanse the country of the Jews.[21] I order the cleansing by regions, as a

---

19. Government measures and decrees containing information the authorities wished to keep clandestine were labeled confidential. They were not published in any official journal or other media.

20. It was first published in Benoschofsky and Karsai, *Vádirat a nácizmus ellen*, 1:124–26. The USHMMA RG 52.001M collection contains extensive material from what is sometimes referred to as the "I collection," which was compiled from archival material acquired from both national and regional archives throughout Hungary; cf. Tim Cole, *Traces of the Holocaust: Journeying in and out of the Ghettos* (New York: Continuum International, 2011), 144n22–23.

21. Since at this point no final decision had been made about the deportation of Hungarian Jews, Eichmann and Endre used "cleansing" to mean the transfer of Jews into camps and ghettos.

result of which the Jews, regardless of sex and age, will have to be transported to designated collection camps. In towns and in larger villages, some of the Jews will subsequently be placed in Jewish buildings designated by the law enforcement authorities, as well as into ghettos.

Exemptions are granted to those Jews who are employed at plants, mines, major companies, or estates that are of military importance, and whose immediate replacement would hinder production at the plant. In plants, mines, and companies that are not of military importance, replacement of the Jews must be executed immediately, and the most suitable person from the staff is to be appointed to head the given company, plant, etc., and is to be given full power. These will be determined by the committees appointed by the local governments.[22] But as soon as the possibility of replacement is secured—and regional public administration authorities must strive to make this happen as soon as possible—a custodian, preferably a trained one, shall be selected immediately and appointed to head the plant, factory, etc., and shall be given full responsibility.

[. . .] The collection of the Jews will be conducted by the police with regional authority and the Hungarian royal gendarmerie.

The gendarmerie will provide armed assistance to the Hungarian royal police in towns, if needed. The German security police will be present on the scene as an advisory agency, and smooth cooperation with them must be accorded special importance.[23]

The regional local governments will establish collection camps based on the number of Jews, deciding on appropriate locations and on how many camps should exist. They must report the location of these camps to the state secretary for public safety.[24] [. . .]

In each town and major municipality in which the number of Jews calls for the establishment of separate Jewish buildings, the police authorities should within their own jurisdiction designate these buildings immediately, because only those Jews who are threats to state security will be left behind in the collection camps, while the others will be moved to Jewish houses. Those buildings in which large numbers of Jews live should

---

22. That is, the designations of the new company directors.
23. The Ministry of the Interior issued a decree that ordered the administrative and law enforcement apparatus to cooperate fully with the Germans. Minister of the Interior's Decree 6000/1944 VII. res. on the principles of the cooperation between the Hungarian authorities and German armed forces, April 19, 1944, in Benoschofsky and Karsai, *Vádirat a nácizmus ellen*, 1:187–90.
24. That is, László Baky; see the glossary.

be the ones designated as Jewish buildings. Of these, residents of non-Jewish ancestry should be moved into apartments—of comparable value and rent—which Jews have vacated. The relocations should take place within thirty days after completion of the cleansing campaign so that Jews moved out into collection camps can at that time be immediately moved into Jewish buildings. [. . .]

As the Jews are collected and transported off, local authorities should at the same time appoint committees that will, together with those police and gendarme units present, immediately close and seal each of the apartments and shops of the Jews. The keys will be handed over in a sealed envelope, together with the name and exact address of the Jew in question, to the command of the collection camp. [. . .]

Money and valuables (gold, silver, bonds, etc.) should be confiscated by the aforementioned agencies present, which should turn them over to town authorities and municipal councils in exchange for a short inventory that lists the items, along with a countersignature. The municipal councils must within three days ship these valuables to the branch of the National Bank located in the center of the region being cleansed. These centers are established on a case-by-case basis by the security forces heading the cleansing campaign.

Transfer of prisoners should be carried out on trains and, if needed, by carts provided by order of the town and municipal councils. Jews to be transported can take along only the clothes they are wearing, at most two additional sets of underwear, and at least fourteen days' worth of food per person and, in addition, luggage weighing at most fifty kilograms [110 lbs.], which includes the weight of bed sheets, blankets, and mattresses. Prisoners may not take along money, jewelry, gold, or silver. Collection of Jews should be carried out in the following order: Kassa, Marosvásárhely, Kolozsvár, Miskolc, Debrecen, Szeged, Pécs, Szombathely, Székesfehérvár, and the Budapest gendarmerie districts, as well as the areas within these districts that are under the control of the police authorities, and finally, in the capital Budapest. [. . .]

I have imposed on the Budapest-based Central Jewish Council a requirement to set up immediately, using their own doctors and equipment, auxiliary temporary hospitals in Nyíregyháza, Ungvár, Munkács, and Máramarossziget.[25] These doctors will also be in charge of health services at the collection camps.

---

25. This clause of the decree was never implemented.

In addition, I call the authorities' attention to the fact that all Jewish refugees from foreign states without exception fall in the same category as communists in terms of treatment and must, therefore, without exception be placed in collection camps.

Dubious Jews are also to be transported to collection camps,[26] and their assessment will take place there.

My present decree should be handled with strict confidence, and the authorities as well as those in charge of commanding headquarters are responsible for making sure that no one finds out about the cleansing campaign before it starts. [. . .]

Budapest, April 7, 1944.                                                    László Baky[27]

The decree contained only sparse directions about how and from what sources transportation, food, health care, and securing and processing of Jews' valuables might be covered. The state secretaries' verbal remarks did little to clarify these details.[28] According to one postwar testimony, Endre responded to the concerns of officials participating in the process by saying, "A principle in carrying out the decree is that everything that facilitates the goal is good and everything that hinders it is bad. Nothing should stand in the way or hinder this process. Everything has to be resolved within one's own sphere of authority."[29]

Based on the April 7, 1944, decree, Hungarian authorities began rounding up and concentrating the Jewish population of the northeastern part of the country on April 16. Ten days later, at the April 26 meeting of the Council of Ministers, a new decree was issued regarding the ghettoization process. (This became Prime Minister's Decree no. 1610/1944, effective as of April 28, 1944.) The government had more than one reason to issue a new regulation. First, the April 7 decree did not fulfill the formal legal requirements and also failed to include what definition of the term "Jew" should be used. The April 26 regulation remedied these formal problems, thereby "legalizing" the ghettoization. Second, the new decree stipulated the creation of ghettos instead of ghettos and

---

26. That is, Jews whose legal status was unclear.

27. Since the official appointment of Endre had not yet arrived from Regent Horthy, Baky signed the document.

28. Memorandum prepared by Géza Halász, leading government official in Carpatho-Ruthenia, regarding "the April 7 meeting conducted in the small council room of the Ministry of the Interior concerning the Jewish question," May 27, 1944, HNA, series I, reel 11.

29. Record of Jenő Péterffy's testimony, November 22, 1945, USHMMA RG 25004M, reel 87, 40029, vol. II.

collection camps.³⁰ Third, in contrast to the April 7 confidential regulation, this one was public. It served as a cover-up for the ghettoization process, camouflaging the operation as a measure aimed merely at easing the dire apartment shortage among non-Jews. Therefore an odd charade unfolded at the April 26 meeting of the Council of Ministers. Minister of the Interior **Andor Jaross** justified the necessity of concentrating the Jews in designated settlements by pointing out that the allocation of apartments was unfair and that Jews lived in more favorable conditions than Christians. The decree before the ministers facilitated the authorities' confiscation of Jewish apartments, while Jaross claimed that "no Jew will become homeless as a result of implementation of the decree."³¹ One might have added to this: because they will be rounded up in ghettos and "**yellow-star houses**," and later in collection camps set up in mills, barns, brick factories, and pigsties.

DOCUMENT 3-4: **Prime Minister's Decree no. 1610/1944 on the regulation of certain questions concerning the apartments of the Jews and the designation of their residence,** *Budapesti Közlöny*, **April 28, 1944, 2–3.**³²

*On the utilization of the Jews' apartments*

[. . .]

1. §

For the purpose of assigning apartments and the accommodation of public offices and institutions serving the public interest, one may utilize:

1. the apartment of a Jew who has another apartment either in that same municipality (town) or in another one;

[. . .]

3. the apartment of a Jew whose apartment exceeds the professional and personal needs of those who live there; in case of such utilization, an apartment should be secured for the subject of the utilization that suits their apartment needs, living circumstances, and permanent salary;

[. . .]

---

30. Based on the experiences of the first concentration phase, as of May 9 a specific ban on the placement of Jews directly into collection camps went into effect (radio news file no. 2848, May 9, 1944, HNA K148, fascicle 1200). Henceforth Jews were first placed in ghettos, and they were transported to collection camps only during the concentration phase, prior to deportation.

31. Minutes of the meeting of the Council of Ministers, April 26, 1944, HNA K27, box 260.

32. The document was published in Benoschofsky and Karsai, *Vádirat a nácizmus ellen*, 1:244–49.

*Designating residences for the Jews*
8. §

(1) The chief executive of a local government may order that in municipalities with populations under ten thousand people, Jews are required to move by a fixed deadline to another municipality or town designated by the chief executive.

(2) For those Jews who are required to move under paragraph (1), accommodation in a new place of residence is arranged by the chief constable or the mayor.

(3) A Jew cannot settle in municipalities that fall under paragraph (1).

(4) The present article does not affect the residence of a Jew in a municipality if residence is based on labor service or some other official order.[33]

9. §

(1) The chief executive of the local government may order that in municipalities that do not fall under Article 8, and in towns, Jews may only live in specified parts of the town or municipality, or in specified streets, even in designated houses.

(2) In the case mentioned in paragraph (1), the apartments needed to accommodate the Jews are arranged by the chief constable in municipalities and by the mayor in towns.

10. §

When enforcing Article 9, the chief executive of the local government may also order, in connection with the accommodation of Jews in specified parts of town (streets, houses), that non-Jewish persons vacate the part of the town or municipality (street, house) that has been assigned to the Jews. But non-Jewish persons can only be required to move out if an apartment is available that is appropriate for their living circumstances and permanent salary.

11. §

(1) During the enforcement of the present decree, in cases when Jews have a business, a lease, or any other venture, which as a result of these Jews' removal they cannot continue to personally manage or liquidate, the

---

33. This applied primarily to doctors and pharmacists practicing while they were labor servicemen in small settlements.

head of the municipal council (the mayor) will make a submission to the court of guardians to have a custodian assigned. A designated custodian's duties and rights must conform to the rules laid down in § 28, provision (d) of Act XX of 1877, regulating affairs concerning custody and guardianship.[34]

[. . .]

The process of physically isolating the Jews, launched on April 16, 1944, rested on the two governmental decrees quoted above. It was concluded in late June, with completion of the forced removal of the Budapest Jews into "yellow-star houses." During these two and a half months, the implementation of the process underwent many changes. In the first phase, mainly collection camps were set up. From early May onward, at approximately the same time throughout the entire country, the creation of ghettos became dominant, and their residents were transferred to collection camps just a few days prior to their deportation. Both decrees offered a very broad framework for their practical implementation, which local authorities could fill as they saw fit. For this reason and despite extensive governmental control, ghettoization followed a varied pattern depending on local circumstances. No central orders prescribed how to create the enclosed area, allowing local forces much leeway in carrying out the process.

What followed was like a blitzkrieg against the Jews: between April and June, in only ten weeks, the Hungarians organized 215 ghettos and collection camps. This number does not include approximately 100 to 150 temporary collection sites (typically synagogues, schools, and other community buildings) where Jews were moved for a few days before their transfer to camps or ghettos. During the concentration phase prior to deportation, people were taken from ghettos to collection camps. However, in Carpatho-Ruthenia, Northern Transylvania, northeastern Hungary, and the southern border areas, these

---

34. Initially the government tried to create the legal framework for confiscating Jewish wealth by handling it as a guardianship issue for the property of "absent" citizens. The first step was issuing a decree that concerned the assets of Jews who were "absent" for at least one year. It appointed orphans' courts to manage such property, justifying the decision by saying that "uncertainty about whether the individual who is absent is still alive does not prevent taking [the assets] into custody." See Minister of Interior's Decree 230.900/1944 on the asset management of the wealth of absent Jews, April 10, 1944, in Benoschofsky and Karsai, *Vádirat a nácizmus ellen*, 1:141–42. Article 11 of the above decree was in line with this concept, which the government later dropped. For details, see Gábor Kádár and Zoltán Vági, *Hullarablás. A magyar zsidók gazdasági megsemmisítése* (Budapest: Jaffa, 2005), 222–23.

collection sites were frequently set up first, and people were deported from them directly.[35]

Four models for physically segregating the Jews emerged across Hungary[36]:

1. Complete resettlement in camp-like accommodations outside residential areas: in factories, industrial or agricultural buildings, or other areas (mines, forests) outside a locality. This model was especially common in Carpatho-Ruthenia and Northern Transylvania and existed, for example, in Beszterce, Dés, and Kolozsvár.
2. One, two, or three closed, segregated residential areas, often at the site of the traditional Jewish quarter. The ghetto was often surrounded by barbed wire or some kind of fence. Such examples existed in Balassagyarmat, Debrecen, Eger, Esztergom, Felsővisó, Gyöngyös, Győr, Huszt, Ipolyság, Kaposvár, Körmend, Makó, Máramarossziget, Mohács, Nagyszőlős, Nyíregyháza, Paks, Pécs, Sátoraljaújhely, Szarvas, Szeged, Szentendre, Tótkomlós, Vác, and Veszprém.
3. A combination of models 1 and 2 (for example, in Kassa, Munkács, Nagyvárad, and Szolnok).
4. Separate buildings or separate clusters of buildings. This occurred, among other locations, in Budapest, Kispest, and Székesfehérvár.

In a few places local authorities did not organize the ghetto at all or did not tightly close off the Jewish residential area (for instance, in Baja, Celldömölk, Hódmezővásárhely, or Szekszárd). The reasons and motivations behind these decisions varied. According to the confidential ghettoization decree, those parts of towns more densely populated by Jews were to be designated as ghetto sites. However, subsequent orders—issued to gain popular support and legitimize the operation among non-Jews—generally stipulated that this process should take into account "Christian interests" to the fullest extent possible.[37] Central authorities did not specify how many people the accommodations should hold,

---

35. See the contribution by László Csősz on ghettos, collection camps, and entrainment centers in Hungary, spring-summer 1944, in Joseph Robert White, ed., *The United States Holocaust Memorial Museum Encyclopedia of Camps and Ghettos, 1933–1945*, vol. 3: *The Camps and Ghettos under European Regimes Aligned with Nazi Germany* (Bloomington: Indiana University Press in association with the USHMM, forthcoming).

36. See the categorization in László Csősz, "A Vészkorszak Jász-Nagykun-Szolnok vármegyében" (PhD diss., University of Szeged, 2010), 75.

37. See the minutes of the meeting of the Council of Ministers, April 26, 1944, HNA K27, box 260.

the number of facilities to be set up, or the deadline by which Jews should be moved into ghettos. Nevertheless, they did make one thing clear: considerations of the Jews' "convenience" could not play a role.

The decision makers also paid attention to each other's solutions. Widespread adoption of stricter, harsher measures occurred frequently. Logistical expectations played a role as well: ghettos could not interfere with traffic, day-to-day activities, or military authorities' operations. Moreover, they had to be easy to supervise. The civilian population frequently influenced decisions. The non-Jewish public was very much occupied with the situation of the Jews. Thousands of petitions and reports to the police show how many people were eager to participate in the planning of the ghettos, some out of antisemitic zeal, others with an eye to personal gain. In some places, the Jewish elite also pressured local leaders with whom they had long-standing relationships. Jewish leaders obviously had little room to maneuver, but sometimes, to a certain extent, they could influence the setting up of ghettos through petitions and interventions of their own.[38]

Assigning people to their own apartments in the neighborhoods most densely populated by Jews seemed like a sensible compromise for many municipal leaders. Sometimes they were also allowed to take along furniture and sufficient quantities of food. In this way the process could be carried out swiftly, in accordance with government expectations. But it also meant that many middle-class Jews could keep their high-quality apartments, which often prompted protests from other residents and the militant right-wing press. Many local leaders were accused of creating a "luxury ghetto," a "sanatorium" for the Jews. These voices grew even louder when thousands of people became homeless due to Allied bombings. The twofold influence of the higher state authorities and antisemitic public opinion led many local leaders to make more radical decisions than originally planned. They subsequently reduced the area of the ghetto or made its internal regulations stricter. This shift often forced Jews into areas unfit for human habitation.

During the concentration, subprefects were predominantly in charge of operative decisions in the **counties**. They generally discussed related tasks with their immediate subordinates at special meetings. In cities and towns, these

---

38. See, e.g., the cases mentioned by Tim Cole, "Writing Bystanders into Holocaust History in More Active Ways: 'Non-Jewish' Engagement with Ghettoisation, Hungary 1944," *Holocaust Studies: A Journal of Culture and History* 11, no. 1 (2005): 55–74; László Csősz, "Őrségváltás? Az 1944-es deportálások közvetlen gazdasági–társadalmi hatásai," in *Küzdelem az igazságért. Tanulmányok Randolph L. Braham 80. születésnapjára*, ed. László Karsai and Judit Molnár (Budapest: MAZSIHISZ, 2002), 75–98.

individuals usually included the mayor and the police commander; at the district level, the meetings would often involve the chief constable and the local **gendarmerie** commander. In some locations, participants had to arrive with ghetto plans and maps in hand, which they had had only days to prepare. Because written records of consultations between the relevant administrative agencies were either not created or subsequently destroyed, the minutes from a Debrecen city hall meeting (document 3-5) is a unique document. It survived by accident and turned up among nineteenth-century records on a completely different topic. The minutes reflect the clash of opinions regarding the ghettoization method. The argument between Mayor Sándor Kölcsey and Lajos Bessenyei, former director of the Calvinist secondary school appointed prefect by the Sztójay government, was not about whether the ghettoization should take place but how to carry it out.

DOCUMENT 3-5: **Minutes of the ghetto meeting at the town hall of Debrecen, May 8, 1944, HBCA IV.B.1406.b, box 365, document 21.838/1944.**

Minutes of the ghetto meeting held at the small council room of the town hall on May 8, 1944.
Present: Prefect Vitéz Dr. Lajos Bessenyei, Mayor Sándor Kölcsey, Deputy Mayor József Zöld, Technical Town Councillor Lóránt Kalenda, Police Chief Vitéz Gyula Tóth, police officer Gyula Szabó, retired judge and Head of the Housing Office Lajos Kókai, Attorney General Dr. Gusztáv Reke, Councillor Dr. Bertalan Balla, Councillor Imre Dömsödy, Honorary Councillor József Koller, Chief Public Health Officer István Gärtner, Honorary Councillor Dr. János Ecsedy, Honorary Councillor Dr. Sándor Vadászi, Housing Officer Géza Böszörményi, Population Movement Registrar Keresztély Hütter, Deputy Chief Accountant Kálmán Balogh.
Recorded by Notary Assistant Dr. Béla Menyhárt
Mayor: Describes the individual points of Ministerial Decree 1610/1944.[39] Article 9 is the primary subject of today's meeting. Preliminary actions for segregating the Jews have been implemented by the technical department. Calls on Councillor Kalenda to state his proposal concerning the designation of the relevant part of town.
Kalenda: The first solution would have been to relocate the Jews outside town, in an independent, closed unit, and we would thereby exclude

---

39. See document 3-4.

them from the town. This could be accomplished by building barracks. This solution has been discarded because of the shortage of construction material. That is how the idea came up to designate the western half of the town instead, the area between Csokonai and Széchenyi Streets. Within this area, the majority of real estate owners are Jewish. Their number exceeds 50%. It should be decided whether the area designated for the Jews will be closed off.

[. . .]

Prefect: We have to create a closed-off area, otherwise it is impossible to control the Jews.

[. . .]

Kalenda: The question of the windows overlooking the street must be decided. Should these windows be boarded up?

[. . .]

Mayor: It is enough if the windowpanes are glued at the bottom. This has no significance in terms of Jewish policy.

Chief Public Health Officer: In the ghettos already in operation, authorized leaders have established that from the perspective of the community, it is undesirable for the Jews to be constantly seen.

Prefect: The windows should not open at the bottom.

[. . .]

Chief Officer Tóth: Szepességi Street has to be completely excluded from the relocation, because the brothels at numbers 3 and 33 in this street cannot be relocated anywhere else. Actually, number 33 has been surrendered to the Germans. [. . .] Brothels have a special layout and cannot be moved out. This is a critical issue from the standpoint of security.

[. . .]

Kalenda: States the details based on the register prepared by the technical department. 4 square meters are to be considered for each person.[40]

Chief Public Health Officer: 4 square meters is a lot. In Mátészalka, some live in the attic.

[. . .]

Mayor: What can they take with them? There is no order to this effect. [. . .] They can take what they want, a cabinet, two beds, a small table, etc.

---

40. Approximately forty-three square feet.

Prefect: This already counts as sanatorium accommodation. Resolute action has to be taken or there will be disturbances.

[. . .]

Chief Public Health Officer: There are 50–55 Jewish doctors. Of these, 20 are assigned for Anti-Air Raid Service, their services have to be used continually.

Prefect: No exceptions can be made, everyone who is required to wear the yellow star must go in. A strict order has been issued about this.

[. . .]

The mayor was trying to secure relatively humane and comfortable accommodations and aimed to avoid the sealing of the ghetto. The prefect, however, insisted on adhering to the Ministry of the Interior's directives. He had the support of the chief public health officer of the city, who had previously surveyed several ghettos and camps in the northeast. Those negative examples proved contagious in the sense that radical measures prevailed over more moderate approaches. Eventually in Debrecen, too, the ghetto was established within the city. In a peculiar reversal of the integration process, Jews were pushed back into the quarter where they had settled in large numbers a hundred years before.[41]

Zala was among the counties in which the extreme right had gained more influence than the national average since the mid-1930s. Chief Notary László Hunyadi directed the operation here.[42] In establishing the ghettos, Hunyadi demanded an especially high level of discipline, making it more difficult to sell or hide assets. At the same time, this strictness also interfered with the corruption, plundering, and maltreatment of Jewish residents common elsewhere. He threatened to lock those found guilty up immediately and even prosecute them under martial law.[43]

---

41. Anikó Gazda, "Hajdú-Bihar megye," in *Magyarországi zsinagógák*, ed. László Gerő (Budapest: Műszaki, 1989), 145–48.

42. László Hunyadi (1898–1976), chief notary (deputy prefect) of Zala County, was the main organizer of the local ghettoization. After 1945, he lived undisturbed in the French occupation zone of Germany and served as a broadcast announcer for Radio Free Europe. He was never put on trial or questioned and died in Germany. László Németh and Zoltán Paksy, eds., *Együttélés és kirekesztés. Zsidók Zala megye társadalmában, 1919–1945* (Zalaegerszeg: Zala Megyei Levéltár, 2004), 48–49.

43. See also oral instructions by László Hunyadi at the meeting conducted at the county hall, May 3, 1944, in Németh and Paksy, *Együttélés és kirekesztés*, 389–93.

DOCUMENT 3-6: **Ghetto order of the subprefect of Zala County, May 4, 1944, in László Németh and Zoltán Paksy, eds.,** *Együttélés és kirekesztés. Zsidók Zala megye társadalmában, 1919–1945* (Zalaegerszeg: Zala Megyei Levéltár, 2004), 393–96.

[. . .]
Re: Designating apartments and accommodation for the Jews
Order
Based on the authorization granted by Articles 8–10 of Prime Minister's Decree no. 1610/1944,[44] I order that throughout Zala County the Jews relocate based on the following regulations:

I. into the town of Zalaegerszeg: if they are residents of the Zalaegerszeg, Nova, and Lenti districts,

II. into the village of Tapolca: if they are residents of the Tapolca and Balatonfüred districts,

III. into the village of Keszthely: if they are residents of the Keszthely district,

IV. into the village of Zalaszentgrót: if they are residents of the Zalaszentgrót, Nagykanizsa, Letenye, and Pacsa districts, and finally,

V. into the village of Sümeg: if they are residents of the Sümeg district.

Those Jews moving into the settlements listed above and those already living there must move into the area designated by me, as yet to be determined in detail and specified precisely by the mayor of Zalaegerszeg, as well as the chief constable in charge. The aforementioned local authorities must report to me with precise information about and a detailed description of the area that has already been designated [for Jews] based on the verbal orders I have already issued.

I order that non-Jewish persons should move out of the houses in the areas designated according to the above stipulations, and more generally out of the entire area. The authorities of first instance will, in keeping with the general housing regulations, arrange suitable apartments for those moving out.

The relocations must begin immediately and must be completed by the evening of May 16, 1944. Beyond this deadline, therefore, Jews within the county are allowed to live only within the designated closed areas as well as houses.

---

44. See document 3-4.

I issue the following order concerning the closed areas inhabited by the Jews:

For non-Jewish persons, entering the closed area is forbidden.

Leaving the closed area is allowed only with a permit specifying the person's name and issued by the police authority. In municipalities, the permit is issued by the subprefect, while in the town of Zalaegerszeg, by the state police headquarters. Permits can be granted only in justified cases, when the issuing is inevitably needed for industrial or business activity, making appearances in offices, or in other similar procedures. The permit can be issued on a case-by-case basis, or as a permanent permit. No one can leave the closed areas between 9 p.m. and 7 a.m. The only possible exemption from this prohibition is for the purpose of obtaining urgently needed medication. Leaving the closed area without a permit constitutes a violation of the regulations of police supervision and is to be punished accordingly as an offense and may in addition lead to immediate internment of the offender.[45]

[. . .]

The Jewish Council, headed by the Jewish leader, handles all internal affairs of the closed area. Contact with the authorities will take place exclusively through the Jewish leader.

The Jews being resettled are generally allowed to bring luggage with them weighing [up to] 50 kilograms per person. [. . .]

In the apartments that are freed up because of the resettlement of the Jews, the furniture and other items left behind must be inventoried immediately. The inventorying is carried out by the municipal councils through committees consisting of at least three members. The inventoried furniture and other items must be collected in one room of the apartment, and that room is then to be locked, its door sealed, and its keys are to be placed in an envelope, sealed, with the name [of the former tenant] written on it, and handed over to the council for safekeeping. [. . .]

Food left in the vacated apartments must be sold. [. . .]

Any valuables that were left behind (gold, silver, jewelry, gemstones) must be entered into a separate inventory and, together with the inventory list and a receipt, must be handed over to the closest gendarme unit (police station) for safekeeping. If a safe suitable for storage is available, then the council may also store the items in it until such time as the Hungarian National Bank arranges for their collection. [. . .]

---

45. That is, incarceration.

Throughout the entire process, attention should also be paid to ensuring that everyone refrains from needless and unnecessary unpleasantries, from remarks that are insulting and abusive to the Jews; all officials handling matters should maintain their calmness, objectivity, and sober thinking.
[. . .]
Zalaegerszeg, May 4, 1944
In place of the Subprefect: Chief County Notary

The living conditions in the Zala ghettos were better than elsewhere in the country. Instead of hours, Jews had up to twelve days to move into them, and the amount of space allocated (four to five people per room) and food provisions were relatively more acceptable than in other regions.

## LIFE IN THE GHETTOS

The relatively favorable conditions of the aforementioned Zala ghettos were not at all typical. In terms of crowding and food, the large ghettos and camps in the northeast provided the harshest circumstances. There, individuals were sometimes assigned barely a single square meter (under ten square feet) of living space. The deadline for moving varied enormously: in Carpatho-Ruthenia, Jews were often given just a few minutes, while in other parts of the country, between three and eight days proved more typical.[46]

The authorities did not care much about the accommodations inside a ghetto, considering this issue an "internal matter" of the Jews. Accordingly, the Jewish Councils usually arranged room assignments. Because of intervention by the churches, ghetto residents of the Christian faith were sometimes placed in separate buildings.[47] Segregation could also be based on age, sex, and social and religious-cultural differences.[48] In order to maintain order inside the ghettos, the

---

46. For details about conditions in the various ghettos and collection camps, see Randolph L. Braham and Zoltán Tibori Szabó, eds., *The Geographical Encyclopedia of the Holocaust in Hungary*, 3 vols. (Evanston, IL: Northwestern University Press in association with the USHMM, 2013).

47. Church leaders frequently justified this with antisemitic reasoning. For example, according to a petition by assistant priest Mihály Sarlós on May 14, 1944, "Those who had converted to Christianity are subject to constant harassment and abusive remarks." See Németh and Paksy, *Együttélés és kirekesztés*, 414–15.

48. For instance, a separate street for those over sixty was established (Beregszász), as were separate barracks for men and women (Csepel) and a **Neologue-Orthodox** ghetto (Bonyhád). László Csősz, "A Vészkorszak Jász-Nagykun-Szolnok vármegyében," 148.

authorities often established a Jewish police force equipped with armbands and batons, which guarded the gates and handled conflicts. Their intercession grew common in these crowded spaces, where deprived and despairing people from diverse social and cultural backgrounds inevitably clashed. The antisemitic press naturally gloated over these incidents.[49]

In the city of Kassa the authorities moved Jews into a collection camp in the local brick factory beginning on April 28. Some were originally from the city, while others had been rounded up in neighboring villages and taken to Kassa before being transported to the collection camp. A group of them (physicians, community leaders, other prominent people, and their family members) were moved to the ghetto established on a few streets of the city.[50] A stone wall was erected to segregate this residential quarter from the rest of Kassa. Police officer László Csatáry, commander of the police unit guarding the ghetto, issued the announcement printed in document 3-7 just prior to the deadline for moving into the ghetto.[51]

DOCUMENT 3-7: **Ghetto order of Kassa, May 1, 1944, National Széchényi Library, Placard and Leaflet Collection.**

ANNOUNCEMENT

In the town of Kassa, the Ghetto has been established for the purpose of segregating individuals of the Jewish race as follows:

> Akácfa Street, Zrínyi Street, Pál Luzsénszky Street, Pogány Street, Andor Jaross Street (the section closed off up to the corner of Vas Street), Csányi Street, Székgyár Street (closed-off section), Nádor Street (houses at no. 15 and 17)

---

49. See, e.g., document 3-8.

50. Report of the Jewish Council in Kassa, May 4, 1944, YVA (Archív mesta Košice) 12549–50, Documents of the Mayor of Kassa (Košice), Selected Documents, 14987/1939–44516/1944.

51. In 1945, László Csatáry escaped to Germany and later immigrated to Canada. In 1995 evidence of his role in the Holocaust was discovered, and two years later he was deprived of his Canadian citizenship. In order to escape legal proceedings, he chose to move back to Hungary. Based on information from the Simon Wiesenthal Center, he was taken into custody in July 2012. The Budapest Municipal Court (Fővárosi Törvényszék) placed the suspect under house arrest. In November 2012, the Budapesti Nyomozó Ügyészség (Budapest Investigative Prosecution Office) was conducting an investigation concerning the Csatáry case under the supervision of the Chief Prosecutor's Office (Fővárosi Főügyészség). Since July 2012, László Csatáry has been interrogated several times, but a case had not yet been made against him. The ninety-five-year-old Csatáry was living in Budapest.

I call upon the population of the Christian race living in the Ghetto area to make arrangements immediately at the Kassa mayor's office to move out of the Ghetto area. From today onward, the Ghetto commanding headquarters will not take responsibility for their personal security and for the protection of their assets!

I order that the individuals of the Christian race who are living in the Ghetto area may not have any contact with individuals of the Jewish race, and may not have transactions of any sort with them. Shops, businesses, and workshops in the Ghetto area may not serve Jews; they may not admit Jews into their apartments or courtyards, and they may not transfer—not even in the form of a loan—any food or other items to individuals of the Jewish race.

Individuals of the Jewish race may not spend time in the streets of the Ghetto, and may only keep the courtyard-side windows of their apartments open. Every individual of the Jewish race is required to be in his apartment at all times.

The command headquarters for the Ghetto is located in the house at 15 Nádor Street. Individuals of the Christian race can contact the commander's office directly with petitions, while individuals of the Jewish race can do so through the Jewish Council.

No one may leave the Ghetto without a permit from the authorities at the exit gates designed for this purpose. I forbid the entry of individuals living outside the Ghetto into the Ghetto area! I strictly forbid the shipment into and out of the Ghetto of any packages, letters, money, and other valuables for individuals of the Jewish race.—I forbid the entry of vehicles into the Ghetto area!

If anyone within the population of the Christian race violates the above regulations, I will initiate an internment process unless the person's action falls into a stricter category; if an individual of Jewish race violates the above regulations, I shall implement strict punitive measures.

Kassa, May 1, 1944                                           Ghetto commander

The ban on contact and mail meant that not even Labor Service call-up summons were delivered into the ghetto. For men subject to mandatory military labor service, these call-ups would have constituted their only escape from deportation. The authorities promised to punish not only the Jews: Christians were also required to move out under the threat of disciplinary measures. This approach toward non-Jews was less typical, for the authorities usually tried to win over non-Jewish residents and gave them extended deadlines for moving out.[52]

The testimonies of survivors collected after the war demonstrate without exception the brutality of Csatáry and his men. "In the ghetto, scandalous beatings were everyday affairs, these left several victims dead," one survivor later recalled.[53] Another remembered Csatáry as follows: "Police Inspector Dr. Csatári [sic] beat people with a dog whip. Whenever he felt like it, he went inside a block, and beat everyone he found there with his whip."[54] A third survivor had similarly negative memories of the ghetto commander: "One day, Ghetto Commander Csatáry issued the order that we should dig a trench with our bare hands. Due to the intervention of the Germans this measure was retracted within a few days."[55] Those Jews who came close to the fence of the ghetto were shot immediately.[56] Authorities displayed the corpse of a seventeen-year-old girl who was shot and killed to deter others from trying to "escape."[57]

The article reproduced in document 3-8 was published in the city of Szombathely in western Hungary in late July, weeks after the Jews were deported to Auschwitz. It focused on daily life in the local ghetto. Note the cynical, sarcastic tone with which the author mocks the Jews incarcerated in the restricted area.

---

52. Radio news file no. 2848, May 9, 1944, HNA K148, fascicle 1200.
53. HJA, DEGOB Protocols, no. 418.
54. HJA, DEGOB Protocols, no. 86.
55. HJA, DEGOB Protocols, no. 627. On Csatáry, see also Braham, *The Politics of Genocide*, 1:599; László Karsai and Judit Molnár, eds., *Az Endre-Baky-Jaross per* (Budapest: Cserépfalvi, 1994), 271.
56. Gendarmes were granted the license to use weapons in instances of real or alleged escape attempts. On the June 10 meeting regarding the deportation of Jews in Deportation Zone IV, Endre reiterated that "in cases of mutiny, resistance, and breakout attempts," the gendarmes were entitled to use firearms. Note on the June 10 meeting prepared by the representatives of the town of Kecskemét, in Karsai and Molnár, *Az Endre-Baky-Jaross per*, 522–24.
57. Tamás Csíki, "Abaúj-Torna County," in *The Geographical Encyclopedia of the Holocaust in Hungary*, ed. Randolph L. Braham and Zoltán Tibori Szabó (Evanston, IL: Northwestern University Press in association with the USHMM, 2013), 1:14.

DOCUMENT 3-8: "Jewish Self-government in the Ghetto" (on the Szombathely ghetto), *Vasvármegye*, July 30, 1944, 3.[58]

[. . .]
Now that a thoroughfare has been opened up through the Szombathely ghetto with the rearrangement of the fences, interesting outer signs of Jewish ghetto life have become visible. The Jews collected in the ghetto enjoyed a certain degree of limited "self-government." In their own affairs—especially in terms of maintaining order inside and handling the food-supply situation—they themselves could implement measures. Their executive body was the so-called Jewish Council.

The Jewish Council set up "headquarters" in the Erdős fashion shop in Szenczy Street.[59] Passersby continue to look at the sheets of paper on which the various orders can be read in the shop window. One of them, for example, says:

"Commission for Order.[60] Entry in official matters only."

[. . .]

The Commission for Order must have been a strict "authority," because one could not enter its office except in official matters. It probably did not have much to do, although from time to time the outside world heard about minor clashes taking place, especially during food distribution.

That this could well have been reality is indicated by the following notice, which was put up in the shop window of the Klausz store, on the notice board of the office of the Jewish Council:

"Warning! The council emphatically calls on shoppers to exhibit the greatest degree of discipline during food distribution. The council will, for a specified period of time, exclude from shopping all those who disturb the smooth execution of the distribution by pushing ahead in the crowd, or by being noisy or rude. Sgd. Council. Zalán."[61]

---

58. The document was published in Ágnes Ságvári, ed., *Dokumentumok a zsidóság üldöztetésének történetéhez* [Vas County] (Budapest: Magyar Auschwitz Alapítvány–Holocaust Dokumentációs Központ, 1994), 55–57.

59. Zsolt Bajzik, László Mayer, and István Végső, "Vas County," in Braham and Szabó, *Geographical Encyclopedia of the Holocaust*, 2:1202–3.

60. This means the ghetto police.

61. Ferenc Zalán (1880?–1945?) was a member of the council. Zalán was born in Dióskál and lived with his family in Szombathely before the war. Arrested in July 1944, he spent a week in Auschwitz and was then transferred to the Buchenwald concentration camp system, where he evidently perished shortly before the end of the war. See *USHMM ITS Collection Data Base* (Buchenwald Camp prisoner cards); Yad Vashem, "Central Database of Shoah Victims' Names," www.yadvashem.org.

Indeed, there must have been a bit of noise making during food distribution and the Jews had a chance to experience for themselves that when there is little to be had, people can get into fights over it.

[. . .]

Ghetto life did not last for long, for after barely two months of local collective resettlement, the Jews were transported off.[62] But traces of ghetto life have remained. Szenczy Street has regained its old look, and those Christians who were moved out of the parts of the ghetto that are still closed are probably not intending to return. They have received larger, better apartments elsewhere, in the comfortable former Jewish apartments. (g.d.)[63]

At dawn on May 3, 1944, the ghettoization of Jews began in Northern Transylvania as well. In Nagyvárad, home of the second-largest Jewish community in Hungary,[64] gendarmerie district commander Colonel Tibor Paksy-Kiss was in charge of the operation. Dissatisfied with the pace and efficiency of the process, and with the results of the house and body searches in particular, on May 4 he assigned Lieutenant Colonel **Jenő Péterffy**, commander of the local gendarme training school, to direct the ghettoization. Péterffy was put in charge of the entire local government and law enforcement apparatus.[65] The cadet corps took over guarding and managing the ghetto from the police. By May 9 they finished rounding up the Jews. Péterffy instituted strict ghetto regulations in which he identified no less than eighty different criminal offences. Letters and any form of relations with the outside world were banned. Jews were obliged to take off their caps and stand at attention before any German or Hungarian officer. "Between curfew and reveille the ghetto shall be deserted and mute," ordered Péterffy. Those attempting an escape were executed.[66] In the grand scheme, labor servicemen were not to be deported; only deserters were taken away. However, many fanatics, Péterffy among them, often disregarded

---

62. Local Jews were deported on July 3 and 4 from the collection camp set up at the local engine factory. Bajzik, Mayer, and Végső, "Vas vármegye," 2:1285.

63. The author, Felicián Gondán, hid behind the "g.d." initials.

64. According to the 1941 census, 21,333 Israelites and 750 Christian Jews lived in the city. József Kepecs, ed., *A zsidó népesség száma településenként (1840–1941)* (Budapest: Központi Statisztikai Hivatal, 1993), 122–23.

65. For further details, see the trial against László Gyapay and others, USHMMA RG 25.004M, reel 87, file 40029.

66. The service code actually permitted this only against dangerous criminals. In his postwar trial, Péterffy's defense was that State Secretary László Endre gave an order to this effect at the Marosvásárhely meeting. Endre denied the accusation. It is a fact that on June 10 he gave permission for the gendarmes to use their weapons during the deportation process.

this Ministry of Defense directive and arrested even those labor servicemen who had obtained permission to be on leave.

The commander of the cadet corps devoted most of his attention to seizing Jewish assets. He issued announcements calling on the population to hand in valuables received from the Jews. Afterward, Péterffy obtained the register of Jews considered wealthy from the Financial Directorate. People were dragged into the warehouse of the Dreher beer factory, where ten investigation teams interrogated victims in the offices.[67] E. L.,[68] a Jewish female torture survivor, gave the testimony in document 3-9.

DOCUMENT 3-9: **Survivor testimony on the interrogations in the Nagyvárad ghetto, 1945, at the trial against László Gyapay and his associates, USHMMA RG-25.004M, reel 87, file 40029 (documents of the Romanian Information Service, SRI), 2:19–20.**

[. . .]

I was also in the Nagyvárad ghetto. I personally heard when gendarme Péterffy ordered those inhumane methods of interrogation, which surpassed even medieval methods and were then carried out on the unfortunate ghetto residents.

They took me into the Dreher interrogation unit, and during all this, I saw Gendarme Lieutenant Colonel Péterffy issue commands that were even stricter. I was also beaten severely and was ordered to present my valuables and report all information about where I put all the things.

At the so-called Group 8, I was with Staff Sergeant József or István Horváth,[69] who, based on Péterffy's orders, tortured me with electricity for about a half hour, undressed me completely, tied together my hands and feet, and tied an electric wire to my genitals, and then gave it an electric shock; I fainted twice in a row. At this point, he beat me severely with a rubber baton, and when I was screaming very loudly from the horrible pain, Gendarme Lieutenant Colonel Péterffy issued the order that the filthy Jew should be gagged before she dies like a dog.

The radio was turned up full blast, so the horrible screaming would not be heard in the street. I saw the women as they were stripped naked, electric wires were attached to their genitals, and I saw as they interrogated

---

67. On this, see also **Ferenczy's** May 9, 1944, report, in Karsai and Molnár, *Az Endre-Baky-Jaross per*, 504–6.

68. Initials are used due to the nature of the information disclosed in this document.

69. After the war, József Horváth was sentenced to hard labor for life by the people's court in Kolozsvár (Romania).

girls who were 13 to 15 years old in a similar way. I even saw my brother's wife, Mrs. S. S. She was also horribly tortured with electricity. She was lying in front of me stripped naked, dazed, screaming in an unconscious state that I should tell everything, because she cannot bear all this suffering anymore.

It was usually impossible to recognize people when the victims were released from the Dreher interrogation unit, their bodies were bruised everywhere, their faces were distorted, filled with mortal fear. Many of them would have preferred suicide at that point because they could not bear those various unimaginable forms of physical pain.

Several labor servicemen passed through the Nagyvárad station, these were, by order from Péterffy, held down by force and carried into the ghetto. They were also severely tortured and then deported.

Because Dr. B. O., a physician, saw these tortures before he was taken into the Dreher interrogation unit, he committed suicide out of fear of the torture and died immediately.[70] S. L.'s wife likewise died by committing suicide.

Péterffy's overzealousness apparently proved too much even for the antisemitic public. An investigation was initiated against him after local residents complained to the police. However, this soon ended in an acquittal, and within a few weeks he returned to work preparing the deportation of Jews from Budapest and its vicinity.[71]

The detectives of the gendarme investigation units and the cadets deployed in several locations across the country committed the most severe atrocities during the anti-Jewish campaign. Although witness recollections primarily attribute cruel measures to the gendarmes, members of the police training units were not much gentler.[72] The methods described above cannot be regarded as local excesses, for they were routine throughout the country. The gendarmes combined medieval methods (for example, beating the soles of the feet, which

---

70. The practice of torturing "suspects" in front of their loved ones was common in Kolozsvár, where children were forced to observe their parents being tormented. Here investigators specialized in methods of torture centering on the testicles. In Kolozsvár many Jews went insane as a result of these agonizing ordeals. Dániel Lőwy, *A téglagyártól a tehervonatig. Kolozsvár zsidó lakosságának története* (Kolozsvár: Erdélyi Szépmíves Céh, 1998), 115.

71. Péterffy was arrested after the war. He hanged himself in his Budapest prison cell prior to his extradition to Romania.

72. Csősz, "A Vészkorszak Jász-Nagykun-Szolnok vármegyében," 50–51, 102–4.

became common during the Ottoman period) with modern technology (for example, torturing people with electrical currents).[73]

Information on the details of the ghettoization process and daily ghetto life often made its way out of the restricted areas. The notes excerpted in document 3-10(A–D) survived among the records of the Central Jewish Council.[74] The documents prove that Jewish community leaders in Budapest received information about the anti-Jewish operation on a regular basis through messages coming in from provincial communities.[75]

**DOCUMENT 3-10(A–D): Daily reports from provincial Jewish Councils, May–June 1944, USHMMA RG-39.013M, reel 7 (HJA XX-A, box D 5/1).**[76]

DOCUMENT 3-10(A): **Nagyvárad**

V [May] 7.
Daily report: resettlement into the designated streets began. Letters and packages can be sent through the Jewish Council.
[. . .]
V/14: Daily report: people from Nagyvárad are resettled in the streets designated for this purpose within the so-called large ghetto, while the Jewish population of Bihar County is accommodated in the so-called small ghetto, located at the public sanitation site outside the town. There accommodations are provided in farm buildings and in the apartments of warrant officers, in stables, and in open sheds. The situation in the small ghetto is desperate. Some of those interned there were not allowed to bring anything with them. The food supply is a disaster. The daily ration is 7 dekagrams of bread,[77] one portion of soup at lunch, and black coffee in the evening. The Christian population is not allowed to approach the ghetto at all. A

---

73. For more on the cruelties committed by the gendarmes, see chapter 4.
74. HJA XX-A, box D 5/1, published by Kinga Frojimovics and Judit Molnár, eds., *Gettómagyarország 1944. A Központi Zsidó Tanács iratai* (Budapest: Magyar Zsidó Múzeum és Levéltár, 2002), 5:50–165.
75. See also the correspondence of the provincial Jewish communities and the National Office of Hungarian Israelites in April–May 1944. (In the spring of 1944, parallel to and entwined with the Central Jewish Council's apparatus, the Pest Israelite Congregation and the National Office of Hungarian Israelites carried on its administrative work.) HJA PIH XVI A, box TA 10/4/2.
76. First published in Frojimovics and Molnár, *Gettómagyarország 1944*, 50–165.
77. A total of seventy grams or 0.15 pounds.

few days ago, the gendarmerie took over guard duties from the police, and since then conditions have become substantially worse. The situation in the large ghetto is somewhat more tolerable, although one finds an unbelievable degree of overcrowding there too. Allegedly, the town has taken over responsibility for supplying food beginning on Sunday.

[. . .]

### DOCUMENT 3-10(B): Marosvásárhely

[. . .]

V/14. The Jews of Marosvásárhely, numbering about 10,000 people, were resettled in the brick factory on Koronkai Road, about two kilometers from the town.[78] The women and the children were accommodated indoors[79]; the men are living in tents. There is practically no food. The Jewish Council is operating; its members include, among others, Dr. Erdélyi and Léderer.[80]

V/24. The food provisions and accommodation circumstances for the Jews are unsatisfactory. Some of them are living outdoors, without a roof.

### DOCUMENT 3-10(C): Szatmárnémeti

V.17. [. . .]
The ghetto's perimeter is boarded up with planks. The apartments are divided up; each person gets a space of 160 by 40 centimeters.[81] They were not allowed to take along any money, only luggage weighing fifty kilograms (this was the weight limit on clothing and food combined). Until further measures are implemented, there are no letters and mail; allegedly they are not even delivering call-up summons.[82] They are not allowed to use beds and can lie only on the mattresses and straw sacks that are placed on the ground. The police are watching them. Treatment is bad.

[. . .]

---

78. Approximately 1.2 miles.
79. The "indoor area" was in fact a crumbling factory hall with a caved-in roof and a brick-drying shed without walls.
80. These were Emil Erdélyi and Dezső Léderer. No additional information is available on Erdéyi and Léderer.
81. Equivalent to 63 × 16 inches. This was the smallest recorded space per person in the Hungarian ghettos.
82. Refers to the labor service summons.

DOCUMENT 3-10(D): **Érsekújvár**

Accommodation: a couple of streets were designated as places where Jews cannot live. For now, they can move freely.
 V/11. An order was issued requiring resettlement in the designated streets. The apartments must be occupied by the evening of May 12.
 V/21. The accommodation process in the designated streets and houses has been completed, but the Christian population has not yet moved out. From 10 a.m. until 7 p.m., the Jewish population is allowed to go into town, but they can move freely within the designated area until 9 p.m. Apart from this, those who have businesses can carry on with their professions outside the designated area as well. Apprentices and other employees can do likewise if they possess the appropriate permits. These individuals are allowed to move freely in town before as well as after the established time. The Jewish Council carries out the orders of the authority, and there are no complaints concerning the council's work. Within the designated area, the authorities have issued a permit for a hospital, an epidemic hospital, a maternity home, a child-care center, all with the most modern equipment, which the doctors have provided. A modern, two-story house may be made available for the aged. A Jewish police and a fire department have been organized.
 V/24. Based on recent reports, the situation, which had already been favorable, has improved further. Three–four people assigned to each room. Quite a few Christians still remain within the ghetto area.
 VI/9. Only the residents of Érsekújvár are concentrated here. The population of the district is accommodated in Nagysurány.[83]
 VI/15. The Jews accommodated here, along with the populations of the Galánta and Szenc ghettos, have been transported via Kassa to Katowice. Several people [from this transport] sent letters bearing a Waldsee postmark.[84]

As the foregoing examples show, the conditions in one ghetto (in this case, in Érsekújvár) could be more favorable than in others (for example, in the closed areas in Nagyvárad, Marosvásárhely, or Szatmárnémeti). These differences

---

83. This refers to the Érsekújvár district (*járás*). The center of this unit was the city of Érsekújvár, but administratively it did not incorporate the municipality itself. On the administrative structure of Hungary, see table 4, p. 370.
84. Most of the trains went via Kassa, Tarnów, and Kraków to Auschwitz, so they did not pass Katowice. The postcards sent from the extermination camp on behalf of the victims bore a fabricated geographical name and were part of an attempt to camouflage the ongoing genocide.

made a difference in survival: those who had spent the period prior to their deportation living in relatively good conditions stood a better chance of passing the selection of **Dr. Josef Mengele** and his SS colleagues at Birkenau.

The SS physicians sent Endre Goldstein, a sixteen-year-old boy from Debrecen, to the gas chambers immediately after arrival. The image reproduced in document 3-11 shows him and his father in a workshop in the downtown Debrecen ghetto in May–June 1944.

DOCUMENT 3-11: **Móric Goldstein and his son Endre in the Debrecen ghetto, spring–summer 1944, USHMMPA WS# 08313.**

Shortly after this photo was taken, Móric was drafted into a Labor Service company and perished. His family was deported to Auschwitz, where in addition to his son Endre, his wife Matilde was also murdered immediately. One of Endre's older brothers, Ernő (Ernst), however, survived Auschwitz and several other concentration camps in Germany. After the war he emigrated to the United States.

CHAPTER 4

# DEPORTATIONS FROM THE PROVINCES AND THE FATE OF THE BUDAPEST JEWS

**G**ERMAN AND Hungarian authorities entered into an agreement on April 22, 1944, regarding the total deportation of all Hungarian Jews (except for labor servicemen) to Auschwitz II–Birkenau.[1] On April 28–29, thirty-eight hundred Jews from the Kistarcsa and Bácstopolya internment camps and Budapest prisons were sent to the death camp.[2] On May 15, the first mass transports from Carpatho-Ruthenia left for Auschwitz. Up to July 9, the Hungarians deported 437,000 Jews: 422,000 to 423,000 people were taken to Birkenau and about 15,000 to eastern Austria. Besides the mass transports, the German police and Hungarians also conducted smaller-scale deportations to Auschwitz and camps in Austria between March and late July. By early July, all Jews in the provinces had been deported; Budapest's Jews were scheduled to be taken away in the operation's final phase. However, yielding mainly to international pressure, Regent **Miklós Horthy** finally stood up to the Germans and halted the deportations. The Jews in Budapest were temporarily spared. This chapter includes documents recording the events of these fateful months.

---

1. See Gábor Kádár and Zoltán Vági, *Hullarablás. A magyar zsidók gazdasági megsemmisítése* (Budapest: Jaffa, 2005), 131–40.

2. **Veesenmayer**'s reports to the Reich Ministry of Foreign Affairs, April 27–29, 1944, in Randolph L. Braham, ed., *The Destruction of Hungarian Jewry: A Documentary Account* (New York: Pro Arte for the World Federation of Hungarian Jews, 1963), 1:361, 363.

## DESTRUCTION OF THE PROVINCIAL COMMUNITIES

To carry out the deportations smoothly, the perpetrators divided the country into six deportation zones (see map 3, p. liv). These corresponded mainly to the **gendarmerie**'s regional divisions, the so-called gendarmerie districts.³ The deportations emptied one zone after another. A meeting held on location or in Budapest preceded each operation. At these conferences the Ministry of the Interior and representatives of the **Sondereinsatzkommando Eichmann** (SEK), along with Gendarme Lieutenant Colonel **László Ferenczy** (in charge of German-Hungarian communication), informed local government leaders and law enforcement officials about the tasks ahead. Gendarme or police units were then sent in with men who preferably had experience with deportations (and did not know the victims), in order to concentrate the Jews in collection camps. In the northeastern part of the country, people had for the most part already been herded into such camps during the ghettoization phase.⁴

The collection camps were set up in industrial and agricultural facilities (such as brick factories, warehouses, barns) situated near industrial rail lines, convenient for subsequently transporting people away. Hungarian law enforcement personnel usually performed guard duties. The commander was generally a locally authorized officer of **Adolf Eichmann**'s unit. The camps lacked water or any kind of medical facilities. Many of the deportees did not have a roof over their heads or sufficient food. Within a few days, conditions turned catastrophic: epidemics erupted, and hundreds of people committed suicide.

State Secretary **László Endre** developed the details for the deportation. On average, the trains consisted of forty-five cattle cars. Officially these cars were suitable for transporting forty soldiers. Now at least seventy Jews were crammed inside. Each cattle car had a bucket of water and an empty bucket for bodily needs; doors had to be locked with a chain. Local government officials had to secure a two-day ration of bread for the journey—that is, eighty dekagrams, less than two pounds per person. While the original plan envisioned seventy Jews to a car, Gendarme Captain László Lulay was candid about the real practice: "As many as one hundred of them can go into a car if needed. They can be packed like herrings, for the Germans want tough people. Those who cannot take it will perish. There is no need for fashionable

---

3. The deportation zones were set up as follows: (1) Kassa gendarmerie district, (2) Kolozsvár and Marosvásárhely gendarmerie districts, (3) Székesfehérvár and Miskolc gendarmerie districts, (4) Szeged and Debrecen gendarmerie districts, (5) Szombathely and Pécs gendarmerie districts, and (6) Budapest gendarmerie district.

4. See chapter 3.

ladies over there in Germany."⁵ The Jews from Carpatho-Ruthenia may have experienced the worst situation. In Beregszász, 60 to 110 people were forced into each car; in Ungvár, 70 to 100. In Munkács the numbers sometimes reached 120. The average in Mátészalka proved somewhat more favorable, with 75 people per car, and in Budakalász, 70 to 80 people.

Deportation applied to all Jews, regardless of gender and age, including those in prisons and patients in hospitals and mental institutions. Only those exempt from the antisemitic measures were spared and—in some cases—those with Christian spouses (colloquially called *árjapárja*, an "Aryan's couple"). However, since the status and definition of these two groups were rather unclear, Endre's office and most local authorities did everything to interpret the rules in a restrictive way and to deport as many people as possible. It also happened that the "Aryan's couples" were first freed and then deported a few hours later.⁶

While in the ghetto and again prior to deportation, Jews underwent searches of their luggage and bodies. In hunting for valuables, gendarmes tortured many of them and even assigned midwives and other health-care practitioners to check women's vaginas.⁷ Afterward, they herded the deportees into cattle cars strictly guarded by gendarmes or policemen. Guards shot at the slightest sign of resistance or during any escape attempts, but in fact they had to resort to the measure in extremely few instances.⁸ The trains then set off for Auschwitz II–Birkenau.

A key figure directing the concentration and deportation operations was Gendarme Lieutenant Colonel László Ferenczy, liaison officer between Eichmann's team and the Ministry of the Interior. Ferenczy received daily typed reports from his subordinates stationed on location, which he summarized, supplemented, and sent on to the Ministry of the Interior and the gendarmerie leaders using an automobile messenger service.⁹ The first report was dated May 3, 1944, the opening day of the concentration operation of Deportation Zone II (Northern Transylvania). The first group of reports included in document 4-1 concerns this operation (I/1–6). Reports II/1–2 focus on the deportation that

---

5. Records of the May 12 meeting in Munkács and the June 10 meeting in Szeged. See László Karsai and Judit Molnár, eds., *Az Endre-Baky-Jaross per* (Budapest: Cserépfalvi, 1994), 524, 527.

6. László Csősz, "A Vészkorszak Jász-Nagykun-Szolnok vármegyében" (PhD diss., University of Szeged, 2010), 46–47.

7. On the body searches, see document 6-7.

8. For example, in Munkács. See HJA, DEGOB Protocols, nos. 132, 1132.

9. Presumably State Secretary Endre was actually the author of some of the reports. Zoltán Vági, "Endre László politikai pályája 1919–1945. Szélsőjobboldali elit, közigazgatási apparátus, zsidókérdés" (PhD diss., ELTE, 2003), 343–45.

began in mid-May and provide precise data about its pace and "results." The last report was written on July 9, after the deportation operation was shut down.

DOCUMENT 4-1: **Reports of Gendarme Lieutenant Colonel László Ferenczy, the liaison officer of the Hungarian gendarmerie, to the Sondereinsatzkommando Eichmann, May 3, 1944, USHMMA RG 39.018 (BMTI), disc 15, V-79348.**[10]

Event report no. I/1.
Kolozsvár, May 3, 1944

In the following, I report on the measures I have implemented in connection with the Jewish campaigns carried out in gendarmerie districts IX and X based on order 6163/1944 VII. of April 7, 1944,[11] along with the events of the first day of the gendarme operations:

1.) Within the two districts, collection camps were designated in 10 towns by Mr. State Secretary. [. . .]

The tasks associated with the collection of Jews in these locations and the regions assigned to them are managed by the committees comprised of gendarme commanders and designated field officers, together with the leaders of public administration officials and police authorities, in cooperation with the German advisory agencies assigned to them.

The campaign began at 5 a.m. today—in every location, with the greatest degree of support from the authorities everywhere.

[. . .]

8.) The mood of the population is generally calm and the execution of the campaign was greeted with joy in several places. Here and there residents felt sorry for [the Jews], but this sentiment came mostly from members of the Romanian ethnic minority.[12]

[. . .]

Event report no. 2
Kolozsvár, May 5, 1944.
    [. . .]

---

10. The document was first published in Karsai and Molnár, *Az Endre-Baky-Jaross per*, 497–522.

11. See document 3-3.

12. Jews sometimes received help or sympathy from members of ethnic minorities. While antisemitism was a long-standing tradition among minorities as well, Serbs, Romanians, and Ruthenians also felt threatened by extremist forms of Hungarian nationalism.

14.) The authorities are generally carrying out the tasks associated with the collection of the Jews and their valuables with the greatest degree of cooperation, taking the initiative and demonstrating flexibility. Where mistakes initially arose, they were due to the fact that within some towns, authorities acting in good faith implemented the measures according to their own conceptions and departed from the instructions attached to the orders: they collected all the Jews within a single day and without taking into account that—due to difficulties with material purchases—furnishing of camps and organizing camp life can happen only gradually, as the population of the camps increases daily.[13] Where the authorities implemented the order in this way, difficulties persisted during the first three days.

[. . .]

Event report no. 3
Kolozsvár, May 6, 1944.

[. . .]

14.) In Szatmárnémeti, on May 2, Dr. Oszkár György, a Jewish doctor, used morphine to poison himself and his mother, Mrs. Oszkár György. Mrs. Oszkár György survived, while Dr. Oszkár György stuffed his pajama jacket into his mouth when he regained consciousness and suffocated.

Albert Weisz and his wife, Jews from Szatmárnémeti, hanged themselves and died.

[. . .]

16.) In general, strikingly few valuables were found on the Jews, which suggests that the Jews have hidden their valuables.

When a notice was issued, several Christian families surrendered the valuables they were hiding, but investigation into this matter continues in many places.

[. . .]

Event report no. I/6.
Kolozsvár, May 10, 1944.

[. . .]

2.) Based on an order received from above, the auxiliary commanding headquarters of the army has issued orders for mass call-ups, and the

---

13. Here Ferenczy refers to the events of Marosvásárhely, where within a day or two eight thousand people were herded into the grounds of a factory without any furnishings whatsoever.

call-up notices were addressed so that they could be delivered in collection camps as well.

The local head of the German security police, citing his agreement with the Ministry of Defense, today received an order by telephone from his superiors in Budapest that in areas in which the collection of the Jews is underway, Jews may not be called up for labor service at all.

Given that two contradictory orders concerning the Jewish labor servicemen exist, I have stopped the delivery of call-up notices in the camps until receiving further instructions from above.[14]

3.) In Kolozsvár, a member of the committee in charge of rounding up the Jews and their valuables, Lajos Nagy, a resident of Kolozsvár, a tax bureau official who was supposed to impound items from a Jew, was caught—by the gendarme investigator assigned to work with him—as he took a gold fountain pen, some leather, some money, and various jewelry items that filled a briefcase with the intent to appropriate them for himself.

[. . .]

Event report no. II/1.
Munkács, May 21, 1944
[. . .]

1.) In the aforementioned gendarmerie districts, the transportation of the Jews is carried out from 21 loading stations. Up until midnight of May 21 of this year, 94,667 Jews were deported in 29 trains. The empty trains arriving from the German Reich are brought into the loading stations as early as one day before departure. As a result, the loading of the shipments, their timely departure, and their journey to the border stations have thus far been carried out in a highly ordered fashion, without any interruptions whatsoever. In Nyíregyháza and Munkács, successful use of firearms occurred in two cases during attempted escapes, one in each location.[15]

2.) The accommodation and food provided to the law enforcement units accompanying the shipment are excellent.

---

14. The Ministry of the Interior did everything it could to deport as many Jews as possible. Since the labor servicemen were not deported, Ferenczy (and Endre, of course) tried to block the call-ups completely.

15. "Successful use of firearms" means that the escapee was shot and killed. No accurate data is available on this, but far more deaths occurred than indicated here.

3.) Based on reports coming in from individual loading stations, 13 trains have become superfluous, while Mátészalka, Kisvárda, and Nyíregyháza requested that four additional trains be brought in. By deploying the superfluous trains, the German security police arranged to have the transportation timetable—which had been planned through June 11—condensed.[16] Accordingly, the transports will be modified from now on so that the trains brought in for dates after June 6 will have their departure times adjusted to earlier times in such a way that the transports from gendarmerie districts VIII, IX, and X will be fully completed by June 6.[17]
[. . .]
5.) I caught detective trainee József Kocsis, who was serving at the Munkács police headquarters, as he was about to assist a Jewish girl to escape from the Jewish camp. At the same time, he also wanted to smuggle official documents and valuables out that he had received from Jews in the camp. I had him taken into custody and proceedings were initiated against him.[18]
[. . .]

Event report no. II/2.
Munkács, May 29, 1944

I report the following concerning the deportation of the Jews collected in gendarmerie districts VIII, IX, and X:
[. . .]
2.) [. . .] The German security police's suggestion and express wish has been that the Jews take along at least five days' worth of food per person, for the duration of the journey; this is all the more important, given that upon their arrival in Auswitz [sic], they will go through the selection process and will be transferred immediately from there to various jobs, via trains. [. . .]

---

16. The number of deportees nationwide was eventually less than the preliminary calculations. The refugees from abroad added to the total number (especially in the northeastern part of the country and in Budapest), but not nearly to the extent the authorities assumed based on their own antisemitic paranoia. Officials in charge at the Ministry of the Interior estimated a Jewish population of over 1 million people.
17. Eventually this occurred on June 7.
18. On the rescue operations and the motivations behind them, see chapter 9.

Cleansing campaign no. II/3.

Event report no. 3
Hatvan, June 8, 1944
[. . .]
7.) Dr. Lajos Tóth, a legal clerk in Munkács, had to be interned along with his family, on the one hand, for dishonoring the nation, on the other, because of his public statements concerning the relocation of the Jews and his condemnation of this campaign.
[. . .]
11.) Economic, political, security-related, and ethnic factors arise with the complete removal of the Jews; today in Munkács, for example, they manifest themselves in the following way and bring overall transformations to the city:

a) The black market disappeared—practically overnight. [. . .]
Entrepreneurial initiative is rather lively, despite the shortage of capital. Industry and commerce anticipate with keen interest that the seized Jewish plants, workshops, and store merchandise will be brought into circulation in the Hungarian economy as soon as possible. Healthy and resourceful ideas are in circulation, plans are being made, the culmination of [a new] self-confidence and confident, uninhibited initiative. The oppressive sense of fear stemming from occupying the formerly disadvantaged minority position that Hungarian industrial and commercial enterprise had experienced is absent. The workers are calm and exhibit increased work capacity.[19]

b) One can no longer see Jewish heads bending together in small groups on the streets, as they whisper among themselves, glancing shiftily at the non-Jewish individuals approaching them, concocting yet another poison-filled portion of frightening rumors and propaganda material.
[. . .]

---

19. The board of directors of the Financial Institutional Center, whose members were clearly much better educated in economics than Ferenczy, saw the situation differently. At its meeting on April 26, it was said that ghettoization had resulted in "economic activity being brought to a standstill" in the Kassa gendarmerie district (which included Munkács). See notes from the meeting of the board of directors of the Financial Institutional Center, April 26, 1944, HNA, reel 24,463. For more on the economic impacts of the deportations, see chapter 6.

Cleansing campaign VI

Event report no. 2
Budapest, July 9, 1944

In my last report, I noted the following concerning the deportation of the Jews collected in 2 collection camps in gendarmerie district I of Budapest:

1.) The deportation of the Jews from the areas above began on July 6 and was already concluded by July 8. A total of 24,128 persons of the Jewish race were transported away in 8 trains.

2.) Since the deportation shipments began, from May 14, 1944, until today, a total of 434,351 persons of the Jewish race have left the country in 147 trains.[20]

3.) With the exception of the capital, Budapest, Jewry has been moved out of all areas of the country. At this time, those still in the country include only the labor servicemen, Budapest Jewry, individuals working in military production, and individuals who are hiding, have converted to Christianity, or are living in a mixed marriage.

4.) During the collection and transportation in the area described above, no reports have come in about abuses, assaults, or excesses by the Hungarian law enforcement agencies.

I submit my report to the Gendarmerie Inspector,[21] State Secretaries vitéz László Endre and László Baky, to the head of Department VII of the Ministry of the Interior,[22] and to the central investigation headquarters of the Gendarmerie.

[. . .]

Contrary to Ferenczy's claim about the absence of "abuses, assaults, or excesses," the concentration and deportation in this zone was carried out with the usual brutality. A woman from Pestszenterzsébet remembered the deportation from the Monor collection camp as follows: "They brought decrepit old people in their 70s and 80s out of the pensioners' home. They grabbed one old engineer who had been crippled in the other war, took him out of his wheelchair, and tossed him into the wagon. They called a doctor out to attend to a woman who had gone into labor, but he never showed up. So they just

---

20. German Plenipotentiary Veesenmayer reported 437,402 Jews deported. See Veesenmayer's report to the Reich Ministry of Foreign Affairs, July 11, 1944, in Gyula Juhász et al., eds., *A Wilhelmstrasse és Magyarország. Német diplomáciai iratok Magyarországról 1933–1944* (Budapest: Kossuth, 1968), 881.

21. Army General **Gábor Faragho**.

22. The Public Safety Department, headed by Gendarme Lieutenant Colonel Gyula Király.

threw her into the train as well, where she gave birth there among 80 other people, crammed in so tightly that they practically had to stand on one leg."[23] According to another survivor, "The Budakalász brick factory may have been worse even than Auschwitz."[24] Here, as all over the country, those gendarme and police units assigned to hunt for Jews' hidden valuables committed the most extremely brutal acts.[25] However, in many cases the impulse triggering gendarme brutality had nothing to do with the search for valuables; it was a manifestation of sheer sadism. The so-called Black Saturday of Munkács is a good example of this. On that day gendarmes took the **Orthodox** Jews into their local synagogue, forced them to demolish the interior, beat them, and then shot a few outside the building.[26]

Although present at all stages of the Jews' persecution, law enforcement brutality became heightened in the concentration and deportation phase. Even those Jews incarcerated under relatively bearable ghetto circumstances entered hell once they were crammed into collection camps and then cattle cars. Compared to many other restricted areas of the country, life was relatively "normal" in the Érsekújvár and Zalaegerszeg ghettos.[27] Later, however, when taken from the city ghetto to the Kurzweil brick factory in Érsekújvár, people had to spend a week without water; investigation units beat many of them.[28] The Zalaegerszeg Jews were concentrated in the Grünbaum brick factory along with people from Zala County. Here the gendarmes used investigation methods quite common in Hungary in those weeks: family members were tortured before each other's eyes. Some of them died; others went insane and committed suicide.[29]

The ghettoization and deportation operation, and especially its widespread and open cruelty, triggered a backlash from the neutral diplomatic delegations and from the Christian churches; it also caused some unrest among the general public as well. This was not the only factor that put Regent Horthy in a difficult position. Information about Auschwitz was being shared in an increasingly wider circle.[30] In early June, Horthy composed a memorandum to **Döme**

---

23. HJA, DEGOB Protocols, no. 2248.
24. HJA, DEGOB Protocols, no. 2219.
25. For the brutality of these units, see chapter 6.
26. HJA, DEGOB Protocols, nos. 2, 1533, 1970, 2150, 2902, 2930,
27. See documents 3-6 and 3-10(D).
28. HJA, DEGOB Protocols, no. 1695.
29. István Károly Vörös, "Zala County," in *The Geographical Encyclopedia of the Holocaust in Hungary*, ed. Randolph L. Braham and Zoltán Tibori Szabó (Evanston, IL: Northwestern University Press in association with the USHMM, 2013) 2: 1281.
30. On these factors, see Randolph L. Braham, *The Politics of Genocide: The Holocaust in Hungary* (New York: Columbia University Press, 1994), 2:824–36, 1170–79, 1185–89, 1212–20.

Sztójay that bore a rather reprimanding tone. The letter clearly aimed to avert responsibility for the "excesses" occurring during the anti-Jewish campaign, for which Horthy mostly blamed the state secretaries, primarily Endre. On one occasion Horthy called him a lunatic,[31] though he had signed Endre's appointment as state secretary just three months prior.

DOCUMENT 4-2: **Horthy's memorandum to Sztójay, June 1944, in Miklós Szinai and László Szűcs, eds.,** *Horthy Miklós titkos iratai* **(Budapest: Kossuth, 1962), 450–54.**[32]

Dear Sztójay!

With German troops marching in two and a half months ago and the well-known events limiting Hungarian sovereignty, I wished to retire from exercising the regent's powers entrusted in me by the nation. Although from my own perspective this would have been the most natural solution, after thinking things over a bit, I had to set aside my plan. First and foremost, I had to appoint a government that enjoyed the trust of Germany, so that—in accordance with their promises—we could be freed from the occupation. In addition, I also felt it was a responsibility I had toward my nation that I persevere in my position. Had I done otherwise, the situation thus ensuing would have had unforeseeable consequences, given the extraordinarily difficult circumstances that the country is in today. But I was also aware that this government—having been forced into a situation that leaves no alternatives open—must implement various measures that I do not consider right and for which I cannot take responsibility.

These measures include the handling of the Jewish question in a manner that does not fit the Hungarian way of thinking, Hungarian circumstances, and with respect to these, Hungarian interests.

First and foremost, it is clear that I was in no position to stop either German activities in this regard or steps by the government that were prompted by German wishes; thus, I was forced not to intervene in this matter.[33] I was not informed beforehand about the measures about to be taken; nor did I receive full information afterward about what had

---

31. See Veesenmayer's report to the Ministry of Foreign Affairs, July 6, 1944, in Juhász et al., *A Wilhelmstrasse és Magyarország*, 874–76.

32. Cf. the English-language collection, Miklós Szinai and László Szűcs, eds., *The Confidential Papers of Admiral Horthy* (Budapest: Corvina, 1965), 301–3.

33. Horthy conveniently "forgets" that—not wanting to be involved in the anti-Jewish campaign—he explicitly gave a free hand to the Sztójay government in Jewish matters in the days following the establishment of the cabinet.

occurred. Still, information I have lately been receiving indicates that what has been happening here on this issue has in many respects exceeded what was happening in Germany itself; the activities have been carried out in ways that are brutal and occasionally inhumane to an extent that is unmatched even by the measures carried out by the Germans. Due to past mistakes, we have a greater proportion of Jews, incomparably more than in Germany, and their share in the economy far exceeds that in the German Reich—in terms of their participation in industry, commerce, and especially in engineering, and, moreover, in medical work, which is especially needed in the present war situation. Despite all this, here in Hungary we have had more extreme measures in excluding the Jews from all sorts of participation in the economy than in the German Reich, where shutting them out was accomplished through a process lasting several years. Moreover, in executing these measures, unjustifiable forms of cruelty and inhumanity were often employed that were even unlike the attitude in the German Reich toward especially those Jews who were still of economic use or still needed for indispensable professional work.

[. . .]

It is therefore my express wish that [. . .] in those professions [. . .] where the work of Jews is indispensable and cannot be performed by others at this time, or is needed either in order for the economy to carry on smoothly and without coming to a halt, or to prevent a drop in the desired level of industrial production, no measures be taken against these Jews that would disrupt their work, and these Jews should not be hindered in their work. I wish also that fair distinctions be drawn among Jews in favor of those Jews who have by now converted to the Christian religion. It is also my desire that all steps be taken that are necessary for my exercising—in accordance with my general power to grant clemency, with countersignature from the Hungarian Royal Minister of the Interior—my ability under my right to grant clemency to exempt certain individuals from measures pertaining to Jews in exceptional cases. I have in mind here individuals of special economic value, Jews who earlier had already converted to Christianity, or—while of Jewish ancestry—were already born as members of a Christian denomination, and who have in addition shown significant achievements in the past that make their exemption exceptionally justifiable for reasons of fairness and Christian humaneness.

In order to avoid the continuation of unwarranted excesses, especially cruel and frequently inhumane actions, I also wish that in the Hungarian Royal Ministry of the Interior, supervision of Jewish affairs be taken away from State Secretary Dr. vitéz László Endre and my preliminary approval be sought in the selection of a reliable, suitable person as his replacement. Further, it is my wish that a proposal to remove from his post State Secretary László Baky—who has up to now been in charge of issuing the relevant orders to law enforcement—be submitted to me as soon as possible. These steps are important, for a significant portion of the public views the aforementioned two men responsible for the excessive measures.

[. . .]

The selective antisemitic argument of the text is remarkable. Horthy raises his voice primarily on behalf of Jews "of economic use" for "national" purposes. He does not demand that the deportations be stopped, only that the cruelty be ended. Probably German plenipotentiary Edmund Veesenmayer was not far from the truth when he assumed that "in this letter, the protest is not nearly as important as is the alibi directed toward the English and the Americans, should the war end badly."[34]

Because of the pressure on the cabinet, now coming from Horthy as well, a special meeting of the Council of Ministers was held on June 21. Prime Minister Sztójay called in State Secretaries of the Ministry of the Interior László Endre and **László Baky** to report on the deportations. Both officials read detailed accounts of the "cleansing campaign" aloud. By this time, the majority of Hungary's provincial Jews had been killed. On the previous day the concentration of Jews into collection camps in Zone IV had been completed, and the ghettoization of Jews in Budapest was proceeding at full speed.

Following Baky's short speech, replete with false statements,[35] Endre's longer written report was read out. The text was a medley of truthful information, factual errors, and gross lies. Endre was cynical enough to brag about setting up a "refreshment service exclusively for the Jews" and to give an account of "the Jews" hiding Soviet paratroopers. He proudly took stock of the "accomplishments" of the administrative and law enforcement bodies. Endre made clear that the anti-Jewish operation had been comprehensive: even the mentally ill and dying had been transported off, along with orphans. To fend off accusations of law enforcement brutality, the state secretary resorted to lies.

---

34. See Veesenmayer's report to the Ministry of Foreign Affairs, June 21, 1944, in Juhász et al., *A Wilhelmstrasse és Magyarország*, 870–71.

35. Baky claimed that altogether eighteen Jews died during the deportations, and "these were old and sick." See Baky's report to the Council of Ministers, June 21, 1944, in Karsai and Molnár, *Az Endre-Baky-Jaross per*, 496.

DOCUMENT 4-3: **Report of László Endre on the deportations for the Council of Ministers, June 21, 1944, USHMMA RG 39.018 (BMTI), discs 15–17, V-79802.**

[...]
Medical service in the ghettos is provided by the Jewish doctors at hand. I have emphasized that the Jews, who are not very inclined to maintain cleanliness, should be kept under constant medical supervision to the extent possible, and that epidemics be suppressed in a timely fashion. I have facilitated hospital stays for those who are seriously ill, as well as for women in labor; their diet in the ghetto can be considered satisfactory because under the ghetto order determined by the local authorities, they were allowed to go out during certain hours of the day to visit markets and stores to go shopping.[36]

[...]
Based on an order by His Excellency, the Minister of Justice, Jews required to wear the yellow star are brought in again [to the collection camps] from detention as well as correctional institutions. Mental health institutions, hospitals, sanatoriums, holiday resorts, and other locations in which Jews may be hiding are also being vacated.

In general, the principle employed for the transports and deportation is that these be carried out in a humane way, in keeping with the Christian spirit. Wherever I observed abuse of any sort, I implemented the most thorough inspection and the strictest punishment for offenders; I ordered the organization of the so-called "refreshment service" at train stations and the border exit stations, which is intended to secure to the extent possible the comfort of the deported Jews.[37]

[...]

The ministers accepted the report. Former prime minister **Béla Imrédy**'s remarks were typical: he found the report "extraordinarily interesting" and

---

36. Endre knew full well that no attention whatsoever was being paid to organizing such public supplies and services, including public health facilities. During his trip between April 24 and May 1, he saw the terrible conditions prevailing in the ghettos and collection camps with his own eyes. But even when health care was covered on paper, the measures were not implemented in reality.

37. On May 29, the Ministry of the Interior did indeed order that a temporary kitchen be set up at the Kassa train station to supply food for the transports. But Endre was lying again: this measure was introduced because the Germans demanded it. Moreover, it is doubtful whether any food was ever distributed to deportees at this kitchen. On establishment of the kitchen, see transcript of the mayor of Kassa (May 30), YVA (Archív mesta Košice) 12549–50, documents of the Mayor of Kassa (Košice), selected documents, 14987/1939–44516/1944.

concurred that it was "a huge accomplishment to have gotten rid of the Jews." He was, however, critical of the fact that no written agreement had been made with the Germans about transports leaving the country. With an eye to public opinion in Hungary and abroad, he suggested that the government should distance itself from the brutal methods employed during the deportation and exempt Jews who had converted to Christianity.[38]

Besides Endre's and Baky's reports, the Council of Ministers also talked about the negative international reaction to the events in Hungary. Although the unsustainability of the explanation given by the government and the press was increasingly obvious, the official communications insisted that the Jews were being taken to Germany for work. Authorities justified the herding off of children and the elderly as well by saying that work morale improved if families stayed together. This was an obvious lie. Over the previous years, many seasonal workers had set out for Germany, mostly to perform agricultural labor, but there had never been talk of their families accompanying them. Moreover, in the case of the Jews, most men capable of work were already away doing forced labor. In addition, the deportees included people who were elderly or ill, had physical or mental disabilities, or had no family members. Document 4-4 includes reports on the handing over of a two-year-old girl and a seventy-four-year-old woman to the German authorities for "work."

DOCUMENT 4-4: **Reports by the police chief inspector of the Sárvár Auxiliary Detention House, July 14, 1944, in Elek Karsai, ed., *Vádirat a nácizmus ellen. Dokumentumok a magyarországi zsidóüldözés történetéhez (1944 június 26–1944 október 15. A budapesti zsidóság deportálásának felfüggesztése)* (Budapest: Magyar Izraeliták Országos Képviselete, 1967), 3:180, 185–86.**

*Auxiliary detention house of the Hungarian Royal Police, Sárvár*[39]
*1333/1944*
   TO THE HUNGARIAN ROYAL POLICE HEADQUARTERS
       DETENTION DEPARTMENT
                  Budapest
  This is to inform you that on July 4, 1944, I handed over to the German army, for the purpose of work in Germany, Mária Ágnes Schrey—a Jew

---

  38. Record of the Council of Ministers, June 21, 1944, in László Karsai and Judit Molnár, eds., *A magyar Qusiling-kormány. Sztójay Döme és társai a népbíróság előtt* (Budapest: 1956-os KHT, 2004), 748–52.

  39. This was an internment camp set up in western Hungary for Polish refugees and residents resettled from the Southern Province, primarily Serbs. Mainly Jews were imprisoned there in 1944.

born in 1942, [to] mother Aranka Sablik—interned based on final decision 7233/1944 of the Ministry of the Interior.

Sárvár, July 14, 1944

Head of the detention house:
[illegible signature]
Hungarian Royal Police Chief Inspector

*Auxiliary detention house of the Hungarian Royal Police, Sárvár 1334/1944.*

TO THE HUNGARIAN ROYAL POLICE HEADQUARTERS DETENTION DEPARTMENT

Budapest

This is to inform you that on July 4, 1944, I handed over to the German army, for the purpose of work in Germany, Mrs. Ábrahám Szerebrenik—a Jew born in 1870, [to] mother Johanna Lőwy—interned based on final decision 7233/1944 of the Ministry of the Interior.

Sárvár, July 14, 1944.

Head of the detention house:
[illegible signature]
Hungarian Royal Police Inspector

Many Jews, crammed into cattle cars for transport to "work," tried to contact the outside world. Despite orders forbidding possession of writing materials, many people managed to keep at least the worn end of a pencil, a postcard, or a piece of paper. They threw hastily written messages consisting of just a few lines through cracks in the cattle cars, entrusting them to the goodwill of those who found them. It was up to these people whether the messages reached their addressees, for the "messenger" often had to purchase stamps to mail them. It appears that many strangers were in fact willing to do this. Their efforts were often in vain, for by this time many of the addressees had themselves already been moved into ghettos or deported. Still, quite a few messages asking for help, sending prayers, or expressing concern about the fate of loved ones did reach their destinations and were preserved. Jenő Reich sent the postcard and letter in document 4-5 to his family. Reich was held in the Kistarcsa internment camp and deported to Auschwitz on July 19.[40] He managed to send first a postcard,

---

40. For the details of the Kistarcsa deportation, see document 4-16. Jenő Reich was born in 1893 in Hajdúhadház. He most likely died in Kaufering, a subcamp of Dachau, in early 1945. See *USHMM ITS Collection Data Base Central Name Index*; Yad Vashem, "Central Database of Shoah Victims' Names," www.yadvashem.org.

then a letter to his wife, Margit. Both were thrown out of a cattle car and found by people ready to help by mailing them.

DOCUMENT 4-5: **Jenő Reich's farewell postcard and letter to his family, July 1944, HJA XX-F-II, box D 6/2.**

> [postcard]
> My dears!
> Today is Wednesday, we are packed up and we are leaving. May God be with you, my dear family, may the dear God be with you. Hugs and kisses,
> Daddy [*Aputok*]
> May the hands mailing this postcard be blessed.
> [Sentence in different handwriting on the bottom of the card]: This [postcard] was thrown out [of the cattle car] at the Karácsond [a municipality northeast of Budapest] railway station. It got wet, but I'll try to send it anyway.
>
> [letter]
> My dear wife and children,
> I have already thrown a postcard out of the train, now I'm trying to write a letter. Undoubtedly, we are leaving for a long journey. May God help us to meet each other once again in joy, since a miracle happened on Saturday, so God might help now too.[41] We could not bring anything with us, they took away everything, our rucksacks [illegible] in a cattle car. The destination is Germany, at least this is what we think, but we may get off at Kassa. The guards are German soldiers, they treat us alright. Fortunately, the weather is not that hot. If I could be sure that you won't be hurt, I could endure my own fate under any circumstances. I don't want to make you sad, but I really wish to live with you, may God help us in this. My dear children, take care of your dear mother, and my dear wife, take care of the apples of our eyes, and if God helps us, we will be grateful for Him. I'll write if I'm able to. Till then your dad [*Aputok*] sends his love and kisses.

---

41. Reich refers to Eichmann's aborted attempt to deport the inmates of the Kistarcsa internment camp. On July 14 (Friday), the prisoners were crammed into cattle cars, but before the train left the country, Horthy stopped it and had it turned back. The deportees arrived back at Kistarcsa the next day (Saturday). However, on July 19 Eichmann's Sondereinsatzkommando struck again, and this time they were successful: 1,220 Jews were taken to Auschwitz, among them Jenő Reich. See document 4-16.

Thursday, 10:30 a.m., freight train.
Whoever finds this letter and mails it without envelop and stamp,[42] will be happy for all his life, I'm sure!!

Jenő Reich was murdered in Auschwitz. His wife, Margit, testified in the 1961 Eichmann trial in Jerusalem, where she also showed the card and the letter. The documents can be found in the Hungarian Jewish Archives today.

## THE STRASSHOF DEPORTATIONS

Ninety-seven percent of deportees from the provinces were sent to Auschwitz II–Birkenau. A minor fraction, about fifteen thousand people from Deportation Zone IV, was instead transported to Strasshof, in lower Austria, in late June. They were taken there to work. The decision had grown out of negotiations between Eichmann and the Zionists, led by **Rezső Kasztner**.[43] In early June, Vienna's mayor and SS-Brigadeführer Hanns Blaschke put in a request for laborers to Ernst Kaltenbrunner, head of the Reichssicherheitshauptamt (Reich Security Main Office), to work in military production plants in the area.[44] Kaltenbrunner informed Eichmann, for whom the request was convenient: he could then point to this transport as a concession in his negotiations with the Zionists. (The Strasshof deportations would probably have taken place even if Eichmann had not been in contact with Kasztner and the Zionists.) The Jews were transferred from the Strasshof distribution camp to settlements in the vicinity, where they worked in agriculture or construction, or cleared rubble. There were no selections; families were for the most part allowed to stay together. A number of these people died because of inadequate provisions and

---

42. That is, the person who found it had to cover the expense of mailing the letter.
43. According to the testimony of Edit Csillag, a young Hungarian deportee who worked for the SS office at the distribution camp of Strasshof, they registered 15,011 people deported from collection camps in the provinces, including Debrecen, Szeged, Szolnok, and Baja. HJA, DEGOB Protocols, no. 3628. On the negotiations between the Nazis and Zionists, see chapter 8.
44. For Kaltenbrunner's reply of June 30, in which he informed Blaschke about the arrival of twelve thousand Jews, 30 percent of them fit for work, see Braham, *The Destruction of Hungarian Jewry*, 1:415–16.

illness or were murdered by retreating SS troops, but around 75 percent survived the war.[45]

In preparation for assembling the Strasshof transports, **Jewish Councils** in camps across Deportation Zone IV, including the town of Szolnok, were told to divide camp residents into two groups. Dramatic scenes accompanied this process. For the most part, prominent community members and their family were eligible to be placed into the "privileged" group, along with doctors, engineers, and other specialists. The remaining slots were to be filled by those fit for work and family members of labor servicemen. Because most of the camp residents fell into the latter two categories, difficulties arose in deciding whom to include. Jews had no specific information regarding the destination of the transports, but many suspected that those in the first group would land in better circumstances. Márta Balázs, sixteen years old in 1944, was lucky, for she was assigned to leave on the first train out of Szolnok, along with 2,566 others sharing her fate.

DOCUMENT 4-6: **Memoirs of Márta Balázs, no date (postwar), USHMMA RG 10.207, 36–37.**

[. . .] And then we began hearing news that we would be taken to Germany. Meanwhile, they were also collecting the Jews from the ghettos in the vicinity of Szolnok, so the ghetto was becoming more and more crowded. Gendarmes kept coming and forcing everyone to hand over the money and valuables that they still possessed. News started circulating that there would be two trains leaving. Somehow it was known that one was the "good" train and the other, the "bad" train. The Jewish leaders were compiling lists, which would enumerate separately the notable and the wealthy people, the families of those doing labor service—and the other list consisting of the anonymous crowd. (At the time, we did not yet know that the good train was going to Austria and the bad one to Auschwitz. And, of course, we had no idea about the existence of concentration camps or gas chambers, and I think if we had been told about this sort of thing, we would not have believed it at all.)

---

45. On the Strasshof deportation, see Braham, *The Politics of Genocide*, 2:733–37; Judit Molnár, *Zsidósors 1944-ben az V. (szegedi) csendőrkerületben* (Budapest: Cserépfalvi, 1995), 146–51; Szita Szabolcs, *Utak a pokolból. Magyar deportáltak az annektált Ausztriában 1944–1945* (Budapest: Metalon Manager Iroda, 1991), 25–41. On the fate of Hungarian deportees, see ibid., esp. 41–47 and 84–117.

[. . .] And then the day of entrainment arrived. As I had mentioned, they kept taking away everything even at the last minute, so they took my small suitcase with the poetry book and the eyeglasses. They pulled instruments, pencils, papers from people's hands in the most brutal way, and even if someone packed a bit of salt in a piece of paper, they took that away as well—to this day, I do not know why. Perhaps they wanted to stop us from sending any sort of news about what was happening to us. And then in the midst of great yelling, they pushed and crammed us into a cattle car, 80 people into a space that would at best have fit 40. This meant that we would be sitting on our packages, would pull our legs underneath us. Those who ended up at the wall of the cattle car were the luckiest, for they could at least prop their backs up against it. We young people mostly ended up in the middle of the cattle car and propped our backs up against one another to find a position that was more bearable to hold for days on end. We were given a bucket of water and a toilet bucket; the latter was a normal-sized pail that was supposed to serve the bodily needs of 80 people. There was grating on the windows, and an open crack of just a few inches was left on the door when it was then locked. And all this was in the midst of the June heat. One suffocated from the lack of air, from thirst, and it was awful to pee and poop in front of others, stepping over the heads of others to reach the toilet bucket. A baby was also traveling with us; we placed him near the open crack on the side of the wagon, so at least he [could] get some air. I remember the journey lasting at least 5 days, and by the time we got there, several old people were pulled off the cattle car dead; they could not withstand the ordeals and the thirst.

School director Lipót Madarász, a decorated and disabled veteran of World War I, was also deported from Szolnok. When dividing the prisoners into two groups, the vicinity's Jewish Council assigned Madarász, an ex-serviceman and prominent member of the community, to the first group, the one most Jews believed would go to a preferable destination.[46] However, when he learned that the family he loved the most was on the second train, he joined them.

---

46. See Béla Varga, *A szolnoki zsidóság története, 1840–1944* (Szolnok : Damjanich János Múzeum, Szolnoki Izraelita Hitközség, 1994), 92.

DOCUMENT 4-7: Class picture of the Szolnok Neologue Jewish elementary school, around 1939, from the private collection of Géza Cseh, Szolnok, Hungary. Lipót Madarász is in the center.

A few days later Madarász perished along with many of his students in the gas chambers of Birkenau.

## THE CONCENTRATION OF THE BUDAPEST JEWS

The Ministry of the Interior and Eichmann sought to isolate and concentrate the Budapest Jews as quickly as possible. As the first step toward this goal, fifteen hundred Jewish apartments in Budapest and the vicinity were confiscated within a single day following the large-scale Allied air raids of April 3 and 4. The measure was to provide housing for Christians whose apartments had suffered bomb damage.[47] Authorities instructed the Budapest Jewish Council that

---

47. The initial plan was to hand over five hundred apartments, but soon the Hungarian and the German authorities raised the number to fifteen hundred. On the evictions, see Ernő Munkácsi, *Hogyan történt? Adatok és okmányok a magyar zsidóság tragédiájához* (Budapest: Rennaissance, 1947), 43–50; testimony of Imre Reiner, June 21, 1946, trial of Adolf Eichmann and his associates, BMA IV/17.166/1949; memorandum of László Endre, April 3, 1944, HNA P1434–16-IV/3.

the Jews evicted from their apartments should be relocated roughly between Podmaniczky Street and Rákóczi Road, that is, in Municipal Districts VI and VII.[48] The newspapers also publicized the idea that the ghetto would be established in this location, and Endre himself issued a statement to this effect.[49]

Several members of the council claimed after the war that a central ghetto was not set up until December because Jewish leaders successfully spread a critical rumor: that the Allies were trying to protect the Jewish population. Therefore, if the Jews were resettled in an isolated, closed-off area, the rest of Budapest would fall prey to air raids.[50] Government representatives had frequently dwelled on the absurd theory of cooperation between the Allies and the Jews.[51] During the **Arrow Cross** era, Minister of Religion and Education Ferenc Rajniss tried to convince former Jewish Council member **Sándor Török** that the Jews should attempt to influence the Anglo-Saxon countries: "They should not bomb Budapest, and then, in exchange . . . the Hungarian government would allow a given number of Jews to emigrate."[52]

Endre himself was afflicted by an anti-Jewish paranoia that bordered on insanity. Still, it seems unlikely that the state secretary opted to ghettoize the Jews in individual blocks instead of a fixed ghetto area because of some clandestine alliance of Allied airmen and the Jewish Council. Throughout the country, various ghettoization models arose. In each locale, the ghetto reflected specific local circumstances: the number of Jews, a town's layout, and the interests of the Christian population.[53] Most likely Endre based his decision on these criteria. It probably seemed easier to select buildings with high concentrations of Jewish tenants to begin with and to force the rest of the Jewish population into them than to move all the Christians out of a given part of town and force all the Jews to move there.[54] The fabricated rumor spread by the Jewish Council may have

---

48. Munkácsi, *Hogyan történt,* 129–30.
49. Statement by László Endre, *Magyarság,* April 16, 1944.
50. Samu Stern, *Emlékirataim. Versenyfutás az idővel! A "zsidótanács" működése a német megszállás és a nyilas uralom idején* (Budapest: Bábel, 2004), 323; recollection of Ernő Pető about the activities of the housing bureau of the council (no date), HJA XX-L-1, box D 5/3.
51. See, e.g., László Baky's statement in *Magyarság,* April 9, 1944, in Ilona Benoschofsky and Elek Karsai, eds., *Vádirat a nácizmus ellen. Dokumentumok a magyarországi zsidóüldözés történetéhez (1944 március 19–1944 május 15. A német megszállástól a deportálás megkezdéséig)* (Budapest: Magyar Izraeliták Országos Képviselete, 1958), 1:140.
52. Recollection of Sándor Török, March 17, 1946, HJA, DEGOB Protocols, no. 3643.
53. For the various models, see chapter 3.
54. There is consensus on this in the more recent literature as well. See Tim Cole, *Holocaust City: The Making of a Jewish Ghetto* (New York: Routledge, 2003), 93–95, 115–25.

struck a chord with certain officials, but it is highly debatable whether it had a significant impact on Endre's decision.

As soon as Endre set into motion deportations from the provinces, he began the ghettoization of the Budapest Jews at a fast pace. On May 26, 1944, he instructed Budapest city officials to designate Jewish and non-Jewish buildings by May 31. Once this had been accomplished, he originally intended to give Jews twenty-four hours to move.[55] That the Jewish Council considered the task logistically impossible would not have changed Endre's mind, but the leaders of the Budapest government and financial apparatus also fervently objected to the tight deadline and enormous workload it entailed.[56] Eventually Endre had no choice but to compromise. According to the lord mayor's decree announced on June 16, the relocation of the Jews had to be completed by 8 p.m. on June 21.[57]

In order to reduce the number of those required to move (and thereby save time and cost), the designated buildings' owners and the majority of their tenants had to be Jewish. Apart from this, one social criterion was also taken into account: modern apartments with low maintenance costs were to go to non-Jews. The decree published on June 16 designated 2,639 so-called "**yellow-star houses**."[58]

Over the next days, the population put considerable pressure on the municipal authorities and the Ministry of the Interior. In a short time, about six hundred petitions arrived at Budapest's city hall. A third of these were written by non-Jewish citizens who protested being moved out of their apartments. The petitioners mostly invoked their social status and the expected costs of the move, but they of course echoed and tapped the government's antisemitic reasoning as well, either out of conviction or opportunism.[59] The petition included

---

55. Memorandum of the Social-Political Department of Budapest, May 26, 1944, in Ilona Benoschofsky and Elek Karsai, eds., *Vádirat a nácizmus ellen. Dokumentumok a magyarországi zsidóüldözés történetéhez (1944 május 15–1944 június 30. A budapesti zsidóság összeköltöztetése)* (Budapest: Magyar Izraeliták Országos Képviselete, 1960), 2:113.

56. Letter by the lord mayor of Budapest, Tibor Keledy, to Minister of the Interior **Andor Jaross**, May 31, 1944, in Benoschofsky and Karsai, *Vádirat a nácizmus ellen*, 2:114–18; Keledy's letter to Mayor Ákos Doroghi Farkas, June 1, 1944, in ibid., 2:118–20; memorandum of the Ministry of Finance, June 9, 1944, ibid., 162–64.

57. Lord Mayor of Budapest's order no. 147.501/1944-IX, June 16, 1944, inBenoschofsky and Karsai, *Vádirat a nácizmus ellen*, 2:203–8.

58. Cole, *Holocaust City*, 101–5.

59. Ibid., 131–33, 136–38 and *passim*.

in document 4-8 came from a recently built residential neighborhood favored by the Jewish middle class.[60]

DOCUMENT 4-8: **László Komlósi's letter to the lord mayor of Budapest, June 19, 1944, USHMMA RG 52.001M, reel 16 (HNA, Series I).**[61]

Your Honor!
On behalf of the Christian residents of Szent István Park 25, Municipal District V, we request that Your Honor kindly exempt the building at Szent István Park 25 from being designated as [a] residence for Jews.

The building in question is one of [the] most beautifully situated houses of Budapest, with all low-rent apartments that are ideal for healthful living, with southern exposures, with two to three sunny rooms affording beautiful views of the banks of the Danube, the Rózsadomb,[62] and Margit Island. In this building 30% of the residents are Christian—all of them civil servants and officials with limited financial means[63]—who have unanimously expressed their wish to stay here. We note also that Christian residents have already submitted petitions for the majority of the Jewish apartments; had the designation been delayed by as little as two weeks, one would no longer have found any Jewish residents here.

With deep respect,
Budapest, June 19, 1944.

László Komlósi
Superintendent of the Hungarian National Bank

Dr. vitéz Gábor Farkas
Attorney, Prosecutor of the Hungarian National Bank

As a result of pressure from city residents, a new category was created: houses with mixed residents. In these instances, non-Jews were permitted to remain in "yellow-star buildings."[64]

---

60. Újlipótváros (Municipal District V of 1944 Budapest, Municipal District XIII today).
61. The letter was first published in Benoschofsky and Karsai, *Vádirat a nácizmus ellen*, 2:234.
62. Rózsadomb (Rose Hill) in Municipal District II of Budapest is a residential quarter with villas, inhabited by the upper middle class and the elite.
63. The petitioners wished to appear less affluent that they actually were. Those who could afford to buy or rent real estate at this address could hardly have struggled to make ends meet.
64. Cole, *Holocaust City*, 141–49.

While Christians requested that their residences not be defined as Jewish houses, Jews tried to obtain "yellow-star house" designations for their buildings. The final list consisting of fewer than two thousand buildings was published on June 23, 1944.[65] The deadline for moving in was modified to midnight on June 24.[66] The housing bureau of the Jewish Council completed the seemingly insolvable logistical task by June 25: over ten days, approximately two hundred thousand people were shifted from approximately ten thousand buildings into barely two thousand.[67] Endre had every reason to be satisfied: by the time the deportations from Szeged and Debrecen began, Budapest's Jews had been isolated. One of the greatest obstacles to the deportation from the capital was removed.

On June 21, the same day the list of "yellow-star houses" was finalized, the police commissioner of Budapest sent the order included in document 4-9 to the lord mayor. The goal was the same as in the provinces: to segregate the Jews prior to their impending deportation so they could be supervised and so that no one could escape the process. Authorities ordered immediate registration of all residents of these houses. The order entrusted building supervisors with the task of checking the number of residents against the registers on a daily basis and reporting missing individuals promptly to the police.[68] A strict curfew was ordered, and raids were regularly conducted to confirm that residents were observing the instructions. Jews (rightly) regarded these measures as preparations for the buildings' evacuation.[69] Eventually, deportation was taken off the agenda (at least temporarily), but the authorities continued to subject residents of these houses to the regulations. Later the daily curfew between 2 and 5 p.m. was lifted, and Jews were able to leave the buildings between 11 a.m. and 5 p.m.[70]

---

65. *Pesti Napló*, June 23, 1944.

66. Lord Mayor of Budapest's order no. 148.452/1944-IX, June 16, 1944, in Benoschofsky and Karsai, *Vádirat a nácizmus ellen*, 2:221.

67. *Magyarországi Zsidók Lapja*, June 22, 1944, 1.

68. Many of building supervisors performed this task proactively and enthusiastically, not only out of a sense of duty but, even more so, out of antisemitic zeal or intoxication with their newfound power. Many Jews were executed during the Arrow Cross regime based on information supplied by building supervisors.

69. See the petition of the Budapest Jewish Council addressed to the prime minister, June 22, 1944, in Braham, *The Politics of Genocide*, 2:737–41.

70. Braham, *The Politics of Genocide*, 2:855–57.

DOCUMENT 4-9: **Order by the Budapest chief of the Hungarian Royal Police, June 23, 1944, National Széchényi Library, Placard and Leaflet Collection.**

Chief of the Hungarian Royal Police in Budapest.
7200/fk. eln. 1944

ORDER

Based on my right secured in Article 8 of Act XXI of 1881[71]—in agreement with the Lord Mayor of the capital, Budapest—I order the following:

1. §.

Jews who have been required to wear the distinguishing mark (yellow star) specified in the Prime Minister's Decree 1240/1944 (henceforth: Jews) are permitted to leave the houses designated to them by the Lord Mayor of the capital, Budapest, only between the hours of 2:00 and 5:00 p.m., exclusively for the purpose of medical treatment, maintaining hygiene, and shopping.

2. §.

Jews may not receive visitors and may not conduct conversations through the windows of their apartments facing the street.

3. §.

Within 24 hours, the owner or the supervisor of each Jewish building, together with the air raid commander or the deputy commander,[72] will compile a register of Jewish residents, grouped by floors. The register will be compiled in triplicate, each copy authenticated with both signatures. [. . .]

4. §.

Jews are required to keep their apartments clean in accordance with public health standards.

In apartments inhabited by several Jewish families, the residents of the apartment are required to select among them an apartment supervisor, who will check that the requirements of the previous paragraph are

---

71. This article allowed that in extraordinary circumstances not regulated by the law (immediate danger to life, physical safety, or threat to assets), the police could issue orders (for a specified location and time) to restrict a person's freedom of movement.

72. Air raid commander (*légoltalmi parancsnok*) was not a military position. It was usually filled by a civilian tenant of the house.

observed and who is personally responsible for the cleanliness and order of the apartment.

The building supervisor is required to post the register of the apartment supervisors at the building entrance and is required to replace the register if it is damaged or destroyed.

5. §.

In houses designated for the Jews, the commander (or deputy commander) of the air raid house guard must designate an area, if possible, a segregated one, within the air raid shelter for the non-Jewish residents of the building. Any Jews crowded out of the air raid shelter must be placed in the deepest-lying room within the building.

6. §.

In trams consisting of several cars, Jews are allowed to travel in the last car only.

7. §.

Jews may not go to parks and leisure areas.

8. §.

It is strictly forbidden—at the risk of a prison sentence—to hide Jews or shelter them, for however short a period of time, in either Christian houses or in parts of Jewish houses inhabited by Christians.
[. . .]

My order becomes effective on the day it is posted.
Budapest, June 23, 1944

Chief of Police

Despite all these restrictions, Budapest Jews were allowed to travel, shop, and partake of the amenities of city life (such as attending designated movie theaters and restaurants), even if they were strictly confined in terms of space and time. In all, they found themselves in a far better situation than the residents of provincial ghettos. However, several factors shattered their morale in the summer of 1944. By this time, many of them knew that Jews in the provinces, including their own relatives, were daily being deported by the thousands. The setting up of the "yellow-star houses" and the arrival of (accurate) news about a planned deportation from Budapest triggered despair on a mass scale.

Many who had believed that the integrated Jews of Budapest would not come under threat now confronted for the first time the reality that they too were in mortal danger. Desperation manifested itself in another wave of conversions to Christianity, which were irrational, given the exemption rules and the probation period imposed on such conversions.[73] Between April and July 1944, the number of successful suicides among Jews was over three times the monthly average for the previous year.[74] In August, once immediate danger had passed, these figures dropped significantly. However, during the fall, Arrow Cross terror ushered in another negative turn of events.

These threats registered sharply in the microworld of Éva Weinmann. In June 1944, this fourteen-year-old girl and her family, like tens of thousands of others, were forced to move into a "yellow-star house." The Weinmanns ended up in the one-bedroom apartment belonging to her aunt, where they lived in crowded quarters but under tolerable conditions compared to the ghetto circumstances in the provinces.

DOCUMENT 4-10: **Éva Weinmann's diary, July 23, 1944, USHMMA RG 39.013M, reel 26 (HJA XX-G, box D 6/6).**

> July 23, 1944
> Unfortunately, it is a very sad time that prompts me to write in your pages again, my little diary.
>
> In the fifth year of the war, Europe's peril, Hitler, has also arrived here. As in all other European countries, the persecution of the Jews also began here. It has been going on for 5 months. We are the only ones left in all of Hungary. God only knows where the others are. They took all my friends. One of them was arrested. He was held on Páva Street until now,[75] but unfortunately they took him now. They were in Kistarcsa, but

---

73. For the issue of conversions, see chapter 8.

74. Among the dead buried by the **Neologue** congregation in Pest in June, every eighth person had committed suicide. Viktor Karády, "Desperation and Resistance under the Rise of Fascism and Nazi Rule: Paradoxes of Jewish Mortality in Budapest (1938–1945)," in *Küzdelem az igazságért. Tanulmányok Randolph L. Braham 80. születésnapjára*, ed. László Karsai and Judit Molnár (Budapest: MAZSIHISZ, 2002), 363–64.

75. The internment camps for Jewish refugees were often placed in Jewish community buildings (synagogues, hospitals, etc.), supervised by the police, and maintained by Jewish aid organizations. The Páva Street Synagogue (today the building of the Holocaust Memorial Center) was one of them. Further examples were the Szabolcs Street Jewish hospital, the Jewish orphanage on Columbus Street, and the Rumbach Street Synagogue (all in Budapest). Braham, *The Politics of Genocide*, 1:107.

supposedly they were also taken away from there.[76] My God, please save them from the worst fate, from death! My heart aches so much for them.

We now have a 2-room (or a 1-room) apartment. We live together with Aunt Juliska. She has the bigger room. Ours is somewhat smaller. Thank God we are relatively well. We can shop between 11 and 1 and can be in the street between 11 and 5. Gyöngyi lives nearby, and I always go over to visit her. Pista is in Csepel.[77] Last Sunday he even came home. The poor boys from Kispest were all taken to Serbia.[78] I do not know if I will see them again ever. Frédi (my current idyllic idol), I do not know where and how he is.

This week there was an assassination attempt against that swine H., but unfortunately it was not successful.[79] Even though I also heard that he died, I do not believe it. I am hoping this situation will be over soon. Here where we live, in Rákóczi Road 57,[80] there is an ugly Arrow Cross man. Yesterday he wanted to have all residents taken away.[81] The time will come when he will be beaten to death. If only I could live to see it. A religious conversion fever broke out among the Budapest Jews. Unfortunately we are also among them. I do not want to, but Dad does, so what can I do. What consoles me is that the conversion can take as long as three months, until then, a lot of things can still happen.[82] Here, in the house, the company is not very great. There are 2 ugly 17-year-old boys. 3 good-looking gentile boys, but those pay no attention to me. 2 17-year-old girls.

---

76. Until the German occupation, the Kistarcsa internment camp was one of the major detention sites where refugees, illegal communists, or anybody the authorities found "dangerous" were incarcerated. After March 1944, the Kistarcsa site was the main internment camp for holding Jews arrested in the first days of the occupation.

77. The Csepel Island, located south of Budapest, had a cluster of labor camps set up mainly in factory buildings. They included the Tsuk fur factory, the Mauthner grain-processing plant, the Duna aircraft factory (a.k.a. Horthyliget), Királyerdő, Herminamajor, and Újtelep camps nos. II and III. Reports of the Central Jewish Council on the internment camps, HJA XX-C-1, box D 8/4; testimony of Dr. Tibor Neumann, HJA, DEGOB Protocols, no. 3617.

78. As labor servicemen, they were sent to the copper mines of Bor. On this, see document 2-13.

79. On July 20, 1944, high-ranking military officers executed an unsuccessful assassination attempt against Hitler.

80. This avenue in Budapest separated Municipal Districts VII and VIII.

81. Unlike in the era of the Arrow Cross rule, at this time the Arrow Cross man did not yet have the authority to have the residents of the house taken away. Presumably, he was objecting to the designation of the building as a "yellow-star house."

82. According to the regulation set by the Christian churches, there was a preparation period between registering for conversion and the actual act of christening.

1 22-year-old girl. 1 12-year-old boy and one 9-year-old girl. That is all. Poor Robi was called up by the Population Movement Bureau, and now he was deported along with the Jews. The poor thing is only 15 years old. I feel terribly sorry.[83]

[. . .]

The advertisements in document 4-11 also shed light on the everyday life of the Budapest Jews in the summer of 1944. For them, wearing the yellow star for long months meant that the stigma became part of their daily routine. The writer Ernő Szép observed how much attention his housemates paid to the shade, fabric quality, and cleanliness of the star, all of which conveyed a certain social status.[84] Advertisements, published by the dozens in the journal of the Jewish Council, reflected a similar persistence of pre-occupation normality.

**DOCUMENT 4-11:** Ads published in *Magyarországi Zsidók Lapja* [Journal of the Jews in Hungary], August 3, 1944.

Standard YELLOW STAR
[can be purchased at the firm] Börzsönyi, Lovag Street 14, Municipal District VI, and at Szent István Boulevard 7, Municipal District V. Cash-On-Delivery service available for the provinces.[85]

RELIABLE, orderly cleaning woman is sought for a small, two-member household near the Buda side of Margit Bridge, from 8 a.m. to 12 p.m. Only exempted individuals, who are not required to wear a distinguishing mark, are considered. Offers marked "Serious" to be sent to the journal's offices.

During the relatively peaceful period between August and October, many Jews were allowed to leave their homes to go to work. Although assigned to

---

83. Éva Weinmann survived the Holocaust and died in 1946 due to severe illness.
84. Quoted in Zsófa Bán, "A sárga csillag mint accessoire. Ironikus beszéd Kertész Imre Sorstalanságában," *Múlt és Jövő* 4 (2003): 126–35. Szép (1884–1953) was a well-known and popular poet, playwright, and novelist in pre–World War II Hungary. A Jew, he was rounded up in October 1944 and released on November 6. He survived the siege of Budapest and Arrow Cross rampage, while his two brothers and sister did not. Szép's memoir was first published in 1945. However, the author remained out of favor with the postwar government in Hungary, and his book was only reissued in 1984. See Ernő Szép, *The Smell of Humans: A Memoir of the Holocaust in Hungary* (Budapest: Corvina, 1984), ix–xii.
85. It is quite grotesque that the advertisement regarded members of provincial Jewish communities—which no longer existed—as potential customers.

hard labor such as clearing rubble, they received a small income and tolerable treatment. The opportunity to perform this job fell to Magdolna Pálmai and her friend Klári, depicted in the photograph reproduced in document 4-12 clearing rubble after an air raid in Budapest in September 1944. The two young women became close friends.

DOCUMENT 4-12: **Magdolna Pálmai (on the right) and her friend Klári clearing rubble in Budapest, September 1944, image no. 1012010205385956, CENTROPA (www. centropa.hu).**[86]

---

86. Magdolna Pálmai (b. 1911) had probably been a tailoress before the war, born in Budapest. She was arrested in the city and sent to Dachau in November 1944. She survived the war and lived for a time in the Feldafing displaced persons camp in Bavaria. See *USHMM ITS Collection Data Base Central Name Index*.

Magdolna lost track of Klári when the Arrow Cross took them both to do forced labor in November.[87] On the fifth day of the more than 130-mile-long death march from Budapest to Vienna, they arrived at Gönyü, where the forced laborers were pushed on to barges. By that time they were totally exhausted and famished. Many died of infections or illnesses, froze to death, or were killed by the gendarmes or Arrow Cross guards. Those who could no longer walk, as well as the sick, were left on the barges, where most of them perished. This was the last place Magdolna saw Klári.

## SUSPENSION OF DEPORTATIONS: JULY TO AUGUST 1944

At the end of June, international pressure on Regent Horthy increased. The Allies liberated Rome on June 4, so Pope Pius XII could speak up more bravely than before. On June 25, he sent a telegram to Horthy, asking him to stop the deportations. On the next day, U.S. President Franklin D. Roosevelt sent the regent an ultimatum written in a harsh tone, making the same demand. The **Auschwitz Protocol**, a report about the Birkenau death factory compiled by Jewish escapees from the Auschwitz complex, reached Switzerland.[88] Earlier a copy had been given to Horthy as well. In the second half of June, the Swiss government abolished censorship, and over the next three weeks, more than three hundred reports and articles appeared worldwide about the mass murder of Hungarian Jews. The world press and international diplomacy loudly condemned the government.

The Swedish media also devoted extensive coverage to Hungarian events, making it clear that the incidents were not isolated atrocities but, rather, part of

---

87. The authors have been unable to identify Klári's surname. For the fate of the Budapest Jews during the Arrow Cross regime, see chapter 6.

88. See the Auschwitz Protocol in Henryk Swiebocki, ed., *London Has Been Informed . . .: Reports by Auschwitz Escapees* (Oświęcim: Auschwitz-Birkenau State Museum, 1997), 181–310. Also see Miroslav Karny, "The Vrba and Wetzler Report," in *Anatomy of the Auschwitz Death Camp*, ed. Yisrael Gutman and Michael Berenbaum (Bloomington: Indiana University Press in association with the USHMM, 1998), 556–63; Erich Kulka, "Escapes of Jewish Prisoners from Auschwitz-Birkenau and Their Attempts to Stop the Mass Extermination," in *The Nazi Concentration Camps: Structure and Aims, the Image of the Prisoner, the Jews in the Camps. Proceedings of the Fourth Yad Vashem International Historical Conference*, ed. Yisrael Gutman and Avital Saf (Jerusalem: Yad Vashem, 1984), 414.

an industrial-style mass murder campaign.[89] On June 24, the Swedish Ministry of Foreign Affairs also got hold of the Auschwitz Protocol.[90] On June 30, Horthy received the telegram excerpted in document 4-13 from the Swedish king.[91] Despite its subdued tone, the king made clear that the neutral states knew full well that Hungary was participating in mass murder.

DOCUMENT 4-13: **Telegram from the king of Sweden, Gustaf V, to Regent Miklós Horthy protesting the deportations, June 30, 1944, in Elek Karsai, ed.,** *Vádirat a nácizmus ellen. Dokumentumok a magyarországi zsidóüldözés történetéhez (1944 június 26– 1944 október 15. A budapesti zsidóság deportálásának felfüggesztése)* **(Budapest: Magyar Izraeliták Országos Képviselete, 1967), 3:58.**

> Upon being informed of the extraordinarily harsh and strict measures that your government has been employing against the Hungarian Jewish population, I have decided to turn personally to Your Serene Highness to ask, in the name of humanity, that you interfere on behalf of those among these unfortunate people who can still be saved. In appealing to your good heart, I am prompted by the old friendly sentiments that I have always felt toward Your country, and the honest wish that Hungary preserve its good reputation before all nations.
>
> *King Gustaf*

Ambassador Carl Danielsson and the secretary of the Swedish legation, Per Anger, handed the telegram over to Horthy on July 5. During the meeting, Horthy repeated the usual lies: the Germans bore all responsibility for the "dirty work," reports of the gendarmes' brutality were fabrications, and the deportees were being transported for work. He also added a line typical of selective antisemitic reasoning: he voiced agreement with the removal from eastern Hungary of the "communist elements" who had "infiltrated" the country. But the situation was different, he claimed, in the case of the Jews of Budapest, and so he

---

89. News material from the Hungarian News Agency, July 6, 1944, in Elek Karsai, ed., *Vádirat a nácizmus ellen. Dokumentumok a magyarországi zsidóüldözés történetéhez (1944 június 26–1944 október 15. A budapesti zsidóság deportálásának felfüggesztése)* (Budapest: Magyar Izraeliták Országos Képviselete, 1967), 3:72–74.

90. Report by Envoy Danielsson, June 24, 1944, in Péter Bajtay, ed. *Emberirtásembermentés. Svéd követjelentések 1944-ből. Az Auschwitzi Jegyzőkönyv* (Budapest: Katalizátor Iroda, 1994), 40–43.

91. Gustaf V (1858–1950), king of Sweden from 1907 until his death.

would do all he could to stop deportations from the capital.[92] A few days later he answered the king but stipulated that the contents of his letter could not be made public.

DOCUMENT 4-14: **Regent Miklós Horthy's reply to the king of Sweden, early July 1944, in Elek Karsai, ed.,** *Vádirat a nácizmus ellen. Dokumentumok a magyarországi zsidóüldözés történetéhez (1944 június 26–1944 október 15. A budapesti zsidóság deportálásának felfüggesztése)* **(Budapest: Magyar Izraeliták Országos Képviselete, 1967), 3:59.**

TO HIS MAJESTY GUSTAF V KING OF SWEDEN
Stockholm

I have received Your Majesty's telegram with the greatest degree of understanding. I ask Your Majesty to be assured that I will do all that is within my power in the present situation in order to secure that the fundamental principles of humanity and fairness be upheld. I am greatly moved as I think of the friendly sentiments that Your Majesty fosters toward my country and ask that you preserve those sentiments toward the Hungarian people in these difficult, trying hours.

*Miklós Horthy*
Regent of the Kingdom of Hungary

In addition to increased international pressure, Horthy received a long memorandum from his old confidant, former prime minister **István Bethlen**, in hiding at the time. Bethlen advised him to curb the "inhumane, foolish, and cruel persecution of the Jews, which was so unfitting for the Hungarian character." He expressly recommended the dismissal of Endre.[93] Horthy's family and those near him also tried to persuade him to turn around the politics of the country. Nonetheless, the decisive factor was probably the Germans' continually deteriorating military situation.

On June 26, for the first time since the German occupation, Horthy called together the Crown Council, that is, a joint meeting of the government and the regent. At the meeting, he proposed that the deportations be stopped (at least partially), that Baky be dismissed, and that Endre's control over Jewish

---

92. Report of attaché Per Anger, July 5, 1944, in Bajtay, *Emberirtás-embermentés*, 88–89.
93. Memorandum by István Bethlen, late June 1944, in Miklós Szinai and László Szűcs, eds., *Horthy Miklós titkos iratai* (Budapest: Kossuth, 1962), 458–65.

affairs be ended.⁹⁴ His attempt was of no consequence. In response to international criticism, the Council of Ministers agreed at its meeting on June 28 to an emigration plan for a narrow circle of Jews. None of these proposals actually came to fruition.⁹⁵ The state secretaries remained in their positions and could, without difficulty, carry on with organizing the deportations in the provinces. Meanwhile, Endre, Eichmann, and Superintendent of the Gendarmerie Gábor Faragho worked out the details for deporting Jews from the capital. According to their plan, numerous gendarme units would arrive in Budapest under the pretext of a flag consecration ceremony. Then over a few days, they would shut down the "yellow-star houses" and deport the Jews. The gendarmes accordingly showed up with significant forces in the first days of July. Until then, Horthy had been hesitant and ineffectual, but the appearance of the gendarmes in the capital strengthened his suspicion that Baky was planning a coup. He banned the ceremony and ordered military forces loyal to him to the capital, while ordering the gendarme units out of Budapest.⁹⁶ Therefore it seems that the plan to deport the Budapest Jews fell through primarily because of Horthy's concern for his own position. Meanwhile, transports from Deportation Zone V (see map 3, p. liv) continued without interruption.

Finally, on July 6 Sztójay informed Veesenmayer about Horthy's decision to halt the deportations. The prime minister listed the reasons the regent wished to communicate to the Germans as the background informing his decision. Veesenmayer immediately sent a telegram to Berlin.

DOCUMENT 4-15: **Telegram of Reich Plenipotentiary in Hungary Edmund Veesenmayer to Minister of Foreign Affairs Joachim von Ribbentrop, July 6, 1944, in IMT, NG-5523 (translated from German).**

In response to my telephone inquiry, I have received word from Sztójay just now that the Regent, apparently after consultation with the Hungarian government, has halted further actions concerning Jews [*Juden-Aktionen*]. [. . .] He explained his reasoning:

1. The Hungarian government has established that no special measures were carried out against the Jews in Romania, and the government of

---

94. Draft of a statement by the regent, June 26, 1944, in Karsai, *Vádirat a nácizmus ellen*, 3:3–6.
95. For the contents of the decision, see Braham, *The Politics of Genocide*, 2:875–77.
96. Ibid., 2:838–40.

the Reich has also tolerated that the problem of Jews was treated relatively generously there.

2. In Slovakia, too, there are still thousands of Jews, especially Christian Jews, living under the protection of Tiso,[97] to which the government of the Reich has agreed.[98]

3. It became known through enemy radio broadcasts that the Jewish-Hungarian millionaires arrived in Lisbon; this fact has created a huge sensation throughout Hungary and has raised doubts about the just and consistent treatment of the Jewish question in Hungary.[99] After all, if Jews can with the help of the SS escape to neutral countries, then the Regent as well as the Hungarian government should try to ensure that the special wishes of individual neutral countries are taken into account when alleviating the Jewish question in Hungary. It is through such gestures that they are at the moment trying to blunt the force of the ongoing general anti-Hungarian agitation, all the more so because the neutral states are of great importance to Hungary in other respects.

4. A barrage of telegrams, appeals, and threats has been directed at the Regent and the Hungarian government because of the Jewish question. Thus the Swedish king and the Pope have both sent several telegrams.[100] The Papal Nuncio visits the Regent and Sztójay several times a day.[101] And similar actions are being taken by the Turkish and Swiss

---

97. Jozef Tiso (1887–1947), Slovak politician, was head of the Nazi puppet state from 1939 to 1945.

98. In terms of its Jewish policy, Hungary did pay attention to the moves of its allies, especially those of neighboring states that it regarded as rivals.

99. In May, the SS went behind the Hungarian government's back and confiscated the Manfréd Weiss Works, which was the largest military production plant in central Europe not yet in German hands. In exchange for transferring the shares to the Germans, they allowed the owners of Jewish origin to take their families and immigrate to Portugal. See Gábor Kádár and Zoltán Vági, *Aranyvonat. Fejezetek a zsidó vagyon történetéből* (Budapest: 2001, Osiris), 155–68. After the contract was signed on May 17, thirty-two members of the Weiss and Chorin families were taken to Vienna. They flew in a special Lufthansa plane to Lisbon, arriving on June 25. See Szinai and Szűcs, *Horthy Miklós titkos iratai*, 443–44; Raul Hilberg, *The Destruction of the European Jews*, 3rd. ed. (New Haven, CT: Yale University Press, 2003), 2:886–87. Tensions in German-Hungarian relations arose when the incident became public. From early June on, the Hungarian government made several unsuccessful attempts to protest the deal. See Veesenmayer's report of June 14, 1944, to the Ministry of Foreign Affairs, in Juhász et al., *A Wilhelmstrasse és Magyarország*, 866–67.

100. On the Swedish king, see documents 4-13 and 4-14; the pope was Pope Pius XII (1939–1958).

101. **Angelo Rotta**. On Rotta, see the glossary. The papal nuncio is the head of the diplomatic legation of the Vatican in a particular country.

governments,[102] as well as Spanish dignitaries,[103] and last but not least, several prominent Hungarians.

5. Under strict confidentiality, Sztójay read aloud three secret telegrams that the English and American ambassadors in Bern sent to their governments[104]; these telegrams were decoded by the Hungarian intelligence agency. These describe in detail what happens to Jews deported from Hungary. The telegrams mention that 1.5 million Jews have already been exterminated there, and the same fate awaits the majority of Jews who are being deported now. The following suggestions are made in these telegrams: bomb and destroy the destination of the Jewish transports, and beyond this, destroy the railroads connecting Hungary to this location. Every Hungarian and German public authority who is playing a role in this matter—along with their exact street addresses in Budapest—should be targeted by precision bombing,[105] and a large-scale propaganda effort should let the whole world know exactly what is happening. A further telegram names 70 prominent Hungarians and Germans who carry the primary responsibility.

Sztójay told me that he is personally unmoved by these threats because, in the event of our victory, the whole issue will become uninteresting, and in the alternative scenario, his life will definitely be over. Despite all this, it was clear that these telegrams had made a strong impression on him. I have heard in the meantime that the Council of Ministers has also been informed about these telegrams and that they had a similar effect.

[. . .] The consequences of the most recent bombings—some of which have been extremely severe and damaged residential areas as well—have been rather unpleasant, and there is widespread worry that after the removal of the Jews, Budapest will perish.[106] [. . .]

The weeks after the halting of the deportation were spent in a tug-of-war between Horthy's circle and the Germans allied with the Ministry of the Interior. The Nazis often flashed a promise: provided that the deportations were resumed, Hitler would not raise any obstacles to the emigration of a few thousand Jews—which the government had decided to permit due to international pressure.

---

102. Switzerland (represented by Vice-Consul **Carl Lutz**) and Turkey (by Envoy Şevket Fuat Keçeci) assisted the planned emigration operations by issuing visas.

103. Chargé d'affaires Ángel Sanz-Briz represented Spain in Budapest.

104. Clifford John Norton and Leland Harrison.

105. Operations of such precision were not possible, given the military technology available at the time.

106. One of the most severe bombings in Budapest occurred on July 2 during the day. This was followed by another round of bombings on the night of July 5.

Although Horthy did not want to fulfill the Germans' conditions, the emigration plan remained on the agenda and became one of the departure points for international rescue operations during the Arrow Cross era.[107]

Without the regent's consent and the effective collaboration of the Hungarian authorities, Eichmann could not continue planning any large-scale operations. He did decide, however, that he would send off at least those Jews imprisoned in the internment camps. On July 14, the SS appeared at the Kistarcsa camp, which was supervised by the Hungarian police, and deported the detainees. Upon learning about the incident, the Jewish Council alerted Horthy's circle, the neutral embassies, and the churches. On Horthy's order the train was turned around and the deportation stopped. Five days later, on July 19, Eichmann tried again. This time he succeeded: the SS stormed the camp and sent 1,220 people to Auschwitz. Document 4-16 describes how István Vasdényei, commander of the Kistarcsa camp, remembered the event.

**DOCUMENT 4-16: Excerpts from the recollection of István Vasdényei, no date (probably early 1960s), HJA XX-G, box D 9/2.[108]**

[. . .] Dr. Pál Ubrizsi appears in the door,[109] behind him my officer-in-chief, and Ubrizsi steps up to me, pulls out a sheet, and tells me: here is my authorization from State Secretary Baky for the transportation of all the camp's inmates. I refused, [telling him that] State Secretary Baky has no authority, since the Regent of Hungary already forbade the deportations, and I was informed so by one of the councillors of the [regent's] office, Radnótfay. I will not hand over the prisoners, and I also object against Ubrizsi's person, since I do not negotiate with a low-ranking officer, and [I'm telling him that] he cannot be the representative of the Ministry of the Interior, since the Ministry does not pick his representative from Rökk

---

107. On the negotiations, the emigration, and the German's strategy, see Braham, *The Politics of Genocide*, 2:874–85 and 1125–33.

108. After the German occupation in 1944, local police superintendant István Vasdényei (also Vasdényey) went to exceptional lengths to release or help Jews held in the Kistarcsa internment camp near Budapest under his command. He sought to inform the local Jewish council of German deportation plans. Yad Vashem recognized him as Righteous Among the Nations in 1969. For a summary of his activities during the war, see Israel Gutman, ed., *The Encyclopedia of the Righteous Among the Nations: Rescuers of Jews during the Holocaust: Europe (Part I) and Other Countries* (Jerusalem: Yad Vashem, 2007), 337–38.

109. Ubrizsi, a police officer and Hungarian commander of the Rökk Szilárd Street internment camp, was allegedly the nephew of László Baky. After the war he emigrated to Switzerland and avoided punishment for his Holocaust-era actions.

Szilárd Street.[110] At that point an old internee, Mr. Mandula, runs in [. . .] and shouts that the German SS are setting up a machine gun. The drama unfolded in a second: three platoons of the *Sonderkommando* attack with two machine guns, each man carrying a submachine gun. They break down the big gate facing toward the capital, and [they storm] the corridors of the commander's office and the courtyard. Resistance is out of the question; I had seven men, the guns were at the outer building, and my officer-in-chief confirmed that we are outnumbered, plus there is a Wehrmacht guard in the camp as well. I told Novak and Ubrizsi that the Regent's order forbade the deportation,[111] and they are responsible for acting against the Regent's will. Novak told me he was aware of that, but he still would carry out the deportation upon Eichmann's order. They stormed one of the buildings; they pulled up into the camp with trucks and started to indiscriminately throw people onto the truck. [. . .] You can't describe the bestial brutality with which they treated eighty-year-old people, people on crutches, and hospital patients who had been operated [on] only a few days prior.

[. . .]

On July 24, using similar methods, the SS deported fifteen hundred Jews from the Sárvár internment camp.[112]

Although Horthy had already initiated the dismissal of Endre and Baky in June and the regent was convinced that the latter was organizing an armed coup against him, the two state secretaries retained their positions. (Granted, on July 20, oversight of Jewish-related affairs was taken away from Endre.) The government meeting of August 2 made it clear that the cabinet still wished to continue the deportations.[113] Andor Jaross proposed the transportation of all Budapest Jews with the exception of Jews who had converted to Christianity. The minister of the interior even considered the technical details.[114] This was

---

110. Vasdényey is referring to the internment camp set up in the building of the Budapest Rabbinical Seminary in Rökk Szilárd Street.

111. Franz Novak (1909–1983) was an SS captain who worked for Eichmann's department of Jewish issues at the RSHA. He was the transportation specialist of the Sondereinsatzkommando Eichmann in Hungary. In this position he arranged the railway capacity for the deportation of Hungarian Jews in 1944. After the war several legal proceedings were initiated against him, and in 1972 he was sentenced to a seven-year prison term.

112. Braham, *The Politics of Genocide*, 2:780.

113. Vági, "Endre László politikai pályája 1919–1945," 440–41.

114. Minutes of the meeting of the Council of Ministers, August 2, 1944, HNA K27 box 262.

too much for Horthy: he dismissed Jaross and appointed State Secretary Miklós Bonczos of the Ministry of Justice as his replacement. On August 8, Baky resigned, and two weeks later Endre was relieved of his post as well. The personnel change did not make a substantive difference to the situation. Sztójay informed Veesenmayer that within a week or two the deportations could resume.[115] At the August 10 government meeting, Deputy Minister of Foreign Affairs Mihály Jungerth-Arnóthy, up until then considered relatively moderate, proposed that in order to satisfy the German demands, "50–60 thousand Jews from Galicia seeping into the country" should be deported.[116] On August 19, Minister of the Interior Bonczos promised Eichmann that the deportations could start on August 25. He also told the SEK commander that all Jews were to be deported except three thousand exempted by the regent and those who had converted to Christianity before August 1, 1941.[117] The government, with Horthy's approval, even drafted an agreement with the Germans regarding the resumption of the deportations.

DOCUMENT 4-17. **Draft of a government decree regarding a German-Hungarian agreement on the deportation of the remaining Jews, August 23, 1944, in Elek Karsai, ed., *Vádirat a nácizmus ellen. Dokumentumok a magyarországi zsidóüldözés történetéhez (1944 június 26–1944 október 15. A budapesti zsidóság deportálásának felfüggesztése)* (Budapest: Magyar Izraeliták Országos Képviselete, 1967), 3:451–52 (translated from German).**

> The Hungarian royal government—after obtaining the approval of His Highness, the Regent—is ready, as of August 28, to put at the disposal of the government of the German Reich
>
> *a)* all Jews drafted for labor service whose families are already in Germany (ca. 55,000–60,000)
>
> *b)* Jews with criminal records or Jews representing a danger to the public (this will be established by the Hungarian government),[118] whose presence endangers public order, the general food supply, and the domestic safety of the country,

---

115. Braham, *The Politics of Genocide*, 2:913.
116. Minutes of the meeting of the Council of Ministers, August 10, 1944, HNA K27, box 262.
117. Horst Grell's telegram to the Reich Ministry of Foreign Affairs, August 19, 1944, in Juhász et al., *A Wilhelmstrasse és Magyarország*, 897.
118. Karsai notes that this phrase originally read, "The Hungarian government will establish whether a previous conviction exists."

to be deployed in the German war industry—beginning August 28, 1944.

[...]

The Jews to be placed at the disposal of the German Reich will be handed over to a Hungarian-German joint commission in collection camps located in Hungary, and their deportation and trip to the Hungarian border will be conducted under the supervision of the same.

[...]

II.

The Jews remaining in Hungary will be placed under protective custody outside Budapest, housed in camps, and utilized in the Hungarian war industry.

III.

The Hungarian government asks [the German government] to be entrusted with the further solution and implementation of the Jewish question in Hungarian lands. The Hungarian government would therefore welcome if

1. in order to sustain friendly Hungarian-German relations, the German secret police operating in Hungary—but especially the unit operating under the leadership of SS-Obersturmbannführer Adolf Eichmann—was ordered to leave Hungary

2. *a)* Jews in German custody in Hungary were handed over to the Hungarian authorities. *b)* the camps and prisons set up by the Germans in Hungary and still operating were disbanded, and *c)* the so-called hostages held in them were also handed over to the Hungarian authorities.[119]

The draft suggested deportation of "dangerous" Jews and also specified that the Hungarian authorities would determine who fell into this category. This simply would have enabled the deportation of all remaining Jews. The document, drafted by the Regent's Cabinet Office and sent to the Ministry of Foreign Affairs, was signed by Gyula Ambrózy, the head of the office, one of Horthy's most important confidants.[120] This clearly indicates that the regent approved the draft agreement.

According to the recollections of Budapest Jewish Council leaders, all this was part of a plan they had allegedly worked out with László Ferenczy, who had switched sides and started to act for the benefit of the Jews. Horthy was also

---

119. Point 2/c refers to those non-Jewish politicians, high-ranking officials, and officers who were arrested in the days following the German occupation.

120. See Benoschofsky and Karsai, *Vádirat a nácizmus ellen*, 3:451–53.

informed of the plot. The extremely risky idea was that the Hungarian authorities would seemingly agree to resume the deportations and order the gendarmerie and some military units to the capital. Because the Germans would think that troops were arriving in the city for the deportations, they would not hinder the gathering. At this point, anti-Nazi officers would replace the commanders of the troops, who would turn their weapons against the Germans.[121] It is altogether unrealistic that Horthy, along with the Jewish Council and the extremely compromised Ferenczy, would prepare an armed resistance. Instead, most likely, he simply crumbled again under German pressure and gave his blessing to the continued deportations. In assessing the role of Horthy in 1944, we should take into account this critical detail. The regent again seemed ready to hand over the remainder of the Jews to the Germans—at a time when, even according to his own account, he knew what was going on in Auschwitz.

Meanwhile, Eichmann's office ordered the council to prepare a list of all leaders, as well as data about all council employees.[122] At the same time, the SS-Business Administration Main Office (WVHA), the SS office supervising the concentration camps, anticipated the arrival of ninety thousand new Jewish forced laborers from Hungary.[123] Eichmann's order was obviously a preliminary step in preparing for the deportations.

Changes in the military situation redrew the picture, however. On August 23, upon seeing the successful advance of the Red Army, Marshal Ion Antonescu was overthrown in Bucharest. Romania switched to the Allied side. Horthy responded in an unusually swift and resolute manner: he asked to see Veesenmayer at noon on August 24 and informed the plenipotentiary that he would not resume the deportations. He promised to remove Jews from the capital and put them into camps outside the city.[124]

At this point, a disappointed and angry Eichmann, claiming that his presence in Budapest had become superfluous, asked that his unit be recalled. Heinrich Himmler notified Higher SS and Police Leader Otto Winkelmann

---

121. Stern, *Emlékirataim. Versenyfutás az idővel!*, 334–35; Braham, *The Politics of Genocide*, 2:906–10.

122. Munkácsi, *Hogyan történt*, 219.

123. See SS-Sturmbannführer Burger's report in the WVHA to Gruppenführer Lörner, August 15, 1944, in Office of United States Chief of Counsel for Prosecution of Axis Criminality, ed., *Nazi Conspiracy and Aggression* (Washington, DC: U.S. Government Printing Office, 1946), 3:824–27.

124. Veesenmayer's telegram to the Reich Ministry of Foreign Affairs, August 24, 1944 (no. 2358), in Juhász et al., *A Wilhelmstrasse és Magyarország*, 900.

by telegram that, for the time being, the deportations were off.[125] Yet again, it became clear that the "Final Solution," though important to the Germans, was by no means their first priority. In the catastrophic military situation, Berlin did not want to risk losing Hungary's loyalty.

With the Germans growing uncertain, Horthy gained more room to maneuver. The regent dismissed the Sztójay government and, on August 29, appointed a (partially) new cabinet, to be headed by General **Géza Lakatos**, whom he asked to make preparations for Hungary's exit from the war. This brought a change in Jewish policies as well. With the German pressure eased and the most rabid pro-Nazi forces losing ground, the Hungarian authorities took the deportation of the remaining Jews off the agenda. Thus Jews in the capital were no longer in immediate danger. Many prisoners were released from the Kistarcsa internment camps, and the detention sites on Csepel Island were shut down.[126] In an important symbolic gesture during the Jewish High Holidays in the fall, Minister of the Interior Miklós Bonczos allowed the Budapest Jews crammed into the "yellow-star houses" some free movement.[127] But on October 15, this state of relative calm dissipated again.

---

125. Veesenmayer's telegrams to the Reich Ministry of Foreign Affairs, August 24, 1944 (no. 2366), and August 25, 1944 (n. 2379), in Braham, *The Destruction of Hungarian Jewry*, 2:480–81.

126. Jenő Lévai, *Zsidósors Magyarországon*, 2nd ed. (Budapest: Magyar Téka, 1948), 284; Frigyes Brámer, "Zsidó túszok—Kistarcsa 1944 'B' Pavilon," in *Évkönyv, 1973/1974*, ed. Sándor Scheiber (Budapest: Magyar Izraeliták Országos Képviselete, 1974), 350–51; János Fóthy, *Horthyliget: a magyar Ördögsziget* (Budapest: K. Müller, 1945), 87–89.

127. *Magyarországi Zsidók Lapja*, September 14, 1944, 3.

## CHAPTER 5
# The Arrow Cross Regime

PRIOR TO the German occupation in March 1944, Regent **Miklós Horthy** had already sought ways for Hungary to pull out of its alliance with the Germans. This became a major trigger for the occupation. Increasingly frequent meetings between unofficial Hungarian delegates and the western Allies took place during 1943, held in neutral countries such as Switzerland, Sweden, and Turkey. The outlines of a possible agreement had begun to emerge. Horthy and Prime Minister **Miklós Kállay** believed that a separate peace agreement with the British and Americans could protect Hungary from both Hitler and Stalin. Although the regent secretly agreed to the Allies' cease-fire conditions in October 1943, this gesture had only theoretical significance: the German occupation in March 1944 and the rapid Soviet advance made implementing the agreement impossible.

In September 1944 the advancing Red Army crossed the Hungarian border. Now Horthy and a small circle of his followers tried to break the Hungarian-German alliance and exit the war. Since the Soviet troops were already in the country, Horthy had to drop the plan of surrendering to the western Allies, and his delegate signed a clandestine cease-fire in Moscow on October 11. Four days later, on October 15, the regent tried to turn against Berlin openly, but the Germans, well informed of his plans, thwarted the attempt. They forced Horthy to resign and transfer power to **Arrow Cross Party** leader **Ferenc Szálasi**, who held out on Hitler's side until the very end. This chapter centers on the fate of Jews during the Arrow Cross regime in Hungary. Chapter 7 covers the story of those deported to the Nazi concentration camp system in the spring and summer of 1944.

## THE TAKEOVER

Horthy's unsuccessful attempt to exit the war took place on October 15, 1944. He had planned to announce his decision at the Crown Council meeting in the morning,[1] informing the nation in a radio broadcast. The proclamation was first read out over the Hungarian radio at 12:30 p.m.

DOCUMENT 5-1: **Hungarian News Agency broadcast of Miklós Horthy's proclamation on the cease-fire, October 15, 1944, in Magda Ádám et al., eds.,** *Magyarország és a második világháború. Titkos diplomáciai okmányok a háború előzményeihez és történetéhez,* **2nd ed. (Budapest: Kossuth, 1959), 479–80.**

> On this day, His Serene Highness the Regent addressed the following speech to the Hungarian nation:
> [. . .]
> Today, every sober-minded individual will recognize beyond a doubt that the German Empire [Reich] has lost this war. Governments that are responsible for their countries must draw the consequences, for as the great German statesman Bismarck once said: a nation cannot sacrifice itself on the altar of loyalty to an alliance.[2] In full awareness of my historic responsibility, I must take every step to avoid further unnecessary bloodshed. A nation that would, with a servile attitude and in order to protect foreign interests, turn its soil—which it had inherited from its fathers—into the site of rearguard battles, would lose the world's respect.
> It is with sadness that I must note that the German Empire, for its part, long ago reneged on its loyalty as an ally to us. For an extended period now, despite my wishes and will, the German Empire has been sending portions of the Hungarian military into battle further and further outside the borders of the country. [. . .][3]
> Simultaneously, the German political police also entered the country and arrested numerous Hungarian citizens, among them, several members of the legislative body and the minister of the interior of my government at the time; and the only way that the prime minister could avoid arrest

---

1. That is, the meeting of the Council of Ministers and the regent.
2. Otto von Bismarck (1815–1898), the German statesman, was first chancellor of Germany after its unification in 1871.
3. In fact, Hungarian military units were always deployed with Horthy's consent.

was by fleeing to a neutral embassy.[4] I appointed the Sztójay government upon receiving the firm promise by the leader of the German Empire that he would stop the incursions against and restrictions on Hungarian sovereignty, provided that I appoint a government trusted by the Germans.[5] But the Germans did not keep their promise. Under the protection of the German occupation, the Gestapo employed the methods that it had followed elsewhere and began dealing with the Jewish question in the familiar way, one that goes against what humane behavior demands.[6] As the war approached the borders of the country and even made its way into the country, the Germans again promised appropriate help. However, they did not keep this promise either, in the way and to the extent they committed. As they were retreating, they turned the country into sites of looting and destruction.[7] [. . .]

I have therefore informed the local representative of the German Empire that we are signing a preliminary ceasefire with those who have been our enemies until now,[8] and I am stopping all hostile action toward them.[9]

[. . .]

I have duly instructed the leadership of the Hungarian military. The troops must, in accordance with their oaths and the general order that I simultaneously issued, obey the commanders appointed by me.

I call upon every Hungarian with a sense of honor to follow me on the sacrifice-filled road to salvaging the Hungarian people.

Horthy.

---

4. In the hours following the occupation in March 1944, the Gestapo arrested Minister of the Interior Ferenc Keresztes-Fischer, as well as numerous other prominent politicians and senior officials. Prime Minister Miklós Kállay sought shelter at the Turkish embassy. After he voluntarily left his asylum in October, he was arrested and deported to the Mauthausen concentration camp and later to Dachau.

5. The Germans did actually promise Horthy that once the "Jewish question" was solved in Hungary, they would return sovereignty to the country.

6. The ghettoization and deportation was carried out not by the Gestapo but by the Hungarian government's very own administrative and law enforcement agencies.

7. The Germans followed a scorched-earth policy: they endeavored to blow up every bridge and any industrial facilities and machinery that they could not take with them.

8. **Edmund Veesenmayer.**

9. The wording of this sentence was crucial: the Hungarian verb tense used here could be present and future as well. Neither was actually accurate, since the cease-fire agreement had been already signed. However, avoiding mention of this, the proclamation did not call for an immediate cease-fire.

However, the coup was weakly prepared and even more weakly implemented. The German secret service thwarted Horthy's plan. SD agents kidnapped his only son, Miklós Junior, a leader of the preparations to leave the war, and took him to Germany.[10] Other members of the conspiracy failed to act in unison. Pro-Nazi elements within the Hungarian officer corps quickly took control of key army units. Horthy's general order to the troops did not contain specific instructions for ceasing engagement with Soviet troops or turning against the Wehrmacht.[11] The pro-German majority of the general staff adhered to the standpoint that the anti-Russian fighting should continue and passed orders to this effect on to their troops.[12] Many officers sided with the Arrow Cross. By nightfall, the Nazis were in full control. Hungarian radio aired Arrow Cross leader Szálasi's general order to fight on the side of Germany until the very end.[13]

## THE ARROW CROSS MOVEMENT: ITS LEADER AND IDEOLOGY

Founded by Ferenc Szálasi, a former officer in the Army General Staff, the Arrow Cross Party–Hungarist Movement gained considerable popularity in the second half of the 1930s.[14] The party constituted the right-wing extremist, militant opposition to the Horthy regime. Because of this, authorities imprisoned Szálasi in 1938–1940 and disbanded his party (then called the National Socialist Hungarian Party–Hungarist Movement). These steps had the opposite effect to that intended. Szálasi was elevated to the status of a martyr, and his newly formed party became increasingly popular. In the 1939 elections, the Arrow Cross Party collected 21.6 percent of the list-based votes, gaining twenty-nine

---

10. For details about the events of October 15, see, e.g., Károly Vigh, *Ugrás a sötétbe* (Budapest: Akadémiai, 1979), 123–36.
11. Miklós Horthy's general order, October 15, 1944, in Magda Ádám et al., eds., *Magyarország és a második világháború. Titkos diplomáciai okmányok a háború előzményeihez és történetéhez* (Budapest: Kossuth, 1959), 485–86.
12. Randolph L. Braham, *The Politics of Genocide: The Holocaust in Hungary* (New York: Columbia University Press, 1994), 2:947–52.
13. Szálasi's proclamation was first broadcast on the radio at 6:25 p.m. See Vigh, *Ugrás a sötétbe*, 147.
14. The party, which on several occasions fell into pieces or absorbed other groups, existed under several names between 1935 and 1944.

seats in parliament.¹⁵ The party probably enjoyed even greater support than this, but the government successfully prevented many Arrow Cross candidates from running in the election by imposing an enormous financial requirement. In some places, the regime even used law enforcement personnel against them.

Szálasi's ideology, Hungarism,¹⁶ was greatly influenced by Nazism. Still, it was—in historian István Deák's words—a genuinely domestic product. Szálasi envisioned the restructuring of society based on a unified national socialist ideology, with a single-party leadership. Although he rejected Marxism, his economic ideals—radical anticapitalism and a centrally steered, partially nationalized, plan-based state and economy—have been likened to bolshevism (and, indeed, nazism).¹⁷ His anticlericalism neatly coexisted with strong Christian messianism. A fanatical Jew hater, Szálasi saw the Jews lurking behind every phenomenon he deemed pernicious.

Szálasi kept written records of his activities and ideas throughout his career. Of these, two documents have come to light only recently: the *Hungarista Napló* (Hungarist Journal) containing documents from the Arrow Cross (Hungarist) movement, and his journal, written during his years in prison (1938–1940 and 1945–1946).¹⁸ Szálasi apparently also kept a private diary between 1940 and 1945. A fragment of this, the so-called Notebook C, was uncovered in late 2008 in the uncatalogued section of the Hungarian Jewish Archives.¹⁹ It contains Szálasi's handwritten notes from the critical period between September 1943 and July 1944. The whereabouts of Notebooks A and B remained unknown until early 2012, when they appeared in Israel. The journal entry included here is from December 1943 (Notebook C) and suggests the flavor of Szálasi's bombastic and confused rhetoric.

---

15. György Földes and László Hubai, eds., *Parlamenti választások Magyarországon 1920–1998* (Budapest: Napvilág, 1999), 199. In the 1939 elections in most electoral districts, citizens could cast their votes for both party lists and individual candidates.

16. The expression was first used by Catholic bishop Ottokár Prohászka (1858–1927), leading advocate of the ideology of conservative antisemitism at the end of the nineteenth century.

17. Miklós Lackó, *Nyilasok, nemzetiszocialisták, 1935–1944* (Budapest: Kossuth, 1962), 46–52.

18. Elek Karsai, "*Szálasi naplója.*" *A nyilasmozgalom a II. világháború idején* (Budapest: Kossuth, 1978); Péter Sipos, ed., *Szálasi Ferenc börtönnaplója, 1938–1940* (Budapest: BFL-Filum, 2007); Elek Karsai and László Karsai, eds., *A Szálasi per* (Budapest: Reform, 1988).

19. Head archivist of the Hungarian Jewish Archives, Zsuzsanna Toronyi, found "Notebook C." László Karsai published it as "Reflektor a sötétbe. Szálasi Ferenc naplója, 1943 szeptember 15–1944 július 18—I. rész," *Beszélő* 9, no. 3 (2009), 54–76.

DOCUMENT 5-2: **Ferenc Szálasi's diary (Notebook C, entry no. 915), USHMMA RG 39.013M, reel 69 (HJA XIX-Benoschofsky, box A 6/2).**

[. . .]
    915. Under liberalism, the peasant, the worker, and the intellectual—who were no longer that, but were instead wage slaves—would, when commanded, kill emperor, king, their own children, parents, themselves, and all this for a wage: for a starvation wage and blood wage. The only way they could secure their daily bread was through everyday moral, intellectual, and material blood sacrifices. They would do anything that was demanded of them by leaders who had become vile, worthless rascals due to the Jewish poison, and who had settled into the swamp of their filthy love of convenience. And when the Jews demanded or forcibly took from this stratum of leaders and leaders like them, without further ado, their power and rule, the change of owners was tolerated; because the peasant, the worker, and the intellectual—the trinity of the clod of earth,[20] the work, and the blood, lying on the sacred and disgraced soil of the Motherland—were unconscious, helpless, stripped of all means of power. It was the struggle of the national socialist worldview—which culminated in Hungarism—that brought back to life these three: the peasant, the worker, and the intellectual, and sent to death all that had until then been a destructive, annihilating force. Hungarism accorded a sense of self-respect to these three, so they could appreciate their lives, and squeeze out of it all the prosperity and life-security that their nationalist and socialist community means and provides. Seeing clearly, judging correctly, and acting swiftly: this is the vital basis for all Hungarist prosperity and life-security.
    [. . .]

The radical draft bills concocted by the Arrow Cross authorities in the spring of 1945 yield insight into how Szálasi's Hungary would have looked if Hitler had won the war. Gay people would have been sterilized, and marriage between a "barren" and a fertile person would have been banned. Furthermore, marriage would have become obligatory for fertile, adult single men and women, with severe penalties for those who did not comply.[21]

---

    20. "Clod of earth" (*rög*) was a central expression in Szálasi's racial philosophy representing the ancient, agrarian Hungarian "values" and also appearing in fabricated terms like the "reality of the clod of earth" (*rögvalóság*), and so forth.
    21. Krisztián Ungváry, "Kik azok a nyilasok?" *Beszélő* 8, no. 6 (2003), 65.

## DEPORTATIONS RESUMED: THE DEATH MARCHES

Following the Arrow Cross takeover on October 15, chaos reigned in the streets of Budapest. Quickly armed Arrow Cross units herded Jewish labor servicemen onto Danube bridges and shot them so they fell into the river. In Népszínház Street and on Teleki Square, a few Jews managed to obtain weapons, adding sporadic resistance to the mix. With help from the Germans, the Arrow Cross militiamen put down the revolt swiftly and retaliated by killing Jews in the neighborhood. The Arrow Cross units often consisted of youth aged fifteen or sixteen. The killing began in the provinces as well. During the first few days, unbridled terror raged. Afterward, the Arrow Cross leaders themselves tried to put an end to the mayhem. Outright looting and killing in the streets of the capital served neither their nor the Germans' interests. Arrow Cross minister of the interior **Gábor Vajna** issued an announcement calling on everyone to refrain from acting against the Jews arbitrarily. He stated that the government would take care of "solving the Jewish question." The perpetrators of the murders were exempted from all criminal prosecution.[22]

The terror unleashed was not the only blow against the Jews. Deportations resumed as well. At dawn on October 20 Arrow Cross militiamen began rounding up Budapest Jews capable of working from the "**yellow-star houses.**" The following day, the new minister of defense, General **Károly Beregfy**, ordered every Jewish man aged sixteen to sixty and every Jewish woman aged sixteen to forty to fulfill a military labor service requirement.[23]

DOCUMENT 5-3: **Decree of Minister of Defense Károly Beregfy on the forced labor of Jewish men and women, October 21, 1944, USHMMA RG 39.013M, reel 25 (HJA XX-F-1, box D 6/1).**

ANNOUNCEMENT

Based on my right established in Article 124 of Act II of 1939,[24] I will utilize Jewish men between the ages of 16 and 60, and Jewish women between the ages of 16 and 40, for the purpose of the national defense labor service.[25]

---

22. Braham, *The Politics of Genocide*, 2:952–56.
23. Decree by Beregfy, October 21, 1944, in Elek Karsai, ed., *"Fegyvertelen álltak az aknamezőkön . . . " Dokumentumok a munkaszolgálat történetéhez Magyarországon* (Budapest: Magyar Izraeliták Országos Képviselete, 1962), 2:643–44.
24. This article stipulated that the minister of defense had the authority to order Jewish men and women to perform labor services.
25. On the labor service, see chapter 2.

I summon Jewish men born between 1884 and 1928, and Jewish women born between 1904 and 1928, to report for their labor service at 8 a.m. on October 23, 1944—the men should appear at the new horserace track on Kerepesi Road and the women at the KISOK sports field on Erzsébet királyné Road.[26]

Those Jews required to report include all those who are exempted, are living in a mixed marriage, or are members of a Christian denomination. Exceptions are: wives, children, and parents of those who are performing actual military service; those who belong to the retired personnel of the Hungarian Royal Army, their wives, children, and parents; Jewish persons who have been working in the armaments industry under a special arrangement, their wives, children, and parents; as well as Jews who are foreign citizens. Only those Jews may be considered foreign citizens who possess a valid passport.[27]

All Jewish men and women required to report must bring warm clothes, sturdy shoes, a blanket, a metal cup, utensils, cooking pots suitable for communal cooking, personal hygiene articles, a backpack, and enough food for three days.

The building commanders and building supervisors are in charge of ordering Jews in their buildings to report for labor service. In cases where Jews required to report fail to do so or return to their residence, the building commanders and supervisors are required—under penalty of arrest—to report them to the nearest police station.

Jews who are required to report and fail to obey the summons will be subject to the harshest form of punishment.

Budapest, October 21, 1944

*Károly Beregfy*
Minister of Defense

The punishment for negligent non-Jews or those caught intentionally assisting Jewish fugitives was immediate execution without trial.[28]

---

26. The track was in Municipal District VIII; the sports field belonged to the National Center for Secondary School Sports Clubs (KISOK), Municipal District XIV, Budapest.

27. This point clarified that Jews holding various **protective documents** other than actual passports were not exempt from the **labor service** obligations. However, neutral legations later freed many Jews holding not passports but other types of protective papers.

28. Éva Teleki, *Nyilas uralom Magyarországon* (Budapest: Kossuth, 1974), 146–47, and see, e.g., the murder of Sára Salkaházi (document 9-13). For other instances of the execution of non-Jews for aiding Jews, see Szabolcs Szita, "Az 1944–1945 évi polgári, diplomáciai és katonai embermentés történetéhez," in *Magyarország 1944. Üldöztetés-embermentés*, ed. Szabolcs Szita (Budapest: Nemzeti Tankönyvkiadó, 1994), 2:68.

Over the next few days, twenty-five thousand men and ten thousand women were taken away. People rounded up through raids and call-ups were initially ordered to dig antitank ditches around Budapest. Then, beginning on November 6, 1944, the deportations commenced. Most Jews were sent off toward the western border on foot. The major collection site for the deportees was a brick factory in Municipal District III (Óbuda). The Arrow Cross guards regularly beat and robbed these men and women, several of whom committed suicide.[29] Put in groups of two to four thousand people, the survivors were forced to march, carrying all their belongings, some twenty miles per day on the main road connecting Budapest to Vienna. They received hardly any food or water on the journey. They spent nights in barns or out in the open. The beatings and lootings continued. Those who tried to flee or grew weak and fell behind were mercilessly shot.[30]

Besides the Jews rounded up in Budapest, the government "relinquished" seventy **Labor Service** companies (approximately fourteen to fifteen thousand people) to the Nazis.[31] At the German (that is, the former Hungarian-Austrian) border, the Hungarian authorities handed people over to German agencies (the SS, SA, and Organisation Todt). In several places Arrow Cross men assisted in guarding them. The deportees were forced to do construction work without adequate accommodations, clothing, or food. With disease and physical abuse rampant, the death rate soared. Near the front lines, German and Hungarian units murdered on-site several thousand people who could no longer keep up with the work.[32] In the early spring of 1945, the Nazis sent the rest on death marches across the Alps to various concentration camps, predominantly to Mauthausen and from there to Gunskirchen.[33] U.S. troops liberated survivors there in early May 1945.

In November to December 1944, the Arrow Cross government herded a total of fifty thousand people to the western border or to the Reich by foot or by train. Diplomats of neutral countries (primarily Switzerland, Sweden, and the Vatican) did all they could to save the deportees. They followed the rows of marching men and women, bringing real or false protection documents with them (some filled out for a specific individual, some still blank). Using a range

---

29. See, e.g., HJA, DEGOB protocols, nos. 136, 1649, 1954.
30. See, e.g., HJA, DEGOB protocols, nos. 167, 194, 730, 1308, 1638, 1765, 2629.
31. Minister of Defense's Decree no. 975, M 42/1944, October 26, 1944, in Karsai, *"Fegyvertelen álltak az aknamezőkön,"* 2:653–57.
32. This occurred, for example, in Kőszeg, where they even tried to set up a gas chamber in the interest of killing more efficiently. HJA, DEGOB Protocols, nos. 1768, 1895.
33. Szabolcs Szita, *Haláleröd. A munkaszolgálat és a hadimunka történetéhez, 1944–1945* (Budapest: Kossuth, 1989), 59–89. See map 4, p. lxiv.

of pretexts, they tried to pull as many people as possible out of the ranks. The diplomats also protested to Szálasi, objecting to the inhumane conditions.

DOCUMENT 5-4: **A report by two representatives of the Swiss embassy on the death marches, November 28, 1944, in Randolph L. Braham,** *The Politics of Genocide: The Holocaust in Hungary* **(New York: Columbia University Press, 1994), 2:967–69.**

> The first groups traveled along the main transport routes [highways], but the later ones used side roads [alternate routes]; they usually covered the 200–220 kilometers [125 to 138 miles] to Hegyeshalom[34] in 7 to 8 days. Those who became sick on the way were often shot dead by the escort personnel, or they were left behind in abandoned agricultural sheds where they stayed without medical help; only in rare cases were arrangements made for feeding them, and even then they got at most a portion of watery soup every day. The start-off of the marching groups was always staged in such a way that they would arrive at Hegyeshalom between 11 A.M. and 12:00 noon. We emphasize that the groups of people marching on foot received at most 3 to 4 portions of soup throughout the entire duration of the foot march, but usually went several days without receiving any food at all.
> [. . .]
> At Hegyeshalom we found the deportees in the worst imaginable condition. The endless labor of the foot march, the almost total lack of food, made worse by the torturing steady fear that they were being taken to the extermination chambers in Germany, have brought these pitiful deportees to such a state that all human appearances and all human dignity have completely left them. Their condition cannot be compared with that of any others who were brought down by physical privations and suffering. The denial of the most elementary human rights, the fact that they were usually totally at the mercy of the brutally behaving escorts, who in practice could do whatever they wanted with them—from spitting in their face through slapping and beating to shooting—left the mark of these horrors on the unfortunate victims. Human dignity can be preserved even among the poverty-stricken and the suffering, as long as there are legal rights; but this dignity is lost when one is totally deprived of one's rights and at the mercy of someone else. We emphasize this because one can feel the beginning of an aversion to the unhappy victims under these

---

34. A town on the Hungarian-German (formerly Austrian) border.

circumstances, even among otherwise well-inclined persons. All social conventions, results of civilization and progress, cease completely among these people. The people—women as well as men—satisfy their bodily needs in front of each other and of strangers, feelings of shame having totally left them. The feeling of the deportees in Hegyeshalom was more satisfactory. They were fed twice daily, and as a result of our visit and our intervention the situation has apparently improved even more. Their accommodations, however, were very poor even in Hegyeshalom, since even there the people were put up in sheds on straw bedding. But the straw was already so worn from several preceding transports that it was filthy and unquestionably infected.

## SZÁLASI'S FINAL PLAN AND THE BUDAPEST GHETTOS

The protests of neutral powers had a far-reaching effect. Longing more than anything for international recognition of his reign, Szálasi was ready to respect the wishes of the diplomatic corps to a certain extent.[35] Their protests thus played a major role in persuading him to stop the marches gradually two to three weeks after their launch.[36] In mid-November, he also attempted to develop a framework for a more moderate Jewish policy based on differentiated categories of Hungarian Jewry.[37] On November 17, 1944, he introduced general rules regulating the situation of the country's Jews. The memorandum, intended as a final decision on the matter, actually attempted to legitimate operations already underway and decisions his government had already made.[38] It set up a total of eleven categories of Hungarian Jews, which were then classified into six larger groups based on their planned fates and assigned residences. The plan based on special categories disappointed the hard-line Nazis: **Adolf Eichmann** called for deporting all Jews as soon as possible.

According to Szálasi's plans, Jews belonging to categories 1, 5, and 6 would be forced to leave the country by a specified deadline, although, given

---

35. On the intervention of the neutral states, see chapter 9.
36. Teleki, *Nyilas uralom Magyarországon*, 146–50; Braham, *The Politics of Genocide*, 2:963–69.
37. The papal nuncio and the Budapest delegates of the neutral states firmly protested as soon as the first anti-Jewish operations transpired. Then, on November 17 (for the second time since August), they wrote a joint letter in a harsh tone, protesting the resumption of the deportations. Braham, *The Politics of Genocide*, 2:1222–23.
38. For details on Szálasi's Jewish policies, see the Introduction.

the foreign political and military conditions at the time, this was completely unrealistic. The plan was to send those in category 2 to Germany. Members of category 3 would be put in ghettos until their departure, and those of the Christian faith would be placed in separate buildings. Jews in category 4 were exempt from ghettoization but were still not considered equal citizens with the same rights as non-Jewish Hungarians.

DOCUMENT 5-5: **Szálasi's "final plan" concerning the Jews, November 17, 1944, in NARA, T-120, reel 4664 (translated from German).**[39]

Memorandum
Regarding the Leader of the Nation's resolutions on November 17, 1944, concerning the final regulation of the Jewish question in Hungary.
The Hungarian Jews are to be categorized into the following 6 groups:
1./ Jews in possession of foreign protective passports[40]
These Jews must be collected at the latest by 4 p.m. on November 20, 1944, in the buildings designated by the Hungarian Royal Ministry of the Interior, the so-called Palatinus-Houses.[41] [. . .] The departure of these Jews depends, on the one hand, on developments in the diplomatic relations between the Hungarian government and the government of the states concerned and, on the other hand, on the transport method agreement between the government concerned and the German government. [. . .]
2./ Jews loaned to the German government who are able to work, the German government intends to employ them in the interest of the joint warfare. These Jews will perform labor service to benefit the Hungarian nation. They will be handed over individually (with their names marked) to the German government; the Hungarian Royal Minister of the Interior will send a delegation,[42] a permanent committee, to Germany for them; one member of this committee is the joint delegate to the International Red Cross and the embassies and consulates concerned. The task of this

---

39. Theodor Horst Grell, an official from Veesenmayer's staff, sent the document from Budapest to Berlin. The Hungarian original and its German translation differed in certain points from the Hungarian text that the Arrow Cross authorities handed over to the **Jewish Council**.

40. That is, Jews possessing protective documents (not just passports) issued by foreign diplomats.

41. The southwestern blocks of Újlipótváros (in 1944–1945 part of Municipal District V, but today District XIII), on the Pest side of Margit Bridge.

42. Gábor Vajna; see the glossary.

committee is to keep a registry of Hungarian Jews performing labor service in Germany after October 16, 1944, and to maintain contact between the German and Hungarian governments for this purpose.[43]

These Jews are subject to a labor requirement that is intended to benefit the Hungarian nation. The Hungarian state, in agreement with the German government, permits them to fulfill their labor service requirement abroad. In the case of Jews who are performing labor service abroad, the Hungarian state will make a decision during the general resolution of the European Jewish question, in accordance with European considerations. Until then, how they are treated will depend on their behavior.

3./ <u>Jews who remain in Hungary will have to be concentrated in ghettos</u>, on the recommendation of the Minister of the Interior. [. . .]

a./ Jews on loan /see 2/./, whose transportation for labor service could not yet take place for some reason;

b./ Children, the elderly, and anyone who for some reason is unfit for transportation, or is unable to walk /pregnant women, those who are ill, etc./.

c./ Those Jewish children who are staying in children's homes under the protection of the International Red Cross, as well as the personnel supervising them.

d./ Jews of the Christian faith, for whom separate buildings must be assigned within the ghetto, to be marked with a cross; Christian Jews wear a patch instead of the Jewish star and have their own council.[44]

[. . .]

The ghetto has four gates facing the four directions of the compass.

There is only one circumstance under which Jews may leave the ghetto, specifically, when Jews on loan who are subject to labor service requirement are being deported.

4./ <u>Jews who possess an exemption document:</u>

[. . .]

These Jews are exempted from regulations concerning racial policies and property laws, as well as other "Jewish Laws," decrees, and resolutions.

---

43. It is not clear whether Szálasi wanted to track what was happening with the Hungarian Jews after they were handed over to the Germans or this point was included exclusively to please the neutral diplomatic corps. Szálasi was actually less enthusiastic about the deportations than **Sztójay**. Still, the Arrow Cross government did not track those tens of thousands eventually deported in November and December.

44. This patch was evidently never introduced. Officially the Christian Jewish Council set up in July did not cease to exist. See chapter 8.

They may not participate in the political, economic, and social life of the country.[45]

5./ Church officials, priests, and nuns enjoy complete exemption, but based on an agreement between the Minister of Foreign Affairs,[46] the Minister of Culture,[47] and the church authorities concerned, they must be segregated within monastic quarters and transferred and admitted abroad within a limited period of time.

6./ Jews of foreign citizenship and Hungarian Jews who have been entered into the register of the National Central Authority for Controlling Foreigners (KEOKH)[48] by 2 p.m. on November 17, 1944, are required to leave the country by December 1, 1944.

Despite Nazi protests, the Arrow Cross gradually did stop the death marches by late November and, in accordance with Szálasi's plan, began organizing the ghettos in Budapest.

Two ghettos were created for the Jews remaining in the capital. Those under the protection of neutral states (Sweden, Switzerland, the Vatican, Spain, and Portugal) or the International Red Cross were placed into the so-called international ("small" or "protected") ghetto created between November 12 and 20 in buildings under the neutral embassies' protection.[49] This was not a fixed, fenced-off area like the large ghetto. On paper, it housed 15,600 protected individuals, but the diplomatic missions had in fact issued protection letters to many more. Many forged protection documents were in circulation as well, and those holding them also had to be admitted into the international ghetto. Beyond this, many people moved in without any papers at all.[50] According

---

45. The range of exempted individuals was originally specified in Prime Ministerial Decree no. 1730/1944. See *Budapesti Közlöny*, May 13, 1944, 1–2. By July 31 the Ministry of the Interior had accepted only 550 applications for exempted status. In June Horthy had expressed his wish to grant exemptions himself. Still, not until August was a decree issued entrusting the regent to give special exemptions to Jews with extraordinary merits in the arts, science, or economy. See Prime Ministerial Decree no. 2040/1944, *Budapesti Közlöny*, August 22, 1944, 1. Szálasi's rules previously established for exemptions were made stricter, and the eight thousand or so exemption certificates issued up to then were revised. At first, Szálasi reduced this number to one-tenth the original, but eventually he agreed to exempt a total of only seventy individuals. Teleki, *Nyilas uralom Magyarországon*, 143. For details on the system of exemptions and its modification over time, see Braham, *The Politics of Genocide*, 2:900–906.

46. Baron Gábor Kemény.
47. Ferenc Rajniss.
48. On KEOKH, see chapter 2.
49. On the protection by the neutral delegations, see chapter 9.
50. Jenő Lévai, *Zsidósors Magyarországon*, 2nd ed. (Budapest: Magyar Téka, 1948), 323–24.

to Swedish diplomat **Raoul Wallenberg**'s report, thirty-five thousand people were living in the "protected" ghetto by mid-December.[51] After Szálasi's government realized that international recognition was beyond reach, it ordered the international ghetto dissolved in early January. Wallenberg intervened to halt its closure. However, at the same time representatives of the neutral states were themselves organizing the transfer of the small ghetto's occupants into the larger one, hoping this would ease provisioning and protecting them.[52]

In mid-November, the Arrow Cross Ministry of the Interior had simultaneously begun concentrating the other Jews scattered across Budapest, residents of "yellow-star houses," into the single, closed "large ghetto." The initial plan had been to select a location outside the city.[53] Eventually, however, the ministry designated a site in Municipal District VII, the area most densely populated by Jews. Setting the ghetto up there would involve relocating the fewest people: more than half of its buildings were already "yellow-star houses."[54] The government tried to find apartments as quickly as possible for evicted Christians. Unlike in the summer of 1944, when the "yellow-star houses" were initially set up, tenants could no longer influence decisions about their buildings' classification. Every Christian had to move out when ordered or face arrest.[55]

Authorities published the decree ordering the Jewish population to move into the ghetto on December 2. The ghetto was sealed on December 10.[56] By January 8, 1945, its population had risen to close to seventy thousand.[57] At the ghetto population's peak, an average of five people lived in one room, including front rooms, kitchens, and smaller rooms.[58] A new decree published on December 23 ordered Jews living in hiding to move into the ghetto within

---

51. See document 9-16.

52. Braham, *The Politics of Genocide*, 2:975–76.

53. Veesenmayer's telegram to the Ministry of Foreign Affairs, October 26, 1944, in Randolph L. Braham, ed., *The Destruction of Hungarian Jewry: A Documentary Account* (New York: Pro Arte for the World Federation of Hungarian Jews, 1963), 2:519.

54. Tim Cole, *Holocaust City: The Making of a Jewish Ghetto* (New York: Routledge, 2003), 210–12.

55. Ibid., 214–15.

56. Minister of the Interior's Decree no. 8935/1944, November 29, 1944, in Braham, *The Politics of Genocide*, 2:977–79.

57. According to the report of the ghetto administration, on that day 62,949 adults and 6,759 children lived in the ghetto. Muster roll of the ghetto, January 8, 1945, HMC Gy-13, box 13, 2011.398.

58. According to the Jewish Council's documentation, the ghetto included 243 apartment buildings that had 4,513 apartments with 18,970 rooms. Reports on the buildings, apartments, and rooms in the large ghetto, December 28, 1944, HMC Gy-13, box 13. If we do not count those rooms that were not suitable for accommodation due to their size or function (pantries, toilets, and bathrooms), then some 13,868 rooms were probably continuously inhabited.

twenty-four hours or risk particularly harsh penalties. Many had already done so, irrespective of the decree: their reserves had run out, or they felt safer in the ghetto than in the outside world.

The Arrow Cross militia and the police placed the closed-off area under tight control. The Jewish Council handled most affairs inside the fence, including organization of food supplies and other public services. The Jewish ghetto police maintained public order.[59] Because of the growing population, shrinking rations, and difficulties in obtaining supplies, a problem that had become chronic during the Soviet army's siege of Budapest over the winter, the ghetto faced severe shortages of food, water, and fuel.[60] The International Red Cross, Jewish welfare institutions, and young Zionist resistance fighters attempted to bring relief.[61] Hygiene provisions sank to a dangerously low level. In the ghetto's makeshift health-care facilities, shortages of medicine, beds, and equipment were ubiquitous. Because of these conditions, Arrow Cross atrocities, and suicides of residents, the daily death rate in the ghetto reached ten times the average in times of peace.[62]

The report in document 5-6 records an example of the Arrow Cross terror in the ghetto. The author is **Béla Berend**, former chief rabbi of Szigetvár, a small town in southern Hungary. He became a member of the Budapest Jewish Council in May 1944. His role and activities prompted heated debates after the war.[63] Berend had a tense relationship with traditional Jewish community leaders because of his Zionist views and his criticism of the Jewish elite, stating that they had greatly distanced themselves from the masses. In 1944 Berend fostered relations with the leaders of the Hungarian Ministry of the Interior and the chief advocate of race-protectionist ideology, **Zoltán Bosnyák**. In his own words, he was experimenting with the "Zionization of antisemitism." He considered the "Jewish question" a worldwide problem that only the emigration of all Jews to a new motherland could solve. In accomplishing this agenda he

---

59. In the first days of January, the ghetto police force was approximately seven hundred strong. See supply account of the ghetto police, January 8, 1945. See also the name list of the ghetto police in HMC Gy-13, box 13, 2011.398.

60. On day-to-day life in the ghetto, see the administrative and other documents of the Jewish Council, HJA XX-A, boxes D 10/1, D 9/1, and D 9/3.

61. Braham, *The Politics of Genocide*, 2:985–90. For details on the young Zionists, see chapter 8.

62. Jenő Lévai, *Fekete könyv a magyar zsidóság szenvedéseiről* (Budapest: Officina, 1946), 262.

63. For details, see Braham, *The Politics of Genocide*, 1:486–89.

considered the rabid antisemites of the Ministry of the Interior his allies, since they also wished to get the Jews out of Hungary.[64]

Many Jews considered Berend a traitor. Others simply thought him a lunatic. It seems likely that during the spring and summer months, he built up private relations with the Ministry of the Interior, informing **László Endre**'s office about the goings-on in the Jewish Council. Nevertheless, during the siege of Budapest in the winter months, he worked tirelessly, risking his own life on behalf of the Jews suffering in the large ghetto: he held religious services and buried the dead. He also maintained good relations with the Arrow Cross commander of Municipal District VII, to whom he could effectively turn for protection. Document 5-6 gives an account of an Arrow Cross attack in Wesselényi Street in the large ghetto. Several similar actions took place in both ghettos in the weeks before liberation.

DOCUMENT 5-6: **Jewish Council member Rabbi Dr. Béla Berend's report to the council on Arrow Cross atrocities, January 12, 1945, USHMMA RG 39.013M, reel 7 (HJA XX-A, box D 9/3).**

Budapest, January 12, 1945

REPORT

On this day (January 12, 1945) at about 9:30 a.m., on behalf of the Jewish Council, in conjunction with the committee of the Hungarian Royal State Police and the Arrow Cross Party, I surveyed the buildings at Wesselényi Street 27–29, where I established the following during the hearings conducted by the mixed [Police–Arrow Cross] committee:

On January 11, 1945, Thursday, at about 22:45 in the evening, a group consisting of 6–8 armed individuals entered Wesselényi Street 27, some wearing Arrow Cross Party armbands, some wearing Honvéd uniforms,[65] some German uniforms. They headed straight to the air raid shelter, and they subjected the Jews they found down there to assault and verbal abuse. They then launched a search and body search, saying they were searching for firearms. They took away small objects such as fountain pens, watches, matches, etc. At first, they fired warning shots into the air with a machine gun, and then they shot, one after the other, the majority of those they found there, in such a way that 26 women, 15 men, and 1

---

64. See Krisztina Munkácsi, "Berend Béla főrabbi népbírósági pere," *Századok* 130, no. 6 (1996): 1525–52.

65. That is, regular Hungarian military uniforms.

small child were shot to death at Wesselényi Street 27. Most of them were shot in the head.

In the same building, they entered apartment I.5, where they executed the married couple they found lying in their bed in the kitchen in a similar fashion.

At the building at Wesselényi Street 29, the looting and murder took place under largely similar circumstances. The disturbance here left one victim dead. It appears that the looters were subsequently interrupted.

Claims by the witnesses who survived and were wounded reveal that the terror group must have consisted of 15 members and that they split up as they went into the two buildings simultaneously, to carry out their bloody misdeed.

The representative of the State Police and the delegate of the Arrow Cross Party launched the investigation—which they claim will be successful—and have promised the most severe form of punishment.

Dr. Berend
Chief Rabbi, Council Member.

Besides the shortage of food, water, fuel, and other basic items, another severe problem in the besieged town was the maintenance of public sanitation and burial of the dead. Initially, murdered Jews were taken to graveyards. By late December the Soviets had advanced as far as the cemetery, forcing the ghetto authorities to find space within the tight confines of the ghetto for mass graves.

DOCUMENT 5-7: **Service ticket issued by the Budapest ghetto police, January 17, 1945, USHMMA RG 39.013M, reel 7 (HJA XX-A, box D 9/3).**

Commanding headquarters, District I[66]
Service Ticket
One of our policemen is lying dead in front of Wesselényi Street 9 and Heroes' Temple[67]; he has been shot; his name is Ignác Lampel, resident

---

66. The ghetto in Pest was divided into ten districts (*körzet*), headed by district aldermen selected by the Jewish Council. They had extensive administrative tasks and authority to enforce laws in the ghetto. For the territorial distribution and the leaders of the districts, see the list of district leaders compiled by the Jewish Council, HMC Gy-13, box 13, 2011.398.

67. "One of our policemen" refers to a member of the ghetto police. Temple of Heroes: the smaller synagogue erected next to the **Neologue** Great Synagogue in Dohány Street (1929–1931); the name refers to the victims of World War I.

at Wesselényi Street 4. Please arrange for the transportation of the dead, since we have no one at our disposal.

January 17, 1945  Deputy Commander, District I
József Fonyó

The dead were interred in the garden of the Dohány Street Synagogue and in Klauzál Square, the center of the ghetto.[68]

DOCUMENT 5-8: **Order by the Jewish Council about the burial of the dead in the ghetto, January 4, 1945, USHMMA RG 39.013M, reel 7 (HJA XX-A, box D 9/3).**

Order<br>
Concerning the burial of the dead in the ghetto.

The building supervisors arrange the burial of those who die in the ghetto by registering the deaths occurring in their buildings.

[. . .]

Once a day they will report with a written summary of the deaths at the appropriate district headquarters. It is the building supervisor's duty to arrange the digging of the graves and the burial of the dead in the area designated for the district in Klauzál Square. The graves are to be dug two meters [6.5 feet] deep and should be placed tightly next to one another, without gaps. Three corpses at most may be buried in each grave, with a layer of earth at least ten centimeters [3.9 inches] thick separating them. Hospital supervisors will arrange for the burial of those who die in hospitals, in the manner described above. Ghetto police staff must report corpses found in the streets at the appropriate district headquarters, and the district headquarters will arrange the burial as described above.

[. . .]

Budapest, January 4, 1945

Burial Department<br>
of the Interim Board<br>
of the Association of Jews in Hungary[69]

Because of the shortage of space, the frozen ground, and the lack of workers, this method became less and less feasible. Corpses were subsequently piled

---

68. See the name lists of the deceased buried in Klauzál Square and in the courtyard of the Dohány Street synagogue, HJA PIH-XIII-A, box B 7/1.

69. That is, the Jewish Council. See chapter 8.

up in community buildings (for example, in the ritual bath in Kazinczy Street) and their courtyards. On the day of liberation, their number had risen past three thousand. Numerous unburied dead also lay strewn across the streets.[70]

There were several makeshift hospitals in the large ghetto, but the major health institution was located just a few steps from the eastern ghetto gate at Wesselényi Street 44. Originally a school building, it was outfitted as a hospital after the Germans seized the Jewish community's Szabolcs Street hospital with all its modern equipment and the Jewish Council had to organize a healthcare system from its own resources. Apart from the sick and the wounded, the hospitals also admitted those experiencing social hardship (e.g., helpless elderly people, people with small children, the blind) and those fleeing the ghetto. However, as the excerpts in document 5-9 show, these institutions also sometimes closed their doors to avoid overcrowding. The number of patients rose to several times the Wesselényi Street hospital's capacity. Two people were assigned to a bed; crowds lay on the ground in corridors and the stairwells. Because of shots into the building from the outside, the hospital rooms often lacked windows or heating. There were not enough instruments or supplies of medicine or bandages. There was no electricity or water for people to clean themselves or to operate the toilets. The overcrowded state of the hospitals posed an enormous risk of epidemics.[71]

During Arrow Cross rule, many health-care institutions came under the protection of the International Red Cross, in the hope that this would keep the Arrow Cross gangs at bay. Doctors and other hospital employees lived in the hospitals and operating rooms, enduring the harsh conditions and attacks, heroically caring for the sick and wounded, and assisting in births. The hospitals also treated and saved Hungarian and German soldiers, even armed Arrow Cross men, and in some places this secured their protection. The liberation of the ghetto by no means spelled an end to all the suffering. Food provisions and overall conditions improved extremely slowly. For several weeks the death rate remained as high as it had been during the siege.[72]

Document 5-9 excerpts the 1945 testimony of the wife of Lajos Lévy (1875–1961), the physician in chief of the Wesselényi Street hospital. Lévy was a prominent medical expert, one of the five founders of the Psychoanalytical Association of Hungary, and one of the first physicians to use an EKG in the

---

70. Braham, *The Politics of Genocide*, 2:990–93, 997–1003.

71. For the history of and the conditions in the Wesselényi Street hospital, see Imre Strausz, "Egy zsidó kórház 1944-ben. Emlékezés-vázlat ötven év múltán," *Múlt és Jövő*, no. 4 (1994), 48–60.

72. HJA, DEGOB Protocols, nos. 3596, 3608, 3621, and 3623.

country. Before the German occupation he led the Szabolcs Street institution (the so-called Jewish Hospital), and later he became the head of the main ghetto hospital. He survived the Holocaust and emigrated to England in 1955, where he died in 1961. His wife, Katalin Freund, spent the ghetto weeks with him in the Wesselényi Street building.

DOCUMENT 5-9: **Testimony of Mrs. Lajos Lévy (née Katalin Freund), 1945, USHMMA RG 39.013M, reel 4 (HJA, DEGOB Protocols, no. 3596).**

[. . .]

In November it becomes more and more dangerous to walk in the street; so the majority of the doctors, among them the head of the hospital, are forced to move into the hospital.

The order to move, and the vision of the ghetto [. . .] diminished the vigor and courage of those who were less resistant. Besides this, many lost their relatives: women and men being called up and taken for work and deported. The hospital had insufficient capacity to deal with a second wave of suicides. They had to expand [its facilities] into the antechamber of the temple and into the bride's room.[73] A shockingly grim sight: the row of unconscious people lying along the center aisle of the temple. Some are regaining consciousness and are returning back to life; some were in deep sleep, journeying toward death. In the weak beam of light, there is an even grimmer sight: the doctor is sitting at the head of the row (he himself is a refugee from the provinces); he would not leave his position for a minute, watching, giving injections, fighting for each and every life.

Meanwhile, outside, Jews are trying to find their places; those who received protection from the Swiss, Swedish, or Papal delegates are crammed into the buildings of the so-called international ghetto. Others occupy the apartments within the designated area of the ghetto. The Wesselényi Street hospital lies just outside this area. There is great fear of the fate expected inside the ghetto, so being admitted to the hospital is again considered a kind of shelter, especially since the hospital has been placed under the protection of the International Red Cross. As the deadline for moving into the ghetto approaches, the fight for admission to the hospital grows fiercer. Restrictions have to be respected at the hospital;

---

73. The temple refers to the hospital's synagogue. The bride's room refers to a room attached to the synagogue where the bride gets ready for her wedding (in Hungarian: *araszoba*).

they cannot admit those who are within the age group that is subject to compulsory labor service.⁷⁴ Still, the hospital is quickly filling up, so it becomes necessary to set up new emergency hospitals.

[. . .]

As the siege intensifies, Arrow Cross atrocities do as well. Proof of this is the string of patients who escaped from the banks of the Danube, having been shot in the back of the neck. During one night, they bring in 4–5 people who have been shot, and they report on the fate of the other 200 unfortunate people. Entire families are wiped out at once in this manner. Victims who have been shot are rescued and carried in from various locations, not just the Danube, but also from the ghetto itself, from other parts of the city, from the street.⁷⁵ Around this time, there are attacks on certain Jewish houses; for example, there is a massacre in the air raid shelter of one of the houses in Wesselényi Street. 46 innocent Jews died there, among them a couple, both teachers at the Israelite High School for Girls.⁷⁶

[. . .]

The hospital gates are kept shut by a firm hand when another wave of people reaches them, seeking admission: this is when the residents of the Swedish and Swiss protected houses are being escorted into the ghetto by the Arrow Cross men.⁷⁷ Sad processions of people marching past in front of the hospital.

[. . .]

In the days before the Soviet army arrived, the Arrow Cross militia, in cooperation with certain German units, prepared to massacre the Jews living in the large ghetto. Pál Szalai, a police contact of the Arrow Cross and confidante of Wallenberg, immediately informed Major General Gerhard Schmidhuber, commander of the Wehrmacht forces defending Pest. Schmidhuber thwarted

---

74. Men between sixteen and sixty and women between sixteen and forty. See document 5-1.

75. Due to the inexperience of the Arrow Cross militiamen, a couple of people were not lethally wounded at the mass execution sites. Others escaped by jumping into the Danube.

76. The sentence is presumably about the mass murder committed on January 11, 1945, at Wesselényi Street 27–29, in which forty-five victims died. See document 5-6.

77. The Arrow Cross militiamen were bringing Jews in from the international ghetto already in early December, but this account is most likely about the moves affecting close to ten thousand people conducted on January 5 and 6. Braham, *The Politics of Genocide*, 2:975–76.

the massacre.[78] The Soviets reached the international ghetto on January 16 and liberated the large ghetto two days later, on January 18. Jews who had survived on the Buda side of the city were not liberated until February 13.[79]

## TERROR OUTSIDE THE GHETTOS

The Arrow Cross terror struck not just the ghettos: many times Jews outside the confined areas were in even graver danger. The attacks in and outside the ghettos intensified, especially after Red Army units surrounded Budapest in late December 1944 and the Arrow Cross leadership left the capital. From then on, the fate of Jews in Budapest rested in the hands of those mid- and low-level Arrow Cross leaders who remained in the city.

The Arrow Cross militia remaining in Budapest largely consisted of newly joined supporters. These included people fired up by propaganda, driven by greed, or intoxicated by sudden power, members of the lower middle class, blue-collar workers, young people, and common criminals. Everyone had to take part in the cruelty; brutality against the Jews became a loyalty test of sorts. The Arrow Cross men mostly organized their operations randomly, independently of orders from above. Their combat value was otherwise minimal, and they tried to keep away from actual battles in any event. This riffraff hunted for deserting soldiers and labor servicemen, communists, alleged saboteurs, and traitors and conducted regular raids in and outside the ghettos. Unlike in the spring and summer, when the situation of Jews and gentiles diverged sharply, their fates now shared many common elements.

In these weeks of terror, the plundering and blackmailing of Jews became an everyday routine. Buildings protected by the neutral diplomatic corps and the Red Cross became frequent targets of raids, during which the Arrow Cross often looted, raped, and tortured their victims. Since most adult men were in Labor Service units and additional thousands had been dragged off for forced labor, the majority of the victims were women, youths, the elderly, and the sick. Initially, those killed were placed in mass graves, but more and more often, Arrow Cross men shot their victims so that they would fall into the Danube. On several occasions, they attacked headquarters of diplomatic missions, Jewish

---

78. Krisztián Ungváry, *Budapest ostroma*, 5th rev. ed. (Budapest: Corvina, 2005), 242; József Szekeres, *A pesti gettók 1945 januári megmentése* (Budapest: Budapest Főváros Levéltára, 1997).

79. Budapest is located on the two sides of the Danube. The west side is Buda; the east side is Pest.

and Christian social institutions, child-care centers, and hospitals.[80] These buildings, too, came under the protection of the International Red Cross, like the ghetto hospitals. On January 12, 1945, the Arrow Cross attacked the Maros Street hospital, then two days later, the sanatorium in Városmajor Street. On the Pest side of the city, the Red Army had already liberated the ghetto, when on January 19 the Arrow Cross units went on to attack the Alma Street nursing home in Buda, killing most of the patients and staff—altogether about 320 people.

Document 5-10 excerpts the testimony of a survivor of the January 14 attack, Mór Halpern. He recalled that the Arrow Cross militia first showed up at the sanatorium on January 13, under the pretext of checking identification documents. Halpern insisted on the building's protected status, and this persuaded the intruders to retreat. The following day, however, fifteen armed men surrounded the building.

**DOCUMENT 5-10: Testimony of Mór Halpern given to the Committee Investigating Nazi and Arrow Cross Atrocities, April 8, 1945, USHMMA RG 52.001M, reel 13 (HNA I).**

[...]

Upon seeing the lethal seriousness of the situation, I intervened again, but this time more forcefully and energetically than on the previous day. I cited the fact that on the previous day, the authorities had accepted the document certifying protection by the International Red Cross, containing the agreement between the Szálasi government and the International Red Cross, according to which the Arrow Cross Party would also recognize the protection.[81] In response, the leader of the Arrow Cross men, an alleged sergeant whose chief assistant was his son, replied that the Szálasi government did not recognize any form of protection; not from the Swiss, not from the Swedes, not from the Red Cross; they recognized only Jews.

---

80. See document 5-10.

81. Minister of Foreign Affairs Baron Gábor Kemény saw the delegates of the International Red Cross on October 19, 1944, and promised to acknowledge the Red Cross protection of various institutions. These twenty-two hospitals and other humanitarian institutions were granted extraterritoriality. The Ministry of Foreign Affairs informed the Ministry of the Interior about this decision on October 28. János Botos, "'Inter arma caritas.' Embermentő tevékenység a Vöröskereszt Nemzetközi Bizottságának közreműködésével (1944 nyara–1945 eleje)," in *Magyarország 1944. Üldöztetés-embermentés*, ed. Szabolcs Szita (Budapest: Nemzeti Tankönyvkiadó, 1994), 2:187–90.

I emphasized again that the hospital was under the protection of the Red Cross. The reply was that Jews were hiding there under the protection of the International Red Cross. I asked him to make it possible for me to get in touch with the delegates of the Red Cross, and he was on the verge of complying, but influenced by his son, he eventually turned down my request. There was no point in telling him that this only used to be a Jewish hospital but no longer was, since it was now a specifically Red Cross hospital. He reproached me, saying that based on the information that he [had] gotten next door, he knew with certainty that we were a Jewish hospital. It was not difficult to figure out that this piece of certain information must have come from the adjacent János Sanatorium, which, for the sake of its own de-Jewification,[82] had swiftly transferred 17 Jewish patients into our hospital before the tragedy took place, and during the siege, they had even denied us access to water.

After this, identity checks began. First, they checked the personnel. Jews were grouped separately in the office, and Christians were taken to a room in the basement. Jewish employees were taken upstairs in front of a wood storage shed and were executed by a firing squad. Afterward, ambulatory patients were lined up in the lounge, and they were also executed in front of the wood storage shed. Finally the Arrow Cross men came around to the patients, going into the rooms one by one and shooting to death sick people lying in their beds. It must have been around 7:00 in the evening when this massacre, which is unprecedented in world history, came to an end. The next day they came again and checked if any of those who had been executed were still alive. I recall that about 4 of them were still alive; the Arrow Cross men put bullets into them again, to do a thorough job. The number of victims was about 150, and they were robbed afterward, in accordance with typical Arrow Cross conduct. Then the entire hospital was looted; specifically, they took all the bedding and linens, kitchen pots and utensils, medicine, and every piece of movable equipment that could be named. I must note that the population of the area also participated in this shameful act, for they carried off each and every item that they could lay their hands upon in every direction. On January 17, the hospital was set on fire. The executed patients and employees all burned inside. Rooms 4 and 27 did

---

82. In this context the term refers to the János sanatorium's efforts to get rid of its Jewish patients.

not burn down, but the corpses were taken away from here, by whom and to where, I do not know.

I do not wish to relate anything else about this matter.

## JEWISH VOICES FROM THE ARROW CROSS ERA

The author of the diary entries excerpted in document 5-11(A), Lilla Ecséri (1928–1986), lived through the Arrow Cross rule as a member of a Jewish middle-class family in Budapest. She had converted to the Catholic faith. Like Éva Weinmann,[83] Anne Frank, and many others who were persecuted, she kept a diary. Her entries indicate that by early September, a hopeful outlook had replaced the fears she experienced in the shadow of the spring and summer deportations. Lilla announced joyously that the danger of deportations had passed, and she ventured that the war could be over soon. She was studying English with her friends.

DOCUMENT 5-11(A): Lilla Ecséri, Budapest, diary entry for October 15 and 16, 1944, in Lilla Ecséri, *Napló, 1944* (Budapest: T-Twins, 1995), 27–29.

*Oct. 15, 1944: CEASE-FIRE!*
Today Hungarian Radio announced during Horthy's speech that the country has agreed to a ceasefire with the U.S.A. For the Russians are already at Szolnok.[84] 3 days ago Bandi was sent home from Kecskemét along with his entire Labor Service company.[85] Now there are lots of boys in the building. Besides Bandi, there is Laci Surányi, the two Fischer boys, and the labor servicemen constantly keep coming. We were overjoyed when we heard about the cease-fire, in the afternoon; there was a gathering at Gabi Szalvay's; it was pretty boring. But now the mood is very bad, because they are afraid of the Germans. To be honest, I am not interested in politics, and I am not as terribly happy as one is supposed to be. I worry only about myself and am exasperated by the thought that nobody fancies me, and I don't know if I will ever become somebody. I am more than 16 years old and have not had

---

83. See document 4-10.
84. A town about sixty miles southeast of Budapest; the Red Army occupied it on November 4.
85. A town close to Szolnok; the Red Army occupied it on November 1.

a proper admirer. Soon, within a week, the war will be over, and I can try to get into the acting academy, where I have just heard they do not require a high school diploma. In the morning I was overjoyed, but my mood transformed into a rather bad mood, and I have a feeling that now something will really happen.

Oct. 16

Today we already have a Szálasi government. The Arrow Cross men have occupied the radio station, and they are now broadcasting inspirational speeches: "Fight till the last drop of blood!" They call Horthy a traitor and are using racial slurs for Jews again. After the rejoicing yesterday, there is now terrible panic through the entire building. I am completely calm and unmoved observing the whole thing. I am convinced that we will survive this whole thing. But if not (which I consider unlikely), the most they will do is take me away and kill me. But I am convinced they won't do that. For in that case I would most likely not be this calm. I will definitely have stories to tell to my grandchildren (assuming I have grandchildren). We are expecting the Russians any day or hour; they are 50 kilometers from Budapest.[86]

[. . .]

A radical turn did take place by evening. Arrow Cross militiamen began killing their enemies, primarily Jews. At the end of October, Lilla was herded off along with thousands of Jewish women to work on fortifications near the capital. Fortunately, she was not taken toward the western border from there but allowed to return to Budapest. There she survived the siege of the city, while constantly fleeing and hiding. Her diary accompanied her throughout these trials. Lilla turned to writing to escape the hardships and constant danger of this period. In the end she lost several family members, including her mother. She lived to experience the liberation in a Budapest hospital.

---

86. At this time the front was about ninety miles from Budapest (not about thirty, as Lilla estimated); by the end of October, this distance had shrunk to approximately sixty miles.

DOCUMENT 5-11(B): **Photograph of Lilla Ecséri, no date, private collection.**

Like Lilla, Hilda Löbl (b. 1913) survived the Holocaust in Budapest. After being confined into a "yellow-star house" in June, she was rounded up by the Arrow Cross on November 10 and taken to the Óbuda brick factory. According to her 1946 memoirs, the Arrow Cross men were ready to send her and hundreds of others westward, when "a gentleman from the embassy arrived there, vehemently argued with the Arrow Cross, and virtually smuggled us out of the brick factory." The unnamed diplomat might have been Raoul Wallenberg or **Carl Lutz**. Hilda and her family were taken to a building protected by the Swiss embassy, but this was just a temporary asylum.

DOCUMENT 5-12(A): **Excerpts from the memoirs of Hilda Löbl, March 1946, private collection.**

[. . .] And then came the raids. The buildings were occupied by the Arrow Cross men and the police, and those who did not have a protective document or whose documents were found forfeited were deported. Before long, it was our turn. A few comrades escaped; others obtained protective documents; only I and another girl were unable to get one. She escaped; I stayed. I knew that if I did not hide, I would be taken away. I hid in the closet; it had a drawer where I spent three hours. I was not welcomed [by the tenants of the rooms where the closet was]; they did not want to let me in; everyone feared for their own lives. However, I was persistent, and I managed to escape this raid. I was lying in the closet, and a meter from me there stood a policeman. I felt the creaking of his boots in my brain. When eventually I could climb out, I was soaking wet from the sweat. [. . .] [Finally,] I have received a great protective document with a French stamp from my aunt. I have erased her name and typed in [brother] Sanyi and his whole family. Mom had a fake one; we could not obtain another one for her. So far we were okay. We escaped two raids with these documents, but the third one is the worst memory of my life. Their building was overlooking our window. I was about to eat the tomato soup sent to me by [sister] Manci when I noticed that their whole building was being raided. I was so scared I forgot to swallow the soup. And all of a sudden I see Dad walking down the stairs with a bag; then Sanyi carries down the stroller; Mom takes down the baggage, and [then] comes Manci with Pista on her arm; both are deathly pale; Pista was sick with a 40 degree [104 Fahrenheit] fever. Mom does not look at me; only Manci stops at the window of the hall; Pista is waving goodbye to me. And I'm standing there, rooted to the ground, scratching the window. I should run there to help! Time has frozen.
    [. . .]

Hilda's family eventually made its way back to the (relative) safety of the protected building. Hilda left the house she was hiding in; using false papers, she posed as a non-Jewish refugee from the provinces and worked in a soup kitchen. She pretended to be hard of hearing and mentally disabled so that she would have time to think if suspicious authorities posed questions. She ultimately survived. The picture reproduced in document 5-12(B) shows her and her husband, Mihály Kádár, in 1941.

DOCUMENT 5-12(B): **Photograph of Hilda Löbl and Mihály Kádár, 1941, private collection.**

Mihály served as a labor serviceman on the eastern front. He escaped and returned home after the war. His family was deported from the provinces and murdered in Auschwitz.

## CHAPTER 6
# Plunder

FOLLOWING THE German occupation, the Hungarian government immediately set out to rob Jews of their property. In the spring of 1944, the government carried out in full the "changing of the guard" that Hungarian antisemites had demanded for decades. Tens of thousands of Jews lost their jobs: they could no longer work, for example, as lawyers, actors, or state employees, nor could they attend universities. Jews found their businesses summarily "Aryanized," their shops, warehouses, and inventories sealed, and their trade licenses revoked. In Budapest alone, the authorities seized over eighteen thousand shops owned by Jews and handed many of them over to Christian competitors. The state confiscated Jewish bank accounts, cash, shares, bonds, insurance policies, and works of art. Ghettoization and deportation deprived Jews of their apartments, houses, furniture, movable property, and livestock. The authorities and the civil population plundered synagogues and community buildings. In the ghettos and collection camps, people were subject to brutal torture so that they would surrender their hidden valuables. The members of the **gendarmerie** unscrupulously plundered Jews locked up in cattle cars during the deportations as well. They demanded jewelry and money for even a sip of water from people suffocating in the summer heat in the overcrowded cars.

The plunder continued in Auschwitz II–Birkenau. The deportees' baggage was taken from them on the "**Jewish ramp**." Those capable of working lost their last belongings in the camp bath, while those sentenced to death left all their possessions in the rooms of the crematoria where they undressed. Prisoners employed in the **Sonderkommando** pulled gold teeth and fillings from the mouths of those who had been gassed. After careful sorting, German authorities distributed deportees' valuables among the guards, Waffen-SS divisions, and German civilian population back in the Reich. Money, foreign currency, bonds, jewelry, and gold, including gold bars cast from gold in teeth, made their way to the SS-Business Administration Main Office (WVHA) and from there to the German Reichsbank. Much of the gold and jewelry was sold in Switzerland. The Nazi regime returned some of the money received in exchange to the SS via the German budget. The genocide was thus self-financing: the victims paid the costs of their own murder. The Nazis used the property of the Jews to lengthen the war and sustain the apparatus entrusted with their annihilation. The combined sum of assets stripped from the Hungarian Jews deported to Auschwitz is estimated at 57 million Reichsmarks, which at the exchange rate of the time amounted to approximately US$23 million.[1]

Meanwhile, back in Hungary, authorities sent massive quantities of originally Jewish-owned valuables westward during the systematic plunder of the country by the **Arrow Cross** and the Germans between October 1944 and March 1945. Of the approximately 600,000 to 700,000 tons of valuables (merchandise, machinery, raw material, movable property, agricultural and industrial products, vehicles, and so forth) shipped out of the country, 100,000 to 150,000 tons had originally been in the possession of Jews.[2] One of the trains sent to Austria became infamous as the "**Gold Train**," its freight worth US$6.5 to $13 million.[3] The documents in this chapter illuminate the key measures, agencies, and beneficiaries of the plundered fortune of the Jews.

---

1. For the detailed calculation, see Gábor Kádár and Zoltán Vági, *Self-financing Genocide: The Gold Train, the Becher Case and the Wealth of Hungarian Jews* (Budapest: Central European University Press, 2004), 124–35. For an overview of the expropriation of the European Jews between 1933 and 1945, see Martin Dean, *Robbing the Jews: The Confiscation of Jewish Property in the Holocaust, 1933–1945* (New York: Cambridge University Press in association with the USHMM, 2008).

2. For details about the transports of plundered Hungarian goods to Germany, see Gábor Kádár and Zoltán Vági, *Hullarablás. A magyar zsidók gazdasági megsemmisítése* (Budapest: Jaffa, 2005), 333–44.

3. For the history of the Gold Train, see Kádár and Vági, *Self-financing Genocide*, 281–370. On the American aftermath of the Gold Train affair, see the website of the Hungarian Gold Train Settlement at www.hungariangoldtrain.org/index_en.php (accessed August 26, 2012).

## THE MACHINERY OF PLUNDER: THE PROCESS AND AGENCIES

By appropriating 20 to 25 percent of the national wealth from the Jews, the government of **Döme Sztójay** expected solutions to two major problems. One was the destitute state of the Hungarian economy. War expenses were eating up an increasingly higher proportion of the national income: in 1942, they consumed 27.8 percent, in 1943, 35.1 percent, and in 1944, 44.1 percent. In addition, Nazi Germany was deeply in debt to Hungary: by March 1944, Berlin owed Budapest about 1.2 billion Reichsmarks (2 billion pengős).[4] This was close to one-third the 1944 Hungarian state budget of 6.14 billion pengős.[5] After March 19, the Germans tightened their grip even more, burdening the Hungarian government with the sizable costs of the occupation.

The government aimed to solve social problems in Hungary. The Sztójay government lowered the retirement age from sixty-five to sixty years. For household employees it introduced mandatory old-age, disability, and widow and orphan insurance. It also improved the retirement insurance system for miners, and the financial situation of teachers. The government expanded the circle of those receiving an additional benefit for raising children and provided reduced insurance costs for those working in agriculture.[6] There were no additional resources for these measures in the crumbling budget: the cabinet intended to fund these steps using Jewish property.

The Prime Minister's Decree no. 1600/1944, issued in April and excerpted in document 6-1, was the basic initial document for the state appropriation of Jewish assets.[7] The Ministry of Finance intended it as the first step in the comprehensive regulations it ultimately envisioned.

---

4. Christian Gerlach and Götz Aly, *Das letzte Kapitel. Der Mord an den ungarischen Juden 1944–1945* (Stuttgart: DVA, 2002), 214.

5. The temporary Hungarian government's memorandum to the Allied Control Committee, March 9, 1945, HNA XIX-J-1-k KÜM Vegyes 1945–1964, box 38.

6. See, e.g., Prime Minister's Decrees no. 2500/1944 and no. 3000/1944, *Budapesti Közlöny*, July 2, 1944, 2, and Decree no. 239.900/1944 of the Ministry of the Interior, in *Magyarországi Rendeletek Tára, 1944* (Budapest: Belügyminisztérium, 1948), 1139–40.

7. For a more detailed analysis of the implementation of the decree, see Kádár and Vági, *Hullarablás*, 223–26, 233–34.

DOCUMENT 6-1: **Prime Minister's Decree no. 1600/1944 on the registration and confiscation of Jewish property, April 16, 1944,** Budapesti Közlöny, **April 16, 1944, 1–3.**

[. . .]

1. §

(1) When this decree goes into effect, all Jews residing within the country are required to register all their assets by April 30, 1944, at the local financial directorate. In the case where a person occupies several residences, registration is required at the financial directorate where income and property taxes have been imposed or should be imposed.[8] Registration under Article 9, concerning commercial or industrial companies (factories, shops) must occur at the financial directorate of the region where the general income tax and corporate assets tax have been imposed or should be imposed. The registration should include the market value of the property holdings at the time this decree takes effect. The registration must be made on the official form available at the municipal council (in towns, at the mayor's councils, and in Budapest, at municipal district councils).

(2) In cases involving minors or persons under legal guardianship, the registration must be made by the legal representative or guardian of the person. In accordance with Article 1 of Prime Minister's Decree no. 1990/1942 (*Comprehensive Digest of Hungarian Decrees*, p. 714), for those who are hindered in addressing official business, those who are absent, or are prevented from registering their assets for any other reasons, the registration must be made by the person in charge of managing the assets.

(3) All property must be registered, with the exception of items for personal use: items of furniture, clothing, as well as household items. The aforementioned items must also be registered if their combined value exceeds 10,000 pengős[9]; if these property items serve the needs of other relatives living in a shared household, then the exemption value limit is increased by 3,000 pengős per relative. However, in all cases, artworks,

---

8. On the financial directorates, see document 6-3.
9. This indicates a sizable value; 10,000 pengős equaled roughly US$2,000 at the time. On the last official exchange rate (dated March 1941), see Jürgen Schneider, Oskar Schwarzer, and Markus A. Denzel, *Währungen der Welt II. Europäische und nordamerikanische Devisenkurse 1941–1951* (Stuttgart: Franz Steiner Verlag, 1997), 503.

carpets, silver items, and other luxury items are subject to the registration requirement.[10]

(4) All persons, Jewish as well as non-Jewish, who are in possession of Jewish property items entrusted to them on any grounds whatsoever are subject to the registration requirement.[11]

[. . .]

5. §

(1) All Jewish-owned items made of pure platinum, platinum alloys, pure gold or gold alloys—including all kinds of gold coins, as well as broken gold and all forms of scrap gold—gold compounds, mined and sediment gold, as well as artifacts and jewelry made entirely or partially from platinum or gold, as well as gemstones and pearls, must be reported and deposited in accordance with the provisions of 4. §.

(2) The provisions of the present article do not apply to the wedding bands of Jewish married (or engaged) couples, as long as the rings are without gemstones or pearls.[12]

[. . .]

13. §

The provisions set forth for the Jews in the present decree must be implemented for every general partnership, limited partnership, as well as limited liability company that has at least one Jewish partner (in the case of a limited partnership, limited partners also count). The report must list what share the Jewish partner holds in the assets (income) of the partnership.

[. . .]

---

10. For details about the fate of artworks stolen from the Jews and related policies of the Hungarian government, see László Mravik, ed., *The "Sacco di Budapest" and Depredation of Hungary, 1938–1949: Works of Art Missing from Hungary as a Result of the Second World War* (Budapest: Hungarian National Gallery for the Joint Restitution Committee at the Hungarian Ministry for Culture and Education, 1998); Gábor Kádár and Zoltán Vági, "Művészet és népirtás. A Műkincskormánybiztosság működése és a magyar zsidó műtárgyak elrablása, külföldre hurcolása, 1944–1945," in *Küzdelem az igazságért. Tanulmányok Randolph L. Braham 80. születésnapjára*, ed. László Karsai and Judit Molnár (Budapest: MAZSIHISZ, 2002), 317–56.

11. This provision also served to prevent the transfer of assets and use of gifts, mock contracts, and other attempts to rescue property.

12. Thus the state sequestered only the more valuable wedding rings. Of course, authorities did not adhere to this during the ghettoization and deportation process and confiscated all jewelry, regardless of this measure.

It soon became clear that the hastily prepared provisions were inadequate and impossible to carry out due to organizational obstacles and severe time limits.[13] The decree was published on the same day that ghettoization in Carpatho-Ruthenia began (April 16), so many Jews taken into ghettos and collection camps did not even have a chance to report their holdings. The decree replaced the instructions pertaining to assets of the confidential ghettoization decree (see document 3-3) in several places.[14] The severe anomalies of the implementation of decree 1600/1944 forced local authorities to modify its central directives. Despite these hardships, it remained the "legal" basis for the plunder of Jews until November 1944, when the Arrow Cross nationalized Jewish property (see document 6-8).

Another landmark step in the "Aryanization" process was the April 21 publication of a decree by the minister of commerce and transport stipulating the sequestration of commercial firms' inventory and equipment. The following day, shops and workshops were prohibited from opening their doors, their owners permitted only to give merchandise to clients who had previously ordered it. They performed these transactions under restrictive circumstances, with shutters lowered halfway and their businesses only open between 7 and 9 a.m.[15] Prior to this, authorities had already tried to halt Jews' attempts to hide inventory and equipment or to transfer items to someone else; for instance, sale and gift transactions were invalidated retroactively. In their antisemitic zeal, the leaders of some regional governments did not wait for orders from above. Overstepping their jurisdiction, they had already initiated the closing of the Jewish shops, as the newspaper article in document 6-2 attests.

---

13. For example, the decree did not apply to Jewish ventures operating in a cooperative or a joint stock company form or to other legal entities, including foundations and associations. Circular letter of the Federation of Industrialists, April 22, 1944, in Ilona Benoschofsky and Elek Karsai, eds., *Vádirat a nácizmus ellen. Dokumentumok a magyarországi zsidóüldözés történetéhez (1944 március 19–1944 május 15. A német megszállástól a deportálás megkezdéséig)* (Budapest: Magyar Izraeliták Országos Képviselete, 1958), 1:223–24. Thus, the decree did not apply to the largest companies and nonprofit organizations. The government created the legal framework for the confiscation of these entities later, often in an ex post facto manner after the owners and stockholders of such companies and organizations were deported. Kádár and Vági, *Hullarablás*, 225–26.

14. According to Prime Minister's Decree no. 1600/1944, the securities, cash, and jewelry had to be deposited at financial institutions affiliated with the Center for Financial Institutions, while Confidential Decree 6163/1944 specified the Hungarian National Bank for this purpose.

15. Minister of Commerce and Transport's Decree no. 50.500/1944 on the sealing of inventories and shop equipment of Jewish merchants, *Budapesti Közlöny*, April 21, 1944, 2–3.

DOCUMENT 6-2: **Press report on the sealing of Jewish shops,** *Somogyi Ujság*, **April 8, 1944.**

Thursday Afternoon. Jewish Shops Sealed across Kaposvár
Inventories of Merchandise to Be Compiled after the Holidays.[16]

Thursday afternoon, following the example of Veszprém, Nagykanizsa, and several other provincial towns like ours, authorities sealed the Jewish shops across Kaposvár on orders of the mayor.[17] Everywhere, the sealing of shops was carried out in a most orderly manner. The owners handed over the keys to their shops, acknowledging that entering the sealed shops qualifies as unlawful entry.[18]

The sealing of shops was carried out on the mayor's order and authorized by the minister of commerce in agreement with the Kaposvár police. The radical procedure undertaken by government officials was necessary because it has been confirmed that several of the Jewish merchants have taken advantage of the freedom they still have and for several days have been transferring large quantities of merchandise for storage with acquaintances in Kaposvár, as well as outside the town, employing various tricks. Christian Hungarian public opinion uniformly supports the mayor's order, for the circumstances mentioned above completely justified his action.

Compiling of inventories of the merchandise in Jewish shops will begin after the holidays. Arrangements about what will be done with the inventoried goods have yet to be made. For now, the plan is to allocate these goods to aid potential bombing victims. Until further instructions, the public should purchase items they need from Christian shops.

Thus far 127 Jewish shops have been closed down in Kaposvár.[19]
We do, however, call attention to the fact that certain shops relocated

---

16. Easter fell on April 9–10 in 1944. The Thursday mentioned in the article was April 6. Kaposvár is a town in western Hungary and seat of Somogy County.

17. Following an order from the German commanding headquarters, Jewish shops in Veszprém were closed two days after the occupation. See Anna Gergely, "Veszprém County," in *The Geographical Encyclopedia of the Holocaust in Hungary*, ed. Randolph L. Braham and Zoltán Tibori Szabó (Evanston, IL: Northwestern Press in association with the USHMM, 2013), 2:1230.

18. Despite frequent attempts to hide merchandise and otherwise rescue valuables, the majority did obey the administrative provisions for closing the shops in an orderly fashion.

19. In Kaposvár, where slightly more than 7 percent of the population was Jewish, about one-third of shops were closed down (127 out of 388). Antal Andrássy, "A város az ellenforradalmi rendszer idején (1919–1944)," in *Kaposvár. Várostörténeti tanulmányok*, ed. József Kanyar (Kaposvár: n.p., 1975), 370; Tamás Kovács, "Somogy County," in Braham and Szabó, *Geographical Encyclopedia of the Holocaust*, 2:822–23. Taking into account the size and significance of the businesses, the impact was even more severe than this number suggests.

into apartments and have until now escaped the attention of the authorities.

The financial directorates ultimately proved the key agencies in the state appropriation, inventorying, and safekeeping of Jewish assets. Each generally covered approximately one **county**, and its sphere of competence also included the towns and cities in the area.[20] At first the directorate personnel conducted the administrative work associated with reporting assets. Subsequently, following a central government decision in early May, the directorates took charge of the entire plundering process.[21] Processing Jewish assets constituted such an excessive burden that numerous civilian assistants (for example, secondary and elementary school teachers, white-collar employees) were also assigned to help the finance officials. In addition, firefighters and even **levente** units consisting of youth aged sixteen to twenty also participated in the work. If further help was needed, civilian assistant police forces (municipality policemen, air raid assistants, and others) aided the authorities. Where even this level of assistance proved unsatisfactory, politically reliable civilians and occasionally local supporters of the Arrow Cross Party took on the task.

The reports excerpted in document 6-3 reflect the problems the financial directorates faced in implementing the central and local orders regarding the sequestration and inventorying of Jewish property. One of the most significant obstacles was the parallel ambition of the occupying German authorities to carve out the largest possible portion for themselves. Although officially the Germans considered the robbing of the Jews an internal matter for Hungary,[22] in practice, they also systematically and extensively plundered the victims. The Germans instructed the Central **Jewish Council** in the days following the occupation to survey the movable property and real estate of all the Jewish congregations.[23] **Adolf Eichmann**'s unit unscrupulously looted Jewish property across the country. Members of other German organs stuffed their storage trunks with

---

20. Zoltán Magyary, *Magyar közigazgatás. A közigazgatás szerepe a XX. század államában. A magyar közigazgatás szervezete, működése és jogi rendje* (Budapest: Magyar Királyi Egyetemi Nyomda, 1942), 260, 265–66.
21. Kádár and Vági, *Hullarablás*, 235–36.
22. Gerlach and Aly, *Das letzte Kapitel*, 175–76.
23. For the circular letter and incoming questionnaires regarding congregations' assets, see Kinga Frojimovics and József Schweitzer, eds., *Magyarországi zsidó hitközségek 1944 április. A Magyar Zsidók Központi Tanácsának összeírása a német hatóságok rendelkezése nyomán. I. rész: Adattár* (Budapest: MTA Judaisztikai Kutatócsoport, 1994).

works of art. On countless occasions, Wehrmacht and SS units all over the country stole Jewish assets.

These otherwise extensive robberies diminished in comparison to the operation orchestrated by SS-Obersturmbannführer **Kurt Becher**, Himmler's economic envoy. Becher blackmailed the Jewish owners of the Weiss Manfréd group, thus securing for the SS one of Europe's largest armament complexes. In addition, all of the owners' shares in other companies were subjected to Himmler's control. The scope of the robbery thus extended far beyond military production, transferring a full range of other Jewish-owned industrial establishments, real estate, and financial institutions to the SS. Small wonder that the Sztójay government did all it could to invalidate the deal—unsuccessfully.

DOCUMENT 6-3: **Confidential reports of the Szolnok Financial Directorate, June 3 and June 13, 1944, JNSZCA VI. 101. b., box no. 1, document no. 60/1944, 60/1/1944.**

[June 3, 1944]

[. . .] There are so many Wehrmacht and SS units in the town of Szolnok that the Jewish apartments have to be used to accommodate them, given that the units cannot be placed in schools or other public buildings.[24] Before inventorying could start, the committee in charge of issuing the Germans' military apartments simply seized the apartments of the wealthiest Jews based on the name registry they obtained from the Jewish congregation, and they are using these apartments to this day. The committee also carried furniture and other valuables from one apartment to another, acting on its own authority to the extent that local authorities (police headquarters, city hall) were completely helpless against the committee. Nor could the Financial Directorate do anything inside these confiscated apartments, because they claimed that they were taking care of the inventorying themselves and were not willing to allow anyone into these apartments. [. . .]

Unfortunately, I must point out that the German army was not the only claimant seeking Jewish items. I kept receiving claims from certain Hungarian Royal Military units, bureaus, and levente homes, which are requesting unbelievable numbers of items, furniture, along with billiards; a library with Hungarian classics; a piano, ping-pong table, violin, cello,

---

24. The town of Szolnok in eastern Hungary was a key transportation junction for shipments heading east. It was common for several thousand German soldiers to use the rest station set up there.

carpets, etc. I ask for instructions on what actions to take regarding this matter.

[. . .] Concerning municipal inventorying, the situation varies from one municipality to the next. There are municipalities (Jászberény, Kunszentmárton) where the local government has allowed the Jews to take some of their furniture to the ghetto. Moreover, in Jászberény, the Jews emptied their apartments completely, so the finance guard found only empty apartments on the premises.[25] In other locations, Jews were not allowed to take even the most basic items of clothing into the ghetto, and now there are constant requests coming in for carrying items out of the sealed Jewish apartments. Concerning apartment claims, there were so many of them in Szolnok—everybody requested a Jewish apartment, if possible, a furnished one—that I had no choice but to make arrangements with the municipal housing bureau that apartment claims should not be granted until the inventorying by our bureau has taken place, because, of course, the claimants all insisted that the inventorying was a matter of urgency. Break-ins have already been on the agenda for some time now.[26]

[June 13, 1944]

[. . .] With all due respect, the undersigned contacted the town authorities as a result of the ministry meeting held on April 29 of this year, appointed the inventorying committees from members of the finance guard and the official witnesses delegated by the town, and began its work, specifically, the inventorying of goods, and began placing them in a safe location.[27] The undersigned has also asked the town authorities not to satisfy any claims for Jewish apartments until the inventories are finished and the safe storage of the furniture of the apartments is resolved.

---

25. The finance guard was the law enforcement branch of the financial administration system. Finance guards were armed employees of the financial directorates. In Jászberény, where the former mother-in-law of the mayor was among those forced into the ghetto, the moving process was carried out in a relatively considerate manner. It is nonetheless an exaggeration, though, that the Jews were actually allowed to take along all their furnishings, for space inside this ghetto was as tight as in other ghettos. László Csősz, "A jászsági zsidóság a Vészkorszakban," *Jászsági Évkönyv* 14 (2006), 90–101.

26. On the day prior to the writing of this report (June 2), a severe American air raid attack hit Szolnok, leaving several hundred families without shelter.

27. Fifteen such committees were established in Szolnok, a city with about fifteen hundred Jewish residents. The committees began inventorying the Jewish apartments, shops, and warehouses on May 24. JNSZCA, VI. 101. b., box 1, document no. 18/1945.

Unfortunately, it proved impossible to carry out the inventorying methodically and in a topographic sequence, because there were too many applicants for Jewish apartments. The German military especially hindered systematic work when they repeatedly issued the requests in short intervals and demanded not only that Jewish apartments be evacuated but also that Jewish shops be emptied in periods too short to make the execution of the order workable.[28] When I objected, the military official in charge stated on several occasions that these cases were not about Jewish assets, because everything belonged to the Hungarian state, and fulfilling their requests and supplying them with what they need was the duty of the Hungarian state. They also added that if we did not carry out the evacuation by the deadline, they would forcibly open the premises and throw into the street whatever items were inside.[29]

[. . .]

Despite the increased number of employees and working hours, the financial directorates' tasks far exceeded their capacity. The reports included in document 6-3 reflect the many difficulties encountered. Szolnok was not the only place where the conduct of inventorying was chaotic. A typical example is the Budapest regional financial directorate, which submitted a question to the municipalities under its jurisdiction inquiring "who inventoried the movable properties in the abandoned Jewish apartments?"[30] Nevertheless, even under these circumstances, directorates prepared hundreds of thousands of inventories of property and assets across Hungary. The list in document 6-4 includes the movable property of a Jew from Újkécske. In this village in Pest-Pilis-Solt-Kiskun County, assets were surveyed between May 20 and 23, 1944.[31]

---

28. Apart from residential real estate and rented estates, the Germans also impounded factories and warehouses, along with large quantities of merchandise, equipment, and instruments. JNSZCA, V. 606. c., box 29, document no. 5218/1944, V. 573. a, boxes 1042 and 1035, document nos. 5676 and 2995/1944.
29. On the plunder committed by the German authorities, see Kádár and Vági, *Hullarablás*, 345–72.
30. Letter by the Budapest regional financial directorate to the municipal councils, June 20, 1944, in Elek Karsai, ed., *Vádirat a nácizmus ellen. Dokumentumok a magyarországi zsidóüldözés történetéhez (1944 június 26–1944 október 15. A budapesti zsidóság deportálásának felfüggesztése)* (Budapest: Magyar Izraeliták Országos Képviselete, 1967), 3:12.
31. Zoltán Vági and István Végső, "Pest-Pilis-Solt-Kiskun County," in Braham and Szabó, *Geographical Encyclopedia of the Holocaust in Hungary*, 2:803–4.

DOCUMENT 6-4: **Inventory of items in a Jewish apartment of Újkécske, May 23, 1944, Archives of Bács-Kiskun County, V-386, box 14.**

Inventory

Recorded in Ujkécske, on May 21, 1944, at Szent Imre Square 4, regarding the belongings of Sándor Acél, a Jew. The undersigned committee members are present, as is Ferenc Radácsy, Hungarian royal financial officer on behalf of the State Treasury.

[. . .]

1 pc dining room cupboard
2 pcs wooden bed with mattress
1 pc dining table
1 pc wooden sink
6 pcs dining chair
1 pc cabinet
1 pc 3-piece cabinet set
1 pc cabinet with a mirror
4 pcs armchair
1 pc round table
1 pc table
4 pcs chair
1 pc iron washstand
1 pc bookshelf
3 pcs plant container
1 pc sofa
1 pc three-legged table
1 pc bookstand
1 pc two-legged table
1 pc woven furniture set (1 table, 3 chairs, 1 divan)
1 pc chandelier with 4 lights
5 pcs oil painting
4 pcs framed embroidery in
29 pcs picture frame with glass
9 pcs ornamental cushion
61 pcs book
2 pcs brass curtain rod
5 pcs vase
2 pcs statue
2 pcs ornamental plant container
1 pc tray
1 pc large soup bowl, porcelain
1 pc platter for serving meat, porcelain
2 pcs soup bowl
1 pc pastry dish
6 pcs soup dish
6 pcs dinner plate
5 pcs small plate
1 pc sauce dish
1 pc saltshaker
6 pcs bone china plate
1 pc sauce dish
2 pcs sugar holder
1 pc tea pitcher
2 pcs polished glass platter
20 pcs glass plate
1 pc wine set
22 pcs glass
15 pcs liquor glass
1 pc glass platter
2 pcs bread container
1 pc saltshaker

9 pcs ornamental plate
2 pcs ornamental plate
1 pc smoking set
2 pcs tin tray
1 pc grater
10 pcs embroidery
1 pc mirror
1 pc whisking bowl
3 pcs candleholder
1 pc mortar with pestle
2 pcs egg cup
10 pcs pickle jar
25 pcs of glass, mixed
1 pc milk pail
1 pc strainer
2 pcs milk holder
1 pc meat grinder
2 pcs frying pan

1 pc pasta strainer
18 pcs tableware
4 pcs porcelain bowl
1 pc butter dish
8 pcs porcelain plate
1 pc half-liter [bowl]
1 pc glazed mug
2 pcs funnel
7 pcs pan
2 pcs pan lid
1 pc pot
1 pc down feather duvet
2 pcs down feather pillow
1 pc bed cover
1 pc clock
1 pc nightstand lamp
1 pc lamp shade

[...]
Ujkécske, May 23, 1944

Committee members:
Zoltán Ferency [signed]
János Cseh [signed]
Sándor Nyul, Gendarme Lance Sergeant [signed]

The authorities not only wanted to seize the assets of Jewish citizens down to the last spoon and wineglass but also wished to make sure Jews had paid all their taxes before being deported. They therefore collected taxes for 1944 in advance. They even authorized local authorities to obtain access to sealed assets in order to collect taxes owed.[32]

---

32. Draft of Minister of Finance's Decree no. 135.740/1944 VII on the collection of tax debts of the Jews, May 18, 1944, in Ilona Benoschofsky and Elek Karsai, eds., *Vádirat a nácizmus ellen. Dokumentumok a magyarországi zsidóüldözés történetéhez (1944 május 15–1944 június 30. A budapesti zsidóság összeköltöztetése)* (Budapest: Magyar Izraeliták Országos Képviselete, 1960), 2:62–64.

DOCUMENT 6-5: **Notice to Jewish taxpayers from the mayor of Veszprém,[33] May 8, 1944, National Széchényi Library, Placard and Leaflet Collection.**

From the Mayor of the City of Veszprém
No. 2838/1944
NOTICE TO JEWISH TAXPAYERS!

I warn every person considered Jewish under Articles 9 and 16 of Act XV of 1941 that they are required to pay their taxes at the town cashier based on the calculations of the town tax bureau and risk the most severe consequences if they do not comply within 48 hours,[34] that is, by Thursday noon, and pay all taxes that are due by December 31 of this year.

[. . .]

Because the process of calculating taxes has not yet been completed for the current year, they are to pay the entire year's taxes based on the final determination made for the previous year.

Veszprém, May 8, 1944

Dr. Lajos Tekeres [signed]
City Councillor, Deputy Mayor

Thus, even after death, Hungarian citizens labeled Jewish continued to pay taxes to the state that had sent them to their demise.

A similarly cynical measure made Jews pay for their own ghettoization and deportation. Long before the German occupation, a proposal emerged in extremist race-protectionist circles that taxation of Jews should finance their removal. The 1944 anti-Jewish campaign was indeed "self-financing." No independent budget existed for the plunder, ghettoization, and deportation. The Ministry of Finance's account (number 157.880) at the Postal Savings Bank partially covered the costs and was replenished from the sale of Jewish assets. This account also indirectly covered the daily salaries of the gendarmes,[35] as well as "transportation costs" for the deportees and the expense of building fences around the ghettos.[36] The costs of the campaign were significant. Once the

---

33. A town in western Hungary.

34. Act XV of 1941 was the so-called Third "Jewish Law." See document 1-3. The reason for the urgency was that the authorities wanted to collect the taxes before the impending establishment of the ghetto.

35. Usually the given municipality first paid the costs, then submitted the invoices to the government, which reimbursed the expenses from the "Jewish account."

36. For the implementation of the concept of the self-financing genocide in Hungary, see Kádár and Vági, *Self-financing Genocide*, 135–42.

deportations began, the receipts listed trips as long as 500 kilometers (about 310 miles), each with several thousand "passengers." The forced moves to the ghettos and collection camps, as well as the deportations, eventually cost several million pengős.

DOCUMENT 6-6: **Record on the reimbursement of railway transportation costs incurred by the Hungarian State Railways during the deportation of the Jews of Hódmezővásárhely, June 2, 1944, USHMMA RG 52.001M, reel 79 (HNA, Series I).**

Protocol

Recorded in Hódmezővásárhely on June 2, 1944, at the Financial Department of the town concerning the cost of railway transportation of deporting the Jews,[37] to be reimbursed to the Hungarian Royal State Railways.

The following are present:

On this occasion, representing the Hungarian Royal State Railways, Sándor Szentandrási, an officer of the Railways, appeared in person and presented, along with the original documentation, the transportation costs incurred when the Jews were deported, specifically, 2.1 pengős per person, altogether 1,547 pengős and 70 fillérs.[38] He requests that this sum be issued to the Hungarian Royal State Railways.

The record has hereby been read and endorsed by the undersigned.

Date: as above

Margit Nagy on behalf of the Hungarian State Railways
Rapporteur Sándor Szentandrási

The government did everything in its power to seize Jewish property and assets, which it considered part of the national wealth. To reach this goal, the cabinet willingly deployed any means possible at every juncture. In every single collection camp and most ghettos, gendarme investigative units conducted brutal interrogations. Transported Jews were obliged to hand in all their money and valuables. The gendarmes and policemen regularly tortured the more affluent or influential Jews. Sadism was an everyday routine. In Seregélyes, the gendarmes beat the bare breasts of women with rubber hoses.[39] Members of the

---

37. On June 2, 1944, 737 local Jews were taken from Hódmezővásárhely, located in southern Hungary, to the neighboring city of Szeged, nineteen miles away.

38. A fillér was a monetary unit worth 0.01 pengő.

39. Miklós Vincze, *Min múlt az élet. Embersorsok a Holocaustban* (Budapest: Fővárosi Könyvkiadó, 1996), 60.

Nagyvárad unit stripped the Jews, beat them with rubber batons, and sent an electric current through the uteruses of women while family members had to look on. Many died from the torture.[40] In Dés, people were whipped, lashed, and clubbed, often as their loved ones, parents, and children were forced to watch. The gendarmes maltreated the Jews with such force that half their clubs broke. They simply broke off many peoples' gold teeth.[41] The Kolozsvár detectives specialized in torture focusing on testicles. In Székesfehérvár, the general repertoire included hitting their hands and feet.[42] In Kolozsvár and Szászrégen, the ordeal drove several people insane.[43] Others were simply beaten to death. For instance, the elderly Mrs. Jakab Berkovics was tortured three times before she died. In Miskolc many people were forced to drink salty water. Other victims were hung upside down and then beaten. Many of them died; others suffered nervous breakdowns.[44] The members of the fifty-strong gendarme unit operating in Salgótarján beat the soles of Jews' feet with rubber truncheons. Four pregnant women were tortured half to death. Within a few days, sixteen people had died from the interrogations there.[45]

At the planning meetings held prior to the deportations, government participants received clear instruction that they must conduct invasive body searches to check for valuables.[46] Due to a severe shortage in health-care

---

40. See also document 3-9; HJA, DEGOB protocols, no. 5; Randolph L. Braham, *The Politics of Genocide: The Holocaust in Hungary* (New York: Columbia University Press, 1994), 1:644.

41. Ágnes Hegyi, "Dés zsidó közösségének virágzása és hanyatlása," in *Tanulmányok a holokausztról III*, ed. Randolph L. Braham (Budapest: Balassi, 2004), 173, 184.

42. Anna Gergely, *A székesfehérvári és Fejér megyei zsidóság tragédiája (1938–1944)* (Budapest: Vince, 2003), 160.

43. Dániel Lőwy, *A téglagyártól a tehervonatig. Kolozsvár zsidó lakosságának története* (Kolozsvár: Erdélyi Szépmíves Céh, 1998), 115; Zoltán Tibori-Szabó, "Csík vármegye zsidósága a betelepüléstől a megsemmisítésig," in *Tanulmányok a holokausztról III*, ed. Braham, 132.

44. Tamás Csíki, *Holokauszt Borsod vármegyében* (New York: Graduate Center of the City University of New York, 2003), 18.

45. Ernő Munkácsi, *Hogyan történt? Adatok és okmányok a magyar zsidóság tragédiájához* (Budapest: Rennaissance, 1947), 84–85.

46. In the Endre-Baky-Jaross trial, no one admitted to issuing the order, but in their testimonies, the mayors and police officers concurred that they had received specific instructions about this matter at the meeting from State Secretaries Endre and **Baky**. Testimony of László Endre, December 18, 1945, in László Karsai and Judit Molnár, eds., *Az Endre-Baky-Jaross per* (Budapest: Cserépfalvi, 1994), 75. Testimony of László Baky, December 19, 1945, in ibid., 103; investigation materials on Gendarme Sergeant Major László Utassy, Staff Sergeant Mátyás Vörös, and Mrs. Ferenc Wittmann and her accomplices, JNSZCA, Documents of the Office of the People's Prosecutor, boxes 1 and 3, nos. 155/1947 and 73/1947.

employees, doctors and midwives (or nurses) were also assigned to carry out the task. The postwar trial of the former deputy police superintendent of the Pécs ghetto in Baranya County generated the court decision in document 6-7, which reveals some of the special costs borne by Jewish women and girls in the face of officially sanctioned greed.

DOCUMENT 6-7: **People's court trial documents on body searches in the Pécs ghetto, 1949, in Ágnes Ságvári, ed.,** *Dokumentumok a zsidóság üldöztetésének történetéhez* **[Baranya County] (Budapest: Magyar Auschwitz Alapítvány–Holocaust Dokumentációs Központ, 1994), 24–30.**

[February 18, 1949]

(Court decision in the case against Jenő Borbola, police commissioner in Pécs:)[47]

The midwives and midwife trainees carrying out the examinations did so in an unclean, downright harmful and dangerous way. It has happened that after reaching into the rectum or menstruating vagina of a woman, they would, without washing their hands, reach into the vagina or rectum of another woman. It also happened that girls were torn.[48] All this was aggravated by the fact that during the body searches of women, the police, though not present, peeped in or looked inside.[49] Characteristically, they were not checking the rectums of men for gold and jewelry. [. . .]

---

47. Jenő Borbola had closely followed the directives put forth at the meeting. The policemen and their assistants hunted for hidden valuables and often forbade people from taking along food, children's toys, or personal items (which were not prohibited by the decrees). They stripped the victims of their personal documents, saying that "they would no longer need them anyway." Commentary to the people's court decision in the Jenő Borbola's case, February 18, 1949, BCA, Pécs People's Court no. 325/1947–13, 24–29.

48. That is, young girls' hymens were torn.

49. Gendarmes and policemen often personally participated in the procedure or were present in the room during the process. In doing so, they actually violated the service regulation, which called for the internal body search of people accused of crimes to be conducted in private rooms, one by one, and carried out by doctors or trained women. On this, see the wartime gendarmerie textbook: Árpád Toldi, ed., *A bűnügyi nyomozás* (Budapest: Stádium, 1941), 46–47.

[October 5, 1949]
(Excerpt from Protocol No. Nb.575/1946-21 of the People's Court of Pécs:)
Protocol
   Prepared based on the public hearing held on October 5, 1949, at the People's Court in Pécs, concerning the criminal case initiated against Mrs. Aladár Bajos for a war crime and also a crime against the people.
   I completed my midwife training in 1941 and worked as a midwife at the maternity clinic in Pécs. In the summer of 1944, I do not remember the exact date when we received a request from the gendarmerie at the clinic that we should send fifteen midwives to perform body searches on those to be interned. One day, the chief midwife came into our room where there were the three of us and said that because there are not enough trainees and midwife trainees, I would also have to go. I immediately reported that I had been on a 24-hour shift, was tired, and wanted to leave. They objected to my assignment, so I also went to Assistant Professor Gábriel, asking him for help in getting out of the assignment. But the professor told me I had to go, and if I did not want to, then I was not fulfilling my duty and I should consider my refusal as my notice to terminate my employment.[50]
   Afterward, ten of us went to the Lakics Barracks,[51] but we had only two pairs of rubber gloves between us. I therefore did not perform any internal, vaginal examinations of the women, only assisted them in undressing.
   [. . .]

   Similar body searches were conducted in numerous ghettos and camps. In Székesfehérvár, ten women used altogether two pairs of rubber gloves to examine the vaginas of several hundred women. In Makó, five liters of water were used for hand washing during the examination of about five hundred women.[52]

---

   50. Those who did not appear risked losing their jobs and could expect disciplinary proceedings and a fine. In exchange for the "work," they received payment, however. In Pécs, for example, midwives received 50 pengős per day for their "highly responsible and exhausting work." Judit Molnár, "Two Cities, Two Policies, One Outcome: The De-Judaization of Pécs and Szeged in 1944," *YVS* 32 (2004), 121.
   51. A cavalry garrison within the Pécs residential area, this was where the collection camp site was designated for local Jews and those from the vicinity.
   52. See Judit Molnár, *Zsidósors 1944-ben az V. (szegedi) csendőrkerületben* (Budapest: Cserépfalvi, 1995), 141.

In Zalaegerszeg, thirteen midwives and seven nurses "examined" Jews for four days.[53] In Székesfehérvár, even six-year-old girls underwent the torturous process.[54] In Tiszaföldvár, the midwives conducted the body searches ruthlessly, occasionally gloating over the victims' misfortune. "Up to now, you were the ladies, filthy Jews; now it will be us," one midwife said, according to survivor recollections.[55] In Szászrégen—and elsewhere—the brutal methods tore girls' hymens, and inspection with dirty hands often resulted in infections.[56] In Dés, a fifteen-year-old girl developed sepsis as a result her examination.[57] The summer of 1944 marked one of the all-time moral low points in Hungarian history: the state sent its officials to brutally enter little girls' vaginas in search of "the national wealth" they might have hidden there.

The **Géza Lakatos's** government that came to power in late August 1944 took deportation of the remaining Jews and the atrocities described above off the agenda, but the devastating economic measures continued. The Lakatos cabinet faced severe anomalies during the processing and redistribution of Jewish property and attempted to remedy the problem. One measure altered the definition of "Jewish company" as laid out in Article 13 of Prime Minister's Decree no. 1600/1944 (see document 6-1). Originally, every company with at least one Jewish partner was considered Jewish. The Lakatos government's new decree, published on September 29, turned the definition around and declared that companies with "at least one non-Jewish partner" were *not* considered Jewish,[58] exempting in this way an unknown (yet obviously large) number of companies from the plundering regulations. The shops and factories of the companies freed from these regulations were obliged to reopen upon the request of the non-Jewish member, and a non-Jewish owner was assigned to head the company. Clearly economic rationality and the recognition that the previous policies had failed were behind this move.

---

53. Mayor's report, August 16, 1944, in Ágnes Ságvári, ed., *Dokumentumok a zsidóság üldöztetésének történetéhez* [Zala County] (Budapest: Magyar Auschwitz Alapítvány–Holocaust Dokumentációs Központ, 1994), 54–55.

54. Gergely, *A székesfehérvári és Fejér megyei zsidóság tragédiája*, 162.

55. See survivor testimonies, 1945, investigation material on Gendarme Sergeant Major László Utassy and Staff Sergeant Mátyás Vörös, JNSZCA, Documents of the Office of the People's Prosecutor, no. 73/1949.

56. Tibori-Szabó, "Csík vármegye zsidósága a betelepüléstől a megsemmisítésig," 132.

57. Hegyi, "Dés zsidó közösségének virágzása és hanyatlása," 173.

58. Prime Minister's Decree no. 3250/1944 on the utilization of the business (industrial) inventory of goods and raw materials, as well as other assets of the Jews, *Budapesti Közlöny*, September 27 and 29, 1944.

The Lakatos government made no attempt to create a uniform national law regulating the entire process. Only after the Arrow Cross seized power on October 15–16 was such a regulation passed. **Ferenc Szálasi**'s government nationalized Jewish assets in one fell swoop through a single legal act.

**DOCUMENT 6-8: Prime Minister's Decree no. 3840/1944 on the nationalization of Jewish assets,** *Budapesti Közlöny***, November 3, 1944, 2.**

The Hungarian Royal Ministry orders the following:
*1. The assets of the Jews being transferred to the state*
1. §.
(1) All assets of the Jews, as assets of the nation, are transferred to the state. These assets must be used to cover expenses associated with warfare, war damages, war aid and care,[59] and also the costs of executing laws concerning the Jews.

(2) All arrangements to do with the transfer of assets that fall under Paragraph (1) are made by the special government commissioner appointed for this purpose, a position under the supervision of the Ministry of the Interior.[60]

(3) The following items are not transferred to the state based on Paragraph (1):

*a)* artifacts intended for religious worship and for domestic worship: articles of clothing worn during religious events by individuals in charge of conducting religious ceremonies; prayer books, religious relics, family portraits, sepulchers, sepulcher vaults[61];

*b)* private correspondence and other writing of Jews; schoolbooks and school equipment of Jews and members of their households;

---

59. War aid and care (*hadigondozás*) was the system of state subsidy provided to the families of people in the service.

60. Among the special government agencies established for handling Jewish assets, the most important was the Government Commissioner's Office for Handling Material and Financial Affairs of the Jews, which was created in early June 1944 and headed by Albert Turvölgyi, department head of the Ministry of Finance. In November, the Arrow Cross government appointed **Árpád Toldi** to head the office, which at this point was already under the auspices of the Ministry of the Interior. Toldi later became the commander of the so-called Gold Train transferring the Jewish property to Austria. Kádár and Vági, *Hullarablás*, 258–67.

61. Even though this point stipulated that liturgical objects would not be nationalized, a vast amount of Judaica was confiscated and loaded onto the so-called Gold Train.

*c)* any medication and medical equipment needed for an illness or physical disability of Jews and members of their households;

*d)* the wedding bands of Jewish married (or engaged) couples;[62]

*e)* food provisions and heating and lighting supplies to cover two weeks for Jews and members of their households;[63]

*f)* cash in an amount not exceeding a combined sum of 300 pengős per household, plus an additional 100 pengős for each family member;

*g)* in amounts not exceeding the regular needs of Jews and their household: domestic and kitchen furniture, pots, cooking utensils and tableware, clothing and personal items, required bedding and linens, as well as tools and other equipment needed in the profession that a Jew may pursue.

(4) There is no exemption preventing transfer to the state of the following: based on the previous paragraph, the abandoned assets of Jews and items that have been removed from their custody or disposal or, in addition, items mentioned in (g) above that contain platinum, gold, silver, precious stones, or pearls.

[. . .]

The laws created by the government of the collapsing Arrow Cross state had nothing to do with reality: by this time, state and party agencies were plundering Jewish property without any restrictions whatsoever. In the territories under military threat, the government gave complete freedom to local authorities to distribute Jewish assets among the population at their own discretion.[64] Meanwhile special Arrow Cross and German agencies organized the large-scale looting of the whole country, directing tens of thousands of trucks, freight cars, and barges westward loaded with Jewish and non-Jewish property. The Nazi plunder of Hungary continued until the very last German troops left the country in April 1945, only to be replaced by Soviet looting. This latter, of course, did not spare those Jewish assets left in Hungary that had not been taken to the Reich in the preceding months.

---

62. In this respect the Szálasi government was more "generous" than the Sztójay cabinet, for the latter allowed Jews to keep their wedding rings only if they did not contain any precious stones or pearls. See document 6-1.

63. The law contained no guidance about who would be responsible for supplying provisions (food, etc.) for the Jews after two weeks had passed.

64. Record of the interministerial meeting, October 31, 1944, HNA K498, fasc. 3.

## THE EFFECTS OF PLUNDER: WINNERS AND LOSERS

Following the German occupation, many Hungarian Jews sought to salvage their property and assets. Jewish men and women streamed to the banks, attempting to convert their deposits into cash. They also tried to sell off their valuables or bury them for safekeeping. Many sought out acquaintances who would (either selflessly or out of greed) take items for safekeeping, collaborate in the mock sale of property, or otherwise rescue and preserve assets. The government tried to halt such attempts early on: on April 6, 1944, the head of Department VII (Public Security Section) of the Ministry of the Interior issued a confidential decree.

DOCUMENT 6-9: **Circular Decree of the Ministry of the Interior on the prevention of the hiding of gold and valuables by the Jews, April 6, 1944, NCA V. 83, box 15.**[65]

Hungarian Royal Minister of the Interior
Number: 6138
VII. res., 1944

Strictly confidential! Immediate attention required! To the Subprefect of every county. To the Commissioner of the Hungarian Royal Police both in Budapest and in the provinces. To the Hungarian Royal Police Border Headquarters and those in charge of the police branch offices.

It has come to my attention that in various feigned transactions Jewish persons are handing over their gold items, jewelry, and valuables to non-Jewish persons—for storage, or for the purpose of placing the items on the market and splitting the profits, or through some other transactions involving payment or in the form of a feigned gift.

In accordance with Article 3 of Prime Minister's Decree no. 1270/1943 on restricting the flow of gold: gold items, etc. may not be placed on the market, and more generally, speculation on and accumulation of gold, gold items, and jewelry is prohibited. Gifts may not exceed the manner and magnitude of customary gift giving in social life.

I hereby instruct you to order the authorities and agencies under your command to maintain the strictest surveillance over the affairs of Jewish persons and those non-Jewish persons contacted for the aforementioned purpose—these affairs are in violation of the decree mentioned and are

---

65. First published in Benoschofsky and Karsai, *Vádirat a nácizmus ellen*, 1:120–22.

a matter of crucial public interest, which must be protected. The police must swiftly investigate and initiate proceedings against the speculators. In accordance with the instructions of Prime Minister's Decree no. 1270/1943, perform your activities firmly and swiftly. Beyond the criminal procedure prescribed in the decree, in accordance with both Prime Minister's Decree no. 8130/1939 and, concerning the execution thereof, Minister of the Interior's Decree no. 760/1939, police supervision or arrest and detainment carried out by the police must be initiated immediately against the offenders and their accomplices.

[. . .]

By decree of the Minister:
*Vitéz Gyula Király*
Gendarmerie Colonel

The call had to be repeated several times throughout the country. Everywhere the press covered the issue in great detail, chastising those who were "hiding the treasures greedily amassed by the people of Judea."[66] non-Jews hiding Jewish property became a mass phenomenon in Hungary in 1944. For instance, on May 6, in his report from Kolozsvár, Gendarme Lieutenant Colonel **László Ferenczy** informed his superiors that "once they were called upon to do so, several Christian families turned in the Jewish valuables that were hidden in their homes, but there are still ongoing investigations in many places."[67] According to a gendarme report dated May 30, 1944, "It has already been ascertained that many people from wide-ranging sectors of society have ventured to hide Jewish assets" throughout the country, and "it is expected that in the future, public security agencies will continue to learn of a number of further incidents of this sort."[68] In Nagyvárad, more than two thousand people, around 3 percent of the Christian population, were accused of hiding Jewish property. According to postwar testimony by **State Security Surveillance** head **Péter Hain**, fifty to sixty reports on this issue were filed each day at the office of the so-called Hungarian Gestapo.[69]

---

66. *Jász-Nagykun-Szolnok Megyei Lapok*, May 27, 1944, 1. Despite the "deterrent examples" listed in the articles and the government calls threatening further investigations and retribution, many people were still willing to take the risk.

67. Ferenczy's report, May 6, 1944, in Karsai and Molnár, *Az Endre-Baky-Jaross per*, 503.

68. Gendarme Report Summary no. kt. 8929/1944 B, May 30, 1944, HNA Series I, reel 12.

69. Testimony of Péter Hain, December 27, 1945, in Karsai and Molnár, *Az Endre-Baky-Jaross per*, 278.

Although non-Jews hid a large number of assets for Jews, out of varying motivations, the state sequestered the property for the most part.[70] The government used the assets not just to finance the anti-Jewish campaign but to cover the costs of certain social measures. The circle of beneficiaries of expropriation went far beyond this, however. State social and health institutions, churches, and organizations loyal to the government, such as the **Order of Vitéz**, received some of the land and property in exchange for a very small sum.[71] Alongside such "legal" robbery, organized and carried out by the government, state officials' plunder for private purposes became frequent.[72] Hain's State Security Surveillance led the way. Hain and his men confiscated large sums of money during arrests of Jews. Rather than handing the cash over to the financial authorities, they simply embezzled it. Their acts of plunder, their brutal interrogation methods, and their night-time revelries gained such notoriety that in June of 1944 Hain was removed from his post.[73]

Hundreds of thousands of private individuals also sought to profit from the ghettoization and deportation of Jews. Throughout the country, the population filed petitions requesting clothes, shoes, bedding, and furniture seized from their Jewish neighbors. Virtual sieges targeting apartments, shops, and goods also began. With corruption flourishing, theft became an everyday affair. Many citizens broke into the former ghettos and plundered abandoned houses where Jews had lived. While much of this behavior went unpunished, in Balassagyarmat, a town of twelve thousand, for example, the authorities initiated proceedings against eight hundred locals for breaking into the former ghetto.[74] In Kaposvár, a team of twenty-five people plundered sealed Jewish apartments for days. In

---

70. See document 6-9.

71. László Csősz, "Land Reforms and Race Protection: The Implementation of the Fourth Jewish Law," in *The Holocaust in Hungary: A European Perspective*, ed. Judit Molnár (Budapest: Balassi, 2005), 189–90.

72. In Gyergyószentmiklós, for example, two noncommissioned officers broke into a sealed Jewish apartment and stole suitcases full of valuables; in Nagykároly, silver cutlery was found in the possession of a financial officer. Ferenczy's reports, May 7 and 10, 1944, in Karsai and Molnár, *Az Endre-Baky-Jaross per*, 504, 506.

73. For details about Hain and the operation of the State Security Surveillance, see the glossary; Kádár and Vági, *Hullarablás*, 282–85; Szabolcs Szita, *A Gestapo Magyarországon* (Budapest: Korona, 2002), 160–78.

74. Árpád Tyekvicska, ed., "Adatok, források, dokumentumok a balassagyarmati zsidóság holocaustjáról," in *Nagy Iván Történeti Kör évkönyve* (Balassagyarmat: Nagy Iván Történeti Kör, 1995), 111.

Dés, residents also looted Jewish properties.⁷⁵ In Beregszász, no less than 10 percent of the sealed apartments suffered break-ins.⁷⁶

DOCUMENT 6-10: **Photograph of local residents plundering furniture and other valuables left behind in a provincial ghetto, summer or autumn 1944, HJA, T 65.686.**

From the spring of 1944 onward, the fate of Jewish property permeated public discussion, spurring continual excitement across a wide social spectrum. Newspaper articles and public announcements by the authorities stressed unflaggingly that the confiscated property belonged to the state. It would be carefully inventoried, pending a decision about its ultimate use or distribution. The government did not want to provide free goods as subsidies, for it feared that such measures could lead to inflation. The treasury wished to receive additional revenue from the Jewish wealth; free-for-all giveaways were not on the agenda.

---

75. Szita, *A Gestapo Magyarországon*, 132; Hegyi, "Dés zsidó közösségének virágzása és hanyatlása," 173.

76. Veesenmayer's report, June 27, 1944. See Randolph L. Braham, ed., *The Destruction of Hungarian Jewry: A Documentary Account* (New York: Pro Arte for the World Federation of Hungarian Jews, 1963), 2:615.

Minister of the Interior **Andor Jaross** made this point clearly in two speeches on May 16, 1944, in Nagyvárad. He succinctly and clearly summarized the principles and objectives of the government with respect to the solution of the "Jewish question" and the redistribution of assets taken from the Jews. He considered it a primary task of his ministry that "every internal enemy be completely undermined and, if needed, extirpated." He clarified that the ghettoization of the Jews (by then complete in Nagyvárad) was merely a first step toward a thoroughgoing and final "solution." While admitting to and justifying barely camouflaged mass murder, he also threatened those helping the Jews, as well as the "neutral" public that was less enthusiastic about the government's policy. In addition, Jaross outlined two major objectives of the government's economic policy: implementing social measures and carrying out macroeconomic stabilization, both to be accomplished by utilizing the confiscated property.

DOCUMENT 6-11: **Speech of Minister of the Interior Andor Jaross in Nagyvárad,** *Magyarság*, **May 18, 1944, 5.**[77]

[. . .] I warn every Hungarian person and family that today every neutral position, every half-hearted opinion, every doubt, suspicion, and worry that can be named mean the support of the internal enemy. To those who today feel and think it appropriate that their responsibility is to protect their so-called fellow humans, I have this to say: you must immediately and forever choose between two options—either you are willing, in the interest of 13.5 million Hungarians,[78] to follow policies and pledge solidarity with them, or you can choose instead to pledge allegiance to a few hundred thousand people who have never belonged to the Hungarian community. (A new round of loud applause.)

[. . .] Our goal cannot be to protect the law at all costs. Our goal is to serve life and to show the achievements of life. (Great approval and applause.) In public administration procedures, I am not interested in whether a certain law has been followed. What I am interested in is whether through the implementation of laws, I have elevated the social

---

77. The same article in *Magyarság* covered both speeches.

78. In 1941, the population of Hungary stood at 14.7 million. József Kepecs, ed., *A zsidó népesség száma településenként (1840–1941)* (Budapest: Központi Statisztikai Hivatal, 1993), 32. Jews and other minorities made up at least one-fourth of this number, and 77.4 percent of the population declared Hungarian to be their mother tongue. Miklós Zeidler, *A revíziós gondolat* (Budapest: Osiris, 2001), 221.

standard, whether I have helped improve our public health, promoted economic development and brotherly cooperation, which are needed throughout the entire Hungarian world and in all the diverse aspects and varieties of life.

[. . .] Today I saw a new Nagyvárad opening up before me in the May sunshine. I saw a new nationalist Nagyvárad, in which there were no Jews in the streets. I saw for myself that the Jews had been segregated in the city.[79] The city has solved this problem and I was reassured to see that the solution meets the requirements of our age. But this problem is not yet over. We have to remove every contaminant, every possible source of infection from the nation's blood and circulatory system. In this respect, the government keeps going further, step-by-step. I do not want to provide all the details—you should watch events as they unfold.

I emphasize that the wealth that Jews, with all their greed, managed to collect in property, treasures, and valuables in the liberal era has ceased to belong to the Jews and now belongs to the Hungarian nation.[80]

But this wealth cannot simply be presented as gifts—it cannot be used to honor certain national achievements. It must enrich the nation in its entirety; it must be built into the circulatory system of the national economy so that all honest working Hungarians can have their share of it.

In this city it is not only the surface, the street view, that must change,[81] but also the way people think, those Hungarians' way of thinking that has not changed up to now.

Perhaps my words have been harsh and firm, but please believe me that it is only with a firm soul that is willing to make sacrifices that this nation can attain a better future. Total war knows no mercy. The heart must not falter, even when there are falling bombs and the clamor of weapons around us. It is not only Hungarian soldiers who have a great

---

79. The Nagyvárad Jewish community was rather large and affluent. In 1941, those belonging to the Israelite religion made up almost 23 percent (21,333 people) of the population. The "Jewish Laws" affected an additional 750 Christians of Jewish origin. Kepecs, *A zsidó népesség száma településenként*, 122. On their fate in 1944, see Dezső Schön et al., eds., *A tegnap városa. A nagyváradi zsidóság emlékkönyve* (Tel Aviv: Láháv, 1981); Dániel Lőwy, "Bihar County," in Braham and Szabó, *Geographical Encyclopedia of the Holocaust in Hungary*, 1:214–33.

80. Jaross is referring to the era during the Austro-Hungarian Empire (1867–1918) when the large-scale economic rise and cultural and political integration of the Jews took place.

81. Antisemitic authorities wanted to get rid of the external signs of Jewish presence, so they set out to remove certain shop signs and advertisements, and in some places they began tearing down synagogues.

duty to stand firm. Total war also demands that everyone assume the responsibility abroad as well as here at home.

[. . .]

Despite such warnings, the number of petitions submitted to government offices and the number of illegal attempts to appropriate Jewish property (through thefts, break-ins, apartment occupations) did not drop. Official pronouncements in the matter were partly ineffectual because it had become clear to everyone that the representatives of the authorities were leading the way in the plunder. The chaotic circumstances of this period enhanced the nepotism and corruption so typical of the state administration.[82] Incidents like the one mentioned in the letter of complaint reproduced in document 6-12 became quite common. Thwarted expectations of quick and easy wealth caused further frustration.[83] Throughout the country, spontaneous rallies of non-Jewish citizens erupted; the military and the police could barely contain groups of people charging toward their coveted goal.[84]

DOCUMENT 6-12: **Complaint of Mrs. Imre Gréczi regarding the auctioning off of Jewish assets, June 2, 1944, USHMMA RG 52.001M, reel 12 (HNA, Series I).**

Protocol.

Recorded in Kassa on June 2, 1944, in the official room of the Hungarian Royal Financial Directorate, concerning the following:

Those present:

From the financial directorate: Dr. Kálmán Nagy, Financial Secretary

Mrs. Imre Gréczi, born Erzsébet Dudás, resident of 6 Rákóczi Boulevard, Kassa, wife of a Honvéd staff sergeant[85]

Mrs. Imre Gréczi appeared without being summoned and reported the following:

On the afternoon of June 1, my husband and I were walking to city hall to inquire about having an apartment assigned to us, because that

---

82. Kádár and Vági, *Hullarablás*, 248–58; László Csősz, "Őrségváltás? Az 1944-es deportálások közvetlen gazdasági–társadalmi hatásai," in *Küzdelem az igazságért. Tanulmányok Randolph L. Braham 80. születésnapjára*, ed. László Karsai and Judit Molnár (Budapest: MAZSIHISZ, 2002), 92–97.

83. Gerlach and Aly, *Das letzte Kapitel*, 197–98.

84. Of the "paupers and irresponsible elements" besieging the ghetto in Nagyvárad, eighty-one individuals were imprisoned. *Új Nagyvárad*, July 6–7, 1944, 7.

85. The Hungarian Defense Force.

same morning they would not talk to me at the Housing Bureau,[86] saying that they were busy at the moment, and they even closed the doors in my face.

On the afternoon of June 1, my husband and I walked to city hall, and in the corridor of city hall, the office messenger stopped us, saying that it was not possible to go up to city hall at the time because a meeting was being held in City Councillor Ruttkai's office. At this point, my husband firmly warned the office messenger that he should allow us upstairs at my own risk [sic], and we went up to the second floor to Councillor Ruttkai's office and the adjacent room. My husband—I should note—was wearing his uniform. About 30–40 people were standing out in the hallway in front of the anteroom to Councillor Ruttkai's office, and the door of the anteroom was open. All of them were town officials. We were standing at the edge of the crowd and saw that somebody in the room was standing on the table, picking up two packages of linens, then a carpet, and yelled out the asking price. For example, "tablecloth, seats 12, with napkins, asking price 15 pengős," and he was also yelling that "there is no need to drive up the price because the auction is among ourselves." He was also yelling, "Duvet cover, asking price 7 pengős, with blanket cover!" They drove the price up to 30 pengős. We looked into the room and saw that there were lots of carpets, linen of all sorts.

A female officer from the crowd asked me who I was, because only officials were allowed to stand there. And then I told her, "I am also the wife of a soldier; I have the same right to Jewish stuff as you do, or else why didn't you take the Jewish stuff to the slums, into the jungle." The female officer retorted, "You will not get anything anyway; go away; you should be ashamed of yourself for coming here," and she even pushed me. As the man standing on the table saw this scene, he also rebuked me: "Get lost; only officials are allowed to be here." At this point, we left city hall.

[. . .]

While many people tried to lay their hands on Jewish assets in the midst of such feverish scenes, the "Aryanization" of prestigious, high-income professions (such as medicine, engineering, and the law) was likewise an important goal for antisemitic middle-class groups. Among other specialist white-collar professionals, physicians made the most radical demands. Back in 1920, student movements at the medical schools had already proven forceful advocates of

---

86. For the flood of petitioners for Jewish apartments, see document 9-4.

the *numerus clausus*. Dissatisfied with the advantages afforded by the "Jewish Laws," members of the National Association of Hungarian Physicians (MONE) did everything in their power to get rid of perceived Jewish competition—and did so paying no heed to the public health requirements of the population.[87] MONE demanded that using the quotas set in the "Jewish Laws," the number of practicing Jewish physicians be cut radically across the areas reannexed between 1938 and 1941. This restriction threatened to collapse the health-care system: in the Upper Province region, three-fourths of all doctors were subject to the "Jewish Laws," while in Northern Transylvania, the restrictions affected almost half of all doctors. For this reason, Minister of the Interior Ferenc Keresztes-Fischer, who oversaw health services, implemented administrative measures to thwart MONE's efforts. A similar clash took place in 1942, when the **Labor Service** called up thousands of Jewish doctors at the urging of radical politicians. The Ministries of Defense and the Interior eventually intervened to stop the practice, which had generated a severe shortage of physicians.

Following the German occupation, MONE put pressure on the government to discharge Jewish physicians from labor service, which meant their deportation. Knowing this would lead to the immediate collapse of the health-care system, the cabinet did not fulfill the request.[88] However, due to the zeal of **László Endre** and certain local authorities, many Labor Service physicians were deported as well. The report in document 6-13, written twelve days after the mass deportations began, indicates the tragic consequences of this development.

DOCUMENT 6-13: **Report of the public health officer of Máramaros County to the Ministry of the Interior, May 27, 1944, USHMMA RG 52.001M, reel 8 (HNA I).**[89]

>Dear Hungarian Royal Minister of the Interior!
>
>Balatonlelle.
>
>With due respect, I report that in the area comprising Máramaros County, the 28 organized municipal and district physician positions have been mostly filled by doctors who are Jewish labor servicemen—due in

---

87. For details about this issue, see Mária M. Kovács, *Liberalizmus, radikalizmus, antiszemitizmus. A magyar orvosi, ügyvédi és mérnöki kar politikája 1867 és 1945 között* (Budapest: Helikon, 2001), 151–64.
88. Ibid., 163.
89. First published in Elek Karsai, ed., *"Fegyvertelen álltak az aknamezőkön . . ." Dokumentumok a munkaszolgálat történetéhez Magyarországon* (Budapest: Magyar Izraeliták Országos Képviselete, 1962), 2:520–22.

part to the partial vacancies in these positions and also because doctors appointed to these posts have been called up for military service.

As a result of the complete removal of the Jews, the following situation has arisen: of 28 municipal and district physician positions, 17 public health officer positions remained vacant, and the public health service was thus largely paralyzed. This situation was reported to Your Excellency via telegram on May 23, 1944, by the subprefect of the county. I myself requested via telephone from the Hungarian Royal Ministry of the Interior department XVI that doctors be assigned to provide municipal and district physician services, and also reported the vacant positions to the same department via telegram. At the same time, the subprefect of the county also submitted to Your Excellency a proposal about eliminating the shortage of doctors, pointing out that there was an impending danger of epidemics and that inpatient care in hospitals had been interrupted. The obstetrics unit of the state public hospital is indeed presently without a head physician because the man who had filled the position of head physician of obstetrics has been called up for military service, and the chief radiologist is likewise fulfilling his military service, and we cannot manage to replace them at present.

Only 3 Christian private physicians are left across the county; of these, 2 are married female dentists, and 1 doctor is a retired hospital head physician, specializing in gynecology and obstetrics. [. . .]

The difficulties of the shortage of doctors are aggravated by the fact that transportation has worsened.

In addition to the large number of typhoid fever cases during the spring months, new diseases have now appeared in several municipalities across the county, and because of the shortage of doctors, keeping certain areas under surveillance has become impossible.

Your Excellency, in the light of the above, I respectfully request that you assign a physician experienced in public health service to aid the Hungarian Royal Chief Public Health Officer, in order to adequately cover the increased number of crucial basic tasks. I also respectfully request that steps be taken to assign at least 10 physicians to fill some of the 17 empty municipal and district physician positions, so that medical services can be provided in the endangered areas.

[. . .]

Máramarossziget, May 27, 1944.

Dr. Imre Barka
Hungarian Royal Chief Public Health Officer

Similar reports pleading for interventions and relief arrived from all parts of the country. The most severe situations unfolded in the reannexed areas, primarily in Carpatho-Ruthenia (for instance, in Máramaros and Ung counties), where the majority of the doctors were Jewish. However, on the draft requesting that Jewish doctors and pharmacists, who were indispensable for basic care, be allowed to remain, László Endre himself scribbled, "On the contrary! Put them in ghettos and camps right away!" The lack of experts forced the Jew-hating prefect of Borsod County to exempt Jewish doctors and chemists from deportation. Removal of certain other white-collar professionals (such as veterinarians and engineers) also caused major difficulties. In some areas, especially in the underdeveloped northeastern regions, only a few businesses remained once the Jews were forced to close their stores. Even in parts of the country with a rather low proportion of Jews (2 to 3 percent), the absence of merchants and other professionals could still be felt, and some business branches were hit quite hard.[90]

## SYNAGOGUES INTO STOREHOUSES

As everywhere else in Europe, in Hungary "Aryanization" consisted of two phases: (1) plundering and then (2) processing and redistributing the goods. The state realized the first phase fully, confiscating all valuables belonging to its Jewish citizens, from factories and precious artworks to the smallest furniture or household items. However, execution of the second phase was fragmented. The government failed both to create a comprehensive legal framework and even to execute the decrees it eventually had drawn up. There were four major reasons for this redistribution deficit: lack of time, deficiencies in the legal framework for the "Aryanization" process, administrative wars among Hungarian authorities about spheres of competence, and initiatives by the German occupiers also claiming Jewish assets.[91]

The authorities managed neither to store properly nor to distribute this massive amount of plunder, lacking the time and personnel. As with some other aspects of the seizure of Jewish property, no central regulation was ever

---

90. See Csősz, "Örségváltás," 76–78.
91. For details about each of the reasons, see Kádár and Vági, *Self-financing Genocide*, 75–111, and Gábor Kádár and Zoltán Vági, "The Economic Annihilation of the Hungarian Jews, 1944–1945," in *The Holocaust in Hungary: Sixty Years Later*, ed. Randolph L. Braham and Brewster S. Chamberlin (Boulder, CO: East European Monographs, 2006), 77–88.

instituted for sealing and safeguarding the appropriated assets. As the ghettoization operation started across the entire country, public administrators encountered obstacles and had to regulate property issues arising during the process at their own discretion.[92] As with the designation of the ghettos,[93] authorities inventoried and stored assets regionally in ways that varied from one locale to the next.

The Nagyvárad mayor's order, adopted by various other municipalities, set up committees comprising city officials and policemen and entrusted them with the ghettoization process and the confiscation of valuables.[94] By contrast, in Vas County, authorities required the Jews forced out of their homes to inventory any movable property they left behind.[95] In Sopron, the gendarmerie took charge of sealing the ghetto apartments of Jews transferred to collection camps; town officers were not allowed near them.[96] In some places, the assets were taken to the gendarme or police stations or to central warehouses (often set up in synagogues). Elsewhere, the valuables were locked up in one of the rooms of a vacated apartment. The regent's commissioner of the Carpatho-Ruthenian military operations zone (prompted by the plundering and large-scale seizures by the army) ordered authorities to collect Jewish property in synagogues.[97]

Prominent Jewish photographer and businessman Béla Liebmann (1899–1996) took the photo represented in document 6-14(B). A decorated veteran of World War I, Liebmann was drafted for labor service in 1944. Returning to his home at the end of the war, the photographer documented huge stockpiles of confiscated goods still stored in the city's synagogue.

---

92. Kádár and Vági, *Hullarablás*, 234–35.
93. See chapter 3.
94. László Csősz, "'Keresztény polgári érdekek sérelme nélkül . . . ' Gettósítás Szolnokon 1944-ben," *Századok* 134 (2000), 658–59.
95. Szombathely ghettoization order, May 9, 1944, in Ságvári, *Dokumentumok a zsidóság üldöztetésének történetéhez* [Vas County], 41.
96. Letter by the Sopron mayor to the prefect, July 10, 1944, GyMSCA IV. 1404. b, box 490.
97. Confidential order no. 162/1944, April 13, 1944, HNA, Series I, reel 11.

DOCUMENT 6-14(A). Confiscated Jewish items piled up in the Szeged synagogue, 1945, Móra Ferenc Museum (Szeged), USHMMPA WS# 18745.

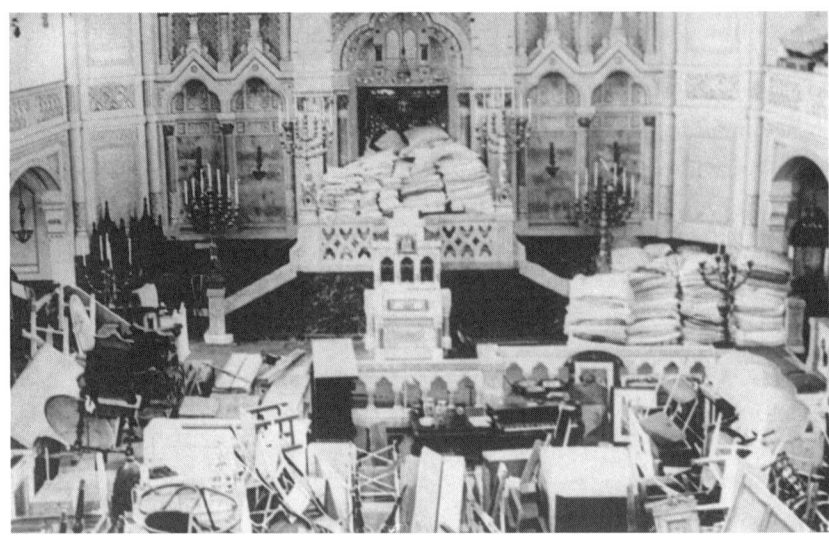

DOCUMENT 6-14(B): Shoes belonging to members of the Jewish community of Szeged in the city's synagogue. Photograph by Béla Liebmann, 1945, USHMMPA WS# 18749.

Most of the owners of the property piled up in the local synagogue never returned to Szeged. Liebmann's twelve-year-old daughter Flóra and wife Szenka were murdered. After being deported to Strasshof, Austria, they had been sent to a labor camp at Weissenbach an der Triesting. Retreating SS troops executed them in the middle of April 1945 in a stone quarry near Sulzbach.[98] Liebmann remarried in Szeged and reestablished his photography business, but in 1951 the communist state confiscated his equipment, store, and house.

---

98. Szabolcs Szita, *Utak a pokolból. Magyar deportáltak az annektált Ausztriában 1944–1945* (Budapest: Metalon Manager Iroda, 1991), 179.

## CHAPTER 7
# IN THE NAZI CAMPS

IN THE YEAR following the German occupation, authorities sent more than half a million Hungarian Jews to various camps. From Tillé in northern France to Tallinn in Estonia, from Lešnica in Serbia to Kiel on the Baltic shores of Germany, deportees and labor servicemen ended up in a total of about six hundred concentration and forced labor camps, factories, and production plants scattered across Europe. Most of them did not live to see the Allies' victory. In the months following the liberation, thousands more died from disease, as well as from the consequences of starvation and brutal treatment suffered in Nazi camps.

Nearly 430,000 were deported to Auschwitz II–Birkenau and 15,000 to Austria (Ostmark). The Nazis soon transported those designated for slave labor at Birkenau to every major concentration camp. These deportees were taken northward and eastward as far as Warsaw and Stutthof and even to Riga in Latvia. After the evacuation of the Auschwitz complex beginning in January 1945, the SS marched tens of thousands of prisoners (among them a number of Hungarians) to Gross-Rosen, Stutthof, Neuengamme, Bergen-Belsen, Sachsenhausen, and other camps.

During the "individual operations" (*Einzelaktionen*), the German Sicherheitspolizei sent thousands from Hungary to Mauthausen and its auxiliary camps. After the **Arrow Cross** coup d'état, the Szálasi government handed over around fifty thousand Jews to the Germans. They fell victim to the death marches headed toward Austria. At first they were ordered to work on fortification construction; the Nazis later transported them away from the front lines into the Mauthausen camp complex (Gunskirchen, Gusen, Ebensee, Melk, and so forth). Other **Labor Service** companies entered German territories with the retreating Hungarian army, and some were taken to France. At the end of 1944, the Arrow Cross authorities sent the last group of deportees—thousands of Jews—to the camps. This chapter follows the trails of those deported into the Nazi concentration camp system, primarily focusing on the center of the Hungarian Jewish Holocaust experience at Auschwitz II–Birkenau but showcasing documents from other camps as well.

## AUSCHWITZ GETTING READY

In the spring of 1944, the Auschwitz death factory was operating at half-steam. Over the first four months of the year, transports became markedly scarcer; a mere twenty-five thousand new prisoners arrived. In March the SS stopped the expansion of the camp.[1] Visiting Birkenau, **Adolf Eichmann** was stunned to note neglected crematoria and delays in construction of the new "**Jewish ramp**" (*Judenrampe*). But the situation changed overnight with the decision to deport the Hungarian Jews. Beginning on May 1, vacations and leaves for SS staff in Auschwitz were banned. Complaints by the Reich Security Main Office (RSHA) and Eichmann led to the dismissal of the Auschwitz complex commander, Arthur Liebehenschel—whom many considered "liberal"—as well as Birkenau commander Fritz Hartjenstein.[2] The Nazis put SS-Obersturmbannführer Rudolf Höss, founder of the camp, in charge of murdering the Hungarian Jews.

Höss had just one week to prepare Birkenau for the operation. He appointed Richard Baer to run Auschwitz I and made Josef Kramer—who later gained notoriety as head of the Bergen-Belsen camp—commander of Birkenau. He accelerated the construction of the new railway line and ramp leading directly to the crematoria. The survivors of the April deportations from Hungarian internment camps and prisons were assigned to work on construction projects. Höss expanded the membership of the ***Sonderkommando***, the Jewish special commando in charge of cremating the corpses, as well as the

---

1. Correspondence of the Auschwitz *Kommandantur* and the Zentralbauleitung, March 29–April 7, 1944, USHMMA RG 11.001M03, reel 24/83 (Zentralbauleitung der Waffen-SS und Polizei in Auschwitz).

2. Der SS-Standortälteste Auschwitz, Standortbefehl no. 14/1944, May 8, 1944, USHMMA RG 15.167M, reel 3 (Proces Rudolfa Hoessa).

so-called *Kanadakommando*, which processed the valuables brought in by the deportees.³

Höss was aware that despite the completion of four new crematoria in 1943, equipped with dressing halls, gas chambers, and furnaces, the camp's cremation capacity was insufficient for the envisioned destruction of 1 million Hungarian Jews. He desperately needed a specialist in burning. Therefore, he dismissed the commander of the crematoria and recalled SS-Hauptscharführer **Otto Moll** from the Gleiwitz subcamp. In 1942, Moll was in charge of exhuming and cremating corpses buried in mass graves before the Birkenau crematoria went into operation.⁴ As Moll took over the Birkenau extermination zone, he realized that the smaller-capacity Crematoria IV and V had been out of use for half a year at that point.⁵ After examining the buildings he ordered them renovated. To increase the gassing and cremating capacities, he reactivated the former Polish peasant house that operated as a temporary gas chamber in 1942–1943 (known as the "little white house," or Bunker 2). He also ordered giant burning pits dug.⁶ Meanwhile, Eichmann's deputy in Berlin, Rolf Günther, ordered Zyklon B gas from the Waffen-SS. Through the end of May, a total of 990 kilograms of the lethal insecticide arrived in Auschwitz.⁷

Once the first transports from Hungary arrived at the camp, the SS-Business Administration Main Office (WVHA), the SS authority controlling Auschwitz, had camp staff sign the statement in document 7-1. It was needed because an

---

3. Danuta Czech, *Auschwitz Chronicle, 1939–1945* (New York: Henry Holt, 1997), 621–23. On April 23, the *Sonderkommando* consisted of only ninety people. On May 12, the *Sonderkommando* staff already had 218 members. On May 16, the day when the first Hungarian mass transports arrived, there were 318 members, and on July 28, this number had risen to 903. Arbeitseinsatz Reports, Auschwitz-Birkenau, between April 20 and July 28, 1944, ABSM, D-AuII-3a, 30276–30461.

4. Moll's testimony in Landsberg, April 29, 1946, USHMMA RG 15.167M, reel 3.

5. Jean Claude Pressac and Robert Jan van Pelt, "The Machinery of Mass Murder at Auschwitz," in *Anatomy of the Auschwitz Death Camp*, ed. Yisrael Gutman and Michael Berenbaum (Bloomington: Indiana University Press in association with the USHMM, 1998), 237.

6. Ota Kraus and Erich Kulka, *Halálgyár* (Budapest: Kossuth, 1958), 232–33; Pressac and van Pelt, "The Machinery of Mass Murder," 237–38; Eric Friedler, Barbara Siebert, and Andreas Kilian, *Zeugen aus der Todeszone. Das jüdische Sonderkommando in Auschwitz* (Lüneburg: zu Klampen, 2002), 184. On the renovation work, see the correspondence between the Silesian Bauinspektion der Waffen-SS und Polizei, the SS-WVHA Amtsgruppe C, the Auschwitz Zentralbauleitung, and private companies, May 9–31, 1944, USHMMA RG 11.001M.03, reel 43/393.

7. Receipt by DEGESCH written for SS-Obersturmführer Kurt Gerstein, along with correspondence about shipment, March 13–June 9, 1944, Eichmann trial 1994, T37/184.

internal investigation of the SS in 1943 had revealed numerous abuses: guards were murdering inmates without permission, corruption was flourishing, and prisoners' gold, money, and valuables were being stolen in massive quantities. Now the WVHA wanted to make sure that the staff in Auschwitz would act with strict discipline during the mass murder of the Hungarian Jews.

DOCUMENT 7-1: **Statement of responsibility by SS-Unterscharführer Arthur Breitwieser about his participation in the operation against the Hungarian Jews, May 22, 1944, USHMMA RG 04.006M (Records of Nazi Concentration Camps), reel 2, Auschwitz, 34 (translated from German).**

Uscha. [Unterscharführer] Breitwieser, Arthur[8]
Statement of Responsibility
1.) I am aware, and have today been informed, that should I acquire Jewish property of any sort through unauthorized means, I will be condemned to die.[9]
2.) With respect to every measure to be carried out in connection with the evacuation of the Jews, I must maintain unconditional confidentiality, even with my comrades.[10]
3.) I hereby commit myself and my work capacity entirely toward the task of executing these measures in a swift and smooth manner.
[signed] Breitwieser SS-Uscha
Auschwitz, May 22, 1944.

The death camp was ready for the largest genocidal operation in its history.

---

8. Johann Arthur Breitwieser (1910–1979) served in Auschwitz between 1940 and 1945. In the summer of 1941, he received training in the use of Zyklon B (*Desinfektor*), and he subsequently worked in the warehouses. After the war, the Americans captured him and handed him over to Poland. He was sentenced to death in the Auschwitz trial in Kraków for assaulting and reporting prisoners. His death sentence was commuted to life imprisonment, and he was then released in 1959. He left for West Germany, where he was arrested on June 9, 1961. In the Auschwitz trial in Frankfurt he was charged with participating in the first gassing operation carried out in the basement of Block 11 of the Auschwitz Gestapo in the fall of 1941. On August 19, 1965, he was acquitted for lack of evidence and released.

9. The threat of death did not deter the SS personnel from stealing. Moreover, the wealth of the Hungarian Jews killed and robbed during Operation Höss led to a proliferation of corruption the likes of which had never been seen before. See, e.g., Wiesław Kielar, *Anus Mundi: Five Years in Auschwitz* (London: Allen Lane, *1981*), 264–65.

10. Considering the call for secrecy, it is rather surprising that SS members created two complete photo albums in the weeks after the statement above was signed. See document 7-2.

## ON THE "JEWISH RAMP" OF AUSCHWITZ II–BIRKENAU

The overwhelming majority of Jews deported from Hungary ended up in Auschwitz. Some trains covered the distance in one and a half to two days, while passengers on the slowest trains remained squeezed into the extremely crowded cattle cars for four to five days. Typically they arrived at Birkenau's "Jewish ramp" after a three-day journey.[11] Under such circumstances many people died in the summer heat.[12] Losses were especially common in the transports from Ungvár. In one car, for example, ten out of the ninety Jewish passengers died, among them several children; of eighty-one people put into each of two other cars, one old woman died, and one child went insane.[13] Deaths were common even in less crowded transports.[14] An average of forty to fifty people died during each trip. In the 150 transports arriving from Hungary, some six to seven thousand Jews had died by the time they arrived at Birkenau. Since removing the dead was forbidden, those still alive traveled in the heat accompanied by decaying corpses.

In Auschwitz, a few SS men and prisoners of the "Kanada" work unit awaited the arrivals. The latter emptied the cattle cars, moved the crowd along, and arranged the men and women into separate rows of five, lining them up for selection. They often shouted at the deportees, pushed them, tore packages out of their hands, and made cynical comments concerning the newcomers' fate. Still, these prisoners saved thousands of lives. Aware that young mothers would be sent to the gas chambers if they held children in their arms, they gave the boys and girls to elderly arrivals, who faced a certain death sentence. Similarly, they tried to separate young people fit for labor from parents incapable of working. And even though they risked their own lives, they whispered warnings to the Hungarian Jews that during the selection older men and women should claim to be younger, while youths should lie and claim to be older.[15]

Soon after disembarking, the deportees were marched in front of an SS man, who decided their fate. Looking for healthy people between sixteen and forty, the Germans immediately set aside those obviously unfit for work: older people and children. In unclear cases, a doctor inquired about a deportee's age

---

11. The case of the Huszt transports is a good example of just how random the duration of journeys was. HJA, DEGOB Protocols, nos. 127, 202, 1135, 1727, 1860.
12. HJA, DEGOB Protocols, no. 180.
13. HJA, DEGOB Protocols, nos. 161, 163, 213.
14. HJA, DEGOB Protocols, nos. 1940, 153.
15. For example, HJA, DEGOB Protocols, nos. 1135, 1413.

and profession and about possible illnesses. The physician then waved the prisoners along, their fate decided. Those deemed incapable of working were sent to the gas chambers immediately. This happened to approximately 300,000 to 345,000 Hungarian Jews,[16] including two little boys, Sril (Israel) and Zelig Jákob (Jakab). Hungarian authorities deported the Jákob family from Carpatho-Ruthenia. They arrived at the ramp in the early morning of May 26, where an SS man took the picture reproduced in document 7-2. Note the boys' typical Hungarian coats and hats.

DOCUMENT 7-2: **Photograph of Sril (or Israel) (left) and Zelig (right) Jákob upon arrival at the Birkenau extermination camp, May 1944, courtesy of YVA (photo album FA268/49).**

The SS murdered Sril and Zelig in the gas chambers immediately after their arrival. Their sister Lili (Lenke), father Mordechai, and two older brothers were selected for work. Lili refused to follow orders and tried to join her mother

---

16. For the number of Hungarian Jews murdered in Auschwitz immediately after their arrival, see the Introduction.

Esther and two younger brothers. However, an SS guard pushed her back into the line of prisoners selected to work, stabbing her in the arm. She became prisoner no. A-10862. In December 1944, Lili was transported to a clothing factory in Silesia, then to a munitions plant; she finally ended up in Mittelbau-Dora, where thousands of prisoners perished while working on the construction of a large underground factory. She fell ill with typhus. American troops, liberating the camp on April 9, found her lying near death in the camp infirmary.

Lili, weighing less than ninety pounds, later looked for clothes in the camp and found a photo album wrapped in striped pajamas. She was shocked to recognize her own family members and other acquaintances, including the chief rabbi of Bilke in the photos. The *Auschwitz Album*, as it is known today, contains around two hundred photographs taken by two SS officers. They had received special permission to record the arrival of the transports and the process of extermination, from the railroad ramp to the entrance of the crematoria.[17] These photos may represent the most important and detailed visual account of the mass murder process conducted at the Nazis' largest extermination camp.

Lili returned to Bilke after the war, where she came to realize she was the only survivor from her family. The Nazis had murdered more than twenty of her relatives. She subsequently moved to the town of Munkács, where she married a survivor and childhood friend. In 1948 they emigrated to the United States. Starting life anew, she had two children and two grandchildren and passed away in 1999 at the age of seventy-three. She donated the *Auschwitz Album* to Yad Vashem.[18] The picture of her brothers taken at the ramp has become one of the best-known images of Auschwitz.

## THE MASS MURDER OF HUNGARIAN JEWS

Many other transports preceded and followed the one that carried the Jákob family to Auschwitz. On some days five to six Hungarian transports arrived. The SS physicians on duty performed selection for fifteen to twenty thousand people over a twenty-four-hour span. They deemed at most 20 to 30 percent of

---

17. The other series of photographs from these months portrayed the lives of SS personnel. Taken by SS-Obersturmführer Karl Höcker, adjutant to the camp commander, the images were acquired by the United States Holocaust Memorial Museum in January 2007.

18. On the postwar history of the album, see Gideon Greif, "The 'Auschwitz Album'— the Story of Lili Jacob," in *The Auschwitz Album: The Story of a Transport*, ed. Israel Gutman and Bella Gutterman (Jerusalem and Oświęcim: Yad Vashem and Auschwitz-Birkenau State Museum, 2002), 136.

the deportees fit for work and sent the rest to the gas chambers. The furnaces operated uninterruptedly, day and night, with tall flames escaping the chimneys. Often, the schedule was so tight that prisoners dragged one transport's dead out of the gas chambers as the next group undressed outdoors and another transport arrived at the ramp. The Nazis' main problem: they were killing more people in the gas chambers than they could burn in the furnaces. The crematoria simply could not keep up with the task.

For this reason, crematoria commander SS-Hauptscharführer Moll returned to the method that proved effective back in 1942: he had pits for burning dug. *Sonderkommando* prisoners lined up three rows of corpses, one on top of the other, in each pit. They doused the bodies with gasoline and alcohol, then set them on fire. But this method led to special difficulties, for human fat melting in large quantities from the bodies hindered the burning process. For this reason, members of the *Sonderkommando* dug sloped canals into the pits, then used buckets to bail the liquid and poured it over the dead bodies in small quantities to enhance the burning process.[19] To keep the operation secret, a thick hedgerow closed the pits behind Crematorium V off from view.

The members of the *Sonderkommando* witnessed the Hungarian Jews' last moments. According to Slovak survivor Filip Müller, these unfortunates "struggled along the dusty roads, exhausted and in low spirits, mothers pushing prams, taking the older children by the hand. The young helped and supported the old and sick."[20] Having spent three to four days in cattle cars, they were very thirsty; the SS promised they would receive tea or soup after the "bath." Müller recalled, "This pre-programmed suffering was deliberately aimed at paralyzing the ability to notice things and the will to resist."[21] First the *Sonderkommando* accompanied the Hungarians to the undressing rooms, then to the gas chambers. They answered the deportees' questions, heard their cries, and saw their deaths. During the gassings they collected the victims' baggage; later, they searched their bodies for hidden objects and then burned them in the furnaces of the crematoria or in the outdoor burning pits. In the summer of 1944 around nine hundred prisoners served on this special squad. With a few exceptions, they were mainly Jews deported from Poland, Greece, Slovakia, and Hungary.

---

19. For a detailed discussion of the digging and operation of the burning pits, see Filip Müller, *Eyewitness Auschwitz: Three Years in the Gas Chambers* (Chicago: Ivan R. Dee in association with the USHMM, 1999), 126–32.

20. Born in 1922 in Sered, Slovakia, Filip Müller was deported to Auschwitz in 1942 and worked in the *Sonderkommando* for two and a half years. He survived the October 1944 revolt and was taken to Mauthausen in early 1945. He was liberated around Wels. See Müller, *Eyewitness Auschwitz*; USHMM ITS Collection Data Base.

21. Müller, *Eyewitness Auschwitz*, 133–35.

Several *Sonderkommando* survivors later mentioned a young **Orthodox** Jew in his thirties from Poland serving in the unit. While due to the psychological and physical torture some *Sonderkommando* men behaved like human robots and others went mad, lost their faith, became aggressive, drank, or spoke in vulgarities, this man maintained his composure and religious convictions even in the crematoria. He refrained from eating meat and tried to keep kosher.[22] During the Jewish holidays he delivered religious ceremonies during which, lacking wine, he blessed tea.[23] He tried to keep his comrades' spirits up as well. He was also active in the *Sonderkommando*'s resistance group and collected information about the mass killings. After the war a few records, prepared and hidden by *Sonderkommando* members in order to document Nazi crimes, were unearthed around the crematoria. The same unknown person had written some of the Yiddish manuscripts. Only decades later was their author identified: the religious young man, Leib (Leyb or Lejb) Langfuss (or Langfus), the *dayan* (member of the rabbinical court) of the Polish town Maków-Mazowiecki (b. 1910).[24] He arrived in Birkenau on December 10, 1942. The Nazis murdered his family in the gas chambers and soon transferred him to the *Sonderkommando*. In his notes, Langfuss recorded the murder of the Hungarian Jews as well.

DOCUMENT 7-3: **Notes of *Sonderkommando* member Leib Langfuss on the murder of the Hungarian Jews, in Bernard Mark, *The Scrolls of Auschwitz*, ed. Isaiah Avrech (Tel Aviv: Am Oved, 1985), 206, 208.**[25]

*Particulars*
[. . .]
Two Hungarian Jews asked the Sonderkommando: "Shall we say the Confession?" He replied in the affirmative. They then pulled out bottles of brandy, and drank happily raising their bottles in a toast to life (Lechaim). They actively persuaded the Sonderkommando to drink with them. The

---

22. Miklós Nyiszli, *Mengele boncolóorvosa voltam* (Budapest: Magyar Lajos Alapítvány, 1994), 144–45.
23. Recollection of former *Sonderkommando* member, Eliezer Eisenschmidt in Gideon Greif, *We Wept Without Tears: Testimonies of the Jewish Sonderkommando from Auschwitz* (New Haven, CT: Yale University Press, 2005), 247.
24. The documents were signed with a coded abbreviation: A.J.R.A. After much research it was decoded as a hint about the author's Hebrew name: Arje Jehuda Regel Arucha. The last two words, *Regel Arucha*, mean the same as *Langfuss* in German: "long foot."
25. The exact fate of Leib Langfuss (1910–1944) is unknown, but the last entry in his diary is dated October 26, 1944. See also Hermann Langbein, *People in Auschwitz* (Chapel Hill: University of North Carolina Press in association with the USHMM, 2004), 201–2.

man was ashamed and refused to drink. They persisted: "You have to avenge our blood. You have to live. So . . . to life!" They appealed to him: "We understand how you feel . . . " And he drank with them. While drinking, the man became very emotional and burst out weeping. He ran into the crematorium and sobbed bitterly for a long time: "Comrades! We have burned enough Jews. Let us destroy everything, and ourselves as well, for the Sanctification of the Name!"

In midsummer,[26] 100 young men from Hungary were brought to be shot to death. They undressed and stood naked in the courtyard of Crematorium #1.[27] Their heads were shaven, with only a stripe of hair running down the middle of their heads. Then Oberscharführer Moosfeld came and commanded them to move to #2.[28] From the gate of one crematorium to the other runs a road some 60 meters long [197 feet], parallel to a public highway. He posted the commandos in two columns,[29] to guard the naked Jews, lest they run to the public road. Thus, totally naked, they were rushed all the way with clubs waving above their heads. Driving them were the Kommandoführer and the German kapo.[30] When they reached the other side, they were jammed into a small room and taken out one by one for execution.[31]

[. . .]

In the last days of May 1944, a transport arrived from Koszyce.[32] The deportees included the old *rebbetzin* of Strapkov who was already 85 years

---

26. The summer of 1944.

27. It was actually Crematorium II, on the left side of the Jewish ramp (*Judenrampe*) in Birkenau.

28. On SS-Oberscharführer **Erich Muhsfeldt** (elsewhere Mussfeldt, Mussfeld, or Mußfeld), see the glossary and Wacław Długoborski and Franciszek Piper, eds., *Auschwitz, 1940–1945: Central Issues in the History of the Camp* (Oświęcim: Auschwitz-Birkenau State Museum, 2000), 3:237; Josef Marszalek, *Majdanek: The Concentration Camp in Lublin* (Warsaw: Interpress, 1986), 130–43; Tomas Kranz, *Die Vernichtung der Juden im Konzentrationslager Majdanek* (Lublin: Pánstwowe Museum na Majdnaku, 2007), 62–63. "#2" was actually Crematorium III, facing Crematorium II, on the right side of the ramp.

29. Members of the *Sonderkommando*.

30. The *Kommandoführer* was an SS man in charge of a crematorium and the *Sonderkommando* unit serving in it. The *Kapo* mentioned here was probably a German prisoner named Karl Konvoent, who was killed by the *Sonderkommando* prisoners during the revolt on October 7, 1944.

31. These killings were usually committed by Muhsfeldt.

32. Koszyce: the city of Košice in today's Slovakia; in Hungarian: Kassa. Hungary reannexed the city in 1938. Between May 16 and June 3, 1944, 15,707 Jews were deported from Kassa to Auschwitz in five transports.

old.³³ She said: "Only now do I see the extinction of the Jews of Hungary. The government permitted significant portions of the Jewish communities to escape. But when the Jews asked the advice of their rabbis, they calmed them. The Rabbi of Belz said that the Jews of Hungary would know nothing worse than fear.³⁴ Until the bitter day suddenly came when the Jews were thrown into hell. Oh yes, the heavenly ones concealed it from them but at the last minute they alone escaped to the Land of Israel; they saved their own souls, leaving their flocks to be slaughtered. Lord of the Universe! In the last moments of my life, I ask You to forgive them for the desecration of Your Name!"

[. . .]

The murder of the Hungarian Jews speeded up preparations for an uprising. Langfuss, knowing it was a suicide mission, volunteered to blow up a crematorium. However, due to communication problems, his team did not manage to execute its mission during the October 7 uprising, and he stayed alive. Two weeks later, the SS started burning the camp's records, then November 25 commenced dismantling of the larger crematoria. The next day the SS performed the last selection of the *Sonderkommando*; Langfuss was among the hundred people chosen to die. In the final entry of his notes, he requested that the person who found them publish them under the title "The Horrors of Murder." According to Filip Müller and Miklós Nyiszli, he gave a passionate speech to his fellows after the selection, telling them not to question God's reasons: "Even if we could, by some chance, save our lives, what use would that be to us now? . . .

---

33. *Rebbetzin:* the rabbi's wife; Strapkow: the town of Stropkov in today's Slovakia; in Hungarian: Sztropkó. The identity of this woman is not clear. Research has established that the "miracle rabbi" Avraham Shalom Halberstam (1856–1940), who served as the chief rabbi in Stropkov from 1897, moved to Kassa in the early 1930s. During the Holocaust, his son and successor, Rabbi Menachem Mendel Halberstam (1873–1954), also left Stropkov for Hungary.

34. Belz is a town in western Ukraine famous for its Hasidic rabbi dynasty. During the Holocaust, a Hungarian counterintelligence officer smuggled the fourth rabbi of Belz, Aharon Rokeach (1880–1957), and his half-brother, Mordechai Rokeach (1902–1949), into Hungary. Their family, left behind, was killed by the Nazis. In Budapest, the Hungarian Jews welcomed them warmly, but soon the Gestapo started to look for them again. With the help of the Zionists, they obtained special certificates to travel to Palestine. Mordechai read Rokeach's farewell speech publicly to thousands of Jews who had gathered; the text of the speech was printed and circulated in Budapest. Rokeach predicted rest and tranquility for the future and said that "only good and kindness will pursue" the Hungarian Jews. They left in January 1944. Two months later the Sondereinsatzkommando Eichmann arrived in Budapest.

We should be alone, without a family, without relatives, without friends, without a place we might call our own, condemned to roam the world aimlessly. For us there would be neither rest nor peace of mind until one day we would die in some corner, lonely and forsaken. Therefore, brothers, let us now go to meet death bravely and with dignity!"[35] When Langfuss finished, there was complete silence. Soon the SS took the prisoners away and killed them.

Even though the October 7 uprising was the most significant attempted revolt, it was not the only instance of resistance in Birkenau in 1944. Members of some Hungarian transports also tried to defy the Nazis. In late May, women from Szolyva waiting at the (real) bath began to smell burning human flesh and noticed bodies being thrown into the burning pits in the distance. The women threw down their packages and picked up stones. Fearing a rebellion, the SS soldiers spent hours trying to calm them. One of them reasoned as follows: "You are not going to believe the tale that in 1944, the Germans would be burning people?" The SS could only restore quiet by touring the entire camp with one of the women so that she could see the prisoners living there for herself.[36]

Because the crematoria were running at full capacity, thousands were herded into the so-called Bunker 2, a former Polish peasant house converted into a temporary gas chamber and reactivated in 1944. In front of the building, which the *Sonderkommando* simply called the "pyre," Eckardt, an ethnic German SS man from Hungary, greeted and tried to calm the newly arrived Jews, promising them water. Other times the Nazis did not bother to deceive the victims. They beat the frightened Jews and chased them into a primitive wooden barracks, where they had to undress very quickly. Afterward, the Jews were herded into the thatch-roofed house with peeling plaster, where death awaited them.[37] Toward the end of the operation, as Zyklon B supplies ran low, victims faced an even more terrible death: some, still alive, were pushed into burning pits dug behind Bunker 2.[38]

In Auschwitz, a number of prisoners fell victim to various pseudoscientific medical experiments as well. SS physicians sterilized numerous Hungarian Jewish women in the camp. Dr. Carl Clauberg injected a caustic substance into

---

35. See Müller, *Eyewitness Auschwitz*, 161–62; Nyiszli, *Mengele boncolóorvosa voltam*, 146.
36. Gábor Kádár and Zoltán Vági, "Magyarok Auschwitzban," *Holocaust Füzetek* 12 (1999), 113.
37. Jean-Claude Pressac, *Auschwitz: Technique and Operation of the Gas Chambers* (New York: Beate Klarsfeld Foundation, 1989), 171–78; see also Długoborski and Piper, *Auschwitz, 1940–1945*, 3:134–43.
38. Pressac, *Auschwitz*, 177; see also Müller, *Eyewitness Auschwitz*, 125–43.

their uteruses or fallopian tubes, often without an anesthetic.[39] In many cases, this led to an inflammation of the peritoneum or the ovaries. Other women found out only much later that the "vitamin injections" administered by SS doctors had rendered them infertile. The physicians who left Auschwitz in early 1945 moved to the Ravensbrück camp, continuing their experiments there for several months. Their last victims were young Hungarian Roma girls deported in the late fall of 1944 from Hungary.

Among the SS physicians, **Josef Mengele** gained the most notoriety. He carried out selections on the ramp, collected several hundred Jewish and Roma twins, and later conducted painful experiments on dozens of these children. Dr. Miklós Nyiszli (1901–1956), a Jewish pathologist from Nagyvárad, may have known Mengele better than any other prisoner: for half a year he was forced to perform autopsies on Mengele's victims and assist him in his pseudo-medical experiments. He saw the massacre of the Hungarian Jews, as well as the murder of survivors of the so-called Gypsy camp, the Łódź and Theresienstadt ghettos, as well as of the last of Slovakia's Jews in the camp. He survived the *Sonderkommando* revolt, the subsequent retaliations and selections, and, finally, the evacuation of Auschwitz and the chaos of the war's last months. Later Nyiszli published his memoirs in Hungarian in Romania and Hungary and in English in the United States. In the past decades further editions have appeared in various languages.[40] The book served as evidence during the Nuremberg trial against the German chemical industry conglomerate I. G. Farben. However, Nyiszli gave his very first recollection in the summer of 1945, when he spoke to representatives of the Hungarian Jewish aid organization **National Committee of Hungarian Jews for Attending Deportees (DEGOB)**.

---

39. See, e.g., Robert Jay Lifton and Amy Hackett, "Nazi Doctors," in *Anatomy of the Auschwitz Death Camp*, ed. Yisrael Gutman and Michael Berenbaum (Bloomington: Indiana University Press in association with the USHMM, 1998), esp. 306–7.

40. The original Hungarian title was *Dr. Mengele boncolóorvosa voltam az auschwitzi krematóriumban* (*I Was Dr. Mengele's Pathologist in the Crematorium of Auschwitz*). A U.S. translation was titled *Auschwitz: A Doctor's Eyewitness Account* (New York: Frederick Fell, 1960). One of the more recent editions has been *Im Jenseits der Menschlichkeit. Ein Gerichtsmediziner in Auschwitz* (Berlin: Dietz, 1992). Nyiszli, born in Somlyo, had obtained a medical degree from the German university in Breslau. He resumed his medical practice after the war and testified in Nuremberg in 1947 at the I. G. Farben trial, one of the "Subsequent Nuremberg Trials" conducted by U.S. occupation authorities in Germany. See also Robert Jay Lifton, *The Nazi Doctors: Medical Killings and the Psychology of Genocide* (New York: Basic Books, 1986), 350–51, 358–78 *passim*.

DOCUMENT 7-4: **Testimony of Dr. Miklós Nyiszli, July 29, 1945, USHMMA RG 39.013M, reel 5 (HJA, DEGOB Protocols, no. 3632).**

Recorded on July 29, 1945, in the DEGOB office. Dr. Miklós Nyiszli, a Jewish physician from Nagyvárad, and DEGOB officers István Heimler and Mrs. László Fischer are present.

On May 22, 1944, along with 26 of my colleagues (all district doctors), I was sent from the Aknaszlatina ghetto to Auschwitz.[41] Following the selection I was sent to the right and, after a 24-hour stay in Auschwitz, I was transferred to Buna,[42] with a *Häftling* population of 14,000.[43] I had been working for about 12 days there in Construction Company 197, when the chief medical officer of the Buna camp, an SS-Hauptsturmführer summoned all physicians to appear before him. We lined up, all 50 of us. They told us that professional pathologists could volunteer for light work. Out of the 50 physicians, two of us stepped forward. I was all the more eager to volunteer since I had already realized that I would break sooner or later doing the heavy cement work. Following a thorough interview, both of us were accepted. I had studied medicine in Germany and had practiced as a pathologist for many years. I had no problem being hired for the position, nor did my colleague, who had worked in a medical school in Strasbourg.[44] Within one hour, accompanied by two armed SS

---

41. Aknaszlatina was located in Máramaros County in Northern Transylvania, which was reannexed to Hungary in 1940. The Jewish physicians in the area were deported along with the other local Jews. The transport, consisting of 3,371 people, crossed the Hungarian border at Kassa on May 25, 1944, and arrived in Auschwitz-Birkenau after four days of travel. Randolph L. Braham, *The Politics of Genocide: The Holocaust in Hungary* (New York: Columbia University Press, 1994), 1:598, 2:1403.

42. By 1944, Auschwitz had developed into a vast camp complex. It consisted of three major parts: Auschwitz I was the administrative center, Auschwitz II (Birkenau) was the main extermination site, and Auschwitz III (Monowitz or Buna) was the hub of industrial production.

43. *Häftling* (German): prisoner. Nyiszli received the tattoo number A-8450 on May 29. Two thousand Hungarian Jews deemed fit to work were registered in Birkenau on this day and received registration numbers A-7741 through A-9740. Female prisoners, including Nyiszli's wife and daughter, were placed in Sector BIIc, the Hungarian female transit camp (*Durchgangslager*). Czech, *Auschwitz Chronicle*, 636. The men were transported to Monowitz, a few kilometers away, where they worked on the construction of a synthetic rubber plant for I. G. Farben. Prisoners called this camp Buna, a reference to the synthetic rubber that it was supposed to produce.

44. Nyiszli later revealed the name of his fortunate colleague, Dr. Robert Levy, who also survived Auschwitz. Miklós Nyiszli, *Orvos voltam Auschwitzban* (Bucharest: Literary Publishers, 1964), 209.

guards, we were put in a luxury-level Red Cross ambulance. To my horror, we were driven to the courtyard of Crematorium I in Auschwitz,[45] where our documents were handed over to the commander of the crematorium, Oberscharführer Mussfeld.[46] We were immediately given thorough instructions as to what we could and could not look at here. Then we were led into a separate, furnished, clean room, and Oberscharführer Mussfeld said that the room had been assigned to us by Dr. Mengele[47]; we got a separate room, while the crematorium staff lived on the second floor. There were 200 staff members of the so-called *Sonderkommando*.[48] Right away, the Oberscharführer obtained a full set of clothing and underwear of excellent quality for us, taken from gassed transports. Dr. Mengele arrived a few hours later and subjected us to another interview lasting circa one hour. He then gave us our first assignment: it involved the medical examination of selected individuals who had some form of abnormal development. We took measurements of these people; then Oberscharführer Mussfeldt shot them in the head with a "Kleinkaliber," that is, a 6 mm gun, after which we were ordered to perform an autopsy and prepare a very precise autopsy report. Subsequently, we applied chloride of lime to the abnormally developed corpses and sent the thoroughly stripped, cleaned, and packed bones to the Anthropological Institute in Berlin-Dahlem. These experiments were sporadic, until one day at midnight SS officers woke us and led us to the dissecting room, where Dr. Mengele was already waiting for us. In the workroom next to the autopsy room were Gypsy twins, altogether 14 of them, under SS guard; they were sobbing bitterly. Without saying a word, Dr. Mengele prepared a 10-cm$^3$ and a 5-cm$^3$ syringe. From one box, he took out evipan; from another he placed chloroform in 20-cm$^3$ vials on a table. Then the first twin sibling was brought in, a young girl of around 14. Dr. Mengele ordered me to undress her and place her on the autopsy table. Then he administered an intravenous injection of evipan in the right arm. After the child lost consciousness, he felt for the left heart ventricle and injected 10 cm$^3$ of chloroform. The child was dead after a single convulsion, and Dr. Mengele had her taken to the morgue. The murder of all 14 twin siblings was carried out in a similar way that night. Dr. Mengele asked us how many autopsies we

---

45. Nyiszli was assigned to Crematorium II, which stood at the left end of the Birkenau ramp.
46. On SS-Oberscharführer Erich Muhsfeldt, see the glossary.
47. On Mengele, see the glossary.
48. See the glossary.

could undertake per day. He thought we could carry out 7–8 of them. In response we replied that to do precise scientific work, we could dissect on average four corpses a day. He agreed to that.

We received subjects for our scientific autopsies either from the camp or from recently arrived transports. During May, June, and July [1944], an average of 3–4 Hungarian transports arrived at the Auschwitz *Judenrampe*.[49] The selections were performed in shifts, with Dr. Mengele and Dr. Thilo taking turns.[50] The selection decisions were based on the ability to work and were occasionally quite erratic. As part of the selection process, newly arrived transports were divided into two groups—one to the right, the other to the left. The right side meant life; the left side meant the crematorium. In terms of percentages, 78 to 80 percent were sent to the left: children, mothers with young children, the elderly, pregnant women, the handicapped, disabled war veterans. In a few minutes, the crowd on the left started to move slowly to the left, carrying their hand luggage.[51] The crematoria were around 200 meters [218 yards] from the *Judenrampe*, and the crowd of circa 2,000 people on the left passed through the gate to Crematoria 1, 2, 3, or 4, as instructed. Once inside the crematorium, they descended 10–12 concrete steps and entered an empty, underground concrete-lined room that could fit 2,000 people. The first row halted at the entrance, but once they read the signs "Disinfection" and "Bath" printed in all major languages, they were reassured and descended down the steps. They were immediately ordered to undress; there were

---

49. See the glossary.

50. Heinz Thilo (1911–1945), SS lieutenant, head physician of the hospital sector of Auschwitz-Birkenau, sent numerous Jews to the gas chambers. Fearing retribution, he committed suicide on May 13, 1945.

51. According to Rudolf Höss, the numbers of those deemed fit or unfit to work fluctuated wildly, but on average, 25 to 30 percent of the Jewish transports were assigned to labor. The rest were gassed on arrival. See Rudolf Höss, *Death Dealer: The Memoirs of the SS Kommandant at Auschwitz*, ed. Steven Paskuly (New York: Da Capo Press, 1996), 35. We are cognizant of the selection data of the first two transports arriving from Hungarian internment camps: 29 percent of the 3,800 individuals were deemed fit for work (i.e., 484 men and 616 women), while 71 percent, or 2,698 people, were executed. See Czech, *Auschwitz Chronicle*, 618. According to the report prepared by the German Ministry of Foreign Affairs, about one-third of the approximately three dozen transports of Hungarian Jews arriving through May 24 were deemed fit to work. See Eberhard von Thadden's report to the Reich Ministry of Foreign Affairs, May 26, 1944, in Randolph L. Braham, ed., *The Destruction of Hungarian Jewry: A Documentary Account* (New York: Pro Arte for the World Federation of Hungarian Jews, 1963), 1:387–89. Chief of the WVHA Oswald Pohl wrote to Himmler that about half the Hungarian Jews fit for work were women. See Pohl's telegram to Reichsführer-SS Himmler, May 24, 1944, in Braham, *The Destruction of Hungarian Jewry*, 1:378–79.

benches and numbered hooks to hang clothes along the walls of the room. As part of its careful deception strategy, the SS reminded everyone to memorize their hook number to make sure they would easily find their clothes after the bath. The crowd would have been calm, although the fact that men, women, and children were made to undress in front of each other caused some disturbance. After about 10 minutes, the crowd of 2,000 was herded—by this time, with rougher handling than before—into the next concrete room that had a 2,000-person capacity. There were no furnishings here, not even a window. This was the gas chamber. The heavy oak doors were slammed behind them, the lights were turned off, and in a few minutes, a luxury car with the Red Cross insignia drove up. A doctor with the rank of captain and his assistant unloaded four metal containers weighing circa 1 kg [2.2 lb.] each. They removed the four concrete lids covering the ventilation shafts leading to the underground bunker, put on their gas masks, punctured the top of the metal containers, and dumped the bean-like, purplish-reddish, or rather red wine-colored chlorine pellets into the four vent holes. Then they immediately covered the openings with the concrete slabs.[52] On one occasion I overheard as the SS doctor urged his assistant: "Gib schon das Fressen den Juden!"[53] Upon contact with air, the pellets generated chlorine gas that caused the cruelest death by suffocation within 5 to 10 minutes. After thirty minutes, the ventilators were switched on, members of the *Sonderkommando* on duty opened the door of the gas chamber, and 2,000 corpses lay covered in blood (from bleeding noses) and feces. Instead of being scattered evenly on the bunker floor, they were piled up on top of each other one story high, explained by the fact that the chlorine gas reached the upper layers with some delay. The *Sonderkommando* washed the corpses with a hose, and the bodies were

---

52. The description refers to the underground gas chambers of Crematoria II and III and the gassing operations that took place there. In 1943 these gas chambers were 210 square meters (2,260 square feet) in size, and up to two thousand people could be forced into them at one time. Later on, the gas chamber of Crematorium II was divided in two by a brick wall, so it became suitable for killing smaller transports. The two smaller crematoria (IV and V) each had three to four gas chambers; the ruins in Birkenau indicate that their combined area was 236.78 square meters (2,548.68 square feet). See Długoborski and Piper, *Auschwitz, 1940–1945,* 3:165–68. The gas chambers of Crematoria III and IV were at ground level; SS personnel would climb a ladder to throw the gas in through the windows. A poison developed originally as an insecticide, hydrogen cyanide (Zyklon B), was used for the gassing. When these pellets came in contact with air at about 27º C (87º F), the hydrogen cyanide converted into a poisonous gas that caused death when inhaled.

53. "Give the feed to the Jews already." SS personnel often used similarly cynical remarks or obscenities during the gassings.

then loaded into a freight elevator and transferred to the furnace room. The room had 15 furnaces, each equipped with its own electric ventilator.[54] A trained staff member dragged the corpses by hooking the crooked end of a walking cane into their mouths. Three bodies were stacked in each furnace at a time, which took twenty minutes to incinerate the bodies into ashes. Before the cremation, the dentist commando removed gold teeth from the dead bodies. The so-called "ash commando" was responsible for periodically removing the ashes and crushing the bones that were not fully burned. Once a week the ashes were transported off by truck and dumped into the nearby Weichsel (Vistula) River.

On November 17, 1944, burning in the crematoria was banned all over Poland, and no inmates were gassed after that date.[55] However, to eliminate living eyewitnesses to the darkest secrets of the political SS,[56] members of the 846-member *Sonderkommando* from Crematoria I, II, III, and IV were executed between 1:30 and 2:30 p.m. the same day.[57] The victims included one hundred Hungarian Jews, as well as forty Russian military officers; the rest were Jews from France, Holland, Belgium, and Poland. As physicians, we also lay there among our comrades before the machine guns, but Dr. Mengele—whose racial biology work had not been completed yet—took us from among those condemned to die. We continued our work quietly in the deserted crematorium until January 18, 1945,

---

54. The furnace room of Crematoria II and III was on the ground floor of the building. Five large furnaces stood in the room. Each had three incinerator openings, allowing three corpses to be burned at a time.

55. In late October/early November 1944, Himmler banned gassing in Birkenau. After November 2, those unfit for work were shot to death in smaller groups. For details about the end of the gassing, see Gábor Kádár and Zoltán Vági, *Self-financing Genocide: The Gold Train, the Becher Case and the Wealth of Hungarian Jews* (Budapest: Central European University Press, 2004), 225–31.

56. Nyiszli is referring to the camp Gestapo here, officially called the Political Department (Politische Abteilung).

57. Nyiszli mixes up dates and events. According to one surviving report, 874 people were working in the *Sonderkommando* on August 30, 1944. In late September, two hundred people were transported off and then killed in the clothing disinfection room (*Entwesungskammer*) of the Auschwitz main camp. On October 7, upon hearing news of another round of selections, the *Sonderkommando* members of Crematorium I and II revolted. Over the next two days, the Nazis killed 451 of the *Sonderkommando*, so their numbers fell to 212. On October 10, the Gestapo arrested thirteen *Sonderkommando* workers; thereafter, a reinforcement of thirty people was added to the work group. The last round of selections took place on November 26, 1944. Following this, the *Sonderkommando* operated with about one hundred people until the January evacuation. See Długoborski and Piper, *Auschwitz, 1940–1945*, 4:117, 120, 245, 248–49; Czech, *Auschwitz Chronicle*, 724–29.

without any more gassing and executions taking place there, at which point the Russians broke through the German front line at Varanovice and Kraków and by midnight had pushed forward within 6 km [3 to 4 miles] of Auschwitz. The SS fell into an awful state of disarray; they took us into the camp, where they abandoned us, leaving us entirely to our own devices. Once there, mixed in with a crowd of circa 4,000 inmates, no one knew that we were members of the *Sonderkommando*. The same night, unfamiliar SS guards took us on a forced march (run) to Mauthausen.[58]

## DEPORTED TO OTHER CAMPS

The survivors of the selection on the *Judenrampe* served as a workforce reserve for the Nazi war industry. If another camp or industrial plant needed slave laborers, transports assembled from these prisoners were created. In this way, the SS sent tens of thousands of Hungarian Jews from Auschwitz to other camps.

A fourteen-year-old Hungarian boy, Imre Kertész, was one of them. He was born in Budapest in 1929. In the summer of 1944, his father reported for labor service; he never returned. Imre was sent to work in a military production plant in nearby Csepel (today, Municipal District XX of Budapest). Meanwhile, on June 30, 1944, the roundup of Jews and their transfer to collection camps had begun in the vicinity of the capital. During one raid, police ordered Kertész and his fellow workers, wearing the yellow star, to get off the bus as they headed for work. They were placed in the collection camp set up at the Budakalász brick factory, where about eighteen thousand people were crowded together. Although Regent **Miklós Horthy** ordered a stop to the deportations on July 6, Hungarian authorities deported another 24,128 Jews to Auschwitz over the next three days. Imre Kertész was on board one of the trains that set out from Budakalász. The transport arrived in Auschwitz after a three-day journey. According to reigning selection practices, the fourteen-year-old Imre should have been sent to the gas chamber. He had a Jewish worker on duty at the ramp to thank for saving his life. When the worker found out Kertész's age, he whispered to the boy, if asked, to say he was sixteen. Kertész was thus classified as fit for work and placed in the camp. Due to a great need for labor in the Reich, he and his fellow inmates did not even receive tattoos; they left the camp on yet another train within three days.[59]

On July 15, the SS sent Kertész on a transport together with 2,499 other prisoners. According to surviving transport documents, the prisoners were placed

---

58. Nyiszli was eventually liberated at the Ebensee camp.
59. For an account of the changing tattooing system at Auschwitz, see Długoborski and Piper, *Auschwitz, 1940–1945*, 2:22–23.

on one of two lists: a numbered register of one thousand names and another list containing fifteen hundred names. The registers included two men named Imre Kertész: one born on July 28, 1894, the other, the teenager deported from Budakalász.[60] After arriving at the Buchenwald concentration camp the next day, four prisoners on the list died, and two Polish half-Jews were added to the group; the rest were sent to Buchenwald subcamps. The younger Kertész ended up in the Wille camp, while the older man went to the Magdeburg camp.[61]

DOCUMENT 7-5: Transfer document of Imre Kertész and 2,499 other prisoners from Auschwitz to Buchenwald, July 1944, USHMMA Acc. 1996.A.0342, NARA, Selected records relating to concentration camps from Buchenwald, reel 147 (translated from German).

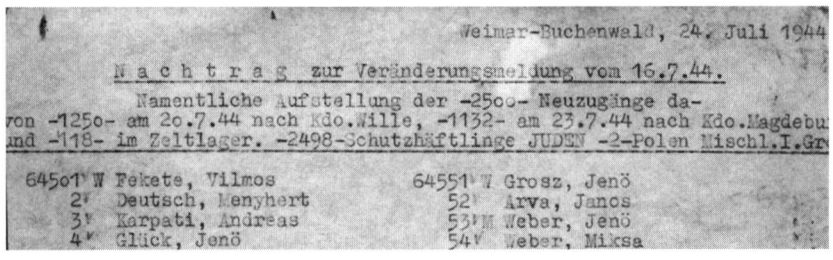

[. . .]

---

60. Kertész was born on November 9, 1929. However, the list specifies his birth date as June 10, 1927. The explanation for this is that Kertész survived the selection by claiming to be two years older. The discrepancies in the month and day are most likely due to typing errors. See Transportliste, ungarischer Juden nach KL Buchenwald, Auschwitz II, July 14, 1944, YVA, ITS Basic Documents, Auschwitz, reel 2.

61. See Nachtrag zur Veränderungsmeldung von 16.7.44, Weimar, Buchenwald, July 24, 1944, USHMMA, Acc. 1996.A.0432 NARA Captured German Records Collection, Buchenwald, reel 147. The list refers to the Buchenwald subcamps by placing the letters W, M, and Z in front of certain names. Wille, a Buchenwald subcamp (also known as Tröglitz, Rehmsdorf, or Gleina), was operating in the vicinity of the German town of Zeitz. Between May and October 1944, about ten thousand prisoners were working there, many of them Hungarian Jews. On this camp, see Franka Bindernagel and Tobias Bütow, "Tröglitz," in *The United States Holocaust Memorial Museum Encyclopedia of Camps and Ghettos, 1933–1945*, vol. 1: *Early Camps, Youth Camps, and Concentration Camps and Subcamps under the SS-Business Administration Main Office (WVHA)*, ed. Geoffrey P. Megargee (Bloomington: Indiana University Press in association with the USHMM, 2009), 429–31.

```
64841'Z  Mattersdorfer, Sandor     64901' M  Weltner, Vilmos
   42'   Mattersdorfer, Matijas       2'     Vajda, Wilhelm
   43' M Rosenberger, Miksa           3'     Veltner, Endre
   44' W David, Lajos                 4' W   Deutsch, Hermann
   45'   Goldmann, Jenő               5'     Klopfer, Laszlo
   46' M Weisz, György                6'     Klopfer, Sandor
   47'   Weisz, David                 7'     Helfgott, Emil
   48'   Weisz, Sandor                8'     Heisler, Lajos
   49'   Weisz, Adalbert              9'     Apfelbaum, Tibor
   50' W Kantor, Gyula               10' M   Rosenfeld, György
   51' M Szeidler, Andor             11' W   Dornfeld, Otto
   52'   Sonnenfeld, Tibor           12'     Herczog, György
   53'   Weisz, Istvan               13'     Erdös, K Frigyes
   54' W Goldstein, Eugen            14' M   Schlecker, Tomas
   55'   Fischer, Jozsef             15'     Weisz, Emmerich
   56'   Adler, Adolf                16' W   Grossmann, Dezsö
   57'   Friedmann, Andor            17'     Klein, Ferenc
   58'   Fleischer, Julius           18'     Frater, Albert
   59' M Pollak, Dezsö               19'     Karfinger, Ferenc
   60' W Keleti, Tibor               20' M   Schwartz, Marton
   61'   Fischbein, Laszlo           21' W   Kertesz, Imre
   62'   Berger, Tomas               22' M   Stern, Bela
```

[. . .]

The young boy, number 64921 on this list, grew continuously weaker in the Wille tent camp. On the verge of death, he was taken back to Buchenwald, where U.S. troops eventually liberated him. He returned to Budapest to learn that his father had died in the Labor Service. In 1975 he published a novel titled *Fatelessness* (*Sorstalanság*) based on his experience during the Holocaust. Translated into several languages, the book gained worldwide fame after Kertész won the Nobel Prize in literature in 2002.

Although most Hungarian Jewish deportees entered the concentration camp system in Auschwitz, this was not at all the only gate to their ordeals in the Nazi camp universe. The remainder of documents in this chapter focus on the major camps Hungarian Jews arrived in besides Auschwitz. One such location was Bergen-Belsen in northwestern Germany. Originally it served as a prisoner of war camp that the SS intended to use as a "special camp" with multiple functions.[62] The first Hungarian Jews arrived there from the Netherlands. The 1,684 passengers of the "**Kasztner** train" followed them in early July 1944

---

62. See *The United States Holocaust Memorial Museum Encyclopedia of Camps and Ghettos, 1933–1945*, vol. 1, 277–88; Eberhard Kolb, *Bergen-Belsen: From "Detention Camp" to Concentration Camp, 1943 to 1945* (Göttingen: Vandenhoeck & Ruprecht, 1986).

and were placed in a separate part of the camp.[63] (They did not have to work and got better food rations than other prisoners; thus only a couple of severely ill people died there. As a result of the Zionist-Nazi negotiations, the first group of 318 people crossed the Swiss border in late August, while the majority was allowed to follow them in early December.[64]) In the fall of 1944 more Hungarian Jews arrived from Auschwitz and its subcamps. In the spring of 1945, when Mittelbau-Dora and other camps were being shut down, thousands more arrived in an extremely weakened state, due to the hard physical work and starvation they had endured. Most likely over ten thousand Hungarian Jews ended up in Bergen-Belsen in the spring of 1945.

Emil Weisz, deported from Budapest toward the end of 1944, arrived at the Bergen-Belsen camp in 1945. While being deported, the fifty-year-old man managed to hold on to several sheets of paper. These included a copy of a letter he had written to Regent Miklós Horthy in September 1944 requesting—in vain—that he be exempted from anti-Jewish measures based on his service in World War I. Weiss persistently and regularly wrote a camp diary on these sheets, which document 7-6 excerpts.

**DOCUMENT 7-6: Emil Weisz's concentration camp diary, January–April 1945, USHMMA RG 39.013M (HJA XX-G, box D 6/6).**

[. . .]

Bergen-Belsen. Entering, I see starving Jews; they say everything will be taken away from us [. . .] Lice, it would be nice to bathe [. . .] I am on good terms with 2–3 people; I barely know 15–20 people; I am not interested in them. My tooth hurts [. . .] I have obtained some butter. What will I eat when I get home? I go for walks in the yard a lot. I am beginning to feel hungry most of the time. I gradually sell my valuables. For bread. [. . .] A couple of people die each day. There is always a great deal of excitement during the evening distribution. I am always hungry [. . .] The group of people is quite a mixture; there are a lot of fights with people beating each other up. I look at my pictures a lot [. . .] Tomorrow the entire camp will go without food, as a punishment; this is all we needed.

---

63. On the Kasztner case, see chapter 8.
64. The members of Kasztner's group lived under better conditions here than other prisoners: they wore civilian clothing and did not have to work, and their families were not separated. On the Kasztner passengers' stay in Bergen-Belsen, see, e.g., Yehuda Bauer, *Jews for Sale? Nazi-Jewish Negotiations, 1933–1945* (New Haven, CT: Yale University Press, 1994), 145ff.; Ladislaus Löb, *Dealing with Satan: Rezső Kasztner's Daring Rescue Mission* (London: Jonathan Cape, 2008), 121–64.

I/9. Today at 8:30 there is lineup in the yard. It is very cold. At noon, the news goes around that the evacuation order is here. We will see if it is true. [. . .]

I/11. Lineup in the morning; I am terribly cold; I put on the other pair of pants as well; it is much better this way.

I/14. Yesterday I bought the beetroot dinner for three cigarettes; for once an evening when I did not go to sleep hungry. I pray three times a day; my dear Rózsika,[65] you would be pleased with me. [. . .] There is not a single day that goes by when I do not look at the pictures. Nice memories from times long past. I have been walking less for a few days now, lying down more. [. . .]

I/15. [. . .] On two occasions, women came to the barracks next door; members of the first group were mostly from Teleky Square,[66] who were brought a few days later on foot from Budapest, starting in mid-November. [. . .] I had them look for you and the family; fortunately I got no reply; I am starting to feel much calmer thinking that you are not here next door; hopefully you are not in a similar camp either? It makes my suffering unbearable that I do not know where you are; oftentimes I feel that you managed to get out of the ring and you are at home in our apartment.[67] [. . .] Here, everyone says that one should not spend time over this question; we cannot change a thing, and it only makes the [. . .] mood worse. [. . .]

I/21. [. . .] Here all of us are like animals, that is, how we line up impatiently in front of the cauldron, as though it were a trough; and we could kill for food. And what are you doing, my darling? How are you getting by?

I/25. At night, several thousands of Hungarian women between 16 and 40 years old arrived from Auswitz [sic] (Silesia). [. . .]

II/1. [. . .] I am still starving; I would not pay attention to the physical agony that comes with it, but my legs and arms have less strength, and this is a problem because I want to remain strong in order to see you again at home. [. . .]

II/25 [. . .] It is 3 o'clock in the afternoon. I have just been to the doctor; without me asking any questions, he told me that I did not look good and that I should try to sell something for food. [. . .] How long do I have to starve; when will we finally have a human life? [. . .]

III/7. I had a very bad day yesterday. My legs were very weak; I was dizzy, and I was extremely exasperated. [. . .]

---

65. Mrs. Weisz, née Rózsa Hirschfeld.
66. Correct spelling: Teleki. Large square in Budapest, one of the roundup sites during the Arrow Cross era.
67. That is, the ring of Arrow Cross or police units back in Budapest.

III/18. [. . .] Last night they shot a 25-year-old beet thief, and we narrowly escaped getting far worse treatment for the entire camp as a punishment. [. . .]

III/19. Now there is talk that poor Hegyesi is near death; how tragic. His wife and daughter are in the women's camp nearby and do not suspect the shadow of tragedy. [. . .] 3 in the afternoon. Poor Hegyesi died in the morning. [. . .]

IV/6. Because of my great weakness, I spend all day lying down. I am without bread all day; I have some reserves, but I am saving them. There is enough food in the camp to last only four days, and who knows what will happen afterward? [. . .]

IV/18. My condition is the same; today, the wound was bleeding again a bit, and I still have not received fresh bandages. [. . .] I very much long to be living with you, my darling, my sweet little one; it would be so good.

Weisz arrived in Bergen-Belsen at a time when the camp's conditions had drastically deteriorated: less and less food was delivered, while the number of prisoners increased steadily. The death rate from starvation, disease, and murder eventually reached three to five hundred people each day until British troops liberated the camp on April 15. The deplorable conditions they found required special measures: they set fire to barracks to combat epidemics, deployed bulldozers to push the numerous dead into mass graves dug by SS guards, and disinfected surviving prisoners one by one. But for many prisoners, this help came too late. During the war, fifty thousand people died in the camp, and during the weeks following the liberation, at least fourteen thousand more perished despite the most attentive care. Emil Weisz was most likely among them.

All in all at least eight to nine thousand Hungarian Jewish women ended up in the Ravensbrück concentration camp, north of Berlin. Six of them arrived before February 1943. Between October 1943 and March 1944, at least 139 others followed from Germany, Belgium, the Netherlands, and probably France as well. They were Hungarian citizens who had been living in these countries and were deported as "foreign Jews" (*ausländische Juden*) on the order of Gestapo chief Heinrich Müller.[68] For instance, on February 7, 1944, sixty-three women and children were registered from the "Hungary-special shipment from the Westerbork camp"; their male relatives—husbands, sons, fathers, and brothers—went to Buchenwald. The Nazis later shipped some of these women

---

68. Judith Buber Agassi, *Jewish Women Prisoners of Ravensbrück: Who Were They?* (Oxford: One World, 2007), 57–84. See also Bernhard Strebel, *Das KZ Ravensbrück. Geschichte eines Lagerkomplexes* (Paderborn: Ferdinand Schöningh, 2003), 126–32.

to Auschwitz, while others perished in Ravensbrück or one of its subcamps from typhus or starvation. In the second half of 1944, another seven thousand Hungarian Jewish girls and women arrived. The non-Jewish prisoner functionaries often treated them inhumanely. A Polish block leader said to one of them, "All the Jews will die, and I will laugh!"[69] Due to a shortage of space, camp authorities placed Hungarian prisoners outside in tents despite the cold winter. The death rate soared, and fellow prisoners carried many corpses, frozen stiff, to the crematoria.[70] At least 290 Hungarian Roma women and girls were deported to Ravensbrück toward the end of 1944. Carl Clauberg and Horst Schumann, medical doctors who had fled Auschwitz, continued their sterilization experiments on them at the camp.[71] Edith Bacher, a deportee to Ravensbrück, wrote the letter excerpted in document 7-7 to the father of her friend Lilly after the end of the war, telling him about the circumstances of Lilly's death.

DOCUMENT 7-7: **Edith Bacher's letter, 1945, USHMMA RG 39.013M (HJA XX-F-II, box D 6/6).**

> Dear Doctor,
> I am embarrassed indeed to have waited until now to contact you, for I have been in Pest since June, but you must believe that all this was because I did not want to cause pain. I thought, however, that by now most likely you have heard about the fate of poor Lilly, or at least in the time that has elapsed, you have at least gotten used to the thought. Also, I would not have been able to look you up in person in any case because I have been ill, confined to bed ever since I came home [. . .]
> As you probably know from my mother already, I knew Lilly well from earlier. So we already greeted each other as acquaintances in Gödöllő as soon as we met, and we stayed together until the end. From Gödöllő,

---

69. "Alle Juden werden sterben und ich werde lachen!" Cited in Linde Apel, *Jüdische Frauen im Konzentrationslager Ravensbrück 1939–1945* (Berlin, Metropol, 2003), 172–73, and cf. 162–65.

70. Agassi, *Jewish Women Prisoners of Ravensbrück*, 88–121, 196; Strebel, *Das KZ Ravensbrück*, 130–32.

71. On the persecution of the Hungarian Roma in 1944–1945, see, e.g., László Karsai, *Cigánykérdés Magyarországon 1919–1944. Út a cigány holocausthoz* (Budapest: Cserépfalvi, 1992); Gyula Purcsi Barna, *A cigánykérdés "gyökeres és végleges megoldása": tanulmányok a XX. századi "cigánykérdés" történetéből* (Debrecen: Csokonai, 2004); Szabolcs Szita, ed., *Tények, adatok a cigányok háborús üldöztetésének tanintézeti feldolgozásához* (Budapest: Magyar Auschwitz Alapítvány–Holokauszt Dokumentációs Központ, 2000). On the fate of Roma victims in Ravensbrück, see Strebel, *Das KZ Ravensbrück*, 134–38.

we went to Isaszeg, where we dug trenches under the terrifying supervision of the Arrow Cross men.[72] [. . .] As the Russians were approaching, they herded us together one night within minutes using hand grenades and the butts of their rifles and began herding us backward toward Pest. [. . .] From the Óbuda brick factory,[73] we set out on foot on the road leading to Vienna. We covered about 40 kilometers [25 miles] each day and slept in the open at night at sports fields or cattle markets—this is how we reached the German border at Hegyeshalom the second week of November.[74] [. . .] Lilly was already weak by then; the long walking was difficult for her; if I remember correctly, she did not even have proper shoes. At Zürndorf the Germans took us off the trains and took us to Ravensbrück via Buchenwald. Lilly [. . .] and I met again in front of the disinfection building; she looked even worse and complained of diarrhea. [. . .] We were put in the same block. You must already have heard of "*appell.*"[75] In the morning, we stood motionless from 4:30 to 8, in snow and frost, and then we were herded out to the fields for work. We were also there in the open, working in the cold until the evening, without gloves, stockings, caps, wearing just summer rags. The woman in charge of our block was awful.[76] They tortured us in every way they could. They beat us before *appell*, before we went out into the freezing cold, poured cold water all over us at the door on purpose, so the water would freeze on us. Lilly and I often stood next to each other during *appell*. She was in very bad shape, extremely weak, with constant diarrhea. She also had a hard time mentally; she cried a lot and constantly said that she would not be able to make it through. Physically and mentally she was among those with the fewest reserves. I tried to console her a lot. [. . .] Her shoes hung on her feet in shreds; that is how she stood in the snow for hours; and then she gave me a photograph that she somehow managed to salvage in the bath by putting it in her shoes; she wanted me to continue hiding it in my shoes, which were in better condition at the time. The photo portrayed a little boy. Each morning, I saw Lilly in a worse and worse

---

72. Along with many thousands of fellow victims, Edith and Lilly were dragged off to work on fortifications in the vicinity of Budapest based on the order of Arrow Cross Minister of Defense **Károly Beregfy**. See document 5-3.

73. The main concentration site of the capital during the so-called death marches was the Nagybátony-Újlak brick factory in Óbuda.

74. On the November death marches, see document 5-4. See also map 4, p. lxiv.

75. *Appell* (German): roll call. In concentration camps, roll calls were a widespread practice, which meant that the prisoners had to stand upright for hours, regardless of the weather or their own often extremely weak condition.

76. That is, a prisoner who had been assigned to supervise fellow prisoners.

condition. She had indescribable diarrhea; eventually, she could hardly stand on her feet. When I last saw her she could no longer walk, but she was still forced to go out for *appell*. And then she lay unconscious, and I heard the next day that she died. [. . .] I continued hiding the picture in my shoe, but on January 15, when I was transported for work at the factory, they disinfected me again and took everything from me again, and then unfortunately they took the picture Lilly had entrusted to me. [. . .] I have been lying ill ever since I returned.

It hurts me very much to have to tell you about such horrible things; please forgive if I have caused too much pain, but I thought that if we were discussing this, complete honesty would be better, knowing for certain, no matter what it is like [. . .]

I send many greetings with genuine compassion, and please believe me that I also think a lot about your Lilly.

Edith Bacher

Death marches and evacuation transports reached the Ravensbrück camp in 1945, bringing further hundreds of Hungarian Jewish women. In the last months, the Nazis executed thousands of prisoners, many of them from Hungary, in different shootings and in the gas chambers. The former chief of the Birkenau crematoria, SS-Hauptscharführer Otto Moll, directed certain gassings.[77]

As Lilly and Edith's story shows, Buchenwald was an important destination for Hungarian Jews. In the summer of 1944, the Nazis transferred ten to eleven thousand of them, including the fifteen-year-old Imre Kertész (see document 7-5), from Auschwitz to Buchenwald, the camp near Weimar, Germany. Most of them were unregistered prisoners classified as fit for work. In early June 1944, two thousand Hungarian Jewish men arrived in the camp. On June 18, another transport of one thousand men reached Buchenwald. At the end of the month, 434 more people were added. In early July, a transport consisting of two thousand Hungarian women came in. Of the latter, 266 women died during the journey due to bombings. In mid-July, two Hungarian transports arrived, each with about twenty-five hundred people. Most of the Hungarian Jews were crammed into tents, and everyone had to work. In the fall and winter of 1944, the Germans transferred another eleven thousand Auschwitz prisoners (among them several thousand Hungarian Jews) to Buchenwald and its subcamps. Others—among them Lilly and Edith—arrived during the November-December deportations from Hungary. The last arrivals during the camp complex's collapse in early 1945

---

77. Testimony of former *Schutzhaftlagerführer* Johann Schwarzhuber cited in Strebel, *Das KZ Ravensbrück*, 479.

included survivors of foot marches and train rides transported under terrible conditions from other concentration camps. During Christmas of 1944, the Budapest Gestapo sent another 1,913 Jews.[78] At least fifteen thousand Hungarian Jews were sent to Buchenwald; thousands of them perished in the camp.[79]

The Mauthausen camp complex in Austria was among the most extensive in the Nazi web of concentration camps. After the occupation, German authorities deported the first Hungarian Jews, most of them from the provinces, to Mauthausen in April 1944. A group consisting of "prominent" persons followed: Jewish and non-Jewish anti-Nazi politicians, intellectuals, industrialists, and businessmen arrested by the Gestapo. They were first taken to various prisons in Budapest and then to the Oberlanzendorf internment camp in the 23rd District in Vienna. In May and June, seventy-five hundred Hungarian Jews were transferred to Mauthausen from Auschwitz; the majority were assigned to labor subcamps, where they died by the hundreds due to hunger and exhaustion. Guards murdered many others. At the end of that year, additional groups ended up in Mauthausen, arriving with the so-called death marches organized by the Arrow Cross authorities. In the last months of the camp's existence, deportees evacuated from Auschwitz and the remnants of Labor Service units joined them. The Nazis gassed hundreds and sent many labor servicemen on to Gunskirchen, where they died by the hundreds.[80]

Document 7-8 shows the Mauthausen prisoner registry card (*Häftlings-Personal-Karte*) of one of the "prominent" persons deported from Hungary: Jewish industrialist and member of the Upper House of parliament Leó Buday-Goldberger (1878–1945). The Goldberger family was typical of Jewish entrepreneurs who in the nineteenth and early twentieth centuries had built up extremely successful industrial and financial companies and contributed a great deal to the modernization of Hungary. The Goldbergers owned an extensive textile factory complex and were among the most respected citizens and benefactors of Óbuda.[81] Unlike most of the industrial and financial tycoons of Jewish origin, family members did not convert to Christianity. Buday-Goldberger himself played an important role in Jewish community life.[82] The German

---

78. Szabolcs Szita, *Magyarok az SS ausztriai lágerbirodalmában* (Budapest: MAZSÖK, 2000), 7.

79. On the history of Buchenwald, see Evelyn Zegenhagen, "Buchenwald," in *The USHMM Encyclopedia of Camps and Ghettos, 1933–1945*, 1:290–95.

80. On the Mauthausen camp complex, including the Gunskirchen subcamp, see *The USHMM Encyclopedia of Camps and Ghettos, 1933–1945*, 1:899ff.

81. Óbuda was an independent municipality until it became part of Budapest in 1873.

82. For the history of the family, see Kinga Frojimovics et al., *A zsidó Budapest. Emlékek, szertartások, történelem* (Budapest: MTA Judaisztikai Kutatócsoport, 1995), 1:75–78.

police arrested him immediately after the occupation and on March 26, 1944, deported him to an internment camp in Vienna, where the Viennese branch of the Gestapo took over his custody and transported him to the Mauthausen concentration camp on May 5. This is why the prisoner registry card indicates "Stapo Wien" as the authority sending Buday-Goldberger to the camp; as the reason for his arrest, the card listed "Hungarian Jew" (Ung.Jude).

DOCUMENT 7-8: Image of Mauthausen prisoner registry card of Leó Buday-Goldberger, HJA XX-C-5, box I 5/3.

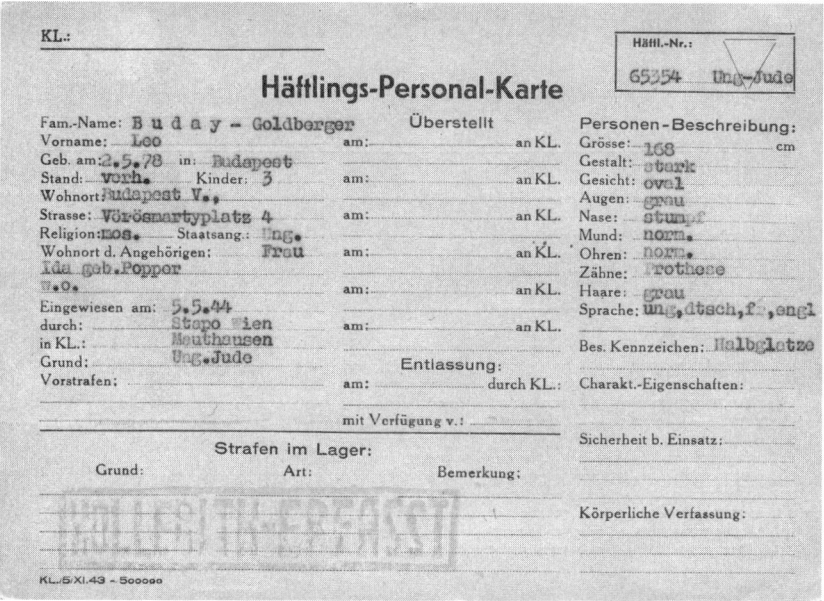

Buday-Goldberger starved to death just after his sixty-seventh birthday. He died on the day of the liberation by U.S. troops in May 1945.[83] In all, a total of twenty-five thousand Hungarian Jews arrived in Mauthausen in 1944–1945; of these, eight to nine thousand perished in the camp and its satellite camps. If we count those who died immediately after the liberation, the number of Hungarian dead in Mauthausen exceeds ten thousand.[84]

---

83. Szita, *Magyarok az SS ausztriai lágerbirodalmában*, 53–64.
84. On the fate of the Hungarian Jews in Mauthausen, see Szita, *Magyarok az SS ausztriai lágerbirodalmában*.

## CHAPTER 8
# JEWISH RESPONSES TO PERSECUTION

RESEARCH ON Jewish responses to persecution has generally centered on the issue of resistance. Did a given Jewish community show resistance toward the policy of genocide? If so, in what form? If not, why? The most obvious manifestation of resistance (and the one traditionally recognized as the only form) was armed opposition to the Nazis and their henchmen. In 1944–1945, conditions in Hungary were not in place for the development of armed Jewish resistance. The reasons were manifold: most young men served in **Labor Service** units under tight military guard, there existed no noteworthy non-Jewish armed resistance to lean on, and the anti-Jewish campaign unfolded at an unprecedented speed.[1] In Hungary unarmed attempts at survival (going into hiding and hiding others, bribing the authorities, ignoring their orders and instructions, forging documents, and fleeing) stood in the foreground and constituted the essence of organized as well as individual resistance.[2] This chapter sheds light on the ways Jewish individuals and groups reacted to the joint Hungarian-German attempt to destroy them and their communities.

---

1. For the analysis of these factors, see Gábor Kádár and Zoltán Vági, "Compulsion of Bad Choices—Questions, Dilemmas, Decisions: The Activity of the Hungarian Central Jewish Council in 1944," in *Jewish Studies at the Central European University*, ed. András Kovács and Michael Miller (Budapest: Central European University Press, 2009), 5:71–89.

2. On the question of resistance and the historiography of the problem, see Dan Michman, *Holocaust Historiography: A Jewish Perspective: Conceptualizations, Terminology, Approaches and Fundamental Issues* (London: Vallentine Mitchell, 2003), 217–48; Yehuda Bauer, *Rethinking the Holocaust* (New Haven, CT: Yale University Press, 2001), 143–66.

## PATTERNS OF INDIVIDUAL JEWISH RESPONSES

As in other occupied countries, the vast majority of Jews in Hungary accepted increasingly sharp persecution measures in a seemingly passive manner. They typically exhibited a traditional respect for the law and authorities. Accordingly, most of them obeyed the ever harsher discriminatory measures. Many Jews considered the sequence of disenfranchisement and persecution merely temporary. They remained hopeful that the Allies would win and thought that after the defeat of the German Reich their lives would return to normal.

At the same time, regional and temporal differences impacted resistance opportunities and inclinations. During the 1944 summer deportations in the provinces, few chances arose to flee and hide. The speed at which authorities carried out the deportations mitigated against much resistance to new regulations and rules. The vast majority of the Christian population remained aloof or showed animosity toward their Jewish neighbors. Jews also lacked viable escape routes. Except in some remote northeastern regions, the country had no impenetrable forests and marshes. Due to aggressive anti-Jewish operations in the previous years, neighboring Romania, Slovakia, and Serbia offered no refuge for persecuted Jews. German and Hungarian forces had sealed the borders anyway. At most a few thousand people managed to escape the country.

Of course, this does not mean that no one opted for individual resistance, self-rescue, or flight. Dozens of provincial ghettos and collection camps reported individual, family, or small group escapes. Poorly integrated **Orthodox** and Hassidic Jews in reannexed regions orchestrated many of these attempted getaways, while the more Magyarized **Neologues** of **Trianon**-era Hungary seemed less inclined to run.[3] Still, flight never became a general phenomenon during the mass deportations from the provinces. By contrast, tens of thousands of Jews in the capital chose opposition to the authorities and abandoned the path of "legality" during the **Arrow Cross** era a few months later. The sheer size of the capital, the rapid disintegration of public order and law enforcement capabilities, and the successful rescue work of neutral embassies proved a great help for many. The non-Jewish population's willingness to engage in rescue activities also increased considerably compared to the period of deportations from the provinces.[4]

---

3. For instance, information on similar collective or individual escape attempts from Huszt, Nagyszőlős, Iza, Munkács, Érsekújvár, Aknaszlatina, and Csillaghegy exists as well. See HJA, DEGOB Protocols, nos., 28, 45, 588, 1097, 1139, 1538, 1695, 1744, 2367. For other stories, see Randolph L. Braham, *The Politics of Genocide: The Holocaust in Hungary* (New York: Columbia University Press, 1994), 1:572–710, 2:711–805, esp. 1:598, 2:1403.

4. On this, see chapter 9.

The diary entries excerpted in document 8-1 offer reflections about the reactions, mood, mind-set, and hopes of Jews in the weeks following the German occupation. They were penned by a law student in his early twenties, Gyula Eörsi (1922–1992), who kept his diary up until the Arrow Cross takeover in October 1944. He survived and went on to become an internationally recognized lawyer, university professor, and member of the Hungarian Academy of Sciences.

**DOCUMENT 8-1: Gyula Eörsi's diary entries for May 8 and 14, 1944, Eörsi family collection.**

V.8 [1944].

It has been exactly two months since I wrote. There is an explanation for this. I doubt I will be able to write for quite some time. Our private life has been suspended. Where are the girls, the kisses, the boring love affairs, teenage-style philosophy? Where is all the worry these days about an exam, where is all the worry about a poem—where is the person these days? A person who lives life leisurely, who is free, whose brain is not oppressed by fear, someone who just jokes and kids around, all sweaty, just laughs and shows off, plays the hero? Where are those who are theoretically "studying" heroism these days, steadfastness, historical times, those who claim they cannot be crushed? People are snatched up in the street—you would not believe this is happening if you did not see it—they snatch them up because each day, they have to arrest 150 people [. . .] Can you imagine it, as someone who has grown up under the protective shield of public security, a well-functioning police and legal order, who has learned: *nullum crimen sine lege*?[5] Can you imagine that while you are walking the streets (by the way, let me inform you, my son,[6] incidentally, that on the left side of one's chest, near the heart, you continuously wear a yellow star, a stigma), so you are in the street, wearing the yellow star, and all of a sudden, a detective approaches you and you are transported off to Germany? They take away your property and declare it national property, and you, my son, would protest in vain, for you are a communist because you were

---

5. He cites a phrase from Roman law here: "no crime without a law" (i.e., holding someone accountable for an action is possible only if the action was defined as a crime according to extant laws).

6. In his diary, Eörsi calls his imaginary conversation partner "my son."

born a Jew.[7] Your apartment becomes everyone's apartment, your money becomes everyone's money, but still, you are the communist, and you are the one wearing the yellow star. You suddenly wake up in the middle of the night and see that everything is engulfed in flames, the entire street; you run out to the open corridor around the courtyard that used to be the peaceful spot for the domestic staff to gossip (granted, Bözsi is no longer here, for Jews are not supposed to keep a maid[8]; they are supposed to live in filth, or they themselves are supposed to do the cleaning. They do not have to cook anyway, because Jews do not receive butter, eggs, or fat), so you run out to the open corridor, where an incendiary bomb crashing down with a sharp whistle chases you right back inside; you are caught in a war; it is not just your enemies who are your enemies,[9] your compatriots are likewise your enemies; they take away all that you have and herd you, along with ten thousand others, to a brick factory, to the ghetto, without food or water—let the typhoid fever come and take its toll. So there is nothing to write about; the troubles of love, the joys of leisure time belong to the good old world (now you are happy if you are able to work); these days you are not allowed to think of meeting up with your circle of friends or calling those who are more successful with the girls extroverted party boys—oh, where is all that now? These days, sheer existence is at stake; we are becoming tougher, more prepared, nobler; we learn to appreciate the bourgeois lifestyle, public security, the law, human dignity, the importance of little things. We will become naked and militant, like we used to be during olden times in the ghetto and in the jungle.

No, I won't write; the Germans have come into Hungary.

V. 18.

Well, things are not going well for us, that much is certain, but still, the previous page was written in a typical evening mood. I do indeed miss the Island,[10] going out for a hike, and we constantly live under some pressure, but we have gotten used to the pressure even though we are very tense anticipating the next round of ordeals, and one way or another, we are psychologically preparing ourselves for them. The

---

7. Eörsi refers to the constant antisemitic propaganda element that identified Jews as communists.

8. See Prime Minister's Decree no. 1200/1944 on the prohibition on non-Jewish employees in Jewish households, *Budapesti Közlöny*, March 31, 1944, 1.

9. This is a reference to the Allies, who were bombing Budapest.

10. Margit Island, an island in the Danube in the heart of Budapest.

pessimist is painting the tragedy of sealed trains headed toward Germany and the final experience of the gas chambers; this is how he is preparing himself, and in his masochism, he is feeling quite alright. The optimist is also expecting the next obstacle, so he can confidently overcome that, too, taking it in a sportsmanlike fashion. It feels as though the yellow star has been around forever; it is part of one's outfit, just like the coat lapel is. Being "hunted prey" is no longer a novel experience but has become a permanent state, a way of life; by now, this state has become bearable even if it lasts through eternity; through it all, one can still be happy or unhappy. Our instincts have developed, but of course we plan for the future, a future in which all this is in the distant past, a document; one way or another, we are planning for it. There are some who are already hanging those responsible, drawing blood, recording and memorizing things; their black list is fattening up, and so are they; the future holds such pleasure, this hanging, having people shot to death, a bloody world—from the perspective of the hunter, it will be such an annoyance when someone runs off and is available only in effigy[11]; what a joy it's going to be to tick off names on the list: this, that, and the other have also gotten "the punishment they were due"....[12] [...]

One peculiarity of Eörsi's diary lies in the May 18 entry's mention of the gas chambers. It is very surprising that three days after the launch of the mass deportations, he possessed information about them. This is all the more astounding since Jews' unawareness of the fate awaiting them was a main factor working against resistance tendencies during that summer. The Nazis strove to keep their genocidal operations secret and had instituted wartime censorship in Hungary as elsewhere. Stories and fragments of information about mass murders nonetheless still reached many people well before 1944. From the summer of 1941 onward, thousands of Hungarian soldiers and labor servicemen watched as certain German units and Baltic and Ukrainian militias killed Jewish communities en masse on the eastern front. One labor serviceman reported in 1945, "I became acquainted with every variety of suffering. I was eyewitness to the execution of many Jewish families."[13] Already in the summer of 1941, several

---

11. That is, figuratively or symbolically (from Latin).
12. Indeed, many sought opportunities after the war to fulfill their justified thirst for revenge. This sentiment later drove many Jews to enter the ranks of the police, which were primarily in communist hands. See chapter 10.
13. HJA, DEGOB Protocols, no. 204.

Hungarian Jewish labor servicemen had witnessed the Kamenets-Podolski massacre, and some even took photographs.[14] During 1941–1942, some two or three thousand survivors of the 1941 summer deportations fled back to Hungary, and many gave detailed accounts of their experiences.[15] Polish and Slovakian refugees hiding in Hungary often tried to warn Hungarian Jews of the fate awaiting those who fell into the German hands. Eörsi might have been in touch with them and credited their words.

During the anti-Jewish campaign following the German occupation, the Hungarian authorities did everything to hide the truth from their victims. They rested their propaganda on two basic lies. First, they emphasized that they were removing Jews from the border regions for military reasons, a favorite theme of right-wing extremist newspapers.[16] They also repeatedly emphasized that they were transporting the deportees for work—within Hungary. The deception generally proved effective. At the same time, some suspected what lay ahead once they detrained at the Birkenau "**Jewish ramp**."[17] These were scarce exceptions. Most deportees had no clue about where they had landed. A postwar remark by journalist Lajos Farkas summed it up: "At the time, the name Auschwitz did not yet mean anything to us."[18]

László Kovács (b. 1931), author of the memoirs excerpted in document 8-2, was also unaware of what awaited him when the Hungarian authorities deported him and his family from Nyíregyháza to Auschwitz. His recollections of his ghetto days shed light on a unique feature of the Holocaust in Hungary: the deported population included far fewer men than women. The government had called up most men for compulsory labor service either prior to or during

---

14. See, e.g., the photos taken by Gyula Spitz and Dr. Béla Somló, both of whom served as military truck drivers. USHMMPA WS# 28214–28217, and Hungarian National Museum Photo Archives, nos. 49258–49260. Image no. 28215 is published in this book as document 2-7.

15. For example, HJA, DEGOB Protocols, nos. 129, 594, 748, 1344, 2067, 2767.

16. See, e.g., *Magyarság*, April 30, 1944, 13.

17. For example, the husband of S. D. had been in touch with refugees back in Hungary, and he "knew from the Poles what would happen to them and he was in a state of deep despair." See HJA, DEGOB Protocols, no. 473. S. H. was deported from Munkács and recalled that his father said, "'This is the end for us.' And then he came up to us and said quietly: 'Let's say farewell to each other,' and he hugged our little siblings with tears in his eyes. My father had heard about the horrors of Auschwitz over the radio," presumably from listening illegally to Allied radio programs. See HJA, DEGOB Protocols, no. 2476/B.

18. HJA, DEGOB Protocols, no. 1530. A native of Gyula, Farkas (b. 1903) was a prominent leftwing journalist in Budapest before the war. Arrested in April 1944, he was forced to work in a factory and a brickyard, before being sent to Auschwitz and then a camp in Bavaria, where he became gravely ill. He was liberated by U.S. troops in 1945.

the ghettoization.[19] Already before 1944, the absence (and in many cases, the deaths) of most fathers or adult sons had become a defining experience in many Jewish families. After the "Jewish Laws" caused men to lose their employment and undermined them economically, a unique form of "emancipation" emerged. The relations between the sexes, gender roles, and the division of labor began to change.[20] This phenomenon manifested itself in 1944 as well. Inside the ghetto, women occupied central roles in the organization of food supplies, cleaning, and everyday life. They arranged education for the children, as well as public kitchens and sleeping accommodations.[21]

In the ghetto the role and status of children also changed. The radically new situation meant not only defenselessness but also greater independence and more adult tasks. László Kovács, for example, twelve years old at the time, snuck out of the ghetto on several occasions to obtain food and firewood on his own, causing his mother a great deal of worry. Parents rarely attempted to place their children with Christian families, even if they had the opportunity to do so. Either out of fear or uncertainty about their children's chances, only a few risked separating from their sons and daughters. Children thus shared their parents' fate. Of the young teenage boys who remained in the ghettos, few survived.[22] László Kovács was one of them.

---

19. For example, in the main ghetto in Veszprém, only 30.8 percent of the residents (193 out of 627) were males. Similar data are found in other eastern European ghettos, but in Hungary the percentage of females was greater than elsewhere. Tim Cole, "A Gendered Holocaust? The Experiences of 'Jewish' Men and Women in Hungary, 1944," in *The Holocaust in Hungary: Sixty Years Later*, ed. Randolph L. Braham and Brewster S. Chamberlin (Boulder, CO: East European Monographs, 2006), 49–52.

20. For a European analysis of the phenomenon, see Raul Hilberg, *Perpetrators, Victims, Bystanders: The Jewish Catastrophe, 1933–1945* (New York: HarperPerennial, 1993), 126–30. The Hungarian ghettos existed for only a few weeks, and therefore these changes were far less spectacular or visible in documentation than in the case of Polish ghettos.

21. On what the Holocaust meant for Jewish women, see, e.g., Dalia Ofer and Lenore J. Weitzman, eds., *Women in the Holocaust* (New Haven, CT: Yale University Press, 1998), especially the introduction and chapters 9, 19, and 20. For the case of Hungary, see Cole, "A Gendered Holocaust?"

22. In 1941, children and youth under age twenty comprised 20 percent of Hungarian Jews; of these, seventy-five to eighty thousand lived in the reannexed areas, and eighty to eighty-five thousand lived in the provinces and Budapest. The Holocaust primarily affected the first two areas, and almost nine-tenths of the children living there were murdered, while in Budapest "only" 55 percent of them perished. Up until the German occupation in 1944, at most 4,000 to 5,000 of the 165,000 Jewish children were killed. A year later, a maximum of thirty to thirty-five thousand were still alive. Kinga Frojimovics, *Szétszakadt történelem. Zsidó vallási irányzatok Magyarországon 1868–1950* (Budapest: Balassi, 2008), 375.

DOCUMENT 8-2: László Kovács's memoir of life in the ghetto, in László Kovács, *Tanú vagyok. Életrajzi töredékek* (Nyíregyháza: Szabolcs-Szatmár-Bereg Megyei Önkormányzat Levéltára, 2004), 41–45.

[. . .]

While still back home, in the courtyard of the Jewish school, we were grouped together with three families with whom we had been good friends for years (it was no coincidence). The children (three boys, three girls) were of similar ages to us, good friends of ours. Each of the four families got out of the schoolyard without the head of the family. We had no knowledge about the men, and neither did any of the other three families.[23] The four mothers converted the four broken families into a large family of 12. Because our mothers kept track of accommodation distributions, they were positioning themselves (and us kids) in such a way that indeed all twelve of us were assigned to the house at Kossuth St. 38, to one of the sparsely furnished rooms looking over the courtyard. And of the twelve members of this large family, eleven fell victim to the brown terror.[24] I was the only one to survive.

Despite the fact that there was very little furniture, there was hardly any room in there, so our mothers decided that we should move out everything; they cleaned up, scrubbed the floor. The furniture that we kept in the room included a table, chairs, a bookshelf on the wall, and a coat rack. The rest was placed on the porch. At night, the table and the chairs were also put there. At this time, it did not occur to us what would have happened to us in these conditions during the winter. Thanks in part to our mothers, despite the ever-changing spring weather, none of us got sick during our period of resettlement. During the days that followed, we all learned to take turns eating from a plate held in our hands, without a table, standing up or sitting on the stone tiles of the porch. It seems like a small thing—we children learned to appreciate single-course lunches at that point. How good it was—if there was any!

---

23. Nyíregyháza's Jews were at first collected in the courtyard of the great synagogue. Some of them were herded off to the Varjúlapos internment camp, including families regarded as foreign, individuals considered politically "unreliable," and many renowned local citizens. The others were placed in the town ghetto. Like a number of others, László's father was separated from his wife and children at this point.

24. That is, the Nazi terror, the Holocaust.

Even without furniture, the room, about 4 meters by 4 [13 feet by 13], was very small for holding 12 people, especially during bedtime. [. . .]²⁵

On the second day before bedtime, the four mothers called every child into the room and closed the door. [. . .] They treated the children as equal partners as they gave us their motherly advice, instructions. My heart still sinks when I recall our conversation from sixty years ago; I remember its contents only: the future is entirely unknown and unpredictable for all of us. Because of this, we must do all we can for one another, help one another and those who are in even greater need than us. If for any reason some of us are separated from the others, they should not give up but should try to keep going, remain honest! You should not give in, be brave! Do not ever forget what happened to your fathers, how your families were broken up, how they treated us, and how they are still treating us! When you grow up and have families, tell them what happened, what they did to us, honest, law-abiding Hungarian citizens, just because we were Jews! Finally: keeping clean is a basic human need at least as important as meals. [. . .]

One of the little ones asked that we stop calling the mother of another child "Mrs.," saying that we should instead add *anya* [mother] to their first name. This is how I came to have *anya* Mariska, *anya* Anci, *anya* Lili, and *anya* Magda as mothers. If the children wanted to address the four of them at once, then they were the four mothers. (This is what we called them!) And if they wanted to address only their own mother, they would call her *anya* [mother.]

[. . .]

We, the four boys, caused many problems. We did not behave well. At times even the girls were naughty, but during our period of captivity, there was never a slap on the face or any other physical punishment. Now, much later, I can imagine the mind-set of the four mothers, which was made worse by the fact that they saw their children destitute and starving.²⁶

[. . .]

---

25. The degree of crowding was even greater in some other buildings in the Nyíregyháza ghetto.

26. The families without food received help from other Jews facing similar fates. Later on, the central ghetto kitchen was also established, where the goal was to cook for all needy people using food obtained by the **Jewish Council** and supplied (in meager quantities) by the authorities.

Mother Lili established study groups for the school-age ghetto children in our courtyard. My sister Éva helped her, along with the other girls in our large family. At first it was just the children living in our house, but later on, children living in neighboring houses also came over. The four mothers considered it important that the children be kept busy, they should not spend their time idly, and at the same time, it was a way for them to also tolerate the destituteness and starvation better.

[. . .]

László survived Auschwitz, Buchenwald, a death march, and Theresienstadt, where Allied troops eventually liberated him. His mother and sister perished in the Stutthof camp, and the Nazis also murdered the other members of the "large family" described in document 8-2.

While Hungarian authorities transported László Kovács and more than 437,000 other Jews from the provinces, **Miklós Horthy**'s decision to halt the deportations in early July temporarily saved Budapest's Jews. Yet behind the scenes, negotiations about resuming the campaign continued. The tragedy of provincial Jewish communities and the efforts of the Christian churches on behalf of Christian converts prompted a wave of conversions during the summer.[27] By August this trend had abated somewhat, but the leaders of the Jewish communities still confronted huge numbers of Jews converting to the Christian faith. The article in document 8-3 appeared in the official journal of the Jewish Council, the *Magyarországi Zsidók Lapja*, reflecting the perspective of Jewish community and religious leaders—Neologue and also to some extent Orthodox—on this phenomenon.[28]

---

27. The number of conversions to Christianity, which had for the most part steadily decreased after a 1938 peak, reached a historic high following the German occupation (by mid-September, the number was twenty times higher than for 1933). Even before this, 60 percent of the conversions took place in Budapest. According to the 1941 census, there were over 17 percent Christians among the Budapest citizens considered Jewish by the discriminatory laws. Viktor Karády, "Zsidótörvények és életfeltételek a szociális jelzők tükrében (1938–1943)," in *Zsidóság, asszimiláció, polgárosodás. Tanulmányok*, ed. idem (Budapest: Cserépfalvi, 1997), 158–59.

28. Despite the article condemning religious conversions, after the war the Jewish Council was accused of favoring Christian converts and failing to react "to the counterpropaganda of those streaming into the churches." See the People's Court on the Jewish Council's case, second day of hearings, in Mária Schmidt, ed., *Kollaboráció vagy kooperáció? A budapesti Zsidó Tanács* (Budapest: Minerva, 1990), 439.

DOCUMENT 8-3: "During the Lull in the Wave of Conversions," *Magyarországi Zsidók Lapja*, August 10, 1944, 1.

Authorized officials of the Christian churches have unanimously taken a stand against conversions to Christianity that are undertaken in order to gain advantages, unaccompanied by conviction. The papers have been publishing reports and articles that cast scorn on those who are lining up to leave the Jewish faith without any spiritual basis, merely with the aim of obtaining a baptismal certificate for themselves and thereby presumably safety.[29]

While it may be part of our mission to weigh in on this matter, we wish to avoid it. We do not restrict freedom of conscience for anyone, but we do of course unfailingly adhere to our principles concerning religious commitment. We note, however, that a certain amount of propaganda has been present in this case as in others. We cannot emphasize enough that as far as we are aware, no one can expect any kind of preferential treatment or advantage from leaving the Jewish religion.[30] All those who leave their religion at present will at most generate new spiritual problems to add to the doubts and spiritual crises that have already become so numerous. Nowadays there is even more of a need for each of us to remove every disturbing doubt from our souls and inner lives, every ambiguity, every problem that may upset the balance of our souls and add to their uncertainty. To counteract this, we can derive strength from tradition, from connecting in all ways to our forebears and the past, all forms of deep-rooted and ingrained religious belief, every prayer and synagogue moment, and in general, everything that brings us closer to the Almighty and bolsters our faith in Him in our souls and our hope for His help.

Converting to Christianity involves more than just outer trappings. This question has an inner side to it as well. We need only look around

---

29. The fundamental claim of the article was the same as the objection often voiced by Christian church leaders against those trying to convert to Christianity to escape persecution. On the attitudes of the churches to the conversions, see chapter 9.

30. Although the Christian churches received numerous promises from the government that Jews of the Christian faith would be treated more favorably than the Israelites, those who converted in 1944 did not get preferential treatment of any kind in the end. Of course, the Jews who viewed conversion as a last escape route could not have known this at the time, even though the "Jewish Laws" defined Jews as people who had converted after 1919 (see chapter 1).

us to see that this question has disturbed the balance among the residents of certain designated buildings, undermined the harmony within certain families, and raised questions and ammunition for disputes that are not at all suited for promoting harmony and agreement.[31]

Unfortunately, our propaganda in this issue is very circumscribed; due to the restrictions on freedom of movement, even life in the temples has been interrupted.[32] We therefore call on everyone to stand by our side as volunteer advocates of the Jewish stance and list for fellow residents and family members all the objections to thoughtlessly and rashly switching one's religion, objections that reveal the moral shortcomings of the question.

Let us maintain our trust in the help of our Almighty God, and let us draw strength from the ancient teachings of our Jewish religion!

## STRATEGY OF THE JEWISH COUNCIL

Though themselves severely restricted in their movements and actions, members of two groups had a much broader scope of activity than "ordinary" Jews: the Central Jewish Council in Budapest and the Zionists in Hungary. After arriving in Budapest on March 19, 1944, **Adolf Eichmann** straightaway sent his two confidants, Hermann Krumey and Dieter Wisliceny, to the headquarters of the Pest Israelite Congregation. They called in all the community leaders and rabbis for the next day. After frantically phoning Hungarian officials, prominent Jews were shocked to find that their network of connection had collapsed overnight. They were completely isolated. Most of their influential friends and supporters had already fallen into Gestapo hands or gone into hiding. Whenever the Jews turned to the Hungarians for help, they got the same disappointing response: the Germans must be obeyed.[33] On the morning of

---

31. The writer Ernő Szép observed that the Jews stuck in the **"yellow-star houses"** were divided along religious as well as social lines. Not only was there tension between Israelites and Christian converts (Szép thought the latter often behaved like "Jewish antisemites"), but conflicts also frequently arose between recent and longtime converts. Ernő Szép, *Emberszag* (Budapest: Osiris, 2000), 20.

32. A curfew was in effect from late June, the time when the "yellow-star houses" were established, except between the hours of 2 and 5 p.m. and, later, between 11 a.m. and 5 p.m. The **Lakatos** government allowed free movement for the Jews for the period of the Jewish High Holidays in early fall.

33. Munkácsi, *Hogyan történt*, 14–15. See Niszon Kahán's recollections in Judit Molnár, *Csendőrök, hivatalnokok, zsidók. Válogatott tanulmányok a magyar holokauszt történetéről* (Szeged: Szegedi Zsidó Hitközség, 2000), 179.

March 20, the **Sondereinsatzkommando Eichmann**'s (SEK) representatives and the Jewish leaders met for the first time. Krumey and Wisliceny employed a strategy successfully used before. Trying to calm everybody down, they assured them that there would be no deportations. Those who obeyed what restrictions there would be need not fear for their lives or their assets.[34] At the same time, the two SS officers announced that while religious and community life could carry on undisturbed, every Jew fell under the Gestapo's purview.

The SEK ordered the Jews to establish a central body by the next day.[35] The Nazis only set up the framework, gave orders, and left the implementation to the Jews, who knew the local conditions better. Therefore Eichmann's men did not assign specific people to the Jewish Council. But the Sondereinsatzkommando insisted on the participation of community leaders, deeming it essential that the new leadership have continuity and appear "legitimate" to the Jewish population. Therefore, they specifically emphasized that in addition to **Neologue** and Orthodox Jews, Zionists should sit on the council.

The Jewish Council's status and jurisdiction were controversial.[36] Officially, the Hungarian authorities ignored its existence. After a month, the government placed the body under its own legal control and changed its name from Central Council of Hungarian Jews to Interim Executive Board of the Association of Jews in Hungary.[37] (Later, as a result of pressure from Christian churches, authorities established a separate organization for Christian Jews.) Theoretically, the Jewish Council had a national sphere of competence, but in practice it operated only in Budapest. In the provinces, local Hungarian (and occasionally German) authorities also set up such councils with memberships ranging from two to ten participants. These operated for a few weeks only and naturally ceased to exist with the deportation of the Jews—among them, the council members.

---

34. Munkácsi, *Hogyan történt*, 16; Samu Stern, *Emlékirataim. Versenyfutás az idővel! A "zsidótanács" működése a német megszállás és a nyilas uralom idején* (Budapest: Bábel, 2004), 303–4.

35. On the circumstances under which the council was established, see Kádár and Vági, "Compulsion of Bad Choices."

36. On the history and activities of the Jewish Council, see Braham, *The Politics of Genocide*, 1:446–710, 2:711–1018; Molnár, *Csendőrök, hivatalnokok, zsidók*, 131–81; Kádár and Vági, "Compulsion of Bad Choices," 71–89; Michman, *Holocaust Historiography*, 159–75; Frojimovics, *Szétszakadt történelem*, 335–48.

37. Prime Minister's Decree no. 1520/1944 on the self-government and representation of the Jews, *Budapesti Közlöny*, April 22, 1944, 1–2. To simplify the description, the body is called Jewish Council in this volume.

The council served primarily to maintain contact between the occupying authorities and the Jews, that is, to convey orders swiftly and fulfill them unconditionally. It comprised mainly the leaders of the largest Neologue community, the Pest Israelite Congregation, but it also included Orthodox and Zionist members.[38] Until the Arrow Cross era, three people shaped its strategy and policy: President **Samu Stern**, a businessman, banker, and president of the National Office of Hungarian Israelites and the Neologue Pest Israelite Congregation; Ernő Pető, an attorney and vice president of the Pest Israelite Congregation[39]; and Károly Wilhelm, an attorney and elder of the Pest Israelite Congregation.[40]

The council's strategy rested on two pillars. One was, in Stern's words, "running a race against time." Council members hoped that the Allies would defeat Nazi Germany before the deportation was completed. The expectation was not completely unfounded, but it ultimately turned out to be unrealistic in the face of the most effective deportation operation of the Holocaust. The other pillar was the deep conviction, shared by many Jewish leaders across German-dominated Europe throughout the war, that any large-scale revolt or policy of disobedience would inevitably lead to the decimation of the whole community.

This strategy implied complete fulfillment of orders from Hungarian and German authorities and constant reassurance of the Jewish population in the official journal, which also entailed demanding total compliance and

---

38. Besides Stern, Pető, and Wilhelm, the members of the first council set up on March 21 included Dr. Samu Csobádi (attorney, president of the Neologue Buda Israelite Congregation), Fülöp Freudiger (factory owner, president of the Budapest Autonomous Orthodox Congregation), **Dr. Samu Kahán-Frankl** (rabbi, president of the Central Office of the Autonomous Orthodox Israelite Denomination of Hungary), and Dr. Niszon Kahán (one of the leaders of the Hungarian Zionist Alliance, representing the Zionists).

39. Ernő Pető (b. 1882–?) trained as a lawyer in Budapest. In addition to his practice as an attorney, he became involved in the community work of the Pest Israelite Congregation. As of 1941, he was appointed vice president of the organization. In 1955 he immigrated to Brazil, where he died in the late 1960s. See Ernő Pető's letter to Lajos Marton, May 22, 1956, USHMMA RG 52, box 72. Large portions of the document appear in Randolph L. Braham, ed., *Hungarian Jewish Studies* (New York: World Federation of Hungarian Jews, 1973), 3:49–74.

40. Károly Wilhelm was born in 1886 in Kassa. After graduating as a lawyer, he worked for the Budapest Stock Exchange. His firm represented the legal interests of large industrial companies, such as the sugar factory of the Hatvany-Deutsch family. In 1941 he was appointed a member of the governing committee of the Neologue Pest Israelite Congregation. After the war he became director-in-chief of the Hungarian Sugar Industry Trust. In 1948 he immigrated to Switzerland, where he died in 1951. For information on Wilhelm, see Braham, *The Politics of Genocide*, 1:498n11.

cooperation.[41] Of course, this was not the council's own initiative. Under strict censorship, the newspaper had no choice but to publish the lies of the Germans and the government. For example, the first issue reassured readers that "no one is arrested for being Jewish, and if certain arrests are necessary, they are carried out for a different reason."[42] A good illustration of this strategy was the announcement published on the front page of the April 6, 1944, issue, a statement that also appeared on posters.

DOCUMENT 8-4: **Announcement of the Central Jewish Council, in *Magyar Zsidók Lapja*, April 6, 1944, 1.**

BROTHERS AND SISTERS!

The Central Council of Hungarian Jews was created by order and appointment of the Hungarian authorities.[43] Its members are those men who—in the years of peace—were elected by the Jewish public to lead the religious institutions.[44]

The Central Council is the only body of the Hungarian Jewry that is recognized by the authorities. Its scope covers every member of the Israelite denomination, as well as those who count as Jewish based on the most recent decrees.[45]

The Hungarian authorities negotiate exclusively with the Central Council, informing it about orders concerning Jewry throughout the country. The lives of each and every member of the Central Council are at risk if these orders are not carried out precisely. The lives of all those who do not fulfill the orders of the Central Council are also at risk.

Brothers and sisters! The Hungarian Jews are required to enforce implementation of the measures introduced by the authorities through its own agencies. Therefore, the Central Council is not an authority, but an executive body of the authorities.

---

41. For a detailed analysis of the Jewish Council's official journal, the *Journal of Hungarian Jews* (later *Journal of Jews in Hungary*), see Gábor Kádár, "A magyarországi zsidók lapjának története (1944 március–október)" (MA thesis, ELTE, 2001).
42. *Magyar Zsidók Lapja*, March 23, 1944, 1.
43. The first sentence of the text was already at variance with reality. During the first months of the occupation, the Hungarian authorities played no role in and had no influence over the activities of the council and even declined contact with the council.
44. On the composition of the Jewish Council, see the glossary.
45. That is, Israelites and converts.

The Central Council cannot allow the disobedience of some individuals to thwart the execution of the orders it receives; should this happen, then a misfortune unlike anything seen before would descend on the entire community![46]

When called upon by the Central Council, everyone is required to appear as directed. The Central Council has been granted unlimited executive rights and responsibilities over all intellectual and material assets and even the labor capacity of every Jew. All of you are agents of the Central Council, women, girls, men, and boys alike. You should recognize that even the gravest steps taken by the Jewish Council are based on measures introduced by the authorities and that the survival of the individual as well as the entire community depends on their precise execution.[47]

May God be with us all and give us the strength and ability to fulfill our task faithfully.

The Central Council of Hungarian Jews

An integral element of the council's strategy was the frequent submission of pleas and petitions to the authorities. Informed within a few days about the ghettoization operation that began on April 16, by April 19 it had already compiled a petition to Prime Minister **Döme Sztójay** requesting that the events be "investigated." The petition came to nothing and went unanswered, as did other requests subsequently submitted to the leaders of the operation.[48] The

---

46. The council wanted to indicate to readers that it was not creating the rules but merely acting as an executive body. This declaration was needed because in the first days of April a bombing raid hit Budapest, and the right-wing extremist propaganda blamed the Jews for it, saying they were the ones giving signals to the Allied planes. The Jews had to hand over fifteen hundred Jewish apartments to Christian bombing victims within twenty-four hours. The task of acquiring the apartments was assigned to the Jewish Council, and the Housing Office led by Rezső Müller accordingly carried out the order. This operation was, of course, bad for the "popularity" of the council.

47. The newspaper issue went on listing anti-Jewish orders for several pages, calling attention to the importance of obeying the authorities' orders, including wearing the yellow star as prescribed.

48. The letters were transferred to State Secretary László Endre, who did not respond to any of them. In his postwar trial, he claimed to have ordered investigations for every one of the complaints submitted by the Jewish Council, but this was a lie. The Christian member of the council, Sándor Török, sent an individual submission to Endre in mid-June, in which he requested that Jewish children of the Christian faith be spared. Endre scribbled a slashed zero on the document, thereby indicating to his subordinates that the submission should be ignored. See letter of **Sándor Török** to the government, June 14, 1944, HNA P1434, fascicle 18, file VI/20.

Jewish Council submitted the petition included in document 8-5 after the mass deportations had already gotten under way.

DOCUMENT 8-5: **Petition of the Central Jewish Council to Minister of the Interior Andor Jaross, May 26, 1944, HNA P 1434, fascicle 17, file V/26.**

Honorable Hungarian Royal Interior Minister!
Your High Excellency!
As the Interim Executive Board of the Association of Jews in Hungary[49]—the legally appointed representative body of the Jews at this time—we dare approach Your High Excellency with the following humble petition:

[. . .] We respectfully present the information that those Jews who on March 19, 1944, and on subsequent days were arrested at the train stations and at customs border checks were taken to the internment camp in Kistarcsa.[50] They were either arriving in Budapest or returning to the provinces, or attempting to cross outlying customs checkpoints of Budapest. Four weeks ago, these people, about two thousand of them, were transported abroad to an unknown destination.[51] [. . .]

The fact that only those able to work because of their age and health were selected for the transports has given a glimmer of hope to their relatives in the midst of their anxiety, for they were left thinking that their family members were transported abroad for work.

Over the past few days, however, many tens of thousands of Jews were deported again from the northeastern regions, including Abaúj and Szabolcs counties. These deportations took place in Munkács, Máramarossziget, Beregszász, Szeklence, Nyíregyháza, Kassa, Ungvár, etc., and are still being carried out at a rapid pace.[52] Whereas only individuals fit for work were taken abroad with the first aforementioned Kistarcsa transport, in recent days in the towns just mentioned, no

---

49. That is, the Jewish Council.
50. That is, the administrative border of the capital.
51. The letter refers to the transport of thirty-eight hundred Jews who were deported to Auschwitz from the Kistarcsa and Bácstopolya internment camps and prisons on April 28–29.
52. The mass deportations began on May 15 from Gendarme District VIII (Deportation Zone I). Every single **county** and settlement mentioned in the document belonged to this zone. Two to five trains per day passed through the Kassa border crossing on the way to Auschwitz.

such selection was made among the many tens of thousands of people deported. Elderly people, even those over eighty years old, were put on the trains and deported. Moreover, in one town—we have been informed it was Beregszász—the very first people taken to the railway station were Jews housed at the home for the elderly. Even infants were taken away. The fact that with these transports the deportations of the Jews was carried out without regard for age, sex, health condition, and therefore the capacity to work causes extraordinary anxiety for relatives who may still remain in the country, as well as for Hungarian Jews as a whole.

[. . .]

On behalf of the hundreds of thousands of members of Hungarian Jewry, we profoundly entreat your High Excellency and ask you with great urgency to kindly put an end to these deportations, which are being carried out at an extraordinarily swift speed; in view of the present swift means of transportation, all Jews from northeastern Hungary will otherwise face deportation within just a few days.

We must also raise the issue that the deportation itself is taking place under circumstances that subject deportees to great peril en route. Seventy people are typically forced into a single freight car, but we have received reports of instances of even greater overcrowding.

Given this overcrowding and the increasingly warmer weather these days, it is not merely the health but in fact the lives of the deportees that are in grave danger, for they are transported in closed, airless freight cars. Again, we must emphasize the fact that not only healthy, young individuals but also elderly and sick people, as well as children, some of them babies, are placed into these cars.

[. . .]

It is with great humility that we turn again to Your High Excellency requesting that you intervene to stop these deportations as a matter of priority and urgency and that you remedy the complaints and eliminate the grievances resulting from the life-threatening overcrowding, inadequate food supplies, and deficient health care. Jews under our purview are already in a tragic and severe situation. Given this fact, the deportations pain us greatly. In our desperate astonishment over the events, the Hungarian Jews can turn only to Your High Excellency, expecting, with pleading hopefulness, that their tragic fate will take a turn for the better, and their current dreadful state will be eliminated.

Awaiting your protective, swift, and benevolent assistance, we remain humble servants of Your High Excellency.

Budapest, May 26, 1944

On behalf of the Interim Executive Board
of the Association of Jews in Hungary:
President [Samu Stern]

The text provides a clear illustration that the Jewish leaders were incapable of reassessing their relationship with the authorities. It also shows that loyalty and obedience to the law still governed their decisions, despite the fact that the Sztójay government aimed at their community's destruction. The letters and pleas conveyed information about the suffering of the Jews to the very leaders who had caused this suffering. Samu Stern addressed the above petition to Minister of the Interior **Andor Jaross**, head of the ministry in charge of ghettoization and the deportations. Jewish leaders could hardly have fostered any illusions about Jaross, for several days earlier he discussed the "solution to the Jewish question" explicitly in a speech that appeared in the press.[53] Provincial Jewish Councils followed a similar strategy of submitting various petitions to the local governments. Their requests appealed to humanity and patriotism, and they also compliantly offered their services, preempting any demands made by the authorities. The Jewish Council of Hajdúszoboszló offered the labor of every single community member who was fit to work. Jews in Nyíregyháza asked merely that instead of the "severe sentence that means the very end," they be granted mercy and allowed to "stay crowded into the tightest place possible, confined to just two–three streets of the town."[54]

The inexplicable delay in dealing with the **Auschwitz Protocol**, a detailed account of the mass murder in Auschwitz, further exemplified the Budapest Jewish Council's controversial strategy. The council probably obtained this document in May 1944 but had certainly seen it by the beginning of June at the latest.[55] Weeks passed before anything happened with the information. Eventually the Zionists sent this critical document to Switzerland, after which the world press published it far and wide. For a time the Jewish Council did not even pass the documents on to those from whom they hoped for help: Horthy

---

53. See document 6-11.

54. HBCA V.B. 474/b., fascicle 232, file 4813/1944, and SzSzCA V. B. 186, fascicle XI., file 700/1944.

55. For questions regarding the protocol, see Braham, *The Politics of Genocide*, 1:703, 2:824–40; Sándor Szenes, *Befejezetlen múlt. Keresztények és zsidók, sorsok* (Budapest: n.p., 1986), 53–62, 109–26, 189–217.

and his circle. Tellingly most council members remained conspicuously silent about the document in their postwar testimonies.[56]

The council itself sometimes also engaged in underground activities. For a time it gave financial and logistical help to the Zionists in their negotiations with the Nazis behind the Hungarian government's back.[57] Council members made contact with the relatively insignificant Hungarian resistance.[58] Through **Raoul Wallenberg**, they sent a letter to the Swedish king, soliciting help.[59] When assessing the council's acts, we also have to note that the council went to enormous effort to organize the provisioning and housing of the (predominantly Budapest) Jews. In addition, the leading trio (Stern, Pető, and Wilhelm) stayed the course: while one of the Orthodox council members, Fülöp Freudiger, escaped to Romania and the other, Samu Kahán-Frankl, resigned and went into hiding, the Neologue leaders did not follow their example, although they had the means to do so.[60]

Despite this, after the war left-wing Zionists accused Stern and his circle of collaborating with the Nazis. Already ardent opponents of the conservative Jewish elite prior to 1944, they called together an unofficial "people's tribunal" in order to investigate their activities. The Zionists' accusations included, among other things, collaboration, corruption, and betrayal of the "Jewish masses."[61] Document 8-6 excerpts a statement submitted by Stern's confidant Ernő Pető to

---

56. Kádár and Vági, "Compulsion of Bad Choices," 88–89.
57. Kasztner report, YVA, 015H/35; Recollection of Hansi Brand, USHMMA RG 52, Randolph L. Braham Collection, box 72.
58. Braham, *The Politics of Genocide*, 2:1134–35.
59. Mária Ember, *Wallenberg Budapesten* (Budapest: Városháza, 2000), 22. See also the recollections of Samu Stern, HJA, DEGOB Protocols, no. 3627, and Ernő Pető's letter to Lajos Marton, May 22, 1956, USHMMA RG 52, Randolph L. Braham Collection, box 72.
60. With the wealth and connections of Stern's circle, they could probably have followed Freudiger if they had wanted. In an interview conducted by Professor Braham in the early 1970s, Freudiger claimed to have offered Stern the chance to escape with him. However, the president found abandoning the sinking ship unthinkable. Randolph L. Braham's interview with Fülöp Freudiger, October 10, 1972, USHMMA RG 52, Randolph L. Braham Collection, box 72. Fülöp Freudiger (1900–1976), head of the Budapest Autonomous Orthodox Congregation (as of 1939), was one of the most influential Hungarian Orthodox leaders. After the war he lived in Israel and testified in the Eichmann trial. For Freudiger's recollections, see Fülöp (Philip) Freudiger et al., "Report on Hungary: March 19–August 9, 1944," in *Hungarian Jewish Studies*, ed. Randolph Braham, 3:75–146; Fülöp Freudiger, "Five Months," in *The Tragedy of Hungarian Jewry: Essays, Documents, Depositions*, ed. Randolph L. Braham (New York: Columbia University Press, 1986), 237–87.
61. For the protocol of the hearing at the "people's tribunal," see Béla Zsolt, *Fehér könyv* (Budapest: n.p., 1945).

the Screening Committee of the Bar Association.[62] Although not created during the "people's tribunal" proceedings, it contains a prominent council member's responses to the charges he faced in the immediate postwar era.

DOCUMENT 8-6: **Testimony of Jewish Council member Ernő Pető, May 28, 1945, USHMMA RG 39.013M, reel 28 (HJA XX-L-1, box D 5/3).**

[. . .]
The question arose: why did we accept our roles when we already knew about the fate of the Jews—the Polish and Slovakian Jews?[63] We have also posed this question to ourselves, and we saw that we had just two paths ahead of us. If we did not accept this role, then we had to go into hiding right away, because as members of the resistance, we would most certainly have been dragged away by the Germans.[64] We could not continue the struggle that we had been pursuing for years, especially since 1938, and, we might say, even since 1921, when the *numerus clausus* was instituted[65]—the struggle aimed at protecting the interests and legal equality of the Jews.

[. . .]
Before the German occupation, the Jews placed their trust in us, entrusted us, as their elected representatives, with the protection of their interests; we felt it would be cowardly and contemptible of us—now that the danger had escalated—to leave our positions, attempting to secure our own safety, while entrusting to others the public interests that until then we believed we had been honestly defending.

I must raise the question: what would have come from our resignations? Either the Germans, or the government of the time, would have installed its own people instead of representatives of the Jews. Could one

---

62. Every person who had performed a state or public task during the war had to justify his or her conduct before the screening committees set up in 1945.

63. Following the war, members of the Jewish Council made no attempt to deny that they had known what was going on in Nazi-occupied Europe. In his 1946 memoirs, Samu Stern admitted that he understood the Nazi agenda: "I knew about their deeds in all occupied countries of Central Europe and I knew that their activity was a long string of plundering and murder. [. . .] I knew their habits, acts, their dreadful reputation." Recollection of Samu Stern, HJA, DEGOB Protocols, no. 3627.

64. Indeed, over the first few days, the Germans carried off many prominent Jews. However, the president of the Hungarian Zionist Alliance, **Ottó Komoly**, refused his appointment to the Jewish Council and still was not arrested. Molnár, *Csendőrök, hivatalnokok, zsidók*, 163.

65. It was actually 1920; see the glossary.

have expected them to defy their executioners and reach concessions [for the Jews]? We knew that we had embarked on a superhuman and dangerous task, and all we could remain hopeful about was that the Red Army was already approaching the borders of the country and that we could postpone the deportations until the time when their arrival would liberate the country and, in it, the Jews who had suffered the most. Along with everyone else, we also hoped that this would come about much sooner than it did in the end. <u>Our past compelled us to accept positions on the council, and our honor compelled us to stay in our posts as long as there remained the slightest glimmer of hope that there was something we could do for the Jews.</u>

There were council members who put their personal safety ahead of other interests and left the country.[66] Because they "fled," the whole Jewish community was enraged, and the press wants to hold them responsible for this now. It is held against us that we stayed, and it is held against them [those who fled] that they did not do so.[67]

The fact that we remained in our difficult positions can be justified by one consideration only, and this is that by delaying the deportations, <u>we managed to save two hundred thousand Jews in Budapest until the arrival of the Red Army</u>. This result of our struggle is a historic achievement, and I hope that by uncovering our actual operations, the Honorable Committee will also form an accurate picture of them.[68]

Samu Kahán-Frankl disappeared,[69] and we had no information about him until the liberation. Did this help anything? There were those, like Fülöp Freudiger, who fled the country without any prior notice, and this was seen by many Jews as outrageous and despicable. Our president only received his resignation letter after he had fled.[70] Our resignation would have served only to increase the Jews' exasperation and fear, and perhaps—we may say this without being presumptuous—their situation would have been worsened by our departure. We had to carry out our work in part

---

66. Pető is referring to Samu Kahán-Frankl and Fülöp Freudiger.

67. Pető's outburst provides an effective summary of the trap created by a compulsion of bad choices (i.e., a situation in which the council members were forced to decide among alternatives that all had negative outcomes).

68. Members of the council spread this legend in order to protect themselves. They basically played no role in the halting of the deportations. On the real reasons, see chapter 4.

69. As mentioned, Rabbi Samu Kahán-Frankl resigned his membership on the council in the summer of 1944 and went into hiding in Budapest, while Fülöp Freudiger and his family fled to Romania.

70. Samu Stern.

secretively so that the informants and secret police who filled our headquarters would not betray us.[71] Therefore, certain operations required only one or two members of the council to have knowledge of them. We had to accept the odiousness of this because we were convinced that we should rescue as many Jews from the terror of deportation as possible and put off, postpone those measures that would have served to prepare or to carry out the deportations.[72]

[. . .]

## ZIONIST RESPONSES

Besides the council, just one other Jewish group in 1944–1945 reacted to the events with organized strategies: the Zionists. Although its membership was very small, the group's influence far exceeded its size. Between the two world wars, Zionism had been a marginal, factious movement in Hungary, rejected by the majority of Jews. It gained strength from 1939, due largely to the influx of Zionist activists from the reannexed Transylvania, Upper Province, and Carpatho-Ruthenia. Hungarian Zionists numbered an estimated two thousand to sixty-five hundred before the reannexation and from ten to twelve thousand afterward. Zionist refugees from territories under Nazi occupation consisted primarily of young people with extensive organizational and resistance experience.[73] The movement operating in Hungary in 1944–1945 had three major subgroups: the **Budapest Relief and Rescue Committee (Rezső Kasztner**'s group), the young Zionists, and the Palestine Office. They followed different strategies, but all three rejected the Jewish Council's politics of waiting and delaying, built on legality, loyalty, and obedience.

Ottó Komoly, an engineer, and Rezső Kasztner, a lawyer and journalist from Kolozsvár, headed the Budapest Relief and Rescue Committee, established in early 1943. Jenő (Joel) Brand and his wife, Hansi, assumed important roles

---

71. Pető is primarily talking about Rabbi **Béla Berend**. On Berend, see the introduction to document 5-6.
72. Perhaps the most severe accusation against the Jewish leaders was that they did not inform the Jews about the impending mortal danger and their sole concern was to rescue themselves, their families, and their friends, while assisting in the Nazis' deception campaign.
73. For a summary of the data, see Attila Novák, *Átmenetben. A cionista mozgalom négy éve Magyarországon* (Budapest: Múlt és Jövő, 2000), 199. For the most comprehensive biographical summary, which contains 420 short portraits of the Zionists operating in Hungary, see David Gur, *Brothers for Resistance and Rescue: The Underground Zionist Youth Movement in Hungary during World War II* (Jerusalem: Gefen, 2007).

on the committee,[74] which became an important link in carrying information across borders to and from the Zionists. Kasztner and his colleagues played the key role in supporting and hiding Jews who fled to Hungary to escape the events raging in Nazi Europe. International Jewish organizations (the Jewish Agency for Palestine and the American Jewish Joint Distribution Committee) provided the funds for their operations.[75] After March 1944, Rescue Committee members quickly decided to seek contact and negotiate with everyone who could significantly influence the fate of Hungary's Jews. Committee president Ottó Komoly took it upon himself to foster contacts with the Hungarian authorities; Rezső Kasztner and Jenő Brand took on the difficult and controversial task of negotiating with Eichmann's unit.

Surprisingly enough, the SS was open to negotiations. Kasztner and his colleagues did not know, however, that Reichsführer-SS Heinrich Himmler was seeking to start separate peace talks with the western Allies behind Hitler's back. Therefore, he was ready to get in touch with the Zionists through his underlings, based on the absurd assumption (fully compatible with Nazi ideology) that the road to Allied leaders led through "world Jewry." As a result of the negotiations Kasztner conducted first with Eichmann, then with Himmler's personal envoy, SS-Obersturmbannführer **Kurt Becher**, the so-called Kasztner train left Budapest on June 30, 1944. It transported its passengers to a special section constructed inside the Bergen-Belsen camp in northwestern Germany. After subsequent negotiations between the Nazis and the Jews, the first "Kasztner Jews" (more than three hundred people) reached safety in

---

74. After the war Jenő (Joel) Brand (1907–1964) settled in Israel with Hansi (née Hajnalka Hartmann; 1912 –1995), who was also instrumental in the committee's activity. Both testified at the Eichmann trial. See obituary for Joel Brand, *Jewish Telegraphic Agency*, July 15, 1964; Yechaim Weitz, "Hansi Brand (Hartmann)," http://jwa.org/encyclopedia/article/brand-hansi (accessed December 2, 2012).

75. For details about the 1944 activities of the Rescue Committee, the Nazi-Jewish negotiations, and the Kasztner affair, see Braham, *The Politics of Genocide*, 2:1058–148; Yehuda Bauer, *Jews for Sale? Nazi-Jewish Negotiations, 1933–1945* (New Haven, CT: Yale University Press, 1994), 172–209; Gábor Kádár and Zoltán Vági, *Self-financing Genocide: The Gold Train, the Becher Case and the Wealth of Hungarian Jews* (Budapest: Central European University Press, 2004), 209–44; Molnár, *Csendőrök, hivatalnokok, zsidók*, 183–97. For a sizable bibliography of the literature on the topic, see Randolph L. Braham and Julia Bock, eds., *The Holocaust in Hungary. A Selected and Annotated Bibliography: 2000–2007* (New York: Columbia University Press, 2008), 143–50; Randolph L. Braham, ed., *The Holocaust in Hungary: A Selected and Annotated Bibliography, 1984–2000* (New York: Columbia University Press, 2001), 143–47; Attila Novák, "An Unknown Hungarian Writer on the Overture to the Era of Terror: The Memoirs of Ernő Szilágyi," in *The Holocaust in Hungary: A European Perspective*, ed. Judit Molnár (Budapest: Balassi Kiadó, 2005), 250–51.

neutral Switzerland in August 1944. The rest (around 1,370 people) followed in December. After the SS halted Jewish emigration from the Nazi-controlled territories in October 1941, this was the first sizable group allowed to leave the territory of the Third Reich.

The diary entries of Ottó Komoly, president of the Hungarian Zionist Alliance and the Budapest Relief and Rescue Committee, offer a glimpse into the negotiations surrounding the preparation of the Kasztner operation from the perspective of one of its central players. Komoly participated in compiling the list of those granted permission to leave the country. The work started in late April. As soon as news of the Nazi-Jewish deal spread, scores of people besieged the Zionist organization. The original agreement covered about six hundred people, but as negotiations proceeded the number grew to almost seventeen hundred. The Rescue Committee compiled the list based on discussions with Orthodox and Neologue community leaders, as well as the young Zionists. Komoly wrote the diary entries presented in document 8-7 during this period.

DOCUMENT 8-7: **Ottó Komoly's diary entries for April/May 1944, USHMMA RG 52.030*01 (YVA, P 31/44).**

April 25, [1944,] Tuesday
Got up after 7. In the morn[ing], Szilágyi mistakenly sends Lea to me with a message addressed to S. At Lila's Mrs. Kósa in the aft[ernoon].[76] At my place, Dr. Horovitz and Dr. Ödön Szabó with his wife and child, regarding aliyah matters. From 4:15 to 8:30 at the Information Office,[77]

---

76. Ernő Szilágyi (Cvi) (1898–1973), businessman, Zionist leader, and president of the Pro-Palestine Association of Hungarian Jews, was the closest colleague of Rezső Kasztner. For his biography and actions, see Novák, "An Unknown Hungarian Writer," 219–46. Lea Komoly (later Fuerst) was born in 1921 in Virovitica, Yugoslavia, the daughter of Ottó Komoly. Arrested in April 1944, she managed to secure a place on Rezső, or Rudolf, Kasztner's "rescue train" to Switzerland in the summer of 1944. She remained in Switzerland for the rest of the war and immigrated to Palestine in 1945. See *USHMMA ITS Collection Data Base*, and for details on Lea's Swiss sojourn, see USHMMA 58.001M, reel 465 (Swiss Refugee Records).

77. The Information Office was set up in the Síp Street center of the Pest Israelite Congregation, which operated as the headquarters of the Jewish Council. The office served as a de facto cover institution for the Kasztner group and the young Zionists. A Zionist activist later said that "orders were given on the third floor [i.e., in the office of the council] and we tried to sabotage them on the ground floor." Mihály Salamon, *"Keresztény" voltam Európában, Pesti riportregény a nyilas időkről* (Tel Aviv: Népünk, n.d.) 50. However, this step also shows that Stern and his circle were sometimes and to a certain extent ready to evade the Hungarian authorities.

exhausting wait and meetings. Home at 8:45 (Kasztner and Brand looked for me while I was gone, in addition, Dr. Herzog and Dr. Steckl. Handbag making.[78] Went to bed after 12. (The situation now is that my name is included on the list submitted. I feel a terrible moral disgust.)[79] I got back the stamped exemption document today.[80]

May 2, [1944,] Tuesday
Got up at 6:30. P[ost]card to Zsuzsi Fried. In the afternoon, Dr. Kasztner informs me that the Germans have granted permission for a transport of 600,[81] they demand a list, etc. Perhaps it can leave at the end of next week. P[alestine] O[ffice] aft[ernoon] meeting in I. 28[82]: the task of preparing the list: me and Szilágyi (a terrible siege) [of people pressing to be on the list]. Home by 9:30. Went to bed at around 11:30. Constant fatigue; the anxiety and stress have gotten to me terribly; I cannot bear the constant siege of people, the unavoidable injustice that comes with the selection. (In the *Esti Újság* [Evening Newspaper], the ord[er] re[garding] exempt s[tatus] has been published.)[83]

The final list included family members of the committee's leaders, prominent members of the community selected by the committee, renowned

---

78. "Lea's bag made out of cloth, gold coins of Napoleon." (The footnote is part of the original document.) Since by this time the authorities had impounded much of the money that Jews had in cash and in bank deposits, many people rescued and hid their property in gold coins.

79. Upon the urging of his colleagues and friends, Komoly was also put on the list. The decision created a severe moral conflict for him. "I could never set foot on the land of Eretz Israel, if at this time I were to choose saving my own life," he told his wife, based on a testimony she gave subsequently. Eventually, they both stayed. Their daughter, Lea, was put on the train, like Kasztner's relatives. By contrast, other Zionist leaders, including Ernő Szilágyi and Niszon Kahán, boarded the train. Judit Molnár, "'Vajon megtelnek-e följegyzéseimmel e könyv lapjai?' Komoly Ottó naplója (1944)," in *Küzdelem az igazságért. Tanulmányok Randolph L. Braham 80. Születésnapjára*, ed. László Karsai and Judit Molnár (Budapest: MAZSIHISZ, 2002), 485–86.

80. As a highly decorated military officer of World War I, Ottó Komoly was exempted from the requirement to wear the yellow star.

81. The number chosen in the negotiations was six hundred because this was the number of entry permits to Palestine that had arrived shortly beforehand in the Palestine Office, the number based on the quota set by the British.

82. This was most likely the number of the room in which the meeting took place.

83. Prime Minister's Decree no. 1530/1944 concerning the review of certain exemption documents involving the Jews, *Budapesti Közlöny*, April 30, 1944.

intellectuals, the 150 wealthy individuals who secured the money paid for the Germans, foreign refugees, Zionist youth, and orphaned children.[84] The major provincial congregations also sent in their own lists, based on which hundreds of people were pulled out of the ghettos and collection camps. Paradoxically, the Zionists thus ended up saving a number of renowned Hassidic and Neologue rabbis, some of Zionist ideology's implacable enemies.[85]

The Kasztner case provoked strong emotions worldwide, its effects reverberating to this day. According to his critics, Kasztner colluded with Eichmann, hiding from the Jewish community the reality that deportations led to total annihilation. In exchange, Eichmann placed no obstacles in the way of the Rescue Committee's operation. Kasztner rescued several prominent Jews and his own family and friends, while the majority went to their death without resistance, his critics charge.[86] Others see Kasztner as a hero who, risking his own life, attempted the impossible. He could not have saved all Hungarian Jews but did at least manage to rescue close to seventeen hundred people from nearly inevitable death. Many sharing this opinion believe that survivors of the eastern Austrian labor camps owe their lives to Kasztner as well.[87]

The second Zionist group worth noting is the young Zionists, members of the **Hehalutz** movement, the *halutzim*. Numbering a couple hundred, they carried out significant activities against the regime—with a handful of exceptions, unarmed.[88] Jewish youth who had fled from Slovakia and Poland between 1942 and 1944 assumed leading roles. For the most part, they came without their families, had nothing to lose, and had grown accustomed to living in an environment of illegality. The Zionist youth adapted quickly to extreme situations and the physical and psychological hardships of living and working outside the law. These attributes were obviously linked partially to their ages, which ranged from eighteen to twenty-six. In view of the prevailing conditions at the time, the young Zionists, the group perhaps most suited for armed resistance due to

---

84. Kasztner report, YVA, 015H/35, I/130–34.

85. For example, Joel Teitelbaum and Kornél Heves, rabbis from Szatmár and Szolnok respectively. See László Csősz, "A Vészkorszak Jász-Nagykun-Szolnok vármegyében" (PhD diss., University of Szeged, 2010), 153–54.

86. Hannah Arendt clearly condemned the activities of Kasztner and his group. Hannah Arendt, *Eichmann in Jerusalem: A Report on the Banality of Evil*, 2nd rev. ed. (New York: Penguin, 1976), 132–33. Subsequent historical analyses contradicted this summarily dismissive opinion and ventured to provide a more nuanced analysis of the situation.

87. See documents 4-6 and 4-7.

88. Historian and former resistance fighter Zvi Erez identified six armed resistance cases, five of which were defensive acts. Interview with Zvi Erez, in István Gábor Benedek and György Vámos, *Tépd le a sárga csillagot* (Budapest: Pallas, 1990), 40.

its members' age range, experiences, and networks, understandably saw little sense in taking up arms.[89]

Following the German occupation, they went about rescuing, hiding, and providing false documents primarily for their own friends and family members.[90] They assisted many people in reaching Slovakia, Romania, and the territories of the former Yugoslavia. According to Asher Cohen's estimates, about seven thousand people made it across the Romanian border alone.[91] The young Zionists performed their bravest actions following the Arrow Cross takeover. Often wearing Arrow Cross uniforms and weapons, they showed forged documents to save people from the hands of the Arrow Cross militiamen. They also made substantial contributions to the child rescue operations of the International Red Cross.[92] Among the most prominent leaders and members of the *halutzim* were Márton Elefánt (Hebrew name: Mose Alpan), Rafael Friedl (Rafi Benshalom), Imre Herbst, Perec Révész, József Mayer, Endre Grósz (David Gur), and Ernő Teichmann (Efra Agmon).[93]

*Halutz* resistance fighter David Gur, born in 1926, grew up in a small village in eastern Hungary near the Romanian border. He joined the underground leftist Zionist Hashomer Hatzair movement in 1943. Following the March 1944 German occupation, he went into hiding in Budapest. His group tried to help persecuted Jews as well as non-Jewish resisters by forging thousands of protective passports, birth certificates, and other documents. During his daring missions, Gur sometimes posed as an Arrow Cross militiaman. In the picture reproduced in document 8-8, probably taken in November or December of 1944, he wears an Arrow Cross armband and carries a pistol. The fact that

---

89. The commonly held opinion is eloquently expressed in this proverbial remark by one of the young Zionists: "I don't want a kibbutz in Palestine to be named after me, I want to live in it." See Ávihu Ronén, *Harc az életért. Cionista ellenállás Budapesten—1944* (Budapest: Belvárosi, 1998), 33.

90. See, e.g., HJA, DEGOB Protocols, no. 3106.

91. Asher Cohen, *The Halutz Resistance in Hungary, 1942–1944* (Boulder, CO: Social Science Monographs, 1986), 99.

92. See chapter 9.

93. For their biographies and 1944 actions, see Gur, *Brothers for Resistance and Rescue*. On the Hehalutz resistance, see Cohen, *The Halutz Resistance in Hungary*; Ronén, *Harc az életért*; Salamon, *"Keresztény" voltam Európában*; Benedek and Vámos, *Tépd le a sárga csillagot*; Rafi Benshalom, *We Struggled for Life: The Hungarian Zionist Youth Resistance during the Nazi Era* (Jerusalem: Gefen, 2001); László Karsai, "Lőni vagy túlélni?" *Beszélő* (July–August 1999), 104–15; Attila Novák, "Ellenállás vagy önmentés? Adalékok az 1944-es magyarországi cionista ellenállás problémájához," *Századok* 1 (2007), 143 –66; Robert Rozett, "Jewish Armed Resistance in Hungary," in *Genocide and Rescue: The Holocaust in Hungary, 1944*, ed. David Cesarani (Oxford: Berg, 1997), 135–45.

Arrow Cross gangs did not have official uniforms and remained quite disorganized supported his missions. In December Gur was arrested, along with his staff. Gendarme detectives brutally interrogated and tortured him. His Zionist comrades came to his rescue at the end of December. Gur eventually survived the war and emigrated to Israel, where he lives in Ramat-Gan with his family.[94]

DOCUMENT 8-8: **Photograph of young Zionist resistance fighter David Gur, winter 1944, USHMMPA WS# 94470.**

---

94. Gur, *Brothers for Resistance and Rescue*, 121–22.

Besides the Kasztner group and the *halutzim*, the Zionists' Palestine Office also followed an independent strategy for the Jews remaining in Hungary. Established to coordinate emigration to Palestine, it became an important Zionist center. Like the Rescue Committee, it included representatives of various Zionist groups. Headed by **Miklós Krausz**, the office resolutely opposed the strategy of the Kasztner group, rejecting the option of negotiating with the Nazis. For this reason Krausz sought and forged relations with several diplomatic legations. His activities became particularly important in the summer of 1944. He had the Palestine Office relocated into the so-called **Glass House** at Vadász Street 29 (Budapest) and managed to have it placed under Swiss diplomatic protection. Although eventually nothing came of the emigration opportunities he sought, the Glass House still provided shelter for several thousand Jews and became one of the primary bases of *halutz* underground activity. However, after a while, his personal relations with some young Zionist leaders deteriorated, and he banned them from the Vadász Street house.[95] Nevertheless, young Zionist leaders deemed undesirable could still freely enter the Glass House. Ultimately Krausz's action with the most impact was his arranging for the Auschwitz Protocol to reach Switzerland, after it had been in the Zionists' possession for a long time.

## THWARTED APPEALS

In the spring and early summer of 1944, both the Jewish Council and the Zionists had obtained a great deal of direct information about the persecution of the Jews in the provinces.[96] By the end of June, it became clear that traditional means and strategies would lead nowhere. At this point, some young employees of the Jewish Council decided to issue a memorandum to the Hungarian public. They shared their plan with the Jewish Council, whose members were unwilling to assume the risk of illegally disseminating the document. Instead, the council entreated the government with yet another pleading letter.[97] Following the fail-

---

95. Testimony of Eszter Eppler, February 27, 1945, HJA, DEGOB Protocols, no. 3615. See also the testimony of Márton Elefánt, HJA, DEGOB Protocols, no. 3619.

96. They included, e.g., young people working at various departments of the Jewish Council.

97. See the memorandum of June 22, 1944, of the Jewish Council, in Elek Karsai, ed., *Vádirat a nácizmus ellen. Dokumentumok a magyarországi zsidóüldözés történetéhez (1944 június 26–1944 október 15. A budapesti zsidóság deportálásának felfüggesztése)* (Budapest: Magyar Izraeliták Országos Képviselete, 1967), 3:35–37.

ure of this attempt, members of the group that had initiated the memorandum—Sándor Somló, Ernő Munkácsi, Rabbi Fábián Herskovits, Fülöp and Jenő Grünvald[98]—began reproducing and disseminating the illegal document. Many members and sympathizers of the Zionist movement assisted with the distribution. In early August 1944, Hungarian authorities arrested many of the participants, who were then freed in early fall during the temporary atmosphere of détente that followed the appointment of the Géza Lakatos government.[99]

Document 8-9(A) excerpts the original text of the memorandum,[100] of which two thousand copies were produced and distributed. Document 8-9(B) is another illegal leaflet authored by the same circle of people, but we have no clear information as to whether the more strongly worded texts were distributed at all.[101]

DOCUMENT 8-9(A–B): Illegal leaflets of the Jewish underground, summer 1944.

DOCUMENT 8-9(A): USHMMA RG 39.013M, reel 26 (HJA XX-F-II, box D 6/4).

COPY OF A LETTER

The Hungarian Jews turn to Christian Hungarian society and raise their voices with a plea in the eleventh hour of their tragic fate. They turn to those with whom they have lived together for a millennium, in good times and bad, in the country where our ancestors, fathers, and grandfathers lie buried.

We did not say a word when we were plundered, lost our civil dignity and respect. And we did not resort to protest when we were thrown out of our homes either. However, it is now about our bare lives. Moreover—and it hurts to even write this sentence—it is about the lives of only those Jews who remain.

---

98. Ernő Munkácsi (1896–1950) was secretary of the Pest Jewish Congregation and an employee of the Central Jewish Council; in the postwar years he was executive director of the National Office of Hungarian Israelites. Fábián Herskovits (1907–1982), a rabbi, became one of the leading rabbis of the country after the war; in 1950 he emigrated to Israel.

99. Recollections of Ernő Munkácsi, *Új Élet*, July 11 and 18, 1946; Karsai, *Vádirat a nácizmus ellen*, 27–32, 34–37; HJA, DEGOB Protocols, no. 3581.

100. Munkácsi published the text with minor modifications after the war. Munkácsi, *Hogyan történt*, 121–23. According to his account, there was more than one version.

101. Braham, *The Politics of Genocide*, 2:1133.

We must make clear to Hungarian society that for weeks now, hundreds of thousands of Hungarian Jews have been deported abroad under tragic and cruel circumstances that are unparalleled in world history.

[. . .][102]

Hungarian society would not be able to watch all these monstrosities idly and without being moved if it had known about them. However, experience shows that the majority of Hungarians do not know about these horrors, particularly since the press remains silent about them.[103]

[. . .]

Will it be historically justifiable that almost six percent of the Hungarian citizens, almost a million people, were doomed to deportation and death without a trial and sentence?

Nowadays we do not have the time nor, <u>particularly, the chance</u> to defend ourselves against one-sided charges, but we face those charges head-on. Even if we made mistakes, they were no particular fault of ours, but arose from that economic system that had prevailed in the world, including Hungary, for a century, and in which all productive forces (Christian and Jewish alike) participated.

[. . .]

The Hungarian nation might see it as appropriate to cast the Hungarian Jewry from its own midst, but how can the chivalrous Hungarian nation endure the cruel extermination of the helpless elderly, babies, unarmed defenseless people, and invalid veterans who lost their sight and limbs in the war?

A way should be found for the remaining few hundred thousands of Hungarian Jews to emigrate if neutral states were contacted. [. . .]

We beg Hungarian Christian society to protect our children, defenseless women, all of us who are awaiting complete destruction.

We believe in the fairness of the Hungarian nation, which expects and claims justice from the world's nations,[104] and which cannot let this terrible death of the innocent happen.

---

102. In the next six paragraphs the pamphlet describes the brutal details of the ghettoization and deportation.

103. Of course the authors realized that the horrors of the ghettoization and deportation were widely known in Hungary.

104. The authors refer to the popular and widely used slogan pertaining to the nullification of the **Trianon peace treaty**: "Justice for Hungary."

But if our pleas are futile, then all we ask for from the Hungarian nation is to put an end to our suffering in our own country, instead of putting us through the horrors of deportation, so that we can be buried in our motherland.

DOCUMENT 8-9(B): **Elek Karsai, ed., *Vádirat a nácizmus ellen. Dokumentumok a magyarországi zsidóüldözés történetéhez (1944 május 26–1944 október 15. A Budapesti zsidóság deportálásának felfüggesztése* (Budapest: Magyar Izraeliták Országos Képviselete, 1962) 3:34.**

*Hungarians!*
Do not soil the pure armor of Hungarian chivalry!

You must recognize this: all Jews in the Hungarian provinces, the villages and towns, about half a million people, have been put on death trains and transported abroad, where they died in gas chambers and crematoria. This end awaits the Jews of the capital, about 200,000 people.

The entire Hungarian nation must assume responsibility for this before the tribunal of history.[105]

End the awful massacre. Christian mercy and Hungarian decency demand it.

Let them place us, who have been pushed out of their homes, into labor camps until the end of the war, at which point we can be resettled outside the country.

And if our voices are not heard, shoot us in piles here, in the Hungarian motherland; let us then rest in the soil of our birthplace.

One author and distributor of the leaflet in document 8-9(A) was teacher and historian Fülöp Grünvald, who worked as an official of the Jewish Council's Housing Department. He was born in 1887 and educated in Budapest. Beginning in 1919 he taught in one of the schools run by the Pest Israelite Congregation. Like many community employees, he began working for the Jewish Council after the March 19, 1944, German occupation of Hungary.

---

105. In contrast to the pamphlet that was eventually copied and distributed, this text contained an outright threat.

DOCUMENT 8-10: Certificate issued by the Central Jewish Council proving that Fülöp Grünvald (erroneously spelled Grünwald in the document) is an employee of the council, April 1944, USHMMA RG 39.013M, reel 25 (HJA XX-F-1, box D 6/1).

No. 2583
**Identification.**
The signatory, the Central Council of the Hungarian Jews, certifies that
*Philipp Grünwald*
Resident in Budapest, *XIV.* district
*Hungária Ring* Street (Lane), No. *131*,
_____ floor, works in the administration of the Central Council.
CENTRAL COUNCIL OF THE HUNGARIAN JEWS.
[stamped and signed (illeg.)]

Arrested as an author of the leaflet, Grünvald was released after the fall of the Sztójay government. He survived the Holocaust and became a professor at the Rabbinical Seminary of Budapest and director of the Hungarian Jewish Museum.

The above-mentioned Grünvald circle probably also compiled the letter in document 8-11. Unlike those in document 8-9(A, B), this one appealed to the Jews.

**DOCUMENT 8-11: Illegal leaflet of the Jewish underground, summer(?) 1944. Elek Karsai, ed.,** *Vádirat a nácizmus ellen. Dokumentumok a magyarországi zsidóüldözés történetéhez (1944 május 26–1944 október 15. A budapesti zsidóság deportálásának felfüggesztése)* **(Budapest: Magyar Izraeliták Országos Képviselete, 1967), 3:32–33.**

*My Beloved Jewish Brothers and Sisters!*

It is with a deep feeling of sympathy that we turn to you now in these days of our final, lethal danger.

Be strong and determined to face anything, come what may. Be worthy of the long rows of our martyr heroes. We have been disappointed in our leaders: they fled in a state of fear, disgracefully, or begged for an exemption document.[106] Even the leaders of the Zionist movement—forgetting about a national shared fate—set up Aliyah lists in their shrewd,[107] crafty way.[108]

We have been left to our own devices. All of you Jews: lift your hearts. We are not luring you into a refugee's life, only toward a better, more honorable end. We have a worthier death for you, for your children, your elders, and your women.

Let us not be like a herd that is being taken to the slaughterhouse.[109] Do not let them carry us far away, to foreign lands under the most horrible conditions, to places where we end up in gas chambers and crematoria regardless.[110]

---

106. The text refers to the members of the Jewish Council.
107. These were lists of possible immigrants to Palestine.
108. This remark refers to the Kasztner operation.
109. This is a reference to the famous passage in the Book of Isaiah: "He was led as a lamb to the slaughter/And as a sheep before its shearers is silent/So he opened not his mouth." (Isaiah 53:7). In the context of the mass murder of Jews, the metaphor was probably first used by Abba Kovner, one of the leaders of the Vilna ghetto resistance, in late 1941 and 1942. On Kovner and his manifesto, see document 9-6, in Jürgen Matthäus, with Emil Kerenji, Jan Lambertz, and Leah Wolfson, *Jewish Responses to Persecution*, vol. 3: *1941–1942* (Lanham, MD: AltaMira Press in association with the USHMM, 2013).
110. In the original, a partially illegible remark added by hand here condemns the "renegades" who were seeking to be baptized.

But do not commit suicide either, as—unfortunately—so many of our brothers and sisters have already done. No! We have no sense of guilt that would drive us to death; it is just that we have committed a great sin against our Jewish existence.[111]

Let us go out into the streets! Our motto should be:

"We are not getting on the death train! Shoot us in piles right here!"

With our sacrifice, let us consecrate the name of the Eternal God and let us gain honor for renewing the Jewish people. Let us show bravery!

We profess, with the half-armed hero Trumpeldor[112]: if they spring from a national sentiment, bravery and honor are worth more than life.

*Adonai, hei ozer lonu.* The Lord help us.

---

111. The remark refers to the widespread thought that the persecution of the Jews was brought about by the secularization and assimilation process. This was mainly an Orthodox standpoint. Oddly enough, this memorandum, authored in Neologue circles, echos the same concept.

112. Joseph Trumpeldor (1880–1920) was one of the leading figures in the Zionist settlement movement in the early twentieth century in Palestine. He was killed in a fight with Arabs.

# CHAPTER 9
## Non-Jewish Reactions

ACCORDING TO the 1941 census, 14.68 million people lived in Hungary. More than 94 percent of them were non-Jewish. In 1944 the vast majority of this population passively observed the maltreatment of their Jewish compatriots. Only a small minority stood up against the persecution. The number of those civilians who actively participated in the Holocaust by reporting and abusing Jews was likewise small. In 1944–1945, thousands delivered food and messages to the ghettos and collection camps and rescued their friends or complete strangers. Thousands of others reported the Jewish neighbors they envied, the boss they hated, or people they knew nothing about. Tens of thousands visited the board fence of the ghetto to peer inside or voiced content at seeing crowds herded toward the train station; at the same time tens of thousands most likely pitied the Jews' plight. But millions simply lived their lives, went to work, and tried to get by under the deteriorating conditions of war. They paid no attention to the tragedy unfolding around them. This chapter showcases the responses of non-Jews to the Holocaust: the various patterns of behavior by non-Jewish Hungarians, the role of the Christian churches, and rescue attempts made by the neutral diplomatic corps.

### BYSTANDERS: COLLABORATORS AND BENEFICIARIES

Unlike in occupied Polish and Soviet territories, the population unleashed no antisemitic outbursts during the ghettoization and deportations in Hungary.

This may seem surprising in the light of the fact that since 1848 several antisemitic waves of atrocities had swept across the country, all tied to historical and economic crises or changes of power (1848, 1881–1885, 1918–1920). Several reasons lay behind this phenomenon. Between 1938 and 1944, the Hungarian population grew accustomed to the state controlling all actions and measures against the Jews. Moreover, in the spring of 1944, the **Döme Sztójay** government surpassed even the wildest dreams of the most radical antisemites by deporting the entire Jewish population in the provinces within eight weeks. Plundering had been an important element of the pogroms of the previous decades, but in 1944 the state organized the robbery. And significantly, until the very end of 1944, no vacuum of state power existed, and public order remained stable.

Nevertheless, the lack of mass violence by the population does not mean that anti-Jewish activism was not present. This attitude often took the form of plans and suggestions submitted to the government regarding the "desirable" handling of the "Jewish question." It was clear even to the average citizen that State Secretary **László Endre** was a key figure in the implementation of the anti-Jewish operation. His populist appeal during his time as a subprefect had already made him extraordinarily popular among the common people.[1] As state secretary, he thus received hundreds of denunciations, petitions, and proposals in connection with "solving the Jewish question."[2] In addition, documents submitted to other government organs on this issue often landed on his desk. The authors of these letters served as Endre's eyes and ears. He did not need to rely only on the text of the official reports but could also use such unsolicited yet useful volunteer informants to find out what was going on in the country, what average people were thinking, and what problems remained to be "solved" in the realm of Jewish affairs. Army colonel Gyula Lootz, who addressed Endre as an "old friend," submitted the proposal excerpted in document 9-1.

**DOCUMENT 9-1: Excerpts from Gyula Lootz's proposal to László Endre on retaliation against the Jews, May 8, 1944, HNA P 1434, fascicle 17, file V/8.**

1. A desire has arisen that in return for each terrorist attack [air raid], 10–20,000 Jews (starting with the richest) should be summarily herded into collection camps. Those who are fit to work should be transported to labor camps, where they would work exclusively for bomb victims. The

---

1. See document 2-2.
2. See the letters written to Endre in HNA P 1434, fascicles 16–19.

financial resources needed for setting up the collection and labor camps should be provided by the Jewish congregations. And once their capacity to work has been exhausted, they should be destroyed.³

2. Another solution would be that after each terrorist attack, as many Jews (starting with those of the highest social rank) as Christians whose lives were lost should be rounded up and executed. Their assets should benefit bomb victims, and their names should be published in neutral newspapers abroad. If the number of deaths is low, then a good many times that number of Jews should be executed. This way, terrorist attacks would grow fewer and would even stop altogether. If despite these measures they do not cease, then the Jews will be destroying themselves in this way. Anyway, the Jews have declared that if the tables turn, they are going to burn the cross on the foreheads of Christians, so why spare them now? [. . .]

Besides these proposals, citizens also sent denunciations and letters offering information to the Hungarian and German police. According to the memoir of **Samu Stern**, president of the Central **Jewish Council**, Germans told him that "there was not a single country in which they were greeted with as many filed reports as in Hungary."⁴ At the same time, the commander of the Budapest Gestapo unit, SS-Sturmbannführer Alfred Trenker, recalled in an interview well after the war conducted by Hungarian historian Péter Gosztonyi, "Of course, over the first days, we were flooded with reports. . . . But in terms of quantity? Well, it was the usual volume."⁵ But Trenker could not have known the precise number of reports filed with **Adolf Eichmann**'s office or had information about the volume of reports sent to the so-called Hungarian Gestapo, the **State**

---

3. The theme of Jews as agents of a "fifth column" collaborating with the enemy was a favorite in the antisemitic press and public discourse. According to this, the "red herds" besieging the eastern front, as well as the Anglo-Saxon "terror bombers," were all under the Jews' direction, while their coreligionists living in Hungary performed sabotage in the hinterland with secret radio broadcasts and other tactics. Many believed these widespread slanderous claims. The Jews ordered to clean up the debris following the bombings were subject to threats and insults on a regular basis. On the latter, see Moshe Élijáhu Gonda, *A debreceni zsidók száz éve. A mártírhalált halt debreceni és környékbeli zsidók emlékére* (Tel Aviv: Debreceni Zsidók Emlékbizottsága, n.d. [1970]), 248.

4. Samu Stern, *Emlékirataim. Versenyfutás az idővel! A "zsidótanács" működése a német megszállás és a nyilas uralom idején* (Budapest: Bábel, 2004), 311.

5. Péter Gosztonyi, *Légiveszély, Budapest. Szemelvények Magyarország II. világháborús történetéből* (Budapest: Népszava Kiadó, 1984), 100.

**Security Surveillance** led by **Péter Hain**.[6] The average Hungarian citizen was in fact more likely to turn to the Hungarian authorities than to the Germans.

DOCUMENT 9-2: **Anonymous denunciation filed with the police, no date (late 1944/ early 1945), HNA P 1434, fascicle 19.**

> To the Head of the Political Department of the
> Hungarian Royal State Police.
> I call the attention of the Political Department to tram transportation conductor Nándor Mikes (resident of Thököly Street 14),[7] who is carrying hundreds of pounds of food into the ghetto. After all, his wife is Jewish. And he brings letters out of the ghetto by the Jews; he is their go-between, and of course they pay him very well for his services. In all respects he is an anti-Hungarian, pro-Jewish, pro-Russian who cannot wait to see the Russians arrive. It is high time that such a crooked, stray rascal got the punishment he deserves.[8]
>
> A patriot.

These reports were often motivated by greed. Many informants had Jewish property in their sights. Although the government tried to dispel expectations that everyone would get his or her share of the Jewish assets right away, the anti-Jewish measures obviously presented a unique opportunity to get rich. According to many postwar explanations, mainly the **Arrow Cross** riffraff had scrambled to seize Jewish assets. But in reality, members of the middle class and intellectual stratum (among them doctors, civil servants, teachers, and priests) also distinguished themselves in the quest for Jewish property. Despite the slogans of the antisemitic campaign, the most valuable apartments and movable property did not go to indigent groups or those who had become homeless. They instead landed in the hands of a middle segment, a social class with greater finesse in lobbying for its interests, more information, more connections, and more capital at the outset. Members of this sector also aimed at moving into enterprises formerly owned or run by Jews and sought to seize all the shops, merchandise, and equipment of their onetime Jewish competitors.

---

6. See Zoltán András Kovács, *A Szálasi-kormány belügyminisztériuma. Rendvédelem, állambiztonság, közigazgatás a nyilas korszakban* (Máriabesnyő-Gödöllő: Attraktor, 2009), 142–60; Szabolcs Szita, *A Gestapo Magyarországon* (Budapest: Korona, 2002), 160–74.

7. Municipal District VII of Budapest.

8. The punishment for those who committed "crimes" similar to those described in this document was discharge, internment, and torture.

DOCUMENT 9-3: **Petition by sound amplification entrepreneur Géza Nagysötétági Macskásy, April 27, 1944, in Ilona Benoschofsky and Elek Karsai, eds.,** *Vádirat a nácizmus ellen. Dokumentumok a magyarországi zsidóüldözés történetéhez (1944 március 19–1944 május 15. A német megszállástól a deportálás megkezdéséig)* **(Budapest: Magyar Izraeliták Országos Képviselete, 1958), 1:262–64.**

Sound amplification design office of sound amplification entrepreneur Géza Nagysötétági Macskásy
No. 44914

Budapest, April 27, 1944

With deep respect, I request that you kindly transfer to me the company (at present closed) listed in the attached statement, along with all business equipment.[9]

The justification for my petition is as follows:

I have been working in the sound amplification, gramophone, and newsreel profession for fifteen years and I have met with the greatest public satisfaction. In the beginning, I entered this profession with a brave and strong hand. I was at a great disadvantage, facing a 100 percent Jewish majority. I had to sacrifice my wealth in the struggle, but the fight was successful, because by establishing a well-constructed Hungarian sound engineering company, I managed to secure a foundation for revival movements.[10]

I did not strive to achieve financial and moral success during the past fifteen years but rather devoted all I had exclusively to the solution of this task.

It is only natural that I was and still am subject to retaliation: I was not and still am not receiving merchandise from the large companies on the other side, and they threaten me if I try to expand.[11] Without sufficient merchandise or space, I can barely survive at present: because of the complete ban on public gatherings, my speakers have been lying

---

9. The petition concerned a total of four companies (see the appendix to the petition).
10. That is, far-right movements. According to the appendix of his submission, he assisted in setting up thousands of meetings and speeches by the right-wing extremists during this period. He thereby aided the careers of various university student leaders as well as several right-wing politicians, including Prime Ministers **Gyula Gömbös** and **Béla Imrédy**. See Ilona Benoschofsky and Elek Karsai, eds., *Vádirat a nácizmus ellen. Dokumentumok a magyarországi zsidóüldözés történetéhez (1944 március 19–1944 május 15. A német megszállástól a deportálás megkezdéséig)* (Budapest: Magyar Izraeliták Országos Képviselete, 1958), 1:264–65.
11. The petitioner refers to Jewish firms.

untouched in my warehouse for two years. It would be the one true acknowledgment of my work—which has been justified by history—to have my aforementioned wish fulfilled.[12]

I feel that I have fought through the Hungarian resurrection from [Prime Minister] Gömbös until today, have cleared the path from elements that do not belong here, have sacrificed 15 years of nights and days, my assets, my freedom, and my health. I made my equipment available during the occupations and suffered financial harm during the second air raid.[13] I created a Hungarian profession, and beyond this, I gave up on even the slightest degree of financial success: my request therefore seems justified.

Even now I am still not seeking private gain; I wish, as always, to serve the interests of the public. I would like my company—which to the present day remains the only Christian company in the profession—to become stronger so that I can even more successfully and securely solve even greater tasks of the internal affairs of the future with my company, which is popularized effectively and which I intend to expand. I know that today a huge crowd can only be led with a well-equipped and strong newsreel company, and I aim for this and this alone. I ask for your help in realizing this goal, and I am looking forward to a favorable outcome in this matter.

I remain with Hungarian respects,

*Macskásy*[14]

To the respected

Alderman of Municipal District VII.

Budapest

---

12. While Macskásy portrays himself as a selfless "fighter" who rejects financial gain and works exclusively for the sake of a noble goal—and assigns blame to "plutocratic" capital—he wanted exclusive control over the market. The petition reveals that the company was put in a tough position primarily because of the 1942 ban on political meetings. Despite this (eleven days after Jewish assets were reported for registration and five days after businesses were closed down), he still blamed Jewish companies, which he thought were still restricting his development and threatening him.

13. Between 1938 and 1941 the Hungarian army took over the reannexed territories amid formal celebrations. The Christian companies monopolized the organization of these events and meetings, for Jewish businesses were excluded from public procurements. The second air raid took place in early April 1944.

14. Like the vast majority of petitioners, Macskásy was unsuccessful in the end. On June 2 the petition was placed into the archives, labeled "until relevant regulations are issued."

[attachment]

April 27, 1944
ELECTRIC SOUND
Budapest, Municipal District XI.,
Zámori Street 11.
468-700.

I would like to receive: "Tonalit" Ltd., Rottenbiller Street 32, in Municipal District VII; the movie technology equipment company of Ferenc Adler, Erzsébet Boulevard 9–11; the movie company of Ferenc Heller, Akácfa Street 5; the "Rex" theater equipment company of Henrik Weiss, Municipal District VII, Akácfa Street 7.

Claims of having been victimized were a recurring theme in petitions of this sort. It was a typical assertion that the former Jewish owner had tried to undermine the Christian petitioner in onerous ways. This gave the submissions a "moral" tone: petitioners purported only to be seeking "their due." For example, a dentist in Szeged, Ferenc Végh, claimed that his Jewish colleague had inflicted a "major financial loss" on him and, moreover, that the dentist's office being sought had originally belonged to Végh, who was "suddenly forced to leave it" because of the Jewish colleague's unpleasant behavior.[15] The author of the petition reproduced above argued his case in a similar vein.

The chase for Jewish property quickly extended to the housing and real estate market. The apartment shortage was one of the severest social problems at the time. Great numbers of people believed the government propaganda that characterized ghettoization as fundamentally about a fairer distribution of apartments.[16] Many citizens "illegally" moved into now empty Jewish apartments and houses, but the majority put their trust in the "legal" channels for gaining such assets. Throughout the country, tens of thousands of people submitted petitions to local government officials requesting Jewish real estate.[17] The greatest push occurred in the capital, where the "prey" included

---

15. Ferenc Végh's petition to the mayor of Szeged, May 4, 1944, HNA, Series I, reel 32.

16. At a meeting of high-ranking officials of the Ministry of the Interior, it was stated that "issuing the vacated Jewish apartments to workers and clerks whose hearts are in the right place [i.e., who are politically loyal] and who are presently living in poor-quality apartments, and to Hungarian families, in order of their merit" was marked as an important task in connection with ghettoization. Note on the meeting of April 19, HNA, Series P1434, fascicle 16, file IV/19.

17. One can find hundreds of such petitions in the surviving documents of virtually all regional local governments. See, e.g., the Documents of the Mayor of Jászberény, JNSZCA V-73, boxes 672–76; Documents of the Mayor of Szolnok, JNSZCA V-474, boxes 502–6; Documents of the Mayor of Gyöngyös, HCA V-173, boxes 43–78.

twenty-eight thousand apartments, and where many people had lost homes due to the air raids. Despite calls by the press and authorities to wait, many petitions came in even before the process of setting up the "**yellow-star houses**" began.[18]

The newspaper *Új Magyarság* (New Hungariandom) published the article excerpted in document 9-4 after the forced move of Jews into "yellow-star houses" was complete and the number of people competing for Jewish apartments had grown to new levels. City leaders in Budapest approached the cabinet, for the unfolding situation had become unsustainable: "Under the double pressure of connections being deployed at higher levels and impatient petitioners,[19] they could not provide a moral guarantee that matters would be resolved in a reassuring way."[20] In order to avoid total chaos, the government created a commissioner's office in charge of apartment affairs, which received five to six thousand petitions daily.[21] The situation was similar in the provinces, where residents put enormous pressure on town halls. In mid-July the subprefect of Komárom County wrote a letter to the Ministry of the Interior, urging that the ban on apartment allocations be lifted, for people were "besieging my own authority as well as the chief constable's office on a daily basis, pressing the authorities with such requests in other districts as well."[22] A similar siege took place in Miskolc and Ózd.[23]

---

18. "For Now, People Cannot File Requests for the Vacated Apartments," *Pesti Hírlap*, June 18, 1944, printed in Ilona Benoschofsky and Elek Karsai, eds., *Vádirat a nácizmus ellen. Dokumentumok a magyarországi zsidóüldözés történetéhez (1944 május 15–1944 június 30. A budapesti zsidóság összeköltöztetése)* (Budapest: Magyar Izraeliták Országos Képviselete, 1960), 2:231.

19. The remark refers to the fact that high-ranking public administration officials and law enforcement officers tried to use their influence to obtain Jewish apartments for themselves and their friends and families.

20. Minutes of the meeting of the Council of Ministers, July 5, 1944, HNA, Series I, reel 1.

21. Christian Gerlach and Götz Aly, *Das letzte Kapitel. Der Mord an den ungarischen Juden 1944–1945* (Stuttgart: DVA, 2002), 202.

22. Letter of the subprefect of Komárom County to the Ministry of the Interior, July 12, 1944, HNA Series I, reel 11.

23. Tamás Csíki, *Holokauszt Borsod vármegyében* (New York: Graduate Center of the City University of New York, 2003), 20–21, 24.

The newspaper *Dunántúl* reported that the housing office in Pécs was "barraged" with petitions.[24]

DOCUMENT 9-4: **"The Civilian Population Should Not Storm the Housing Bureau,"** *Új Magyarság*, **June 29, 1944.**[25]

The housing bureau of the capital [Budapest] has been overrun by such massive crowds of people that highly undesirable mob scenes have developed. City leaders have on several occasions asked the public not to rush to the housing bureau, for the assignment of apartments is suspended until further notice. Final instructions about access will be issued within a few days for those entitled to claim apartments. Aerial terror attacks greatly hinder this work, because the first task of the housing authority is to secure apartments for those who have lost their homes through bomb damage. The mayor has announced that the accommodation of those who have become homeless because of the air raids falls under the jurisdiction of the municipal district council in the area of the apartment that was made uninhabitable. The municipal district councils have already received instructions to the effect that by utilizing the abandoned Jewish apartments, they should arrange for accommodations for bomb victims without delay.[26]

[. . .]

---

24. Judit Molnár, "'Hazafias tisztelettel.' Zsidók és nem zsidók Pécsett a holokauszt idején," in *Tanulmányok a holokausztról II*, ed. Randolph L. Braham (Budapest: Balassi, 2002), 265.

25. First published in Benoschofsky and Karsai, *Vádirat a nácizmus ellen*, 2:335–36.

26. No matter what the propaganda said, actual needs were secondary during the distribution of apartments. Social hierarchy, nepotism, and state interests weighed far more heavily. The best apartments were given to loyal civil servants, police and gendarme officers, clerks, influential intellectuals, priests, and decorated military officers who had served on the front line. Only after they had been taken into account were those who truly needed apartments considered: disabled war veterans, bombing victims, and poor families with many children. People had to pay a fee in exchange for the apartments and the furnishings. László Csősz, "Őrségváltás? Az 1944-es deportálások közvetlen gazdasági–társadalmi hatásai," in *Küzdelem az igazságért. Tanulmányok Randolph L. Braham 80. születésnapjára*, ed. László Karsai and Judit Molnár (Budapest: MAZSIHISZ, 2002), 89–92.

The mayor has firmly asked the public of the capital to avoid approaching the housing bureau with questions relating to apartments, because the bureau cannot accept such petitions. The inventorying of abandoned Jewish apartments is under way, and satisfactory steps will be taken within a short time to address those claiming these apartments.[27]

[...]

According to reports that have come in to City Hall, in some instances people have moved into empty Jewish apartments without a permit. City leaders warn the public that they should not move into any apartments without a permit, and those who do so will face severe punishment and will have to pay a fine. [...][28]

The economic hardships suffered by the population and the scarcity of apartments due to bombings offer only a partial explanation for the chase after Jewish property. Many petitioners, desiring to switch from a comparatively good housing situation to an even better one, submitted petitions without any legal ground whatsoever, in some cases probably deceiving the housing authorities.[29]

The hope of many people to gain a share of Jewish property contributed to the general lack of support for the persecuted. The deportations financially benefited many people who would otherwise not have wished for the victims' death. Those who raised their voices or acted on behalf of Jews went against their very own material interests. Other factors contributed to a largely indifferent public mood and the numb passivity of the non-Jewish population. Allied air raids, the destruction of homes, and growing food shortages played their part. The Allies first bombed Hungary severely in April 1944. In the following months tens of thousands died in subsequent campaigns. Moreover, civilian casualties, together with increasing propaganda about enemy air force activities

---

27. The petitioners typically designated the specific apartment or shop they wanted to occupy or provided a wish list.

28. Despite severe threats by the authorities on several occasions, breaking into and robbing sealed real estate, as well as illegal occupation of apartments, remained a widespread phenomenon. Csősz, "Őrségváltás," 95. Those who committed such crimes under blackouts were subject to martial law proceedings and, in extreme cases, faced a death sentence.

29. *Nagyvárad*, June 15, 1944, 2. In Nagyvárad, proceedings were initiated against several local officials who submitted apartment petitions with false data.

(for example, stories about the Allies dropping exploding children's toys) helped foster an antisemitic mood, since the press identified the Jews with the "air force terrorists." After twenty-five years of intense goading, the charges fell on fertile ground.

A coordinated media campaign played a major part in the implementation of the operation against the Jews. Waged over the radio and in the press, it deployed other propaganda materials, such as posters and flyers, continually inciting hatred. It frequently depicted collaboration with the authorities as a patriotic act and called on the population to report all attempts to rescue assets or people as "a duty every member of the community had toward his nation and race."[30] Document 9-5(A–B) shows that these manipulation strategies were accompanied by increasingly frequent threats toward those citizens who disapproved of the antisemitic persecution or merely sympathized with the Jews. At the same time, the intensity of the propaganda also suggests that many people did express their sympathy for them.

Following the German occupation of Hungary, only those newspapers could remain operational that suited the ideological taste of the new government. Alongside these, the regime launched a new weekly, *Harc* (Struggle), devoted entirely to the "Jewish question" and modeled on the Nazi weekly *Der Stürmer*. Published between May and December 1944 as the official newspaper of the Hungarian Institute for Research of the Jewish Question, this new organ strove to provoke its readers with pseudoscientific articles and racist cartoons and caricatures. Its editor in chief and the head of the institute was **Zoltán Bosnyák**, an advocate of race-protectionist ideology, as well as a friend and protégé of State Secretary for the Press **Mihály Kolosváry-Borcsa** and State Secretary László Endre. Bosnyák's institute was not legalized until 1944, but he nonetheless maintained an office at the Pest County Hall, with Endre's special permission. He even received a permanent allowance from the **county** budget. Between 1935 and 1944, Bosnyák published no fewer than fifteen books and a great many articles on the "Jewish question."[31]

---

30. *Jász Hirlap*, June 3, 1944.
31. For a bibliography of the works by Bosnyák, see Mihály Kolosváry-Borcsa, *A zsidókérdés magyarországi irodalma* (Budapest: Stádium, n.d [1943]), 106–7.

DOCUMENT 9-5(A–B): **Propaganda materials lashing out at solidarity with the Jews, summer 1944.**

DOCUMENT 9-5(A): *Harc*, June 3, 1944.

> [On the poster in the upper right corner: THEY ARE WASHING UP, WASHING AWAY!]
> DO NOT FORGET ANYTHING, BROTHER!
>
> Do you remember this poster?
>
> They would still want to stress their innocence; they would still want to wash up.
>
> Do you feel sorry for them? Do you remember what the Jewish-Bolshevik executioner company of Béla Kun did to you in 1919 . . . They still want to be washing up, washing things away. Do not let them! Do not pity them![32]

---

32. Appealing to the popular (and realistic) fear of the Soviets, one of the most compelling antisemitic arguments invoked the leadership of the 1919 communist dictatorship, whose members were overwhelmingly of Jewish descent. Although it was widely known that the "Lenin boys" did not spare Jewish citizens either, this did not keep antisemitic propagandists from calling the events of 1919 "Jewish terror."

DOCUMENT 9-5(B): **Leaflet of the far-right Eastern Frontline Comrades' Association,**[33] **summer 1944, HBCA IV.B. 1406/b., document 26.607/1944.**

Our children are torn apart by the dozens by the rag dolls thrown at us by the English.[34]
<u>Are you aware that this degradation of war is a Jewish idea?</u>
And we still see you walking with somebody wearing a yellow star? Be ashamed and don't forget that this is our <u>last warning</u>!

Eastern Frontline<br>Comrades' Association

It is not clear how much the average citizen knew about the real goal of the anti-Jewish operations. By 1942–1943, the Hungarian leadership certainly had a full understanding of what the Nazi Jewish policy meant in practice.[35] While detailed information never reached ordinary citizens, Allied radio broadcasts or accounts of men who had been on the front line informed many about the mass murders. Even if most people did not believe such news, they probably became at least somewhat suspicious upon seeing masses of people—for the most part unfit for work—transported out of Hungary, apparently never to return. Telltale remarks in newspaper articles and petitions indicate that many people knew or suspected the real consequences of the operation.

The 1944 diary of writer and journalist Sándor Márai (1900–1989) also proves this point. His work occupies a special place in the literature on the Holocaust in Hungary. A Christian intellectual, Márai carefully considered the behavior and responsibility of society, especially the middle class, in the upheaval of that year. His direct experiences of the ghettoization and deportation in the provinces inspired his thinking. Very few surviving sources from the era provide such a detailed, critical report of events as they unfolded. Márai belonged to those few among the intellectual elite who firmly rejected anti-Jewish policies and public discourse from the very beginning. Besides his Catholicism, humanism, and cosmopolitanism, he also had a personal reason

---

33. The Eastern Frontline Comrades' Association (KABSZ) was established in 1943 as a semimilitary organization of the Hungarian Renewal Party, which at the time played a right-wing extremist opposition role. Péter Sipos, ed., *Imrédy Béla a vádlottak padján* (Budapest: Osiris-Budapest Főváros Levéltára, 1999), 58.
34. This alludes to the alleged dropping of bombs disguised as children's toys by Allied planes.
35. Randolph L. Braham, *The Politics of Genocide: The Holocaust in Hungary* (New York: Columbia University Press, 1994), 2:806–23.

for his oppositional stance: the Jewish ancestry of his wife, Ilona Matzner.[36] Following the German occupation, the Márai family left their Budapest home and moved to a village in the vicinity, taking with them Márai's Jewish sister-in-law and her family. From there, they went to Losonc in May,[37] attempting to free Márai's father-in-law from the Kassa ghetto, where the diary entries excerpted in document 9-6 were written.

**DOCUMENT 9-6: Diary entries of writer Sándor Márai, summer of 1944, in Sándor Márai, *Napló* (1943–1944) (Budapest: Révai, 1945), 261–83.[38]**

X. has been in the Kassa ghetto for a week.[39] In his first three letters, he describes what is happening in the camp, where there is no water, no latrines, no buildings, only open sheds without walls, and where fifteen thousand people have been herded together for over five days.[40]

The ghettos are set up everywhere, it is compulsory in every Hungarian town with a population exceeding ten thousand. Jews from the vicinity are also herded into these ghettos.[41] In Losonc, they began moving Jews this morning. As I am writing, carts rattle noisily by underneath my window on which miserable people are pushing their penurious, ragged things.

I feel like Josephus Flavius when Titus and Vespasian sent him under the walls of Jerusalem to see and describe the destruction of Jerusalem.[42] If I survive this, I will write it down.

---

36. Ilona ("Lola") Márai (née Matzner; 1899–1986) married Sándor (also Alessandro Grosschmid) in 1923, and they lived in various cities throughout Europe before the war. The couple again left Hungary after the war and later moved permanently to the United States. *USHMM ITS Collection Data Base Central Name Index*; U.S. social security death index.

37. A small town at the Hungarian-Slovakian border.

38. Márai published a memoir in English but not his diaries: *Memoir of Hungary, 1944–1948* (1972; Budapest: Corvina in association with Central European University Press, 2000).

39. Samuel Matzner (1868–1944) had served in the military as a young man and subsequently become a publisher. He was active in social welfare work, as was his wife, Ilona Márai's mother, Irén (née Moskovic; 1879–1934). Irén became a bookstore owner in the last decade of her life. See Štefan Kolivoško et al., *Slovník Židovských osobností Košíc a okolia* (Košice: Verejná knižnica Jána Bocatia v Kožiciach, 2001), 101–2; Hungarian Marriages Database (www.jewishgen.org/databases/Hungary).

40. See document 3-7.

41. On the ghettoization, see chapter 3.

42. Here, Márai is referring to Roman Jewish historian Flavius Josephus's work titled *The Jewish War*. The province of Judea rebelled against Roman rule in 66 CE, and the uprising was put down in 70 CE, with the occupation of Jerusalem.

[. . .]

Nothing helps: everything must be experienced in person, on our own bodies. That is how we will understand it in reality. All that we have heard about the fate of Polish, Austrian, German Jews over the years was just a hazy image. But when I first saw a man being taken away to a truck by two Gestapo soldiers—on Vörösmarty Square[43] in Budapest—I understood reality. And now that men, women, children bearing yellow stars are marching along in front of my window, carrying their meager packages, to live crammed together, five thousand of them, tens of thousands of them, headed toward some uncertain fate—and I am afraid it is not really uncertain!—as they are leaving behind their homes, their work—why?!—to vegetate in shacks and barracks on the edge of town, with food to last them two weeks, without money and earnings—why?!—now I finally understand. All this has to be seen, in person.

The human soul does not have a genuine power to imagine things. Only reality has imaginative power.

It is shameful to be alive. It is shameful to be walking in the sun. It is shameful to be alive.

[. . .]

A cold May. I am shivering in the sun.

There is nothing to talk to people about. Just as it is impossible to argue with a drunken man or with lunatics: the Hungarian middle class has gone mad and has gotten drunk over the Jewish question. The Russians are at Kőrösmező,[44] the English and the Americans are above Pest, and this society is delirious and furious and does not and cannot talk about anything else except the Jews.

[. . .]

X. was deported to Poland. The prefect, to whom I sent a letter requesting that they not take the seventy-six-year-old man but leave him in the ghetto, wrote a few lines of rejection. He wrote that there was nothing he could do. But if he cannot do anything, then why does he not resign?[45]

---

43. Large square in downtown Budapest (in 1944 Municipal District IV, today Municipal District V).

44. Municipality in Carpatho-Ruthenia, on the border of Hungary and the General-gouvernment.

45. The addressee is Péter Schell, prefect of Abaúj-Torna County and minister of the interior between October 12 and 16, 1944. The authorities received similar pleading petitions by the hundreds but did not respond to most of them in writing.

In each car, there were eighty people travelling with two buckets of water. The mortality rate en route is close to twenty. One car took six days to get from Nagyvárad to Kassa. The cars are sized to fit forty people or six horses. The eighty people cannot lie down or sit down in them.

[. . .]

In the town of L.,[46] a Jewish physician, A., was taken away to a labor camp,[47] his five-year-old child was taken to Poland in a railway car, along with other ghetto residents; but the doctor's office remained in place. He was a classmate of mine. He furnished his office with modern equipment, with an X-ray machine, an electrocardiogram. All these are quite rare in the countryside. Two people were competing for the office and the equipment: the local public health officer and an internist. The robbers could not agree, the dispute became a matter of chivalry, a duel.

That is because we are a chivalrous people, real gentlemen, you know.[48]

[. . .]

## BYSTANDERS: SOLIDARITY AND RESCUE

Non-Jews' willingness to engage in rescue showed a spatial and temporal pattern similar to that of Jewish self-rescue. During the deportations in the provinces, such efforts remained scarce, whereas later, in the Arrow Cross era, rescue efforts increased markedly in Budapest. In the spring and summer, due to the authorities' proceeding at lightning speed, non-Jewish bystanders could not have improved the victims' situation significantly. But the brutal scenes struck a chord with many people. Despite the propaganda campaign that dehumanized and criminalized the victims and painted their removal as an act of national self-defense, the brutality unleashed and the sight of children, elderly, and sick people being herded off shocked many people. The leaders of the Christian churches received large numbers of petitions in response.[49] Typically, the authors of these requests did not contest the legitimacy of the anti-Jewish operation;

---

46. Losonc.

47. On the labor service of Jewish physicians and its consequences, see document 6-13.

48. The remark is sarcastic and refers to the fact that medieval traditions and principles, including military and knightly virtues, were central to the self-image of Hungarian nationalists of the era.

49. Letter of Catholic bishop Lajos Shvoy to Cardinal **Jusztinián Serédi**. Quoted in Anna Gergely, *A székesfehérvári és Fejér megyei zsidóság tragédiája (1938–1944)* (Budapest: Vince, 2003), 208.

they merely questioned its methods and raised their voices on a selective basis (for example, on behalf of children).⁵⁰ At the same time, the propaganda was often so successful that helping and showing mercy created a severe personal conflict for many people.⁵¹ Even so, shock at the sight of cruelty inevitably created some sense of sympathy toward the Jews.

The significance of this sentiment increased during the Arrow Cross era, when authorities also terrorized the non-Jewish population. In Budapest, tens of thousands of non-Jewish deserters and political persecutees went into hiding. The hunt for the Jews could thus dovetail with the suffering of the Christian population. The most integrated Jewish community lived in Budapest, embedded in a "mixed" professional, business, and family network. These ties also augmented rescue activity. Some people had already begun preparing for the postwar period: they hid persecuted individuals in order to gain some favor and secure the transfer of their position and assets. Accordingly, rescue activities in the capital rose significantly as compared to the provinces during the summer.⁵² Following the Arrow Cross takeover, many thousands of Jews had gone into hiding in the capital with or without false documents, supported by Christian Hungarians, despite the fact that by this time helping Jews was punishable by death. Up until that point, those who had circumvented the persecution of the Jews had "merely" risked internment and prison.

Several factors inhibited rescue activities. Indifference, antisemitic propaganda, the silence of the churches, and the lack of organized resistance were certainly among them. Citizens and authorities had grown accustomed to anti-Jewish administrative measures and laws. Antisemitism now permeated the law enforcement agencies, the military, and the country's public administration. Finally, the punishment meted out to those who dared support the Jews

---

50. See, e.g., petition anonymously submitted by "Christian residents of Paks," June 1944, in Ágnes Ságvári, ed., *Dokumentumok a zsidóság üldöztetésének történetéhez* [Tolna] (Budapest: Magyar Auschwitz Alapítvány–Holocaust Dokumentációs Központ, 1994), 37.

51. According to Vilmos Apor, bishop of Győr, "[. . .] our congregations do not know what to believe within the flood of deception coming from official sources. In the confessional boxes they raise the question: is it permissible to feel sorry for those poor, abused Jews." Letter of Apor to Cardinal Jusztinián Serédi, June 17, 1944, in Sándor Szenes, *Befejezetlen múlt. Keresztények és zsidók, sorsok* (Budapest: n.p., 1986), 234.

52. Among the individual Jewish rescue initiatives within Hungary acknowledged by Yad Vashem as acts of righteousness among gentiles, only 15 percent fall into the period of deportations from the provinces. Most such operations took place in Budapest following the Arrow Cross takeover. Sári Reuveni, "A Világ Igazai Magyarországon," in *A Világ Igazai Magyarországon a második világháború alatt*, ed. Kinga Frojimovics and Judit Molnár (Budapest: Balassi, 2009), 12.

played a part. These factors jointly created a context in which it took considerable courage to help a fellow citizen. Despite this, several thousand Hungarian policemen, soldiers, civil servants and officers, gendarmes, and common citizens decided not to sit passively by and watch the persecution of the Jews.[53]

One of them rescued Mrs. Lázár Berkovics, a thirty-year-old housewife in the city of Huszt.

**DOCUMENT 9-7(A): Extract from the testimony of Mrs. Lázár Berkovics, July 12, 1945, HJA, DEGOB Protocols, no. 1216.[54]**

[. . .]

At the beginning of April 1944, I was put in the ghetto in Huszt,[55] and I stayed there for the whole time. My family and I were even put on trains there. I was expecting a baby at that time. I was one of four pregnant women in that cattle car into which 70 people were crammed. In Királyháza,[56] a sergeant named István Kulcsár freed the four of us; I should note that he already wanted to help us escape from the Huszt ghetto, but he did not succeed there. The train stood in Királyháza for a long time; that is how he managed to do it. From Huszt, he followed the train by bicycle to Királyháza, where he reported for duty. He did not want money for his help, but we would not have been able to pay him anyway, because we were poor.[57]

[. . .]

---

53. For a comprehensive collection of Hungarian rescue cases, see Kinga Frojimovics and Judit Molnár, eds., *A Világ Igazai Magyarországon a második világháború alatt* (Budapest: Balassi, 2009).

54. After the sergeant helped her escape from the transport, she obtained false papers. Returning to Budapest, she worked briefly before being sent to Wiener Neustadt, just south of Vienna, where she gave birth and remained until the end of the war. After the war, she returned to Budapest.

55. This was one of the major ghetto and entrainment centers in Carpatho-Ruthenia.

56. A village about 16 kilometers (10 miles) southwest of Huszt.

57. Several dozen Hungarian army officers and soldiers were awarded the Yad Vashem title "Righteous Among the Nations." Most of them protected and hid labor servicemen working in the army. The events described here were exceptional in many ways. Although the officer did utilize the influence of the uniform, he far overstepped his sphere of jurisdiction. The women did not have protected status, so freeing them had no "legal" basis. Personal acquaintance with the victims and financial or other interests can also be excluded as factors.

After her rescue from the deportation train, Mrs. Berkovics escaped to Budapest. Following the Arrow Cross takeover in October 1944, she was rounded up and deported to a labor camp in Wiener Neustadt, Austria. There she received good treatment compared to other prisoners. She was hospitalized and gave birth to her child. Ultimately, she survived the war.

Ignác Berkovits (not related to the aforementioned Mrs. Berkovics), a thirty-year-old electrician from Aknasugatag, was taken to the Bárdfalva ghetto in April 1944.

DOCUMENT 9-7(B): **Extract from the testimony of Ignác Berkovits, June 30, 1945, HJA, DEGOB Protocols, no. 182.**[58]

[. . .] After about three–four weeks, we were forced to walk to Máramarossziget—this is one of my most dreadful memories. This horrible march—in which I, too, was involved—reminded me of Jud Süss.[59] There were about two thousand of us: women, children, everyone carrying big colorful packs on their backs. A train came in just then, and I met several acquaintances who all loved me, and it hurt me to have them see me like this. There were also several Christians who wanted to hide me and promised to provide me with food until this situation was over. But I wanted to share the fate of my parents and my older sister, and I could not bring myself to part with her two beautiful children who were quite young. [. . .]

Berkovits's story reveals that there were more Hungarians willing to hide people than actual instances where this happened. Denunciations and blackmail thwarted some of their efforts. Nor was it uncommon for victims themselves to turn down help because they did not want to leave their families. The SS murdered Ignác's entire family at Auschwitz. Due to his profession, he survived the death camp. The Soviet army liberated him in Silesia.

---

58. Ignác Berkovits (b. 1913) was an electrician and mechanic from a family of some means. He returned from labor service in Russia around the time that the Germans entered Hungary; he was sent to the ghetto in Bárdfalva and a few weeks later on a forced march of several thousand people to Máramarossziget. From there he was sent to Auschwitz-Birkenau by train, for a time serving in the **Sonderkommando**. In mid-January 1945, he was evacuated to Landeshut and another camp, all the while working as an electrician. Berkovits was liberated by Russian troops, but his entire family perished in the war.

59. A 1940 Nazi film adaptation of Lion Feuchtwanger's novel with a similar title. A notorious scene depicts the pogrom-like expulsion of the Stuttgart Jews.

The Schönberg sisters also survived the ordeals owing to the rescue activity of their nanny, Frantiska Prva. When the Germans occupied Hungary in March 1944, oil refinery owner Sándor Schönberg and his wife Hela (née Weinberg) from Csap (in Carpatho-Ruthenia) realized the terrible danger they faced and decided to hide their daughters, seven-year-old Renáta (document 9-8, on the right) and six-year-old Szilvia (left), under assumed identities. Frantiska Prva bravely risked moving with the girls to the village of Lajosmizse, not far from Budapest.

DOCUMENT 9-8: **Photographs of Renáta and Szilvia Schönberg and their rescuer, Frantiska Prva, 1946, USHMMPA WS# 45878.**

Not recognized as Jews, Renáta and Szilvia ultimately survived the war. However, the Nazis murdered their parents in Auschwitz. After the war the girls emigrated along with their aunt, Bella Zwiebel, living in Sweden and Canada before settling down in the United States.[60]

---

60. The aunt who survived found the girls after the war and took them to Nyíregyháza, where they remained until 1946. Frantiska chose to return home rather than to move on with them. See donor's file, USHMMPA WS# 45878.

Many times non-Jews provided help in exchange for material gains. If caught, they faced prison.[61] Although the moral value of selfless help is obviously higher than that of well-paid rescue, many Jews undoubtedly survived because some people risked punishment for money. The extreme right-wing press frequently reported on such cases. Of course, when reading these articles, one has to keep in mind that the journalists wished to overemphasize the role of money or sometimes to distort the story completely, since the concept of Jews "corrupting" gentiles fit well with antisemitic propaganda and stereotyping.

**DOCUMENT 9-9(A): News reports from the extreme right-wing press about rescue attempts in 1944, *Magyarság*, June 29, 1944.**

<u>Kassa Police Uncovered Attempt to Help Jews Escape</u>
Kassa, June 19

The Kassa police have just now completed an investigation of a criminal organization that was helping Jews escape. Jolán Asztalos, a 24-year-old private clerk from Rákospalota,[62] Mrs. István Nyitrai, born Aranka Straub, from Budapest, Ilonka Szilágyi, a 24-year-old milliner from Budapest, all of them of Christian origin, and Erzsébet Werber, a 32-year-old Jewish resident of Budapest, a taxidermist by profession, had been commissioned by Budapest resident Ilona Mezei to conspire in helping her brother-in-law, 47-year-old whitewash merchant Sándor Freymann, and his wife to escape from the Jewish camp at the Kassa brick factory using false documents.

The false documents were shipped by Andor Freymann, a 21-year-old Jewish resident of Kassa, who was already hiding in Budapest in order to avoid the Labor Service. The women involved in the incident each received an advance payment of 1,500 pengős. The three Christian women were engaged in conspicuous merriment in Kassa; one of them gave 100 pengős to the Gypsy violinist. This brought them to the attention of the police. They were arrested and that was when the Jewish escape attempt was revealed. The three women and Sándor Freymann were handed over to the Kassa prosecutor's office.

---

61. This is what happened, for example, to those Debrecen clerks who assisted in the issuing of false documents about ancestry. Disciplinary proceedings against István Varga and his associates, summer 1944, HBCA IV.B. 1406/b, document 4928/1945. Their Jewish collaborators were deported to Auschwitz.

62. A small town in the vicinity of Budapest, today part of the capital city's Municipal District XV.

DOCUMENT 9-9(B): "The World of the Yellow Star," *Függetlenség*, June 11, 1944.

[. . .]

The Slovakian border is just three kilometers [1.8 miles] from Léva.[63] These days, many Jews are trying to flee to Slovakia in order to avoid complying with orders pertaining to the Jews. The Léva police arrested Mrs. Izrael Treitel and her two children because they wanted to flee with the help of József Závódszky from Nyitra and Mrs. János Bognár from Léva. Of course, Mrs. Izrael Treitel was loaded with diamonds and gold, and she even obtained false documents and was also carrying money in excess of 5,000 pengős. She and the two people assisting in her escape were arrested, taken to Budapest, and then interned.[64]

[. . .]

Without the enthusiastic, coordinated, and efficient collaboration of the two hundred thousand Hungarian clerks, policemen, and gendarmes, German Eichmanns and Hungarian Endres would have been incapable of accomplishing their goals. Still, even within the ranks of the police and bureaucrats, some defied the policy of genocide. As with rescue operations initiated by the population and by diplomats, interventions by non-Jewish officials on behalf of Jews occurred more frequently during the Arrow Cross era. Here, primarily members of the police mounted rescue efforts: they secured armed protection for diplomats involved in such operations or used their weapons to prevent massacres by the Arrow Cross. There were few rescuers in the ranks of the gendarmes, but a handful did exist, including Gendarme Sergeant Major László Endre, who was unrelated to the state secretary of the same name. The Jews he saved gave the statements excerpted in document 9-10(A, B) to record his rescue activity.

---

63. A small town on the border of Hungary and Slovakia.

64. Romania and Slovakia were two possible destinations for escape during the summer of 1944. Up until 1942 both advocated a radical antisemitic policy, which cost hundreds of thousands of lives. Following the turn in the war, the murderous operations were stopped owing to political considerations. Crossing the northern and the southeastern border from Hungary in the spring and summer of 1944 constituted a chance to stay alive. Compared to other parts of the country, the forested mountainous areas of these borders were favorable for flight. At the same time, border guards anticipated the appearance of refugees and arrested quite a few people.

DOCUMENT 9-10(A): **Statement about the rescue activities of Gendarme Sergeant Major László Endre, 1945, HMC, Rescuers' Personal Files, file 250.**

April 15, 1945

Statement

I, Zsuzsanna Gábor, of the Israelite religion, resident at Csillaghegy,[65] Rákóczy Street 5, hereby declare that on December 6, 1944, former Csillaghegy Gendarme Noncommissioned Officer László Endre recognized me on the local tram, and because I did not have a place to stay or hide, he hid me in the Csillaghegy house of József Kováts from the Arrow Cross on Pozsonyi Street up until the time when the Russians came in, and on several occasions he had food sent to me at this address. He did all this without getting anything in return for his help, simply out of a philanthropic duty.

Zsuzsanna Gábor

[. . .]

DOCUMENT 9-10(B): **Statement about the rescue activities of the Gendarme Sergeant Major László Endre, 1945, HMC, Rescuers' Personal Files, file 250.**

To the respected
Mr. László Endre

<u>Csillaghegy</u>
Uri Street 13.

Dear Good Sir Officer!

[. . .]

I cannot find fitting words to adequately thank you for the goodwill you displayed toward me, your act manifesting a noble human heart.

Last year, toward the evening of November 6, you appeared like a guardian angel at the "Tungsram"[66] holiday resort, where along with thousands of others, I was waiting for what was to come in a dazed state, having almost reconciled myself to the fate of being herded back for forced labor first toward Austria and then to Germany, at the mercy of the insane beasts of the regime of the time.[67] It was sheer coincidence that you were

---

65. A small town in the vicinity of Budapest, today part of the capital's Municipal District III.
66. The Hungarian electricity company.
67. On the "death marches," see chapter 5.

there, sought me out among hundreds of thousands of people, and pulled me along with four others out of the crowd and brought us out of there, thereby risking your job as well as your own life and the lives of your family. Later on you found me a place in Csillaghegy, and while I was in hiding, you tried to give me courage for life ahead through encouraging messages during the hours of despair.

[...]

Csillaghegy, January 30, 1945.

Yours faithfully,<br>Jenő Kalmár

Sergeant Major Endre carried out ghettoization orders in the most humane manner possible.[68] If the Jews locked up in the ghetto needed a travel permit to obtain **protective documents**, he often gave it to them. The evening before the deportation, Endre personally warned the Jews and announced that anyone could flee during the night, for he would tell his men to halt their guard duties temporarily. Some took advantage of this opportunity to escape. Endre helped others flee the ghetto himself. He saved the lives of many (Jewish and non-Jewish) Polish refugees as well when he refused to hand over to the Gestapo a list of people in the nearby refugee camp. In the winter of 1944, Endre helped dozens of Jews escape the death marches. He also hid them, thereby risking his own life and the safety of his family. All in all, he rescued about three to four hundred people, including small children, labor servicemen and refugees, Hungarians and Poles, and people persecuted for political or racial reasons. In 1951, during the communist dictatorship, his gendarme past resulted in his discharge from the police—without a pension. László Endre died in 1971.[69]

Rescue during the Holocaust was a complex phenomenon, and even some people holding outright antisemitic views ultimately saved some Jewish lives. One such person was writer László Németh (1901–1975). From the early stages

---

68. Yad Vashem denied Sergeant Major László Endre the title "Righteous Among the Nations" based on the consideration that as a member of the executive apparatus, he took part in the ghettoization and deportation process. Letter of Sári Reuveni to Szabolcs Szita, December 29, 1996; letter of Mordecai Paldiel to Szabolcs Szita, July 27, 1997, HMC, Rescuers' Personal Files, file 250.

69. On the life and actions of Sergeant Major László Endre, see HJA, DEGOB Protocols, nos. 505, 3496, 3590, 3604, 3642; Zoltán Vági, "Csillaghegyi csendőrtörténet," *Remény* 3 (1998), 47–53; HMC, Rescuers' Personal Files, file 250.

of his career onward, Németh, a leading figure of the so-called folk movement,[70] had criticized the role of the Jews in Hungarian literature and culture. In his view, in this multiethnic country, assimilating aliens ("shallow Hungarians") were pushing the "native" (in his words, the "deep Hungarian") majority into an intellectual and economic minority status. Yet Németh's thinking was at variance with a Nazi-style race theory. On several occasions, he emphasized that he used the concept of race in an intellectual and moral sense. His writings clearly denounced all violent forms of antisemitism.[71] All this hardly diminishes the responsibility of the writer, who repeated his arguments in an even more extreme form in the summer of 1943 following the persecution in neighboring countries and with Hungarian Jews experiencing discrimination and partial disenfranchisement through antisemitic legislation.

DOCUMENT 9-11(A): **Speech by László Németh in 1943, in *Szárszó, Az 1943. évi balatonszárszói Magyar Élet-tábor előadás- és megbeszéléssorozata*, 3rd ed. (Budapest: Püski, 1993), 46–47.**

[. . .] The capitalist system—to which the West owes its high-level industrial civilization and prosperity—has, as we have seen, thrust the Hungarian people even deeper into its fate, similar to the fate of colonized aboriginal peoples. We also need not belabor the point that bringing in or reverting to an Anglo-Saxon style of capitalism would virtually, within hours, diminish the share of the Hungarians in the national wealth. But it is perhaps less obvious that the socialist system carries similar dangers, perhaps even greater ones. Imagine a socialist state in which the free peasants

---

70. The folk movement shared similarities with the German "*völkisch*" ideology, but its racist elements were less prominent. The representatives of this intellectual movement emerging in the early 1930s were of the opinion that the alternative for Hungarians stuck between the Western bourgeois democracies undergoing a crisis and the radical, statist, collectivist (cooperative-fascist or communist) ideologies would be a unique "third way." They rejected the **Horthy** regime, which was built on a political deal between the landowning aristocracy and the industrial and banking elite, but they also opposed its liberal and leftist opposition, the so-called urban stance. By "urban," they meant Jews or pro-Jewish gentiles. For more information on the so-called folk-urban debate, see Péter Nagy Sz., ed., *A népi-urbánus vita dokumentumai 1932–1947* (Budapest: Rakéta, 1990); János Gyurgyák, *A zsidókérdés Magyarországon* (Budapest: Osiris, 2001), 554–80.

71. One of his critics provided a fitting label for Németh's views, calling them "a modern mixture of vulgar antisemitism and sophisticated humanism." Lajos Hatvany, "A szellem különítményesei," *Újság*, May 27, 1934, cited in Nagy Sz., *A népi-urbánus vita dokumentumai*, 94–105.

were herded into a *kolkhoz*,⁷² the craftsmen had to work in large, communal workshops, the intellectuals were under the tightest surveillance, and that in this state, those under surveillance were Hungarians and those in charge of surveillance were Bushmen or Tibetans. Well, do you not think that this socialist state would hardly be better off than in the darkest era of serfdom, even if it formally respected the principles of socialism? You know all too well that I am not thinking of Bushmen and Tibetans.

I, of all people, have the right to say a few words about the Jewish question, in part because for four years I remained almost completely silent about it. Undoubtedly, it was world history that brought the Jewish question back to us in a form more extreme than ever before. [. . .] If the situation had remained as it was in 1937: there would be no Jewish question in Hungary thirty years from now; Jewry would evaporate over the test tubes of childless affluence. Since then, everything has reactivated the Jews. Primarily the "Jewish Laws," which did not allow Jews to be Jewish; they had to rent Jews from the "early Christian" middle class.⁷³ Assimilated half- and quarter-Jews were forced among the Jews by stigmatization.⁷⁴ Their money was needed to organize the newspapers of the resistance.⁷⁵ Former legitimists,⁷⁶ adherents of race protectionism and clericalism, were forced under their supervision. And now there comes a peace for which they will act as prompters, possibly even becoming its appointed saviors.⁷⁷ When it comes to the Jewish question, I have never made generalizations. My reviews and writings prove this quite well. But it is entirely natural that over these four or five years, against the modest adherent of culture, a Jewry that is thirsty for revenge and devoid of self-criticism must have

---

72. *Kolkhozes* were agricultural farming collectives in the Soviet Union, theoretically organized on a voluntary basis. After the war, this model was introduced in occupied eastern Europe when it came under Soviet rule.

73. This expression was used widely at the time to designate people of non-Jewish racial origin; it of course had nothing to do with early Christianity. Németh refers to the so-called **stróman** system here.

74. He condemned the "Jewish Laws" not because of their discriminatory nature but because they stalled the process of assimilation and, through persecution, reinforced what he called the "worst, revengeful features" of the Jews.

75. Németh is primarily referring to the conservative, anti-Nazi newspaper *Magyar Nemzet*, published between 1938 and 1944 and financed by the richest, Jewish capitalist enterprise in Hungary, the Chorin-Kornfeld-Weiss group.

76. Legitimism was a conservative political movement that promoted the Habsburgs' return to the Hungarian throne. Its representatives rejected the policies of both the extreme right and the left wing.

77. On the situation of Jews in the postwar communist dictatorship, see chapter 10.

grown far stronger. Those who do not realize that Shylock is after the heart have a deaf ear when it comes to hearing how the knives are being sharpened.[78]

[. . .]

In the 1944 edition of the essay (as well as subsequent ones), Németh omitted the last sentence of the paragraph cited above. However, he never publicly retracted what he had said in his speech. At the same time, in 1944 Németh, a committed antisemite, provided shelter in his apartment for the Jewish poet Zoltán Zelk.[79] Document 9-11(B) gives an account of this, pointing out the paradoxical situation: Németh, whose pre-1944 influence was partially responsible for the general antisemitic sentiment of the Hungarian intellectual elite and therefore the wide-scale acceptance of the persecution of the Jews, sheltered one of "his victims" during the Holocaust.

DOCUMENT 9-11(B): **Memoir of István Vas on László Németh's rescue activity in 1944,[80] in István Vas, *Nehéz szerelem III. Összegyűjtött Munkái* (Budapest: Szépirodalmi, 1984), 13:259.**

[. . .] Illyés arranged for Zoltán [Zelk] to stay in László Németh's house on Rózsadomb,[81] where Zoltán hid away for four days. [. . .] Granted, the host was also hiding away at the time—at Illyés's. Still, it was with

---

78. Shylock, a Jewish usurer, is a character in William Shakespeare's play *The Merchant of Venice*. He loans money to his non-Jewish opponent on the condition that if he is not repaid in time, he can collect "a pound of flesh" from the body of the debtor. Mentioning Shylock was far more than an unfortunate accident, for this was a recurring metaphor in Németh's writing. He used it for the first time in 1934 against a group of liberal Jewish intellectuals criticizing his views, deploying the term to designate a group among Jews he called "racists," who ruled the "nationwide network of Jewish sensibility." László Németh, *Sorskérdések* (Budapest: Magvető-Szépirodalmi, 1989), 94–101.

79. Zoltán Zelk (1906–1981) was a poet and literary translator.

80. István Vas (1910–1991) was a poet, writer, and literary translator. Although Vas had converted to Catholicism in 1938, he was persecuted under the anti-Jewish laws and conscripted into the labor service during the war. He was freed with the help of friends and survived the war in underground Budapest. He wrote of his experiences in his memoir *Azután* (1990). See Susan Suleiman and Eva Forgacs, eds., *Contemporary Jewish Writing in Hungary: An Anthology* (Lincoln: University of Nebraska Press, 2003), 53; "Vas, István," *YIVO Encyclopedia of Jews in Eastern Europe*, www.yivoencyclopedia.org/article.aspx/Vas_Istvan (accessed on May 3, 2012).

81. Gyula Illyés (1902–1983) was a writer, poet, and participant in the folk movement along with László Németh. Rózsadomb was an affluent residential quarter of Budapest.

László Németh's knowledge that Illyés was having Zoltán hide there [. . .] This is where Illyés's wife, Flóra,[82] visited Zoltán—bringing him some cigarettes. She found him sitting on the floor, a couple of issues of *Tanú* spread about him[83]—he had found them in the bottom of the bookshelf. Flóra asked if he liked what he had read. "Well, it looks to me like Laci has played a bit of a part in bringing about that he has to be hiding me here right now," Zoltán responded.[84] Through this improvised paradox, he gave what is perhaps the most succinct characterization of the interconnections between Hungary's intellectual and political life, and especially of the final consequences of László Németh's style of thinking.

## THE CHURCHES

The position taken by the major Christian churches (Roman Catholic, Calvinist, and Lutheran) on the "Jewish question" derived from their anti-Judaic heritage rooted in religious and theological traditions. The churches played a key role in helping anti-Jewish public discourse gain ground and influence. Their leaders, also members of parliament, supported most antisemitic laws. Still, by 1941 they refused to vote for the "Race Protection Law," primarily because it affected tens of thousands of members of their own churches who were of Jewish ancestry. Thus the state's legislation grossly violated church autonomy, including the sanctity of marriage and baptism.[85] Moreover, many church leaders found Nazi ideology's anti-Christian neopaganism and race theory unacceptable.[86]

Loyalty to the pro-Nazi government, together with some careful strategizing, defined church attitudes following the German occupation. From information garnered in previous years, high-level church leaders had some idea about the essence of the "Final Solution." They were well-informed about the cruel methods of the anti-Jewish campaign within the country and, as of May 1944, even had a

---

82. Flóra Kozmutza (1905–1995) was a psychologist.
83. *Tanú* was László Németh's periodical, which he wrote and edited all by himself (1932–1937).
84. Laci is a diminutive of the first name László.
85. Speech by Cardinal Jusztinián Serédi in the Upper House, in *Az 1939. évi június hó 10-ére hirdetett országgyűlés képviselőházának naplója* (Budapest: Athenaeum, 1942), 2:283–85.
86. István Deák, "The Peculiarities of Hungarian Fascism," in *The Holocaust in Hungary: Forty Years Later*, ed. Randolph L. Braham and Bela Vago (New York: Columbia University Press, 1985), 44–45.

copy of the **Auschwitz Protocol**.[87] Church leaders thus increased their protests, while simultaneously seeking to maintain their customary forms of communication and steer clear of serious conflict with the government. They also refrained from informing their congregations and lower-level priests about unfolding events.

Those against taking a public stand to protest the anti-Jewish operation reasoned that an open confrontation with the state could potentially incite an anticlerical campaign and result in the loss of state subsidies and other privileges.[88] Leading church officials also factored in the reactions of antisemitic members of their own congregations and were reluctant to endanger their image as the patrons of "Christian Hungary." Many found it impossible to shed their antisemitic prejudices and reevaluate their long-standing political stance. Any objections they raised cited not discrimination and persecution against Jews as such but the inhumane methods employed to enforce them. In many cases they limited their protests to advocacy for Jews of the Christian faith.[89] The churches never came forth with a unified, joint public protest. At the same time, several prelates, including Catholic bishops Áron Márton and Vilmos Apor, bravely and clearly voiced condemnation in their sermons during the deportations.[90]

---

87. See the interviews with Reverend **József Éliás** and Gennaro Verolino, diplomat of the Vatican. Szenes, *Befejezetlen múlt*, 55–74; Péter Bokor, *Végjáték a Duna mentén. Interjúk egy filmsorozathoz* (Budapest: RTV-Minerva, 1982), 116–20; Walter Laqueur, *The Terrible Secret: Suppression of the Truth about Hitler's "Final Solution"* (New York: Henry Holt and Co., 1998), 54–58.

88. Tamás Majsai, "A protestáns egyházak az üldözés ellen," in *Magyarország 1944. Üldöztetés-embermentés*, ed. Szabolcs Szita (Budapest: Nemzeti Tankönyvkiadó, 1994), 153–54. On the question of how realistic this scenario was and the extent to which it justified the churches' strategic decisions, see Paul A. Hanebrink, *In Defense of Christian Hungary: Religion, Nationalism, and Antisemitism, 1890–1944* (Ithaca, NY: Cornell University Press, 2006), 219.

89. Instead of taking a clear (and risky) position, the churches opted for a middle stance between the persecuted and the persecutors. For the analysis of this strategy, see István Bibó, "Zsidókérdés Magyarországon 1944 után," in *Zsidókérdés, asszimiláció, antiszemitizmus. Tanulmányok a zsidókérdésről a huszadik századi Magyarországon*, ed. Péter Hanák (Budapest: Gondolat, 1984), 154–55. See also Hanebrink, *In Defense of Christian Hungary*, 218–21.

90. On the activities of Márton, see László Virt, *Nyitott szívvel. Márton Áron erdélyi püspök élete és eszméi* (Budapest: Teleki László Alapítvány–XX. Századi Intézet, 2002), 100–106; on Apor's efforts, see his letters written to Cardinal Serédi between April 12 and June 22, 1944, in Jenő Gergely, "A katolikus püspöki kar és a konvertiták mentése (Dokumentumok)," *Történelmi Szemle* 27, no. 4 (1984), 597–99, 607. His intervening letters written to members of the government are published in József Horváth, *Apor püspök élete és halála* (Munich: Apor Emlékbizottság, 1984), 103–6, and see also 55–59, 62–63; for his biography, see Erzsébet Szolnoky, *Fellebbezés helyett. Apor Vilmos püspök élete és vértanúsága* (Szeged: Szent Gellért Egyházi Kiadó, 1990), 129–49, 133–47. On efforts by other church leaders, see Jenő Gergely, "A magyar katolikus püspöki kar, az Apostoli Szentszék és a Soá," in *Magyar megfontolások a Soáról*, ed. Gábor Hamp, Özséb Horányi, and László Rábai (Budapest: Balassi, 1999), 94–110.

Some church leaders tried to exert pressure on the government behind the scenes.[91] The Hungarian cabinet had a fundamental interest in maintaining good relations with the churches. Therefore, it tried to satisfy protesting church officials with minor concessions to Jews of the Christian faith,[92] which in no way improved the situation of the Christian Jews. Nonetheless, pressure from high-ranking priests clearly played some role in the regent's decision to stop the deportations in July 1944.[93]

A few Christian social organizations carried out effective relief work for those suffering persecution, including the **Good Shepherd Committee**,[94] a Protestant organization, and the **Holy Cross Society**, a Catholic body. At the same time, the Christian denominations refused to make the conditions for conversion more lenient, and the Lutherans even made them stricter.[95] Moral condemnation of those looking at Christianity "merely" as a shelter from persecution was widespread.[96] Therefore, very few clergymen, for example, Albert Bereczky and his colleagues, dared to stray from the strict rules and baptize anyone who approached them.[97] However, these acts only had some psychological importance, for exemption rules did not spare those who converted in 1944.

Christian leaders long declined to take a public stand against the persecution of the Jews. The head of the Catholic Church, Archbishop of Esztergom Jusztinián Serédi, hoped to get results from behind-the-scenes negotiations.

---

91. Braham, *The Politics of Genocide*, 2:1176–77, 1184–85.

92. For example, a Christian Jew (**Sándor Török**) was also included in the Jewish Council, and later on, a separate council was set up for Jewish Christians as well; see chapter 8.

93. Opinions on this are summarized in Hanebrink, *In Defense of Christian Hungary*, 219. For more details about the halting of the deportations, see chapter 4.

94. See Gábor Sztehlo, *In the Hands of God* (Budapest: Gábor Sztehlo Foundation for the Help of Children and Adolescents, 1994).

95. The Calvinists further restricted conversion conditions with a regulation issued on July 1, 1943. Those converting from non-Christian denominations were required to pursue a whole year of religious studies. The Lutheran bishops made the same move during the rush to convert: instead of the previous requirement of one month, they prescribed at least half a year of religious education. See Gábor G. Tarján, "Ezer bűnnel megterhelve. A református egyház és a zsidókérdés," *Új Forrás*, no. 1 (1984): 65–72; record of the meeting of Lutheran bishops, May 26, 1944, HNA, Series I, reel 180.

96. For example, Imre Révész, the Calvinist bishop of Debrecen who otherwise held moderate views, rejected petitions requesting that the church become active, take a stand, and ease the conversion rules. His justification was that the rules had to be obeyed, and public opposition would jeopardize the success of ongoing nonpublic negotiations with the government. Béla Síró, "A debreceni zsidóság a Vészkorszak idején," in *Történeti Tanulmányok IV*, ed. Zsuzsa L. Nagy and Géza Veress (Debrecen: KLTE Történelmi Intézet, 1995), 162.

97. Majsai, "A protestáns egyházak az üldözés ellen," 172–73.

However, by mid-June, influenced by repeated orders from the Vatican and pressure from some Catholic bishops, he consented to have the Council of Bishops issue a joint pastoral letter condemning the deportations. A pastoral letter, an open letter addressed by a prelate to the priests of his diocese or to the entire congregation, typically contains directives concerning correct behavior in certain periods of the liturgical year or in particular situations. After lengthy rounds of preparations and negotiations, the council wrote the document on June 29, 1944. Meanwhile, between June 11 and 28, close to one hundred thousand additional people, or on average about fifty-five hundred per day, were deported. By the end of June, the authorities had already sent more than three hundred thousand Jews to Auschwitz. Publishing the letter and reading it out in every Catholic church would have sent a very strong message to Hungarian society and government and probably would have drawn international attention as well. Compared to communications up until then, the text of the pastoral letter firmly condemned the machinery of genocide, but it also contained serious antisemitic remarks and charges.

DOCUMENT 9-12: **Pastoral letter of Archbishop Jusztinián Serédi on behalf of the Hungarian Catholic Council of Bishops, June 29, 1944, in Randolph L. Braham,** *The Politics of Genocide: The Holocaust in Hungary* **(New York: Columbia University Press, 1994), 2:1180–82.**

[...]

Now therefore, our dear believers, we, the members of the Hungarian Council of Bishops, hereby fulfill our duty in these fateful times in defense of the innocent, by raising our protesting chief-pastoral voices in God's name against the type of warfare and bombardments condemned by Christian ethics. The destruction of the homes of peaceful citizens remote from any strategically significant site, the machine gunning of peaceful women and children from low-flying airplanes, the crippling of innocent children by the throwing of explosive toys: all these are acts which warfare claiming honesty cannot allow.

But we must also point out that when in this horrible world war God's help is so badly needed, when we ourselves should carefully avoid any word or act that would draw God's wrath upon us and our nation, we see with unspeakable sadness that in Christian Hungary a series of measures have been taken that are against the laws of God. To you, our dear believers, we need not list in detail the measures which are well known to you along with the manner of their execution, and which violate or even deny the inherent rights of some of our fellow citizens, even some who are together with us, members of our holy faith, only because of their origin. And all this without the determination of individual guilt and judicial decree. You could truly only understand all this, if the same deprivation of rights happened to you.

As the Chief Pastor of our believers as ordered by God, all partisan politics has been far from us, is still far from us, and will continue to be so, as well as any group interest or any individual interest. We also have no doubt that a part of Jewry has had a guilty subversive influence on the Hungarian economic, social and moral life. It is also a fact that the others did not stand up against their coreligionists in this respect. We do not dispute the fact that the Jewish question must be resolved in a legal and just manner. Therefore we do not object, but actually hold it desirable, that in the economic system of the country the necessary measures be taken and the rightfully objectionable symptoms be remedied. However, we would neglect our moral and pastoral duty if we did not make very certain that the just shall not suffer, and our Hungarian fellow citizens and Catholic believers not be offended merely because of their origins; therefore we have endeavored for several months through oral and written negotiations to protect the just generally, and especially our fellow citizens and believers made victims of recently issued injurious measures: we have asked for the modification, and as it were, the repeal, of the injurious orders themselves.

[. . .]

But now, when we see with great shock that our negotiations have been almost without success, especially in the most important respects, we solemnly disavow our responsibility. But in defense of the divine laws and by this means we also ask the competent authorities, recognizing their responsibility to God and history, to urgently remedy the injurious measures. These measures not only cause legal insecurity at this time of fighting for the existence of the nation, but they also disturb the unity of the nation, turn the common opinion of the Christian world against us, and more importantly they turn God against us.

[. . .] Be careful that by approval or promotion of the objectionable acts, you do not take the horrible responsibility upon yourselves before God and mankind. Do not forget that the true well-being of the homeland cannot be served through injustice. Pray and work for all our Hungarian co-citizens without exception, mainly for our Catholic brethren, for our Catholic Church, and for our beloved Hungarian homeland.

[. . .]

The text reveals much about the attitude of Catholic Church leaders. Tellingly, the lines that detail the suffering of the Jews do not mention the word "Jew," whereas the next paragraph (listing their alleged sins) does. The document, supposed to convince the public not to participate in persecution, fully supported the anti-Jewish legislation and contained most clichés dispensed by antisemitic propaganda.

While the Protestant churches' attitude did not differ qualitatively from that of the Catholics,[98] the senior Calvinist bishop, **László Ravasz**, and Lutheran bishop Sándor Raffay urged—in vain—that the three denominations act jointly. By the end of June, like Serédi, László Ravasz had also written a pastoral letter condemning the deportations, but his did not contain antisemitic remarks. The government would have found loud church condemnation of the deportations extremely unpleasant. Therefore, one cabinet member dissuaded the Protestant and Catholic leaders from going public with their pastoral letters. The minister deployed a classical mixture of false promises of concessions for Christian Jews and baseless threats: he argued that public criticism could lead to the fall of the government and an Arrow Cross takeover. As a result, the Catholic and Protestant leadership read neither pastoral letter to the public. Instead, both issued meaningless statements about their attempts to negotiate with authorities in the realm of Jewish affairs.[99] The delay meant that no one who might have been rescued was left in the provinces.

Following the Arrow Cross takeover, Christian rescue activities did in fact intensify significantly, especially at the middle and lower levels. Several thousand people found shelter in almost fifty convents and in the buildings of numerous Christian organizations. Members of several Hungarian and foreign orders of monks and nuns and other church-affiliated individuals protected the

---

98. For example, in their proposal submitted to the government on June 20, they protested the idea that "it should be the ardent members of our church who should suffer punishment for the Jewish mentality, with which they have solemnly broken their connections." Jenő Lévai, *Szürke könyv a magyar zsidók megmentéséről* (Budapest: Officina, n.d. [1946]), 61–63.

99. For details on the Christian churches' policies, see circular letter by Cardinal Jusztinián Serédi to the members of the Council of Bishops, July 9, 1944, in Gergely, "A katolikus püspöki kar és a konvertiták mentése," 613–16; interview with András Zakar, secretary to the cardinal, in Szenes, *Befejezetlen múlt*, 129–85; Braham, *The Politics of Genocide*, 2:1170–204; Albert Bereczky, *A magyar protestantizmus a zsidóüldözés ellen* (Budapest: Református Traktátus Vállalat, 1945), 12–23; Lévai, *Szürke könyv a magyar zsidók megmentéséről*, 58 and *passim*; Majsai, "A protestáns egyházak az üldözés ellen," 151–62; Tamás Majsai, "A magyarországi református egyház és a holokauszt. A nyilvános tiltakozás története," *Világosság* 36, no. 5 (1995): 50–80.

persecuted with great courage and resourcefulness, often sacrificing their own lives. The martyrs rescuing Jews included the head of the Scottish Mission to Budapest, Jane Haining, who was deported to Auschwitz; Archdeacon Ferenc Kálló, army chaplain; and Sister Sára Salkaházi.[100]

Sára Salkaházi belonged to the Society of Sisters of Social Service, a Catholic order established in Hungary in 1923. Led by **Margit Slachta**, the society took a stand against right-wing extremist ideology and the persecution of the Jews as early as the first years of the war. Sára Salkaházi, head of the National Association of Catholic Working Women and Girls, was a leading figure of the rescue operations in 1944.[101] In 1943 she pledged to sacrifice her life for the persecuted if necessary. Following the German occupation, the order hid Jews in every one of its buildings in Budapest and the provinces, concealing altogether about one thousand people. On December 27, 1944, based on a report filed with the authorities, Arrow Cross militiamen raided the residence headed by Salkaházi.[102] She was about to return to the building and, on seeing the guards, could have kept her distance. Instead, she walked straight up to the commander, who was checking identification documents, to speak for her wards. The militiamen arrested her, along with a Christian teacher and four Jews hiding on the premises. Document 9-13, a passage from an eyewitness's statement, recalls the circumstances of the arrest.

**DOCUMENT 9-13: Postwar eyewitness report on the arrest of the Catholic sister Sára Salkaházi, in Károly Hetényi-Varga,** *Papi sorsok a horogkereszt és a vörös csillag árnyékában*, **2nd ed. (Budapest: Új Ember–Márton Áron, 2004), 141.**

> The chapel door sprang open all of a sudden, and Sára was standing there, with the Arrow Cross men behind her. "Let me in here for a moment!"

---

100. See Nicholas Railton, *Jane Haining and the Work of the Scottish Mission with Hungarian Jews, 1932–1945* (Budapest: n.p., 2007), 29–77; Károly Hetényi Varga, "A magyar katolikus egyház az üldözöttekért (1944–1945)," in *Magyarország 1944. Üldöztetésembermentés*, 121–23, 133–49; interview with Károly Hetényi Varga, in Szenes, *Befejezetlen múlt*, 221–59.

101. Sára Salkaházi (Schalkház) (1899–1944) was designated by Yad Vashem as Righteous Among the Nations in 1972. On her life, see Ilona Mona and Elemér Szeghalmi, *Vértanú kortársunk: Salkaházi Sára élete és munkássága* (Budapest: Ecclesia, n.d. [1990]); Máté Hídvégi, ed., *Boldog Salkaházi Sára. Emlékkönyv* (Budapest: Szent István Társulat, 2006); János P. Szőke, "Boldog Salkaházi," *Vértanúink-hitvallóink* 12, no. 47 (December 2006).

102. Municipal District IX of Budapest, 5 Bokréta Street.

she said, but she already broke away from them and came forward, all the way to the tabernacle. Two Arrow Cross men followed her. I still did not understand what was happening. Sára knelt down on one knee, and I could see from the side the eternal flame at the altar lighting her face. This made an impression on me that I could not quite put into words, but I definitely remember thinking to myself, "My God! Sára is a saint!" The two Arrow Cross men were also stunned by the sight, and for a few moments there was complete silence. I already suspected at that time what all this was about and that Sára would be taken away for hiding the Jews. I began intensely praying for her. Just a few seconds passed before one of the Arrow Cross men, the grim-looking one, grabbed her and yelled at her, "Let's go already! You can pray more at night!" Then she stood up, but with peace. This was a miraculous apparition of sorts. She wanted to bend her knee once more, but they forcefully pulled her up and took her away.

That same day, the Arrow Cross militiamen herded all the people arrested at the residence to the banks of the Danube and shot them so they would fall into the icy water. According to one witness's recollection, before the fusillade, a short, black-haired woman (Salkaházi) "turned to her executioners with an inexplicable calmness about her [. . .] and then knelt down, and lifting her eyes to the sky, she made the sign of a broad, big cross."[103] Pope Benedict XVI beatified her in 2006.

## INTERVENTION AND THE INTERNATIONAL COMMUNITY

The international community made efforts to assist the Jews and other victims of Nazism prior to 1944.[104] From the summer of 1944 onward, however, a coordinated, intensive series of rescue operations assisted tens of thousands of people. Half the diplomats awarded the Yad Vashem honorary title "Righteous

---

103. Quoted in Mona and Szeghalmi, *Vértanú kortársunk*, 90.
104. See, e.g., the work of the Emergency Rescue Committee. On the history of the committee, see the memoirs of the head of the organization: Varian Fry, *Surrender on Demand* (Boulder, CO: Johnson Books, 1997).

Among the Nations" received it in recognition of their activities in Budapest at the turn of 1944–1945.[105]

By 1943 it already seemed probable that the Axis Powers would lose the war. This brought a shift in neutral states' attitudes and U.S. policy. President Franklin D. Roosevelt established the War Refugee Board, a U.S. government agency, in January 1944, in large part through pressure and financial support from Jewish organizations. The board played a key role in the launch of several new diplomatic initiatives. Central among these was the effort to rescue the last major Jewish community left in Hitler's Europe: the Jews of Budapest.[106] The turn in the war, American support, and public pressure emerging in response to press reports on the deportations motivated the neutral states (especially Switzerland and Sweden) to embark on broader rescue operations.

Increasing tension with the Vatican and other neutral states played a significant role in Regent Miklós Horthy's decision to stop the deportations in early July. Yet their more expansive rescue activities emerged only afterward. Horthy wanted to improve the country's dramatically deteriorated international image, so the government began heeding the demands of neutral diplomatic missions. Establishment of the "protected Jew" status meant that a neutral country could confer immunity on a given person in whose safety it had an interest.

The representatives of the major neutral diplomatic corps (from the Vatican, Sweden, Portugal, Spain, and Switzerland) first issued a statement in order to stop the resumption of deportations on August 21, 1944.[107] Following the Arrow Cross takeover, their activities intensified. They pressured **Ferenc Szálasi**'s government, issued an ever-growing number of protective documents, and took personal risks to rescue people from death marches and mass executions. Their actions resulted in the setting up of the so-called international or protected ghetto of safe houses for Jews holding (real or fake) protective documents.[108] The nature of the diplomats' activities also underwent a qualitative change. Confronted with a formally illegitimate government, they no longer

---

105. This constituted fourteen awardees out of a total of twenty-seven. Reuveni, "A Világ Igazai Magyarországon," 16.

106. On U.S. policies concerning refugees and the "Jewish question," see David S. Wyman, *The Abandonment of the Jews: America and the Holocaust, 1941–1945* (New York: Pantheon Books, 1984); Richard Breitman and Alan M. Kraut, *American Refugee Policy and European Jewry, 1933–1945* (Bloomington: Indiana University Press, 1987); David S. Wyman, ed., *America and the Holocaust*, vol. 8 (New York: Garland, 1990). On efforts to help Hungarian Jews, see Henry L. Feingold, *Bearing Witness: How America and Its Jews Responded to the Holocaust* (Syracuse, NY: Syracuse University Press, 1995), 141–68.

107. Braham, *The Politics of Genocide*, 2:914–15.

108. On the international ghetto, see chapter 5.

insisted on adhering to traditional diplomatic methods and, where necessary, resorted to fraud, forgery, and suborning corruption. They far exceeded their original instructions and their governments' restricted objectives. Tens of thousands of people ultimately owed their lives to these diplomats.

Among heroic rescuers in Hungary, the name of **Raoul Wallenberg** is the most widely known. Just as important was the vice consul of the Swiss embassy, **Carl Lutz**.[109] Switzerland represented the interests of the citizens of several states at war with Hungary, including the United States and Great Britain. This made it possible for the embassy to pursue negotiations regarding emigration to Palestine, which was under British control at the time, and to issue emigration documents. The vice consul managed to persuade the Hungarian government and German plenipotentiary **Edmund Veesenmayer** to agree—at least theoretically—to an emigration quota of seven thousand people. Although the operation came to naught, the selected Jews were exempted from the deportations. "Emigration to Palestine" became one of the fundamental components of and models for the emerging system of diplomatic protection set up later by the neutral delegations and the International Red Cross (IRC).

A critical feature of the diplomatic intervention proved to be the issuing of a range of protection letters or protective passes. These gained particular significance after October 15, 1944, when the Budapest Jews again faced mortal danger. Because Szálasi strongly desired international recognition for his government, he therefore sought good relations with the neutrals. Once it became clear, however, that these countries were unlikely to acknowledge the Arrow Cross regime, the influence of the embassies diminished considerably. For this reason (and because of the devaluation of protective documents through forgery on a large scale), armed Arrow Cross men became increasingly less inclined to accept documents certifying the holder's protected status. By the time of the Budapest siege, protected individuals as well as the people assisting them stood in lethal danger.

Document 9-14 reproduces one of the first protective documents issued by the Department of Foreign Interests at the Swiss legation and signed by Vice Consul Carl Lutz. The letter stated that the bearer of the document, Maria Magdalena (Magda) Grausz, worked for the embassy as a housemaid. Grausz survived the siege of Budapest under Swiss protection. After the war, Lutz divorced his wife and married Magda. He also adopted her daughter, Agnes.

---

109. For details about Lutz's activities and career, see Theo Tschuy, *Dangerous Diplomacy: The Story of Carl Lutz, Rescuer of 62,000 Hungarian Jews* (Grand Rapids, MI: William B. Eerdmans, 2000); Alexander Grossman, *Nur das Gewissen—Carl Lutz und seine Budapester Aktion* (Wald: Im Waldgut, 1986).

DOCUMENT 9-14: Protective letter (*Schutzbrief*) issued by the Swiss legation in Budapest to Maria Magdalena Grausz, July 1, 1944, USHMMPA WS# 45647.

SCHWEIZERISCHE GESANDTSCHAFT
ABTEILUNG FÜR FREMDE INTERESSEN
BUDAPEST

BUDAPEST,
V., SZABADSÁG-TÉR 12
TELEPHON 129-510
129-519

AKTENZEICHEN: UNSER
IHR

Es wird hiermit bestätigt, dass

Frau Maria Magdalena GRAUSZ

Hausangestellte bei Herrn Konsul C.Lutz, Leiter der Abteilung für fremde Interessen der Schweizerischen Gesandtschaft ( I.Verböczy utca 1.), ist.

Budapest, den 1. Juli 1944.

SCHWEIZERISCHE GESANDTSCHAFT
Abteilung für fremde Interessen:
i.A.
Vizekonsul.

Ezennel igazoljuk, hogy

GRAUSZ Maria Magdalena asszony

háztartási alkalmazott C.Lutz konzul urnál, a Svájci Követség Idegen Érdekek Képviselete hivatalának vezetőjénél ( I.Verböczy utca 1.).

Budapest, 1944 julius 1.

SVÁJCI KÖVETSÉG
Idegen Érdekek Képviselete:
m.h.
alkonzul.

Besides issuing thousands of protective documents, Lutz placed several dozen buildings under diplomatic protection. These included the so-called **Glass House** in Vadász Street. In doing so, he aided the work of the Palestine Office, led by **Miklós Krausz**, as well as the young Zionist activists.[110] Following the Arrow Cross takeover on October 15, Lutz regularly violated his own mandate in order to rescue as many people as possible. It is no coincidence that when the other key figure of the rescue, Sweden's Raoul Wallenberg, arrived in Budapest in July 1944, he visited Lutz as one of his first tasks. He developed his own strategy following the model of the Swiss rescue operation.[111]

The head of the legation, Carl I. Danielsson, initially directed the Swedish embassy's relief and rescue work. At first, the embassy issued a limited number of temporary passports (*Provisoriskt Pass*) to prominent figures with Swedish connections.[112] Later, following the example of the Swiss, the Swedish also issued protective passports and letters. Document 9-15, issued (in Hungarian and German) by the Swedish embassy and signed by Danielsson, attested to the status of Dr. József Katona as a person protected by the embassy until his "repatriation" to Sweden. Born in 1909 in Zalaegerszeg and a graduate of the Rabbinical Seminary of Budapest, Rabbi Katona survived the Holocaust in the capital.

---

110. On the activities of the Zionists, see chapter 8.

111. Mária Ember, *Wallenberg Budapesten* (Budapest: Városháza, 2000), 26–28; Tschuy, *Dangerous Diplomacy*, 182.

112. On the provisional passports, see Paul A. Levine, *From Indifference to Activism: Swedish Diplomacy and the Holocaust, 1938–1944* (Uppsala: Uppsala University Library, 1998), 268–73.

DOCUMENT 9-15: **Protective passport (*Schutzpass*) issued by the Swedish embassy to Rabbi József Katona, September 15, 1944, USHMMPA WS# 67062.**

After the war Dr. Katona became a leading rabbi of the Dohány Street Synagogue. He died of a heart attack in September 1959 while delivering a memorial speech in the synagogue on the hundredth anniversary of the temple's consecration.[113]

Upon receiving information about the mass deportations after mid-May 1944, Danielsson coordinated with the Red Cross and Jewish organizations in planning a large-scale rescue operation.[114] This coincided with the objectives of the War Refugee Board, which aimed to launch its humanitarian mission in Budapest via Swedish diplomatic channels. The Swedish government appointed Raoul Wallenberg for the task. Although the thirty-two-year-old had no prior experience as a diplomat (he was an architect by profession and later worked as a businessman), this work suited him well. Many of his family members had been involved in diplomatic missions. In 1936 he spent half a year in Palestine, where Jewish refugees first told him about the real face of Hitler's regime and the persecution of the Jews. In 1941 he established a joint commercial company with a Hungarian Jew, and he had visited Hungary several times before 1944. Wallenberg arrived in his new role on July 9, 1944, and took over rescue affairs. The broad and effective network of connections he developed in the capital included, apart from neutral diplomats and Jewish leaders, some Hungarian and German officials as well. During the Arrow Cross era, Wallenberg became a leading figure in diplomatic rescue efforts.

Wallenberg and his coworkers directed an apparatus consisting of several hundred people. He issued thousands of protective documents and provided food for Jews living in about thirty Swedish **protected houses**. He also participated in securing provisions for the large ghetto. He constantly risked being arrested or killed as he rescued people from the death marches and transports sent westward in November and December 1944.

---

113. On the passing of Dr. Katona, see Ferenc Katona, "'Oltárra ne sújts vassal!'—Emlékeim a Zsinagóga századik évfordulójáról," in *A Dohány utcai Zsinagóga 150 éve. Tudományos konferencia a Dohány utcai Zsinagógáról* (Budapest: Gabbiano, 2010), 28–44.

114. Report of Ambassador Danielsson to the Swedish Ministry of Foreign Affairs, June 25, 1944, in Péter Bajtay, ed., *Emberirtás-embermentés. Svéd követjelentések 1944-ből. Az Auschwitzi Jegyzőkönyv* (Budapest: Katalizátor Iroda, 1994), 79–81.

DOCUMENT 9-16: **Reports of Raoul Wallenberg to the Swedish Ministry of Foreign Affairs regarding the rescue activity of the Swedish embassy, July–December 1944, in Raoul Wallenberg, *Letters and Dispatches* (New York: Arcade Publishing in association with the USHMM, 1995), 236–37, 257–58, 262–63, 265–67.**

[July 18, 1944].[115]
 [. . .]
 Most people you speak to are ashamed of what is happening and maintain that these brutalities are not being committed by Hungarians but only by Germans. However this is not true. Hungarian anti-Semitism is deeply rooted. Positive intervention is usually limited to helping friends by providing food and hiding places. Many deplore the persecution of the Jews, pointing out that it is costing the Hungarians sympathy abroad and that they risk being treated more harshly than Romania in the event of peace, since Romania's policy toward its Jewish population is known to have become more lenient of late. It would appear, however, that this awareness is limited to the leaders of industry.[116] There is a certain amount of speculation regarding the punishment awaiting those who have taken an active part in these criminal actions.

 I might mention, in this connection, that the presence of Jews is sometimes thought to constitute protection against bombing raids. Those who hold this view appear to believe that the scattering of the Jews into about 2,600 Jewish houses all over Budapest, instead of concentrating them in ghettos, is a deliberate act and that this is also the reason why the Jewish workforce has been forbidden to seek shelter during air raids.
 [. . .]

---

115. Wallenberg's first report demonstrates that he had obtained a great deal of information about the deportations and a clear sense of the rescue's conditions and limits. During this period, the overarching goal for diplomats was to develop a system of protection and include as many people in it as possible. They obtained an exemption from wearing the yellow star for individuals under Swedish protection and began moving them into separate buildings. See also Wallenberg's report of August 6 and Danielsson's report of September 6, 1944, in Bajtay, *Emberirtás-embermentés*, 123–26.

116. Wallenberg is referring to the Manfréd Weiss affair; see chapter 4.

[September 29, 1944].[117]

[. . .]

After September 16 no new applications will be accepted.[118] The section may now close down as soon as the present applications for protective passports—around 8,000—have been decided. Our plans are to issue a total of 4,500 protective passports, of which 2,700 have already been distributed.[119]

It goes without saying that it is very difficult to distribute the remaining number fairly.

We have been told that people have sometimes made financial sacrifices to secure a protective or a provisional passport. We have discovered that certain individuals not employed by the section—among them some unscrupulous lawyers—have taken advantage of the precarious situation of the Jewish population and exacted large fees to handle the application for a protective passport. They have claimed to have connections among the staff.[120]

[. . .]

---

117. This report was written in a transition period. The deportation of the Budapest Jews was taken off the agenda. With cautious optimism, the Swedes decided on a gradual reduction of Wallenberg's department. It looked as though Wallenberg, whose mission was planned to last two months, would soon be able to return to Stockholm. After September 16, the embassy did not accept any more petitions for protection letters. At the same time, the Swedish diplomats kept tabs on unfolding events so they could revive their activities in the case of another anti-Jewish operation. See the report of Kálmán Lauer, in Ember, *Wallenberg Budapesten*, 122–29; on Wallenberg's report of September 12, 1944, see Paul A. Levine, "One Day during the Holocaust: An Analysis of Raoul Wallenberg's 'Budapest Report' of 12 September 1944," *Holocaust Studies* 11, no. 3 (winter 2005), 88–91; for an analysis of the latter document, see 91–97.

118. That is, for protective documents.

119. Eventually the number of protective documents issued by the Swedes exceeded this number. See the name lists of those officially receiving Swedish protective documents in HJA XX-F-II, box D 6/3. The lists consist of more than ten thousand names.

120. The illegal trade in real and fake documents was a flourishing business in Hungary in 1944–1945. Not only were these papers issued by the neutral corps on the "market," but so were military identity books, birth, death, marriage, baptismal and residence certificates, rations cards, and so forth. The most bizarre type of document available was a medical certificate proving that the bearer's foreskin had been removed not for religious reasons (i.e., he was not Jewish) but due to genital health problems. This could be a lifesaver for many Jews, since in the Szálasi era the Arrow Cross militia often identified Jews in hiding by checking if males were circumcised or not. For a detailed description of this "market," see Tivadar Soros, *Masquerade: Dancing around Death in Nazi-Occupied Hungary*, ed. Humphrey Tonkin (1965; New York: Arcade, 2001).

[October 22, 1944].

Since my last report the situation regarding the Hungarian Jews has deteriorated considerably.[121]

[. . .]

During the first night of the [Arrow Cross] putsch, several individual arrests were made, and there were several pogrom acts, in the course of which some 100–200 persons are estimated to have been killed.[122] Several Jewish houses were also emptied by Arrow Cross troops and the occupants taken away to detention centers. These [people] have largely been allowed to return, but a couple of hundred appear still to be missing.

[. . .]

The events of the 17th were disastrous for the section.[123] We lost the entire staff, plus a car which had been placed at our disposal free of charge, as well as some keys to locked rooms, cupboards, etc. I spent the whole of the first day in streets filled with bandits, on a lady's bicycle, trying to straighten everything out. Day two was spent moving staff members in imminent danger by car to safer hiding places and hauling food to them in a sack. Today only about ten staff members are missing, while some thirty have not yet come to work. One of the section's larger areas has been co-opted by the embassy to house the Swedish colony.[124]

[. . .]

---

121. On October 12, 1944. Raoul Wallenberg, *Letters and Dispatches* (New York: Arcade Publishing in association with the USHMM, 1995), 260–61.

122. On the events of October 15–16, see chapter 5.

123. October 17.

124. The Arrow Cross takeover redrew the picture in a flash. Yet again, direct rescue became a primary objective. Unlike most other diplomatic missions, the Swedish embassy remained in Budapest with all its employees. Once the "Jewish department" was reorganized after some disarray following the coup, Wallenberg and his colleagues strove to rescue protected individuals who were being herded off on death marches. Wallenberg's large-scale operations outraged the Arrow Cross as well as the Germans. In mid-December, the Swedish ambassador to Berlin protested at the German Foreign Office that he had gotten word that Eichmann swore "to shoot Wallenberg, that Jewish dog." The Germans did not deny the claim but merely sought to trivialize it. On this, see the reports of the Swedish embassy, December 15–23, 1944, in Bajtay, *Emberirtás-embermentés*, 169–76.

[December 12, 1944]

Since the last report the situation of the Hungarian Jews has further deteriorated.

Probably in the vicinity of 40,000 Jews, of whom 15,000 men from the Labor Service and 25,000 of both sexes [were] seized in their homes or in the street, have been forced to march on foot to Germany. It is a distance of 240 kilometers [149 miles]. The weather has been cold and rainy ever since these death marches began. They have had to sleep under rain shelters and in the open. Most have only been given something to eat and drink three or four times. Many have died.

[. . .]

The Jews are collected in a central ghetto intended to house 69,000 Jews, but which will probably house more than this number, as well as in a ghetto for foreigners [designed] for 17,000, already containing 35,000, of whom 7,000 [are] in Swedish houses, 2,000 in houses belonging to the Red Cross, and 23,000 in Swiss houses.[125] Thousands of people under Swiss and Vatican protection are taken away from here to the central ghetto or to deportation areas. The Jews live 4–12 to a room in the ghettos, the Swedish houses having the best conditions.[126]

[. . .]

The Jews are mostly very poor, as they are only allowed to take with them what they are able to carry during their repeated moves. Supplies will soon be disastrously low.

[. . .]

The Organization[127]

After the deadly blow dealt in October, the section has again grown rapidly. The staff now numbers 335, in addition to some 40 doctors, house governors, etc. All these people and about the same number of family members are living in the section's buildings. There are ten offices and dwellings, of which one [is] in the foreign ghetto.

Two hospitals have been established and improvised, respectively, with a total of 150 beds.

---

125. That is, the so-called international ghetto.
126. On the ghettos, see chapter 5.
127. By *organization*, Wallenberg means the section of the embassy dealing with rescue and its Hungarian employees.

A soup kitchen has been started.
[. . .]
A large part of the section's correspondence has been destroyed.[128]
[. . .]

On January 17, 1945, Wallenberg set out to cross the front lines to reach the Soviet command headquarters in order to negotiate further rescue operations. Suspecting him and his companion of spying, the Soviets arrested them and secreted them to a Moscow jail. Soviet authorities would not admit their responsibility in Wallenberg's disappearance for a long time. The postwar communist dictatorship even attempted to divert responsibility for Wallenberg's disappearance to Jewish leaders, claiming that members of the Jewish Council executed him. Moscow officials eventually revealed that Soviet troops had actually arrested the Swedish diplomat. The Soviets long maintained that Wallenberg died of a heart attack in his prison cell in Moscow in 1947.[129]

On a much smaller scale than the Swiss or the Swedish embassy, other neutral diplomatic bodies also joined the rescue operations. In previous years, Franco's Spain had already demonstrated its diplomatic independence by letting refugees pass through its borders (in part tacitly) and by granting citizenship to Jews of Spanish origin. At the end of November 1944, the Spanish government recalled its representative, Ángel Sanz-Briz. However, by that time, he had issued twenty-three hundred passports and protective documents.[130] Spain's agreement to admit five hundred Jewish children from Hungary provided major momentum for subsequent operations. Although never executed, the transfer did facilitate the child rescue action of the International Red Cross. From the end of November 1944, Italian tradesman **Giorgio Perlasca** took over work at

---

128. The date of the last report signaled the beginning of the most difficult interval for the embassy. After it became public that the Swedes did not acknowledge the Szálasi government, the Arrow Cross would no longer spare those protected by the embassy, even turning against its employees. Wallenberg and his colleagues often put their own lives on the line during their work.

129. Wallenberg's activities have spawned an extensive literature. For a selected bibliography, see Szabolcs Szita, ed., *Raoul Wallenberg emlékezete. Bibliográfiák* (Budapest: Ex Libris, 2007); Randolph L. Braham, ed., *The Holocaust in Hungary: A Selected and Annotated Bibliography, 1984–2000* (New York: Columbia University Press, 2001), 156–61; Randolph L. Braham and Julia Bock, eds., *The Holocaust in Hungary: A Selected and Annotated Bibliography: 2000–2007* (New York: Columbia University Press, 2008), 152–56.

130. Iván Harsányi, "A budapesti spanyol követség által az 1944. évi üldözések idején védelemben részesített magyar zsidók névsora," *Holocaust Füzetek*, no. 3 (1993), 46.

the embassy. Completely illegally, he posed as the Spanish representative. His brave and efficient bluff led to the rescue of hundreds.[131]

The Portuguese legation also began granting diplomatic immunity to individuals. Yielding to American pressure, Turkey issued some protective documents as well. Finally, the Salvadorian consulate based in Geneva sent nationality certificates to Hungary, which were likewise accepted as protective documents. Transylvanian Hungarian Jewish businessman and diplomat **Georges M. Mantello** orchestrated the operation behind the scenes.

Even though the reality of mass extermination had been clear, the International Red Cross's actual rescue activity began only after the Arrow Cross takeover. Before that, the IRC, insisting on legal formulas, considered the deportations a matter of Hungarian internal affairs. Headed by Swiss delegate Friedrich Born, an extensive network of institutions developed for the protection of the Jews. Zionist leader **Ottó Komoly** headed Section A, originally set up to protect Jewish children. **Gábor Sztehlo**, a Lutheran, directed Section B, intended to shield Jewish children who had converted to Christianity. This network extended IRC protection to about six thousand children in over fifty children's homes, as well as to a dozen food warehouses, twenty-two hospitals and smaller health institutions, and selected buildings in the ghetto.[132] The Swedish Red Cross, headed by Valdemar Langlet, organized rescue operations independently of the IRC and, to some extent, independently of the Swedish embassy as well. The organization issued about four thousand protective documents, and its leaders rescued and hid numerous people.[133]

Document 9-17 was issued by the International Red Cross and signed by the head of the IRC delegation in Hungary, Friedrich Born. The bearer of the document, Dr. László Benedek (1906–1974), was a chief physician at the Wesselényi Street makeshift hospital during the ghetto period.[134]

---

131. On his life and actions, see Enrico Deaglio, *The Banality of Goodness: The Story of Giorgio Perlasca* (Notre Dame, IN: University of Notre Dame Press, 1998).

132. Jean-Claude Favez, *The Red Cross and the Holocaust* (Cambridge: Cambridge University Press, 1999), 233–50; János Botos, "'Inter arma caritas.' Embermentő tevékenység a Vöröskereszt Nemzetközi Bizottságának közreműködésével (1944 nyara–1945 eleje)," in *Magyarország 1944. Üldöztetés-embermentés*, 185–211.

133. Nina Langlet, *A svéd mentőakció, 1944* (Budapest: Kossuth, 1988).

134. For his recollections, see HJA, DEGOB Protocols, no. 3608.

DOCUMENT 9-17: **Protective document issued by the International Red Cross for Dr. László Benedek, September 7, 1944, HJA XX-F-1, box D 6/1.**

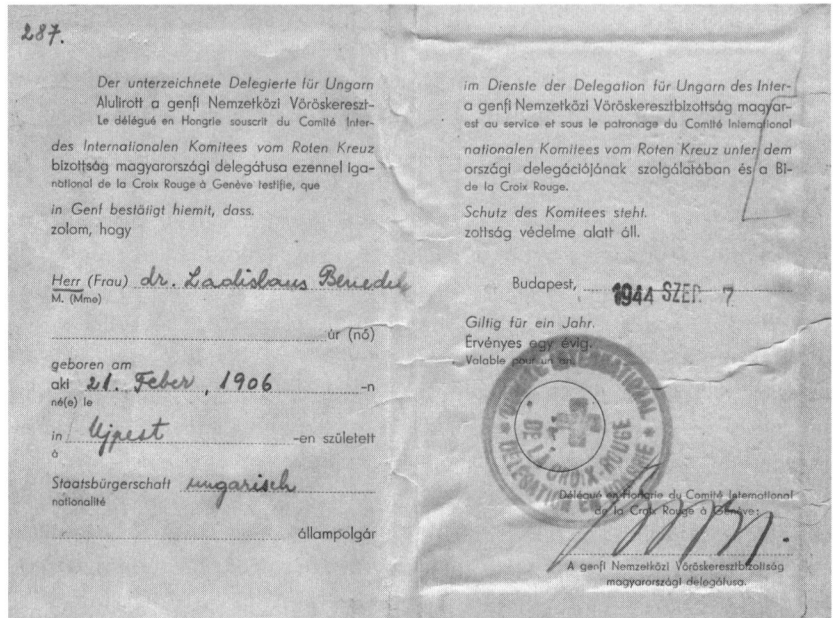

After the war Benedek became an influential figure in Jewish public life. He supported the communist government in introducing total control over the community's institutions. Despite that, during preparations for the 1953 anti-Zionist show trials, he was—among other community leaders (**Lajos Stöckler, Miksa Domonkos**)—arrested and tortured by the communist political police. Sentenced to three years, Benedek was released in December 1954. He left the country in 1956.[135]

Although continually informed about the march toward the "Final Solution" from 1941 onward, Pope Pius XII nonetheless declined to protest publicly for a long time. Only after the liberation of Rome on June 4, 1944,

---

135. Géza Komoróczy, *A zsidók története Magyarországon* (Pozsony: Kalligram, 2012), 2:1015.

did he become more active, raising his voice on behalf of the Hungarian Jews.[136] However, his delegate to Budapest, Papal Nuncio **Angelo Rotta**, had been protesting the anti-Jewish measures since the end of March 1944. Rotta had access to the government even after the Arrow Cross takeover. Backed by the prestige of the Vatican, he exerted ever more pressure on Szálasi. The tangible results of his activity took the form of several thousand protective documents distributed (as blank forms) among the Jews herded off in death marches, saving many from deportation.[137]

Alongside these initiatives, international Protestant organizations also conducted efforts to rescue the Hungarian Jews. The Geneva-based center of the ecumenical movement played an important role in passing the Auschwitz Protocol on to Switzerland and in the subsequent press campaign.[138] It supported aid operations and exerted pressure on the leaders of the Hungarian Protestant churches.[139] However, the latter—comprising, for the most part, adherents of the era's pro-Axis policy and supporters of the anti-Jewish legislation—did not wish to take advantage of the additional rescue options afforded by international aid.[140]

---

136. For an outline of the politics of the Vatican during the Holocaust and related readings, see Carol Rittner et al., *The Holocaust and the Christian World: Reflections on the Past, Challenges for the Future* (New York: Continuum, 2000), 126–47. See also Owen Chadwick, *Catholicism and History: The Opening of the Vatican Archives* (Cambridge: Cambridge University Press, 2009); Michael Phayer, *Pius XII, the Holocaust, and the Cold War* (Bloomington: Indiana University Press, 2008); Hubert Wolf and Kenneth Kronenberg, *Pope and Devil: The Vatican's Archives and the Third Reich* (Cambridge, MA: Belknap Press of Harvard University Press, 2010).

137. On the rescue activities of the Budapest nuncio, see Lévai, *Szürke könyv a magyar zsidók megmentéséről*, 16–18; Antal Meszlényi, ed., *A magyar katolikus egyház és az emberi jogok védelme* (Budapest: Szent István Társulat, 1947), 21–30; John F. Morley, "*Pope Pius XII, Roman Catholic Policy, and the Holocaust in Hungary: An Analysis of Le Saint Siège et les victimes de la guerre, janvier 1944–juillet 1945*," in *Pope Pius XII and the Holocaust*, ed. Carol Rittner and John K. Roth (London: Leicester University Press, 2002), 154–74.

138. The central organization of the movement, the World Council of Churches (WCC), was formally established in 1948. The central figure of the rescue operations was W. A. Visser't Hoof (1900–1985), who later became secretary general of the WCC.

139. For example, it was through their coordinated effort that the aid sent by the American Methodists, a half million pengős, reached Protestant organizations cooperating with the International Red Cross.

140. For details, see Tamás Majsai, "A magyarországi református egyház és a 'svájci' ökumené a Soáh idején," in *The Holocaust in Hungary: Fifty Years Later*, ed. Randolph L. Braham and Attila Pók (New York: Columbia University Press, 1997), 457–509. On the attitude of the Hungarian Calvinists, see Tamás Majsai, "Bíborosok és püspökök a zsidómentés barikádharcában," *Budapesti Negyed* 3, no. 2 (1995), 176–80.

## CHAPTER 10
# JEWS IN POSTWAR HUNGARY

SURVIVORS OF the Holocaust, hoping for a normal life after years of madness in Hungary, were disappointed. The Hungarian Communist Party gradually extended its control over the country after 1945, relying on the Soviet army for support. Using illegal and violent means, the communists undermined their major opponent, the Independent Smallholders' Party, which achieved a landslide victory in 1945 with 57 percent of the vote. In 1947, the communists won the election through fraud. By the second half of 1948, the Hungarian Workers' Party, created through a merger of the Communist and Social Democratic parties, no longer had any opponents. Backed by the Soviets and in line with Stalin's expectations, the single-party system was born. Hungary became a Soviet satellite state. Years of total communist dictatorship began under **Mátyás Rákosi**. The state once again began brutally oppressing its citizens, Jews and Christians alike. The population's desperation broke out in the 1956 anti-Stalinist revolution and battle for freedom. The Soviet army put down the revolt. Moscow appointed a new leader, János Kádár, who established a dictatorial system that slowly and gradually eased up until the 1989–1990 fall of the communist empire. The change of regime and creation of a multiparty parliamentary democracy marked the beginning of a new era for Hungary and its Jewish community. This chapter focuses on the situation for Jews and the memory of the Holocaust in postwar Hungary.

## LIBERATION

Out of the 760,000 to 780,000 Hungarian citizens labeled as Jewish in 1944, only about 250,000 survived the Holocaust. The largest survivor group included those people liberated in Budapest: close to seventy thousand in the large ghetto and around fifty thousand in the international ghetto and in hiding. Jewish survivors of the concentration camps and former labor servicemen numbered altogether about 100,000 to 130,000 people.[1]

László Keller was one of them. He and another prisoner known as Feri ended up in Waldlager V Ampfing, a subcamp of Dachau/Mühldorf, in the last weeks before the liberation. The prisoners worked on building an underground aircraft factory in the forest. Many of them perished due to poor housing and a lack of food, as well as the inhumane treatment meted out by the camp commander and prisoner functionaries. The U.S. Army finally liberated Ampfing on May 2, 1945.[2] A day later, Public Health Team No. 2 of the U.S. Third Army arrived at the camp and described what they saw:

> Here on double-deck wooden beds—mere wooden slabs covered with filthy straw—were gaunt shadows of men with shaved heads, showing their ulcerated legs, the unhealed whiplashes across their backs. They all had pale faces and puffy ankles, the protein-deficient flesh that was unable to recuperate from even minor wounds. Numbers were tattooed on their forearms or across their chests. [. . .] On both sides of a rectangular space were triple shelves, bare wooden planks. In the center, three wooden poles supported the ceiling. At the far end a nude skeleton sat on a barrel with a plank across it. He was supported by another skeleton who was standing; rather, they leaned against each other in order not to fall down. Bloody excrement was spattered around the barrel. We walked around the planks on the muddy floor. The shelves were filled with what had been men.

---

1. Randolph L. Braham, *The Politics of Genocide: The Holocaust in Hungary* (New York: Columbia University Press, 1994), 2:1298–300.

2. On Ampfing, see *The United States Holocaust Memorial Museum Encyclopedia of Camps and Ghettos, 1933–1945*, vol. 1: *Early Camps, Youth Camps, and Concentration Camps and Subcamps under the SS-Business Administration Main Office (WVHA)*, ed. Geoffrey P. Megargee (Bloomington: Indiana University Press in association with the USHMM, 2009), 501; HJA, DEGOB Protocols, nos. 114, 1530, and 2977. Leslie (Les, László) Keller (1927?–1998) lived in the ghetto of his hometown, Nagyvárad, for a brief period from May 1944 before his deportation to Auschwitz. In January 1945 he was sent on to Dachau and then to the subcamp Waldlager V Ampfing. Feri may have been Szeged native Ferenc Isaak Weiszfeiler (a.k.a. Volgyi) (1912?–1980), who arrived in Dachau in November 1944. See *USHMM ITS Collection Data Base Central Name Index.*

Their bodies were naked or only partly covered by a scrap of tattered, dirty, gray blanket. Their bodies were no more than skin stretched over bone; their knees were the thickest portion of their legs. Their shaved heads hung limply, eyes staring out of hollow sockets, noses abnormally prominent against the fleshless faces. Mouths were open, dry, red. [. . .] Some had enough strength to turn and extend their hands in our direction; some just lay, staring with unseeing eyes and barely breathing.³

DOCUMENT 10-1: László Keller (left) and a fellow prisoner named Feri (right) in the Ampfing concentration camp after the liberation, May 4, 1945, USHMMPA WS# 67871.

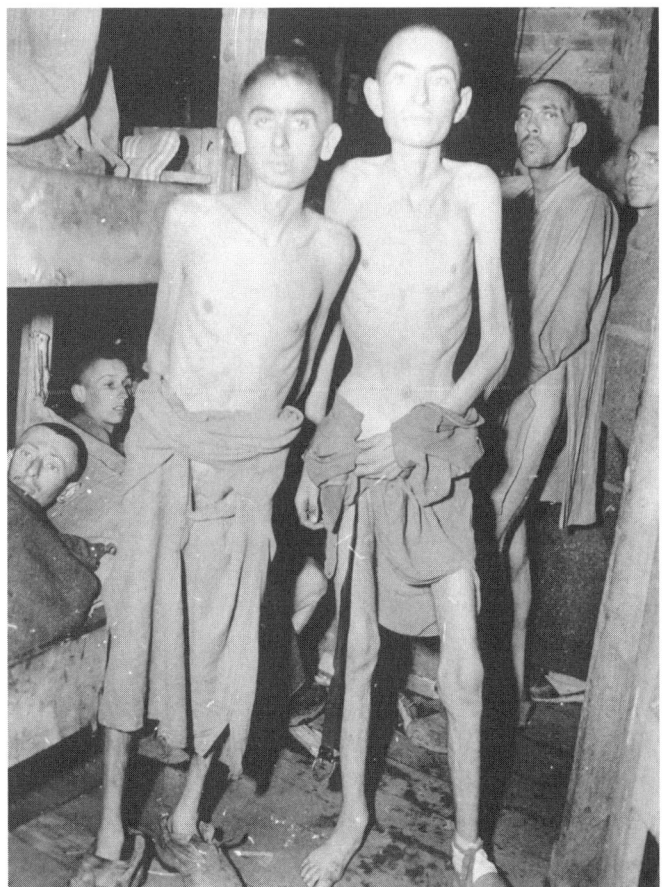

---

3. Michael B. Shimkin, "An Incident at Ampfing," *Scientific Monthly* 63, no. 4 (October 1946): 285–86.

Close to the end, a typhus epidemic broke out, claiming the lives of many prisoners in Ampfing. Keller and Feri both survived beyond liberation; Keller ultimately emigrated to the United States.

The Red Army liberated Pauline Fabri, another survivor, in Budapest.[4] She took detailed notes of her life between November 16, 1944, and January 18, 1945, and included them in the memoirs she penned after the liberation in 1945–1946, while still in Budapest. **Arrow Cross** authorities had forced Pauline to leave the home she had owned for thirty years and move to a "**yellow-star house**" at the end of June 1944. They deported her mother and younger brother's family from the provinces to Auschwitz. Pauline survived Arrow Cross rule and the siege in buildings protected by Swiss and Swedish diplomats. Her memoirs provide a detailed account of the hardships facing the Jewish community of Budapest just before and after liberation. Having lost several family members and nearly all of her possessions, she was among those who sought an opportunity to leave the country immediately. After some unsuccessful attempts, she acquired permission to immigrate to the United States, settled in New York, got married, and had two sons.

DOCUMENT 10-2: **Memoirs of Pauline Fabri, Budapest, June 1945–January 1946, USHMMA Acc. 2007.168 Pauline Widder Fabri diary.**

> January 12, 1945, Friday, at night [when] I was watching the fires from the staircase I heard clearly on the reinforced loudspeakers of the Russian radio as if it were a message from Heaven: "The battle for Budapest is nearing its end."[5] I darted to my roommates with the news. On this Friday I noted: "I have no food." Margit gave me a few beans of roasted ersatz coffee and we were chewing them and then I ate a tiny bit of the minuscule piece of chocolate that I always carried in my pocket to stave off [. . .] actual starvation.
>
> January 14, 1945, Sunday [. . .] The important thing was, when will the Russians come into our building, when will we be liberated? [. . .] Since Christmas we were waiting for them daily with trepidation, but the thing dragged on. We set dates. When we saw that Budapest wasn't occupied on the second day of Christmas, we said, they certainly mean Russian

---

4. Pauline (Paula) Fabri (née Widder; 1883–1956) was born in Boldogkőváralja (today in northeastern Hungary). See donor file, USHMMA Acc. 2007.168.

5. In the original the words are given in German (translator's comment).

Christmas or again they are thinking of New Year,[6] but of course they want to take it on Russian New Year.[7] We thus waited, hoped for them, in the meantime watching the strengthening or weakening of the bombardment, arguing whether this or that was an incoming or outgoing explosion. [. . .] The pessimist considered each explosion outgoing; the optimist incoming.

[. . .] It was the night of January 15 to the 16th, when I became aware that someone was banging on the apartment door. The engineer who slept in the entrance hall [. . .] opened the door and spoke French with someone. I immediately connected and yelled out loud: the Russians are here! Some 12 people slept in the room; they all jumped up and in the next moment a young Russian soldier came in carrying his lamp. This was an historic moment! We all jumped up, surrounded him, caressed him, and all but embraced him. [. . .]

January 16th, 1945 [. . .] The apartment was in an indescribable condition.[8] Everything from the closets [was] on the floor, whatever [the soldiers] left there and couldn't carry away. Valuable and worthless paper, rags, china, glass shards. Goods were lying ankle deep on the floor. There were no windows, doors were wide open, water frozen in the bathtub. Of the huge quantity of food which I had left there, hardly anything was left, because the German-Hungarian soldiers lived there. Even so we did not dare to touch anything because it could well have been bloody or infected with lice.

[. . .]

Mrs. Fenyő[9] did not have to sleep in the apartment partly because of the still audible firing but mostly because of the Russians who at the moment still attacked the houses at night, shot their way in if they were not admitted, and tried to carry off the women. [. . .]

Nonetheless, the night was very active and scary, when I heard banging on the door downstairs. It didn't seem to stop, so the house guard finally had to open it and I heard them as they were walking through the hallways with the drunken Russian soldiers, stopping in front of our door, explaining that there was nobody in there. I remember I thought this

---

6. January 7.
7. January 13.
8. This was the apartment in the "yellow-star house" in which Pauline left her belongings and furniture when she was forced to move to another designated building.
9. An acquaintance of the Fabri family.

was the end of me and I tied a babushka over my head in order to look even more ancient.[10] Women thought to walk around with babushkas on, which made them look as ugly and unkempt as possible, was a life-saving strategy even in the daytime, and they were right.

For Jews in Hungary, the Soviet victory meant liberation and instant cessation of the immediate lethal danger they had faced. Nonetheless, for the civilian population as a whole, the end of the fighting resulted in a new series of ordeals. Soviet troops brought inordinate suffering to the country. They killed thousands of civilians, raped tens of thousands of girls and women,[11] and took hundreds of thousands of Hungarians to labor camps in the Soviet Union, in which tens of thousands of them died.[12]

The Soviet authorities did not distinguish between captured labor servicemen and Hungarian soldiers.[13] Troops carried off thousands of concentration camp survivors to Soviet POW camps, many of whom never returned home.[14] Looting, abusive Soviet soldiers inquired about neither their victims' religion and ancestry nor their war experiences. For example, the soldiers who liberated Hungarian-Israeli writer Ephraim Kishon also robbed him and then took him away for forced labor.[15] Hilda Löbl, who was hiding in the capital during the Arrow Cross era, recalled the day when she tried to tidy up her looted and partially bombed apartment: "There are drunk [Soviet] soldiers coming in and shooting randomly [. . .] I have to hide in the cabinet again. I sit there and feel a great pang. I am hiding from the Russians, I must hide—me? Us?"[16]

---

10. Headscarf (Russian, literally "grandmother").

11. Several eyewitness accounts of these crimes are quoted and discussed by Krisztián Ungváry, *Budapest ostroma*, 5th rev. ed. (Budapest: Corvina, 2005), 281–95.

12. Tamás Stark, "Magyarok szovjet kényszermunkatáborokban," *Kortárs*, nos. 2–3 (2002): 81. According to recent reserach, a total of 550,000 Hungarian POWs and civilians ended up in Soviet camps (including Jewish labor servicemen), where about 65,000 of them perished. See Éva Mária Varga, *Magyar hadifoglyok és internáltak a Szovjetunióban az oroszországi levéltári források tükrében (1941–1956)*. PhD diss., ELTE, 2008, 126.

13. László Karsai, *Holokauszt* (Budapest: Pannonica, 2001), 222.

14. After the war, **Miksa Domonkos**, a former employee of the **Jewish Council**, estimated the number of former labor servicemen in the Soviet Union at twenty-five thousand, but this number did not include those who had been dragged off from Hungary. A Jewish Telegraphic Agency report estimated the number of Hungarian Jewish women taken to Soviet camps at about ten thousand. Eugene Duschinsky, "Hungary," in *The Jews in the Soviet Satellites*, ed. Peter Meyer et al. (Syracuse, NY: Syracuse University Press, 1953), 392–95.

15. Ephraim Kishon, *Hogy volt? A nagy lebőgés oknyomozó története* (Budapest: Officina Nova, 1992), 12–15.

16. The recollection of Hilda Löbl is in the possession of and translated by the authors.

## THE DIMENSIONS OF DESTRUCTION

Between 1941 and 1945, the German Nazis and their Hungarian collaborators murdered about half a million people, two-thirds of the Jewish population living in the wartime territory of Hungary.[17] At least 300,000 to 345,000 were murdered in the gas chambers upon arrival in Birkenau. Tens of thousands of additional men, women, and children perished due to starvation, epidemics, maltreatment, pseudomedical experiments, slave labor, and "selections" throughout the web of the Nazi ghettos and concentration camps.[18] The Statistical Department of the Hungarian Representation of the World Jewish Congress estimates that 78 percent of the Jews in provincial regions of **post-Trianon Hungary** perished. In Budapest, this figure stood at 52 percent.[19] After the war, the survivors reorganized less than half the congregations, which encompassed only a fraction of their original membership.[20] Moreover, many of them soon dissolved again because of emigration and migration to the capital and a few other large cities. These centers offered more protection, social support, and job opportunities for survivors. Therefore, the urban concentration that had long characterized Hungarian Jewish life during the modern era increased even further. Some 150,000 Jews still lived in Hungary in 1949, with 75 percent of them in Budapest.[21]

The Jewish community's profile had drastically altered through the years of war and persecution: rebirth appeared a distant prospect. Far more women than men remained among the survivors. Furthermore, youth under age

---

17. For the estimates ranging from 440,000 to 564,000, see Tamás Stark, *Zsidóság a vészkorszakban és a felszabadulás után 1939–1955* (Budapest: Magyar Tudományos Akadémia Történettudományi Intézete, 1995), 76–89, and Braham, *The Politics of Genocide*, 2:1295–301.

18. For the number of Hungarian victims in various concentration camps, see chapter 7.

19. Braham, *The Politics of Genocide*, 2:1299–301.

20. In 1948, out of 275 congregations of post-Trianon provinces, 185 (67 percent) had fewer than one hundred members. Kinga Frojimovics, *Szétszakadt történelem. Zsidó vallási irányzatok Magyarországon 1868–1950* (Budapest: Balassi, 2008), 378.

21. The 1949 census found 133,862 people of Jewish religion (75,721 women and 58,141 men) in Hungary, out of whom 101,259 lived in the capital. József Kepecs, ed., *A zsidó népesség száma településenként (1840–1941)* (Budapest: Központi Statisztikai Hivatal, 1993), 7. If we consider the number of converts and the fact that in 1949 probably quite a few Jews did not want the census to show their religion, we can estimate the total Jewish population at about 150,000.

twenty had practically disappeared: four out of five Jewish children had perished.[22] However, some regional differences within this general picture emerge. In Budapest and those few other communities partly spared deportation to Auschwitz, the survival rate of women, children, and the elderly was much higher. In most of the provinces, by contrast, former labor servicemen constituted the largest (and sometimes the only) survivor group. The survivor population now contained many widows, widowers, and orphans, and the traditional extended family networks had been largely destroyed.[23] Many survivors suffered from severe physical ailments and mental disturbances and depended on healthcare assistance and social aid.[24] Their assets had for the most part fallen prey to state and private theft and the destructive force of the war. The partial revival of the Hungarian Jewish communities and institutions would thus have been impossible without the extensive help of international Jewish organizations, especially the American Jewish Joint Distribution Committee.[25]

The Jewish communal infrastructure had been dismantled: hundreds of synagogues, prayer houses, and community buildings had been looted or destroyed.[26] The famous **Orthodox** synagogue in the eastern Hungarian city of Mád, built in the late 1790s, shared this fate. Ninety percent of Mád's Jews were murdered during the Holocaust. The survivors, a mere thirty or forty people, revived the community after the war, but in the 1950s it ceased to exist altogether. The picture reproduced in document 10-3 shows Dávid Teitelbaum

---

22. Only 21.4 percent of them survived. László Csorba, "Izrealita felekezeti élet Magyarországon a vészkorszaktól a nyolcvanas évekig," in *Hét évtized a hazai zsidóság életében*, ed. László Bányai et al. (Budapest: MTA Filozófiai Intézet, 1990), 1:63.

23. In Budapest, half of the children and youth died; in the provinces, 87 percent perished. Of those over sixty, 90 percent in the provinces and 31 percent in Budapest did not survive. Frojimovics, *Szétszakadt történelem*, 374–75; Braham, *The Politics of Genocide*, 2:1299; Viktor Karády, "Szociológiai kísérlet a magyar zsidóság 1945 és 1956 közötti helyzetének elemzésére," in *Zsidóság az 1945 utáni Magyarországon* (Paris: Magyar Füzetek, 1984), 71. On the so-called Strasshof deportation and the chances for survival there, see document 4-6.

24. István Kulcsár, "A maradék zsidóság lelki keresztmetszete 1946-ban," *Thalassa* 5 (1994): 334–36.

25. Besides the Joint, other international and Hungarian organizations and government bodies also played an important role, including the Jewish Agency, the Hebrew Immigrant Aid Society (HIAS), the Red Cross, the **National Committee of Hungarian Jews for Attending Deportees (DEGOB)**, the **Government Commissariat for Repatriation**, and the Office of People's Care. Csorba, "Izrealita felekezeti élet Magyarországon," 1:65.

26. On the destruction of community property (synagogues, cemeteries, archives, libraries, liturgical objects, etc.), see Csorba, "Izrealita felekezeti élet Magyarországon," 1:66, and esp. Zsuzsanna Toronyi, ed., *Zsidó közösségek öröksége* (Budapest: Magyar Zsidó Levéltár, 2010).

amid the ruins of the Mád synagogue, holding destroyed Torah scrolls in his hands. Teitelbaum descended from a prominent local family instrumental in the erection of the building.

DOCUMENT 10-3: **Dávid Teitelbaum in the destroyed Mád synagogue, 1946–1947, HJA XXII-IV.65.**

The Mád synagogue was partially rebuilt at the end of the 1970s. Completely renovated soon after 2000, it became one of the region's tourist attractions. No Jewish community remains in Mád today.

In the immediate postwar years, the remaining and reviving Jewish communities had to face more than the obvious challenges (poverty, survivors' physical and psychological difficulties, a destroyed community infrastructure, and so forth). The new situation also gave rise to new halachic (religious legal) questions. Was it permissible to sell a synagogue if the majority of a community had perished and the few remaining survivors were unable to sustain the building? What should happen to those thousands of women whose husbands had disappeared but who lacked clear evidence that the men had died (according to halachic law they were still bound by the marriage).[27] Another group

---

27. On these problems, see Frojimovics, *Szétszakadt történelem*, 407–16.

of such questions cropped up around commemoration of the victims: for instance, **Neologue** and Orthodox Jews could not agree on the proposed date for a memorial day.[28]

The Sárbogárd Jewish community wished (as did many other revived congregations) to erect a memorial bearing the victims' names. Soon the question arose about whether a Jewish religious community could appropriately list the names of those who had converted to Christianity but were murdered because of their Jewish roots. Religious Jews, regardless of whether they were part of the Neologue or Orthodox communities, usually condemned conversion deeply.[29] The Neologue congregation of Kecskemét titled the registry of the converts the *Registry of the Deceased*, indicating that they were "dead" to the community.[30] In 1944 the Budapest Jewish Council published in its official journal numerous articles against the conversions. However, many converts had obviously shared the Israelites' fate and been murdered by the tens of thousands between 1941 and 1945 because of their Jewish origins. The Sárbogárd Jewish community wanted a sound answer to this question and sent its inquiry about the issue to both the Neologue and the Orthodox rabbis. Their answers follow in document 10-4(A, B).

DOCUMENT 10-4(A): **Letter of the Central Office of the Autonomous Orthodox Israelite Denomination of Hungary to the Sárbogárd Jewish community, September 19, 1947, USHMMA RG 39.013M, reel 107 (HJA XV-B Sárbogárd, box TA 6/5/5).**

To the Orthodox Israelite Congregation
Sárbogárd.

In response to your inquiry, we inform you that we presented your request to the rabbinical council. The decision has been made that the names of those who converted due to fear of deportation, labor service, or other threats to life can be put on the memorial.

With a coreligionist's greetings,
Central Office of the Autonomous Orthodox Israelite
Denomination of Hungary

[signed] Samu Kahán-Frankl[31]
President

---

28. Ibid., 408–9.
29. For Jewish attitudes toward conversions, see Miklós Konrád, "Vallásváltás és identitás. A kitért zsidók megítélésének változásai a dualizmus korában," *Századok* 144, no. 1 (2010): 3–46.
30. *Halottak jegyzéke*, HJA XV-B Kecskemét, box E 6/3.
31. For Kahán-Frankl, see the glossary.

DOCUMENT 10-4(B): **Letter of the National Association of Rabbis to the Sárbogárd Jewish community, January 9, 1948, USHMMA RG 39.013M, reel 107 (HJA XV-B Sárbogárd, box TA 6/5/5).**[32]

> To the Presidium of the Sárbogárd Israelite Congregation
> Sárbogárd
> In response to your inquiry about whether it is permissible to commemorate those Jews who converted to Christianity in 1936–1940 on the memorial of the victims of the Labor Service and deportation, we inform you that, while these people's act was inappropriate from a religious point of view, their names can still be listed on the memorial. We have to assume that since they must have been convinced that their apostasy was unsuccessful, they retrospectively regretted it and considered themselves members of the Jewish people. The time of their conversion was the time of severe persecutions.
> With a coreligionist's greetings,
> National Beth Din
> [signed] Dr. Ernő Róth[33]
> President

The Neologue rabbis drew the line at 1936. It is unclear why they picked that year, for Hungary's anti-Jewish legislation was launched in 1938. It might have been a simple mistake in the letter. The memorial plaque could not name anyone who had converted before that date, though. We do not know exactly how many of the converted Hungarian Jews who died during the Holocaust had changed religions before 1936 (or 1938). Their number probably amounted to thousands.[34] The Orthodox rabbis' reasoning is similar but not identical to that of their Neologue counterparts. The memorial could list the names of those who converted not for religious conviction but out of fear. The Orthodox did not indicate a precise date but mentioned the life-threatening factors that had come into play, such as deportation and induction into the **Labor Service**. Obviously they did not include anti-Jewish legislation as an "acceptable" reason to convert. Therefore their decision was—understandably—stricter than that of the Neologues.

---

32. This rabbinical council included Neologue and Status Quo rabbis. Frojimovics, *Szétszakadt történelem*, 407.

33. Dr. Ernő Róth (also Abraham Naftali Zwi Roth, 1908–1991), an eminent scholar of Jewish religious law (*Halakha*), member of the Pest Jewish community, and director of the Rabbinical Seminary, eventually left Hungary in the autumn of 1956, along with thousands of other Jews. See Kinga Frojimovics et al., *Jewish Budapest: Monuments, Rites, History* (1995; Budapest: Central European University Press, 1999), 212.

34. For the legal definition of "Jew" and the conversions, see chapter 1.

## TO LEAVE OR TO STAY?

One of the most pressing dilemmas facing survivors after liberation was whether to stay in the country or to emigrate. A U.S. Army officer tried to convince sixteen-year-old future Nobel laureate Imre Kertész not to return to Hungary. Kertész thanked him and then went back to Budapest to find his family. Unlike him, many people liberated outside Hungary never returned. After living in displaced persons (DP) camps or hospitals for months and even years, they decided to stay away for good. Others, hoping for a new beginning, went home. Many people, who had considered themselves "Jewish Hungarians" before the persecution, felt that they could never make Hungary their home again. Some became Zionists, leaving for Palestine (as of 1948, Israel). Others also chose emigration but headed west (to Great Britain, the United States, or Canada).

Alexander (Sándor) Feuer was among those who decided to emigrate to the United States. The Hungarian authorities deported him from the Transylvanian city of Szatmárnémeti, where he had been born in 1929, to Auschwitz in May 1944. Feuer survived the selection and was sent to perform slave labor in the Kaufering camp system, from which he escaped a few days before liberation. After the war he spent some time in a DP camp and a children's home in Germany. He left for American shores from Bremen, Germany, in September 1947.

DOCUMENT 10-5: **Embarkation card issued to Alexander Feuer indicating his place on the SS *Marine Flasher*, USHMMPA WS# 02110.**

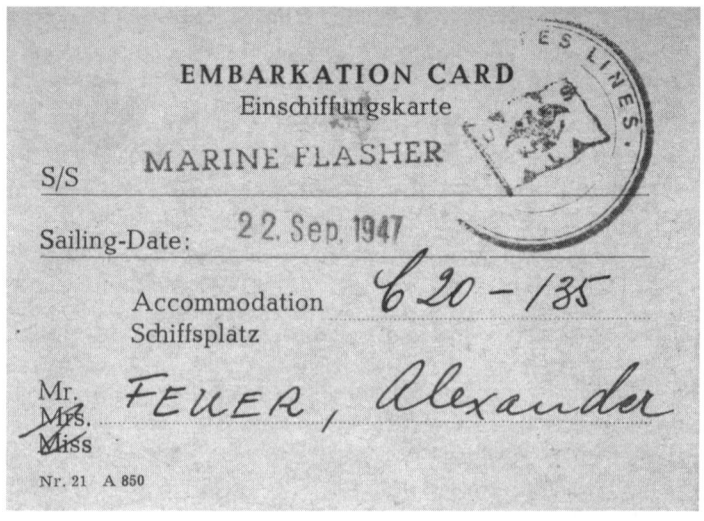

Through 1957, thirty to fifty thousand Jews left Hungary for various destinations. Nevertheless, proportionately far fewer Jews emigrated from Hungary in this period than from Czechoslovakia, Romania, Bulgaria, or Poland,[35] perhaps because most survivors came from Budapest. In the capital, the integrated and acculturated Neologue tradition had always had strong roots. Thousands thus stayed in Hungary, hoping for a new beginning and expecting the system that replaced **Miklós Horthy**'s regime to ensure a normal life for them. Many of them tried to forget everything and refused to talk to their children about their Jewish ancestry and the traumas they had endured.[36]

## REHABILITATION, RESTITUTION, POGROMS

The political system established in postwar Hungary under Allied control was initially a multiparty, parliamentary democracy before transforming into a communist dictatorship in 1948 to 1949. The newly formed Interim National Government of Hungary took significant steps that furnished hope among many survivors for at least partial reconciliation.[37] According to the armistice agreement signed in Moscow in January 1945, one of the government's first tasks was to revoke the anti-Jewish legislation of the past years. In March 1945, it issued Prime Minister's Decree 200/1945, which declared all anti-Jewish laws null and condemned the persecution of the Jews.[38] Legally, the Jews became equal citizens again. The first freely elected government (1945 to 1947) followed this line: high-ranking politicians issued frequent public declarations against antisemitism.[39] In the summer of 1946, the Ministry of Religion and Education issued a special decree stipulating that schools had to deal with the topic of "contemptible antisemitism." Symbolically, Prime Minister Ferenc

---

35. Karády, "Szociológiai kísérlet a magyar zsidóság," 63, 104.

36. On the survivors' trauma-management mechanisms and identity issues, see Viktor Karády, *Önazonosítás, sorsválasztás. A zsidó csoportazonosság történelmi alakváltozásai Magyarországon* (Budapest: Új Mandátum, 2001), 77–96, 263–95.

37. The Interim National Government was set up in December 1944 in the Hungarian territories occupied by the Soviet army. It was a coalition established on an anti-Nazi platform but was politically very heterogeneous. It included, for example, a Holocaust perpetrator in the person of the former head of the **gendarmerie**, **Gábor Faragho**, but also the communist Imre Nagy.

38. Prime Minister's Decree 200/1945, May 17, 1945, *Magyarországi Rendeletek Tára, 1945* (Budapest: Szikra, 1946), 1:28–30.

39. See, e.g., the declarations of President Zoltán Tildy (*Kis Ujság*, May 28, 1946) and Prime Ministers Ferenc Nagy (*Magyar Nemzet*, August 5, 1946) and Lajos Dinnyés (*Magyar Nemzet*, June 17, 1947).

Nagy personally supervised the restoration of two destroyed synagogues.[40] This and subsequent governments had a threefold duty in their approach to Jewish survivors: legal rehabilitation, economic and financial compensation and restitution, and the protection of Jews from postwar antisemitism. Of these, we can assess only one component, their legal rehabilitation, as more or less successful.

The most important element of the legal rehabilitation was Act XXV of 1946 (document 10-6). The parliament, the site in previous years of fiercely antisemitic exhortations, passed a law that firmly and clearly condemned the persecution of the Jews and took steps toward economic rehabilitation as well. However, these latter provisions remained far from complete.

DOCUMENT 10-6: **Act XXV of 1946 condemning the persecution of the Jews, November 15, 1946,** in *1946. évi törvényczikkek* **[Acts of 1946] (Budapest: Franklin, n.d.), 104–8.**

> 1. § (1) The National Assembly of Hungary solemnly states the following, concerning all the orders based on foreign influence and measures of the former regime that deprived a part of the population of the country—on account of their Israelite religion and Jewish origin—of their rights, violated their human dignity, and eventually led to the annihilation of most of them, largely in foreign camps: these orders and measures go against the eternal principles of humanity, the moral convictions of the Hungarian people, and the spirit of the Hungarian law. It is with utter contempt that the National Assembly condemns these orders and measures.
>
> (2) Remembering those decrees and orders of democratic governments, which revoked all the barbaric regulations of foreign origin that relied on faulty reasoning to support racial persecution, unfairly punishing a valuable and patriotic part of the population, orders that restored legal equality and thereby established the legal grounds for reparations: the National Assembly simultaneously expresses the appreciation and gratitude of the Hungarian people to all those who bravely defied external and internal intimidation and selflessly stood on the side of their persecuted fellow human beings, all those who were willing to make sacrifices and thereby saved many thousands of human lives from destruction.[41] With this, the resistance of the entire Hungarian people has been expressed,[42]

---

40. Csorba, "Izrealita felekezeti élet Magyarországon," 1:85.
41. On the Hungarian population's rescue efforts, see chapter 9.
42. With this illogical twist, the law projected the bravery of those few who actually defied the Nazis on all of Hungarian society.

which stood in the way of the reactionary regime, preventing the thoroughgoing implementation of the national socialist brutality of racial persecution up until the German occupation and state violence became complete.[43] This resistance has made it clear that the Hungarian people do not identify with racial persecution.

[. . .]

The act's indisputable merit was that it condemned the persecution of the Jews. However, it formed part of the false narrative according to which Hungarian society had heroically resisted the Nazis and their Hungarian henchmen and anti-Jewish legislation had resulted from foreign intervention. As we have seen in chapter 1, while it is true that the Nazi Nuremberg laws served as a model for the 1941 Third "Jewish Law," until 1941–1942 Nazi Germany had exerted no pressure on Hungary to pass antisemitic legal measures. The discriminatory legislation launched in 1938 was a genuine product of Hungarian politics. Furthermore, the Hungarian parliament passed one of the first antisemitic laws in interwar Europe (the so-called ***numerus clausus***) in 1920. Hungary, like most nations in postwar Europe, was not ready to confront its responsibility. (Similarly, for example, Austrians long held to the myth that they were "Hitler's first victims.") In addition, Hungarian domestic policy makers had always had an eye on the peace negotiations at the end of the war and hoped to create a positive international picture of Hungary. Therefore, the government made serious efforts to show the world that Hungary's interwar political elite, a handful of Arrow Cross lunatics, Nazi Germany, and the ethnic Germans of Hungary were alone responsible for what had happened during the war.

The work of the **people's courts**, the legal bodies that tried those charged with war crimes, reflected this effort. In addition to holding the guilty responsible, the courts also aimed at discrediting the entire Horthy regime. In the legal and procedural sense, the people's courts' measures raised a number of questions. They automatically classified simple members of the pro-Nazi, ethnic German social organization (Volksbund), as well as Hungarian Germans conscripted by the Waffen-SS, as potential war criminals, regardless of whether they had joined these organizations or troops voluntarily or under pressure. A similar policy applied to a large number of bureaucrats promoted after **Ferenc**

---

43. The "reactionary regime" meant Horthy and his consecutive governments. According to the text, the Hungarian people had prevented the ghettoization and deportation of the Jews before the German occupation. However, it was Horthy and a small circle of politicians who, as of the spring of 1942, defied German demands. This was, of course, impossible to integrate into the narrative of the law, according to which the country's few leaders acting on foreign orders had carried out the persecution of the Jews.

**Szálasi**'s seizure of power, regardless of whether these people had committed any crimes. In some cases the interrogators beat and tortured a defendant, forcing a false confession.

These deficits notwithstanding, the people's courts called to account many of those responsible for the disenfranchisement and persecution of the Jews, providing significant moral compensation for the survivors. Between 1945 and 1950, the courts tried about 60,000 people, finding around 27,000 guilty; first instance courts sentenced to death 477 people, of whom 189 were actually executed.[44] Among them were four prime ministers: **Béla Imrédy**, who played a major role in preparing and passing the "Jewish Laws"; **László Bárdossy**, premier at the time of the Kamenets-Podolski and Újvidék massacres; the head of the 1944 collaborationist government, **Döme Sztójay**; and Arrow Cross "Leader of the Nation" Ferenc Szálasi. Gallows awaited the state secretaries in charge of the deportations, **László Endre** and **László Baky**, and also their former boss, Minister of the Interior **Andor Jaross**. Other dramatis personae of the Hungarian Jews' destruction were executed as well: for example, the liaison officer between **Sondereinsatzkommando Eichmann** and the Hungarian authorities, Lieutenant Colonel **László Ferenczy**; the head of the "Hungarian Gestapo," **Péter Hain**; and Arrow Cross mass murderer and former monk András Kun. Many war criminals, former members of murder squads, and Arrow Cross Party servicemen also received capital punishment.[45] Some Hungarian perpetrators were tried and sentenced outside Hungary.[46]

The trials generally did not focus on the Holocaust, although the courtroom proceedings mentioned the antisemitic legislation, looting,

---

44. See László Karsai, "The People's Courts and Revolutionary Justice in Hungary, 1945–46," in *The Politics of Retribution in Europe: World War II and Its Aftermath*, ed. István Deák, Jan T. Gross, and Tony Judt (Princeton, NJ: Princeton University Press, 2000), 233–51.

45. Besides the trials, about forty thousand people were interned without being convicted, and sixty-two thousand public servants were dismissed. Two hundred thousand ethnic Germans, held collectively guilty for war crimes, were expelled from the country. All in all, close to four hundred thousand people (about 10 percent of Hungarian men and 4 percent of the entire population) suffered some kind of punishment. Postwar political cleansing was more severe than in some other European countries. At the same time, lynchings and other illegal punishments inflicted upon real or alleged collaborators were a rarity in Hungary, unlike, for example, in France or Italy. For details, see István Deák, "Elnyomás vagy megtorlás? Háborús bűnösök perei a második világháború utáni Magyarországon," in *2000*, no. 3 (1998): 6–10.

46. For example, the perpetrators of the Újvidék massacre (e.g., Ferenc Feketehalmy-Czeydner, József Grassy, and Márton Zöldi) were executed in Yugoslavia. Many former members of the Hungarian law enforcement and administration bodies in Transylvania were sentenced and executed in Romania.

disenfranchisement, and deportation of Jews many times. The hearings placed more emphasis on Hungary's role in World War II, its relations with Germany, and the destruction of the country during the Arrow Cross regime.[47] In the new system's narrative, the Hungarian nation in its entirety was a victim, leaving no real room for showcasing the uniqueness of Jewish suffering.[48] As the communists gradually took over, these trials gave ever less weight to anti-Jewish persecution. The focus turned from war criminals to "enemies of the people," as the communists labeled their opponents. Still, many survivors felt that after a long wait, they were finally getting some justice.

While the legal rehabilitation of Jews was soon complete, restitution of their looted assets remained far from satisfactory. Due to the postwar economic crisis and strained social climate, consecutive governments did not risk the political explosion and immense loss of popularity that implementation of a real restitution process for formerly Jewish-owned property would have produced. However, the men steering Hungarian foreign policy perceived that wide-scale financial restitution might help improve the country's international image and even lead to a more favorable outcome in the peace negotiations. This question ultimately played no role in Hungary's treatment in Paris, but it nonetheless pushed the government to implement restitution measures. Many members of the new political elite thought it imperative to find some solution to the problem of plundered Jewish assets. Moreover, Article 27 of the 1947 Peace Treaty of Paris obliged Hungary to return property confiscated from Jews after September 1, 1939. As a result of all these factors, more than two hundred laws and decrees passed and issued from 1945 to 1948 aimed at restoring, even partially, the looted assets of Jews.[49]

The regulations proved highly controversial. In the summer of 1946, the umbrella organization of the Neologue communities, the National Office of

---

47. For the analysis of the Sztójay trial from this aspect, see László Karsai and Judit Molnár, eds., *A magyar Qusiling-kormány. Sztójay Döme és társai a népbíróság előtt* (Budapest: 1956-os KHT, 2004), 70–84.

48. The war crime cases were largely over by the early 1950s. The last of such trials occurred in the late 1960s and early 1970s. In the most important of these late cases, former members of the Arrow Cross group of Budapest's Municipal District XIV were sentenced in the summer of 1967. Three defendants were executed, while the others received long prison sentences. For the details, see József Sólyom and László Szabó, *A zuglói nyilasper* (Budapest: Kossuth, 1967).

49. See the laws and decrees issued in 1945–1946, in Endre Déry et al., *A fasizmus üldözötteit védő jogszabályok 1945–1946* (Budapest: American Jewish Joint Distribution Committee Magyarországi Bizottsága, 1946).

Hungarian Israelites,[50] summarized the main problems with the legislation and how the compensation and restitution process was put into practice.

**DOCUMENT 10-7: Memorandum of the National Office of Hungarian Israelites on restitution and compensation issues, summer 1946, HJA XXIV-A (XXIII-5-b), box 3.**

[. . .]

The Hungarian government has never denied that the spirit of antisemitism continues to exist since the liberation. If we consider the fact that during hard times the Jews gave their property for safeguarding to those Christians who were (or were assumed to be) philosemites, and that after the liberation those returning asked for the items back, it is not baseless to presume that antisemitic thought has infected additional masses of people. Old antisemites did not learn and did not change, and many of those obliged to give the property back became antisemites.

The Hungarian government realized this and therefore very cautiously began the process of compensating Jews' material claims and grievances by passing laws and issuing decrees. The government assumed that continuously issuing acts favoring Jews would result in the increase of antisemitism. It is the peculiar misfortune of Jewish fate that this strange attitude cannot be labeled as completely without foundation. Jews are not able to reclaim their assets, looted movable property, apartments, [or] workshops without triggering the revenge and fury of disadvantaged non-Jews, and thus these Jews unwittingly increase antisemitism.

The government's aforementioned attitude is reflected in all the decrees and laws that have been issued since the liberation to rehabilitate the Jews legally and make redress for their losses and grievances. From the regulations regarding land reform and industry and trade,[51] through the restoration of licenses, settlement of apartment and shop disputes, etc., one might sense an involuntary negative compromise with the situation [by the government].[52] In the meantime, the interests of non-Jews

---

50. In 1950 it was merged into the new, unified Jewish umbrella organization, the National Representation of Hungarian Israelites.

51. If a plot of land was given to a farmer from the agricultural proletariat, the original Jewish owner could not reclaim it. Déry et al., *A fasizmus üldözötteit védő jogszabályok*, 37–38.

52. If a formerly Jewish-owned asset was "an object of essential everyday use," and the new owner did not actually steal it during the Holocaust, he or she could keep the item and was not obliged to give it back to its original owner. See ibid. Both examples show that the new regulation's tendency to allow for exemptions essentially led to the legalization of state robbery committed during the war.

who had come into possession [of formerly Jewish property] are given the greatest possible consideration, as are their investments and their future positions.

[. . .]

Based on this assessment, it is not surprising that according to the May 1946 joint declaration of the Jewish organizations, "the General Assembly of the Hungarian Jews regretfully establishes that the various decrees aiming at legal rehabilitations of Jews [. . .] contain such conditions that deprive the majority of Hungarian Jews from regaining their property and rights."[53] The problematic regulation did lead to a myriad of lawsuits. According to a 1947 estimate, close to one hundred thousand cases arose nationwide in which a survivor tried to get back the property that he or she had handed over to an acquaintance for safeguarding during the Holocaust.[54] Journalist József Pál calculated that in Budapest alone police investigated about sixty thousand ownership claims. He suggested that these cases added at least fifty thousand people to the ranks of postwar antisemites.[55]

Antipathy caused by efforts of Jews to reclaim their assets also served a psychological function, retroactively "justifying" previous anti-Jewish attitudes and looting. These property issues played a significant role in the outbursts of antisemitic violence after the war. In 1945 to 1947 several anti-Jewish atrocities of varying severity occurred in one of the largest waves of mass ethnic violence in modern Hungarian history. Apart from traditional anti-Jewish prejudices, economic and financial conflicts, political strife, and social tensions fueled these events. Many people did not want or were unable to give back formerly Jewish-owned real estate and assets obtained in various ways during the war. The economy of the war-torn country was sinking into a state of crisis never seen before, worsening the social climate. The country was in ruins: according to government sources, Hungary had lost 55 to 62 percent of its prewar national wealth.[56] Cash transactions had practically ceased, and one could only pay for goods and services with foreign currency, gold, or other goods and services. Extreme poverty fueled anger in a country that, in accordance with old patterns, found a ready scapegoat for all ailments in the Jews.

Politics further exacerbated the tension. As we have seen, antisemitism had deep roots in the political arena; perhaps only the Social Democratic Party was

---

53. *Új Élet*, May 9, 1946.
54. *Kis Ujság*, August 31, 1947.
55. *Haladás*, December 15, 1945.
56. Note on Hungary's wartime losses, HNA, KÜM Békeelőkészítő, reel 12,415, title 17, 115–20 and 177–98.

largely devoid of this strain. The communists wanted to increase their own membership and admitted en masse former, less prominent members of the Arrow Cross Party—the small fry—who tried to disguise their actions and prevent others from remembering their participation through newly acquired party membership. Moreover, Arrow Cross and communist ideologies were not nearly as dissimilar as many thought.[57]

Of several antisemitic incidents cropping up in this period, some twenty cases escalated into mass violence, plunder, devastation, or murder. The atrocities peaked between February and August 1946. Two factors explain this timing: Hungary was experiencing one of the largest-scale periods of inflation in world history (at the end of July 1946, prices increased on average by 158,486 percent every day).[58] Furthermore, food shortages also escalated in this period: before the harvest of 1946 a large part of the population in rural and urban areas alike faced famine.

The other factor was nakedly political: after their defeat in the free elections in November 1945, the Communist Party planned a counterattack against their strongest rivals, the Smallholders, in the spring of 1946. Attempting to refute the label "Jewish party" through demonstrative action against the "capitalists," communists incited the public against black marketers and price speculators. This accusation was used at a communist-organized incident in the summer of 1946 in Miskolc, when a mob of young factory workers lynched a Jewish mill owner and his production manager. The Jewish police officer interrogating the perpetrators was beaten to death after the rioters stormed police headquarters.[59] Local political conflicts led to a pogrom in another industrial center, Ózd, in February 1946. On hearing rumors of an alleged assassination attempt against a local communist leader (a former member of the Arrow Cross Party), ironworkers raided and robbed Jewish houses and stores.[60]

As a symptom of the increasingly antisemitic public mood, a modern interpretation of the old blood libel surfaced, intertwined with other allegations against the Jews. A prejudice-fuelled mass hysteria swept over the eastern part

---

57. For details on this, see Krisztián Ungváry, "Kik azok a nyilasok?" *Beszélő* 8, no. 6 (2003): 58–68.

58. Ignác Romsics, *Magyarország története a XX. században* (Budapest: Osiris, 1999), 304–5.

59. On the riots in Miskolc, see János Pelle, *Az utolsó vérvádak. Az etnikai gyűlölet és a politikai manipuláció kelet-európai történetéből* (Budapest: n.p., 1996), 189–247; Éva Standeisky, *Antiszemitizmusok* (Budapest: Argumentum, 2007), 159–73.

60. *Haladás*, March 7, 1946.

of the country in May and June 1946.[61] The most serious incident took place in Kunmadaras. Anti-Jewish violence grew out of a conflict over the people's court trial of a popular local schoolteacher, János Nagy, indicted for giving an antisemitic speech in May 1944. Many local citizens sided with Nagy and decided to attend the court hearing held in the neighboring town of Karcag. Halted by police at the town border, however, the mob went back to Kunmadaras. The protesters soon turned against local Jews. A rumor also spread that Jews in Karcag had made sausages out of Christian children. Fuelled by the frightening rumors, the population attacked the Jews on the following day. Document 10-8 excerpts the report of Communist Party representative Kálmán É. Kovács, sent from Budapest to investigate the case.

DOCUMENT 10-8: **Excerpts from a report by Kálmán É. Kovács to the chief secretariat of the Hungarian Communist Party on the pogrom in Kunmadaras, May 27, 1946, APH I. 274, fascicle 11, no. 64.**

[. . .]

The following day, [May] 21, was a market day in Kunmadaras. Many more people than usual were swarming through the marketplace and they were discussing yesterday's events in an agitated manner. Abruptly, a rumor began circulating that the Jews were abducting the Christian children in the village and murdering them. The pogrom began. At first [the mob] beat up the Jews in the marketplace. Then they went from door to door and dragged [the Jews] out of the houses and stores. In the meantime, they looted some of the stores. Altogether, they beat up 17 Jews. Two Jews died, two were seriously wounded. Women from among the lumpenproletariat as well as men, gypsies, and schoolchildren took part in the riot.[62]

[. . .]

---

61. Csorba, "Izrealita felekezeti élet Magyarországon," 1:81. In 1946–1947, only in the Debrecen region were nineteen people from several localities put on trial for spreading rumors about ritual murder and cannibalism committed by Jews and for inciting violence against them based on those false allegations. See HBCA XXV.1, boxes 26–39. For details about communist-era anti-Jewish attitudes and about postwar pogroms, see, e.g., Standeisky, *Antiszemitizmusok*, 131–73, and Pelle, *Az utolsó vérvádak*.

62. A term coined by Karl Marx in the middle of the nineteenth century, *Lumpenproletarier* (German, literally "ragged proletariat") refers to the lowest stratum of the working class, people who according to Marxist ideology lack class consciousness and are therefore useless in the proletariat's struggle for power.

After the pogrom, the Smallholders' Party summoned an interparty meeting chaired by Gergely Takács.[63] They submitted a proposal [for a communiqué] on behalf of the Smallholders in which they expressed regrets for the events, but [decided that] Jews had to leave the village in six hours. Because the chairman of the trade union and the secretary of the Communist Party objected to the proposal, the draft of the minutes was torn up, and the Smallholders' Party submitted a new proposal, according to which Jews had to leave the village in 24 hours. When this one was rejected as well, the Smallholders modified the proposal and suggested that those Jews who could integrate into the Hungarian community should be allowed to stay. The chairman of the trade union and the secretary of the Communist Party expressed their concern about this proposal as well. However, when the representative of the Women's Alliance, whose husband is Jewish, backed the proposal and twice suggested it should have been accepted, the proposal was passed by the interparty meeting.

[. . .]

The final decision accepted by the participants called upon those Jews in the community who were "not willing to integrate into the democratic life of the municipality to leave the village for their own good, because the [local organizations of the political] parties could not guarantee their safety."[64] In this way, despite the "selective" antisemitic tone of the final draft, rival political parties compromised about holding the victims responsible for the events. Most of the approximately seventy survivors in fact left Kunmadaras after the pogrom. The murderers, as well as local leaders accused of inciting the violence, were put on trial and sentenced to long prison terms that same year.[65] As a sign of the rapidly changing political atmosphere, the trial of the Miskolc rioters, which began only three months later, took a different turn. Because most of the defendants were Communist Party members or sympathizers, the communist-dominated police and people's court dismissed the charges and released all suspects.[66]

---

63. Local chairman of the Smallholders' Party.
64. Minutes of the people's court trial, July 25, 1946. Quoted in Standeisky, *Antiszemitizmusok*, 148.
65. Verdict of the National Council of People's Courts, November 30, 1946, JNSZCA IV. 407, doc. 6791/1947.
66. *Kis Ujság*, April 9, 1947.

## JEWS, COMMUNISTS, ZIONISTS

The large number of Communist Party members among rioters and the party's involvement in antisemitic instigation reflect the controversial relationship between Jews and the communist movement. Quite understandably, many Hungarian Jews turned to left-wing parties in the immediate postwar years. They relied on the communists and social democrats to fight consistently against the legacy of the Horthy regime. Large numbers of Jews joined both parties, despite the fact that their rank and file (especially in the case of the communists) included many antisemites. Several survivors became committed communists based on the reasoning that once the proletariat attained power on an international scale, the "Jewish question" and antisemitism would disappear.

The newly organized public administration and law enforcement needed a skilled workforce, but many civil servants and officers, compromised by participation in the previous regime's apparatus, had been dismissed or were being held in penal institutions. Their positions opened up for Jews who had lost government jobs during the Horthy regime. Many entered the ranks of the communist secret police, seeking to avenge the deaths of family members and friends.[67] A foremost goal of the authorities was to catch and sentence war criminals, so they willingly relied to some extent on Jewish members of the police apparatus. These policemen obviously did not share in the guilt of the recent past, nor did they maintain private contacts with suspects. In this way, many Jews found employment in law enforcement organizations or attained key positions in the state apparatus.[68] Five functionaries of Jewish origin became prominent figures in the Communist Party (and the Stalinist regime between 1949 and 1953): Mátyás Rákosi, Ernő Gerő, Mihály Farkas, Gábor Péter, and József Révai.[69] The apparently strong overrepre-

---

67. The overwhelming majority of members of the police forces were, of course, non-Jewish, but the number of officers of Jewish origin was much higher in key positions, for instance, among detectives and members of the political investigation unit, and therefore their participation was more "visible." For example, at the police station in Karcag, four out of sixty-seven officers were Jewish: the deputy commander, a rapporteur, and two detectives. List of policemen in Karcag, March 6, 1945, JNSZCA XXVII, 413 (1945–1946), box 2.

68. Karády, "Szociológiai kísérlet a magyar zsidóság," 110–53.

69. It is important to add that these "Jewish" politicians sharply rejected their Jewish identities, just as their predecessors in the 1919 Hungarian communist leadership had. We should also not forget that there were many Jewish intellectuals among the anti-Stalinist opposition as well. Kata Bohus, *Jews, Zionists and Rootless Cosmopolitans: The Hungarian Communist State and the "Jewish Question" in a Comparative Perspective (1956–1969)* (PhD diss., Central European University, in progress), 12.

sentation of politicians of Jewish origin in the regime's higher echelons created the false popular impression that the dictatorship was actually the Jews' revenge for the Holocaust. The propaganda of the interwar years, blurring Jewry and communism, was not completely forgotten either.

Despite the antisemitic perception that regarded the regime as a form of "Jewish rule," the communist dictatorship hit most Jews just as hard (and even harder in some sectors) as other Hungarians. The new government, of course, took restitution of plundered assets off the table. Moreover, those who had regained stores and enterprises after the war lost them again with the nationalization of many properties.[70] Between 1948 and 1953 the communist regime arrested many representatives of the "Horthy regime's ruling classes" and took them to designated places of residence and work camps without proper trials. (These actions were not connected to the operation of the people's courts mentioned above.) At least 30 percent of those evacuated were Jews, including former businessmen, prominent entrepreneurs, and others.[71]

As it became a Stalinist dictatorship, the growing communist power destroyed Jewish communities as independent public entities. Two factors defined postwar Jewish community politics: the enormous destructive impact of the Holocaust and the altered political conditions. The Pest (as of 1950, the Budapest) Israelite Congregation, which had been the most significant community in Hungary before 1944, gained even greater importance due to the wartime destruction of provincial Jewish communities. Since the predominantly Neologue Budapest Jews had the highest survival rate in the country, Orthodox influence decreased. However, this did not mean that the pre-Holocaust Neologue elite strengthened its leading position. Former Jewish Council member **Lajos Stöckler** became head of the Pest Israelite Congregation; he had strongly opposed the "elitist" politics of **Samu Stern** and his circles during the war. In addition, the rapidly ascending influence

---

70. On state appropriation of properties and frauds connected with Jewish-owned assets committed by the communist government, see Gábor Kádár and Zoltán Vági, *Hullarablás. A magyar zsidók gazdasági megsemmisítése* (Budapest: Jaffa, 2005), 380–91.

71. András Kovács, "Magyar zsidó politika a háború végétől a kommunista rendszer bukásáig," in *A másik szeme. Zsidók és antiszemiták a háború utáni Magyarországon*, ed. András Kovács (Budapest: Gondolat, 2008), 112.

of the Zionist factions also became visible in the official Jewish leadership.[72] However, when Moscow turned against the new Israeli state and decided to eliminate Zionism within its sphere of interest, the Stalinists dismantled the Zionist movement in Hungary, too. The official Jewish community led by Lajos Stöckler was loyal to the communist government and instrumental in destroying the Zionist institutional network that had emerged after the war. The arrest of the main Zionist leaders marked the end of the movement in May 1949.[73]

As part of its endeavor to create a totalitarian system, the communist government decided to take complete control of all religious organizations, including those of the Jewish community. After nationalizing all religious schools in 1948, the government decided in 1949 to forcibly unify the various Hungarian Jewish religious branches (Neologue, Orthodox, **Status Quo Ante**) into one body. A new umbrella organization, the National Representation of Hungarian Israelites, came into being. The idea of unification emerged among Jewish leaders in the years prior to 1950, but the communist state finally compelled the various communities to enter into an agreement. Most of the Jewish leaders, especially the Orthodox, sharply opposed the decision but eventually yielded to overwhelming pressure.[74]

---

72. The reasons behind the sharp increase in the Zionists' mass support were twofold. They were the sole group that had performed organized resistance in 1944–1945. Moreover, their ideology defying assimilation and promoting a genuine Jewish national politics was attractive to many survivors, who felt that Hungarian society had brutally denied their pre-Holocaust efforts to integrate and assimilate. See Kovács, "Magyar zsidó politika," 94–98; Attila Novák, *Átmenetben. A cionista mozgalom négy éve Magyarországon* (Budapest: Múlt és Jövő, 2000), 23–43. On the eve of the Zionist Congress of 1946 in Basel, ninety-five thousand shekels (quasi-membership fees) were sold in Hungary. These numbers show that the majority of the approximately150,000-strong Hungarian Jewish population supported the Zionists, while 10 to 25 percent were actual members of the movement. See Kovács, "Magyar zsidó politika," 97. The membership of the Zionist Alliance grew continuously: in October 1948 it stood at fifteen thousand, while in March 1949 the number reached forty-one thousand. Novák, *Átmenetben*, 167.

73. Novák, *Átmenetben*, 172.

74. The Orthodox rabbis had actually formulated a secret declaration in Hebrew among themselves stating that they had agreed to the unification only under pressure and would at the very first possible opportunity declare their consent null and void. Géza Komoróczy, *A zsidók története Magyarországon* (Pozsony: Kalligram, 2012), 2:997–98.

DOCUMENT 10-9: Photo taken at the unification congress of the Jewish religious branches in Budapest in February 1950, HGA XXII-IV/57, image no. 02171.

The February 1950 unification conference took place in the banquet hall of the Pest Israelite Congregation at 12 Síp Street, the very hall where Hermann Krumey and Dieter Wisliceny, **Adolf Eichmann**'s henchmen, had assembled the Jewish leaders in March 1944 to inform them of the Nazis' demands. Only six years later, pictures of Lenin, Stalin, and Hungarian communist dictator Mátyás Rákosi gazed down from the wall, while Minister of Religion and Education Gyula Ortutay delivered his ceremonial speech.[75] But some of the old faces were also present. Sitting to Ortutay's left is former Jewish Council member Lajos Stöckler, who became the head of new organization. On the minister's right is **Samu Kahán-Frankl**, another member of the Jewish Council in 1944. Rabbi Kahán-Frankl represented the Orthodox voice in the council as well as in the new umbrella organization formed by the communists.[76] This

---

75. The political atmosphere is exemplified by the fact that right after the event, Ortutay was forced to resign, probably because of the ill-considered words of his speech about the protection of religious freedom. Duschinsky, "Hungary," 470.
76. He soon left the country. Duschinsky, "Hungary," 469–70.

constellation, along with the menorah and the Torah curtain looming in the background, reveals a great deal about the situation of the Jews, particularly the Jewish leadership, in Hungary's postwar era.

The remaining members of the Jewish leadership could not avoid criminal proceedings based on false charges, a phenomenon typical of communist regimes. The government arrested and tortured several community leaders—for example, Lajos Stöckler and former chief secretary of the congregation Miksa Domonkos (who both showed great courage during the Holocaust).[77] As a special favor to the Soviet kidnappers of **Raoul Wallenberg**, the government wanted to prove the absurd claim that Stöckler and Domonkos had shot the Swedish diplomat. In 1953, with Mátyás Rákosi leading the way—following an initiative by Moscow and similar campaigns in other Eastern Bloc countries—the regime began preparing several spectacular anti-Zionist, antisemitic trials.[78] Following Stalin's death in March 1953, however, Moscow stopped its anti-Jewish proceedings, so the Hungarians canceled them as well.

## THE 1956 REVOLUTION AND FIGHT FOR FREEDOM

On October 23, 1956, a mass demonstration in Budapest, held to show sympathy for a Polish workers' strike brutally put down the previous June, turned into an increasingly anti-Stalinist uprising. In order to prevent Hungary from leaving the pro-Soviet alliance, the Soviet army invaded the country on November 4. Hundreds of tanks sent by Marshall Zhukov, who had occupied Berlin in 1945, now stormed the Hungarian capital. The fighting claimed around 2,000 Hungarian lives, while 1,540 Soviet troops were wounded and 720 killed. The members of the "reform communist" government leading the takeover, including Prime Minister Imre Nagy, were arrested and later executed. A Kremlin appointee, János Kádár, assumed power. Soviet troops did not withdraw from Hungary until after the 1989–1990 collapse of the Eastern Bloc.[79]

In light of the pogrom waves of the nineteenth and twentieth centuries and the popular view that the communist dictatorship represented Jewish rule, it is surprising that antisemitism was not a major factor of the revolution. Nevertheless, with the disruption of public order at the end of October 1956,

---

77. Kovács, "Magyar zsidó politika," 106–15.
78. On these trials, see Zvi Y. Gitelman, "The Evolution of Soviet Anti-Zionism: From Principle to Pragmatism," and Theodore H. Friedgut, "Soviet Anti-Zionism: Origins, Forms and Development," in *Anti-Zionism and Antisemitism in the Contemporary World*, ed. Robert S. Wistrich (New York: New York University Press, 1990), 11–25, 26–45.
79. The last Soviet troops left Hungary in June 1991.

antisemitic attacks reappeared.[80] For example, after breaking into a pub in Hajdúnánás and drinking up all the brandy, a mob beat several Jews and looted numerous Jewish houses and stores. The revolutionary committee stopped the riot—by arresting a few Jews.[81] Still, many eyewitnesses (Jews and non-Jews alike) and historians examining the events agree that antisemitism was a marginal phenomenon during the revolution.[82] The new authorities usually tried to step up measures against such outbursts. However, the escalating events incited fear in many Jews, particularly those who remembered the disorder and violence of 1944. These fears also explain why a disproportionate number of Jews left Hungary after the revolution.[83]

Some revolutionaries came from Jewish backgrounds. Among them were the chief of staff of the revolution's army, István Kovács, the leader of one of the main Budapest resistance groups, László Nickelsburg, and an editor of revolutionary newspapers, Miklós Gimes. Another prominent Jewish figure in the events of 1956 was István Angyal. The Hungarian authorities deported Angyal, born in 1928, and his family to Auschwitz in 1944, where his mother and sister were murdered. After the war he began university studies in Hungarian literature and history, but in 1949 he was expelled for expressing an opinion in a public debate opposing the official communist party line. In 1956 Angyal became the leader of an armed resistance group in Budapest. After Soviet and Hungarian communist forces put down the revolution, authorities arrested him in April 1958 and sentenced him to death. His case went to the People's Court Council of the Supreme Court, which was to deliver the final verdict.[84] Document 10-10 is a supporting letter, sent by the National Representation of Hungarian Israelites to the court, requesting a pardon for Angyal by invoking his suffering during the Holocaust. The leadership of the organization at

---

80. The report prepared by the National Representation of Hungarian Israelites in January 1957 listed twenty-four antisemitic incidents in the country, mostly in the initial phase of the revolution. Most of the atrocities took place in the northeastern part of the country, roughly in the same areas as in 1945 to 1947. See János Gadó, "Összegyűjtöttük és regisztráltuk—antiszemita atrocitások 1956-ban," *Szombat* (October 1992).

81. On this riot and other antisemitic incidents of 1956, see Standeisky, *Antiszemitizmusok*, 174–221.

82. For a summary of opinions about popular antisemitism in the 1956 Revolution, see Bohus, *Jews, Zionists and Rootless Cosmopolitans*, 9–12.

83. Out of some two hundred thousand refugees, about twenty to thirty thousand were Jewish. Varga László, "'Zsidókérdés' 1945–1956," *Világosság* 33, no. 1 (1992): 67. Kovács, "Magyar zsidó politika," 116–17.

84. For the details of Angyal's life, see László Eörsi, *Angyal István (1928–1958)* (Budapest: Noran, 2008).

the time fully collaborated with the communist powers. (One of the signers, President Endre Sós, was in fact an undercover informant for the communist secret service.[85]) With communist retribution for the uprising in full swing, terror was at a high point. Under these circumstances, such a letter constitutes a significant example of Jewish solidarity.

DOCUMENT 10-10: **Letter of the National Representation of Hungarian Israelites to the People's Court Council of the Supreme Court, November 27, 1958, HJA XVI-B, box TB B/309.**

Budapest, November 27, 1958.
To the People's Court Council of the Supreme Court
Budapest

As the supreme body of the Hungarian Israelite denomination, we appeal to the People's Court Council of the Supreme Court, requesting a decision in the case of István Angyal that recommends him for pardon and submits a clemency plea to the President's Council of the Hungarian People's Republic. We join the clemency plea of István Angyal's attorney, and we also request that the President's Council of the Hungarian People's Republic change the capital punishment of István Angyal into a prison sentence for life.

It is not our task to judge the gravity of István Angyal's deeds, but we are aware that he committed serious crimes. However, we still request a pardon, since this young man already suffered a great deal in his youth: he was taken to the Auschwitz deportation camp as an adolescent and he had to witness the murder of his mother and sister by Hitler's fascists.

We plead for mercy for him due to the tribulations he suffered in Auschwitz. We plead mercy for him on behalf of his unfortunate father and little child. We plead mercy for him because of the memory of his mother and sister murdered in Auschwitz.

Sincerely,
National Representation of Hungarian Israelites/
/László Jenő// Jenő Schück// Endre Sós/
Chairman    Rabbi    President[86]

---

85. Komoróczy, *A zsidók története Magyarországon*, 2:1002.

86. Chairman László Jenő (1913–1985); Endre Sós (1905–1969) was a writer and journalist, as well as the president of the Budapest Israelite Congregation.

The clemency plea was rejected: the People's Court Council of the Supreme Court sentenced Angyal to death, and he was executed on December 1, 1958.

## THE KÁDÁR ERA AND BEYOND

During the Kádár era in Hungary (1957–1989), the situation of Jewish communities gradually improved. Despite being pushed into the background and strongly controlled by the state, religious life (Jewish and Christian alike) survived. In contrast to the era between 1949 and 1956, when memory of the Jews' persecution was thrust into oblivion, memoirs, literary pieces, and even a few scholarly works about the Holocaust appeared in print beginning in the late 1950s.[87] Of course, this did not represent the advent of freedom of research or publication. Authorities permitted Holocaust-related scholarly research selectively. Drawing lessons from the 1956 Revolution, János Kádár adhered to a policy of keeping the social peace by any means possible.[88] He thought talking and writing about the Holocaust and the "Jewish question," not to mention Hungarian involvement in the destruction of the Hungarian Jews, could stir up emotions in an undesirable way. It is indicative of the situation that Randolph L. Braham published the definitive, groundbreaking account of the Holocaust in Hungary in the United States in 1981.[89]

The fall of communism in 1989–1990 and the dawn of parliamentary democracy in Hungary brought new opportunities and challenges for Jewish institutions, Holocaust survivors, and their descendants. Scholarly and public interest

---

87. Randolph L. Braham, ed., *The Hungarian Jewish Catastrophe: A Selected and Annotated Bibliography*, 2nd rev. ed. (New York: Social Science Monographs and Institute for Holocaust Studies, City University of New York, 1984), lists several works published in Hungary between 1945 and 1984.

88. Kádár's attitude was best summarized by his statement on the desirable Hungarian approach to the Eichmann case in 1960: "It is not good to turn these terrible fascist issues into an exclusively Jewish question [. . .] Eichmann not only murdered Jews; there were others, too. This is not a Jewish question; this is a question of fascism and antifascism." Quoted in András Kovács, "A holokauszt emlékezete és a magyar társadalom: a holokausztmúzeum fogadtatása a magyar közvéleményben," in *Tanulmányok a holokausztról IV*, ed. Randolph L. Braham (Budapest: Presscon, 2006), 289.

89. Braham, *The Politics of Genocide*. Columbia University Press published the second revised U.S. edition in 1994. The Hungarian editions appeared in 1988 (Budapest: Gondolat) and in 1997 (Budapest: Belvárosi). Braham himself was a survivor of the Holocaust in Hungary. He served in the labor service on the eastern front, while most of his family members were deported from Dés (Transylvania) and killed in German concentration camps. Braham immigrated to the United States in January 1948 aboard the same ship (the SS *Marine Flasher*) that had brought Alex Feuer to America a few months before. See document 10-5.

also focused increasingly on the events of the twentieth century. After forty years of suppressed public debate, a series of heated discussions commenced about the "Jewish question" and the interpretation of such historical traumas as the **Trianon Peace Treaty**, World War II, the Holocaust, and the communist era.[90]

In the two decades following the democratic transition, the Hungarian political elite in general has consistently condemned what happened to Hungarian Jews during the war. The decisions of consecutive governments resulted in the establishment of a National Holocaust Memorial Day, commemorated in parliament and schools since 2000, as well as the opening of the new permanent Hungarian exhibition at the Auschwitz-Birkenau State Museum and the inauguration of the Holocaust Memorial Center in Budapest, both in 2004. The Holocaust Memorial Center is the only government-financed Hungarian institution focusing exclusively on Holocaust education, remembrance, and research. A memorial site dedicated to the approximately half million victims from Hungary who perished during the Holocaust, the institute houses a permanent exhibition titled *From Deprivation of Rights to Genocide* and a historical collection containing objects, photos, and archival documents pertaining to the Holocaust. Furthermore, Hungary joined major international initiatives for the commemoration of the Holocaust, such as the Stockholm Declaration, and supported establishment of the intergovernmental Task Force for International Cooperation on Holocaust Education, Remembrance, and Research in 1998. Since initiation of a "March of the Living" in 2002, thousands of people, including high-ranking politicians from both sides of the moderate political spectrum, commemorate the victims.

One of the clearest governmental declarations condemning the Hungarian state's and intelligentsia's role in the genocide came from Minister of Education Bálint Magyar, delivered at the opening ceremony of the permanent Hungarian exhibition at the Auschwitz museum, entitled *The Citizen Betrayed*.

DOCUMENT 10-11: **Speech of Hungarian Minister of Education Dr. Bálint Magyar at the opening of the permanent Hungarian exhibition at Auschwitz on April 15, 2004, published in** *The Citizen Betrayed: In Memory of the Victims of the Hungarian Holocaust* **(catalog of the permanent exhibition of the Hungarian National Museum in the Auschwitz-Birkenau State Museum) (Budapest: Magyar Nemzeti Múzeum, 2006), 17–19.**

It all began with words.

Not with the banging of train doors, or the swearing of gendarmes, and not even with the laments of the tortured. These were not the first

---

90. For these, see Braham, *The Politics of Genocide*, 2:1353–65.

sounds. It began with the careful words and fluid sentences of refined gentlemen, politicians, journalists, economists and statisticians. In newspaper articles, books, scholarly research, in speeches at political gatherings, in trains of thought that were easy to grasp and which, for every woe, offered explanations about "damaging Jewish influence" and the "alien parasites sucking at the Hungarian spirit."

Deportation did not begin with the cattle wagons. Quite the opposite: the train standing in the Hungarian station in 1944 was the penultimate stage; the first step on the road towards it was the acceptance of the ideology discriminating between people on the basis of their race.

[. . .]

It is hard to understand how the Hungarian state could reject, stigmatize, and rob hundreds of thousands of its citizens before sending them to their deaths. Even if there were many thousands, perhaps many tens of thousands of brave men and women who risked their lives to save those being persecuted,[91] it is still hard to comprehend the fact that the majority of Hungarian society observed the Calvary of its compatriots passively, while many were only too glad to grab the Jews' assets. It is hard to understand that what happened was not the private act of a handful of criminals but rather the culmination of a lengthy process, one for which the Hungarian political elite, intelligentsia and a significant portion of society were responsible.

[. . .]

For us Hungarians, Auschwitz means mourning of the dead and also the responsibility that is not easy to live with. What happened was not our crime, but it is we who have to confront it. We cannot comfort ourselves with the fact that Jews were also annihilated in other countries. [. . .]

There is and cannot be such a thing as collective responsibility: descendants cannot be held responsible for actions 60 years ago. But there is such a thing as personal responsibility. Our responsibility to remember, and to express, loudly and clearly, that the tragedy which occurred in 1944–1945 was the accumulation of many hundred thousands of

---

91. By January 2011 Yad Vashem had granted the title "Righteous Among the Nations" to 764 Hungarians. See Yad Vashem, "The Righteous Among the Nations," www1.yadvashem.org/yv/en/righteous/statistics.asp#detailed (accessed April 25, 2012). The number of rescuers is probably much higher. In Budapest alone, many thousands of Jews were in hiding during the Arrow Cross era. That required approximately a similar number of non-Jews to support or help them. For rescue efforts by non-Jews during the Holocaust, see chapter 9.

individual compromises, jealousies, cowardices, crimes and animosities, over many decades.

If we must not keep quiet about something, we must talk about it. Talk about it openly and freely. So let us be open about what happened in Hungary 60 years ago. Let us tell our children, the next generation, that six decades ago Hungarians persecuted, humiliated and murdered other Hungarians on the basis of an evil and mindless ideology. I will tell my daughter that her great-grandfather's family, Margit Schwarcz, Lajos Grósz and Aunt Bözsi Kurtág, all died here at Auschwitz. We all have to do this so that those particular coded or unmistakable words should never again lead to the banging of doors on cattle trains.

It must be an indelible part of national memory that the Holocaust was also a Hungarian tragedy, for its every tenth victim—that is more than half a million Hungarian Jews and Roma—were killed as Hungarian citizens. We must never forget that every third victim of the largest Nazi extermination camp was deported from Hungary by the Hungarian authorities under the orders of a Hungarian government that assisted the Nazis.

[. . .]

The sixtieth anniversary of the Holocaust in Hungary, April 2004, was the most widely marked Holocaust commemoration ever experienced in Hungary, and to a certain extent, it was a moment of grace. The political and intellectual elites were seemingly unified for the commemoration or at least did not voice disturbing opinions. Sociological research showed that the commemorations, articles, books, and television shows dealing with the history of the Holocaust had reached large groups across Hungarian society: knowledge of the events had grown significantly.[92]

However, this positive atmosphere quickly diminished. Political turmoil starting in 2006 and the 2008 economic crisis brought shocking changes. In a general cultural paradigm shift, the extreme right, isolated and despised only a few years earlier, shed its underground status and became a mainstream trend that provided a new cultural identity for many. The Internet has provided its most vibrant forum. The main features of this far-right culture include anticapitalist economic ideas, xenophobia, notions of white supremacy, homophobia, an antiurban and anti-Western ethos, and antidemocratic, autocratic political

---

92. Mária Vásárhelyi, "Holokauszt a családtörténetekben," in *Tanulmányok a holokausztról IV*, 284–86.

attitudes. Central elements also include fierce antisemitism, anti-Israeli sentiments, and open Holocaust denial.

According to empirical research by sociologist András Kovács, the number of radical antisemites in the Hungarian population grew from 9 to 20 percent between 2003 and 2011, peaking in 2010 at 22 percent.[93] (These numbers do not include those holding "moderate" anti-Jewish views, the number of whom varied between 15 and 22 percent in this period.) At the same time the percentage of those who refused to respond to survey questions radically decreased (from 17 to 3 percent). This series of data shows that the number of radical antisemites probably had not doubled; rather, far more people simply dared to express antisemitic sentiments. Kovács calls this the "Jobbik effect," referring to the extreme right political party that had gained close to 17 percent of the vote in the 2010 election and resorted to openly antisemitic and anti-Roma messages. Mainstream unwillingness to adopt antisemitic public speech has declined continuously. A new, educated, younger generation of political antisemites has appeared, legitimizing open use of anti-Jewish hate speech and Holocaust denial.

According to Kovács's research, in 2011 20 percent believed in a Jewish conspiracy controlling Hungary's economy and politics; 12 percent favored legalizing discrimination against the Jews, including forcing them to leave the country. The data also show that in election years, the combined number of radical and "moderate" antisemites increased (with 2010 representing the peak, at 44 percent), which shows that manipulating anti-Jewish sentiments remains a favored campaign method in the political arena. Data relevant to the memory of the Holocaust show that between 2003 and 2011, the number of those who felt the "topic of the persecution of the Jews should be taken off the agenda" had grown from 42 to 58 percent. In 2003, 4 percent expressed the view that Nazi Germany had not operated gas chambers; in 2011 this figure stood at 7 percent. The ratio of those who believed the "Jews" wished to benefit financially from their suffering was 35 percent in 2003, rising to 45 percent in 2011.[94]

---

93. Kovács defines a radical antisemite as a person who not only holds several strong anti-Jewish stereotypes but connects very strong emotions to these views and would be ready to discriminate against Jews as well.

94. For Kovács's data, see András Kovács, *The Stranger at Hand: Antisemitic Prejudices in Post-Communist Hungary* (Leiden: Brill Academic Publishers, 2011); "Az antiszemita nyelv legitimmé vált a közbeszédben," interview with András Kovács in *Szombat*, January 4, 2012, www.szombat.org/?l1=news&l2=plug_news&l3=showNews&id=4214 (accessed April 25, 2012).

Some observers went so far as to call Budapest "Europe's capital of antisemitism."[95] Others, however, pointed out that despite this dangerous political turn, Jewish communities still enjoy firm state support and recognition and are not subjected to political or cultural suppression or direct threats. According to a journalist who reported from Budapest in 2010, "I saw this myself at Chanukah when I munched on latkes at a Friday night Oneg Shabbat, sampled doughnuts at a sit-down dinner for Holocaust survivors, joined 20-somethings at a riotous klezmer/hip-hop gig, and just missed witnessing the foreign minister, Budapest's mayor, and other VIPs help light a big menorah set up in the center of town."[96]

Hungarian Jews indeed have been spared physical violence at home since 1956. However, recent political and social developments have caused a general feeling of discontent in the Jewish community. The most perilous phenomenon is the pervasive hatred toward Hungary's largest ethnic minority, the Roma. Anti-Roma prejudices deeply permeate society: they have even made inroads with social strata that otherwise do not sympathize with the far right. Racist feelings culminated in a series of hate crimes in 2008–2009, which included racially motivated killings. Six Roma, a five-year-old boy among them, were murdered by an armed group, several others were wounded, and entire communities were intimidated.

The birth of a pluralist, democratic state after 1989 brought about several positive phenomena as well, and these have prevailed, despite the negative developments described above. Hungary, today the homeland of one of the largest Jewish communities in central Europe, has witnessed a vivid Jewish revival in the period following the fall of the communist regime.[97] After decades of suppression and silence, religious and ethnic consciousness could be expressed openly. A number of the children and grandchildren of Holocaust survivors have found their way back to their Jewish identity, sometimes entailing a religious turn as well. The network of Jewish cultural, educational, and religious institutions has grown stronger and more extensive. Apart from the traditional

---

95. Erich Follath, "Europe's Capital of Anti-Semitism: Budapest Experiences a New Wave of Hate," *Der Spiegel International*, October 14, 2010, www.spiegel.de/international/europe/0,1518,722880,00.html (accessed April 25, 2012).

96. Ruth Ellen Gruber, "Could Hungarian Anti-Semitism Get out of Control?" *JTA*, December 21, 2010, www.jta.org/news/article/2010/12/21/2742260/could-hungarian-anti-semitism-get-out-of-control (accessed April 25, 2012).

97. This is the sixth-largest Jewish community on the continent and the thirteenth largest in the world. See "The Jewish Population of the World," Jewish Virtual Library, www.jewishvirtuallibrary.org/jsource/Judaism/jewpop.html (accessed April 25, 2012).

or Neologue and Orthodox communities, the Chabad Lubavitch movement (a branch of modern Hasidism) and two new Reform congregations have appeared on the scene.[98] The wider Jewish community social infrastructure includes schools, ranging from nursery schools to higher educational institutions, as well as cultural and community centers, weekly and monthly journals, publishing houses, and a museum and archives.

Beyond this, several nongovernmental organizations established to strengthen Jewish community life and identity include organizations dedicated to Holocaust remembrance and education and combating antisemitism and intolerance. Jewish history and culture have become popular and frequent topics of research and art, as well as public discussion. The number of scholarly publications, memoirs, and literary works published about contemporary Jewish history and the Holocaust has grown considerably in the last two decades.[99] Every year several concerts, films, plays, and other artistic performances connected to Jewish traditions and culture take place. These events have attracted many non-Jewish spectators as well. The Jewish Summer Festival is one of Budapest's largest and most fashionable cultural events. Clubs, pubs, workshops, hummus bars, and kosher stores also testify to the presence of vital cultural traditions, as well as an assertive and open-minded urban intelligentsia and youth strongly committed to preserving the open, receptive, and culturally diverse character of Hungarian society.

The geographic center of this vibrant Jewish life is the Seventh District of Budapest, where the headquarters of the major Judaic religious branches and communities, most of the important synagogues, and kosher shops and restaurants can be found in a relatively small area. In the symbolic focal point of this center stands one of the largest Jewish temples in the world, the Dohány Street Synagogue, consecrated in 1859. When the Jewish community in Pest decided in 1845 to build the temple and follow the modern liturgy, Jews still lived in Hungary as second-class subjects, merely tolerated at the periphery

---

98. The Sim Shalom Progressive Jewish Congregation and the Bet Orim Reform Jewish Congregation. These are "Reform" congregations in the twentieth- and twenty-first-century American sense of the word, and they have little to do with the nineteenth-century religious reform in Europe.

99. See Randolph L. Braham, ed., *The Holocaust in Hungary: A Selected and Annotated Bibliography, 1984–2000* (New York: Columbia University Press, 2001); Randolph L. Braham and Julia Bock, eds., *The Holocaust in Hungary: A Selected and Annotated Bibliography, 2000–2007* (New York: Columbia University Press, 2008).

of society. Fifty years later, in 1895, having attained complete legal equality, entered into the mainstream of the Hungarian modernization project, and accumulated significant intellectual and financial wealth, hundreds of thousands of Jews felt that they had found a home. At the service held in the synagogue in May 1896 to celebrate the thousand-year anniversary of the establishment of the Hungarian state, notable Jewish figures, successful industrialists, entrepreneurs, and bankers, many wearing the traditional garb of the Hungarian nobility, listened to the patriotic sermon delivered by Neologue chief rabbi Sámuel Kohn.[100] Five decades later, in January 1945, the bodies of hundreds of Jews murdered in the Budapest ghetto lay strewn across the garden of the synagogue. Today they are buried in mass graves in the garden, their names engraved on a memorial plaque. This topography encapsulates 150 years of history: the majestic synagogue and the mass graves in its garden reflect the ascent, catastrophe, and revival of the Hungarian Jewish community.

---

100. Sámuel Kohn (1841–1920) was an early historian of the Jews in Hungary, early rabbi of the Dohány Temple, and one of the founders of Budapest's Rabbinical Seminary. See Frojimovics et al., *Jewish Budapest*, esp. 115–16.

DOCUMENT 10-12: **The Dohány Street Synagogue's garden and the northern wall of the building, October 2012. Courtesy of Christine Schmidt.**

# Tables

**TABLE 1:** U.S. Army Equivalents of SS Ranks[1]

| | |
|---|---|
| *Reichsführer-SS* | General of the army |
| *Oberstgruppenführer* | General |
| *Obergruppenführer* | Lieutenant general |
| *Gruppenführer* | Major general |
| *Brigadeführer* | Brigadier general |
| *Oberführer* | Rank between Colonel and Brigadier general |
| *Standartenführer* | Colonel |
| *Obersturmbannführer* | Lieutenant colonel |
| *Sturmbannführer* | Major |
| *Hauptsturmführer* | Captain |
| *Obersturmführer* | First lieutenant |
| *Untersturmführer* | Second lieutenant |

---

1. Information drawn from Raul Hilberg, *The Destruction of the European Jews*, 3rd. ed. (New Haven, CT: Yale University Press, 2003), 3:1299.

**TABLE 2:** Changes in the Number and Percentage of Israelites within the Hungarian Population[1]

| Year of Registration | Total Population | Number of Israelites | Percentage of Israelites |
|---|---|---|---|
| 1720–1735 | 1,769,422 | 12,219 | 0.7 |
| 1787 | 6,468,327 | 80,783 | 1.3 |
| 1805 | 6,888,890 | 126,620 | 1.8 |
| 1825 | 8,801,255 | 191,475 | 2.3 |
| 1830 | 8,894,906 | 203,220 | 2.3 |
| 1840 | 9,693,744 | 240,252 | 2.5 |
| 1846 | 9,724,126 | 258,832 | 2.7 |
| 1850 | 9,308,629 | 339,816 | 3.7 |
| 1869 | 11,215,555 | 510,389 | 4.6 |
| 1880 | 13,749,603 | 624,826 | 4.5 |
| 1890 | 15,162,988 | 707,961 | 4.7 |
| 1900 | 16,838,255 | 831,162 | 4.9 |
| 1910 | 18,264,533 | 911,227 | 5.0 |
| 1920* | 7,990,202 | 473,355 | 5.9 |
| 1930* | 8,668,319 | 444,567 | 5.1 |
| 1941** | 14,683,323 | 725,007 | 4.9 |

\* Within the territory of the country after the 1920 **Treaty of Trianon (post-Trianon Hungary)**.
\*\* Within the extended territory of the country from 1941 to 1944.

1. László Varga, "Zsidó bevándorlás Magyarországon," *Századok* 1 (1992): 66.

**Table 3:** Territorial Expansion of Hungary, 1938–1941

| Event | Date | Area Gained (in Square Miles) | Population (1941) | Israelite Population[1] (1941) |
|---|---|---|---|---|
| First **Vienna Award** | November 2, 1938 | 4,605 | 1,062,022 | 67,876 |
| Occupation of Carpatho-Ruthenia | March 1939 | 4,656 | 694,022 | 78,087 |
| Second Vienna Award | August 30, 1940 | 16,642 | 2,577,260 | 164,052 |
| Occupation of the Southern Province | April 1941 | 4,430 | 1,030,027 | 14,202 |

---

1. The figures include only persons of Jewish religion and not Christians of Jewish origin. In 1941, approximately one hundred thousand Hungarians of Jewish ancestry belonged to Christian denominations but fell under the jurisdiction of the anti-Jewish laws.

**TABLE 4:** Administrative Structure of Hungary in 1944

| Name of Administrative Unit | Head of Public Administration | Type of Law Enforcement |
|---|---|---|
| Capital city of Budapest (Budapest *székesfőváros*) | Lord mayor (*főpolgármester*) Mayor (*polgármester*) | Police |
| *Kerület*: 14 municipal districts | Municipal district alderman (*kerületi elöljáró*) | Police |
| *Törvényhatósági jogú város*: 20 cities | Mayor (*polgármester*) | Police |
| *Vármegye*: 41 counties | Prefect (*főispán*) (formal head) Subprefect (*alispán*) (actual control) | See below |
| *Közigazgatási kirendeltség*: 3 administrative regions (in Carpatho-Ruthenia) | Regent's commissioner (*kormányzói biztos*) (for the administrative regions) | |
| *Megyei város*: town | Mayor (*polgármester*) | Police |
| *Járás*: district | Chief constable (*főszolgabíró*) | Gendarmerie |
| *Község*: village | Notary (*jegyző*) | Gendarmerie |

**TABLE 5:** Number of Jewish Congregations in Post-Trianon Hungary and Carpatho-Ruthenia after World War II[1]

| Year | Number of Congregations in Post-Trianon Hungary |
|---|---|
| Pre–World War II | Close to 700 |
| 1945 | 112 |
| 1946 | 288 |
| 1948 | 279[2] |
| 1949 | 256 |
| 1950 | 170 |
| 1958 | 78 |
| 1975 | 75 |

---

1. Kinga Frojimovics, *Szétszakadt történelem. Zsidó vallási irányzatok Magyarországon 1868–1950* (Budapest: Balassi, 2008), 374–78; Géza Komoróczy, *A zsidók története Magyarországon* (Pozsony: Kalligram, 2012), 2:913, 1138.

2. These consisted of 275 in the provinces and 4 in Budapest.

**TABLE 6:** Concordance between Hungarian and Non-Hungarian Place Names

| Hungarian | German | Romanian | Ruthenian | Serbian | Slovakian | Ukrainian |
|---|---|---|---|---|---|---|
| Aknaszlatina | — | Slatina | Solotvyno | — | Slatinské Doly | Solotvyno |
| Bácstopolya | — | — | — | Bačka Topola | — | — |
| Beregszász | Bergsass | Bereg | Berehovo | — | Berehovo | Berehove |
| Beszterce | Bistritz | Bistriţa | — | — | — | — |
| Bilke | — | — | Bilki | — | — | Bilki |
| Csap | — | — | Chop | — | Čop | Chop |
| Cservenka | Tscherwenka/ Rotweil | — | — | Crvenka | — | — |
| Csíkszereda | Szeklerburg | Miercurea Ciuc | — | — | — | — |
| Dés | Desch/Burglos | Dej | — | — | — | — |
| Érsekújvár | Neuhaus | — | — | — | Nové Zámky | — |
| Felsővisó | Oberwischau | Vişeu de Sus | — | — | — | — |
| Galánta | Gallandau | — | — | — | Galanta | — |
| Gyergyószentmiklós | Niklasmarkt | Gheorgheni | — | — | — | — |
| Huszt | — | Hust | Khust | — | Chust | Khust |
| Ipolyság | Eipelschlag | — | — | — | Šahy | — |
| Iza | — | — | Iza | — | — | Iza |
| Kassa | Kaschau | — | — | — | Košice | — |
| Királyháza | — | — | Korolevo | — | — | Koroleve |
| Kolozsvár | Klausenburg | Cluj | — | — | — | — |

| Hungarian | German | Romanian | Ruthenian | Serbian | Slovakian | Ukrainian |
|---|---|---|---|---|---|---|
| Kőrösmező | — | — | Yasinia | — | — | Yasinia |
| Léva | Lewenz | — | — | — | Levice | — |
| Losonc | Lizenz | — | — | — | Lučenec | — |
| Máramaros | — | Maramureş | — | — | — | — |
| Máramarossziget | Marmaroschsiget/ Siget | Sighetu Marmaţiei | Sigit | — | Sihoť | Sigit |
| Marosvásárhely | Neumarkt (am Mieresch) | Târgu Mureş | — | — | — | — |
| Munkács | Munkatsch | Muncaci | Mukachevo/ Mukachovo | — | Mukačevo | Mukacheve/ Mukachiv |
| Nagykároly | Grosskarol/ Grosskarl | Carei | — | — | — | — |
| Nagyszőlős | — | Seleuşu Mare | Syvlyush/ Vynohradovo | — | (Veľký) Sevluš | Vynohradiv |
| Nagyvárad | Grosswardein | Oradea | — | — | — | — |
| Nyitra | Neutra | — | — | — | Nitra | — |
| Pozsony | Pressburg | — | — | — | Bratislava | — |
| Retteg | Retteneck | Reteag | — | — | — | — |
| Rimaszombat | Grossteffelsdorf | — | — | — | Rimavská Sobota | — |
| Rozália | — | Rozavlea | — | — | — | — |
| Sajkásvidék | — | — | — | Šajkaška | — | — |

(*Continued*)

**TABLE 6:** Continued

| Hungarian | German | Romanian | Ruthenian | Serbian | Slovakian | Ukrainian |
|---|---|---|---|---|---|---|
| Szolyva | Schwalbach | — | Svalyava | — | — | Svalyava |
| Szászrégen | (Sächsisch) Regen | Reghin | — | — | — | — |
| Szatmárnémeti | Sathmar | Satu Mare | — | — | — | — |
| Szeklence | — | — | Sokyrnytsa | — | Sekernice | Sokyrnytsia |
| Szered | — | — | — | — | Sered nad Váhom | — |
| Székelyföld | Szeklerland | Ținutul Secuiesc | — | — | — | — |
| Turócszentmárton | Turz–Sankt Martin | — | — | — | Turčiansky Svätý Martin | — |
| Ungvár | Ungwar/Ungarisch Burg | Ujhorod | Uzhgorod | — | Užhorod | Uzhgorod |
| Újvidék | Neusatz | — | — | Novi Sad | Nový Sad | — |
| Vágújhely | Neustadt an der Waag | — | — | — | Nové Mesto nad Váhom | — |
| Zsolna | Sillein | — | — | — | Žilina | — |

# List of Documents

## 1: Laws against the Rule of Law

### The "Jewish Laws"

Document 1-1: Pronouncement of fifty-nine leading intellectuals and artists protesting the First "Jewish Law," *Pesti Napló*, May 5, 1938, 2.

Document 1-2: Act IV of 1939 on the Limitation of Jewish Expansion in Public and Economic Spheres (Second "Jewish Law"), in Miklós Degré and Alajos Várady-Brenner, eds., *Magyar Törvénytár. 1939. évi törvényczikkek* (Budapest: Franklin, 1940), 129–48.

Document 1-3: Act XV of 1941 on the Modification and Amendment of Act XXXI of 1894 on Marriage Law and the Necessary Related Race Protection Regulations (Third "Jewish Law"), in Miklós Degré and Alajos Várady-Brenner, eds., *Magyar Törvénytár. 1941. évi törvényczikkek* (Budapest: Franklin, n.d. [1942]), 63–65.

Document 1-4: Act XV of 1942 on the Jewish-Owned Agricultural Lands and Forests, in Miklós Degré and Alajos Várady-Brenner, eds., *Magyar Törvénytár. 1942. évi törvényczikkek* (Budapest: Franklin, n.d. [1943]), 93–98.

### The Impact of the Antisemitic Legislation

Document 1-5(A): István Domonkos, recollections of the impact of the discriminatory laws on individuals, 2004–2005, CENTROPA (www.centropa.hu).

Document 1-5(B): Portrait of Péter Domonkos, image no. 1011222232160678, CENTROPA (www.centropa.hu).

Document 1-5(C): Dr. Róbert Pap (1945), recollections of the impact of the discriminatory laws on individuals, HJA, DEGOB Protocols, no. 3560.

Document 1-5(D): Ernő Galpert, personal recollections of the impact of the discriminatory laws on individuals, 2003, CENTROPA (www.centropa.hu).

Document 1-5(E): Portrait of Ernő Galpert, image no. 1012150900158492, CENTROPA (www.centropa.hu).

## 2: Discrimination, Radicalization, and the First Mass Murders

### Bureaucratic and Illegal Antisemitism before 1944

Document 2-1: City regulation and the attached statement of reasons, issued by the Rimaszombat municipal authorities, June 1941, YVA RG M 48, fascicle 3166, ŠOKA Rimavská Sobota, Documents of the Mayor of Rimaszombat, document 4400/1941.

Document 2-2(A): Letter written by János K. (last name illegible) to the subprefect of Pest-Pilis-Solt-Kiskun County, László Endre, spring 1941, Pest County Archives IV/408/B, document 29.877/1941.

Document 2-2(B): Order of the subprefect of Pest-Pilis-Solt-Kiskun, No. 27.845/1941, May 1941, USHMMA RG 39.013M, reel 71 (HJA XXIV/C, box A 5/1).

Document 2-3: Minutes of a meeting of the Bihar County authorities, March 28, 1942, HBCA IV.B. 1406/b, box 284, document 16.978/1942.

### The First Mass Murders

Document 2-4: Photograph of a Jewish community representative at a commemorative event celebrating the reannexation of Northern Transylvania by Hungary, 1940 (Courtesy of FORTEPAN).

Document 2-5: Decree of the Minister of the Interior, July 12, 1941, USHMMA RG 39.018M, disc 45, V-122.405 (HAHSS, file V-122.405).

Document 2-6: Report of István Weiss on the activity of Putnok chief constable Imre Mogyoróssy in 1941, February 26, 1946, HBCA XXV.1, file 257/1947.

Document 2-7: Photograph by Gyula Spitz of Jews being taken to the execution site in Kamenets-Podolski, August 1941, USHMMPA WS# 28215 (courtesy of Ivan Sved).

Document 2-8: Testimony of Julia Kolb about the Újvidék massacre (1945), USHMMA RG 39.013M (HJA, DEGOB Protocols, no. 761).

### Labor Service

Document 2-9: Introduction to and articles of Act XIV of 1942 on the Modification and Extension of Act II of 1939 on National Defense and Act IV of 1938 on the Recognition of the Achievements of Combat Veterans of the 1914–1918 World War, in *1942. évi Országos Törvénytár* (Budapest: Magyar Királyi Belügyminisztérium, 1943), 76–89.

Document 2-10(A): Memoirs of Minister of Defense Vilmos Nagybaczoni Nagy (1947), published in Vilmos Nagybaczoni Nagy, *Végzetes esztendők*, 2nd rev. ed. (Budapest: Kossuth, 1986), 99, 126, 132, 168.

Document 2-10(B): Decree of Minister of Defense Vilmos Nagybaczoni Nagy, December 19, 1942, in Elek Karsai, ed., *"Fegyvertelen álltak az aknamezőkön . . ." Dokumentumok a munkaszolgálat történetéhez Magyarországon* (Budapest: Magyar Izraeliták Országos Képviselete, 1962), 1:178–84.

Document 2-11: Diary entries of a Hungarian officer serving on the eastern front lines, November–January 1943, USHMMA RG 39.013M, reel 71 (HJA XXIV/C, box A 5/4).

Document 2-12: Sentence of the people's court in the city of Győr regarding the crime committed by Corporal Ferenc Varga and Private István Suri, August 2, 1945, in Elek Karsai, ed., *"Fegyvertelen álltak az aknamezőkön . . ." Dokumentumok a munkaszolgálat történetéhez Magyarországon* (Budapest: Magyar Izraeliták Országos Képviselete, 1962), 1:83–88.

Document 2-13: Miklós Radnóti, "Fourth Razglednica," private collection, Mrs. Miklós Radnóti.

Document 2-14: Photograph of labor serviceman Aladár Barber in 1944, USHMMPA WS# 10030 (courtesy of Charles and Herma Ellenboghen Barber).

## Hungarian-German Relations and the "Jewish Question"

Document 2-15: György Ottlik's report to the Ministry of Foreign Affairs, October 10, 1942, HNA, Series K 64, fascicle 96, item 41, file 437/1942.

Document 2-16: Regent Miklós Horthy's letter to Adolf Hitler, May 7, 1943, in Miklós Szinai and László Szűcs, eds., *Horthy Miklós titkos iratai* [Confidential Papers of Miklós Horthy] (Budapest: Kossuth, 1962), 391–400.

Document 2-17: Report by Edmund Veesenmayer, representative of the German Foreign Office, on the political situation in Hungary, December 10, 1943, IMT, NG-5560 (translated from German).

## 3: Blitzkrieg against the Jews

### Stigmatization

Document 3-1: Prime Minister's Decree no. 1240/1944 on the distinguishing mark of the Jews, *Budapesti Közlöny*, March 31, 1944, 3.

Document 3-2: Wedding portrait of Imre Rosner and his wife, Klára Krausz, 1944, USHMMPA WS# 27410.

## Setting Up the Ghettos

Document 3-3: Minister of the Interior's Confidential Decree no. 6163/1944 on designating the residence of Jews, April 7, 1944, USHMMA RG 52.001M, reel 11 (HNA I).

Document 3-4: Prime Minister's Decree no. 1610/1944 on the regulation of certain questions concerning the apartments of the Jews and the designation of their residence, *Budapesti Közlöny*, April 28, 1944, 2–3.

Document 3-5: Minutes of the ghetto meeting at the town hall of Debrecen, May 8, 1944, HBCA IV.B.1406.b, box 365, document 21.838/1944.

Document 3-6: Ghetto order of the subprefect of Zala County, May 4, 1944, in László Németh and Zoltán Paksy, eds., *Együttélés és kirekesztés. Zsidók Zala megye társadalmában, 1919–1945* (Zalaegerszeg: Zala Megyei Levéltár, 2004), 393–96.

## Life in the Ghettos

Document 3-7: Ghetto order of Kassa, May 1, 1944, National Széchényi Library, Placard and Leaflet Collection.

Document 3-8: "Jewish Self-government in the Ghetto" (on the Szombathely ghetto), *Vasvármegye*, July 30, 1944, 3.

Document 3-9: Survivor testimony on the interrogations in the Nagyvárad ghetto, 1945, at the trial against László Gyapay and his associates, USHMMA RG-25.004M, reel 87, file 40029 (documents of the Romanian Information Service, SRI), 2:19–20.

Document 3-10(A–D): Daily reports from provincial Jewish Councils, May 1944, USHMMA RG-39.013M, reel 7 (HJA XX-A, box D 5/1).

Document 3-10(A): Nagyvárad

Document 3-10(B): Marosvásárhely

Document 3-10(C): Szatmárnémeti

Document 3-10(D): Érsekújvár

Document 3-11: Móric Goldstein and his son Endre in the Debrecen ghetto, spring–summer 1944, USHMMPA WS# 08313.

# 4: Deportations from the Provinces and the Fate of the Budapest Jews

## Destruction of the Provincial Communities

Document 4-1: Reports of Gendarme Lieutenant Colonel László Ferenczy, the liaison officer of the Hungarian gendarmerie, to the Sondereinsatzkommando Eichmann, May 3, 1944, USHMMA RG 39.018 (BMTI), disc 15, V-79348.

Document 4-2: Horthy's memorandum to Sztójay, June 1944, in Miklós Szinai and László Szűcs, eds., *Horthy Miklós titkos iratai* (Budapest: Kossuth, 1962), 450–54.

Document 4-3: Report of László Endre on the deportations for the Council of Ministers, June 21, 1944, USHMMA RG 39.018 (BMTI), discs 15–17, V-79802.

Document 4-4: Reports by the police chief inspector of the Sárvár Auxiliary Detention House, July 14, 1944, in Elek Karsai, ed., *Vádirat a nácizmus ellen. Dokumentumok a magyarországi zsidóüldözés történetéhez (1944 június 26–1944 október 15. A budapesti zsidóság deportálásának felfüggesztése)* (Budapest: Magyar Izraeliták Országos Képviselete, 1967), 3:180, 185–86.

Document 4-5: Jenő Reich's farewell postcard and letter to his family, July 1944, HJA XX-F-II, box D 6/2.

## The Strasshof Deportations

Document 4-6: Memoirs of Márta Balázs, no date (postwar), USHMMA RG 10.207, 36–37.

Document 4-7: Class picture of the Szolnok Neologue Jewish elementary school, around 1939, from the private collection of Géza Cseh, Szolnok, Hungary. Lipót Madarász is in the center.

## The Concentration of the Budapest Jews

Document 4-8: László Komlósi's letter to the lord mayor of Budapest, June 19, 1944, USHMMA RG 52.001M, reel 16 (HNA, Series I).

Document 4-9: Order by the Budapest chief of the Hungarian Royal Police, June 23, 1944, National Széchényi Library, Placard and Leaflet Collection.

Document 4-10: Éva Weinmann's diary, July 23, 1944, USHMMA RG 39.013M, reel 26 (HJA XX-G, box D 6/6).

Document 4-11: Ads published in *Magyarországi Zsidók Lapja* [Journal of the Jews in Hungary], August 3, 1944.

Document 4-12: Magdolna Pálmai (on the right) and her friend Klári clearing rubble in Budapest, September 1944, image no. 1012010205385956, CENTROPA (www.centropa.hu).

## Suspension of Deportations: July to August 1944

Document 4-13: Telegram from the king of Sweden, Gustaf V, to Regent Miklós Horthy protesting the deportations, June 30, 1944, in Elek Karsai, ed., *Vádirat a nácizmus ellen. Dokumentumok a magyarországi zsidóüldözés történetéhez (1944 június 26–1944 október 15. A budapesti zsidóság deportálásának felfüggesztése)* (Budapest: Magyar Izraeliták Országos Képviselete, 1967), 3:58.

Document 4-14: Regent Miklós Horthy's reply to the king of Sweden, early July 1944, in Elek Karsai, ed., *Vádirat a nácizmus ellen. Dokumentumok a magyarországi zsidóüldözés történetéhez (1944 június 26–1944 október 15. A budapesti zsidóság deportálásának felfüggesztése)* (Budapest: Magyar Izraeliták Országos Képviselete, 1967), 3:59.

Document 4-15: Telegram of Reich Plenipotentiary in Hungary Edmund Veesenmayer to Minister of Foreign Affairs Joachim von Ribbentrop, July 6, 1944, in IMT, NG-5523 (translated from German).

Document 4-16: Excerpts from the recollection of István Vasdényei, no date (probably early 1960s), HJA XX-G, box D 9/2.

Document 4-17. Draft of a government decree regarding a German-Hungarian agreement on the deportation of the remaining Jews, August 23, 1944, in Elek Karsai, ed., *Vádirat a nácizmus ellen. Dokumentumok a magyarországi zsidóüldözés történetéhez (1944 június 26–1944 október 15. A budapesti zsidóság deportálásának felfüggesztése)* (Budapest: Magyar Izraeliták Országos Képviselete, 1967), 3:451–52 (translated from German).

# 5: The Arrow Cross Regime

## The Takeover

Document 5-1: Hungarian News Agency broadcast of Miklós Horthy's proclamation on the cease-fire, October 15, 1944, in Magda Ádám et al., eds., *Magyarország és a második világháború. Titkos diplomáciai okmányok a háború előzményeihez és történetéhez*, 2nd ed. (Budapest: Kossuth, 1959), 479–80.

## The Arrow Cross Movement: Its Leader and Ideology

Document 5-2: Ferenc Szálasi's diary (Notebook C, entry no. 915), USHMMA RG 39.013M, reel 69 (HJA XIX-Benoschofsky, box A 6/2).

## Deportations Resumed: The Death Marches

Document 5-3: Decree of Minister of Defense Károly Beregfy on the forced labor of Jewish men and women, October 21, 1944, USHMMA RG 39.013M, reel 25 (HJA XX-F-1, box D 6/1).

Document 5-4: A report by two representatives of the Swiss embassy on the death marches, November 28, 1944, in Randolph L. Braham, *The Politics of Genocide: The Holocaust in Hungary* (New York: Columbia University Press, 1994), 2:967–69.

## Szálasi's Final Plan and the Budapest Ghettos

Document 5-5: Szálasi's "final plan" concerning the Jews, November 17, 1944, in NARA, T-120, reel 4664 (translated from German).

Document 5-6: Jewish Council member Rabbi Dr. Béla Berend's report to the council on Arrow Cross atrocities, January 12, 1945, USHMMA RG 39.013M, reel 7 (HJA XX-A, box D 9/3).

Document 5-7: Service ticket issued by the Budapest ghetto police, January 17, 1945, USHMMA RG 39.013M, reel 7 (HJA XX-A, box D 9/3).

Document 5-8: Order by the Jewish Council about the burial of the dead in the ghetto, January 4, 1945, USHMMA RG 39.013M, reel 7 (HJA XX-A, box D 9/3).

Document 5-9: Testimony of Mrs. Lajos Lévy (née Katalin Freund), 1945, USHMMA RG 39.013M, reel 4 (HJA, DEGOB Protocols, no. 3596).

### Terror outside the Ghettos

Document 5-10: Testimony of Mór Halpern given to the Committee Investigating Nazi and Arrow Cross Atrocities, April 8, 1945, USHMMA RG 52.001M, reel 13 (HNA I).

### Jewish Voices from the Arrow Cross Era

Document 5-11(A): Lilla Ecséri, Budapest, diary entry for October 15 and 16, 1944, in Lilla Ecséri, *Napló, 1944* (Budapest: T-Twins, 1995), 27–29.

Document 5-11(B): Photograph of Lilla Ecséri, no date, private collection.

Document 5-12(A): Excerpts from the memoirs of Hilda Löbl, March 1946, private collection.

Document 5-12(B): Photograph of Hilda Löbl and Mihály Kádár, 1941, private collection.

## 6: Plunder

### The Machinery of Plunder: The Process and Agencies

Document 6-1: Prime Minister's Decree no. 1600/1944 on the registration and confiscation of Jewish property, April 16, 1944, *Budapesti Közlöny*, April 16, 1944, 1–3.

Document 6-2: Press report on the sealing of Jewish shops, *Somogyi Ujság*, April 8, 1944.

Document 6-3: Confidential reports of the Szolnok Financial Directorate, June 3 and June 13, 1944, JNSZCA VI. 101. b., box no. 1, document no. 60/1944, 60/1/1944.

Document 6-4: Inventory of items in a Jewish apartment of Újkécske, May 23, 1944, Archives of Bács-Kiskun County, V-386, box 14.

Document 6-5: Notice to Jewish taxpayers from the mayor of Veszprém, May 8, 1944, National Széchényi Library, Placard and Leaflet Collection.

Document 6-6: Record on the reimbursement of railway transportation costs incurred by the Hungarian State Railways during the deportation of the Jews of Hódmezővásárhely, June 2, 1944, USHMMA RG 52.001M, reel 79 (HNA, Series I).

Document 6-7: People's court trial documents on body searches in the Pécs ghetto, 1949, in Ágnes Ságvári, ed., *Dokumentumok a zsidóság üldöztetésének történetéhez* [Baranya County] (Budapest: Magyar Auschwitz Alapítvány–Holocaust Dokumentációs Központ, 1994), 24–30.

Document 6-8: Prime Minister's Decree no. 3840/1944 on the nationalization of Jewish assets, *Budapesti Közlöny*, November 3, 1944, 2.

## The Effects of Plunder: Winners and Losers

Document 6-9: Circular Decree of the Ministry of the Interior on the prevention of the hiding of gold and valuables by the Jews, April 6, 1944, NCA V. 83, box 15.

Document 6-10: Photograph of local residents plundering furniture and other valuables left behind in a provincial ghetto, summer or autumn 1944, HJA, T 65.686.

Document 6-11: Speech of Minister of the Interior Andor Jaross in Nagyvárad, *Magyarság*, May 18, 1944, 5.

Document 6-12: Complaint of Mrs. Imre Gréczi regarding the auctioning off of Jewish assets, June 2, 1944, USHMMA RG 52.001M, reel 12 (HNA, Series I).

Document 6-13: Report of the public health officer of Máramaros County to the Ministry of the Interior, May 27, 1944, USHMMA RG 52.001M, reel 8 (HNA I).

## Synagogues into Storehouses

Document 6-14(A). Confiscated Jewish items piled up in the Szeged synagogue, 1945, Móra Ferenc Museum (Szeged), USHMMPA WS# 18745.

Document 6-14(B): Shoes belonging to members of the Jewish community of Szeged in the city's synagogue. Photograph by Béla Liebmann, 1945, USHMMPA WS# 18749.

# 7: In the Nazi Camps

## Auschwitz Getting Ready

Document 7-1: Statement of responsibility by SS-Unterscharführer Arthur Breitwieser about his participation in the operation against the Hungarian Jews, May 22, 1944, USHMMA RG 04.006M (Records of Nazi Concentration Camps), reel 2, Auschwitz, 34 (translated from German).

## On the "Jewish Ramp" of Auschwitz II–Birkenau

Document 7-2: Photograph of Sril (or Israel) (left) and Zelig (right) Jákob upon arrival at the Birkenau extermination camp, May 1944, courtesy of YVA (photo album FA268/49).

## The Mass Murder of Hungarian Jews

Document 7-3: Notes of *Sonderkommando* member Leib Langfuss on the murder of the Hungarian Jews, in Bernard Mark, *The Scrolls of Auschwitz*, ed. Isaiah Avrech (Tel Aviv: Am Oved, 1985), 206, 208.

Document 7-4: Testimony of Dr. Miklós Nyiszli, July 29, 1945, USHMMA RG 39.013M, reel 5 (HJA, DEGOB Protocols, no. 3632).

## Deported to Other Camps

Document 7-5: Transfer document of Imre Kertész and 2,499 other prisoners from Auschwitz to Buchenwald, July 1944, USHMMA Acc.1996. A.0342, NARA Selected records relating to concentration camps from Buchenwald, reel 147 (translated from German).

Document 7-6: Emil Weisz's concentration camp diary, January–April 1945, USHMMA RG 39.013M (HJA XX-G, box D 6/6).

Document 7-7: Edith Bacher's letter, 1945, USHMMA RG 39.013M (HJA XX-F-II, box D 6).

Document 7-8: Image of Mauthausen prisoner registry card of Leó Buday-Goldberger, HJA XX-C-5, box I 5/3.

# 8: Jewish Responses to Persecution

## Patterns of Individual Jewish Responses

Document 8-1: Gyula Eörsi's diary entries for May 8 and 14, 1944, Eörsi family collection.

Document 8-2: László Kovács's memoir of life in the ghetto, in László Kovács, *Tanú vagyok. Életrajzi töredékek* (Nyíregyháza: Szabolcs-Szatmár-Bereg Megyei Önkormányzat Levéltára, 2004), 41–45.

Document 8-3: "During the Lull in the Wave of Conversions," *Magyarországi Zsidók Lapja*, August 10, 1944, 1.

## Strategy of the Jewish Council

Document 8-4: Announcement of the Central Jewish Council, in *Magyar Zsidók Lapja*, April 6, 1944, 1.

Document 8-5: Petition of the Central Jewish Council to Minister of the Interior Andor Jaross, May 26, 1944, HNA P 1434, fascicle 17, file V/26.

Document 8-6: Testimony of Jewish Council member Ernő Pető, May 28, 1945, USHMMA RG 39.013M, reel 28 (HJA XX-L-1, box D 5/3).

### Zionist Responses

Document 8-7: Ottó Komoly's diary entries for April/May 1944, USHMMA RG 52.030*01 (YVA, P 31/44).

Document 8-8: Photograph of young Zionist resistance fighter David Gur, winter 1944, USHMMPA WS# 94470.

### Thwarted Appeals

Document 8-9(A–B): Illegal leaflets of the Jewish underground, summer 1944.

Document 8-9(A): USHMMA RG 39.013M, reel 26 (HJA XX-F-II, box D 6/4).

Document 8-9(B): Elek Karsai, ed., *Vádirat a nácizmus ellen. Dokumentumok a magyarországi zsidóüldözés történetéhez* (1944 május 26–1944 október 15. A budapesti zsidóság deportálásának felfüggesztése) (Budapest: Magyar Izraeliták Országos Képviselete, 1967), 3:34.

Document 8-10: Certificate issued by the Central Jewish Council proving that Fülöp Grünvald (erroneously spelled Grünwald in the document) is an employee of the council, April 1944, USHMMA RG 39.013M, reel 25 (HJA XX-F-1, box D 6/1).

Document 8-11: Illegal leaflet of the Jewish underground, summer(?) 1944. Elek Karsai, ed., *Vádirat a nácizmus ellen. Dokumentumok a magyarországi zsidóüldözés történetéhez (1944 május 26–1944 október 15. A budapesti zsidóság deportálásának felfüggesztése)* (Budapest: Magyar Izraeliták Országos Képviselete, 1967), 3:32–33.

## 9: Non-Jewish Reactions

### Bystanders: Collaborators and Beneficiaries

Document 9-1: Excerpts from Gyula Lootz's proposal to László Endre on retaliation against the Jews, May 8, 1944, HNA P 1434, fascicle 17, file V/8.

Document 9-2: Anonymous denunciation filed with the police, no date (late 1944/early 1945), HNA P 1434, fascicle 19.

Document 9-3: Petition by sound amplification entrepreneur Géza Nagysötétági Macskásy, April 27, 1944, in Ilona Benoschofsky and Elek Karsai, eds., *Vádirat a nácizmus ellen. Dokumentumok a magyarországi zsidóüldözés történetéhez (1944 március 19–1944 május 15. A német megszállástól a deportálás megkezdéséig)* (Budapest: Magyar Izraeliták Országos Képviselete, 1958), 1:262–64.

Document 9-4: "The Civilian Population Should Not Storm the Housing Bureau," *Új Magyarság*, June 29, 1944.

Document 9-5(A–B): Propaganda materials lashing out at solidarity with the Jews, summer 1944.

Document 9-5(A): *Harc*, June 3, 1944.

Document 9-5(B): Leaflet of the far-right Eastern Frontline Comrades' Association, summer 1944, HBCA IV.B. 1406/b., document 26.607/1944.

Document 9-6: Diary entries of writer Sándor Márai, summer of 1944, in Sándor Márai, *Napló (1943–1944)* (Budapest: Révai, 1945), 261–83.

## Bystanders: Solidarity and Rescue

Document 9-7(A): Extract from the testimony of Mrs. Lázár Berkovics, July 12, 1945, HJA, DEGOB Protocols, no. 1216.

Document 9-7(B): Extract from the testimony of Ignác Berkovits, June 30, 1945, HJA, DEGOB Protocols, no. 182.

Document 9-8: Photographs of Renáta and Szilvia Schönberg and their rescuer, Frantiska Prva, 1946, USHMMPA WS# 45878.

Document 9-9(A): News reports from the extreme right-wing press about rescue attempts in 1944, *Magyarság*, June 29, 1944.

Document 9-9(B): "The World of the Yellow Star," *Függetlenség*, June 11, 1944.

Document 9-10(A): Statement about the rescue activities of Gendarme Sergeant Major László Endre, 1945, HMC, Rescuers' Personal Files, file 250.

Document 9-10(B): Statement about the rescue activities of the Gendarme Sergeant Major László Endre, 1945, HMC, Rescuers' Personal Files, file 250.

Document 9-11(A): Speech by László Németh in 1943, in Szárszó, *Az 1943. évi balatonszárszói Magyar Élet-tábor előadás- és megbeszéléssorozata*, 3rd ed. (Budapest: Püski, 1993), 46–47.

Document 9-11(B): Memoir of István Vas on László Németh's rescue activity in 1944, in István Vas, *Nehéz szerelem III. Összegyűjtött Munkái* (Budapest: Szépirodalmi, 1984), 13:259.

## The Churches

Document 9-12: Pastoral letter of Archbishop Jusztinián Serédi on behalf of the Hungarian Catholic Council of Bishops, June 29, 1944, in Randolph L. Braham, *The Politics of Genocide: The Holocaust in Hungary* (New York: Columbia University Press, 1994), 2:1180–82.

Document 9-13: Postwar eyewitness report on the arrest of the Catholic sister Sára Salkaházi, in Károly Hetényi-Varga, *Papi sorsok a horogkereszt és a vörös csillag árnyékában*, 2nd ed. (Budapest: Új Ember–Márton Áron, 2004), 141.

## Intervention and the International Community

Document 9-14: Protective letter (*Schutzbrief*) issued by the Swiss legation in Budapest to Maria Magdalena Grausz, July 1, 1944, USHMMPA WS# 45647.

Document 9-15: Protective passport (*Schutzpass*) issued by the Swedish embassy to Rabbi József Katona, September 15, 1944, USHMMPA WS# 67062.

Document 9-16: Reports of Raoul Wallenberg to the Swedish Ministry of Foreign Affairs regarding the rescue activity of the Swedish embassy, July–December 1944, in Raoul Wallenberg, *Letters and Dispatches* (New York: Arcade Publishing in association with the USHMM, 1995), 236–37, 257–58, 262–63, 265–67.

Document 9-17: Protective document issued by the International Red Cross for Dr. László Benedek, September 7, 1944, HJA XX-F-1, box D 6/1.

# 10: Jews in Postwar Hungary

## Liberation

Document 10-1: László Keller (left) and a fellow prisoner named Feri (right) in the Ampfing concentration camp after the liberation, May 4, 1945, USHMMPA WS# 67871.

Document 10-2: Memoirs of Pauline Fabri, Budapest, June 1945–January 1946, USHMMA Acc. 2007.168 Pauline Widder Fabri diary.

## The Dimensions of Destruction

Document 10-3: Dávid Teitelbaum in the destroyed Mád synagogue, 1946–1947, HJA XXII-IV.65.

Document 10-4(A): Letter of the Central Office of the Autonomous Orthodox Israelite Denomination of Hungary to the Sárbogárd Jewish community, September 19, 1947, USHMMA RG 39.013M, reel 107 (HJA XV-B Sárbogárd, box TA 6/5/5).

Document 10-4(B): Letter of the National Association of Rabbis to the Sárbogárd Jewish community, January 9, 1948, USHMMA RG 39.013M, reel 107 (HJA XV-B Sárbogárd, box TA 6/5/5).

## To Leave or to Stay?

Document 10-5: Embarkation card issued to Alexander Feuer indicating his place on the SS *Marine Flasher*, USHMMPA WS# 02110.

## Rehabilitation, Restitution, Pogroms

Document 10-6: Act XXV of 1946 condemning the persecution of the Jews, November 15, 1946, in *1946. évi törvényczikkek* [Acts of 1946] (Budapest: Franklin, n.d.), 104–8.

Document 10-7: Memorandum of the National Office of Hungarian Israelites on restitution and compensation issues, summer 1946, HJA XXIV-A (XXIII-5-b), box 3.

Document 10-8: Excerpts from a report by Kálmán É. Kovács to the chief secretariat of the Hungarian Communist Party on the pogrom in Kunmadaras, May 27, 1946, APH I. 274, fascicle 11, no. 64.

## Jews, Communists, Zionists

Document 10-9: Photo taken at the unification congress of the Jewish religious branches in Budapest in February 1950, HGA XXII-IV/57, image no. 02171.

## The 1956 Revolution and Fight for Freedom

Document 10-10: Letter of the National Representation of Hungarian Israelites to the People's Court Council of the Supreme Court, November 27, 1958, HJA XVI-B, box TB B/309.

## The Kádár Era and Beyond

Document 10-11: Speech of Hungarian Minister of Education Dr. Bálint Magyar at the opening of the permanent Hungarian exhibition at Auschwitz on April 15, 2004, published in *The Citizen Betrayed: In Memory of the Victims of the Hungarian Holocaust* (catalog of the permanent exhibition of the Hungarian National Museum in the Auschwitz-Birkenau State Museum) (Budapest: Magyar Nemzeti Múzeum, 2006), 17–19.

Document 10-12: The Dohány Street Synagogue's garden and the northern wall of the building, October 2012. Courtesy of Christine Schmidt.

# Bibliography

THIS SELECTION from a vast and continuously growing number of publications complements the footnote references in the chapters. It is designed to serve as an orientation for further study not as a compilation of all relevant literature. For more comprehensive listings of recent publications, check the bibliographic sections of *H&GS, YVS*, and other journals.

Ádám, Magda, Gyula Juhász, and Lajos Kerekes, eds. *Magyarország és a második világháború. Titkos diplomáciai okmányok a háború előzményeihez és történetéhez* [Hungary and World War II: Confidential Diplomatic Documents on the History and Antecedents of the War]. 2nd ed. Budapest: Kossuth, 1959.

Ancel, Jean, ed. *Documents Concerning the Fate of Romanian Jewry during the Holocaust*. 12 vols. New York: Beate Klarsfeld Foundation, n.d. [1986].

Apel, Linde. *Jüdische Frauen im Konzentrationslager Ravensbrück 1939–1945*. Berlin: Metropol, 2003.

Arad, Yitzhak, Shmuel Krakowski, and Shmuel Spector. *The Einsatzgruppen Reports: Selections from the Dispatches of the Nazi Death Squads' Campaign against the Jews, July 1941–January 1943*. New York: Holocaust Library, 1989.

Arendt, Hannah. *Eichmann in Jerusalem: A Report on the Banality of Evil*. 2nd rev. ed. New York: Penguin, 1976.

Bajtay, Péter, ed. *Emberirtás-embermentés. Svéd követjelentések 1944-ből. Az Auschwitzi Jegyzőkönyv* [Genocide and Rescue: Reports of the Swedish Embassy from 1944: The Auschwitz Protocol]. Budapest: Katalizátor Iroda, 1994.

Bányai, László, László Csorba, Anikó Kis, Ferenc L. Lendvai, Gyula Zeke, Péter Bihari, and Györgyi Tamási, eds. *Hét évtized a hazai zsidóság életében* [Seven Decades in the Life of the Jews in Hungary]. 2 vols. Budapest: MTA Filozófiai Intézet, 1990.

Bauer, Yehuda. *Jews for Sale? Nazi-Jewish Negotiations, 1933–1945*. New Haven, CT: Yale University Press, 1994.

Benoschofsky, Ilona, and Elek Karsai, eds. *Vádirat a nácizmus ellen. Dokumentumok a magyarországi zsidóüldözés történetéhez*. 1. *(1944 március 19–1944 május 15. A német megszállástól a deportálás megkezdéséig)* [The Indictment of Nazism: Documents on the Persecution of Jews in Hungary. Vol. 1: March 19–May 15, 1944: From the German Occupation to the Beginning of the Deportations]. Budapest: Magyar Izraeliták Országos Képviselete, 1958.

———, eds. *Vádirat a nácizmus ellen. Dokumentumok a magyarországi zsidóüldözés történetéhez*. 2. *(1944 május 15–1944 június 30. A budapesti zsidóság összeköltöztetése.)* [The Indictment of Nazism: Documents on the Persecution of Jews in Hungary. Vol. 2: May 15–June 30, 1944: The Concentration of the Jews in Budapest]. Budapest: Magyar Izraeliták Országos Képviselete, 1960.

Benshalom, Rafi. *We Struggled for Life: The Hungarian Zionist Youth Resistance during the Nazi Era*. Jerusalem: Gefen, 2001.

Bezwińska, Jadwiga, and Danuta Czech, eds. *KL Auschwitz Seen by the SS: Höss, Broad, Kremer*, 2nd rev. ed. Oświęcim: Auschwitz-Birkenau State Museum, 1991.

Braham, Randolph L., ed. *The Destruction of Hungarian Jewry: A Documentary Account*. 2 vols. New York: Pro Arte for the World Federation of Hungarian Jews, 1963.

———. *Eichmann and the Destruction of Hungarian Jewry*. New York: Pro Arte for the World Federation of Hungarian Jews, 1961.

———. "The Holocaust in Hungary: A Retrospective Analysis." In *The Nazis' Last Victims: The Holocaust in Hungary*, edited by Randolph L. Braham with Scott Miller, 27–43. Detroit, MI: Wayne University Press in association with the USHMM, 1998.

———, ed. *The Holocaust in Hungary: A Selected and Annotated Bibliography 1984–2000*. New York: Columbia University Press, 2001.

———, ed. *Hungarian Jewish Studies*. Vol. 3. New York: World Federation of Hungarian Jews, 1973.

———. *The Politics of Genocide: The Holocaust in Hungary*. 2 vols. 2nd rev. ed. New York: Columbia University Press, 1994.

———, ed. *Tanulmányok a holokausztról* [Studies on the Holocaust]. 4 vols. Budapest: Balassi, 2001–2006.

———, ed. *The Tragedy of Hungarian Jewry: Essays, Documents, Depositions*. New York: Columbia University Press, 1986.

———, ed. *The Wartime System of Labor Service in Hungary: Varieties of Experiences*. New York: Columbia University Press, 1995.

Braham, Randolph L., and Julia Bock, eds. *The Holocaust in Hungary: A Selected and Annotated Bibliography, 2000–2007*. New York: Columbia University Press, 2008.

Braham, Randolph L., and Brewster S. Chamberlin, eds. *The Holocaust in Hungary: Sixty Years Later*. New York: Columbia University Press, 2006.

Braham, Randolph L., and Attila Pók, eds. *The Holocaust in Hungary: Fifty Years Later*. New York: Columbia University Press, 1997.

Braham, Randolph L., and Zoltán Tibori Szabó, eds. *The Geographical Encyclopedia of the Holocaust in Hungary*. 3 vols. Evanston, IL: Northwestern University Press in association with the USHMM, 2013.

Braham, Randolph L., and Bela Vago, eds. *The Holocaust in Hungary: Forty Years Later.* New York: Social Science Monographs, 1985.
Browning, Christopher R., with contributions by Jürgen Matthäus. *The Origins of the Final Solution: The Evolution of Nazi Jewish Policy, September 1939–March 1942.* Lincoln and Jerusalem: University of Nebraska Press and Yad Vashem, 2004.
Buber Agassi, Judith. *Jewish Women Prisoners of Ravensbrück: Who Were They?* Oxford: One World, 2007.
Carmilly, Moshe, and Michael K. Silber, eds. *Jews in the Hungarian Economy, 1760–1945: Studies Dedicated to Moshe Carmilly-Weinberger on His Eightieth Birthday.* Jerusalem: Magnes Press, 1992.
Case, Holly. *Between States: The Transylvanian Question and the European Idea during World War II.* Stanford, CA: Stanford University Press, 2009.
*The Citizen Betrayed: In Memory of the Victims of the Hungarian Holocaust* (catalog of the permanent exhibition of the Hungarian National Museum in the Auschwitz-Birkenau State Museum). Budapest: Magyar Nemzeti Múzeum, 2006.
Cohen, Asher. *The Halutz Resistance in Hungary, 1942–1944.* Boulder, CO: Social Science Monographs, 1986.
Cole, Tim. *Holocaust City: The Making of a Jewish Ghetto.* New York: Routledge, 2003.
———. *Traces of the Holocaust: Journeying in and out of the Ghettos.* New York: Continuum International, 2011.
———. "Writing Bystanders into Holocaust History in More Active Ways: 'Non-Jewish' Engagement with Ghettoisation, Hungary 1944." *Holocaust Studies: A Journal of Culture and History* 11 (summer 2005): 55–74.
Csősz, László. "Land Reforms and Race Protection: The Implementation of the Fourth Jewish Law." In *The Holocaust in Hungary: A European Perspective*, ed. Judit Molnár, 180–97. Budapest: Balassi, 2005.
———. "A Vészkorszak Jász-Nagykun-Szolnok vármegyében" [The Holocaust in Jász-Nagykun-Szolnok County]. PhD diss., University of Szeged, 2010.
Czech, Danuta. *Auschwitz Chronicle, 1939–1945.* New York: Henry Holz, 1997.
Dean, Martin. *Robbing the Jews: The Confiscation of Jewish Property in the Holocaust, 1933–1945.* New York: Cambridge University Press in association with the USHMM, 2008.
———, ed. *The United States Holocaust Memorial Museum Encyclopedia of Camps and Ghettos, 1933–1945.* Vol. 2: *Ghettos in German-Occupied Eastern Europe.* Bloomington: Indiana University Press in association with the USHMM, 2012.
Déry, Endre, Endre Elbert, Endre Friedmann, and József Vági. *A fasizmus üldözötteit védő jogszabályok 1945–1946* [Laws and Decrees Defending the Persecutees of Fascism, 1945–1946]. Budapest: American Jewish Joint Distribution Committee Magyarországi Bizottsága, 1946.
Długoborski, Wacław, and Franciszek Piper, eds. *Auschwitz, 1940–1945: Central Issues in the History of the Camp.* 5 vols. Oświęcim: Auschwitz-Birkenau State Museum, 2000.
Duschinsky, Eugene. "Hungary." In *The Jews in the Soviet Satellites*, edited by Peter Meyer et al., 373–489. Syracuse, NY: Syracuse University Press, 1953.
Eichmann, Adolf. *Tárgyalástól ítéletig. Feljegyzések a börtönből* [From the Trial to the Verdict: Memoirs Written in Prison]. Budapest: Trifer, 2000.

Favez, Jean-Claude. *The Red Cross and the Holocaust*. Cambridge: Cambridge University Press, 1999.

Friedler, Eric, Barbara Siebert, and Andreas Kilian. *Zeugen aus der Todeszone. Das jüdische Sonderkommando in Auschwitz*. Lüneberg: zu Klampen, 2002.

Frojimovics, Kinga. *I Have Been a Stranger in a Strange Land: The Hungarian State and the Jewish Refugees in Hungary, 1933–1945*. Jerusalem: Yad Vashem, 2007.

Frojimovics, Kinga, and Judit Molnár, eds. "Gettómagyarország 1944. A Központi Zsidó Tanács iratai" [Ghetto-Hungary 1944: Documents of the Central Jewish Council]. In *Magyar Zsidó Levéltári Füzetek* [Publications of the Hungarian Jewish Archives]. Vol. 5, ed. Zsuzsanna Toronyi. Budapest: Magyar Zsidó Múzeum és Levéltár, 2002.

———. *A Világ Igazai Magyarországon a második világháború alatt* [Righteous Among the Nations in Hungary during World War II]. Budapest: Balassi, 2009.

Frojimovics, Kinga, and József Schweitzer, eds. *Magyarországi zsidó hitközségek 1944 április. A Magyar Zsidók Központi Tanácsának összeírása a német hatóságok rendelkezése nyomán. I. rész: Adattár* [Jewish Congregations in Hungary, April 1944: The Census of the Central Council of Hungarian Jews Taken by Order of the German Authorities. Part I: Data]. Budapest: MTA Judaisztikai Kutatócsoport, 1994.

Gergely, Jenő. "A katolikus püspöki kar és a konvertiták mentése (Dokumentumok)" [Catholic Bishops and the Rescue of Converts (Documents)]. *Történelmi Szemle* 27, no. 4 (1984): 580–616.

Gerlach, Christian, and Götz Aly. *Das letzte Kapitel. Der Mord an den ungarischen Juden 1944–1945*. Stuttgart: DVA, 2002.

Grossman, Alexander. *Nur das Gewissen—Carl Lutz und seine Budapester Aktion*. Wald: Im Waldgut, 1986.

Gur, David. *Brothers for Resistance and Rescue: The Underground Zionist Youth Movement in Hungary during World War II*. Jerusalem: Gefen, 2007.

Gutman, Yisrael, and Michael Berenbaum, eds. *Anatomy of the Auschwitz Death Camp*. Bloomington: Indiana University Press in association with the USHMM, 1998.

Gyurgyák, János. *A zsidókérdés Magyarországon* [The Jewish Question in Hungary]. Budapest: Osiris, 2001.

Hanebrink, Paul A. *In Defense of Christian Hungary: Religion, Nationalism, and Antisemitism, 1890–1944*. Ithaca, NY: Cornell University Press, 2006.

Haraszti, György, ed. *Auschwitzi Jegyzőkönyv* [The Auschwitz Protocol]. Budapest: Múlt és Jövő, 2005.

Hilberg, Raul. *The Destruction of the European Jews*. 3 vols. 3rd ed. New Haven, CT: Yale University Press, 2003.

———. *Perpetrators, Victims, Bystanders: The Jewish Catastrophe, 1933–1945*. New York: HarperPerennial, 1993.

Horthy, Miklós. *Memoirs*. New York: Robert Speller & Sons, 1957.

Höss, Rudolf. *Death Dealer: The Memoirs of the SS Kommandant at Auschwitz*, edited by Steven Paskuly. New York: Da Capo Press, 1996.

Ioanid, Radu. *The Holocaust in Romania: The Destruction of Jews and Gypsies under the Antonescu Regime, 1940–1944*. Chicago: Ivan R. Dee in association with the USHMM, 2000.

———. "The Sacralised Politics of the Romanian Iron Guard." In *Fascism, Totalitarianism and Political Religion*, edited by Roger Griffin, 125–59. New York: Routledge, 2005.

Isaacson, Judith Magyar. *Seed of Sarah: Memoirs of a Survivor.* Chicago: University of Illinois Press, 1990.

Isacovici, Salomon, and Juan Manuel Rodriguez. *Man of Ashes.* Lincoln: University of Nebraska Press, 1999.

Juhász, Gyula, Ervin Pamlényi, György Ránki, and Loránt Tilkovszky, eds. *A Wilhelmstrasse és Magyarország. Német diplomáciai iratok Magyarországról 1933–1944* [The Wilhelmstrasse and Hungary: German Diplomatic Documents from Hungary, 1933–1944]. Budapest: Kossuth, 1968.

Kádár, Gábor. "A magyarországi zsidók lapjának története (1944 március–október)" [The History of the Journal of the Jews of Hungary: March–October 1944]. MA thesis, ELTE, 2001.

Kádár, Gábor, and Zoltán Vági. "Compulsion of Bad Choices—Questions, Dilemmas, Decisions: The Activity of the Hungarian Central Jewish Council in 1944." In *Jewish Studies at the Central European University.* Vol. 5, edited by András Kovács and Michael Miller, 71–89. Budapest: Central European University Press, 2009.

———. *Hullarablás. A magyar zsidók gazdasági megsemmisítése* [Robbing the Dead: The Economic Annihilation of the Hungarian Jews]. Budapest: Jaffa, 2005.

———. "Rationality or Irrationality? The Annihilation of the Hungarian Jews." *Hungarian Quarterly* (summer 2004): 32–54.

———. *Self-financing Genocide: The Gold Train, the Becher Case and the Wealth of Hungarian Jews.* Budapest: Central European University Press, 2004.

Kállay, Miklós. *Hungarian Premier: A Personal Account of a Nation's Struggle in the Second World War.* Westport, CT: Greenwood Press, 1970.

Karády, Viktor. *The Jews in Europe in the Modern Era: A Socio-historical Outline.* Budapest: Central European University Press, 2004.

———. *Önazonosítás, sorsválasztás. A zsidó csoportazonosság történelmi alakváltozásai Magyarországon* [Self-Identification, Decisions on Fate: The Historical Tranformations of Jewish Collective Identity in Hungary]. Budapest: Új Mandátum, 2001.

Karsai, Elek, ed. *"Fegyvertelen álltak az aknamezőkön . . ." Dokumentumok a munkaszolgálat történetéhez Magyarországon* ["Unarmed They Stood on the Minefields . . .": Documents on the History of the Labor Service in Hungary]. 2 vols. Budapest: Magyar Izraeliták Országos Képviselete, 1962.

———, ed. *"Szálasi naplója." A nyilasmozgalom a II. világháború idején* ["Szálasi's Diary": The Arrow Cross Movement during World War II]. Budapest: Kossuth, 1978.

———, ed. *Vádirat a nácizmus ellen. Dokumentumok a magyarországi zsidóüldözés történetéhez. 3. (1944 május 26–1944 október 15. A budapesti zsidóság deportálásának felfüggesztése)* [The Indictment of Nazism: Documents on the Persecution of Jews in Hungary. Vol. 3: May 26–October 15, 1944. Suspension of the Budapest Deportations]. Budapest: Magyar Izraeliták Országos Képviselete, 1967.

Karsai, Elek, and László Karsai, eds. *A Szálasi per* [The Szálasi Trial]. Budapest: Reform, 1988.

Karsai, László. *Cigánykérdés Magyarországon 1919–1944. Út a cigány holocausthoz* [The Gypsy Question in Hungary, 1919–1944: The Road to the Gypsy Holocaust]. Budapest: Cserépfalvi, 1992.

———. "The People's Courts and Revolutionary Justice in Hungary, 1945–46." In *The Politics of Retribution in Europe: World War II and Its Aftermath,* edited by István

Deák, Jan T. Gross, and Tony Judt, 233–51. Princeton, NJ: Princeton University Press, 2000.

———. "Reflektor a sötétbe. Szálasi Ferenc naplója, 1943 szeptember 15–1944 július 18—I. rész" [Searchlight into the Darkness: The Diary of Ferenc Szálasi, September 15, 1943–July 18, 1944. Part I]. *Beszélő* 9, no. 3 (2009): 54–76.

Karsai, László, and Judit Molnár, eds. *Az Endre-Baky-Jaross per* [The Endre-Baky-Jaross Trial]. Budapest: Cserépfalvi, 1994.

———. *Küzdelem az igazságért. Tanulmányok Randolph L. Braham 80. születésnapjára* [Struggle for Justice: Studies in Honor of Randolph L. Braham's Eightieth Birthday]. Budapest: MAZSIHISZ, 2002.

———, eds. *A magyar Quisling-kormány. Sztójay Döme és társai a népbíróság előtt* [The Hungarian Qusiling Government: Döme Sztójay and his Associates before the People's Court]. Budapest: 1956-os KHT, 2004.

Katzburg, Nathaniel. *Hungary and the Jews: Policy and Legislation, 1920–1943*. Ramat-Gan: Bar-Ilan University Press, 1981.

*Képviselőházi irományok* [Documents of the Parliament of Hungary]. Budapest: Athenaeum, 1861–1945.

*Képviselőházi Naplók* [Parliamentary Journals for the Parliament of Hungary], Budapest: Athenaeum, 1861–1945.

Kolb, Eberhard. *Bergen-Belsen: From "Detention Camp" to Concentration Camp, 1943–1945*. Göttingen: Vandenhoeck & Ruprecht, 2002.

Konieczny, Alfred. *KL Gross-Rosen*. Wałbrzych: Państwowe Muzeum Gross-Rosen, 2000.

Kovács, András. "Magyar zsidó politika a háború végétől a kommunista rendszer bukásáig" [Hungarian-Jewish Politics from the End of World War II to the Fall of the Communist Regime]. In *A másik szeme. Zsidók és antiszemiták a háború utáni Magyarországon* [The Eye of the Other: Jews and Antisemites in Postwar Hungary], edited by András Kovács, 86–136. Budapest: Gondolat, 2008.

Kovács, M. Mária. *Liberal Professions, Illiberal Politics: Hungary from the Habsburgs to the Holocaust*. New York: Oxford University Press, 1994.

Kranz, Tomas. *Die Vernichtung der Juden im Konzentrationslager Majdanek*. Lublin: Państwowe Muzeum na Majdanku, 2007.

Kraus, Ota, and Erich Kulka. *Halálgyár* [Death Factory]. Budapest: Kossuth, 1958.

Kremer, Johann Paul. "Tagebuch." In *Hefte von Auschwitz* 13. Oświęcim: Verlag Staatliches Auschwitz Museum, 1971.

Lackó, Miklós. *Arrow Cross Men, National Socialists, 1935–1944*. Budapest: Kossuth, 1969.

Langbein, Hermann. *People in Auschwitz*. Chapel Hill: University of North Carolina Press in association with the USHMM, 2004.

Langfus, Leib. "Particulars." In *Amidst a Nightmare of Crime: Manuscripts of Members of Sonderkommando*, edited by Jadwiga Bezwinska and Danuta Czech, 113–22. Oświęcim: State Museum at Oświęcim, 1973.

Lévai, Jenő. *Black Book on the Martyrdom of Hungarian Jewry*. Zürich: Central European Times Publishing Company, 1948.

———. "The Hungarian Deportations in the Light of the Eichmann Trial." *YVS* 5 (1964): 69–103.

Levine, Paul A. *From Indifference to Activism: Swedish Diplomacy and the Holocaust, 1938–1944*. Uppsala: Uppsala University Library, 1998.

———. "One Day during the Holocaust: An Analysis of Raoul Wallenberg's 'Budapest Report' of 12 September 1944." *Holocaust Studies* 11, no. 3 (winter 2005): 84–104.

Löb, Ladislaus. *Dealing with Satan: Rezső Kasztner's Daring Rescue Mission*. London: Jonathan Cape, 2008.

Lozowick, Yaacov. *Hitler's Bureaucrats: The Nazi Security Police and the Banality of Evil*. London: Continuum, 2002.

*Magyar Törvénytár. Corpus juris Hungarici* [Collection of Hungarian Laws]. Budapest: Franklin, 1896–1949.

*Magyarországi Rendeletek Tára* [Collection of Hungarian Decrees]. Budapest: Belügyminisztérium-Szikra, 1939–1946.

Majsai, Tamás. "The Deportation of Jews from Csíkszereda and Margit Slachta's Intervention on Their Behalf." In *Studies on the Holocaust in Hungary*, edited by Randolph L. Braham, 113–63. New York: Columbia University Press, 1990.

———. "A kőrösmezei zsidódeportálás 1941-ben" [The Deportation of Jews to Kőrösmező in 1941]. *A Ráday gyűjtemény évkönyve* [The Yearbook of the Ráday Collections] 4–5 (1984–1985): 59–86, 195–237.

Mallmann, Klaus-Michael. "Der qualitative Sprung im Vernichtungsprozess. Das Massaker von Kamenez-Podolsk Ende August 1941." *Jahrbuch für Antisemitismusforschung* 10 (2001): 239–64.

Marszalek, Josef. *Majdanek: The Concentration Camp in Lublin*. Warsaw: Interpress, 1986.

Megargee, Geoffrey P., ed. *The United States Holocaust Memorial Museum Encyclopedia of Camps and Ghettos, 1933–1945*. Vol. 1: *Early Camps, Youth Camps, and Concentration Camps and Subcamps under the SS-Business Administration Main Office (WVHA)*. Bloomington: Indiana University Press in association with the USHMM, 2009.

Mendelsohn, John, ed. *Final Solution in the Extermination Camps and the Aftermath*. Vol. 12: *The Holocaust: Selected Documents in Eighteen Volumes*. New York: Garland Publishing, 1982.

Molnár, Judit. *Csendőrök, hivatalnokok, zsidók. Válogatott tanulmányok a magyar holokauszt történetéről* [Gendarmes, Officials, Jews: Selected Studies on the History of the Holocaust in Hungary]. Szeged: Szegedi Zsidó Hitközség, 2000.

———, ed. *The Holocaust in Hungary: A European Perspective*. Budapest: Balassi Kiadó, 2005.

———. *Zsidósors 1944-ben az V. (szegedi) csendőrkerületben* [Jewish Fate in the Fifth Gendarmerie District (Szeged) in 1944]. Budapest: Cserépfalvi, 1995.

Morley, John F. "Pope Pius XII, Roman Catholic Policy and the Holocaust in Hungary: An Analysis of Le Saint Siège et les victimes de la guerre, janvier 1944–juillet 1945." In *Pope Pius XII and the Holocaust*, edited by Carol Rittner and John K. Roth, 154–74. London: Leicester University Press, 2002.

Mravik, László, ed. *The "Sacco di Budapest" and Depredation of Hungary, 1938–1949: Works of Art Missing from Hungary as a Result of the Second World War*. Budapest: Hungarian National Gallery for the Joint Restitution Committee at the Hungarian Ministry for Culture and Education, 1998.

Müller, Filip. *Eyewitness Auschwitz: Three Years in the Gas Chambers*. Chicago: Ivan R. Dee in association with the USHMM, 1999.

Munkácsi, Ernő. *Hogyan történt? Adatok és okmányok a magyar zsidóság tragédiájához* [How Did It Happen? Data and Documents on the Tragedy of Hungarian Jewry]. Budapest: Rennaissance, 1947.

Nagy-Talavera, Nicholas M. *The Green Shirts and the Others: A History of Fascism in Hungary and Romania*. Iaşi: The Center for Romanian Studies, 2001.

Nagybaczoni Nagy, Vilmos. *Végzetes esztendők* [Fatal Years]. 2nd rev. ed. Budapest: Kossuth, 1986.

Novák, Attila. *Átmenetben. A cionista mozgalom négy éve Magyarországon* [In Transition: Four Years of the Zionist Movement in Hungary]. Budapest: Múlt és Jövő, 2000.

Nyiszli, Miklós. *Mengele boncolóorvosa voltam* [I Was Mengele's Pathologist]. Budapest: Magyar Lajos Alapítvány, 1994.

Patai, Raphael. *The Jews of Hungary: History, Culture, Psychology*. Detroit, MI: Wayne University Press, 1996.

Pelt, Robert Jan van. *The Case for Auschwitz: Evidence from the Irving Trial*. Bloomington: Indiana University Press, 2002.

Phayer, Michael. *Pius XII, the Holocaust, and the Cold War*. Bloomington: Indiana University Press, 2008.

Piper, Franciszek. *Auschwitz: How Many Perished Jews, Poles, Gypsies . . .* Oświęcim: Auschwitz-Birkenau State Museum, 1996.

———. *Die Zahl der Opfer von Auschwitz*. Oświęcim: Staatliches Museum in Oświęcim-Brzezinka, 1993.

Pressac, Jean-Claude. *Auschwitz: Technique and Operation of the Gas Chambers*. New York: Beate Klarsfeld Foundation, 1989.

Purcsi Barna, Gyula. *A cigánykérdés "gyökeres és végleges megoldása." Tanulmányok a XX. századi "cigánykérdés" történetéből* [The "Radical and Final Solution of the Gypsy Question": Studies on the History of the "Gypsy Question" in the Twentieth Century]. Debrecen: Csokonai, 2004.

Püski, Levente. *A Horthy-rendszer* [The Horthy Regime]. Budapest: Pannonica, 2006.

Railton, Nicholas. *Jane Haining and the Work of the Scottish Mission with Hungarian Jews, 1932–1945*. Budapest: n.p., 2007.

Ránki, György. *1944. március 19. Magyarország német megszállása* [March 19, 1944: The German Occupation of Hungary]. 2nd rev. ed. Budapest: Kossuth, 1978.

Romsics, Ignác. *Magyarország története a XX. században* [The History of Hungary in the Twentieth Century]. Budapest: Osiris, 1999.

Rozett, Robert. "From Poland to Hungary: Rescue Attempts, 1943–1944." *YVS* 24 (1994): 177–93.

Safrian, Hans. *Eichmann's Men*. Cambridge: Cambridge University Press in association with the USHMM, 2010.

Ságvári, Ágnes, ed. *Dokumentumok a zsidóság üldöztetésének történetéhez* [Documents on the History of the Persecution of the Jews]. 19 vols. Budapest: Magyar Auschwitz Alapítvány–Holocaust Dokumentációs Központ, 1994.

Sajti, Enikő A. *Délvidék 1941–1944. A magyar kormányok délszláv politikája* [Southern Province, 1941–1944: The Southern-Slavic Policy of the Hungarian Governments]. Budapest: Kossuth, 1987.

Schmidt, Mária, ed. *Kollaboráció vagy kooperáció? A Budapesti Zsidó Tanács* [Collaboration or Cooperation? The Jewish Council of Budapest]. Budapest: Minerva, 1990.

Sellier, André. *A History of the Dora Camp*. Chicago: Ivan R. Dee, 2003.

Sereny, Gitta. *Into That Darkness: An Examination of Conscience*. New York: Vintage Books, 1983.

Sipos, Péter, ed. *Imrédy Béla a vádlottak padján* [Béla Imrédy in the Prisoner's Box]. Budapest: Osiris–Budapest Főváros Levéltára, 1999.

———, ed. *Szálasi Ferenc börtönnaplója, 1938–1940* [Ferenc Szálasi's Prison Diary, 1938–1940]. Budapest: BFL-Filum, 2007.

Sofsky, Wolfgang. *The Order of Terror: The Concentration Camp*. Princeton, NJ: Princeton University Press, 1999.

Soros, Tivadar. *Masquerade: Dancing around Death in Nazi-Occupied Hungary*, edited by Humphrey Tonkin. New York: Arcade, 2001.

Stark, Tamás. *Zsidóság a vészkorszakban és a felszabadulás után 1939–1955* [Jews during the Holocaust and after the Liberation, 1939–1955]. Budapest: Magyar Tudományos Akadémia Történettudományi Intézete, 1995.

Stern, Samu. *Emlékirataim. Versenyfutás az idővel! A „zsidótanács" működése a német megszállás és a nyilas uralom idején* [My Memoirs: Race against Time. The Work of the Jewish Council during the German Occupation and the Reign of the Arrow Cross]. Budapest: Bábel, 2004.

Strebel, Bernhard. *Das KZ Ravensbrück. Geschichte eines Lagerkomplexes*. Paderborn: Ferdinand Schöningh, 2003.

Swiebocki, Henryk, ed. *London Has Been Informed . . . : Reports by Auschwitz Escapees*. Oświęcim: Auschwitz-Birkenau State Museum, 1997.

Szinai, Miklós, and László Szűcs, eds. *Horthy Miklós titkos iratai* [Confidential Papers of Miklós Horthy]. Budapest: Kossuth, 1962.

Szirtes, Zoltán. *Temetetlen halottaink. Körösmező, Kamenyec-Podolszk, 1941* [Our Unburied Dead: Körösmező, Kamenets-Podolski, 1941]. Budapest: Kopint-Datorg, 1996.

Szita, Szabolcs. *A Gestapo Magyarországon* [The Gestapo in Hungary]. Budapest: Korona, 2002.

———. *Halálerőd. A munkaszolgálat és a hadimunka történetéhez, 1944–1945* [Death Fortress: On the History of the Labor Service and Forced Labor, 1944–1945]. Budapest: Kossuth, 1989.

———. *Magyarok az SS ausztriai lágerbirodalmában* [Hungarians in the Web of the SS Concentration Camps in Austria]. Budapest: MAZSÖK, 2000.

———, ed. *Magyarország 1944. Üldöztetés-embermentés* [Hungary, 1944: Persecution and Rescue]. Budapest: Nemzeti Tankönyvkiadó-Pro Homine-1944 Emlékbizottság, 1994.

Sztehlo, Gábor. *In the Hands of God*. Budapest: Gábor Sztehlo Foundation for the Help of Children and Adolescents, 1994.

Teleki, Éva. *Nyilas uralom Magyarországon* [The Reign of the Arrow Cross in Hungary]. Budapest: Kossuth, 1974.

Toronyi, Zsuzsanna, ed. *Zsidó közösségek öröksége* [Heritage of Hungarian Jewish Communities]. Budapest: Magyar Zsidó Levéltár, 2010.

*The Trial of Adolf Eichmann: Record of Proceedings in the District Court of Jerusalem*. 9 vols. Jerusalem: State of Israel, Ministry of Justice, 1992–1995.

Tschuy, Theo. *Dangerous Diplomacy: The Story of Carl Lutz, Rescuer of 62,000 Hungarian Jews*. Grand Rapids, MI: William B. Eerdmans, 2000.

Ungváry, Krisztián. *Budapest ostroma* [The Siege of Budapest]. 5th rev. ed. Budapest: Corvina, 2005.

———. *A magyar honvédség a második világháborúban* [The Hungarian Army in World War II]. Budapest: Osiris, 2004.

Vági, Zoltán. "Csillaghegyi csendőrtörténet" [A Gendarme's Story in Csillaghegy]. *Remény* 3 (1998): 47–53.

———. "Endre László politikai pályája 1919–1945. Szélsőjobboldali elit, közigazgatási apparátus, zsidókérdés" [The Political Career of László Endre, 1919–1945: Extreme Right-Wing Elite, Administrative Apparatus, Jewish Question]. PhD diss., ELTE, 2003.

Vago, Bela. "The Destruction of the Jews of Northern Transylvania." In *Hungarian Jewish Studies*. Vol. 1, edited by Randolph L. Braham, 171–221. New York: World Federation of Hungarian Jews, 1966.

Vargyai, Gyula. "Így döntöttek. A Magyarország német megszállását eredményező német katonai döntési mechanizmus" [They Decided So: The German Military Decision-Making Process Resulting in the Occupation of Hungary]. In *Magyarország 1944—a német megszállás* [Hungary, 1944: The German Occupation], edited by Gyula Vargyai and János Almási, 7–20. Budapest: Nemzeti Tankönyvkiadó, 1994.

———. *Magyarország a második világháborúban. Összeomlástól összeomlásig* [Hungary in World War II: From Collapse to Collapse]. Budapest: Korona, 2001.

Vértes, Róbert, ed. *Magyarországi zsidótörvények és rendeletek 1938–1945* [Hungarian Jewish Laws and Decrees, 1938–1945]. Budapest: Polgár, 1997.

Vigh, Károly. *Ugrás a sötétbe* [Jump into the Dark]. Budapest: Akadémiai, 1979.

Wallenberg, Raoul. *Letters and Dispatches*. New York: Arcade Publishing in association with the USHMM, 1995.

Weissberg, Alex. *Desperate Mission*. New York: Criterion Books, 1958.

*The White Terror in Hungary: Report of the British Joint Labour Delegation to Hungary*. London: Trades Union Congress and the Labour Party, n.d. [1920].

Wiesel, Elie. *Night*. New York: Bantam Books, 1986.

Witte, Peter, and Stephen Tyas. "A New Document on the Deportation and Murder of Jews during 'Einsatz Reinhardt' 1942." *H&GS* 15, no. 3 (2001): 468–86.

# Glossary

**Arrow Cross, Arrow Cross Party,** Party of **Ferenc Szálasi** (1897–1946). Szálasi was a Hungarian military officer and leader of the most popular right-wing extremist movement during the Horthy regime, from 1939 known as the Arrow Cross Party–Hungarist Movement. As a result of his sharp criticism of the system, Szálasi was imprisoned (1938–1940), and his various parties were dissolved on several occasions, but the movement managed to renew itself each time. Following the German occupation, Szálasi did not get any government appointments, primarily because the Germans considered him an unserious and politically unmanageable character. However, after Horthy's removal in October 1944, the Germans chose to mobilize him and his party. From October 16, 1944, until March 28, 1945, Szálasi was prime minister of Hungary as well as its plenipotentiary head of state, bearing the title "Leader of the Nation." Following the war, he was sentenced to death and executed.

**Auschwitz Protocol** (also Vrba-Wetzler Report) A report based on accounts by prisoners who had escaped from Birkenau—among them Slovak deportees Walter Rosenberg (later Rudolf Vrba) and Alfréd Wetzler—between April and May 1944. It provided a precise description and map sketches of the camp's layout, operation, day-to-day activities, and selection and extermination techniques; it also gave estimates by country of the number of victims up to that point. In Hungary, the illegal Zionist organizations were the first to receive the information, but the protocol soon reached the Central Jewish Council as well as members of the non-Jewish resistance and Regent Miklós Horthy's circles. Through Zionist channels, a copy of the protocol reached Switzerland and both the British and U.S. governments around June 19 or 20, 1944. It was partly in light of this information that in late June these governments began, in the form of threats, to demand that the Hungarian government stop the deportation of Jews.

See Miroslaw Karny, "The Vrba and Wetzler Report," in *Anatomy of the Auschwitz Death Camp*, ed. Yisrael Gutman and Michael Berenbaum (Bloomington: Indiana University Press in association with the USHMM, 1998), 553–69.

**Baky, László** (1898–1946) Hungarian gendarmerie officer, right-wing extremist politician, and member of parliament. He was appointed political state secretary of the Ministry of the Interior by the Sztójay government on March 24, 1944, and was one of the key figures responsible for the deportations. In late August 1944, as the Hungarian government's Jewish policies changed, he was removed from office. Following the Arrow Cross takeover, Ferenc Szálasi appointed him to head the National Security Office, which was in charge of military intelligence. The people's court sentenced him to death in 1946, and he was executed.

**Bárdossy, László** (1890–1946) Hungarian diplomat, ambassador to Romania from 1934 to 1941, and prime minister and minister of foreign affairs from April 3, 1941, to March 7, 1942. During his tenure, Hungary strengthened its commitment to an alliance with Germany more than ever before. He had a share in the Hungarian government's handing over about twenty thousand so-called stateless Jews to the Germans, the majority of whom were killed. Following the Arrow Cross takeover, he became one of the leaders of the National Association of Legislators, consisting of members of parliament loyal to Szálasi. The People's Court found him guilty of war crimes and sentenced him to death. He was executed.

**Becher, Kurt** (1909–1995) German SS officer and businessman and, from 1944 to 1945, a special envoy to Reichsführer-SS Heinrich Himmler in Hungary. He orchestrated the "negotiations" with leading Jewish businessmen, including the owners of one of the largest war industry concerns in central Europe, the Weiss Manfréd Works. He blackmailed them into handing over this large complex to the SS. Becher was also involved in Himmler's attempts to negotiate a separate peace with the western Allies. After the war he was arrested but ultimately not tried. He became one of the wealthiest businessmen in West Germany.

See Gábor Kádár and Zoltán Vági, *Self-financing Genocide: The Gold Train, the Becher Case and the Wealth of Hungarian Jews* (Budapest: Central European University Press, 2004).

**Beregfy, Károly** (1888–1946) Hungarian military officer and commander of the Third Army from 1943 and the First Army from 1944. As a staunch Arrow Cross sympathizer, during the Szálasi regime he was appointed the exclusive leader of the army (serving as both the minister of defense and chief of the General Staff). In May 1945, he was captured by American troops and extradited to Hungary. He was sentenced to death by the People's Court and executed.

**Berend, Béla** (1911–1987) Chief rabbi of Szigetvár and member of the Jewish Council from May 1944 to January 1945. Because of his relations with László Endre and Zoltán Bosnyák, he was suspected of being an informant for the government in the Jewish

Council. While the Budapest ghettos were operational, he carried out rabbinical services in a steadfast, self-sacrificing manner. Following the war, the People's Court found him guilty of collaboration with the Arrow Cross and sentenced him to ten years in prison, but he was acquitted on appeal. Berend emigrated to the United States and changed his name to Albert B. Belton.

**Bethlen, István** (1874–1946) Hungarian conservative politician, large-scale landowner, and prime minister from 1921 to 1931. He orchestrated the period of political and economic consolidation following World War I and represented a moderate right-wing, anti-Nazi, pro-English stance. Though concerned about the "Jewish question," Bethlen rejected Hungary's anti-Jewish laws. He was forced to go into hiding following the German occupation. In the summer of 1944 he wrote a secret memorandum to the regent, calling on Horthy to stop the deportations. He was arrested by Soviet troops in 1945 and died in prison.

**Bosnyák, Zoltán** (1905–1952) Hungarian journalist and race-protectionist ideologue who wrote and edited numerous anti-Jewish books. Tens of thousands of copies of some of his works were printed. A close friend, confidante, and colleague of László Endre, he headed the Hungarian Institute for Research of the Jewish Question from 1943. In 1944, he was editor in chief of *Harc* (Struggle), a weekly modeled on the Nazi *Der Stürmer*. He was found guilty of war crimes, sentenced to death, and executed in 1952.

**Budapest Relief and Rescue Committee** (Vaadat ha' Ezra ve'ha'Hatzalah, or Vaada) An illegal Hungarian Zionist relief organization founded in 1942–1943 for the rescue, hiding, and support of Jews fleeing from neighboring countries. Its most renowned members were Executive Director Ottó Komoly, Executive Vice Director Rezső Kasztner, Jenő (Joel) Brand and his wife Hansi, Mózes (Moshe) Schweiger, and Ernő Szilágyi. Following the German occupation of Hungary in March 1944, the Vaada initiated negotiations with the SS in order to rescue Hungarian Jews.

See Yehuda Bauer, *Jews for Sale? Nazi-Jewish Negotiations, 1933–1945* (New Haven, CT: Yale University Press, 1994).

**bureaucratic antisemitism** Administrative practice used by the Hungarian public administration occasionally in the early 1920s and commonly in the 1930s and 1940s. Antisemitic officials applied existing laws and decrees in a much stricter, discriminatory way against Jews, while non-Jews did not have to abide by the same requirements. See also **illegal antisemitism**.

**county** (*vármegye*) The basic public administration unit of Hungary from the eleventh century onward, today called *megye*. Between 1867 and 1920, Hungary consisted of sixty-three counties, and between the two world wars, of twenty-five. Following the territorial gains during World War II (1938–1941), forty-one counties and three public administration districts were created. From 1945 to 1950, there were again twenty-five counties. Since 1950, their number has been nineteen.

**Csatay, Lajos** (1886–1944) Hungarian army officer and from June 1943 to October 15, 1944, minister of defense with a pro-German stance that gradually turned into moderate anti-Nazism. He was arrested following the Arrow Cross takeover. He and his wife committed suicide in prison.

**Darányi, Kálmán** (1886–1939) Conservative Hungarian politician and prime minister from October 1936 to May 1938. The First "Jewish Law" (Act XV of 1938) was prepared during his tenure. Dissatisfied with his activities, Horthy forced him to resign. Until his death, he remained the president of the Lower House (House of Representatives) of the two-chamber parliament.

**DEGOB** See National Committee of Hungarian Jews for Attending Deportees.

**Domonkos, Miksa** (1890–1953) Hungarian Jewish engineer, World War I veteran, and from April 1944 head of the Central Jewish Council's Technical Department. One of his sons died while performing labor service on the eastern front. During the Arrow Cross regime, Domonkos was one of the large ghetto's leaders, struggling with great resolve to protect Budapest's Jews. Following the war, he became chief secretary of the Pest Israelite Congregation but was arrested based on fabricated charges during the antisemitic campaign of 1953. As a result of prison conditions, he died shortly after his release.

**Eichmann, Adolf** (1906–1962) German SS officer in charge of "Jewish affairs" in the Security Service (Sicherheitsdienst, or SD) from 1935. In 1938, he organized the forced emigration of Austrian and subsequently Czech and German Jews. From 1941, as head of the Jewish Affairs Department (IV/b/4) of the Reich Security Main Office (Reichssicherheitshauptamt), he was in charge of deportations from various European destinations to ghettos and death camps. From March 1944, his special unit (Sondereinsatzkommando Eichmann) arranged for the ghettoization and deportation of the Hungarian Jews. Following the war, he first went into hiding in Germany and later fled to Argentina. Israeli agents abducted him in 1960 and took him to Jerusalem, where he was tried, sentenced to death, and hanged.

See Hans Safrian, *Eichmann's Men* (Cambridge: Cambridge University Press in association with the USHMM, 2010).

**Éliás, József** (1914–1995) See **Good Shepherd Committee**.

**Endre, László** (1895–1946) Hungarian civil servant and antisemitic politician. As subprefect from 1938 to 1944 of the largest Hungarian public administration unit, Pest-Pilis-Solt-Kiskun County, he was the first to ban Jews from markets and public baths, triggering similar antisemitic measures in other counties. Endre held leading positions in several right-wing extremist organizations and in the late 1930s became one of the most influential antisemitic public figures of Hungary. As state secretary of the Ministry of the Interior of the Sztójay government, he initiated and directed the Hungarian Jews' deportation. Eichmann considered him one of his closest friends. He did not participate in the preparation of the Arrow Cross coup, but Szálasi appointed him "government commissioner of civilian public administration in military operations zones." In the spring of 1945, he fled to Austria, where he was arrested. After U.S. authorities handed him over to Hungary, he was sentenced to death and executed.

**Faragho, Gábor** (1890–1953) A Hungarian army general and gendarmerie superintendent who became a key figure in the summer of 1944 deportations. In September of the same year, he headed the cease-fire delegation sent to Moscow and signed the preliminary cease-fire conditions on October 11. During his absence, the Arrow Cross seized power and stripped him of his rank. He avoided being held accountable after the war and even served as minister of public welfare in the postwar anti-Nazi cabinet called the Interim National Government of 1944–1945. He was subsequently expelled from Budapest by the communist government and was forced to live in a designated village.

**Ferenczy, László** (1898–1946) Hungarian gendarmerie officer and from 1944 the liaison officer between Eichmann's Sondereinsatzkommando and the Ministry of the Interior, directing the summer deportations. Following the Arrow Cross takeover, he was placed at the Ministry of the Interior as officer in charge of Jewish matters. In 1946, the People's Court sentenced him to death, and he was executed.

**gendarmerie** Law enforcement agency founded in Hungary in 1881 based on the French model. Its primary tasks were to prosecute crime and maintain order in villages and rural areas. (The police force was in charge of these tasks in towns.) During the Horthy era, due to strong nationalistic and racial indoctrination, combined with its selection process, the gendarmerie became an elite force that served the regime unconditionally. After 1938, in the areas reannexed to Hungary, gendarmes along with the army committed atrocities against ethnic minorities, including Jews. In 1944, the twenty-thousand-strong gendarmerie played a key role in the ghettoization and deportation of the Hungarian Jews. With few exceptions, gendarmes fulfilled and went beyond orders, often committing excesses out of antisemitic zeal and sadism. After the war, the gendarmerie was declared a criminal organization and dissolved. During so-called screening procedures, a gendarme could avoid administrative disadvantages (e.g., cancellation of benefits or pension) only if he could prove active defiance against the Horthy regime.

**Glass House** The glass wholesale store of Artúr Weiss in downtown Budapest at 29 Vadász Street. Beginning in July 1944, it housed the emigration office of the Foreign Interests Department of the Swiss embassy, headed by Carl Lutz. Not only was the building the center of Swiss rescue operations, but Zionist youth organizations also orchestrated their rescue actions from there. The Glass House served as a shelter as well, hiding several hundred Jews by the turn of 1944–1945. The Arrow Cross murdered owner Artúr Weiss.

See Tim Cole, *Holocaust City: The Making of a Jewish Ghetto* (New York: Routledge, 2003).

**Gold Train** A train carrying valuables taken from the Hungarian Jews, sent to Germany in the spring of 1945 under orders of the Hungarian Arrow Cross government. The assets ended up scattered across Austria. The Hungarian commander of the train (see **Árpád Toldi**) took some valuables, and the U.S. Army impounded a significant portion. Most items under French control were returned in 1948 to Hungary, where for the most part the communist authorities embezzled the goods. American soldiers appropriated a small portion of the assets and the bulk was auctioned off and the proceeds handed over to the American Jewish Joint Distribution Committee, the Jewish aid organization. Shortly after 2000, Hungarian survivors filed a lawsuit against the U.S. government for its mishandling of the assets. The lawsuit ended in a settlement.

**Good Shepherd Committee** An organization set up in 1942 by Hungarian Protestant churches to protect the Jewish members of Protestant denominations. Headed by a pastor of Jewish origin, József Éliás, the organization carried out significant rescue work. In May 1944, the Lutheran Church delegated Gábor Sztehlo to the Good Shepherd Committee as its representative.

**Gömbös, Gyula** (1886–1936) Hungarian military officer, right-wing politician, and prime minister from 1932 to 1936. Compared to his former, radically antisemitic program, he pursued moderate politics once he became head of the government: no anti-Jewish laws were passed during that time. However, in the course of his tenure as prime minister, pro-Nazi, radically antisemitic elements gained an ever greater influence in the army and public administration. He was the first foreign head of government to visit Adolf Hitler in 1933.

**Government Commissariat for Repatriation** (Hazahozatali Kormánybiztosság) A state organization responsible for the repatriation and registration of Hungarian POWs, deportees, refugees, and other displaced persons from 1945 to 1947, headed by Sándor Millok, a social democratic politician and survivor of the Mauthausen concentration camp. Working under the auspices of the Ministry of the Interior and jointly with other relief agencies—mainly the International Committee of the Red Cross—the commissariat had its main office in Budapest and several branch offices in the provinces, as well as abroad.

**Hain, Péter** (1895–1946) Police superintendent, personal detective of Regent Horthy, and informant of the German secret services. Following the March 1944 German occupation, he headed the State Security Surveillance. He was relieved of this position in June 1944 because of embezzlement and personal conflicts with German leaders. Following the Arrow Cross coup, he obtained a key position once again as head of the political surveillance department of the Budapest police headquarters, an office with nationwide competence. In 1946, he was sentenced to death and executed.

***halutz, halutzim*** See ***Hehalutz***

***Hehalutz*** (Hebrew: pioneer) This association of Jewish youth aimed to train its members to settle in Palestine. Founded in 1918, it became an umbrella organization for Zionist youth groups across Europe. At its peak between 1930 and 1935, the movement counted one hundred thousand adherents. Hehalutz continued its work from its new base in Geneva during the war.

**Holy Cross Society** Hungarian Catholic organization founded in 1939 to offer material support and legal advice to Catholics who fell under the "Jewish Laws." The society cooperated with Jewish aid organizations, such as the Patronage Office of Hungarian Israelites, and solicited the help of Papal Nuncio Angelo Rotta and Hungarian church leaders, particularly Bishop Vilmos Apor, the organization's primary patron. The society was very active in 1944 in rescue operations until the arrest of its most widely known leader, József Cavallier, and several of his colleagues by the Arrow Cross regime in November. Subsequently, the Good Shepherd Committee took over most of its activities.

**Horthy, Miklós** (1868–1957) Austro-Hungarian admiral and conservative Hungarian politician. After leading the 1919 counterrevolution, he was appointed head of state of the Hungarian Kingdom from March 1, 1920, to October 16, 1944 (in the so-called Horthy era), holding the title of regent. The leitmotif of his foreign policy was the revision of the Trianon Peace Treaty. Following the German occupation (March 19, 1944), Horthy, under pressure from Berlin, appointed the collaborator government of Döme Sztójay and waived his right to ratify laws, thereby "washing his hands": he was neither going to help nor hinder the flood of anti-Jewish regulations and measures. For this reason, he too bears considerable responsibility for the deportation of the Jews from the provinces. In early July 1944, he became active again and stopped the deportations, thereby saving Budapest Jews slated for transportation to Auschwitz. However, he later approved resumption of deportations, which were ultimately thwarted by Romania switching sides in the war in late August 1944. In the radically new military and political situation that arose, Horthy did not want to hand over any more Jews to Germany. He began preparing Hungary's defection from the war, but the Germans forced him to cede power to Arrow Cross leader Ferenc Szálasi on October 15–16, 1944. Horthy testified as a witness during the Nuremberg Trials, but he was not held accountable. He died in Portugal and was reburied in Hungary in 1993.

**illegal antisemitism** A term for various anti-Jewish administrative practices used by the Hungarian public administration in the late 1930s and early 1940s. Under illegal antisemitism, as opposed to bureaucratic antisemitism, officials actually went beyond the existing anti-Jewish laws and decrees and took administrative measures that violated written antisemitic regulations. Illegal antisemitic acts were committed most notoriously by László Endre but also by many other officials, especially in the territories reannexed to Hungary.

**Imrédy, Béla** (1891–1946) Hungarian financial expert, right-wing politician, and prime minister from May 1938 to February 1939. He played a key role in the preparation of the First and Second "Jewish Laws" (Act XV of 1938 and Act IV of 1939) and was the leader of the extreme right-wing, antisemitic Hungarian Life Movement, founded in January 1939. From 1940 on, he led the Hungarian Renewal Party, which split off from the right wing of the governing party. Following the occupation of Hungary, Imrédy became the German's first-choice candidate for prime minister, but Horthy was unwilling to appoint him. From May 23 to August 7, 1944, he served as minister without portfolio responsible for economic affairs in the Sztójay government. Convicted by the People's Court, he was executed.

**Jaross, Andor** (1896–1946) Hungarian politician and advisor to the military public administration in the reannexed territories following the first Vienna Award. In 1940, he became deputy head of the Hungarian Renewal Party, Béla Imrédy's pro-Nazi party attacking the government from the right. As minister of the interior in the Sztójay government (March to August 1944), he was one of the central figures responsible for the disenfranchisement, plunder, and deportation of the Jews. During Szálasi's rule, he was co-president of the parliamentary group supporting the Arrow Cross regime. He was sentenced and executed after the war.

**Jewish Council** Body of Jewish representatives created by the Nazis and their Hungarian collaborators to carry out restrictive and/or genocidal measures against the Jews. Roughly 150 Jewish Councils were set up all around the country in the spring and summer of 1944, predominantly by Hungarian authorities. They operated for only a few weeks and ceased to exist when the deportations started. There was only one exception: the Budapest Jewish Council. On paper all Hungarian Jews were supervised by this body, but its sphere of competence was actually limited almost exclusively to Budapest. The council's personnel, name, and legal status changed several times between March 1944 and January 1945.

> *First Jewish Council:* The Central Council of Hungarian Jews was formed on March 21, 1944, on the order of the Sondereinsatzkommando Eichmann. The members were recruited from the community's pre-occupation elite: President Samu Stern, Ernő Pető, Ernő Boda, and Károly Wilhelm were the leaders of the Neologue Pest Israelite Congregation; Samu Csobádi served as president of the Neologue Buda Israelite Congregation. Rabbi Samu Kahán-Frankl, president of the Central Office of the Autonomous Orthodox Israelite Denomination of Hungary, and Fülöp Freudiger, president of the Budapest Autonomous Orthodox Israelite Congregation, represented the Orthodox. The council also had a Zionist member, Niszon Kahán, leading official of the Hungarian Zionist Alliance.

*Second Jewish Council:* In late April 1944 the government decided to settle the legal status of the council and to draw the body into its own sphere of competence. Prime Minister's Decree No. 1520/1944 (April 22) formed a "new" entity: the Interim Executive Board of the Association of Jews in Hungary. Modifications in personnel accompanied the change of name and legal status. On May 8 Csobádi, Boda, and Kahán were replaced by Rabbi Béla Berend, physician József Nagy, journalist Sándor Török, and János Gábor, an official of the Pest Israelite Congregation.

*Third Jewish Council:* Yielding to pressure from the Christian churches, on July 14 the government created a separate council for converts: the Interim Executive Board of the Association of Christian Jews in Hungary. The body consisted of nine members (György Auer, András Sebestyén, Sándor Török, Sándor Antal, Pál Rózsa, Mihály Kádár, Elemér Tamás, Endre Somló, and Sándor Balassa). It was headed by retired attorney general György Auer, while the executive vice president was Sándor Török, member of the Second Jewish Council. The Christian council existed mainly on paper and its impact was minimal. However, it brought some changes in the Second Jewish Council. With permission from the authorities, Sándor Török left the body to participate in the new formation. He was not the only one to quit: Rabbi Kahán-Frankl resigned and went into hiding. Therefore, on July 22 Ernő Boda, a member of the first council, was reappointed, and a new person was also assigned: Lajos Stöckler. In early August, Fülöp Freudiger escaped to Romania, leaving the council. His place was not filled.

*Fourth Jewish Council:* The Arrow Cross government reshaped the council again on October 22. The fourth council consisted of the following members: Samu Stern (president), Lajos Stöckler (vice president), Béla Berend, István Földes, Ottó Komoly, József Nagy, Miklós Szegő, and Lajos Vas. During Arrow Cross rule, when Stern was in hiding, Stöckler actually headed the council.

Three Jewish Council members were killed during the Holocaust: János Gábor was deported to a German concentration camp, while Miklós Szegő and Ottó Komoly were executed by Arrow Cross militiamen.

*Judenrampe* ("**Jewish ramp**") The railroad platform in Auschwitz II–Birkenau where the deportees got off the cattle cars that had brought them. The so-called old ramp was about half a mile away from the entrance of the camp between 1942 and 1944; those selected as unfit for work were carried by trucks to the gas chambers, while the rest were herded on foot to Birkenau. In May 1944, the railroad feeder line leading into the camp was completed, along with a new ramp encircled by three pairs of rails. The construction was completed by Hungarian Jews. At the end of the ramp and facing one another were Crematoria II and III. As a result, those deemed unfit for work had to walk just a few hundred yards to reach the gas chambers.

**Kahán-Frankl, Samu** (1890–1970) Orthodox rabbi, head of the Central Office of the Autonomous Orthodox Israelite Denomination of Hungary, and member of the Central Jewish Council in 1944. In the summer of 1944 he resigned from his position in the council and went into hiding. After the war he became head of the national Orthodox organization again. He emigrated first to Israel in 1950 and then to New York.

**Kállay, Miklós** (1887–1967) Hungarian landowner, conservative politician, and prime minister from March 1942 to March 1944, who aimed at distancing Hungary from Germany and strove to establish contacts with the western Allies. His domestic policies were characterized by two opposing trends: loud, antisemitic rhetoric together with new "Jewish Laws" on the one hand and resolute resistance to German and far-right demands calling for ghettoization and deportation on the other. Following the German occupation, he fled to the Turkish embassy. After the Arrow Cross coup, he was arrested and deported to a German concentration camp. He was not held accountable after the war. He lived in Italy until 1953 and then emigrated to the United States, where he became a leader of Hungarian emigrants. He died in New York City.

**Kasztner, Rezső** (1906–1957) Hungarian Zionist leader who, as executive vice director of the Zionist Budapest Relief and Rescue Committee (Vaada), played a significant role in hiding and helping Jewish refugees from abroad beginning in 1940. Following the German occupation, he became involved in negotiations with Eichmann and Becher on behalf of the Rescue Committee, facilitating plans for the so-called Kasztner Train, which left the country with close to seventeen hundred Jews aboard. After the end of the war, he immigrated to Israel, where he assumed a public role again. Between 1953 and 1955 his wartime activities were brought into the public limelight through a trial in which Kasztner testified not as defendant but as witness in a libel suit. The government had initiated the trial against a right-wing publicist, Malkiel Grünwald, for making slanderous remarks about Kasztner, a state employee. Kasztner found himself facing an accusation of collaboration, complicity, and treason. The judge sided with Grünwald. In March 1957 Kasztner was shot near his Tel Aviv home by members of a right-wing group and died shortly thereafter. In 1958 the Israeli Supreme Court rehabilitated him.

See Yehuda Bauer, *Jews for Sale? Nazi-Jewish Negotiations, 1933–1945* (New Haven, CT: Yale University Press, 1994).

**Kolosváry-Borcsa, Mihály** (1896–1946) Hungarian journalist and extreme right-wing ideologue. From 1937 to 1945, he worked as editor in chief of *Függetlenség* (Independence). He was appointed chief press officer of the Imrédy government in 1938. From 1939 until December 1944, he served as president of the National Hungarian Press Chamber. He was sentenced to death by the People's Court and executed.

**Komoly, Ottó** (1892–1945) Hungarian Zionist leader, World War I veteran, and from 1940 president of the Zionist Alliance of Hungary. As president of the Budapest Relief and Rescue Committee, he belonged to the centrist Klal Zionists and mediated between the religious Zionists (Mizrachi) and the left-wing Zionists (Ichud Mapai, Hashomer Hatzair). Besides his leading role in the Rescue Committee, he was also one of the leaders of the child rescue operation organized by the International Red Cross. Following the Arrow Cross takeover, he became a member of the Jewish Council. He was killed by Arrow Cross men on January 1, 1945.

**Kozma, Miklós** (1884–1941) Hungarian right-wing politician and head of the army's propaganda department set up by Miklós Horthy in 1919. He served as minister of the interior from 1935 to 1937. As the regent's commissioner of Carpatho-Ruthenia from 1940 to 1941, he was one of the initiators of the so-called Kamenets-Podolski deportation.

**Krausz, Miklós** (1908–1985) Hungarian head of the Palestine Office, a Zionist organization, who carried out rescue activities in close collaboration with the diplomatic corps in Budapest. In the second half of June 1944, he managed to pass the Auschwitz Protocol on to Switzerland, the publication of which played a major role in halting the deportations. Following the war, he immigrated to Israel, where he worked as a civil servant.

**Labor Service** The Hungarian system of public interest labor service was officially established by Act II of 1939 as a part of Hungary's preparations for war. Besides introducing the general system of compulsory military service for all men over age twenty-one, the law aimed at mobilizing those deemed unfit for armed service. Although the law was not discriminatory as such, the regime increasingly used it against those it considered "dangerous from a national security perspective": left-wingers and members of ethnic and religious minorities, among them Romanians, Serbs, Croats, Ruthenians, and Roma, as well as members of smaller denominations who refused armed service on religious grounds, such as Jehovah's Witnesses. However, the majority of labor servicemen were Jews. Tens of thousands of them died during World War II, not only due to enemy attacks but also because of inhumane treatment meted out by their guards. Besides frontline casualties and those who died in Soviet POW camps, thousands of the labor servicemen handed over to the Germans and deported in the fall and winter of 1944 perished in Nazi concentration camps and on death marches.

See Randolph L. Braham, ed., *The Wartime System of Labor Service in Hungary: Varieties of Experiences* (New York: Columbia University Press, 1995).

**Lakatos, Géza** (1890–1967) Hungarian military officer and prime minister from August 29 to October 16, 1944. After Romania switched over to the Allies' side in August 1944, Horthy assigned Lakatos to prepare a cease-fire. Following the Arrow Cross coup, he was arrested by the Germans. In 1945 Lakatos was captured by the Soviets. His assets were seized during the communist dictatorship. He immigrated to Australia in 1965.

**levente** An institution that provided military, physical, and ideological training for Hungarian youth between the two world wars. As of 1921, every boy was subject to levente duty from age twelve to twenty-one (raised to twenty-three as of 1939) or until the start of his military service. Their instructors were ex-servicemen, members of the lower middle class or provincial intellectuals, most of them harboring strong antisemitic sentiments. As a result, in many places the institution turned into a forum for humiliating Jewish youth on a regular basis. Jews were drafted into separate levente units beginning in 1941, and from 1942 onward, they were completely excluded from levente service. The organization was dissolved after the war.

**Lutz, Carl** (1895–1975) Swiss diplomat who from 1942 led the Foreign Interests Department of the Swiss embassy in Budapest. In 1944–1945, he was one of the architects and managers of the system of diplomatic protection provided for Jews. He supervised the Glass House, placed several dozen buildings under Swiss diplomatic protection, and issued thousands of protective documents. He received no Swiss or international recognition after the war but was instead accused of having overstepped his competence. He was rehabilitated in 1958, and in 1964 Yad Vashem granted him the title "Righteous Among the Nations."

**Mantello, Georges M.** (1901–1992) Born György Mandl to an Orthodox Jewish family in Transylvania (presently Romania), he had made a living as a businessman before the outbreak of World War II. Through personal contacts, he was appointed honorary consul of the Republic of El Salvador in 1939. From August 1941, he served as first secretary for the Salvadoran consulate in Geneva, Switzerland. Mantello and his colleagues prepared and issued thousands of Salvadorian protective documents to save endangered Jews throughout Europe. Having been informed about the mass deportations from Hungary and the murder of his own family, he further increased his rescue activity. With the help of his Romanian colleague, Florian Manoliu, he managed to have a copy of the Auschwitz Protocol smuggled to Switzerland. Mantello prepared a summary of the document, and through his connections in Swiss political circles, he distributed the text to the Swiss and international press. Hence, he greatly facilitated the diplomatic pressure inflicted on Regent Miklós Horthy to halt the deportations in July 1944.

**Mengele, Josef, Dr.** (1911–1979?) German SS officer and physician. From 1943, he was one of the lead physicians at Auschwitz II–Birkenau. In the summer of 1944, he supervised the "selection" process on the Birkenau ramp, sending tens of thousands of Hungarian Jews to their deaths, and conducted criminal, pseudomedical experiments. After the war, he went into hiding in Germany before he fled to South America in 1949, where he is believed to have died in 1979.

**Moll, Otto** (1915–1946) German SS NCO in charge of the Auschwitz II–Birkenau "extermination zone" during the summer 1944 mass murder of the Hungarian Jews. He became notorious for his extreme brutality. After the evacuation of Auschwitz, Moll continued his crimes in other concentration camps. He was sentenced to death in the Dachau trial in November 1945 and hanged in 1946.

**Muhsfeldt, Erich** (also Mussfeldt, Mussfeld, or Mußfeld) (1913–1948) German SS-NCO assigned to Auschwitz II–Birkenau in April 1944, where he supervised the work of the *Sonderkommando* for the crematoria. He was sentenced to death by a Polish court in 1947 and executed.

**Nagybaczoni Nagy, Vilmos** (1884–1976) Hungarian army general and minister of defense from September 1942 to June 1943. Because he tried to abolish the hitherto brutal treatment of labor servicemen and made no attempt to satisfy the Germans' military demands in a speedy manner, Prime Minister Miklós Kállay dismissed him under pressure from the Nazis and the Hungarian extreme right. Following the Arrow Cross takeover, he was arrested and taken to Germany. Yad Vashem granted him the title "Righteous Among the Nations" in 1965.

**National Committee of Hungarian Jews for Attending Deportees** (Magyarországi Zsidók Deportáltakat Gondozó Országos Bizottsága, **DEGOB**) One of the key organizations responsible for the repatriation and relief of Holocaust survivors in Hungary. Established in Budapest in March 1945, DEGOB received its financial support from the American Jewish Joint Distribution Committee, the International Red Cross, and the Jewish Agency for Palestine. DEGOB organized twenty-six expeditions in 1945 and managed to repatriate several thousand Hungarian deportees from former Nazi camps throughout Europe. In addition to providing aid for survivors, DEGOB was one of the earliest and largest projects to document the mass destruction of European Jews. It set up a card index of about 150,000 data sets on survivors and victims and recorded thousands of interviews with returning deportees related to their suffering in the preceding years, but mostly in 1944–1945. The earliest document was transcribed on December 12, 1944, before the establishment of DEGOB, while the last one dates from April 13, 1946.

See the DEGOB website at www.degob.org.

**Neologue** A branch of Hungarian Jewry that in the nineteenth century revised religious rules in a liberal spirit, modernized and loosened dietary regulations and dress codes, and changed liturgical traditions. After the 1868–1869 Israelite Congress, the Neologue communities separated from the Orthodox. Neologism was especially strong in the western and southwestern parts of Greater Hungary, as well as in the capital. The largest and most significant Hungarian Neologue community was the Pest Israelite Congregation. The umbrella organization of the Neologue communities was the National Office of Hungarian Israelites.

***numerus clausus*** (Latin: closed number) A phrase referring, in the context of Hungarian anti-Jewish legislation, to Act XXV of 1920. Passed by the parliament of Hungary on September 26, 1920, the act restricted the percentage of Jews and other ethnic minorities admitted to universities and colleges according to their demographic ratio. As a result, the mix of Jews among higher education students fell from over 30 percent in the prewar years to under 8 percent in 1927. In 1928, due to international pressure and political consideration, the discriminatory paragraph regarding ratios of nationalities was replaced by a system of criteria based on the economic and social status of prospective students' parents (Act XIV of 1928). In addition, the condition of "loyalty to the nation and moral character" remained in the law, which left its interpretation up to the discretion of the universities. Since the universities in general stood at the forefront of antisemitic policies, the chances remained high that they would limit the number of Jewish students admitted.

**Order of Vitéz** (members: *vitéz*) An organization established by Horthy in 1920 to reward war veterans loyal to the regime and counterrevolutionaries with a title and a piece of land that could be inherited by the eldest son. Although on paper Jews were not excluded from the order, administrative measures were generally used to prevent those Jews from joining who otherwise fulfilled the criteria. At the same time, the order became one of the primary beneficiaries of the Jewish laws as some of the estates seized from the Jews were given to members. The order was dissolved following the war.

**Orthodox** A branch of Hungarian Jewry that held strongly to established traditions and rejected modernization efforts. After the 1868–1869 congress this branch was organizationally separated from the Neologues. Orthodox communities were most frequent in the eastern and northeastern regions of Greater Hungary. The Central Office of the Autonomous Orthodox Israelite Denomination of Hungary served as their umbrella organization.

**People's Courts** The twenty-four regional courts in post–World War II Hungary (1945–1949) set up primarily for the investigation of war crimes. The members of the People's Courts were predominantly political delegates and generally lacked law degrees. However, the appeals forum (National Council of People's Courts) consisted of lawyers. About sixty thousand people were tried in the People's Courts in the postwar years, and roughly twenty-seven thousand were found guilty. Of these, 477 people were sentenced to death, and 189 were actually executed.

**Perlasca, Giorgio** (1910–1992) An Italian who arrived in Budapest in the early 1940s as a representative of an Italian firm. During the Spanish Civil War, he fought on Franco's side and thus had good relations with the Spanish diplomatic corps. He was arrested following the German occupation. Perlasca managed to avoid internment through his Spanish connections: the Spanish ambassador's deputy, Ángel Sanz-Briz, gave him shelter and documents. When the Spanish diplomatic mission to Budapest finished its Hungarian operations following the Arrow Cross coup, Perlasca assumed the role of Spanish deputy and supervised buildings protected by Spain. He issued thousands of documents with the embassy's stamp, thus saving the lives of many hundreds of people. In 1988, Yad Vashem granted him the title "Righteous Among the Nations."

**Péterffy, Jenő** (1899–1945) Hungarian gendarmerie commander and gendarme cadet corps commander in Nagyvárad from May 1, 1943, and in Galánta after August 20, 1944. He actively participated in the ghettoization and deportation process, ordering his men to treat the Jews in an extremely brutal manner. According to Baky's and Endre's plans, he would have orchestrated and directed the deportation of the Budapest Jews in early July 1944, but Horthy's decision to halt the deportations thwarted the plan. Following the Arrow Cross takeover, he became deputy director of Department XX of the Ministry of the Interior. He was arrested after the war and committed suicide while in pretrial detention.

**Post-Trianon Hungary** The term refers to the territory of the Hungarian Kingdom between June 1920, the Trianon Peace Treaty, and November 1938, the First Vienna Award, which returned to Hungary parts of areas lost after World War I (see map 1, p. xxxvii).

**protected companies** Labor Service companies whose members were under the diplomatic protection of a foreign country in 1944–1945.

**protected houses** Buildings in Budapest assigned in November 1944 as residences for Jews under the protection of neutral states' diplomatic missions. Most of them were in a residential quarter of Budapest called Újlipótváros. The protected houses were theoretically safer than other buildings assigned to the Jews, but in reality Arrow Cross squads also killed many of the people living there.

**protective document** Various certificates, passports, identity cards, and papers issued by the Budapest missions of neutral states (primarily Switzerland, Sweden, and the Vatican) that were supposed to prove to Hungarian and German authorities that the issuing state had special interests vested in the bearer's safety. The issuing of the protective documents—generating a large-scale operation for forging such papers—was a widely used and effective rescue method.

**Rákosi, Mátyás** (1892–1971) Communist politician. Born Mátyás Rosenfeld to a poor Jewish family in southern Hungary (Serbia today), he became a communist while a POW in Russia between 1915 and 1918. After the end of World War II, he became the leader of the Hungarian Working People's Party (MDP). His party assumed absolute power by 1948–1949 with Soviet support, and Rákosi established a Stalinist-style dictatorship in Hungary. As chief secretary of the MDP between 1948 and 1953, and also as prime minister (chairman of the Council of Ministers) in 1952–1953, he created a personality cult for himself and brutally oppressed all the opposition, including his former brothers-in-arms. Following Stalin's death, the Soviets removed him from his post as prime minister in June 1953. After temporarily regaining his influence, he was forced in July 1956 to resign from the party chairmanship. He left for the Soviet Union and died in exile.

**Ravasz, László** (1882–1975) Hungarian Calvinist bishop who served as the quasi-head of the Hungarian Calvinist Church during World War II. As a member of the Upper House, he actively supported and voted in favor of the First and Second "Jewish Laws" (Act XV of 1938 and Act IV of 1939). On the other hand, he opposed the Third "Jewish Law" and the later physical persecution of the Jews as well. In 1944 he was involved in church-operated rescue efforts, primarily assisting Jewish converts to Christianity.

**"Red Terror"** A series of armed operations by the 1919 communist dictatorship launched to punish and intimidate those opposing the communist rule. It led to the deaths of several hundred people.

**Rotta, Angelo** (1872–1965) Papal nuncio, Budapest delegate of the Holy See from 1930 to 1945, and doyen of the diplomatic staff in the interwar period. During the war, he assisted Polish refugees arriving in Hungary. In 1944, he played a major role in rescue activities by intervening vis-à-vis the subsequent Hungarian governments. During the Arrow Cross era, he issued thousands of Vatican protective documents. In the spring of 1945, yielding to pressure from Soviet authorities, the Allied Advisory Commission expelled him from Hungary. Yad Vashem granted him the title "Righteous Among the Nations" in 1997.

*Schutzbrief, Schutzpass* See **protective document**.

**Serédi, Jusztinián** (1884–1945) Archbishop of Esztergom and head of the Hungarian Catholic Church from 1927 until his death. In 1938–1939, he supported laws in the Upper House designed for social and economic discrimination against Jews, but he rejected the "Race Protection Law," the so-called Third "Jewish Law" (Act XV of 1941). He spoke out against persecution of the Jews in a 1944 pastoral letter that was not published at the time and even included antisemitic remarks. He rejected Protestant proposals for issuing a joint pastoral letter. Behind the scenes he intervened with representatives of the government, primarily on behalf of Jews who had converted to Christianity.

**Slachta, Margit** (1884–1974) Catholic nun, one of the leaders of the Christian Women's Camp and the Society of Sisters of Social Service, and the first woman to become a member of parliament in Hungary. In 1941, she approached the minister of the interior, protesting the deportation of Jews considered stateless. In 1944, she carried out significant rescue activities along with the other Social Service Sisters. In 1949, she fled communist Hungary for the United States. Yad Vashem granted her the title "Righteous Among the Nations" in 1977.

**Sondereinsatzkommando Eichmann** (SEK) See *Adolf Eichmann*.

***Sonderkommando*** A special work group, consisting mostly of Jews, operating in the Auschwitz II–Birkenau crematoria. Its workers' main task was to burn the corpses, but they also emptied the gas chambers after the gassings and removed the gold teeth from victims' mouths. The SS killed the members of the *Sonderkommandos* in intervals, replacing them with new arrivals.

See Filip Müller, *Eyewitness Auschwitz: Three Years in the Gas Chambers* (Chicago: Ivan R. Dee in association with the USHMM, 1999).

**State Security Surveillance** Hungarian political police agency created in March 1944, after the German occupation of Hungary. Colloquially referred to as the "Hungarian Gestapo," it was headed by Péter Hain and notorious for its agents' brutal interrogation methods. In the months following its creation, it arrested, robbed, and tortured hundreds of Jews and political persecutees. Due to conflicts with the Ministry of the Interior and the Germans, it was disbanded in early June 1944. After the Arrow Cross takeover in October 1944, the Political Department of the Budapest Police headquarters reactivated many of its former staff (including Hain).

**Status Quo Ante** A Latin term referring, in the context of Hungarian Jewish history, to the branch of Hungarian Jewry affiliated with neither the Neologues nor the Orthodox, but instead favoring the situation prior to the split. This branch of Hungarian Jewry was generally closer to the Orthodox with respect to liturgy and modernization level. The umbrella organization for its congregations was the National Alliance of the Status Quo Ante Congregations.

**Stern, Samu** (1874–1946) Hungarian banker, Neologue Jewish community leader, and president of the Central Jewish Council in 1944–1945. He was elected president of the Pest Israelite Congregation in 1929 and of the National Office of Hungarian Israelites in 1932. Based on his excellent relations with the upper echelons of the political elite, he tried to restrain the increasingly harsh antisemitic policies of successive governments. Following the war, he was charged with collaboration, and an investigation was initiated against him, but the case did not reach trial.

**Stöckler, Lajos** (1897–1960) Hungarian industrialist and member of the Jewish Council from July 1944. During the Szálasi regime, he became de facto head of the council and was very effective in organizing food supplies and providing protection for Budapest ghetto residents. After the war, he became president of the Pest Israelite Congregation and the National Office of Hungarian Israelites. In 1950, Stöckler was appointed head of the National Representation of Hungarian Israelites, the organization sanctioned by the regime. Arrested in 1953 on false charges as part of the "anti-Zionist" campaign, he was convicted but released in 1954. In 1956 he emigrated to Australia.

***stróman*** A Hungarian expression derived from the German word *Strohmann* (strawman). It designated a non-Jewish person who agreed—in exchange for money or other advantages—formally to take over the company or enterprise of Jews who were excluded from economic activities due to the anti-Jewish laws, making it possible for the genuine owner to continue operations.

**Szálasi, Ferenc** See *Arrow Cross*.

**Székely** (Szekler, Secui) Hungarian-speaking ethnic group living in Transylvania, mostly in the eastern part of the region called Székelyföld (Szeklerland, Ţinutul Secuiesc). The Székely enjoyed special privileges and territorial autonomy in the medieval Hungarian Kingdom and maintained a certain level of group and territorial identity to distinguish themselves from Magyars.

**Sztehlo, Gábor** (1909–1974) Hungarian pastor, one of the leaders of the Good Shepherd Committee, and head of Section B of the International Red Cross in Hungary. During Arrow Cross rule, he organized the protection of persecuted children. After the war, he continued working for orphaned children. In 1961, he emigrated to Switzerland, where he continued his pastoral services. Yad Vashem awarded him the title "Righteous Among the Nations" in 1972.

**Sztójay, Döme** (1883–1946) Hungarian army officer, diplomat, and prime minister. Between 1935 and 1944, he served as ambassador to Berlin, an enthusiastic supporter of Nazi politics. After the March 1944 German occupation of Hungary, he became prime minister and minister of foreign affairs from March 22 to August 29, 1944, and orchestrated the plunder and deportation of the Jews. During his short tenure, the cabinet issued close to a hundred anti-Jewish decrees. Jews from the provinces were deported to Auschwitz II–Birkenau, where most were killed, while Budapest Jews were forced to move into "yellow-star houses." Due to Horthy's plan to prepare a cease-fire, the pro-German Sztójay was deposed at the end of August. At the end of the war, the American military authorities captured Sztójay and extradited him back to Hungary. The People's Court found him guilty of war crimes, and he was sentenced to death and executed.

**Teleki, Pál** (1879–1941) Hungarian geographer, right-wing politician, and one of the leaders of the 1919 anticommunist counterrevolution. As prime minister from 1920 to 1921 and again from February 1939 to April 1941, he played a central role in the creation of the so-called *numerus clausus* act (Act XXV of 1920), as well as the Second and Third "Jewish Laws" (Act IV of 1939 and Act XV of 1941). Having failed to halt Hungary's involvement in the Axis attack on Yugoslavia, he committed suicide on April 3, 1941.

**Toldi, Árpád** (1898–?) Hungarian gendarmerie officer and prefect of the city of Székesfehérvár and Fejér County from April 26, 1944. As a determined antisemite and national socialist, he served as the head of Department XI at the Ministry of the Interior from November 1944 and was appointed the government commissioner responsible for confiscating, handling, and redistributing Jewish assets. He subsequently became commander of the so-called Gold Train carrying valuables seized from Jews (see *Gold Train*).

Fleeing to Switzerland, he was arrested by French authorities in the spring of 1945 but not held accountable for his wartime actions. His fate after 1946 is unknown.

**Török, Sándor** (1904–1985) Hungarian writer and Jewish Council member. From 1923, he wrote for various newspapers, such as the *Ellenzék* (Opposition), *Szegedi Napló* (Szeged Journal), and for a time even the right-wing extremist *Magyarság* (Hungariandom). Following the German occupation and a brief internment, he was appointed as a Christian member of the Jewish Council. In July, he became one of the leaders of the Interim Executive Board of the Association of Christian Jews in Hungary (a.k.a. the Christian Jewish Council), established in the summer of 1944. He went into hiding during the Arrow Cross era. After the war, he became a popular writer who received many assignments and wrote numerous novels for children and youth.

**Trianon Peace Treaty** Post–World War I peace treaty signed on June 4, 1920, in the Grand Trianon Palace in Versailles, near Paris. It was signed by the victorious powers and Hungary, the successor state of the Austro-Hungarian monarchy, which had lost the war as one of the Central Powers. As a result of the treaty, Hungary had to cede two-thirds of its territories to neighboring countries (going from 109,000 square miles to 36,000 square miles and from a population of 18.2 million to 7.9 million). About one-third of the lost territories' inhabitants (roughly 3.2 million) were ethnic Hungarians according to the Hungarian census of 1910, including hundreds of thousands of Hungarian-speaking Jews. Hungary lost its access to the sea and most of its natural resources, and its armed forces were cut drastically. Hungarian public opinion bitterly opposed the treaty conditions, and even today Trianon is considered one of Hungary's greatest national tragedies. Revision of the peace treaty was the principal aim of the country's foreign policy in the interwar period, leading Hungary to become the ally of Italy and Nazi Germany in the 1930s and to join the Axis during World War II. Between 1938 and 1941 Hungary regained a part of the territories lost as a consequence of Trianon, but the peace treaty signed in Paris in 1947 reduced Hungarian territory to the pre-1938 borders with minor modifications (see map 1, p. xxxvii).

**Vajna, Gábor** (1891–1946) Hungarian Arrow Cross politician and minister of the interior in Szálasi's government. Anti-Jewish measures belonged within his sphere of responsibility. In March 1945 he fled to Austria, where U.S. troops captured him. The United States extradited him to Hungary, where he was found guilty of war crimes, sentenced to death, and executed.

**Veesenmayer, Edmund** (1904–1977) German diplomat and SS officer. Following the occupation of Yugoslavia in April 1941, he played an important role in the establishment of the Croatian fascist (Ustaša) state. In 1943, based on his repeated visits to Budapest, he prepared two detailed reports on the political and economic situation in Hungary. He was a key figure in the preparations for the occupation of Hungary that took place in the following year. On March 19, 1944, Hitler appointed him Reich plenipotentiary in Hungary. Veesenmayer cooperated with Eichmann in the annihilation campaign against the Hungarian Jews in the spring and summer of 1944. In 1949 he was sentenced to twenty years in prison in the Nuremberg trials, but he was released in 1951.

**Vienna Awards** German and Italian diplomatic decisions designed to settle territorial disputes between Hungary and its neighbor states. According to the First Vienna Award, on November 2, 1938, Hungary reannexed from Czechoslovakia the southern strip of the Upper Province and part of Carpatho-Ruthenia, which had been detached from Hungary by the 1920 Trianon Peace Treaty. On August 30, 1940, the Second Vienna Award returned areas to Hungary that had been under Romanian control since the end of World War I: Northern Transylvania, including the Székely Land. (See table 4, p. 370, and map 2, p. xlii).

**Wallenberg, Raoul** (1912–1947?) Swedish architect and diplomat. He arrived in Hungary in July 1944. As a member of the Swedish diplomatic mission and following an assignment by the War Refugee Board, an American government organization, he provided assistance to Jews. He soon became the force behind Swedish rescue operations, issuing thousands of protective documents and placing numerous Budapest buildings under Swedish protection. Through colleagues as well as personal efforts, he saved huge numbers of people during the Arrow Cross regime. Soviet authorities arrested him in January 1945 and took him to Moscow. Having previously denied involvement in Wallenberg's disappearance, in 1957 the Soviet government issued an official statement that he had died in prison in 1947 due to heart failure.

See Raoul Wallenberg, *Letters and Dispatches* (New York: Arcade Publishing in association with the USHMM, 1995).

**"White Terror"** Reference to the various retaliation operations and pogroms carried out by commandos of officers in the National Army of Miklós Horthy after 1919. Hundreds of Jews fell victim to the "White Terror."

**"yellow-star houses"** Buildings located in Budapest into which Hungarian authorities forced Jews to move in June 1944. Unlike in most provincial settlements, Jews in Budapest were not concentrated in a closed ghetto at that time. Instead, they were ordered to move to about two thousand residential buildings marked with a yellow star. In late November and early December 1944, the Arrow Cross government moved their residents into the large ghetto and the so-called international ghetto.

# Chronology

THIS CHRONOLOGY is meant to provide additional context for the historical events described in this volume. More comprehensive discussions of anti-Jewish measures across Europe in the 1930s and 1940s can be found in specialized studies of the period, such as those referenced in this volume's chapters and bibliography or in the multivolume book series produced by the U.S. Holocaust Memorial Museum, *Jewish Responses to Persecution*. Most of the casualty figures mentioned here are estimates.

## BEFORE 1938

March 1848: A revolution against Habsburg rule occurs in Hungary; anti-Jewish riots follow.

1848–1849: During the War of Independence, the Revolutionary Hungarian Parliament passes a short-lived law on the emancipation of the Jews on July 28, 1849.

1867: The Law of Emancipation of the Jews is passed (Act XVII of 1867), giving Israelites equality in civil and political rights.

1882–1883: In conjunction with the Tiszaeszlár blood libel trial, antisemitic pogroms are staged throughout the country. The National Antisemitic Party is established.

1895: Enactment of the Law of Reception (Act XLII of 1895), granting equal standing to the Jewish religion.

1914–1918: As part of the Austro-Hungarian Empire, Hungary participates in World War I as an ally of Germany (Central Powers).

October–November 1918: Following the collapse of the Austro-Hungarian Empire, a democratic revolution sweeps through Hungary, accompanied by anti-Jewish violence.

March–August 1919: During the 133-day reign of the Hungarian Soviet Republic, Hungary experiences **"Red Terror."**

1919–1921: **"White Terror"** in Hungary is accompanied by antisemitic pogroms.

1919–1920: A counterrevolutionary regime is established; the National Assembly elects Admiral **Miklós Horthy** as regent. He holds the post from March 1, 1920, to October 16, 1944.

June 4, 1920: The **Trianon Peace Treaty** deprives Hungary of more than two-thirds of its territories and close to 60 percent of its population, including 3.2 million ethnic Hungarians.

September 26, 1920: A *numerus clausus* law restricts the number of Jewish students who are admitted to universities (Act XXV of 1920).

1921–1931: A period of political consolidation under Prime Minister Count **István Bethlen**.

1932–1938: The antisemitic, far-right political leader **Gyula Gömbös** is appointed prime minister (1932–1936), succeeded by **Kálmán Darányi** (1936–1938).

## 1938

May 14, 1938: **Béla Imrédy** becomes prime minister (1938–1939).

May 29, 1938: The First "Jewish Law" (Act XV of 1938) restricts the proportion of Jews in certain professions and white-collar positions at major industrial and commercial companies to 20 percent.

November 2, 1938: In the First **Vienna Award**, parts of the Upper Province and Carpatho-Ruthenia are reannexed from Czechoslovakia.

## 1939

January 1939: Hungary joins the Anti-Comintern Pact.

February 16, 1939: Count **Pál Teleki** becomes prime minister (1939–1941).

March 1939: Hungary reannexes the rest of Carpatho-Ruthenia from Czechoslovakia.

March 11, 1939: The Act on National Defense (Act II of 1939) is passed, and the **Labor Service** system is legally established.

May 4, 1939: Under the Second "Jewish Law" (Act IV of 1939), Jewish participation in certain professions is restricted to 6 percent, while other measures restrict the economic opportunities and civil rights of Jews in Hungary.

September 1, 1939: The German attack on Poland marks the beginning of World War II.

## 1940

August 30, 1940: In the Second Vienna Award, Northern Transylvania is reannexed from Romania.

November 1940: Hungary joins the Tripartite Pact created by Germany, Italy, and Japan.

## 1941

April 1941: Hungary participates in the campaign against Yugoslavia. The Southern Province is reannexed. Prime Minister Pál Teleki commits suicide. **László Bárdossy** becomes prime minister (1941–1942).

June 22, 1941: The German attack on the Soviet Union is followed by mass murder of Jews by the Wehrmacht and special killing squads of the SS and German police (*Einsatzgruppen*).

June 27, 1941: Hungary joins the German invasion of the Soviet Union.

Mid-July to mid-August 1941: Some twenty thousand Jews of "uncertain citizenship" are deported to occupied Soviet territory.

August 8, 1941: The Race Protection Law, or Third "Jewish Law" (Act XV of 1941), bans marriage between Jews and Christians and forbids sexual relations between Jewish men and non-Jewish women.

August 27–30, 1941: Einsatzgruppe C and Ukrainian militias slaughter some twenty-three thousand Jews at Kamenets-Podolski, including many thousands of deportees from Hungary.

## 1942

1942–March 1944: About twenty-five to forty thousand Hungarian labor servicemen perish on occupied Soviet territory or in Soviet captivity.

January 4–23, 1942: Hungarian gendarmes and soldiers massacre more than seven hundred Jews and some twenty-five hundred Serbs in Bácska (former Yugoslavia) under the pretext of conducting antipartisan raids.

March 1942: **Miklós Kállay** becomes prime minister (1942–1944).

July 1942: Hungary's Act XIV of 1942 codifies the already existing practice that Jews fulfill their military obligation exclusively through the unarmed auxiliary service (Labor Service).

September 6, 1942: The Fourth "Jewish Law" (Act XV of 1942) forms the basis for confiscating land owned by Jews.

## 1943

April 16–17, 1943: During German-Hungarian talks in Klessheim, Austria, Hitler and Joachim von Ribbentrop confront Horthy about his government's peace negotiations and moderate Jewish policies.

## 1944

March 19, 1944: The Germans occupy Hungary. **Adolf Eichmann** and his deportation experts (**Sondereinsatzkommando**) arrive in Budapest.

March 21, 1944: By order of the Nazi authorities, the Central Council of Hungarian Jews (**Jewish Council**) is created under the leadership of **Samu Stern**, president of the Pest Israelite Congregation.

March 22, 1944: A collaborationist cabinet is formed under the former Hungarian ambassador in Berlin, **Döme Sztójay**; the government makes the political decision to force Hungarian Jews to wear the yellow star and to isolate them physically (ghettoization).

March 31, 1944: By decree, Jews are forced to wear a yellow star (effective as of April 5); a specific ghettoization plan is approved.

April 7, 1944: A confidential decree is issued on the concentration of Jews.

Up to April 13, 1944: German and Hungarian leaders reach agreement about limited deportations (one hundred thousand Jewish men capable of working).

April 16, 1944: Ghettoization/concentration of Jews begins in what later became Deportation Zone I (Carpatho-Ruthenia). A decree on the registration and confiscation of Jewish assets is issued.

April 22, 1944: The Szentkút agreement is reached, entailing a final decision on the comprehensive, total deportation of all Hungarian Jews to Auschwitz.

April 28, 1944: A government decree orders ghettoization of Jews.

May 15, 1944: Mass deportations to Auschwitz by the Hungarian authorities begin (fifteen thousand people are taken to eastern Austria).

June 25, 1944: By this date, the Jews of Budapest are crowded into 1,948 designated buildings ("**yellow-star houses**").

July 6, 1944: Horthy halts the deportations.

July 9, 1944: Deportations end. From May 15 until this date, more than 437,000 Jews have been deported from Hungary.

July 19, 1944: Despite Horthy's decision, Eichmann's unit deports 1,220 detainees of the Kistarcsa internment camp to Auschwitz.

July 24, 1944: Jews from the Sárvár internment camp, about fifteen hundred in all, are deported to Auschwitz.

August 23, 1944: Romania switches over to the Allies' side.

August 24, 1944: Horthy refuses to hand over Budapest Jews to Germany. Eichmann's Sondereinsatzkommando is called back.

August 29, 1944: A new government forms under Horthy loyalist General **Géza Lakatos**.

October 7, 1944: Members of the prisoner ***Sonderkommando*** in Birkenau revolt, and guards kill hundreds of Hungarian Jewish prisoners.

October 15–16, 1944: Horthy attempts to leave the war, and the **Arrow Cross** takes power.

October 26, 1944: The Arrow Cross government of **Ferenc Szálasi** hands over seventy Labor Service companies to the Germans.

November 6, 1944: Forced marches of Budapest Jews to Hungary's western border begin.

November 17, 1944: Szálasi decides to create two ghettos in Budapest.

November 21, 1944: Szálasi halts the "death marches."

December 24, 1944–February 13, 1945: The Soviet army lays siege to Budapest. Arrow Cross militiamen engage in anti-Jewish terror and massacres.

# 1945

January 16–18, 1945: Budapest ghettos are liberated on the Pest side of the city (altogether containing about eighty to ninety thousand Jews).

January 27, 1945: The Red Army liberates the prisoners remaining in Auschwitz.

February 13, 1945: The Red Army liberates the Jews in the Buda side of city.

March 30, 1945: The "**Gold Train**" carrying looted Hungarian Jewish assets and valuables leaves the country.

April 13, 1945: Soviet occupation of Hungary is completed. More than five hundred thousand Hungarian Jews have been killed between 1941 and 1945.

## AFTER 1945

1946: Act XXV of 1946 repeals earlier anti-Jewish laws.

1948–1949: Communist takeover of Hungary.

1953: The leaders of the Hungarian Jewish community are arrested in the context of an "anti-Zionist" showcase trial.

1975: Holocaust survivor Imre Kertész's novel *Sorstalanság* (*Fatelessness*), depicting the experiences of a fifteen-year-old boy in concentration camps, is published.

1989–1990: Communist rule ends.

1992: Act XXIV of 1992 on the partial compensation of material damages to citizens passes, with a view to settling property relations. Act XXXII of 1992 passes, giving compensation to those wrongfully deprived of their life and liberty for political reasons.

1994: The Hungarian government officially apologizes for Hungarian complicity in the Holocaust.

1999: The Hungarian government agrees to establish a Holocaust Memorial Center in Budapest.

2000: The Hungarian government declares April 16 as Hungary's annual Holocaust Memorial Day.

2002: The Nobel Prize in Literature is awarded to Imre Kertész, author of the novel *Fatelessness*.

2004: The permanent exhibition *The Citizen Betrayed: In Memory of the Victims of the Hungarian Holocaust*, opens in Block no. 18 at Auschwitz I (main camp), part of the Auschwitz Memorial. A Holocaust Memorial Center opens in Budapest.

2006: A permanent exhibition, *From Deprivation of Rights to Genocide*, opens at the Holocaust Memorial Center in Budapest.

# Index

Entries that appear in boldface can be found in the Glossary. Page numbers followed by "n" indicate footnotes. Page numbers in *italic* indicate illustrations and photographs. Hungarian place names are used throughout; for non-Hungarian alternatives, see Table 6, p. 372.

Act II of 1939 (Act on National Defense), 46
Act IV of 1939 (Second "Jewish Law"), 6–9, 29n16
Act XIV of 1942, 49–51
Act XLII of 1895, xxxiii
Act XV of 1938 (First "Jewish Law"), xli–xliii, 3–6, 306, 343
Act XV of 1941 (Third "Jewish Law"), 10–13
Act XV of 1942, 13–15
Act XXV of 1920, xxxix
Act XXV of 1946, 342–43
agricultural estates: confiscation of, 13–16; restitution and, 346n51
air raids, 123–24, 287, 291, 320
*államtitkár,* xxixn5
Allies: cooperation of Jews with, rumored, 124, 281n3, 288–89, 320; defection to, lv; negotiations to surrender to, xviii, xix, xlvi, 147; response to deportations, 139
Alma Street nursing home, 170–72
Ambrózy, Gyula, 143

American Jewish Joint Distribution Committee, 266, 336
Ampfing concentration camp, 330–32, *331*
Anger, Per, 135
Angyal, István, 356–58
Anti-Comintern Pact, xli
anti-Roma prejudice, modern, 363
antisemitic legislation: assimilation interrupted by, 304; bans on use of public facilities, 27–30; under Bárdossy, xli–xliii; churches and, 306; current calls for, 362; development of, xliii; under Endre, xlix–l; enforcement of, xvii–xviii; false narrative of, 342–43; impact of, 16–22; in implementation of "Final Solution," xx; opposition to, 3–6; revocation of, postwar, 341; roots of, 2; shopping bans, 25–27; under Teleki, xxxix; types of, 72; on yellow star, 73–76. *See also* "aryanization"; "Jewish Laws"; *specific acts*
antisemitic violence: before 1938, xxxii–xxxiii, xxxv, 2; antisemites opposed to, 303; by Arrow Cross, lxv; during Arrow

425

**426** Index

Cross takeover, 153; Communist Party and, 348–49, 350; under Horthy, xxxvi; police intervention in, lvii; postwar, 347–50; and Tiszaeszlár blood libel case, xxxiii–xxxiv; during the "White Terror," xxxvi. *See also* mass murder
antisemitism: 1956 Revolution and, 355–56; in Austro-Hungarian Empire, xxxiv; in Catholic Church, 309; Holocaust and, xxx; as ideology, 2; of interwar period, xxxviii–xli, 343; political, ideologies of, 2; post-1989, 361–66; postwar declarations against, 341; preoccupation with, 293; prevalence of, 2; prewar, xxxii–xxxiv; propaganda and, 288–89; of radicals, xlv–xlvi; rescue attempts despite, 302–6; roots of, 1–3, 320; Soviet, 355; and state policy, xxxviii–xxxix, 280. *See also* bureaucratic antisemitism; illegal antisemitism
Antonescu, Ion, 61, 144
apartments: redistribution of, 285–88; seizure of, 123, 258, 288n28
Apor, Vilmos, 295n51, 307
Arendt, Hannah, 269n86
*árjapárja,* deportation of, 105
**Arrow Cross:** antisemitic violence by, lix, lxv; during Budapest ghettoization, 131n81; coalition government and, xlix; death marches under, 155–57, 323; deportations under, lxii–lxiii, 153–57, 213–14; executions of, postwar, 344; expropriation by, 282; general violence by, 169–72; in German occupation, 150; ghetto massacre planned by, 168–69; ghettos under, 160–69; ghetto violence by, 163–64, 168; Hungary under, lxii–lxv; ideology of, 150–52; Jewish assets nationalized under, 196–97; Jewish policy of, 157–60; looting by, 197; mass murders under, 155, 168, 169–72, 313, 322; police interference with, lvii; in prewar elections, xlv; protective documents and, 315; raids by, 175; Red Cross and, 169–72; resistance to, 153, 244, 270–71, *271*; sympathy

for Jews and, 295; takeover by, 148–50, 173, 311–13, 322; trials of, postwar, 344
"aryanization": Hungarians and, 64; of Jewish businesses, 177, 205
assets, nationalization of, 196–97, 352
Association of Awakening Hungarians (ÉME), xxxviii
Asztalos, Jolán, 299
auction of Jewish possessions, 204–5
*Auschwitz Album,* 219
Auschwitz (Oświęcim, Poland) concentration camp: deportation to, under Eichmann, xxviii–xxix; economic objectives of, lxin91; evacuation of, lxvi; expansion of, 214–16; gas supply for, 215; medical experiments in, 224–28; Mexico sector, lxi; postwar accounts of, xxviii; proportion of victims from Hungary, lxii; transports from, lxvi, 231–33. *See also* Birkenau camp
Auschwitz II-Birkenau. *See* Birkenau concentration camp
**Auschwitz Protocol,** 134–35, 261, 272, 327
Austria, eastern, xxx, lxvi, 21, 103, 269
Austrian Jews, xxx–xxxi
Austro-Hungarian army, Jews in, xxxii
Austro-Hungarian Empire, xxxiii, xxxiv

Bacher, Edith, 237–39
Bácska, 42–46
Bajos, Mrs. Aladár, 194
**Baky, László:** and deportations, liii, 115, 141–42; dismissal of, 141–42; execution of, postwar, 344; in ghetto planning, 76–79; proposal to remove, 115; as state secretary for political affairs, xlix
Balázs, Márta, 121–22
Baltic region, xxix
Barber, Aladár, *60,* 60–61
Barber, Károly, 61
Bárdfalva ghetto, 297
**Bárdossy, László,** xli, 344
Bartha, Károly, drafting of Jews under, 47–48
Bartók, Béla, 4n7

Báthory-Szűts, Sándor, 31–33
**Becher, Kurt,** 185, 266
Belarus, xxvii
Benedek, László, 325–26, *326*
Benshalom, Rafel (Rafi), xlvii, 270
Bereczky, Albert, 308
**Beregfy, Károly,** 153–54
Beregszász, 105, 259–60
**Berend, Béla,** 162–64, 265n71
Bergen-Belsen concentration camp, 233–36, 266
Berkovics, Mrs. Jakab, 192, 296n54
Berkovics, Mrs. Lázár, 296–97
Berkovits, Ignác, 297
Bessenyei, Lajos, 85–87
**Bethlen, István,** xxxix–xl, 136
Bet Orim Reform Jewish Congregation, 364n98
Bihar County, 31–33
Birkenau concentration camp (Auschwitz II): arrival at, lx–lxi; crematoria of, 215, 220; Hungarian Jews in, lx–lxii; "Jewish ramp" of, xxviii, 217–19; mass murders at, 219–31; photographs of, *218,* 219; plundering in, 177–78; preparation of, lx, 214–16; resistance in, 224, 230n55; selections at, lx–lxi, lxii, 217–18, 228–31; state museum at, 359–61; women at, lxi
blood libel, xxxiii–xxxiv, 348–49
body searches, 105, 192–95
Bognár, Mrs. János, 300
Bonczos, Miklós, 142
Bor, 58–59, 131
Borbola, Jenő, 193
Born, Friedrich, 325
Borsod County, 208
**Bosnyák, Zoltán,** 162, 289
Brand, Hansi, 265–66
Brand, Jenő, 265–66
Breitwieser, Arthur, 216
brick factories, 111–12, 231
Britain. *See* Great Britain
Buchenwald concentration camp, 232–33, 239–40
Budakalász, 105

Budapest: Allied air raids on, 123–24, 139, 287; apartment seizures in, 123, 285–88; concentration of Jews in, 335; deaths in, number, 335; liberation of, 330, 332–34; police interference in, lvii; rescue activities in, 295; resistance in, 244; survivors from, 341
Budapest ghetto (large ghetto): administration of, 162; under Arrow Cross, 160–69; Arrow Cross violence in, 163–64; creation of, 161–62; hospitals in, 166–68; liberation of, 169; massacre planned for, 168–69; mass graves in, 164–66, 365; population of, 161, 323; survivors of, 330. *See also* international ghetto; yellow-star houses
Budapest ghettoization, 123–34; under Arrow Cross, lxiii–lxv, 131n81; reactions of non-Jews to, 125–27
Budapest Jewish Council. *See* Jewish Council
Budapest Jews: conversions of, 130, 131, 252–54; daily life of, 132; deportation of, lv, 137, 141–42, 145; despair of, 129–30; employment of, 132–34, *133*; freedoms allowed to, 129, 145; optimism of, 172–73; and suicide, 130
**Budapest Relief and Rescue Committee,** 265–69
Budapest yellow-star houses. *See* yellow-star houses
Buday-Goldberger, Leó, 240–41, *241*
Bulgaria, xxvii, xliv
**bureaucratic antisemitism:** before 1944, 24–33; definition of, 24; of Hungarian officials, lvi; of KEOKH, 36
burial of dead, in Budapest ghetto, 164–66, 365

Calvinists: conditions of conversion, 308n95–96; deportations condemned by, 311
Carpatho-Ruthenia: antisemitic policies in, xliii; deportations from, 36n35, 105; doctors in, 208; reannexation of, casualties in, 34

Catholic Church, 308–11, 312–13, 326–27
cattle cars, 104–5, 217, 260, 296
Celldömölk, xxxvi
Central Jewish Council. *See* Jewish Council
Chabad Lubavitch movement, 364
Chevra Kadisha (Holy Society), 19
children: body searches of, 195; deaths of, numbers, 336; deportation of, 117–18; in ghettos, 249–52; murder of, 249n22; rescue of, 325
Christian churches: antisemitism of, 306–7; autonomy of, 306; protests by, 307–8; reaction of, 306–13; Third "Jewish Law" and, 10. *See also* Catholic Church; Protestant churches
Christian Jews: conversions, 130, 131, 252–54, 308; in ghettos, 90; after "Jewish Laws," 22; and legal definition of Jews, 9, 12n21; memorials and, 338–39; population of, xlvin44
Christians: in Budapest ghettoization, 125–27; favored under Bethlen, xxxix–xl; ghettos and, 91–93
Christian social organizations, 308
*Citizen Betrayed, The* (Magyar), 359–61
citizenship: certification of, 24; "miscegenation" and, 11n19–20; under Second "Jewish Law," 7
civil service: collaboration of, lvi; Jews in, postwar, 351
Clauberg, Carl, 224–25, 237
Cohen, Asher, 270
collaboration: of gendarmerie, lvii; of Horthy, lviii–lx; Jewish Council accused of, 262–65; legitimized by Horthy, xlviii; by non-Jews, 279–94; occupation based on, xlviii, lv–lviii; propaganda for, 289–91, *290*; in success of "Final Solution," xxix
collection camps: conditions in, 104; for deportations, 82, 104; financing of, 190–91; Jewish assets and, 182; Labor Service summons and, lv; medical care in, 116n36; organizing, 107; planning of, lii, 76–79, 80n30
commemoration, 338–39

Communist Party. *See* Hungarian Communist Party
compensation: for assets, 345–50; for land expropriation, 15; for Újvidék massacre, 45
concentration camps: liberation of, 330–32, *331*; roll calls in, 238n75; used for Hungarian Jews, 213. *See also specific camps*
conversion: of Budapest Jews, 130, 131, 252–54; conditions for, 308. *See also* Christian Jews
crematoria, 215, 220, 229–30
Croatia: collaborators in, xxix; "Final Solution" in, numbers killed during, xxxi; removal of minorities from, xliv
Croats, in Hungarian population, xxxi
Csatáry, László, 91–93
**Csatay, Lajos,** 55
Csepel Island, 131n77, 145
Csíkszereda, 33–34
Csillag, Edit, 120n43
Csillaghegy, 244n3, 301–2
Csobádi, Samu, 256n38
Czechoslovakia, refugees from, 35–36

Dachau concentration camp, 108
Danielsson, Carl I., 135, 317
"Death Gate" (Birkenau), xxviii
death marches: under Arrow Cross, 155–57, 323; from Auschwitz, lxvi; from Bor, 58–59; conditions of, 156–57; in deportations, lxiii, *lxiv*; diplomats and, 155–57; from Máramarossziget, 297; from Óbuda brick factory, 238
Debrecen ghetto, 85–87, 101, *101*
**DEGOB.** *See* **National Committee for Attending Deportees in Budapest**
denunciations, 282
deportations: abuses during, 111–12; Allied response to, 139; under Arrow Cross, lxii–lxiii, 153–57; attempted escapes, 108, 109, 296; from Auschwitz, lxvi, 231–33; awareness of, 273–78; body cavity searches during, 105; cattle cars in, 104–5, 217, 260; of children, 117–18; church

protests against, 308; collection camps for, 82; conditions during, 39, 116, 217; deaths during, xlviii, 115n35, 217; decision-making process and, lii–lv, 61; of doctors, 206–8; of elderly, 117–18; end of, lv, lix, lxiii–lxv; under Endre, l; excuses used for, 117–18; exemptions from, 105; financing, 190–91; German pressure for, 63–67; by Hungarian army, xliv; international reactions to, 117, 134–36, 138–39, 314; Jewish Council and, 255, 259–61; for labor service, lxii–lxiii; murders after, Horthy's awareness of, lix; number of, liii, 103, 109n16; official reports on, 115–17; pace of, lx–lxi, 108–9, 244; planning for, liii, lx; propaganda on, 248; reactions against, 112, 279–80, 288, 309–11, 360; after reannexation, 33; of refugees, 36–40; reports on, 105–11; rescue efforts during, 296, 319–24; resistance during, 244; resumption of, lxii–lxiii, 139–40, 142–43, 153–57; scope of, lii–liii, *liv*; under Second "Jewish Law," 6–7, 9; selection for, 121; from Strasshof, 120–23; suicides during, 107; suspension of, 40, 134–45, 264, 314; warnings of, 302; of women, 248–49. *See also* Birkenau concentration camp
deportation zones, *liv,* 104
Dés, 192, 195
diplomats, 155–57, 314–25
displaced persons (DP) camps, 340
Diszel, xxxvi
Dobossy, Sándor, 28–30
doctors: exclusion of Jews, 205–8; in Labor Service, 52–53; in reannexed territories, 206–8
Dohány Street Synagogue, 165, 365, *366*
Domonkos, István, 17–18
**Domonkos, Miksa,** 18, 326, 355
Domonkos, Péter, 17–18
DP (displaced persons) camps, 340
*dzsentri,* 1n2

Eastern Frontline Comrades' Association, 291n33

economic participation of Jews: in agriculture, 13–16; Horthy on, 114; industrialists, xxxiv–xl; policies on, xliii, 6, 64, 66–67, 110
Ecséri, Lilla, 172–73, *174*
education: in ghettos, 252; of Hungarian Jews, xxxii; Jewish, modern, 364; restricted access to, xxxix, 17
**Eichmann, Adolf:** deportations under, lii–liii, lxii–lxiii; Endre's relationship with, l, li; "Final Solution" under, xxix–xxx; on Hungarian collaboration, lv–lvi; in Kistarcsa deportation, 140–41; resumption of deportations and, 144; speed of Holocaust in Hungary under, xxviii; on state of Auschwitz, 214; Zionist negotiations with, 120, 266. *See also **Sondereinsatzkommando Eichmann***
elderly, deportation of the, 117–18
Elefánt, Márton, 270
El Salvador, 325
ÉME. *See* Association of Awakening Hungarians
emigration from Hungary: deportation resumption and, 139–40; after "Jewish Laws," 22; to Palestine, 315; of survivors, 340–41
Endre, László (gendarme), 300–302
**Endre, László (state secretary):** antisemitic legislation under, ln54, 27–30; background of, xlix; Berend and, 163; in Budapest ghettoization, 124; bureaucratic antisemitism of, 24; cooperation of, xxix; in deportation planning, 104, 115–16; deportations under, l, lii–liii, 141–42; dismissal of, 141–42; on draft exemption for doctors, 208; Eichmann's relationship with, l, li; execution of, 344; "Final Solution" under, xxix–xxx; ghettoization under, l; and ghetto planning, 79n27; Horthy and, 115; influence on antisemitic regulations, 30; Jewish Council petitions and, 258n48; personal antisemitism of, l; popular support for, 280; prosecution of, postwar, 344; as state secretary for public administration, xlix–l

Eörsi, Gyula, 245–47
Erez, Zvi, 269n88
Érsekújvár ghetto, 100
escapes: from deportations, 108, 109; from ghettos, 93n56; Hassidic Jews in, 244; of Jewish Council members, 262; from Labor Service, 56, 57; Orthodox Jews and, 244
ethnic Germans. *See* Germans, ethnic
ethnic minorities: campaigns against, 34; policies against, xliv; sympathy from, 106
exemptions: from Arrow Cross Jewish policy, 159–60; from deportations, 105; from Labor Service, 154, 206, 208; from wearing yellow star, 74, 268n80
expropriation: administration of, 184; attempts to avoid, 198–99; beneficiaries of, 200–202, 282; body searches and, 192–95; condemnation of, 360; during deportations, 81–82, 107; effects of, 198–208; of emigrants, 62; interrogations around, 96; inventories in, 183–84, 185–89; process of, 179–82; public petitions for, 200; and redistribution, 201–5; restitution for, postwar, 345–50; in Újkécske, 187–89. *See also* plundering

Fabri, Pauline, 332–34
Farkas, Gábor, 126
Farkas, Lajos, 248
Farkas, Mihály, 351
*Fatelessness (Sorstalanság)*, 233
Feketehalmy-Czeydner, Ferenc, 42–46, 344
Felvidék, xliii
**Ferenczy, László:** on deportation numbers, liiin71; deportations directed by, 105; execution of, 344; on hiding Jewish assets, 199; reports from, 105–11; resistance by, 144; resumption of deportations and, 143–44
Feuer, Alexander (Sándor), 340, *340*
"fifth column," Jews as, 55, 281n3
financial directorates, expropriation in, 184
First "Jewish Law." *See* Act XV of 1938

folk movement, 303
Fonyó, József, 164–65
food rations, 72n6, 251
forced labor (of Jews). *See* Labor Service
forged documents, 270, 299, 321n119
"Fourth Razglednica," 59
France: collaborators in, xxix; deportations in, 61; Holocaust in, xxviii
Franco, Francisco, 56n94
Freudiger, Fülöp, 256n38, 262, 264, 264n69
Freund, Katalin, 167–68
Freymann, Andor, 299
Freymann, Sándor, 299
Friedl, Rafael. *See* Benshalom, Rafel (Rafi)

Gábor, Zsuzsanna, 301
Galicia, 38–40
Galpert, Ernő, 20–21, *21*
**gendarmerie:** attitudes of, lviiin79; brutality of, 112; in Budapest deportations, 137; collaboration of, lvii; in ghetto security, 93n56; interrogations by, 191–92; plundering by, 177; recruitment in, lvii; in rescue attempts, 300–302; torture by, 97, 191–93
gendarmerie districts, 104
gender roles, 249
gentiles. *See* non-Jews (Hungarian)
German occupation: Arrow Cross in, 150; coalition government during, xlviii–xlix, 71–72; Hungarian bureaucracy in, lvi–lvii; Jewish reactions to, 245–47. *See also* collaboration
Germans: in Hungarian population, xxxi; plundering by, 184–87, 197
Germans, ethnic *(svábs)*, lxvi–lxvii, 63, 344
Gerő, Ernő, 351
Geschke, Hans: in deportation planning, liii; Einsatzgruppe under, xlviii
ghettos: administration of, 94–95; children in, 249–52; conditions in, 90–102, 250–51; establishment of, lii, 76–82; government in, 94–95; Hungarian refugees in, 39; Jewish Council role

in, 90; of Kassa, 91–93; Labor Service summons and, lv; medical care in, 116; police forces of, 91, 162; possessions allowed in, 186; in Szálasi's plan, 159; torture in, 96–98, 191–92; women in, 249

ghettoization: administrators of, 84–90; awareness of, 273–78, 291–94; in Debrecen, 85–87; under Endre, l; financing, 190–91; implementation, 82–90, 302; Jewish assets and, 182; justification for, 80; models of, 83, 124; non-Jews and, 84, 279–80, 285–88; phases of, 82; planning, lii, *liv,* 76–82; of Zala County, 87–90. *See also* Budapest ghettoization

Gimes, Miklós, 356

**Glass House,** 272, 317

gold, 178, 181

Goldberger family, 240

Goldstein, Endre, 101, *101*

Goldstein, Ernő, 102

Goldstein, Matilde, 102

Goldstein, Móric, *101,* 101–2

**"Gold Train,"** 178

**Gömbös, Gyula,** xl–xli

**Good Shepherd Committee,** 308

Gosztonyi, Péter, 281

Government Commissioner's Office for Handling Material and Financial Affairs of the Jews, 196n60

Grassy, József, 43, 45n61, 344

Grausz, Maria Magdalena, 315, *316*

Great Britain, 139

Gréczi, Mrs. Imre, 204–5

Grell, Theodor Horst, 158n39

Grósz, Lajos, 361

Grünvald, Fülöp, 275–76, *276*

Grünwald, Jenő, 273

Günther, Rolf, 215

Gur, David, 270–71, *271*

Gustaf V of Sweden, lvii, 135–36, 138

Gyapay, László, 96–97

Gyarmati, Fanni, 59

Gyémánt, Emil, 56

Gyergyószentmiklós, 200n72

Gyömrő, 27–30

Gyöngyös, xxxv, xxxvi

György, Oszkár, 107

**Hain, Péter,** 199, 200, 344

Haining, Jane, 312

Hajdúnánás, 356

Hajdúszoboszló, 261

Halberstam, Avraham Shalom, 223n33

Halberstam, Menachem Mendel, 223n33

Halpern, Mór, 170–72

*halutzim,* 269–72

*Harc* (Struggle), 289–90

Hartjenstein, Fritz, 214

Hassidic Jews, in escape attempts, 244

Havasalja, 36

Hegyeshalom, 156

Herbst, Imre, 270

Herskovits, Fábián, 273

Heves County, 25–26

higher education: of Hungarian Jews, xxxii; Jewish, modern, 364; restricted access to, xxxix, 17

Hirschfeld, Rózsa, 235n65

Hitler, Adolf, assassination attempt on, 131

HMC. *See* Holocaust Memorial Center

Höcker, Karl, 219n17

Höfle, Hermann, xxviii

Holocaust Memorial Center (Budapest), 359

**Holy Cross Society,** 308

**Horthy, Miklós:** antisemitic legislation under, xxxix–xl; in Budapest deportations, 137; cease-fire under, 148–50, 172; deportations under, lv, 112–15, 137–39, 143–44, 314; on German alliance, 65–67; during German invasion, xlvii; ideology of, xxxviii; international condemnation of, 134–36; in negotiations with Allies, 147; personal antisemitism of, 1; responsibility of, lviii–lx, 112–15, 135–37, 143–44

**Horthy, Miklós, Jr.,** 150

Horváth, József, 96

hospitals, in Budapest ghetto, 165–68

**Höss, Rudolf,** lx, 214–15

Hungarian army: antisemitism of, 34; deportations by, xliv; Jews in, xxxiii; Jews protected by, 41n50; rescue attempts and, 296. *See also* Labor Service
Hungarian Communist Party, 329, 348–49, 350, 351–55
Hungarian Institute for Research of the Jewish Question, 289
Hungarian Life Party (MÉP), xlv, xlviii–xlix
Hungarian National Socialist Party (MNSZP), in coalition government, xlviii–xlix
Hungarian Racial Hygiene and Population Policy Association, xxxiv, xli
Hungarian Renewal Party (MMP), xlv, xlviii–xlix
Hungarian Soviet Republic: establishment of, xxxv; Jews in leadership of, xxxv
Hungarian War of Independence, xxxii–xxxiii
Hungarian Workers' Party, rise of, 329
Hungarism, 151–52
*Hungarista Napló*, 151
Hunsche, Otto, liii
Hunyadi, László, 87–90

I. G. Farben, 225
**illegal antisemitism,** 24–33, 47–48, 52–53
Illyés, Flóra, 306
Illyés, Gyula, 305–6
immigration to Hungary: of European Jews, xxx–xxxi; and wartime refugees, xlvi–xlvii
**Imrédy, Béla,** xlv, 6, 116–17, 344
Independent Smallholders' Party, 329, 348, 350
Information Office, 267n77
insurance system, 179
international ghetto, 160–61, 314, 323, 330
International Red Cross, 166, 169–72, 325, *326*
internment camps, lv, 130n75. *See also specific camps*
Israelite: population after World War I, xxxviii; population over time, 368; use of term, xxx

Istóczy, Győző, xxxiii, xxxiv
Italy, xxïx, xlvi, 61

Jákob, Esther, Lili, Mordechai, Sril, and Zelig, 218–19
János Sanatorium, 171
**Jaross, Andor:** Budapest deportations and, 141–42; and confiscated property, 202–4; in deportation planning, liii; execution of, 344; on ghettos, 80; Jewish Council petitions and, 261; as minister of the interior, xlix
Jászberény ghetto, 186
Jeckeln, Friedrich, 39–40
Jenő, László, 357
jewelry, plunder of, 178
Jewish assets, 180–81, 198–99, 204–5, 209–11, *210*, 345–50. *See also* "aryanization"
**Jewish Council** (Central, Budapest): awareness of "Final Solution," 263n63; in Budapest ghetto, 162; on burial of dead, 165; and Christian converts, 252n28; collaboration charges and, 262–65; on conversion of Jews, 252–54; deportations and, 143–44, 255, 259–61; Domonkos (Péter) in, 18; escape and, 262; establishment of, 254–55; and ghettoization, 98–100, 123–24, 125; jurisdiction of, 255; petitions of, 258–61; resistance by, 144, 262; on yellow star, 74. *See also* Budapest ghetto
**Jewish Councils** (provincial): petitions of, 261; role in ghettos, 90, 94; in Strasshof deportations, 121
"Jewish Laws," 3–16; circumvention of, 16; emigration after, 22; Horthy's endorsement and, lviii; use of term, 3n4. *See also specific acts*
**"Jewish ramp"** (*Judenrampe*), xxviii, 217–19
Jewish refugees, xlvi–xlvii, 7, 36–40, 79, 130n75, 248
Jewish revival, postwar, 363–65
Jews (Hungarian): in 1956 Revolution, 356; under Austro-Hungarian Empire,

xxxiii; categories of, 157–58; as communists, 290, *290*; cooperation with Allies, rumored, 124, 281n3, 288–89, 320; deaths of, numbers, 335; definitions of, 32; demographics, xxx–xxxi, xxxviii; hidden by non-Jews, 297–98, 312; Hungarian identity of, xxxi–xxxii, 22; in law enforcement, 351; legal definition of, 3, 7, 9, 10, 12, 32; military service by, xxxii, xxxiii, 46, 49–50; negotiations with SS, xix–xx; optimism of, xvii–xviii, 22; political participation of, xxxii; proportion of Auschwitz murders, lxii; re-entry to Hungary, 61–62; relationship with postwar Communist Party, 351–55; social mobility of, xxxi–xxxii; unification of branches, 353–55, *354*; voting rights for, 6, 7–8. *See also* Christian Jews; economic participation of Jews

Jews (non-Hungarian): emigration to Hungary, xxx–xxxi; of reannexed territories, 34, *35*

Judaica, confiscation of, 196

*Judenrampe. See* **"Jewish Ramp"**

Jungerth-Arnóthy, Mihály, 142

Kádár, János, 329, 355, 358n88
Kádár, Mihály, 175–76, *176*
Kahán, Niszon, 256n38, 268n79
**Kahán-Frankl, Samu,** 256n38, 262, 264, 338, 354
**Kállay, Miklós,** xvii, xlv–xlvi, 13, 61, 147, 149n4
Kálló, Ferenc, 312
Kalmár, Jenő, 301–2
Kaltenbrunner, Ernst, xlviii
Kamenets-Podolski massacre, 40–42, *42*, 248, 344
Kaposvár, 183–84, 200
Kassa, 204–5, 222–23, 259–60, 299
Kassa ghetto, 91–93
**Kasztner, Rezső,** 120, 265–69
Kasztner group, 233–34, 265–69
Katona, József, 317–19, *318*
Keitel, Wilhelm, 43

Keller, László, 330–32, *331*
Kemény, Gábor, 170n81
KEOKH. *See* National Central Authority for Controlling Aliens
Keresztes-Fischer, Ferenc, 40, 149n4, 206
Kertész, Imre, 231–33, *232–33*, 340
Királyháza, 296
Kishon, Ephraim, 334
Kistarcsa internment camp: deportations from, lv, 118–20, 140–41, 259; release of prisoners from, 145; use of, 131n76
Kocsis, József, 109
Kodály, Zoltán, 4n7
Kohn, Sámuel, 365
Kolb, Julia, 44
Kölcsey, Sándor, 85–87
Kolozsvár, 34, *35*, 108, 192
Komárom County, 286
Komlósi, László, 126
Komoly, Lea, 267n76, 268n79
**Komoly, Ottó,** 265–69, 325
Konvoent, Karl, 222n30
Kőrösmező, 36
Kovács, Alajos, xxxin7, xlvin44, 362
Kovács, István, 356
Kovács, Kálmán É., 349–50
Kovács, László, 248, 249–52
Kováts, József, 301
Kovner, Abba, 277n109
**Kozma, Miklós,** 36
Kramer, Josef, 214
Krausz, Klára, *75*, 75–76
**Krausz, Miklós,** 272, 317
"*Kristallnacht*," compensation tax for, 33
Krumey, Hermann, 254–55
Kulcsár, István, 296
Kun, András, 344
Kun, Béla, xxxv
Kunmadaras, 349–50
Kurtág, Bözsi, 361

labor camps, 280–81, 334
**Labor Service,** 46–61; armed resistance and, 243; under Arrow Cross, 153–54; in Bor death march, 58–59; brutality in, xlvii, 48–49, 52–53, 55–57;

deportations for, lii, liii–liv, lxii–lxiii; doctors in, 52–53, 206–8; exemptions to, 154; requirement for, xliv–xlv, 46; Soviet captivity and, 56n95, 334; summons for, lv, 108; in Szálasi's plan, 158–59; women in, 46n65
**Lakatos, Géza,** lv, 145, 195
Langfuss, Leib, 221–24
Langlet, Valdemar, 325
laws. *See* antisemitic acts
leaflets, illegal, 272–78
legal rehabilitation, postwar, 341–45
Lévy, Lajos, 166–68
Liebehenschel, Arthur, 214
Liebmann, Béla, Flóra, and Szenka, 209–11
Löbl, Hilda, 174–75, *176,* 334
Lootz, Gyula, 280–81
Lorsi, Milkós, 59
Lőwy, Johanna, 118
Lulay, László, 104
Lutherans, 308n95, 311
**Lutz, Carl,** 315–17

Macskásy, Géza Nagysötétági, 283–85
Madarász, Lipót, 122–23, *123*
Mád synagogue, 336–37, *337*
Magyar, Bálint, 359–61
Magyarization, of Hungarian Jews, xxxi–xxxii
*Magyarországi Zsidók Lapja,* 252
Makó, 194
Manfréd Weiss Works, 138n99
**Mantello, Georges M.,** 325
Márai, Sándor, 291–94
Máramaros County, 206–7
Máramarossziget, 259–60, 297
Maros Street hospital, 170
Marosvásárhely, 99, 107
marriages: Arrow Cross proposals for, 152; halachic law on, 337–38. *See also* "miscegenation" laws
Márton, Áron, 307
mass graves, in Budapest ghetto, 164–66, 365
mass murder: under Arrow Cross, 155, 168, 169–72, 313, 322; awareness of, 62–65, 247–48, 263n63, 273–78, 291–94, 306–7; by gassing, 220–24, 228–31; in ghettos, 168; international reactions to, 134–36; in Kamenets-Podolski, 40–42, *42;* of labor servicemen, 48–49; in the Southern Province, 42–46. *See also* Auschwitz; Birkenau concentration camp; ghettos
Mátészalka, 105
Matzner, Ilona and Samuel, 292
Mauthausen camps, 213–14, 240–41, *241*
Mayer, József, 270
medical care: in ghettos, 116, 166–68; and International Red Cross, 166, 170n81; "Jewish Laws" and, 206–8. *See also* doctors
medical experiments: in Auschwitz, 224–28; in Ravensbrück, 237
memorials, postwar: in Budapest, 359; Christian Jews and, 339
**Mengele, Josef,** 225–28
MÉP. *See* Hungarian Life Party
Mezei, Ilona, 299
Mezőszentgyörgy, xxxvi
Mikes, Nándor, 282
military exemption tax, 32–33
military service. *See* Labor Service
"miscegenation" laws: double standards in, 12; under Third "Jewish Law," xliii, 9, 10–13
Miskolc, 192, 348, 350
MMP. *See* Hungarian Renewal Party
MNSZP. *See* Hungarian National Socialist Party
Mogyoróssy, Imre, 38–39
**Moll, Otto,** 215, 239
MONE *See* National Association of Hungarian Physicians
Monor collection camp, 111
**Muhsfeldt** (Mussfeld), **Erich,** 227
Müller, Filip, 220, 223
Munkács: "Black Saturday" of, 112; deportations from, 105, 108, 259–60
Munkácsi, Ernő, 273
Muslim Pomacs, removal of, xliv
Mussolini, Benito, deportations under, 61

Nagy, Ferenc, 341–42
Nagy, János, 349
Nagy, Lajos, 108
**Nagybaczoni Nagy, Vilmos,** 51–55
Nagykároly, 200n72
Nagyvárad: ghettoization of, 95–97; Jewish assets in, 199, 209
Nagyvárad ghetto, 96–97, 98–99, 192
National Antisemitic Party, xxxiv
National Association of Hungarian Physicians (MONE), 206
National Central Authority for Controlling Aliens (KEOKH), 35–36
**National Committee for Attending Deportees in Budapest (DEGOB),** 225
National Holocaust Memorial Day, postwar, 359
nationalization of assets, under postwar communism, 352
National Office of Hungarian Israelites, 345–47
National Representation of Hungarian Israelites, 353–55, *354,* 356–58
naturalization policies, 7
Németh, László, 302–6
**Neologue Jews:** escape attempts and, 244; Hungarian identity of, 22; as majority, xxxviii; official recognition of, xxxii; postwar influence of, 352; on postwar memorialization, 338–39; unification of Jewish branches, postwar, 353–55, *354*
Netherlands, xxviii, xxix, 223, 236
Nickelsburg, László, 356
non-Jews (Hungarian): appeals to, 273–78; "aryanization" and, 64; awareness of, 273–78; benefits of ghettoization for, 285–88; as collaborators, 279–94; impact of "Jewish Laws" on, 16–17; as informants, 281; Jewish assets hidden by, 198–99, 282; Jews hidden by, 297–98; murder of Jews and, lvii–lviii; Nazi opinion of, 67–69; petitions for Jewish businesses, 282–85; rescue efforts of, 294–306; sympathy of, 289–91, 294–95

Northern Transylvania: antisemitic policies in, xliii–xliv; deportations from, 33–34, 105–11; doctors in, 206–8; ghettoization in, 95–97; reannexation of, 34, *35*
Norway, xxix
Novak, Franz, 141
*numerus clausus,* xxxix, 2, 17n32, 343
Nuremberg Laws, 12
Nyíregyháza, 108, 259–60, 261
Nyíregyháza ghetto, 250–52
Nyiszli, Miklós, 223, 225–31
Nyitrai, Aranka (née Straub), 299

Oberlanzendorf internment camp, 240
Óbuda brick factory, 155, 174, 238
occupation. *See* German occupation
Office for Handling Material and Financial Affairs of the Jews, 196n60
Operation Höss, lx
**Order of Vitéz,** 15–16
Organisation Todt: Labor Service and, 49; women in, lxi
**Orthodox Jews,** xxxii, 112, 221, 244, 278n111, 338–39, 353–55, *354*
Ortutay, Gyula, 354
Ottlik, György, 62–65
Ózd, 348

Paksy-Kiss, Tibur, 95
Pál, József, 347
Palestine Office, 272, 317
Pálmai, Magdolna, *133,* 133–34
Pap, Róbert, 19n34
Páva Street Synagogue, 130
Pécs ghetto, 193–94
**people's courts,** 343–45
**Perlasca, Giorgo,** 324–25
*Pester Lloyd,* 62
Pest Israelite Congregation, 352
Pest-Pilis-Solt-Kiskun County, xlix, 24, 28–30, 187
Pétain, Henri-Philippe, 61
Péter, Gábor, 351
**Péterffy, Jenő,** 95–97

petitions: for apartments, 285–88; for Jewish assets, 200; for Jewish businesses, 282–85; by Jewish Council, Budapest, 258–61; by Jewish Councils, 261; against yellow-star houses, 125–27
Pető, Ernő, 256, 262–65
Petschauer, Attila, 48
pits, burning, 220, 224
Pius XII (Pope), 134, 138–39, 326–27
plundering: by Arrow Cross, 197; by Auschwitz staff, 216; in financing the murder of Jews, 178; after gassing, 220; by gendarmerie, 177; by Germans, 184–85, 197; by public, 200, *201,* 204; as state action, 280; by State Security Surveillance, 200. *See also* expropriation
pogroms. *See* antisemitic violence
Pohl, Oswald, lxi
Poland: deportations from, 38–39; "Final Solution" in, numbers killed, xxvii; Holocaust in, speed of, xxviii; refugees from, 35–36
Polish Jews, emigration to Hungary, xxx–xxxi
Pomacs, Muslim. *See* Muslim Pomacs
Portugal, 325
Prohászka, Ottokár, 151n16
propaganda: about Allies, 288–89; on deportations, 248; about Jewish Bolshevism, *290;* and sympathy for Jews, 295
property confiscation. *See* expropriation
protected buildings, 317, 322. *See also* international ghetto; International Red Cross
**protective documents:** forged, 270, 299, 321n119; in rescue efforts, 315–17, *316, 318,* 321, 324–25, *326*
Protestant churches: deportations condemned by, 311; rescue efforts of, 327. *See also* Christian churches
Prva, Frantiska, 298, *298*
Putnok, 38–39

Rácalmás-Kulcs, xxxvi
Race Protectionist Party, in prewar elections, xlv
"Race Protection Law." *See* Act XV of 1941
Radnóti, Miklós, 59
Raffay, Sándor, 311
Rajniss, Ferenc, 12, 124
**Rákosi, Mátyás,** 329, 351
**Ravasz, László,** 311
Ravensbrück concentration camp, 236–39
reannexations to Hungary: doctors and, 206–8; expulsions after, 33; "Jewish Laws" and, 20; map of, *xlii;* refugees in, xlviin45; Vienna Awards in, xli; violence and, 34
Red Army: abuses by, 334; border crossed by, 147; cease-fire with, 148–49, 172; in liberation of Budapest, 332–34
Red Cross. *See* International Red Cross
**Red Terror,** xxxv
Reform Judaism, postwar, 364
refugees, Jewish, xlvii, 7, 35–40, 45, 79, 130n75, 248
rehabilitation, postwar legal, 341–45
Reich, Jenő and Margit, 118–20
religious objects, confiscation of, 196
rescue efforts: by antisemites, 302–6; army in, 296; in Budapest, 295; of Catholic Church, 312–13; by Christians, 311–13; from deportations, 296, 319–24; factors inhibiting, 295–96; gendarmerie in, 300–302; hiding of Jews, 297–98; international, 313–27; for pay, 299; police in, 300; protection documents in, 315–17, *316, 318,* 321; of Protestant churches, 327; of Raoul Wallenberg, 319–24; of Sweden, 317, 319–24; of Switzerland, 155–57, 315–17
resettlement, of Jews, 31–34, 40n47
resistance: to Arrow Cross, 153, 270–71, *271;* in Birkenau, 224, 230n55; in Budapest, 244; during deportations, 244; to German occupation, xlviii; of *halutzim,* 269–71; illegal leaflets, 273–75, 277–78; by Jewish Council, 144; postwar mythology about, 342–43; research on, 243; by Zionists, 270–71, *271*
restitution, postwar, 346–47
Révai, József, 351
Révész, Perec, 270

Ribbentrop, Joachim von, 43, 137–39
Righteous Among the Nations, 140n108, 295n52, 296n57, 302n68, 312n101, 313–14, 360n91
right-wing organizations, in interwar period, xxxviii–xl
Rimaszombat, 25–27
Rokeach, Aharon and Mordechai, 223
Romania: collaborators in, xxix; defection to Allies, lv, 144; deportations in, 61; escape to, 300n64; "Final Solution" in, xxvii, xlvi; Jewish refugees and, 244; removal of minorities from, xliv
Romanians: in Hungarian population, xxxi; in Labor Service, 47
Roma victims, 225, 237, 361
Roosevelt, Franklin D., 134
Rosner, Imre, 74–76, *75*
Rosner, Klara, *75*
Róth, Ernő, 339
**Rotta, Angelo,** 138n101, 327

Sablik, Aranka, 118
Sajkásvidék, 42–46
Salgótarján, 192
Salkaházi, Sára, 312–13
Sanz-Briz, Ángel, 324
Sárbogárd, 338–39
Sárvár, 117–18
Sárvár internment camp, lv, 141
Schmidhuber, Gerhard, 168–69
Schönberg, Hela, Renáta, Sándor, and Szilvia, 298, *298*
schooling, in ghettos, 252
Schrey, Mária Ágnes, 117–18
Schück, Jenő, 357
Schumann, Horst, 237
Schutzstaffel, xix–xx, 185, 367
Schwarcz, Margit, 361
Second Hungarian Army, 47–48
Second "Jewish Law." *See* Act IV of 1939
segregation, 31–33, 83. *See also* collection camps; ghettos; ghettoization
selections: at Birkenau, lx–lxi, lxii, 217–18, 228, 231; data on, 228n51; for Strasshof deportations, 121

Serbia, xxvii, 244
Serbs: campaigns against, 34; expulsion from Hungary, xliv; mass executions of, 43; removal from Croatia, xliv
**Serédi, Jusztinián,** 308–10
Seregélyes, 191
Seventh District of Budapest, 365
sexual intercourse, laws pertaining to, 11–12
Siménfalvy, Sándor, 37
Sim Shalom Progressive Jewish Congregation, 364n98
**Slachta, Margit,** 40
Slovakia: antisemitic laws in, 25n5; collaborators in, xxix; escape to, 300; "Final Solution" in, xxvii, xlvi; Jewish refugees and, 244
Smallholders' Party. *See* Independent Smallholders' Party
Somló, Sándor, 273
**Sondereinsatzkommando Eichmann (SEK),** xviii, xxviii, xlviii, li–lv, 104–11, 119n41, 141, 223n34, 255, 344
*Sonderkommando,* 214–15, 220–24, 230
Sopron, 209
Sós, Endre, 357
Southern Province: ethnic campaigns in, 34; mass murder in, 42–46; purges in, xliv
Soviet army. *See* Red Army
Soviet Union: Hungary under, 329, 355–58; labor servicemen captured by, 56n95, 334; war against, Labor Service in, 47–48
Spain, rescue efforts of, 324
Spitz, Gyula, 41–42, *42*
SS. *See* Schutzstaffel
SS-Business Administration Main Office, 178
statement of reasons, for legislation, 13n26
**State Security Surveillance,** personal plundering by, 200
**Status Quo Ante,** xxxii, 353–55, *354*
**Stern, Samu,** 256, 263n63
Stockholm Declaration, 359
**Stöckler, Lajos,** 352, 354, 355

Strasshof deportations, 120–23
*stróman (strómans),* 16–17, 64
*Südostwall,* lxiii
suicides, 107, 130, 155, 162, 167, 278
Suri, István, 57–58
survivors: in Budapest, 330; demographics of, 335–36; emigration of, 340–41; international aid for, 336
*svábs. See* Germans, ethnic
Sweden: reaction to Hungarian mass murders, 134–36; rescue efforts of, 317, 319–24
Switzerland: Auschwitz Protocol delivered to, 272; rescue efforts of, 315–17
synagogues, 209–11, *210. See also specific synagogues*
Szalai, Pál, 168
**Szálasi, Ferenc,** 147–52, 173; collaboration under, lxv; death marches under, 157; deportations under, lxii–lxv; diary, 151–52; execution of, 344; Jewish assets nationalized under, 196–97; Jewish policy of, 157–60; political aspirations of, lxv
Szászrégen, 192, 195
Szatmárnémeti ghetto, 99
Szeged, 19–20, 209–11, *210*
*székely (székelys),* resettlement in Southern Province, xliv
Székely Land, railroad for, 53–55
Székesfehérvár, 192, 195
Szeklence, 259–60
Szentkút agreement, lii–liii
Szép, Ernő, 132
Szerebrenik, Mrs. Ábrahám, 118
Szilágyi, Ernő, 267n76, 268n79
Szilágyi, Ilonka, 299
Szolnok ghetto, 186
Szombathely ghetto, 93–95
Szombathelyi, Ferenc, 42, 57
**Sztehlo, Gábor,** 325
**Sztójay, Döme:** awareness of mass murders, 62–65; and deportations, 112–15; economy under, 179; execution of, postwar, 344; "Final Solution" under, xviii; on international reactions to deportations, 139; as prime minister, xlviii; social policies of, 179

Takács, Gergely, 350
Tapolca, xxxvi
tax collection, from deportees, 189–90
Teichmann, Ernő, 270
Teitelbaum, Dávid, 336–37, *337*
**Teleki, Pál:** antisemitic legislation under, xxxix; Hungarian Racial Hygiene and Population Policy Association under, xxxiv; as prime minister, xxxivn19; Second "Jewish Law" and, 6; suicide of, xli; Third "Jewish Law" and, 9
Thessalonika, xxvii
Thilo, Heinz, 228n50
Third "Jewish Law." *See* Act XV of 1941
Tiszaeszlár, xxxiii–xxxiv
Tiszaföldvár, 195
*tisztességes,* 11n20
**Toldi, Árpád,** 196n60
**Török, Sándor,** 124, 258n48, 308n92
torture: in expropriation process, 191–92; in ghettos, 96–98
Tóth, Lajos, 110
Treitel, Mrs. Izrael, 300
Trenker, Alfred, 281
trials, postwar, 343–45
**Trianon Peace Treaty,** 345; borders changed by, xxxvi–xxxviii, *xxxvii*; discontent over, xli
Tripartite Pact, Hungary in, xli
Trumpeldor, Joseph, 278n112
"Turanism," xxxiv
Turkey, 325
Turvölgyi, Albert, 196n60

Ubrizsi, Pál, 140–41
Újkécske, 187–89
*Új Magyarság,* 286–88
Újvidék massacre, xlvii, 43–46, 344
Ukraine, xxvii, xxix, 38–40
Ukrainians, removal of, xliv
Ungvár, 105, 217, 259–60

Index **439**

United States, 139, 314
Upper Province: deportations from, 33; doctors in, 206–8; reannexation of, 34
U.S.S.R. *See* Soviet Union

**Vajna, Gábor,** lxii–lxv, 153
Varga, Ferenc, 57–58
Városmajor Street sanatorium, 170–72
Vas, István, 305–6
Vas County, 209
Vasdényei, István, 140–41
**Veesenmayer, Edmund:** on changes in deportation plan, lxiii; emigration negotiations with, 315; on Hungarian disarmament, xlvii; on Hungarians, 67–69; on penalties for Jews, 74; on suspension of deportations, 137–39
Végh, Ferenc, 285
Versailles Peace Treaty, xli
Veszprém County, 183, 190
veterans, World War I, 50–51
victim numbers: in Budapest, 335; children, 336; from deportations, lxvi, 115n35, 217; Hungarian Jews, 335; in Labor Service, 48; from military labor service, xlvii; in reannexation, 34, in Újvidék massacre, xlvii
**Vienna Awards,** xli
Viennese Jews, emigration to Hungary, xxx–xxxi
Visser't Hooft, W. A., 327n138
voting rights, and Hungarian Jews, 6, 7–8

**Wallenberg, Raoul,** 317; disappearance of, 324, 355; on international ghetto, 161; rescue efforts of, 315, 319–24
War Refugee Board, 314
Warsaw, deportation of Jews from, xxviii
WCC. *See* World Council of Churches
Weinmann, Éva, 130–32
Weiss, István, 38–39
Weiss, Mrs. Ödön, 38
Weiss Manfréd Works, 185
Weisz, Albert, 107
Weisz, Emil, 234–36

Weiszfeiler, Ferenc Isaak, 330n2
Welfare Bureau of Hungarian Israelites, 19
Werber, Erzsébet, 299
Wesselényi Street, 163–64
Wesselényi Street hospital, 166–68
**White Terror,** xxxvi
Wilhelm, Károly, 256
Wille camp, 232–33
Winkelmann, Otto, li, liii
Wisliceny, Dieter, xxviiin1, 254–55
women: at Birkenau, lxi; body searches of, 193–95; in ghettos, 249–52
World Council of Churches (WCC), 327n138
World War I, Hungary after, xxxviii–xli
WVHA. *See* SS-Business Administration Main Office

Yad Vashem, 140n108
yellow star: advertisement for, 132; exemptions from, 74, 75, 268n80; legislation requiring, 73–76; reaction to, 245; social status and, 132
**yellow-star houses:** in Budapest ghetto, 161; conditions in, 130–32, 333; establishment of, 123–27
Yugoslavia: Hungarian invasion of, xli; refugees from, 35–36

Zala County, 87–90
Zalaegerszeg, 112, 195
Zalán, Ferenc, 94n61
Závódszky, József, 300
Zelk, Zoltán, 305–6
Zhukov, Marshall, 355
Zionism, 162, 353
Zionists: collaboration accusations by, 262–65; composition of, 265; illegal leafleting by, 272–78; on Jewish Council, 255; negotiations with Eichmann, 120; postwar influence of, 352–53; strategies of, 265–72. *See also halutzim*
Zöldi, Márton, 43, 45n61, 344n46
Zwiebel, Bella, 298
Zyklon B gas, 215, 216n8, 229

# About the Authors

**László Csősz** is senior historian at the Holocaust Memorial Center in Budapest. In 2006–2007 he was a Charles H. Revson Foundation Fellow at the Center for Advanced Holocaust Studies. He received his PhD in history from the University of Szeged in 2011. His scholarly publications include "Land Reforms and Race Protection: The Implementation of the Fourth Jewish Law," in *The Holocaust in Hungary: A European Perspective* (2005), and entries in Randolph L. Braham's *The Geographical Encyclopedia of the Holocaust in Hungary* (2013).

**Gábor Kádár** is senior historian at the Hungarian Jewish Archives, Budapest. In 2003–2004 he was a Charles H. Revson Foundation Fellow at the Center for Advanced Holocaust Studies. He has authored and coauthored numerous studies on various aspects of the Holocaust, as well as three monographs, including a history of the looting of Jewish property in Hungary, *Aranyvonat. Fejezetek a zsidó vagyon történetéből* (2001), and *Self-Financing Genocide: The Gold Train, the Becher Case and the Wealth of Hungarian Jews* (2004). He is a co-creator of the permanent Hungarian exhibition in the Auschwitz-Birkenau State Museum and the permanent exhibition of the Holocaust Memorial Center in Budapest.

**Zoltán Vági**, historian, is deputy director of the Social Conflicts Research Center at Eötvös Loránd University, Budapest. His fields of specialty in Holocaust and comparative genocide studies are Hungarian Jews in Auschwitz-Birkenau and other camps, extreme right-wing movements, interethnic conflicts, and antisemitic violence in eastern Europe. In 2003–2004 he was a Charles H. Revson Foundation Fellow at the Center for Advanced Holocaust Studies. He is author of numerous articles and coauthor of three monographs, including *Self-Financing Genocide: The Gold Train, the Becher Case and the Wealth of Hungarian Jews* (2004) and *Hullarablás. A magyar zsidók gazdasági megsemmisítése* (2005) on the expropriation of Hungary's Jews.